HUMAN RIGHTS IN ONTARIO

Second Edition

by

Judith Keene, LL.B.

of the Ontario Bar

CARSWELL
Thomson Professional Publishing

Canadian Cataloguing in Publication Data

Keene, Judith, 1952-
  Human rights in Ontario

2nd ed.
Includes index.
ISBN 0-459-55676-2

1. Civil rights - Ontario. 2. Ontario. Human
Rights Code, 1981. I. Title.

KE0814.52.K43 1992   342.713′085   C92-093554-0
KF4483.C5K43 1992

CARSWELL
Thomson Professional Publishing

One Corporate Plaza, 2075 Kennedy Road, Scarborough, Ontario M1T 3V4
Customer Service:
Toronto 1-416-609-3800
Elsewhere in Canada/U.S. 1-800-387-5164
Fax 1-800-298-5094

As before, to Dorothy Keene and Doug Ewart

PREFACE

In the nine years since I wrote the first edition of this book, there has been a significant rise in public awareness of human rights issues. It is also painfully obvious that discrimination is still entrenched in our society. There has been little tangible improvement in the situation of people who face injustice because of their race, ancestry or origin, their colour, ethnicity, citizenship or creed, their sex or their sexual orientation, their marital or family status, their handicap, or the fact that they have received public assistance or have been convicted of an offence.

No social change can be accomplished by legislation and government action alone, but there is more for government to do. It is clear that the effectiveness of the Ontario Human Rights Commission has been allowed to decline and that the complaints investigation system is in dire need of improvement. Even more importantly, preventive legislation is clearly overdue, for two reasons. The first is that, in the absence of preventive legislation, a complaint-driven system fights a losing battle trying to keep up with demand, in an era in which large annual budget increases are a thing of the past. The second and more compelling reason is that preventive legislation goes a long way toward removing the burden of achieving equity from those who have already been victimized, and is likely to produce real results for people who have waited too long for justice. The pay equity legislation was a step in the right direction; effective employment equity legislation, with mandatory goals and timetables, is the logical next step, and is eagerly awaited.

Producing this book took far longer than I had expected. It is intended to reflect the law up to May 1, 1991. I hope the reader will forgive errors and omissions which will undoubtedly be found herein, and which are solely my responsibility. Perhaps those who have tried to produce a book while practising full-time will find it easier to be understanding.

Once again, I would like to acknowledge with gratitude the financial assistance of the Law Foundation of Ontario, which, among other benefits, enabled me to avail myself of the research assistance of Sandy Stephens, through the Centre for Research on Public Law and Public Policy at Osgoode Hall Law School. I would also like to thank Mary Bruno for much patient typing, and Carswell for producing this second edition.

As always, I owe more than I can say to Doug Ewart, who in addition to being an encyclopedic legal resource and passionate human rights advocate is, I am proud to say, my very best friend.

Toronto   Judith Keene
February, 1992

TABLE OF CONTENTS

TABLE OF CASES

1

AN INTRODUCTION TO
THE ONTARIO HUMAN RIGHTS CODE

The purpose of this introduction is to set out some general propositions that may be useful in the interpretation of the Ontario *Human Rights Code.*[1] The broad statements herein will be supported by the more detailed section-by-section analysis contained in the chapters that follow.

Human rights legislation has been in force in Ontario since the turn of the century,[2] generally in the form of limited statutes directed to specific practices and specific grounds of discrimination.[3] The first Ontario *Human Rights Code*[4] consolidated the more area-specific previous legislation, and charged the Ontario Human Rights Commission with the implementation of the general Act. The 1962 statute was amended several times;[5] generally, the effect of the amendments has been to widen the scope of the *Code.*

The 1981 *Code,*[6] which came into force on 15 June 1982, was not an amendment but a new Act, which in turn was amended in 1986. The 1981 *Code* introduced new grounds of discrimination: citizenship, family status, handicap, receipt of public assistance and record of offences.[7] The 1986 amendments added protection against discrimination because of sexual orientation, slightly expanded protection against age discrimination, specifically expanded the definition of sex discrimination to include discrimina-

---

1. Amended in 1986: S.O. 1986, c. 64 [now R.S.O. 1990, c. H.19]. While some amendments took effect as of 18 December 1986, sections amending or replacing sections 10, 16, 23 and 40 were not proclaimed until 18 April 1988.
2. See the *Religious Freedom Act,* R.S.O. 1897, c. 306, s. 1 [as reproduced in R.S.O. 1990, c. 1, s. 1].
3. See the *Insurance Act,* R.S.O. 1990, c. I.8, s. 140. See also the *Racial Discrimination Act,* S.O. 1944, c. 51 [rep. 1954, c. 28, s. 19]; *Fair Accommodation Practices Act,* S.O. 1954, c. 28 [rep. 1961-61, c. 93, s. 19]; *Female Employees Fair Remuneration Act,* S.O. 1951, c. 117 [rep. 1961-62, c. 93, s. 19].
4. S.O. 1961-62, c. 93.
5. S.O. 1965, c. 85; 1967, c. 66; 1968, c. 85; 1968-69, c. 83.
6. *Human Rights Code,* 1981, S.O. 1981, c. 53.
7. The previous *Code,* R.S.O. 1980, c. 340, prohibited discrimination on the ground of race, creed, colour, sex, marital status, nationality, ancestry or place of origin.

tion because of actual or possible pregnancy, and dropped a major bar to protection against handicap discrimination.

The 1981 *Code* affected more areas of activity than had previous legislation. Contracts became subject to the *Code*, and occupational associations were added. Protection against discrimination in the provision of goods, services and facilities was no longer limited to places "to which the public is customarily admitted." The 1981 *Code* also introduced specific prohibitions against harassment, constructive discrimination and discrimination because of association.

The 1981 *Code* also made changes to the administration of the Act. The responsibilities of the Ontario Human Rights Commission were extended, and the *Code* addressed more effectively the Commission's capacity to enforce the legislation. The Commission's functions were more clearly delineated, to include intervention in community problems arising from discrimination and the recommendation of "affirmative action" programs. The new *Code* created a race relations division within the Commission.[8]

In regard to the enforcement of the *Code*, the Minister's discretion to refuse to appoint a Board when requested to do so by the Commission was removed by the 1981 *Code*. The Commission was given the authority to combine complaints under certain conditions.

AN OVERVIEW OF THE CODE

The *Code* is divided into five parts; the interrelationship of Parts I and II has implications for the interpretation of the substantive rights set out therein.

Part I sets out the basic rights to equal treatment in the provision of services, goods and facilities, in accommodation, in employment, in membership in a trade union, trade or occupational association or self-governing profession, and in the right to form contracts.[9]

In all of these protected areas, Part I provides a right to "equal treatment without discrimination" on the basis of race, ancestry, place of origin, ethnic origin, citizenship, creed, sex, age, marital status, family status and handicap. Pursuant to a 1986 amendment,[10] freedom from discrimination on the basis of sexual orientation and actual pregnancy or potential for pregnancy[11] is also mandated in all of the above-noted areas. In addition, discrimination because of receipt of public assistance is prohibited in the area of accommodation, and discrimination because of record of offences is pro-

---

8. In 1985, the race relations division was, in effect, transferred to the Ministry of Citizenship and renamed. See discussion, Chapter 8.
9. R.S.O. 1990, c. H.19, ss. 1-9 generally.
10. S.O. 1986, c. 64, s. 18.
11. R.S.O. 1990, c. H.19, s. 10(2).

hibited in the area of employment.[12]

Part I also contains prohibitions against harassment in the areas of accommodation and employment, on the ground of race, ancestry, place of origin, colour, ethnic origin, citizenship, creed, age, marital status, family status, handicap or sex. In addition, harassment on the ground of receipt of public assistance is prohibited in accommodation, and harassment on the ground of record of offences is prohibited in employment.[13] There is also a specific provision prohibiting sexual harassment by anyone "in a position to confer, grant or deny a benefit or advancement" to the person so harassed.[14] Part I also prohibits reprisals, or threats thereof, against anyone who claims and enforces his or her rights, or refuses to infringe another's rights.[15]

The right to equal treatment is broadly worded, and Part I concludes with section 9, which states: "no person shall infringe or do, directly or indirectly, anything that infringes a right under this Part."

Further definitions of actions that are considered to infringe Part I rights are set out in Part II. These include constructive discrimination, discrimination because of association, the publication of representations indicating an intention to discriminate or inciting discrimination, discriminatory employment advertising and employment applications and discrimination by employment agencies.

Part II has four functions. It contains most of the definition clauses.[16] It sets out, for greater clarity the above-noted specific actions which will be held to infringe Part I rights[17] and specific exceptions in respect of actions that would otherwise constitute an infringement.[18] Finally, it provides for a new deemed condition in contracts made with the provincial government in a number of situations. Where a board of inquiry has found employment discrimination in the performance of a government contract, or in the carrying out of a government-assisted project, the government may cancel the contract, loan, grant, etc.[19]

Part III continues the Ontario Human Rights Commission and sets out its functions. It also creates a race relations division of the Commission.

Part IV covers the investigation and settlement of complaints and the procedure through which a board of inquiry may be appointed. It also sets

---

12. Ibid., ss. 2(1), 5(1).
13. Ibid., ss. 2(2), 5(2).
14. Ibid., s. 7(3).
15. See sections 8 and 9. To date, few boards have found a breach of s. 8: see *Karumanchiri v. Liquor Control Board of Ontario* (1987), and see *Noffke v. McClaskin Hot House* (1989), 11 C.H.R.R. D/407 (Ont. Bd. of Inquiry).
16. See s. 10.
17. See ss. 11, 12, 13, 23(1), (2) and (4), 25(1) and (4).
18. See ss. 14(1), 15, 16, 17(1), 18-22, 23(3), 24 and 25(2) and (3).
19. See ss. 25(1) and (4).

out the purpose, and some of the procedures, governing boards of inquiry and contains a section dealing with awards.

Part V includes some additional definitions, a section that states that the Crown is bound by the *Code* and a primacy clause.

THE CODE AS PUBLIC POLICY: PRIMACY AND LIBERAL INTERPRETATION

The *Code's* primacy clause,[20] which took effect in 1984, clearly signals the importance of human rights law in Ontario public policy. It is interesting to note, however, that there is authority for the proposition that human rights legislation takes precedence over other legislation even without a specific statutory provision, and that the Supreme Court of Canada has demonstrated itself willing to interpret human rights legislation liberally and purposively. Professor Pentney, in *Gohm v. Domtar Inc.*,[21] sets out a succinct review of the Court's approach to date, beginning with the judgment of the Court in *O'Malley v. Simpsons-Sears Ltd.*[22]

> The Supreme Court of Canada ruled unanimously that the Code prohibits adverse effect discrimination. Mr. Justice McIntyre, for the Court, began his analysis of the issue by referring to the Preamble to the Code, which enunciates its "broad policy." He described the general approach to the interpretation of human rights laws in the following passage, at pp. 328-9:
>
> > It is not, in my view, a sound approach to say that according to established rules of construction no broader meaning can be given to the Code than the narrowest interpretation of the words employed. The accepted rules of construction are flexible enough to enable the Court to recognize in the construction of a human rights code the special nature and purpose of the enactment (see Lamer J. in *Insurance Corp. of B.C. v. Heerspink* . . .), and to give to it an interpretation which will advance its broad purposes. Legislation of this type is of a special nature, not quite constitutional but certainly more than the ordinary — and it is for the courts to seek out its purpose and give it effect. The Code aims at the removal of discrimination. This is to state the obvious. Its main approach, however, is not to punish the discriminator, but rather to provide relief for the victims of discrimination.
>
> This general principle has been repeated by the Supreme Court of Canada in virtually every human rights decision since 1985, so that today it must be a touchstone to guide all interpretation of these laws: see *Craton v. Winnipeg School Division No. 1*, [1985] 2 S.C.R. 150; *Action Travail des Femmes v. Canadian National Railway Co.*, [1987] 1 S.C.R. 1114; *Robichaud v. Canada*, [1987] 2 S.C.R. 84; *Ville de Brossard v. Quebec Human Rights Commission*, [1988] 2 S.C.R. 279. In the *Action Travail* case (*supra*), Chief Justice Dickson described the "proper interpretative attitude towards human rights codes and acts" at p. 1134:

---

20. S. 47(2). This provision was applied in *Hickling v. Lanark, Leeds & Grenville County Roman Catholic Separate School Board* (1986), 7 C.H.R.R. D/3546 (Ont. Bd. of Inquiry), reversed (1987), 40 D.L.R. (4th) 316 (Ont. Div. Ct.); *Joseph v. College of Nurses (Ontario)* (1985), 51 O.R. (2d) 155 (Div. Ct.).

21. (1990), 12 C.H.R.R. D/161 (Ont. Bd. of Inquiry).

22. (1986), 64 N.R. 161 (S.C.C.)

> Human Rights legislation is intended to give rise, among other things, to individual rights of vital importance, rights capable of enforcement, in the final analysis, in a court of law. I recognize that in the construction of such legislation, the words of the Act must be given their plain meaning, but it is equally important that the rights enunciated be given their full recognition and effect. We should not search for ways and means to minimize those rights and to enfeeble their proper impact.[23]

Exceptions to the Act have been construed correspondingly narrowly. In *Ontario (Human Rights Commission) v. Etobicoke (Borough)*, McIntyre J. stated that "[I]t will be seen at once that under the *Code* non-discrimination is the rule of general application and discrimination, where permitted, is the exception."[24]

"EQUAL TREATMENT WITHOUT DISCRIMINATION"

The term "equal" is addressed in the interpretation section of the *Code* as follows: "equal means subject to all requirements, qualifications and considerations that are not a prohibited ground of discrimination."

It is obvious that the above-noted clause is a qualification, rather than a definition, of the meaning of the word "equal". It does no more than make it clear that any considerations attendant on a decision or practice in areas covered by the *Code* may be applied, as long as a prohibited ground of discrimination is not among those considerations. For example, a landlord may assess a prospective tenant as to trustworthiness in paying the rent, proclivities toward wild parties, etc. However, absent a statutory exception, he or she must not base such a judgment on the applicant's race, sex, religion, etc. An employer is free to canvass an applicant's references or impose a probationary period on a new employee, in order to assess whether the employee demonstrates the appropriate "work ethic." However, absent a statutory exception, if the employer acts on the assumption that the applicant's child care responsibilities or ethnic origin mean, *ipso facto*, that he or she will be unreliable, the employer infringes the applicant's rights under section 5. It is clear that where even one of the "requirements, qualifications and considerations" that go into a decision is the race, sex, creed, etc., of the person involved, the decision-maker has breached the Part I right, in the absence of a statutory exception. The view that liability can exist where motives are mixed is justified, both by the phrase "*without* discrimination" and by a doctrine that began with *R. v. Bushnell Communications*[25] and is well established in human rights case law.[26]

The statutory qualification of the term "equal" is further qualified by

---

23. fn. 21 at 32-34.
24. (1982), 132 D.L.R. (3d) 14 at 19 (S.C.C.).
25. (1973), 45 D.L.R. (3d) 218, affirmed (1974), 4 O.R. (2d) 288 (C.A.).
26. See discussion of "mixed motives" in Chapter 9.

the existence of section 11, which prohibits constructive (otherwise known as unintentional or adverse effect) discrimination. Section 11 makes it clear that discrimination can exist where there are discriminatory consequences, whether or not these are intended. This concept is further discussed below.

Apart from the qualification of the term "equal," the phrase "equal treatment without discrimination" is left undefined in the *Code*. As most Canadian legislation fails to define equal treatment or discrimination, it has been left to tribunals and courts to supply the lack.

For reasons having to do with the wording of the particular statute at issue, early human rights decisions focused on defining the words "discriminate" or "discriminatory," and, not surprisingly, focused on the aspect of differentiation and therefore required the presence of a comparison individual or group. The resulting problem is tellingly illustrated in a 1985 decision of the Manitoba Court of Appeal in *Dakota Ojibway Tribal Council v. Bewza*,[27] in which proof of hostile remarks and actions directed at a Native patron by a motel-keeper failed to establish discriminatory treatment. In *Bewza*, Mr. Justice Twaddle remarked:

> Here the hostility of Ms. Bewza to, and her prejudice against, Indians may or may not have influenced her conduct, but, in the absence of proof that the guests were treated differently from other guests in similar circumstances, she is not guilty of contravention of the Act. Prejudice without discrimination is not wrongful in law."[28]

This kind of problem appears to have been foreseen by Lord Simon in *Post Office v. Union of Post Office Workers:*[29]

> My only reservation from entire agreement is in relation to the word "discriminate"; and I only state such reservation because it is a word which tends to recur in modern statutes. In my view, both of the meanings indicated by my noble and learned friend — (i) treating a person less favourably than he would otherwise be treated, and (ii) treating a person less favourably than others are treated in comparable circumstances — are equally natural meanings of the word. Here the phraseology "penalize or otherwise discriminate against" seems to me to make the former the more appropriate reading.[30]

It appears that tribunals are gradually becoming aware of the danger of requiring that a comparison individual or group be available in all cases so that it is clear that differentiation is going on. In the first Ontario board to deal with sexual harassment by an employer, in a context in which, because of the absence of a specific prohibition of harassment, sex discrimination had to be proved, the Chair dealt with the problem presented by the fact that all of the employees concerned were women.

> Clearly a person who is disadvantaged because of her sex is being discriminated against

---

27. (1984), 7 C.H.R.R. D/3217 (Man. Bd. of Adjud.), affirmed (1986), 37 Man. R. (2d) 207 (C.A.).
28. *Ibid.*, at 218.
29. [1974] All E.R. 229 (H.L.).
30. *Ibid.*, at 239.

in her employment when employer conduct denies her financial rewards because of her sex, or exacts some form of sexual compliance to improve or maintain her existing benefits. *The evil to be remedied is the utilization of economic power or authority so as to restrict a woman's guaranteed and equal access to the work place, and all of its benefits, free from extraneous pressures having to do with the mere fact that she is a woman.* Where a woman's equal access is denied or when terms and conditions differ when compared to male employees, the woman is being discriminated against.[31]

In a later sex discrimination case involving a requirement that female serving staff wait tables naked from the waist up, *Ballantyne v. Molly 'N Me Tavern*[32] the Board addressed the single sex job classification problem as follows:

> In my view, the *Sage Realty* and *Lodger's International* cases are suggestive of one line of interpretation of the Code's provisions which may be helpful in cases of this kind. In any case where, as in *Lodger's* essentially similar work is done by both male and female employees, the imposition of a more burdensome dress requirement on females would constitute an infringement of the Code. It would appear that the language of Section 4(1) (g) is sufficiently broad to embrace a situation of this kind. Nothing in that section suggests that discrimination can only be found where both male and female employees occupy positions having the same job description in the narrow sense. If male and female employees are engaged in roughly similar work, the terms and conditions of their employment should in these respects also be similar. In the present case, it has been noted that at the very least there are male and female employees engaged in essentially similar work, and on this basis, therefore, I would hold that even on the view of the fact taken by counsel for the respondent, discrimination within section 4(1) (g) [now s. 5 (1)] has occurred.
>
> A second point of interpretation suggested by these cases is that where the job in question is in fact held only by female employees, an argument of the kind raised on behalf of the respondent should not succeed unless membership in the female sex is a bfoq for the job in question. Thus, in a case like *Sage Realty* where the employer is in fact hiring only female employees for the position in question, this ought not *per se* to constitute a defence to a claim of discriminatory treatment if in fact the job is one which should by law be made available to both male and female applicants. The facts of *Sage Realty* itself, for example, appear to be a very difficult situation in which to defend membership in the female sex as a bfoq, and it is obvious that if male employees were hired to fill a position, they would not be required to wear the "bicentennial" outfit. If a basis for this assumption were established in evidence, it would be a perverse reading of the Code which would permit a defence to a complaint under Section 4(1) (g) [now s. 5(1)] simply because there were no actual male occupants of the position in question with whom a direct comparison could be made.[33]

In a later racial discrimination case, *Ahluwalia v. Metropolitan Toronto (Municipality) of Commissioners of Police*,[34] the Board addressed the logical consequence of requiring a comparison group in all cases.

> If one argues that the meaning of discriminate in s. 4(1) (g) [of the Ontario Code

---

31. *Bell v. Ladas* (1980), 1 C.H.R.R. D/155 at D/156 (Ont. Bd. of Inquiry).

32. (1982), 4 C.H.R.R. D/1191 (Ont. Bd. of Inquiry).

33. *Ibid.*, at D/1195-6.

34. (1983), 4 C.H.R.R. D/1757 (Ont. Bd. of Inquiry).

now s. 5(1)] is restricted to the sense of being treated differently, such conduct, no matter how offensive to reasonable sensibilities, would not be unlawful so long as the offensive conduct was maintained consistently throughout the workplace.[35]

Insofar as the above noted development of the law by boards of inquiry had to do with a lack of a specific harassment provision in the *Code*, that the problem has now been rectified. However, such phenomena as job ghettoes and the situation encountered in *Bewza* have not disappeared, and such situations require a board to take notice of historical patterns of oppression and in the appropriate situation to explore the idea of the "notional other," that is, the likelihood that if persons other than those of the complainant's race, sex etc. had been present in the disputed situation, such others would be accorded more dignity than was the complainant.

Another inevitable debate concerning the definition of "discrimination" was whether evidence as to the mental state of the actor was necessary. The history of this aspect of human rights laws shows a progression in other jurisdictions from a requirement of proof of actual ill-will or malice to the development of the notion that the social ill to be addressed in human rights law was effect, not intent. In Canada, boards of inquiry adopted the view relatively early that proof of intent to discriminate was not necessary, but appeal decisions took a narrower view. The decision of the Chief Justice for a unanimous Supreme Court of Canada in *Action travail des femmes v. Canadian National Railway Co.*[36] traced the evolution of the law as follows:

> Many of the first anti-discrimination statutes focussed solely upon the behaviour of such individuals, requiring proof of "intent" to discriminate before imposing any sanctions. See W.S. Tarnopolsky, Discrimination and the Law in Canada (Toronto: De Boo, 1982), at pp. 109-122. There were two major difficulties with this approach. One semantic problem was a continuing confusion of the notions of "intent" and "malice". The word "intent" was deprived of its meaning in common parlance and was used as a surrogate for "malice". "Intent" was not the simple willing of a consequence, but rather the desiring of harm.
>
> This imputed meaning was coherent in the context of a statute designed to punish moral blameworthiness. However, as the second problem with a fault-based approach was revealed — that moral blame was too limited a concept to deal effectively with the problem of discrimination — an attempt was made by legislatures and courts to cleanse the word "intent" of its moral component. The emphasis upon formal causality was restored and the intent required to prove discrimination became the intent to cause a discriminatory result. The judgment of the Federal Court of Appeal in *Canadian National Railway Co. v. Bhinder*, [1983] 2 F.C. 531 (C.A.) is an example of this approach (aff'd on different grounds in *Bhinder v. Canadian National Railway Co.*, [1985] 2 S.C.R. 561). The difficulty with this development was that "intent" had become so encrusted with the moral overtones of "malice" that it was often difficult to separate the two concepts. Moreover, the imputation of a requirement of "intent", even if unrelated to moral

---

35. *Ibid.*, at D/1765.
36. (1987), 8 C.H.R.R. D/4210 (S.C.C.)

fault, failed to respond adequately to the many instances where the effect of policies and practices is discriminatory even if that effect is unintended and unforeseen. The stated purpose of human rights legislation (in the case of the Canadian Act, to prevent "discriminatory practices") was not fully implemented. . . .

There can be no doubt that Canadian human rights legislation is now typically drafted to avoid reference to intention. As noted previously, the Canadian *Human Rights Act* is addressed to "discriminatory practices". The *Ontario Human Rights Code*, R.S.O. 1980, c. 340 [now R.S.O. 1990, c. H.19], seeks to uphold the "equal dignity" of all men and women by preventing discrimination.[37]

The Supreme Court has in fact gone further than to remove consideration of motive. In a 1985 case, *O'Malley v. Simpsons-Sears*,[38] it resolved the intent-versus-effect debate by declaring that intention to discriminate need not be proven when it can be demonstrated that a particular action or decision has an adverse effect on a group protected by human rights legislation. The history of this development will be discussed in detail in Chapter 4.

A third issue to be examined in defining discrimination is the importance of the nature of the consequences complained of to the finding of discrimination. Relatively few boards of inquiry have discussed whether the consequences of an impugned action must be "adverse" to be discriminatory, or how adverse they must be. This may be due in part to the fact that the Commission acts as "floodgate," in that it must decide whether a matter should go to a board, and may refuse to deal with a complaint that is "trivial, frivolous, vexatious or made in bad faith."[39]

Obviously there is no such floodgate in respect of cases that have come before the courts under section 15 of the *Charter of Rights*. Further, by their nature, challenges under section 15 of the *Charter* frequently deal with legislation, and legislation by its nature classifies and distinguishes. It is, therefore, not surprising that appellate cases under section 15 lean toward the view that mere differentiation, without adverse consequences, is insufficient to qualify as discriminatory treatment under section 15.[40] In the Supreme Court of Canada decision in *Andrews v. Law Society of British Columbia*[41] the Supreme Court of Canada, McIntyre J., indicated that distinctions are often necessary to promote true equality. He went on to the following short definition of discrimination:

Discrimination may be described as a distinction, whether intentional or not but based on grounds relating to personal characteristics of the individual or group, which has the effect of imposing burdens, obligations or disadvantages not imposed on others, or

---

37. *Ibid.*, at D/4224-6.
38. [1985] 2 S.C.R. 536.
39. *Human Rights Code*, R.S.O. 1990, c. H.19, s. 34(1)(b).
40. See *R. v. Century 21 Ramos Realty Inc.* (1987), 58 O.R. (2d) 737 (C.A.), leave to appeal to S.C.C. refused (1987) 62 O.R. (2d) ix (note) (S.C.C.); *R. v. Le Gallant* (1987), 54 C.R. (3d) 46 (B.C. C.A.).
41. [1989] 1 S.C.R. 143.

which withholds or limits access to opportunities, benefits and advantages available to other members of society. Distinctions based on personal characteristics attributed to an individual solely on the basis of association with a group will rarely escape the charge of discrimination, while those based on an individual's merits and capacities will rarely be so classed.[42]

In *Allan v. Chrysalis Restaurant*,[43] the Divisional Court refused an appeal by the Commission of a ruling by a board of inquiry that appeared to turn in part on whether a uniform requirement for women employees was sufficiently onerous to constitute discrimination. Madame Justice Van Camp ended her brief judgment by quoting with approval a definition of discrimination "given in 14 C.E.D. (Ont. 3rd), Title 74, s. 11, namely: 'differential treatment as a result of which the victim suffers adverse consequences or a serious affront to a dignity'."[44]

On the strength of the few boards of inquiry to have addressed the matter even peripherally, it can be said that they tend to accept that consequences must be averse to be discriminatory, but that most have been willing to extend a subjective interpretation to assessing adversity.

Chairman Cumming in *Hickling v. Lanark, Leeds and Grenville Roman Catholic Separate School Board*[45] declined to pass judgment on the degree of gravity of the effect of denial of a benefit because of handicap:

> If a separate school board denied a Catholic education to a pupil on the ground, for example, of sex, ethnic origin or family status, all the proof in the world that the pupil would get a better education in a non-Catholic system would clearly not avail to make the denial non-discriminatory. The same is true if that denial is based on handicap, which is just as plainly listed as a prohibited ground in section 1 of the Code. The fact that the pupil may as a whole be better off as a result of the denial, or that the school board's intention is to make the pupil better off, is irrelevant to whether the denial is discriminatory.[46]

In *Tomen v. Ontario Teachers' Federation*,[47] the respondent submitted that if the net injury is insubstantial, no finding of discrimination can be made, citing the *Andrews* decision. The board acknowledged as a fact that, despite the impugned rule of mandatory membership in a women's teachers' federation, the complainant was also allowed to be a member of the OPSTF at very little cost. However, the board pointed out that: "The detriment to the complainants is that a portion of money in the form of dues, as a matter of compulsion, goes to an organization whose purposes and cases they do not want to support. Another way of expressing this is to say the

---

42. *Ibid.*, at 174.
43. (1987), 61 O.R. (2d) 460 (Div. Ct.).
44. *Ibid.*, at 463.
45. (1986), 7 C.H.R.R. D/3546 (Ont. Bd. of Inquiry), revised on other grounds (1987), 60 O.R. (2d) 441 (Div. Ct.), affirmed (1989), 67 O.R. (2d) 479 (C.A.).
46. *Ibid.*, at D/3555.
47. (1989), 11 C.H.R.R. D/223 (Ont. Bd. of Inquiry).

complaints have put forward injury to their dignitary interests."[48]

The board rejected the argument that Mr. Justice McIntyre's analysis of effect, as set out in *Andrews*, excluded effects to dignitary interests.[49]

It is suggested that the subjective approach is the one most suited to the objects of the *Code*, particularly given the tendency of society, observable in the history of human rights issues, to discount the importance of rights that go against entrenched custom. Certainly, the *Code* imposes no explicit obligation as to proof of adverse consequences of the impugned action or decision; indeed, in respect of constructive discrimination, the proof adduced may be of "exclusion qualification *or preference*" (emphasis added) of a group identified in the *Code*. Further, as noted, there are safeguards in the statutory scheme that negate any need for an interpretation of the *Code* that adds any requirement as to proof of adverse consequences. The complainant must satisfy the Commission that a complaint is serious enough to be brought before a board. This state of affairs is appropriate, as the Commission is appointed to represent the public interest in freedom from discrimination.

Presumably, the rationale is that the Commission's assessment of the weight of a complaint is perhaps more likely to reflect changing public values than is a legislative provision. The Commission may refuse to appoint a board or to deal with the complaint at all because the complaint is "trivial, frivolous, vexatious" or made "in bad faith." On the other hand, there is nothing to stop the Commission from appointing a board in respect of a novel issue. It is this power which, for example, has enabled human rights commissions to refer to a board complaints against the refusal of a job for "chivalrous" reasons. Where "chivalry" once might have seemed a reasonable consideration in an employment decision, the Commission and boards of inquiry have recognized that it can work economic harm.[50]

The *Code* provides an additional safeguard. If a board should find the complaint insufficiently weighty, it has the power to award costs against the Commission.[51]

STATUTORY MODIFICATION OF THE TERM DISCRIMINATION

By virtue of sections 2(2), 5(2), 7, 11, 12, 13, 23(1), (2) and (4), and 25(1), specific actions which may not otherwise have been considered to fit the rough working definition of discrimination set out above are, by necessary implication, included.

---

48. *Ibid.*, at D/235.
49. See similar views in *Brooks v. Canada Safeway Ltd.* (1989), 10 C.H.R.R. D/6183 (S.C.C.); and *Janzen v. Platy Enterprises Ltd.* (1989), 10 C.H.R.R. D/6205 (S.C.C.).
50. See the cases discussed in the section on sex discrimination in Chapter 3.
51. R.S.O. 1990, c. H.19, s. 41(4).

Sections 2(2), 5(2) and 7 set out the right to be free of harassment because of grounds set out in the *Code*.[52]

Section 11 represents a legislative acknowledgement that, in some circumstances, treating people identically can have a discriminatory effect. The section prohibits "constructive discrimination"; that is, the imposition of a seemingly neutral requirement, qualification or consideration that would effect the "exclusion, qualification or preference" of a group protected by the *Code*. A classic example of constructive discrimination is the imposition of height and weight requirements for a certain job, effectively excluding women and persons belonging to generally small-boned racial groups. The imposition of such a requirement will be considered to infringe the *Code* unless the respondent can either be brought under a statutory exception or establish that the requirement is "reasonable and *bona fide* in the circumstances."[53]

Section 12 prohibits discrimination by association; that is, discrimination "because of relationship, association or dealings with a person or persons identified by a prohibited ground of discrimination." An example of this type of situation is adverse treatment suffered by a person because of his or her marriage to someone of a particular race.[54]

The *Code* also deals with certain publicly displayed representations. Section 13(1) provides:

> A right under Part I is infringed by a person who publishes or displays before the public or causes the publication or display before the public of any notice, sign, symbol, emblem, or other similar representation that indicates the intention of the person to infringe a right under Part I or that is intended by the person to incite the infringement of a right under Part I.

Section 13(2) provides that freedom of expression is not to be interfered with.[55]

Section 23 sets out provisions directed toward non-discrimination in recruiting for employment. The section includes clauses prohibiting discrimination by employment agencies, in employment advertisements and in pre-employment applications and interviews.[56]

Finally, section 25(1) provides that denying employment where the applicant fails to qualify for a discriminatory employment benefit plan, or making employment conditional on qualification for such a plan, infringes the right to equal treatment with respect to employment.[57]

To sum up, it would seem that a functional definition of discrimination

---

52. Harassment is discussed in Chapter 7.
53. S. 11 is discussed in Chapter 4.
54. S. 12 is discussed in Chapter 5.
55. S. 13 is discussed in Chapter 5.
56. This section is discussed in Chapter 5.
57. This section is discussed in Chapter 5.

for the purposes of the *Code* includes, generally, differentiation based on a prohibited ground of discrimination, harassment and the unintentional causation of a disparate impact upon persons protected by the *Code* and, specifically, breach of sections 12, 13, 23(1), (2), (4), or 25(1).

Finally, it should be added that an action that would otherwise constitute discrimination may be found not to infringe Part I rights where the respondent can establish that there is a statutory exception that applies to his or her situation. The exceptions are usually specific and those that limit rights protected by the *Code* are to be construed narrowly. They are found in sections 14(1), 15-17(1), 18-22, 23(3), 24 and 25(2) and (3).[58] All of these exceptions either refer directly to discrimination or are obviously applicable only to whether the right to freedom from discrimination applies in a particular situation.

---

58. See Chapter 6.

2

AREAS IN WHICH DISCRIMINATION IS PROHIBITED

INTRODUCTION

This chapter deals with the scope of the areas and activities affected by Part I, and with the definition for the purposes of the *Code* of services, goods, facilities, accommodation, employment and contracts. The prohibited grounds of discrimination will be discussed in another chapter, as well as the statutory exceptions that affect each area. The exceptions will, however, be briefly listed, in this chapter, at the end of the discussion of each area.

SERVICES, GOODS AND FACILITIES

Section 1 provides that:

> Every person has a right to equal treatment with respect to services, goods and facilities, without discrimination because of race, ancestry, place of origin, colour, ethnic origin, citizenship, creed, sex, age, marital status, family status or handicap.

Section 1 was amended in 1986 to include new grounds of discrimination. It is otherwise identical to the 1981 *Code*. The wording of the 1981 *Code* [now the 1990 *Code*] represented a departure from the wording of the previous *Code* in two important respects. First, there is no longer a clause limiting protection from discrimination to places "to which the public is customarily admitted." Second, the section is much more generally worded than the corresponding section of the previous *Code*.[1]

---

1. Section 2 of the former 1980 *Code* provided as follows:
   "(1) No person, directly or indirectly, alone or with another, by himself or by the interposition of another, shall
       (a) deny to any person or class of persons the accommodation, services or facilities available in any place to which the public is customarily admitted; or
       (b) discriminate against any person or class of persons with respect to the accommodation, services or facilities available in any place to which the public is customarily admitted,
   because of the race, creed, colour, sex, marital status, nationality, ancestry or place of origin of such person or class of persons or of any other person or class of persons."

The Private/Public Distinction

Human rights legislation in many jurisdictions confines its protection, in regard to services, etc., to public places.[2] For this reason there has been considerable case law as to whether a particular service was sufficiently public to attract the protection of the *Code*.[3]

The cases that may well have been responsible for changing the Ontario law are *Ontario Rural Softball Association v. Bannerman*[4] and *Cummings v. Ontario Minor Hockey Association*.[5] Both cases were brought on behalf of outstanding girl athletes who played on, respectively, a junior softball and a hockey team where the other players were boys. In *Bannerman*, the child in question was refused permission to play in "play-downs" conducted by O.R.S.A., which had a practice of segregating its teams according to sex. In *Cummings* the O.M.H.A. refused permission for the girl to be registered as goalie on an all-star team.

Before neither board was there any evidence that there was a physiological reason why girls should not compete with boys in junior sports; indeed, in *Bannerman*, there was empirical evidence to suggest that girls and boys tended to be evenly matched in team sports until approximately the age of fourteen.[6] An argument that boys would somehow suffer unique psychological harm if defeated by girls was deservedly dismissed by the board in *Cummings*.[7] Findings were made in both cases that the girls had been barred from playing on the sole ground of their sex. In both cases the boards found that the "services and facilities" in question were places to which the public was admitted, and that therefore the respondents had breached the *Code*.

Both decisions were overturned by the Divisional Court on the same day. In deciding *Cummings*, Evans C.J.H.C. found that the O.M.H.A. was

---

2. See, for example, the *Canadian Human Rights Act*, S.C. 1976-77, c. 33. s. 5; the *Human Rights Act*, S.N.S. 1969, c. 11, s. 3; the *Individual's Rights Protection Act*, R.S.A. 1980, c. I-2, s. 3; and England's *Race Relations Act*, 1976, s. 20 and *Sex Discrimination Act*, 1975, s. 29.
3. See, for example, *Charter v. Race Relations Bd.*, [1973] 1 All E.R. 512, in which the House of Lords exhaustively considered the nature of a Conservative social club; *Dockers' Labour Club & Institute Ltd. v. Race Relations Bd.*, [1974] 3 All E.R. 592 (H.L.), in which the same scrutiny was applied to a working men's club; *Applin v. Race Relations Bd.*, [1974] 2 All E.R. 73 (H.L.), which dealt with foster care for children.
4. (1978), 21 O.R. (2d) 395 (Div. Ct.), affirmed (1979), 26 O.R. (2d) 134 (C.A.).
5. (1978), 21 O.R. (2d) 389 (H.C.), affirmed (1979), 26 O.R. (2d) 7 (C.A.).
6. *Bannerman v. Ontario Rural Softball Assn.*, (1977), unreported, (Ont. Bd. of Inquiry) p. 17 (transcript).
7. An argument as to "danger of future family stability" was also unsuccessfully adduced: see *Cummings v. Ontario Minor Hockey Assn.* (1977), 29 R.F.L. 259 at 272 (Ont. Bd. of Inquiry), reversed (1978), 7 R.F.L. (2d) 359 (H.C.) affirmed (1979), 10 R.FL. (2d) 121 (C.A.)

indeed providing a "service or facility." He also acknowledged that the arena was a place to which the public was admitted. However, he interpreted the *Code* as containing an additional qualification: "the prohibition is against discrimination in the provision of accommodation, services or facilities *available to the public* in any place to which the public is customarily admitted."[8]

In discussing this decision, the Board of Inquiry in *Wan v. Greygo Gardens*[9] noted:

> In effect, the Divisional Court's reasoning would permit the grossest violations of the intent of the Ontario *Human Rights Code* for it would allow a place to maintain a private status outside the provisions of the *Code* simply by maintaining an admission policy which is blatantly discriminatory.

The *Cummings* appeal was dismissed by the Court of Appeal solely on the basis that the O.M.H.A. was unincorporated. However, the Court of Appeal dealt with the *Bannerman* case, which had been disposed of by the Divisional Court on the basis of its decision in *Cummings*.

The appeal from the decision of the Divisional Court in *Bannerman* was dismissed in a two-to-one decision. All the justices wrote separate opinions. For the majority, Houlden J.A. decided that the O.R.S.A. was not offering a "service or facility," and Weatherstone J.A. decided that the "real reason for the separation of boys and girls [was] overall fairness"[10] in competition. However, what is important to note for the purpose of this discussion is that all three justices declined to follow the interpretation of "available in a place to which the public is customarily admitted" given by the Divisional Court. Houlden and Wilson JJ.A. specifically rejected the approach taken by Evans C.J.H.C. On this point, Madame Justice Wilson, dissenting on other grounds, opined that the *Code* might properly "extend to services which, although not themselves customarily available to the public, are being made available in a place to which the public is customarily admitted."[11] She also pointed out the flaw noted by the board in *Greygo*:

> The submission, it seems to me, if accepted, could also have the effect of defeating the object of the legislation. Is it open to O.R.S.A. to say: "we provide softball for whites and softball for blacks and that is the scope of the service we have decided to provide"? I do not think so. I do not believe that the services provided in a public place can be circumscribed on the basis of the prohibited criteria.[12]

---

8. (1978), 21 O.R. (2d) 389 at 392-3 (H.C.).
9. (1982), 3 C.H.R.R. D/812 (Ont. Bd. of Inquiry).
10. (1979), 26 O.R. (2d) 134 at 152 (C.A.). In using this reasoning, Weatherston J.A. evidently failed to consider the line of cases that establish that where a discriminatory reason is a proximate cause of an action, the *Code* is breached even though there were other reasons for the action. See the discussion in Chapter 9 of "mixed motives."
11. (1979), 26 O.R. (2d) 134 at 142 (C.A.).
12. *Ibid*, at 143.

Possibly in response to the *Cummings* and *Bannerman* decisions, the legislature elected to remove the qualifying phrase from the "services, goods and facilities" section of the 1981 *Code*, and to rely instead on specific exemptions. Ironically, sex-segregated sports were specifically exempted from the provisions of the *Code*,[13] but the Court of Appeal decision in the *Bannerman* case remains an obvious deterrent to any judicial attempt to qualify section 1 other than by reference to a statutory exception or by the definitions accorded the terms "services, goods and facilities."

General Wording

It should be noted at the outset that section 1 contains no limitations regarding whether a good, service or facility is paid for or is free of charge. Stripped of the public/private distinction, goods, services and facilities are clearly to be given the broad interpretation suitable to remedial legislation, and can be interpreted to include virtually anything that can be "provided."

Goods

Murray's New English Dictionary provides a fairly sweeping definition of good, including "something, whether material or immaterial, which it is an advantage to attain or possess." The *Oxford English Dictionary* definition is considerably briefer: "movable property." *Black's Law Dictionary* provides a definition that is obviously influenced by mercantile law. It includes:

Items of merchandise, supplies, raw materials, or finished goods. Sometimes the meaning of "goods" is extended to include all tangible items, as in the phrase "goods and services."

All things (including specially manufactured goods) which are movable at the time of identification to the contract for sale other than the money in which the price is to be paid, investment securities and things in action. Also includes the unborn of animals and growing crops and other identified things attached to realty as fixtures.

There appear to be no published human rights cases that have defined goods; however it is reasonably clear that section 2 would be applicable in respect to all wholesale and retail sales transactions, whether of completed merchandise or of raw materials. The section would also apply to the free distribution of goods, through programs undertaken by charitable agencies, for example.

Services

In the context of section 2, it is obvious that services does not relate to

---

13. R.S.O. 1980, c. 53, s. 19(2), discussed in Chapter 6, was eventually struck down by the Ontario Court of Appeal as offensive to the Canadian *Charter of Rights and Freedoms*, and the subsection was subsequently repealed.

employment, but to the offering or provision of something. The *Oxford English Dictionary* definition of service includes:

> the action of serving, helping or benefitting; conduct tending to the welfare or advantage of another; the duties or work of public servants; the supply of the needs of persons; waiting at the table, supply of foods . . . commodities, the supply . . . of gas or water; accommodation for conveyance or transit.

A case law definition of the term "services" is hard to come by since, in human rights legislation especially, the term is generally coupled with "facilities" and no differentiation is made. However, the term has been used in the case law in a way that corresponds with the O.E.D. definition.

The term service was interpreted by the Supreme Court of Canada in *Gay Alliance Toward Equality v. Vancouver Sun.*[14] In that case, Martland J., writing for the majority, stated that "service refers to such matters as restaurants, bars, taverns, service stations, public transportation and public utilities."[15] It seems clear from his words that Martland J. did not intend to set out an exhaustive list,[16] Furthermore, his observation must be placed in the context of the legislation before him in the *G.A.T.E.* case, which limited

---

14. (1979), 97 D.L.R. (3d) 577 (S.C.C.), hereinafter referred to as the *G.A.T.E.* case.
15. *Ibid.*, at 590.
16. In discussing the *G.A.T.E.* case in *Ontario Human Rights Commission) v. Ontario Rural Softball Assn.* (1979), 26 O.R. (2d) 134 at 142 (C.A.), Madame Justice Wilson expressed this view:

> "Perhaps of paramount importance is the question whether the illustrations given by Martland, J., as to the type of services and facilities covered by s. 3 of British Columbia *Code* are the same type of services and facilities as are covered by s. 2 of the Ontario *Code*. Or are his illustrations premised on the fact that the services and facilities caught by s. 3 of the British Columbia *Code* are limited to those "customarily available to the public"? In other words, is the *Gay Alliance* case distinguishable as far as the generic content of Mr. Justice Martland's illustrations are concerned on the basis of the different wording in the sections?
>
> It seems to me that, while the illustrations given by the learned Justice are the accommodation, services and facilities which the anti-discrimination legislation was initially designed to ensure would be available to all, the case itself illustrates a totally different kind of service, namely, classified advertising in a newspaper, which was found to be within the scope of s. 3 of the British Columbia *Code* as a service "customarily available to the public". I do not think therefore that it would be appropriate to refine too much on Mr. Justice Martland's illustrations. I think the learned Justice refers to them because of their historic significance in the development of the law in this area. I do not think he should be taken to have suggested that the categories of accommodation, services and facilities covered by the British Columbia section are closed.

A similar point of view was expressed by the New Brunswick Court of Appeal in *New Brunswick School District No. 15 v. New Brunswick (Human Rights Bd. of Inquiry* (1989), 10 C.H.R.R. D/6426 (N.B. C.A.), leave to appeal to S.C.C. refused (1989), 104 N.R. 318 (note) (S.C.C.)

"services" to those "customarily available to the public."

In a recent case, the Ontario Supreme Court chose a narrow definition of the term "services." In *Canada Trust Co. v. Ontario (Human Rights Commission)* the trustee of a trust established in 1923 to provide scholarships brought an application to the court for a ruling as to whether the trust violated the Ontario *Human Rights Code* or other public policy. The scholarship created by the trust was, due to the stipulations of the settler, available only to white students, of British nationality or parentage, and Protestant, and less scholarship money was available for female than for male students.

Despite indicating that the *Code* should be given the "widest possible interpretation," quoting definitions of the word "service" which included "the rendering of assistance or aid" and acknowledging that education has been held to be a service, McKeown J. went on to state: "it is my view that this reasoning has not yet been applied to a trust. Therefore, scholarships arising out of a trust are not a service or facility".[17]

No further reason was given for declining to consider why a scholarship should not be considered a service. McKeown, J., ruled that the trust was not invalid on the ground of contravention of the *Code* or public policy.

The Ontario Court of Appeal overturned this decision, with differences in the reasons given by Robbins and Osler, J.J.A. and by Tarnopolsky, J.A.

While not commenting on the definition of a trust as a service, all three justices thought that it was proper for the matter to be dealt with by the courts rather than by a tribunal under the *Human Rights Code*. Tarnopolsky, J.A. made a point of identifying the review of trust documents as an exception to the rule established by the Supreme Court of Canada in *Bhadauria*[18] to the effect that the Code provided the sole route by which claims of discrimination should be litigated.

In an extensive review of the law, Tarnopolsky J.A. set out the rationale for discriminatory trusts being struck down as against public policy. He distinguished contrary British authority decided prior to the passage in 1968 of Britain's *Race Relations Act*. He went on to review the establishment of non-discriminatory public policy from the growth of human rights legislation and the establishment of non-discrimination principles in other legislation and official declarations of government policy to the passage of the *Charter of Rights and Freedoms* and various international covenants.

Finally, Tarnopolsky J.A. pointed out that not all trusts that restrict eligibility are to be considered discriminatory:

---

17. (1987), 61 O.R. (2d) 75, at page 91.
18. *Seneca College of Applied Arts and Technology v. Bhadauria*, [1981] 2 S.C.R. 181.

In my view, these trusts will have to be evaluated on a case by case basis, should their validity be challenged. This case should not be taken as authority for the proposition that all restrictions amount to discrimination and are therefore contrary to public policy.

It will be necessary in each case to undertake an equality analysis like that adopted by the Human Rights Commission when approaching ss. 1 [am. 1986, c. 64, s. 18(1)] and 13 of the *Human Rights Code*, 1981 and that adopted by the courts when approaching s. 15(2) of the *Charter*. Those charitable trusts aimed at the amelioration of inequality and whose restrictions can be justified on that basis under s. 13 of the *Human Rights Code*, 1981 or s. 15(2) of the *Charter* would not likely be found void because they promote, rather than impede, the public policy of equality. In such an analysis, attention will have to be paid to the social and historical context of the group concerned (see *Andrews v. Law Society of British Columbia*, [1989] 1 S.C.R. 143, 36 C.R.R. 193, 34 B.C.L.R. (2d) 273, 25 C.C.E.L. 255, 10 C.H.R.R. D/5719, 56 D.L.R. (4th) 1, 91 N.R. 255, [1989] 2 W.W.R. 289, at pp. 152-53 S.C.R., pp. 201-02 C.R.R. per Wilson J. and p. 175 S.C.R., p. 228-29 C.R.R., per McIntyre J.) as well as the effect of the restrictions on racial, religious or gender equality, to name but a few examples.

Not all restrictions will violate public policy, just as not all legislative distinctions constitute discrimination contrary to s. 15 of the *Charter (Andrews, supra*, pp. 168-69 S.C.R., p. 223 C.R.R., per McIntyre, J.). In the indenture in this case, for example, there is nothing contrary to public policy as expressed in the preferences for children of "clergymen", "school teachers", etc. It would be hard to imagine in the foreseeable future that a charitable trust established to promote the education of women, aboriginal peoples, the physically or mentally handicapped, or other historically disadvantaged groups would be void as against public policy. Clearly, public trusts restricted to those in financial need would be permissible. Given the history and importance of bilingualism and multiculturalism in this country, restrictions on the basis of language would probably not be void as against public policy subject, of course, to an analysis of the context, purpose and effect of the restriction.

In this case, the court must, as it does in so many areas of law, engage in a balancing process. Important as it is to permit individuals to dispose of their property as they see fit, it cannot be an absolute right. The law imposes restrictions on freedom of both contract and testamentary disposition. Under the *Conveyancing and Law of Property Act*, s. 22, for instance, covenants that purport to restrict the sale, ownership, occupation or use of land because of, *inter alia*, race, creed or colour are void. Under the *Human Rights Code*, 1981, discriminatory contracts relating to leasing of accommodation are prohibited. With respect to testamentary dispositions, as mentioned earlier, one cannot establish a charitable trust unless it is for an exclusively charitable purpose (see *Waters, Law of Trusts*, at pp. 601-03 and 626; and *Ministry of Health v. Simpson, supra*). Similarly, public trusts which discriminate on the basis of distinctions that are contrary to public policy must now be void.

A finding that a charitable trust is void as against public policy would not have the far-reaching effects of testamentary freedom which some have anticipated. This decision does not affect private, family trusts. By that I mean that it does not affect testamentary dispositions or outright gifts that are not also charitable trusts. Historically, charitable trusts have received special protection: (1) they are treated favourably by taxation statutes; (2) they enjoy an extensive exemption from the rule against perpetuities; (3) they do not fail for lack of certainty of objects; (4) if the settlor does not set out sufficient directions, the court will supply them by designing a scheme; (5) courts may apply trust property cypres providing they can discern a general charitable intention. This preferential treatment is justified on the ground that charitable trusts are dedicated to the benefit of the community (*Waters, Law of Trusts*, p. 502). It is this public nature of charitable trusts which attracts the requirement that they conform to the public policy against discrimination. Only where the trust is a public one devoted to charity will restrictions that are contrary to the public policy of equality render it void."[19]

Services Provided by Governmental or Quasi-governmental Organizations

A number of services provided by agencies of government have been challenged under human rights legislation.

Taxation Practices

Subsection 10(1)(e) of the *Code* provides that "services" does not include a "levy, fee, tax or periodic payment imposed by law." Yet to be determined is whether this provision is broad enough to encompass not just the imposition of taxes, but all practices effected by regulation, guideline or administrative act that surround levies, fees, taxes or periodic payments.

While the federal *Human Rights Act* does not have an exception comparable to subsection 10(1)(e), it is useful to review one case under that Act, which sets out principles relevant to the scope of the "services" area of the Ontario legislation. In *Bailey v. Canada (Minister of National Revenue)*[20] the complaint under federal human rights legislation was of discrimination on the basis of marital status and sex, with regard to the availability of tax exemptions. The respondent applied for an injunction prior to a board hearing. In refusing the injunction, the federal Court took the view that questions of interpretation of the scope of "services" should be determined in first instance by the tribunal. However, the Court went on to comment on the substance of the case:

> Here there may well be questions of law that may arise on the complaints. There is the issue as to whether the Department of National Revenue, in assessing taxes, is engaged in the provision of services within the meaning of section 5 of the *Canadian Human Rights Act*. There is the question whether, if the Department is engaged in the provisions of services within the meaning of section 5 of the Canadian Human Rights Act. There is the question whether, if the Department is engaged in the provisions of services within the meaning of section 5, the Department is engaged in the provisions of services within the meaning of section 5, the Department's action in applying discriminatory provisions of the *Income Tax Act* is in itself an unlawful discriminatory practice. If so, there is the question whether any of the kinds of relief specified in section 41 would be appropriate or ought to be afforded. This may involve the question whether provisions of the *Income Tax Act* which discriminate on bases prohibited by the *Canadian Human Rights Act* have been *pro tanto* repealed. And there may be others.
>
> With respect to the first questions, which appears to me to be one that goes to the

---

19. *Canada Trust Co. v. Ontario (Human Rights Commission)* (1990), 74 O.R. (2d) 481, at 514-515 (C.A.).

20. (1980), 1 C.H.R.R. D/193 (Cdn. Human Rights Trib.).

jurisdiction of the Tribunal, I am not prepared to accept the broad proposition that in assessing taxes under the *Income Tax Act* the Department of National Revenue is not engaged in the provision of services within the meaning of section 5 of the *Canadian
Human Rights Act*. The statute is cast in wide terms and both its subject-matter and its
stated purpose suggest that it is not to be interpreted narrowly or restrictively. Nor do I
think that discrimination on any of the bases prohibited by the Act cannot conceivably
occur in the provision of such services to the public.[21]

Bailey involved a complaint that the Minister of National Revenue discriminated, on the ground of marital status, in the provision of services customarily available to the public by refusing to allow a "spouse support" tax
deduction by an unmarried woman who was supporting the man with whom
she lived.

The board in *Bailey* dismissed the complaint, despite a finding that the
distinction complained of was unreasonable, following the reasoning expressed by the Supreme Court of Canada in cases where federal legislation
was challenged under the *Canadian Bill of Rights*.[22] However, Chairman
Cumming found that both the administration of the *Income Tax Act* and the
sections challenged constituted "services."

In so finding, the board first considered the dictionary definition of
service, the use of the term in federal legislation, the description of its services published by the ministry and the purpose of the *Canadian Human
Rights Act*. Chairman Cumming went on to differentiate between the administration of the Act, as it involves ministerial discretion, and the following of procedures mandated by that Act. In regard to administration, he
stated,[23]

> I would find that the Canadian Human Rights Act applies to practices of govern-
> ment officials in performing duties pursuant to statutory provisions (which do not in
> themselves discriminate) which provide that such officials shall exercise discretion.

In regard to the discriminatory sections themselves, Chairman Cumming
noted that provision for income tax deductions constitutes an indirect tax
expenditure, and concluded that "these provisions constitute 'services' of
government, just as direct expenditures do."

Insurance Schemes and Other Benefits

In challenges under federal legislation, unemployment insurance has

---

21. *Canada (Attorney General) v. Cumming* (1980), 1 C.H.R.R. D/91 at D/94 (Fed. Ct.).
22. The board cited *R. v. Burnshine*, [1975] 1 S.C.R. 693; *Prata v. Canada (Minister of
    Manpower & Immigration)*, [1976] 1 S.C.R. 376; *Bliss v. Canada (Attorney General)*
    (1978), [1979] 1 S.C.R. 138, which stated that in order to successfully challenge legisla-
    tion under the Canadian *Charter of Rights*, the challenging party must prove that the leg-
    islation was not enacted to achieve a valid federal objective.
23. *Ante*, note 20 at D/214.

been held to be a service.[24] Worker's Compensation has not yet been considered in Ontario; the Prince Edward Island Court of Appeal recently found that such benefits were not "services ordinarily available to the public."[25]

A service "to assist workers to find suitable employment and employers to find suitable workers," established under subsection 139(1) of the *Unemployment Insurance Act*, has been held to be a service.[26]

Income maintenance by way of social assistance benefits has not uniformly been accepted as a service in other provinces, primarily because of the "available to the public" question.

A British Columbia Board of Inquiry confirmed that provision of welfare benefits is a service; interestingly, the provincial Human Rights Council and the respondent in that case agreed upon this point.[27] A Saskatchewan board decision to the effect that welfare was not customarily available to the public, confirmed by the Saskatchewan Queen's Bench, was overturned by the Court of Appeal.[28] It is suggested that the broader interpretation would obtain, in Ontario, both because of the elimination of the public/private distinction and the inclusion in the *Code* of a specific exemption from scrutiny as a "special program," any such programs "implemented by the Crown or an agency of the Crown."[29]

In Ontario, the Assistive Devices Program, established by the Ministry of Health for funding to aid in the purchase of devices that ameliorate the

24. *Morrell v. Canada (Employment & Immigration Commission)* (1985), 6 C.H.R.R. D/3021 (Cdn. Human Rights Trib.); *Corlis v. Canada (Employment & Immigration Commission)* (1987), 8 C.H.R.R. D/4146 (Cdn. Human Rights Trib.); *Druken v. Canada (Employment & Immigration Commission)* (1987), 8 C.H.R.R. D/4379 (Cdn. Human Rights Trib.), affirmed (1988), 9 C.H.R.R. D/5339 (C.A.).

25. *Jenkins v. Prince Edward Island (Workers Compensation Bd.)* (1986), 9 C.H.R.R. D/5145 (P.E.I. C.A.), involved a complaint of discrimination on the ground of marital status. In considering the definition of "services" the Prince Edward Island Court of Appeal found that Workers' Compensation benefits did not constitute a service. At D/5149 the Court said:

> I do not perceive the compensation scheme created under the Act, essentially a plan for no fault liability insurance, as being a service. It is neither administered, or funded, by government.

26. *Morisette v. Employment & Immigration Commission (Canada)* (1987), 8 C.H.R.R. D/4390 (Cdn. Human Rights Trib.).

27. *British Columbia Human Rights Coalition v. British Columbia (Ministry of Human Resources)* (1987), 8 C.H.R.R. D/4275 (B.C. Human Rights Council).

28. *Chambers v. Saskatchewan (Department of Social Services)* (1987), 8 C.H.R.R. D/4139 (Sask. Bd. of Inquiry), affirmed (1987), 8 C.H.R.R. D/4240, (Sask. Q.B.), reversed (1988), 9 C.H.R.R. D/5181 (Sask. C.A.).

29. R.S.O. 1990, c. H.19, s. 14(5).

effects of disabilities, was found to be a service.[30]

Licensing, Registration

There have been no Ontario cases in this area. Two Newfoundland cases found, respectively, that the issuance of hunting licenses and the registration of nursing assistants are services.[31]

Policing, Law Enforcement

There have been no Ontario cases on point, but is is established in Alberta and under the federal *Human Rights Act* that policing is a "service."[32] More recently, the Canadian Employment and Immigration Department was found to be performing a "service" in its efforts to identify illegal immigrants or permanent residents who commit crimes while living in Canada, pursuant to the *Immigration Act.*[33]

Education

Ontario cases have clearly favoured the inclusion of education within the term services, as have most other jurisdictions.[34] To date, primary schools and junior schools have been considered.[35]

Other Services

Other than the activities listed above, the following have been characterized as "services" or "services or facilities":

---

30. *Roberts v. Ontario (Ministry of Health)* (1989), 10 C.H.R.R. D/6353 (Ont. Bd. of Inquiry).
31. *Rogers v. Newfoundland (Department of Culture, Recreation and Youth)* (1988), 10 C.H.R.R. D/5794 (Nfld. Comm. of Inquiry); *LeDrew v. Council for Nursing Assistants (Nfld.)* (1989), 10 C.H.R.R. D/6259 (Nfld. Comm. of Inquiry).
32. *Gomez v. Edmonton (City)* (1982), 3 C.H.R.R. D/882 (Alta. Bd. of Inquiry); *Akena v. Edmonton (City)* (1982), 3 C.H.R.R. D/1096 (Alta. Bd. of Inquiry); *Hum v. Royal Canadian Mounted Police* (1986), 8 C.H.R.R. D/3748 (Cdn. Human Rights Inquiry).
33. *LeDeuff v. Canada (Employment & Immigration Commission)* (1986), 8 C.H.R.R. D/3690 (Cdn. Human Rights Trib.). (Confirmed on this point, but reversed in result (1987), 9 C.H.R.R. D/4479).
34. See *Bloedel v. University of Calgary* (1980), 1 C.H.R.R. D/25 (Alta. Bd. of Inquiry); *Hobson v. B.C. Institute of Technology* (1988), 9 C.H.R.R. D/4666 (B.C. Human Rights Council); *New Brunswick School District No. 15 v. New Brunswick (Human Rights Bd. of Inquiry)* (1989), 10 C.H.R.R. D/6426 (N.B. C.A.); *Calgary (Board of Education) v. Deyell* (1984), 8 C.H.R.R. D/3668 (Alta. Q.B.).
35. *Lanark, Leeds and Grenville Roman Catholic Separate School Board v. Ontario (Human Rights Commission)* (1987), 8 C.H.R.R. D/4235 (Ont. Div. Ct.) affirmed (1989), 10 C.H.R.R. D/6336 (C.A.); *Peel Board of Education v. Ontario (Human Rights Commission)*, (1990), 72 O.R. (2d) 593 (Civ. Ct.); *Sehdev v. Bayview Glen Junior School*, (1988), 9 C.H.R.R D/4881 (Ont. Bd. of Inquiry).

1. The provision of classified advertising space by a newspaper.[36]
2. Restaurants, bars, taverns.[37]
3. Service stations.[38]
4. Public utilities.[39]
5. Public transportation and school bus services.[40]
6. Insurance coverage.[41]
7. Branch banking.[42]
8. The provision of "pick your own vegetables" at a farm.[43]
9. The provision of foster care to children.[44]
10. Hall rental and catering by the Royal Canadian Legion.[45]
11. The operation of a milk marketing board.[46]

Facilities

The *Oxford English Dictionary* defines facilities as "opportunities, a favourable condition, for the easier performance of any action." The *Random House Dictionary* provides a more concrete definition: "something designed, built, installed, etc. to serve a specific function affording a convenience or service."

Without defining facilities, subsection 20(2) of the English *Race Relations Act*, 1976 includes the following examples:

c) facilities by way of banking or insurance or for grants, loans, credit of finance

d) facilities for education

e) facilities for entertainment, recreation or refreshment

f) facilities for transport or travel.

It should be noted that the range of these "facilities" in the English legisla-

---

36. *G.A.T.E.*, *ante*, note 14.
37. *Ibid.*
38. *Ibid.*
39. *Ibid.*
40. *Ibid.*, and see *Simpson & Lane School Bus Ltd. v. Majestic Tours Ltd.* (1986), 44 Alta. L.R. (2d) 265 (Q.B.); and *Bourque v. Westlock School Division No. 37 (Board of Trustees)*, (1986), 8 C.H.R.R. D/3746 (Alta. Q.B.).
41. *Insurance Corp. of British Columbia v. Heerspink* (1977), 79 D.L.R. (3d) 638 (B.C. S.C.) affirmed (1978), 91 D.L.R. (3d) 520 (B.C. C.A.).
42. *Philadelphia Savings Fund Society v. Robert Myers and the Banking Bd. of the Commonwealth of Pennsylvania*, 1979 A. 2d 209 (1972).
43. *Wan v. Greygo Gardens*, (1982), 3 C.H.R.R. D/812 (Ont. Bd. of Inquiry).
44. *Applin v. Race Relations Bd.*, [1974] 2 All E.R. 73 (H.L.).
45. *Singh v. Royal Canadian Legion, Jasper Place (Alberta), Branch No. 255*, (1990), 11 C.H.R.R. D/357 (Alta. Bd. of Inquiry).
46. While the Board in *Janssen v. Ontario (Milk Marketing Board)* (1991), 13 C.H.R.R. D/397, did not specifically deal with the issue, it is presumed that the activity of the Board was considered a service.

tion is limited by a statutory qualification that the facilities be such as might be provided "to the public or a section of the public."

Facilities and services are often linked without distinction in human rights case law. In other jurisprudence, the courts seem to have focused on structures and physical assets constructed to fulfill a particular function.

With or without the services element, facilities have been held to include:

1. Freight and passenger rail transport.[47]

2. Buildings and other structures necessary to load cattle.[48]

3. Dairy farm equipment and cattle.[49]

4. Books, maps, globes and charts.[50]

5. Lockers at a golf club.[51]

6. University athletic facilities, courses and special tutoring.[52]

7. Organized athletic competitions.[53]

8. The crew of a ship.[54]

9. Branch banking.[55]

---

47. *Little Rock and Ft. S. Railway Co. v. Oppenheimer*, 43 S.W. 150 (1897).

48. *St. Mary's & Western Ontario Ry. Co. v. West Zorra* (1910), 2 O.W.N. 455.

49. *Re Bellavista Farms Ltd.* (1951), 1 W.W.R. (N.S.) 600 (B.C. C.A.).

50. *Montana v. Cave*, 52 P. 200 (1898).

51. *Knoll Golf Club v. U.S.*, 1979 F. Supp. 377 (1959); and see *Jones v. Toronto* (1982), unreported (Ont. Bd. of Inquiry), in regard to other aspects of golf club "facilities." It is notable that no Ontario boards of inquiry have dealt with membership restrictions in clubs, although despite widespread instances of discriminatory rules and the clear jurisdiction afforded by the *Code*. A recent appeal of a decision by a Yukon board of inquiry illustrates judicial attitudes that bear a striking resemblance to those evidenced by the Ontario Divisional Court in the *Bannerman* case discussed above. In *Gould v. Yukon Order of Pioneers, Dawson Lodge No. 1* (1991), 14 C.H.R.R. D/176 the Supreme Court of the Yukon Territory found that despite a rule that barred women as members, the board has erred in finding that the respondent club had discriminated. In a judgment clearly heavily based on policy rather than statutory interpretation, the Court found that there was a conflict between the right to be free of sex discrimination and the right, also enshrined in the *Human Rights Act*, to freedom of association, and that the board has not appropriately resolved the conflict.

52. *Bloedel v. University of Calgary* (1980), 1 C.H.R.R. D/25 (Alta. Bd. of Inquiry); *Beattie v. Acadia University* (1976), 72 D.L.R. (3d) 718 (N.S. C.A.).

53. *Cummings v. Ontario Minor Hockey Assn.* (1977), 29 R.F.L. 259 (Ont. Bd. of Inquiry); *Bannerman v. Ontario Rural Softball Assn.* (1977), unreported (Ont. Bd. of Inquiry). *Mcleod v. Youth Bowling Council of Ontario* (1988), 9 C.H.R.R. D/5371 (Ont. Bd. of Inquiry), affirmed (1990), 14 C.H.R.R. D/120 (Ont. Div. Ct.).

54. *Montana v. Cave, ante*, note 50.

55. *Philadelphia Savings Fund Soc. v. Robert Myers and the Banking Bd. of the Commwealth of Pennsylvania, ante*, note 42.

10. Teachers and their services.[56]

11. Ultrasound diagnostic services.[57]

12. A hospital.[58]

As with services, other examples may be inferred from the wording of the exception sections in the *Code*.

For the same reasons as those noted above in the discussion of services, it is reasonable to expect that the interpretation of the term facilities under the present *Code* will be given a fair, large and liberal interpretation.

Exceptions Relevant to Services, Goods and Facilities

The statutory exceptions most likely to affect the right to freedom from discrimination in services, goods and facilities are found in the following provisions:

1. section 14, which provides for "special programs";

2. section 15, which provides an exemption in respect of preferential treatment for those aged sixty-five and over;

3. section 16(1), which provides an exemption for situations in which Canadian citizenship, as a requirement, qualification or consideration is imposed or authorized by law;

4. section 16(2), by which cultural, educational, trade union or athletic activities can be restricted to Canadian citizens and permanent residents;

5. section 16(3), which provides an exemption for requirement respecting Canadian citizehship or domicile with the intention to obtain citizenship, when adopted by an organization or enterprise for the holder of senior executive positions;

6. section 17(1), which provides an exception when the sole reason for the facts giving rise to a complaint by a handicapped person is that the person is incapable of performing or fulfilling the essential duties or requirements attending the exercise of the right because of handicap;

7. section 18, which allows a special interest organization primarily engaged in serving the interests of persons protected by the *Code* to restrict membership or participation to persons who are similarly identified;

8. section 19(1), which maintains those rights or privileges of separate

---

56. *Ibid.*

57. *Manitoba Clinic Holding Co. v. Manitoba (Health Services Commission)* (1985), 36 Man. R. (2d) 124 (Q.B.).

58. *Peters v. University Hospital* (1980), 2 C.H.R.R. D/358 (Sask. Bd. of Inquiry), reversed (1981), 2 C.H.R.R. D/524 (Sask. Q.B.), reversed (1983), 4 C.H.R.R. D/1464.

schools and their supporters that are provided under the *British North America Act* and the *Education Act*;

9. section 19(2), which provides that the *Code* does not affect "the application of the *Education Act* with respect to teachers";

10. section 20(1), which allows the restriction of services or facilities to "persons of the same sex on the ground of public decency";

11. section 20(2), which allows for the enforcement of a minimum drinking age of nineteen years;

12. section 20(3), which allows a "recreational club" to restrict or qualify "access to its services or facilities" or give "preferences with respect to membership dues and other fees because of age, sex, marital status or family status"; and

13. section 22, which allows discrimination on the basis of age, sex, marital status, family status or handicap (where the discrimination is reasonable and *bona fide*) in a contract of automobile, life, accident or sickness or disability insurance, or a non-employment group life insurance contract, or a life annuity.

The exceptions are discussed in detail in Chapter 6.

ACCOMMODATION

Section 2 provides that:

(1) Every person has a right to equal treatment with respect to the occupancy of occupation, without discrimination because of race, ancestry, place of origin, colour, ethnic origin, citizenship, creed, sex, sexual orientation, age, marital status, family status, handicap or the receipt of public assistance.

(2) Every person has a right to equal treatment with respect to the occupancy of accommodation, without discrimination because of race, ancestry, place of origin, colour, ethnic origin, citizenship, creed, sex, sexual orientation, age, marital status, family status, handicap or the receipt of public assistance.

Section 2 was amended in 1986 to include new grounds of discrimination. It is otherwise identical to the original provision in the 1981 *Code*. However, a further statutory provision affecting accommodation was added in 1986. Section 3a [now section 4] provides that:

(1) Every sixteen or seventeen year old person who has withdrawn from parental control has a right to equal treatment with respect to occupancy of and contracting for accommodation without discrimination because the person is less than eighteen years old.

(2) A contract for accommodation entered by a sixteen or seventeen year old person who has withdrawn from parental control is enforceable against that person as if the person were eighteen years old.

The provision was necessary because the *Code*'s definition of age limits protection against discrimination to those eighteen years of age or older, with an upper limit in the area of employment, where protection from discrimination does not extend past age sixty-five.

The *Oxford English Dictionary* defines accommodation as "anything which supplies a want, or affords aid or refreshment, or ministers to one's comfort" and, more specifically, as "room and suitable provision for the reception of people; entertainment; lodgings."

This term by itself involves a fairly wide range of situations; however, it is suggested that it is modified by the term occupancy, which imports in varying degrees the concepts of possession and exclusivity.[59] Generally, then, it would seem reasonable to remove from the ambit of section 2 those types of accommodation that also fit the description of services and facilities. Obviously, residential and commercial tenancies are properly within

---

59. Occupancy is defined in the *Oxford English Dictionary* as "the condition of being an occupant; the fact of occupying; the act of taking, or fact of holding, actual possession, esp. of land (*spec.* in *Law*, the taking possession of something not belonging to any one, as constituting a title to it); actual holding of or residence in a place" *Black's Law Dictionary*, 5th ed. (1979) sets out the following definitions: "Occupancy: Taking possession of property and use of same; said *e.g.* of a tenant's use of leased premises. Period during which person owns, rents, or otherwise occupies real property or premises." "Occupant: Person in possession. Person having possessory rights, who can control what goes on on premises. One who has actual use, possession or control of a thing." Case law definitions of "occupancy" are usually concerned with which shade of meaning, of the many accruing to the term, fits the overall purpose of the statute or other instrument being construed. See: *Edinburgh Int. House v. Edinburgh Assessor*, 1958 S.L.T. 60; *Winicofsky v. Army and Navy Gen. Assur. Assn.* (1919), 88 L.J.K.B. 1111; *Lambert v. Wawanesa Mutual Fire Insurance Co.*, [1945] 1 D.L.R. 694 (C.A.); *R. v. Tao*, [1976] 3 All E.R. 65 (C.A.); *R. v. Dietsch* (1928), 49 C.C.C. 220 (Ont. Co. Ct.); *Toronto (City) v. University of Toronto*, [1946] O.R. 215 (C.A.); *Wheat v. Lacon (E.) & Co.*, [1966] 1 All E.R. 582 (H.L.); *Newcastle City Council v. Royal Newcastle Hospital*, [1959] 1 All E.R. 734 (P.C.); *Paterson v. Gas Light & Coke Co.*, [1896] 2 Ch. 476 (C.A.); *Woodcock v. South West Electric Bd.*, [1975] 2 All E.R. 545.

On more than one occasion, judges have commented on the elasticity of the term: *Paterson v. Gas Light & Coke Co.*, [1896] 2 Ch. 476 (C.A.), *per* Lindley L.J. at 482-3: "The term 'occupier' is ambiguous. In one sense a caretaker is an occupier, but in another sense his occupation is that of some other person." *R. v. Hung* (1946), 85 C.C.C. 308 (Ont. C.A.), *per* Robertson C.J.O. at 313: "The words 'occupy' and 'occupant' have a variety of shades of meaning. No doubt, we commonly speak of the 'occupants' of a dwelling-house, meaning thereby all persons who, at the time, live there. We use the word in even a wider sense when we speak of the 'occupants' of premises, meaning thereby all the persons who happen to be within them at the particular time. Primarily, however, 'to occupy' means 'to take possession', and such wider meanings, while no doubt now well recognised by usage, and proper enough in the right context, are not the only meanings, according even to present common use." *R. v. Wilson*, [1957] O.W.N. 19, *per* Aylen J. at 21 (H.C.): "The word 'occupy', like many English words, has various meanings, depending on how it is used. . . . In one context, therefore, the word 'occupy' may suggest some measure of control, but when it is used in relation to the seat of a motor car, its proper meaning, in my view, is simply 'to fill the dimensions of' the seat; similarly, a person may occupy a pew in a church or a seat in a theatre. So used, the word 'occupy' certainly does not suggest any measure of control."

the ambit of section 2,[60] while the use of a bus-stop shelter or washrooms at a service station, for example, are more properly dealt with under section 1.

Types of use that belong in the middle ground between a ten-minute stay in a bus-stop shelter and the leasing of an apartment are somewhat more difficult to assign with confidence. The issue will inevitably come up, either at the behest of a public assistance recipient who has been discriminated against by, for example, a hotel,[61] or by someone who wishes to invoke protection against harassment, which protection is provided by section 2(2) and is missing from section 1, in other than a residential or commercial tenancy.

There is reason to expect that short-term occupancy accommodation will be included under section 2(1), but that section 2(2) may not extend to short-term occupancy.

In support of the first-noted proposition, the remarks of Mr. Justice Martland in *Gay Alliance Toward Equality v. Vancouver Sun* can be noted: "Accommodation refers to such matters as accommodation in hotels, inns and motels,"[62] Furthermore, there have been several board of inquiry decisions which included hotels, etc., among the public accommodation in which discrimination is forbidden. One of the earliest human rights board decisions in Ontario, *Davis v. Pleasant View Camp*,[63] involved denial of accommodation at rental cottages because the complainants were black. *Organ v. Fletcher*[64], also an Ontario decision, involved cottages. *Chelsea v. Sportsman's Motels*,[65] was decided under the same public accommodation section of the British Columbia *Human Rights Code* that was interpreted by the Supreme Court of Canada in the *G.A.T.E.* case. Thus it seems likely that

---

60. This inference is supported by the inclusion of s. 21 in the *Code*. There are considerable number of cases under s. 3 of the previous *Code*. Residential tenancy cases include: *Gordon v. Papadropoulos* (1968), unreported (Ont. Bd. of Inquiry); *Mitchell v. O'Brien* (1968) unreported (Ont. Bd. of Inquiry); *Walls v. Lougheed* (1968), unreported (Ont. Bd. of Inquiry); *McKenzie v. Gross* (1970), unreported (Ont. Bd. of Inquiry); *Nawagesic v. Crupi* (1978), unreported (Ont. Bd. of Inquiry); *Copenace v. West* (1979), unreported (Ont. Bd. of Inquiry); *Fong v. Taylor* (1982), 3 C.H.R.R. D/636 (Ont. Bd. of Inquiry).

There may have been only two decisions in respect of a commercial tenancy. See: *Blake v. Loconte* (1980), 1 C.H.R.R. D/74 (Ont. Bd. of Inquiry); and *Tabar v. Scott* (1982), 3 C.H.R.R. D/1073 (Ont. Bd. of Inquiry).

61. "Receipt of public assistance" is a "ground" only under s. 2.

62. (1979), 97 D.L.R. (3d) 577 at 590 (S.C.C.). Mr. Jurtice Martland did not include residential and commercial tenancies in the above definition. However, this limitation should have no effect on the interpretation of s. 2, as the B.C. *Human Rights Code* section interpreted in *G.A.T.E.* spoke only of accommodation "customarily available to the public." Commercial and residential tenancies are discussed in another section of the B.C. *Code*.

63. (1962), unreported (Ont. Bd. of Inquiry).

64. (1966), unreported (Ont. Bd. of Inquiry).

65. (1981), 2 C.H.R.R. D/424 (B.C. Bd. of Inquiry). See also *Doucette v. Aberdeen Motel* (1980), 1 C.H.R.R. D/13 (N.S. Bd. of Inquiry).

the protection of section 2(1) applies to hotels, vacation cottages, and any other situation in which the use is such that it can be reasonably described as occupancy.

In section 2(2), which deals with harassment, the term landlord is used. This raises the question of whether the legislature intended to narrow the meaning of accommodation, for the purpose of protection from harassment, to include only residential and commercial tenancies. Whether this effect will be given to the subsection will probably depend on whether tribunals favour the definition given by, for example, the *Oxford English Dictionary*, or the narrower usage common in Ontario statutes such as the *Landlord and Tenant Act*. The *Oxford English Dictionary* defines landlord as:

> Originally, a lord or owner of land; in recorded use applied on *spec.* to the person who lets land to a tenant . . . A person of whom another person holds any tenement, whether a piece of land, a building or part of a building . . . In extended sense: The person in whose house one lodges or boards for payment; one's "host." b. The master of an inn, an innkeeper.

By contrast, landlord is not used in Ontario statutes to denote the owner of a hotel, etc. The operator or manager of such an establishment is generally referred to as an innkeeper or hotelkeeper.[66]

It may be argued that the legislature intended to restrict protection from harassment to those situations when the occupant would find it extremely difficult or distressing to quit the premises. However, it is suggested, given that the legislation is remedial, that it would not be unreasonable to interpret section 2(2) as providing protection from harassment that does not depend on length of stay or degree of exclusivity of possession.

Purchase and Sale of Real Estate

Given the inclusion of the terms occupancy (rather than ownership) and landlord in section 2, it is unlikely that the section will be applied to the problem of discrimination in the purchase and sale of real estate. It is suggested that this matter is properly dealt with under section 3 of the *Code*, which concerns contracts.

Exceptions Relevant to Accommodation

The statutory exceptions that are most likely to affect the right to freedom from discrimination[67] in accommodation are found in the following sections:

---

66. See, for example, the *Innkeepers Act*, R.S.O. 1990, c. I.7, and the *Hotel Fire Safety Act*, R.S.O. 1990, c. H.16.
67. It is highly unlikely that the exceptions in the *Code* will be held to apply in respect of harassment. See Chapter 1 for discussion on this point.

1. section 14, which provides for "special programs";

2. section 15, which provides an exemption in respect of preferential treatment for those aged sixty-five and over;

3. section 16(1), which provides an exemption for situations in which Canadian citizenship, as a requirement, qualification or consideratin is imposed or authorized by law;

4. section 16(2), by which cultural, educational, trade union or athletic activities can be restricted to Canadian citizens and permanent residents;

5. section 16(3), which provides an exemption for requirement respecting Canadian citizenship or domicile with the intention to obtain citizenship, when adopted by an organization or enterprise for the holder of senior executive positions;

6. section 17(1), which provides an exception where the sole reason for the facts giving rise to a complaint by a handicapped person is that the person is incapable of performing or fulfilling the essential duties or requirements attending the exercise of the right because of handicap;

7. section 18, which allows a religious, philanthropic, educational, fraternal or social institution or organization that is primarily engaged in serving the interests of persons protected by the Code to restrict membership or participation to persons who are similarly identified;

8. section 21(1), which allows discrimination on all grounds cited in section 2 in residential accommodation where

   (a) the owner or the owner's family resides in the accommodation, and

   (b) the occupant(s) are required to share a bathroom or kitchen with the owner or the owner's family; and

9. section 21(2), which allows discrimination on the ground of sex, "where the occupancy of all the residential accommodation in the building, other than the accommodation, if any, of the owner or family of the owner, is restricted to persons who are of the same sex".

These exceptions are discussed in Chapter 6.

CONTRACTS

Section 3 provides as follows:

> Every person having legal capacity has a right to contract on equal terms without discrimination because of race, ancestry, place of origin, colour, ethnic origin, citizenship, creed, sex, sexual orientation, age, marital status, family status or handicap.

The section was amended in 1986 to add new grounds of discrimination, but is otherwise unchanged from the version in the 1981 *Code*. In addition, section 3a [now section 4] was added in 1986. The section specifically affects contracts for accommodation by persons aged sixteen or seventeen who have withdrawn from parental control.

To date only one published Ontario board decision has discussed the definition of "contract". *Grant v. Wilcock*[68] involved the sale of a cottage. The board found that the respondent breached the *Code* when he declined to sell because of the race of the would-be buyer.

The board in *Grant* agreed that the right to contract on equal terms may be infringed both in the making of an offer and in the acceptance or rejection of an offer, if any of the steps in the contract process are influenced by discrimination on a prohibited ground. In addition, the board extended the ambit of the provision

> . . . to include the invitation to treat or deal stage of the contractual process, which in many, if not most instances, is begun by an advertisement in a public place or in the news media. Not to extend the reach of s. 3 to the invitation to treat stage, would render the section ineffective in many instances. The ugly face of discrimination often makes a first appearance, when an advertisement is answered by a person who will be the target of discrimination prohibited by s. 3.[69]

Presumably, all types of contracts are affected by section 3; there seems to be no reason why contracts concerned with the subject matter of sections 1, 2, 5 and 6 should be excluded. Section 3 appears to extend the protection of the Code to mercantile and other business contracts, franchises, partnership agreements, loans, grants and guarantees from lending institutions under provincial jurisdiction, insurance contracts[70] and consumer transactions,[71] as well as to the purchase and sale of real estate.

Exceptions Relevant to Contracts

The statutory exceptions most likely to affect the right to freedom from discrimination in contracts are found in the following provisions:

1. section 14, which provides for "special programs";

2. section 15, which provides an exemption in respect of preferential treatment for those aged sixty-five and over;

---

68. (1991), 13 C.H.R.R. D/22.
69. *Supra* at D/125.
70. See *Bates v. Zurich Insurance Co. of Canada* (1985), 6 C.H.R.R. D/2948 (Ont. Bd. of Inquiry), reversed (1987) 58 O.R. (2d) 325 (Div. Ct.). The major case dealing with discrimination in insurance (considered as a "service") is *Heerspink v. Insurance Corp. of British Columbia*, [1982] 2 S.C.R. 145. Exceptions in regard to insurance are discussed in Chapter 6.
71. See, for example, *Quinn v. Williams Furniture Ltd.*, [1981] I.C.R. 328 (C.A.) in which the court of appeal found sex discrimination where a store had a policy of requiring only women purchasers to have their spouses guarantee hire-purchase contracts.

3. section 16(1), which provides an exemption for situations in which Canadian citizenship as a requirement, qualification or consideration is imposed or authorized by law;

4. section 16(2), by which cultural, educational, trade union or athletic activities can be restricted to Canadian citizens and permanent residents;

5. section 16(3), which provides an exemption for requirement respecting Canadian citizenship or domicile with the intention to obtain citizenship, when adopted by an organization or enterprise for the holder of senior executive positions;

6. section 17(1), which provides an exception when the sole reason for the facts giving rise to a complaint by a handicapped person is that the person is incapable of performing or fulfilling the essential duties or requirements attending the exercise of the right because of handicap;

7. section 25(2) which provides that certain employment benefit plans may discriminate on the ground of age, sex, marital status where such plans comply with the *Employment Standards Act* and Regulations. However, employment may not be denied because of failure to qualify in such a plan, nor made conditional on qualifying for inclusion.

8. section 25(3) which provides that certain employment benefit plans may discriminate on the ground of handicap where the distinction is reasonable and *bona fide*. Employment may not be made conditional on qualification in such plans, and an excluded employee must be compensated (sections 25(1) and 25(4)).

The exceptions are discussed in detail in Chapter 6.

EMPLOYMENT

Section 5 provides:

> (1) Every person has a right to equal treatment with respect to employment without discrimination because of race, ancestry, place of origin, colour, ethnic origin, citizenship, creed, sex, marital status, family status or handicap.
>
> (2) Every person who is an employee has a right to freedom from harassment in the workplace by the employer or agent of the employer or by another employee because of race, ancestry, place of origin, colour, ethnic origin, citizenship, creed, age, record of offences, marital status, family status or handicap.

Section 5 was amended in 1986 to include new ground of discrimination. It is otherwise identical to the original provision [section 4] in the 1981 *Code*.

The legislation preceding the 1981 *Code* dealt with all matters specifically relating to employment in one section. Section 4 of the 1980 *Code* covered pre-employment practices,[72] practices during employment[73] and dismissal.[74] The section also dealt with the practices of employment agencies.[75]

While the employment section of the previous *Code* was broad in scope, the wording of the section raised potential difficulties. For example, an employer might discriminate not by refusing employment, but by setting out discriminatory terms and conditions as part of a job offer. In taking this action, the employer was not, strictly speaking, breaching section 4(1)(*a*) of the previous *Code*, which provided that "No person shall . . . refuse to refer or to recruit . . . for employment" because of a prohibited ground of discrimination. Nor could the employer precisely be said to have infringed section 4(1)(*g*), which forbade the employer to "discriminate against any employee with regard to any term or condition of employment," since the applicant in the situation was not yet an employee. To ask a board to make a finding in this situation would indeed have demanded a "fair, large and liberal" interpretation, perhaps one which a board would properly decline to make when deciding a question of jurisdiction.

The present *Code* removes these difficulties. The wording of section 5(1) is very general; it is suggested that matters "with respect to employment" could encompass any employment-related matter, from recruitment to pensions.

In some circumstances, a question may arise as to whether the matter that the complaint is "in respect of" can properly be called employment. It is suggested that in determining this question, board of inquiry will properly rely on dictionary definitions of "employment" and, to some extent, on the law of master and servant. A liberal approach to the subject was taken in *Metropolitan Toronto Board of Commissioners of Police v. Ontario*

---

72. For example, advertising, other forms of recruitment or referral application forms, apprenticeship. Ontario cases dealing with pre-employment practices include: *Shack v. London Drive-Ur-Self* (1974), unreported (Ont. Bd. of Inquiry); *Segrave v. Zellers* (1975), unreported (Ont. Bd. of Inquiry); *Rajput v. Algoma University* (1976), unreported (Ont. Bd. of Inquiry); *Morgan v. Toronto General Hospital* (1977), unreported (Ont. Bd. of Inquiry); *Muccilli v. Ed's Warehouse Restaurant* (1979), unreported (Ont. Bd. of Inquiry).

73. For example, probation, classification, lines of progression and seniority, terms and conditions of employment. See *Kennedy v. Mohawk College* (1973), unreported (Ont. Bd. of Inquiry); *Simms v. Ford Motor Co.* (1970), unreported (Ont. Bd. of Inquiry); *Offierski, Re v. Sklavos Printing* (1981), 2 C.H.R.R. D/457 (Ont. Bd. of Inquiry).

74. See, for example, *Nembhard v. Caneurop Manufacturing Ltd.* (1976), unreported (Ont. Bd. of Inquiry); *Hadley v. Mississauga* (1976), unreported (Ont. Bd. of Inquiry); *Blatt v. Catholic Children's Aid Society of Metropolitan Toronto (Municipality)* (1980), 1 C.H.R.R. D/72 (Ont. Bd. of Inquiry); *Hendry v. Ontario (Liquor Control Bd.)* (1980), 1 C.H.R.R. D/160 (Ont. Bd. of Inquiry); *Cousens v. Nurses' Assn. (Canada)* (1981), 2 C.H.R.R. D/365 (Ont. Bd. of Inquiry).

75. See *Britnell v. Brent Personnel Placement Services* (1968), unreported (Ont. Bd. of Inquiry).

Human Rights Commission.[76] The Ontario Divisional Court held that, since the *Code* was remedial legislation, the applicant police commission could properly be named as respondent to a complaint although it did not have the usual master-servant relationship with a probationary constable. A similar approach was taken in *Nelson v. Gubbins*[77] in which the Supreme Court of British Columbia upheld a board's view that the manager of a townhouse complex was the "servant" of the rental agent, rather than of the owner of the complex, who paid the manager's wages. This analysis was accepted by the British Columbia Court of Appeal.[78]

A recent board of inquiry found that an organization which has social elements was an employer. The Canadian Corps of Commissionaires obtained clients and assigned its members as security personnel for these clients. The board considered this arrangement to constitute employment for the purposes of the *Code.*[79]

In the most recent Ontario Board decision to deal with the definition of "employment," a board found that a member of the supervisory committee of a credit union could be considered neither the employer nor an employee of the credit union. In *Szabo v. Atlas Employees Welland Credit Union,*[80] the issue was whether the credit union, in refusing to hire the son of one of the members of the supervisory committee, could rely on subsection 24(3) of the *Code*.

Labour arbitration cases have, of course, defined employee in the context of decisions about which workers are properly included in a bargaining unit. However, these decisions were made in the light of a requirement to distinguish people in the workplace according to the extent to which they are necessarily dependent on the employer. As such, they reflect restrictions that are unnecessary for the purposes of section 5(1).[81] By contrast, there is a possibility that such restrictions may be considered appropriate to section 5(2).[82]

The *Oxford English Dictionary*, defines employment as "a person's regular occupation; a trade or profession," and employ as "to use the services of (a person) in a professional capacity, or in the transaction of some special business; to have or maintain (persons) in one's service." The

---

76. (1979), 27 O.R. (2d) 48 (Div. Ct.). Also see *Brown v. Waterloo (Region) Commrs. of Police* (1986), 13 C.C.E.L. 45 (Ont. Bd. of Inquiry) — Interim decision.
77. (1979), 106 D.L.R. (3d) 486 (B.C. S.C.), affirmed (1981), 122 D.L.R. (3d) 340 (B.C. C.A.).
78. *Ibid.*
79. *Barnard v. Canadian Corps of Commissionaires* (1985), 6 C.H.R.R. D/2659 (Ont. Bd. of Inquiry).
80. (1988), 9 C.H.R.R. D/4735 (Ont. Bd. of Inquiry).
81. See, generally, Labour Relations Casebook Group, *Labour Relations Law Casebook*, 3d. ed. (1979); Brown and Beatty, *Canadian Labour Arbitration*, (1977).
82. This is discussed below.

Random House Dictionary defines employment as "an occupation by which a person earns a living; business." A similar broad definition is appropriate for the purpose of section 5(1).

As long as a matter is employment-related in this sense, it would seem that the complainant need not be an employee, in the sense used in labour relations law; an independent contractor, for example, might complain under section 5.[83] Nor need the respondent be an employer; a trade union or other vocational association that discriminates in a way that affects access to or continuance of employment, or terms and conditions, can be a respondent to a section 5 complaint.[84]

In regard to unions, it is possible that a union's liability for discriminatory action encompasses responsibility for a discriminatory clause in a collection agreement. In *Mossop v. Canada (Secretary of State)*[85] a bereavement leave policy was specifically defined to apply to only couples of opposite sexes. A homosexual couple successfully challenged the provision on the ground of family status. Although the complainant's union had supported the complainant in grieving his exclusion, the tribunal found the union liable, as well as the employee.

---

83. Contractors of various descriptions have been considered for "employment" protection in other jurisdictions. See *Cormier v. Alberta (Human Rights Commission)* (1984), 5 C.H.R.R. D.2411 (Alta. Q.B.); *Strenja v. Connox Taxi Ltd.* (1981), 2 C.H.R.R. D/585 (B.C. Bd. of Inquiry); *Sharma v. Yellow Cab Co.* (1983), 4 C.H.R.R. D/1432 (B.C. Bd. of Inquiry); and *Pannu v. Prestige Cab Ltd.* (1986), 8 C.H.R.R. D/3911 (Alta. C.A.). In *Chauban v. Minister of Health (Minister of Health, Long Term Care Program)* (1985), 6 C.H.R.R. D/2786 (B.C. Human Rights Council), the long term care program of the Senior Frayer Health District was not found to employ the operator of a personal care home. In *Bugis v. University Hospitals* (1989), 65 Alta. L.R. (2d) 274 (Q.B.), affirmed (1990), 74 Alta. L.R. (2d) 60 (C.A.) the Alberta Court of Queen's Bench ruled that the contractual relationship between a doctor and a hospital was not one of employment. Depending on the circumstances, complainants in a contractual relationship might properly file a complaint under section 3 of the *Code*.

84. There are two ways in which a vocational association might discriminate "with respect to employment." The first is by denying membership, where membership is a prerequisite to employment or to an opportunity for employment. In this case, of course, the vocational association would also be in breach of s. 6. The other areas where discrimination by a vocational association could affect employment is where the association denies a licence, certificate or accreditation that would allow or assist the complainant to obtain employment. The latter situation is discussed in *British Judo Assn. v. Petty*, [1981] I.C.R. 660 (Employment App. Trib.).

Unions were named as respondents in two recent cases: *Gohm v. Domtar and Office and Professional Employees International Union* (1988), Doc. No. 331 (Ont. Bd. of Inquiry) and *Roosma v. Ford Motor Co. of Canada* (1988), 10 C.H.R.R. D/5766 (Ont. Bd. of Inquiry).

85. (1989), 10 C.H.R.R. D/6064 (Cdn. Human Rights Trib.). Reversed for other reasons: 12 C.H.R.R. D/355.

It should be noted that the legislation construed by the Tribunal[86] specifically prohibited both union and employer from entering into a discriminatory collective agreement, so that the union's responsibility was clear, by statute. However, it is arguable that such a specific provision is not needed, given the wording of the Ontario *Human Rights Code*, and it is possible that, rather than attempting to "go behind" a collective agreement in an attempt to judge which party was more responsible for a particular clause, a board would impose joint liability.

It is clear that employers and employees cannot "contract out of" the *Human Rights Code*. In ruling on a case involving mandatory retirement, the Supreme Court of Canada, through Mr. Justice McIntyre, commented:

> Although the *Code* contains no explicit restriction on such contracting out, it is nevertheless a public statute and it constitutes public policy in Ontario as appears from a reading of the statute itself and as declared in the preamble. It is clear from the authorities, both in Canada and in England, that parties are not competent to contract themselves out of the provisions of such enactments and that contracts having such effect are void, as contrary to public policy.[87]

Where a complaint is made under section 5(2), which deals with harassment, it might be argued that the legislature intended to narrow the wide scope of section 5(1). The use of the terms "employee" and "in the workplace" may have been intended to import the restrictive meaning with which the term employee has been invested by labour relations law. The rationale for this narrowing would be that independent contractors are less dependent on the particular employer and workplace for economic survival than are employees and, therefore, need less protection. However, as noted in regard to section 2(2), human rights tribunals are unlikely to read remedial legislation restrictively; it is reasonable to assume that public policy as expressed in the *Code* would favour prohibiting harassment in any employment situation.

Exceptions Relevant to Employment

The statutory exceptions most likely to affect the right to freedom from discrimination[88] in employment are found in the following provisions:

1. section 14, which provides for "special programs";

2. section 15, which provides an exemption in respect of preferential treatment for those aged sixty-five and over;

3. section 16(1), which provides an exemption for situations in which

---

86. *Canadian Human Rights Act*, R.S.C. 1985, c. H-6, s. 10(b).

87. *Etobicoke v. Ontario Human Rights Commission* (1982), 132 D.L.R. (3d) 14 at 22 (S.C.C.).

88. It is unlikely that the exceptions in the *Code* will be held to apply in respect of the right to be free of harassment. See discussion of this point in Chapter 1.

Canadian citizenship, as a requirement, qualification or consideration is imposed or authorized by law;

4. section 16(2), by which cultural, educational, trade union or athletic activities can be restricted to Canadian citizens and permanent residents;

5. section 16(3), which provides an exemption for requirement respecting Canadian citizenship or domicile with the intention to obtain citizenship, when adopted by an organization or enterprise for the holder of senior executive positions;

6. section 17(1), which provides an exception when the sole reason for the facts giving rise to a complaint by a handicapped person is that the person is incapable of performing or fulfilling the essential duties or requirements attending the exercise of the right because of handicap;

7. section 19(1), which maintains those rights or privileges of separate schools and their supporters that are provided under the *British North America Act* and the *Education Act*;

8. section 19(2), which provides that the *Code* does not affect "the application of the *Education Act* with respect to teachers";

9. section 23(3), which allows questions to be asked concerning a prohibited ground of discrimination at an employment interview, where discrimination on that ground is otherwise permitted by the *Code*.

10. section 24(1)(a), which provides that,

    a religious, philanthropic, educational, fraternal or social institution or organization that is primarily engaged in serving the interests of persons identified by their race, ancestry, place of origin, colour, ethnic origin, creed, sex, age, marital status or handicap employs only, or gives preference in employment to, persons similarly identified if the qualification is a reasonable and *bona fide* qualification because of the nature of the employment.

11. section 24(1)(b) which allows discrimination that would otherwise breach section 5 where:

    the discrimination in employment is for reasons of age, sex, record of offences or marital status if the age, sex, record of offences or marital status of the applicant is a reasonable and *bona fide* qualification because of the nature of the employment;

12. section 24(1)(c), which provides that section 5 is not breached where

    an individual person refuses to employ anothe for reasons of any prohibited ground of discrimination in section 5, where the primary duty of the employment is attending to the medical or personal needs of the person or of an ill child or an aged, infirm or ill spouse or other relative of the person;

13. section 24(1)(d), which provides that an employer may grant or withhold employment or advancement in employment to a person who is the spouse, child or parent of the employer of an employee;

14. section 25(2) which provides that certain employment benefit plans may discriminate on the ground of age, sex, marital status or family status, where such plans comply with the *Employment Standards Act* and Regulations. However, employment may not be denied because of failure to qualify in such a plan, nor made conditional on qualifying for inclusion;

15. section 25(3) which provides that certain employment benefit plans may discriminate on the ground of handicap where the distinction is reasonable and *bona fide*. Employment may not be made conditional on qualification in such plans, and an excluded employee must be compensated (sections 25(1) and 25(4)).

The exceptions are discussed in detail in Chapter 6.

OTHER PROVISIONS AFFECTING EMPLOYMENT

In addition to the general right set out by section 5, there are specific statutory duties and prohibitions set out in Part II. Section 23 affects employment advertising, applications for employment, personal employment interviews and employment agencies. Section 25 affects the duties of employers with respect to employment benefit plans. Section 23 and 25 are discussed in Chapter 5. Section 26 is triggered where there is employment discrimination in government-assisted projects, or employment under a government contract.

Discrimination in Employment under Government Contracts and in Government-Financed Projects: Section 26

Section 26(1) provides:

It shall be deemed to be a condition of every contract entered into by or on behalf of the Crown or any agency thereof and of every subcontract entered into in the performance thereof that no right under section 5 will be infringed in the course of performing the contract.

Section 26(2) similarly make absence of discrimination or harassment in employment a deemed condition of every "grant, contribution, loan or guarantee made by or on behalf of the Crown" or a Crown agency.

In respect of both government contracts and government-financed projects, section 26(3) provides that:

Where an infringement of a right under section 5 is found by a board of inquiry upon a complaint and constitutes a breach of a condition under this section, the breach of condition is sufficient grounds for cancellation of the contract, grant, contribution, loan or guarantee and refusal to enter into any further contract with or make any further grant, contribution, loan or guarantee to the same person.

Enforcement of the Section 26 Right

The actual implementation of its rights under section 26(3) by a government ministry or agency is reasonably simple: the agency may cancel the contract, grant, loan, etc., and refuse further dealings. There are, of course, preliminary determinations to be made as to whether such an action is warranted by the circumstances, since the ministry or agency would be liable for breach of contract if its action was unwarranted.

In respect of contracts[89] entered into after proclamation of the *Code*, the only issues that arise in regard to the cancellation will be whether a board has found[90] a breach of section 5 "in the course of performing" the contract or subcontract[91] or "in the course of carrying out the purposes for which the grant, contribution, loan or guarantee was made."[92] In respect of contracts made prior to the enactment of the *Code*, the agency will first need to consider whether section 26 applies to such contracts at all.[93]

Section 26 and Contract Compliance

In providing a potential for the loss of government contract, grant, loan, etc., where the recipient breaches section 5, section 26 constitutes the first effective step toward "contract compliance" with human rights legislation in Canada.[94] It also represents a commitment by the government of Ontario to the effective discouragement of employment discrimination.

---

89. For the purpose of convenience, this term will be used in reference to contracts, subcontracts, grants, contributions, loans or guarantees affected by s. 26.

90. Obviously, a finding by a board is not finally determinative as to whether the *Code* was breached, in all circumstances. The government agency would therefore be well advised to refrain from cancelling a contract until the other party has exhausted its rights of appeal on the issue of liability under s. 5. While s. 26(3) speaks only of the finding of a "board of inquiry," the *Statutory Powers Procedure Act*, R.S.O. 1990, c. S.22, s. 25, provides that an appeal operates as a stay of the order of a board except where the appellate tribunal otherwise orders.

91. See s. 26(1).

92. See s. 26(2).

93. In the unlikely event that an issue should arise concerning a contract that was executed prior to 15 June, 1982, please refer to a review of the issue of retrospective application of the *Code* in the first edition of this book.

94. Section 19 of the *Canadian Human Rights Act*, S.C. 1976-77, c. 33 enables the federal government to make compliance with human rights legislation a consideration of federal contracts:

"The Governor in Council may make regulations respecting the terms and conditions to be included in or applicable to any contract, licence or grant made or granted by Her Majesty in right of Canada providing for

(a) the prohibition of discriminatory practices described in sections 5 to 13; and

(b) the resolution, by the procedure set out in Part III, of complaints of discriminatory practices contrary to such terms and conditions."

While no regulations have been passed under s. 19, a new federal contract or "Program" came into effect in September, 1986. The program is administered by the Canadian Employment and Immigration Commission.

The legislative confirmation of this commitment invites speculation as to how far the Ontario government might go in implementing anti-discrimination policy.

The progress of "contract compliance" in the United States is perhaps a useful comparison. The American evolution of contract compliance is succinctly traced by Professor Tarnopolsky in *Discrimination and The Law*:[95]

> The evolution of "contract compliance" to its present scope and application can be seen as having passed through four phases. The first Executive Order dealing with racial discrimination, was issued by President Roosevelt in 1941 as Executive Order No. 8802. At this initial state, the order merely required that all defence contracts with federal agencies would have to include as a condition of the contract, a stipulation that the contractors not discriminate in employment because of race, creed, colour, or national origin.
>
> The next major stage came in 1953, when President Eisenhower issued Executive Order No. 10,479, which created a Government Contract Committee to enforce the order. The G.C.C. was responsible for supervising compliance and was empowered to receive complaints and to conduct educational programs. However, the agency's power was merely that of attempting voluntary conciliation toward persuading the employer to eliminate discrimination, and the making of recommendations.
>
> The third phase came in 1961, when President Kennedy issued Executive Order No. 10,925. This Order was the first one to go beyond requiring merely the undertaking *not* to discriminate: it mandated a promise that the contractor would take "affirmative action":
>
> > The contractor will take *affirmative action* to ensure that applicants are employed, and that employees are treated during their employment, without regard to their race, creed, colour, or national origin. Such action shall include, but shall not be limited to the following: employment, upgrading, demotion or transfer; recruitment or recruitment advertising; layoff or termination; rates of pay or other compensation; and selection for training, including apprenticeship.
>
> In addition, supervision was placed in the hands of the President's Committee on Equal Employment Opportunities.
>
> Finally, after the enactment of the *Civil Rights Act* of 1964 President Johnson promulgated Executive Order No. 11246 in 1965. This is the order that is currently in force (although subsequent Executive Orders have amplified its scope and application). Executive Order No. 11246 dissolved the Committee on Equal Employment Opportunities, and place the program under the Secretary of Labor who, to carry out the terms of the order, established the Office of Federal Contract Compliance (O.F.C.C.). What is more important, however, is that the order expanded the coverage to require inclusion of the equal opportunity clause not just in the employment concerned with the particular contract, but also, since the clause was to apply "during the performance of [the] contract", to all of the employer's operations. The order also required the inclusion of the clause in federally-assisted projects. To grasp the full scope of this crucial equal opportunity clause, it is reproduced here in full:
>
> > During the performance of this contract, the contractor agrees as follows:
> >
> > > (1) The contractor will not discriminate against any employee or applicant for em-

---

95. (1982), pp. 122-6.

ployment because of race, color, religion, sex, or national origin. The contractor will take affirmative action to ensure that applicants are employed, and that employees are treated during employment, without regard to their race, color, religion, sex or national origin. Such action shall include, but not be limited to the following: employment, upgrading, demotion, or transfer; recruitment or recruitment advertising; layoff or termination; rates of pay or other forms of compensation; and selection for training, including apprenticeship. The contractor agrees to post in conspicuous places, available to employees and applicants for employment, notices to be provided by the contracting officer setting for the the provisions of this nondiscrimination clause.

(2) The contractor will, in all solicitations or advertisements for employees placed by or on behalf of the contractor, state that all qualified applicants will receive consideration for employment without regard to race, color, religion, sex or national origin.

(3) The contractor will send to each labor union or representative of workers with which he has a collective bargaining agreement or other contract or understanding, a notice, to be provided by the agency contracting officer, advising the labor union or workers' representative of the contractor's commitments under Section 202 of Executive Order No. 11246 of September 24, 1965, and shall post copies of the notice in conspicuous places available to employees and applicants for employment.

(4) The contractor will comply with all provisions of Executive Order No. 11246 of Sept. 24, 1965, and of the rules, regulations, and relevant orders of the Secretary of Labor.

(5) The contractor will furnish all information and reports required by Executive Order No. 11246 of September 24, 1965, and by the rules, regulations, and orders of the Secretary of Labor, or pursuant thereto, and will permit access to his books, records, and accounts by the contracting agency and the Secretary of Labor for purposes of investigation to ascertain compliance with such rules, regulations, and orders.

(6) In the event of the contractor's noncompliance with the non-discrimination clauses of this contract or with any of such rules, regulations, or orders, this contract may be cancelled, terminated or suspended in whole or in part and the contractor may be declared ineligible for further Government contracts in accordance with procedures authorized in Executive Order No. 11246 of Sept. 24, 1965, and such other sanctions may be imposed and remedies invoked as provided in Executive Order No. 11246 of September 24, 1965, or by rule, regulation, or order of Secretary of Labor, or as otherwise provided by law.

(7) The contractor will include the provisions of Paragraphs (1) through (7) in every subcontract or purchase order unless exempted by rules, regulations, or orders of the Secretary of Labor issued pursuant to Section 204 of Executive Order No. 11246 of Sept. 24, 1965, so that such provisions will be binding upon each subcontractor or vendor. The contractor will take such action with respect to any subcontract or purchase order as the contracting agency may direct as a means of enforcing such provisions including sanctions for noncompliance: *Provided, however,* that in the event the contractor becomes involved in, or is threatened with, litigation with a subcontractor or vendor as a result of such direction by the contracting agency, the contractor may request the United States to enter into such litigation to protect the interests of the United States.

Further amendments by Executive Order No. 11478 of 1969 established the Office of Minority Enterprise to encourage and supervise what are called "special provision programs" which require prime contractors to allocate portions of contracts awarded to them to minority contractors and sub-contractors.

There have been, to date, no board decisions that address section 26.

VOCATIONAL ASSOCIATIONS

Section 6 provides as follows:

Every person has a right to equal treatment with respect to membership in any trade union, trade or occupational association or self-governing profession without discrimination because of race, ancestry, place of origin, colour, ethnic origin, citizenship, creed, sex, sexual orientation, age, marital status, family status or handicap.

Section 6 was amended in 1986 to include new grounds of discrimination but is otherwise identical to the original provision (s.5) in the 1981 *Code*. The section extends the protection offered by section 5 of the 1980 *Code*, which covered only trade unions and self-governing professions, makes the protection more general and includes more grounds of discrimination.[96] Clearly the section is applicable to employers' and management-level organizations, and any other association having to do with its members' vocations.

To date, only two Ontario boards of inquiry have dealt with allegations of discrimination in which vocational associations have been the sole respondents (other cases have coupled vocational associations with employers).[97] *Joseph v. College of Nurses of Ontario*[98] involved a complaint concerning a disciplinary action taken by the College of Nurses. *Tomen v. Ontario Teachers' Federation*[99] involved a challenge to a by-law of the Federation. The by-law required that a woman teaching mostly at the elementary level must be a member of the Federation of Women Teachers' Associations, while a similarly employed man must be a member of the Ontario Public School Teachers' Federation.

A problem likely to arise in relation to vocational associations, and particularly self-governing professions, is that statutes affecting these asso-

---

96. Section 5 of the 1980 *Code* provided:

"(1) No trade union shall exclude from membership or expel or suspend any person or member or discriminate against any person or member because of race, creed, colour, age, sex, marital status, nationality, ancestry or place of origin.

(2) No self-governing profession shall exclude from membership or expel or suspend any person or member or discriminate against any person or member because of race, creed, colour, age, sex, marital status, ancestry or place of origin."

97. See for example *Gohm v. Domtar Inc. and the Office and Professional Employees International Union, Local 267* (1990), 12 C.H.R.R. D/161.

98. (1985), 51 O.R. (2d) 155 (Div. Ct.)

99. (1988), 10 C.H.R.R. D/5877 (Ont. Div. Ct.), (1989), 11 C.H.R.R. D/97, D/104, D/223.

ciations may impose, or appear to impose, requirements that are discriminatory in themselves or have discriminatory results when implemented. Where this conflict is in fact present, the primacy clause in the *Code*[100] provides a solution.

One decision under the 1980 *Code* suggests that a board should thoroughly review the actual statutory requirements and compare them to the actions taken by the respondent. In *Snyker v. Fort Frances-Rainy River Board of Education*,[101] the complainant, who had been a teacher with the respondent board for several years, was declared "redundant" because of the respondent's implementation of a "Canadians first" policy. The respondent based one of its arguments on the provisions of the Education Act, stating that the Act required "discrimination" on the basis of citizenship. The opposing arguments are summed up in the decision:

> The argument on behalf of the Board may be summarized as follows:
>
> (1) By virtue of Section 145.11 of the *Education Act, 1974*, the Board is required to appoint teachers, "all of whom shall be qualified according to this Act and the regulations."
>
> (2) Regulation 100 under the *Department of Education Act*, R.S.O. 1970, c. 111, provided that:
>
> > 2(1) Every applicant for a permanent teaching certificate under this Regulation shall submit to the Deputy Minister,
> >
> > (a) . . .
> >
> > (b) in the case of an applicant who was born outside the Commonwealth of Nations, evidence that he is a British subject or a Canadian citizen.
>
> (3) Mr. Snyker's "Application For A Permanent Teaching Certificate" dated September 19, 1972 did not comply with the requirement of Regulation 199. Indeed, there is a strong inference that Mr. Snyker sought deliberately to conceal from the Deputy Minister his residence in the United States since the Application Form shows his "Home Address" as simply "Box 93 Island View Rte" without reference to International Falls.
>
> (4) Since the Application to comply with the statutory condition, the certificate could not be granted and was completely invalid.
>
> (5) As a result, Mr. Snyker was not qualified to teach and had to be dismissed by the Board.
>
> Mr. Sopinka responded by arguing that:
>
> (1) the requirement of submitting evidence of Citizenship was merely directory and not a condition precedent to the validity of the certificate. The Deputy Minister would have had Mr. Snyker's entire file before him. The proper inference is, therefore, that the Deputy Minister had noticed that Mr. Snyker was not a Canadian citizen and did not require such proof. This view of the facts is supported by the existence of s. 10(1)(*b*) of

---

100. S. 47(2).
101. (1979), unreported (Ont. Bd. of Inquiry).

the Department of Education Act at the time when the application was considered. The section provided:

10(1) The Minister may

(a) . . .

(b) accept in lieu of any requirement prescribed for a teacher, head of a department, director, supervisor or supervisory officer, or for a candidate for a certificate or for admission to a school, such evidence of experience, academic scholarship or professional training as he considers equivalent thereto:

Moreover, Mr. Green points out, s. 227(3) of the *Education Act, 1974*, provides that "All certificates of qualification are valid for such periods as the regulations prescribe." Since the regulations have never imposed time limitations upon the validity of certificates, their validity continues in the absence of clear words of limitation.[102]

The board of inquiry's response was to assess the actual statutory requirements against the somewhat sweeping nature of the Board of Education's policy. It concluded:

it would be entirely speculative and inappropriate for me to attempt to determine the validity of Mr. Snyker's certificate.

There is no specific statutory provision or regulation compelling the Board to dismiss Mr. Snyker. There is, therefore, no justification for the *prima facie* contravention of section 4(1)(*b*) of the *Code* which has been admitted by the Board.[103]

In *Joseph v. College of Nurses of Ontario*[104] two out of a panel of three judges of the Ontario Divisional Court agreed that a vocational association can breach the Code even while fulfilling its statutory duties.

Exceptions Relevant to Vocational Associations

The statutory exceptions most likely to affect the right to freedom from discrimination in vocational associations are found in the following sections:

1. section 14, which provides for "special programs";

2. section 15, which provides an exemption in respect of preferential treatment for those aged sixty-five and over;

3. section 16(1), which provides an exemption for situations in which Canadian citizenship, as a requirement, qualification or consideration is imposed or authorized by law;

4. section 16(2), by which cultural, educational, trade union or athletic activities can be restricted to Canadian citizens ahd permanent residents;

---

102. *Ibid.*, pp. 7-9.
103. *Ibid.*, p. 10.
104. *Ante*, note 98.

5. section 16(3), which provides an exemption for requirement respecting Canadian citizenship or domicile with the intention to obtain citizenship, when adopted by an organization enterprise for the holder of senior executive positions; .

6. section 17(1), which provides an exception when the sole reason for the facts giving rise to a complaint by a handicapped person is that the person is capable of performing or fulfilling the essential duties or requirements attending the exercise of the right because of handicap.

The exceptions are discussed in detail in Chapter 6.

3

THE GROUNDS OF DISCRIMINATION

INTRODUCTION

The scope of the 1981 *Code* was broadened both by the addition of new grounds of discrimination and by the inclusion of sections specifically prohibiting constructive discrimination and discrimination because of association. Further new grounds were added pursuant to the 1986 amendments.

In this chapter, the grounds of discrimination will be examined in turn. It should be noted that complaints frequently involve more than one ground of discrimination,[1] and that approaches taken by boards in relation to a particular ground may be analogous to other grounds.

Each section of this chapter will examine, where case law is available, cases that define the term used in the legislation, examples of disparate treatment on that ground and examples of constructive discrimination on that ground. It will be notable that case law definition is sometimes unnecessarily unclear and ambiguous, more so for some grounds than for others. This appears to be due to a tendency of boards and courts to allow the question of whether disparate treatment or adverse impact has been visited upon people of a particular age, sex, etc. to be confused with the issue of whether the effect complained of is sufficiently serious to be worthy of redress.[2] This lack of clarity is particularly obvious in allegations of sex, handicap, record of offences and age discrimination, and may reflect the ambiguity within our society concerning the propriety of discrimination on these grounds.

---

1. The frequent adduction of several grounds in a complaint is explained when one considers that the complainant may be characterized according to a number of grounds and that it is often not clear what factor caused the response complained of.
2. See the discussion of whether the impugned treatment or effect must cause adversity to be considered discriminatory in Chapter 1.

RACE, ANCESTRY, PLACE OF ORIGIN, COLOUR AND ETHNIC ORIGIN: THE RACE-RELATED GROUNDS

Race and Colour

Definition

It is extremely difficult to define race for any purpose. In anthropological and biological literature, race is an extremely limited method of classification.[3] Clearly, however, the term is not at all limited in every-day usage.[4] Since human rights legislation is largely concerned with common perceptions about groups held by the general public, it is not surprising that in the *Code*, as elsewhere, there is no definition of race. Thus, the term will be interpreted in its common, broad sense. The limits of the definition are inferable from the many board decisions concerned with race. Generally, the term has to do with physical features strongly associated, by the respondent or a presumptive public, with a particular group.[5] However, in no Ontario decision has a board purported to define race, or exhibited any indication that a narrow definition of the term is appropriate. No complaint has been dismissed because the complainant alleged discrimination on the wrong ground; typically, race, ancestry, colour, place of origin and, less frequently, ethnic origin are cited as grounds in the same complaint.

---

3. See, for example, Mead, *et al.*, ed., *Science and the Concept of Race* (1968).
4. Tarnopolsky, *Discrimination and the Law* (1985), pp. 5-1 to 5-12, provides a wide-ranging discussion of the concept of "race." On the misuse of the term, the author comments (pp. 5-7), "In the light of the above it will readily be seen that the term 'race' is frequently wrongly used in a popular or vernacular context, with reference to such population groups as the Chinese or Germans, who should more accurately be described as 'nations,' or to such language families as Slavic or Semitic, or to such religiously- or culturally-based minority groups as Jews or Gypsies. Moreover, in the United States, for such purposes as miscegenation laws or segregation in such facilities as schools, transportation, property rights, naturalization laws, etc., people have been categorized as being members of the 'Negro race' or 'black race' on the basis of being even fractionally descended from African ancestry. Some of the state laws even went so far as to define a 'Negro' as 'any person who has in his or her veins any Negro Blood whatsoever,' and 'persons of colour' as 'having any blood of African race in their veins'. One of the obvious reasons for these difficulties of any precise categorization has been aptly described in the following: '[O]ne anthropologist estimates that probably less than one-fourth of the Negroes in America are of unmixed descent, and that in respect to alleged Negro physical traits, the average American Negro is as far from the pure Negroid type as he is from the average Caucasoid type. In short, the average American Negro is as much a white man as he is a black man. The label that we give is thus at least half purely social invention. Many times we apply it to people whose *race* is mostly white.'"
5. England's *Race Relations Act*, 1976, s. 3 provides:
   3.(1) In this Act, unless the context otherwise requires —
   'racial grounds' means any of the following grounds, namely colour, race, nationality or ethnic or national origins;
   'racial group' means a group of persons defined by reference to colour, race, nationality or ethnic or national origins, and references to a person's racial group refer to any racial group into which he falls.
   (2) The fact that a racial group comprises two or more distinct racial groups does

Disparate Treatment

Since its inception, complaints of disparate treatment on the grounds of race and colour have made up a large proportion of the Ontario Human Rights Commission's caseload.[6] Most early cases were in the areas of accommodation and employment.[7] A number of early cases involved frank admissions of

not prevent it from constituting a particular racial group for the purposes of this Act. The approach taken by the British Parliament in referring to people's perceptions, however mistaken, of what race is seems appropriate to human rights legislation. A similar approach was taken in *Dakota Ojibway Tribal Council v. Bewza* (1984), 7 C.H.R.R. D/3217 (Man. Bd. of Inquiry) at D/3224, where the board declined to speculate as to whether complainants' status as native Canadians corresponded to anthropological definitions of the term "race": "What is to be determined is whether or not the Respondent discriminated in a prohibited fashion against an individual or group of individuals because the Respondent perceived that person or persons as belonging to a certain racial or ethnic group. Whether or not the party or parties discriminated against objectively did belong to such a group is or ought to be immaterial."

6. In *Life Together*, the Commission's 1977 report on human rights in Ontario, the statistics are given as follows: "In the fiscal year 1976-1977, race-related complaints made up 58 per cent of the Commission's caseload; in 1975-1976, race-related complaints constituted 57 per cent of the caseload. As these statistics make clear, the protection of people from racial discrimination is a major responsibility of the Ontario Human Rights Commission, and one that requires very substantial attention and resources." The Commission's 1981-82 *Annual Report* notes that forty-five percent of the formal cases taken by the Commission are complaints related to race and colour. More recently, the 1988-89 Annual Report of the Commission notes complaints of racial or ethnic origin as the second largest group of complaints (after complaints of discrimination on the ground of handicap).

7. Unreported complaints decided by Ontario Human Rights Commission boards of inquiry previous to the enactment of the 1990 *Code* include: *Khow v. Wonsch Const.* (1963), unreported; *Gordon v. Papadropoulos* (1968), unreported (Ont. Bd. of Inquiry): agreement re apartment rental rejected by respondent, although rental sign remained in window and respondent subsequently offered the apartment to another; *Mitchell v. O'Brien* (1968), unreported (Ont. Bd. of Inquiry): respondent stated that apartment was rented after seeing complainant and subsequently continued to advertise for rental; *Massey v. Castlefield Apartments* (1969), unreported (Ont. Bd. of Inquiry): when complainant appeared, respondent said apartment was rented; apartment continued available; *Harris v. Bouzide* (1971), unreported (Ont. Bd. of Inquiry): respondent denied vacancy upon seeing complainant, then subsequently offered apartment to another applicant; *Anderson v. Mascioli* (1972), unreported (Ont. Bd. of Inquiry): respondent denied vacancy upon seeing complainant, then subsequently re-advertised same apartment; *Matthew v. Seven City Development Co.* (1973), unreported (Ont. Bd. of Inquiry): respondent claimed apartment rented; subsequently continued to advertise; *Maraj v. Kozlovac* (1975), unreported (Ont. Bd. of Inquiry): retroactive increase in rent of complainant's apartment; no comparable rental increase in other apartments; *Morgan v. Toronto General Hospital* (1977), unreported (Ont. Bd. of Inquiry); *Nawagesic v. Crupi* (1978), unreported (Ont. Bd. of Inquiry): respondent told complainant apartment was rented; subsequently rented to someone else.; *Lomer v. Ottawa (City)* (1964), unreported (Ont. Bd. of Inquiry): complaint of discrimination in hiring in respect of application form requesting information as to nationality, citizenship, religion, place of birth, etc.; *Williams v. Ouellette* (1973), unreported (Ont. Bd. of Inquiry); *Rajput v. Algoma University* (1976), unreported (Ont. Bd. of Inquiry).

discriminatory attitudes.[8] More recent cases tend to demonstrate some of the more subtle forms of discrimination; an example can be seen in *Suchit v. Sisters of St. Joseph*,[9] in which a qualified black job applicant was subjected to questions as to whether he might have a "chip on his shoulder" in dealing with white colleagues or subordinates, while being asked little about his education, work history or background. However, there are still instances of more blatant disregard for human rights. In *Shepherd v. Bama Artisans*,[10] a black patron of a restaurant/bar was asked to pay an entrance fee that was double what white persons were asked. He was also left standing in line while white persons behind him in line were permitted entry. Finally, at a point in the evening the manager changed the dance music, cleared the dance floor and readmitted white patrons only. In *Lee v. J. Applebee Food Conglomeration*,[11] an employee left her employment in part because of a workplace atmosphere that included racial slurs both initiated and tolerated by management.

Constructive Discrimination

To date no Ontario boards of inquiry have dealt with instances of constructive discrimination relating solely to race/or colour.

The inclusion of section 11 in the *Code* means that, where the existence of a physical characteristic closely associated with a racial group is a proximate cause of the imposition of a requirement, qualification or consideration, the *Code* may be breached where that requirement, etc., operates so as to exclude, qualify or prefer people of that race. An example of a requirement that may breach section 11 is a height and weight standard used in employment, where this may exclude most members of the finer-boned or small statured races.

Ancestry, Place of Origin

Definition

As with race and colour there has been little definition of ancestry or place of origin by boards of inquiry.

Ancestry was defined in *Cousens v. Nurses' Association (Canada)*:[12]

> The term "ancestry" is here interpreted to mean family descent. In other words, one's ancestry must be determined through the lineage of one's parents through their parents.

---

8. This type of frank discrimination was noted in the following unreported Ontario board of inquiry cases: *Duncan v. Szoldatis* (1968), unreported (Ont. Bd. of Inquiry); *Laws v. Domokos* (1969), unreported (Ont. Bd. of Inquiry); *Tompkins v. Kyryliuk* (1971), unreported (Ont. Bd. of Inquiry); *Jones v. Huber* (1976), unreported (Ont. Bd. of Inquiry); *Copenace v. West* (1979), unreported (Ont. Bd. of Inquiry).
9. *Suchit v. Sisters of St. Joseph* (1983), 4 C.H.R.R. D/1329 (Ont. Bd. of Inquiry).
10. *Shepherd v. Bama Artisans Inc.* (1988), 9 C.H.R.R. D/5049 (Ont. Bd. of Inquiry).
11. *Lee v. T. J. Applebee's Food Conglomeration* (1987), 9 C.H.R.R. D/4781 (Ont. Bd. of Inquiry).
12. (1980), 2 C.H.R.R. D/365 at D/367 (Ont. Bd. of Inquiry).

Place of origin has not been defined in any published decision, although it has been cited as a ground of discrimination in many cases, generally in combination with race, ethnic origin, nationality and/or ancestry.

It is suggested that boards are correct in distinguishing citizenship and place of origin.[13] The latter term was probably intended to cover situations where it is not the complainant's citizenship, but rather characteristics that, to the respondent, are strongly associated with a particular place, that trigger discrimination. For example, an employer who regularly hires black Canadian citizens might refuse to hire a black Canadian citizen with a Jamaican accent because of his assumptions about Jamaicans. This would constitute discrimination on the ground of place of origin.

Presumably, the place in question need not be a country. The term might be extended to a state, province, group of countries or even a city. Furthermore, a person might effect constructive discrimination, contrary to section 11, by such practices as imposing a requirement that candidates for employment originate from non-Communist countries or giving preference to people from tropical countries.

A final point on the subject of place of origin is that it can be distinguished from residency. A person who was born and brought up in Canada, for example, and who is denied a job because he or she has recently spent a short time in the Soviet Union may have been treated unfairly but presumably has not been discriminated against on the ground of place of origin.

Another aspect of the residency distinction is that local employment schemes would not be likely to be affected by the prohibition against discrimination on the ground of place of origin. An employer who, for example, offers jobs to residents of Sudbury only is clearly not discriminating on the ground of place of origin unless he or she denies a job opportunity to a qualified applicant because the applicant was not born in Sudbury.

Disparate Treatment

In an early Ontario case, the board of inquiry specifically noted that, of the several grounds of discrimination cited in the complaint, place or origin was the reason for the adverse treatment in question. This case, *Rajput v. Algoma University*,[14] involved the failure by the respondent to hire the plaintiff for an academic position for which he was highly qualified. A major reason for the refusal was a concern for the Canadianization of the department. Although the complainant was a Canadian, the principal was worried about hiring him because doing so would mean that all three of the

---

13. See *Rajput v. Algoma University* (1976), unreported (Ont. Bd. of Inquiry); *Myszkowski v. British Columbia (Ministry of Transportation and Highways)* (1986), 7 C.H.R.R. D/3321 (B.C. Human Rights Council).

14. *Ante*, note 12.

positions in the department would be held by professors from Pakistan. The board concluded that the true reason for the discriminatory conduct was place or origin, rather than race, colour, or nationality.

In a more recent case, *Bone v. Hamilton Tiger Cats Football Club Ltd.*,[15] a Canadian quarterback was disadvantaged by a rule allowing American-trained quarterbacks to dress for a game without counting toward a quota limiting non-Canadian trained players. The board found discrimination based on either nationality or place or origin.

Recently, an Ontario board of inquiry, without specifically commenting on the point, appeared to accept that discrimination because an employee was not a "Franco-Ontarian" would be discrimination on the grounds of both ancestry and place of origin. However, in that case, *Iancu v. Simcoe County (Board of Education)*,[16] the complaint was dismissed. A similar position had been taken in an earlier case involving language — *Cousens v. Canadian Nurses' Association.*[17] *Cousens* was a complaint of discrimination in employment. In an administrative restructuring, the respondent association had eliminated the complainant's job and replaced it with a similar position. The Association explained to Cousens that it needed someone "fluently bilingual and preferably a Francophone."

In the course of the hearing, the board found that Cousens was competent in his job. It also found that, while Cousens could speak and understand French, he was not "fluently bilingual." On the evidence, the board found that a significant factor in the termination was the fact that the association was feeling pressure from the Order of Nurses of Quebec to provide French language services of good quality. For this reason the association had decided that a Francophone was needed in the position in question. This left the board with the need to determine whether termination because an employee is not "a Francophone" is discrimination on the ground of ancestry.

The board found that to be a Francophone was not necessarily to be of French descent "even in a Canadian context." However, Chairman Ratushny agreed that " 'Francophone' means French-speaking in the sense of having French as one's 'langue maternelle' or 'mother tongue'," and that the term "suggests, at least, a requirement beyond fluency in French. It suggests a person who is completely comfortable in the French language, and familiar with its nuances."[18]

Chairman Ratushny concluded that the respondent had not intended to discriminate against the complainant. However, he found it appropriate to

---

15. (1979), unreported (Ont. Bd. of Inquiry).
16. (1983), 4 C.H.R.R. D/1203 (Ont. Bd. of Inquiry).
17. *Ante*, note 12.
18. *Ibid.*

turn his attention to the consequences of giving preference to a Francophone. He stated:

> Notice must be taken of the reality that most (although not all) of the Francophones in Ontario today have French as their mother tongue because they are of French ancestry. Similarly, most (although not all) of those who are not of French ancestry are not Francophone. As Mr. Cousens stated in his testimony: "I can become bilingual but I could not become a Francophone." In other words, a potential employee can acquire fluency in a language but cannot change his mother tongue.
>
> The issue then boils down to how closely "mother tongue" is associated to "ancestry". Are they sufficiency related that to give preference in hiring on the basis of mother tongue (as opposed to fluency in language) could constitute discrimination on the basis of ancestry?
>
> This Board has concluded that "mother tongue" is, in fact, closely enough associated to ancestry that to give preference in employment to a "Francophone" *could* constitute a contravention of the *Ontario Human Rights Code* on the basis of ancestry.[19]

Given that Cousens was competent in his administrative duties, which were almost exactly the same in the new position, and that he had more facility in French than other senior officers in the association, the board found that the complainant had suffered discrimination on the basis of ancestry.

Constructive Discrimination

Obvious issues in constructive discrimination on the ground of ancestry or place of origin are accent and facility with the language of the majority of the population.

There have been no Ontario cases involving accent. In an Alberta case, *Fazal v. Chinook Tours*,[20] the complainant, a South Asian from Tanzania, had been dismissed from her employment as a travel agent, although she was generally competent at her job. It was established at the hearing that the reason for her dismissal was that customers of the agency had difficulty understanding her over the phone, because of her accent. (Much of Fazal's work was done over the telephone.)

Fazal's working language was English, and this fact was noted by the board. While the respondent adduced the testimony of four clients who had had difficulty understanding Fazal, the Commission was able to produce four clients of the respondent who stated that they had had no such difficulty. In addition, the Commission relied on two expert witnesses, one an expert in linguistics, the other a professor of English, both of whom had tested the complainant and found her competent in the English language. However, in the result, the complaint was dismissed.

As in *Cousens*, the board in *Fazal* found that accent related to more factors than race, ancestry or place of origin. However, the board seemed to

---

19. In this case, nationality was considered synonomous with citizenship.
20. (1981), 2 C.H.R.R. D/472 (Alta. Bd. of Inquiry).

have another reason for dismissing the complaint. The board took the view that discrimination could not exist without specific intention and, seemingly, animosity. The board relied on the fact that witnesses for the respondent had testified that the complainant's accent did not offend them, and that "nothing derogatory was ever said to her by Chinook about her race or colour."[21] While the board briefly mentioned in closing that the respondent had "a legitimate non-discriminatory reason for its actions," this was obviously secondary to its finding that the respondent had not discriminated.

Given the board's reliance on motive, and its clear belief that the presence of any non-discriminatory reason sufficed to legitimize the action, it is highly unlikely that *Fazal* would be considered good law in Ontario.

There has been one Ontario case involving facility with the English language and constructive discrimination. In *Romano v. North York (City) Board of Education*,[22] the board found that the respondent's requirements for English proficiency were unreasonable and not demonstrably related to the requirements for being a school bus driver. However, despite statistical evidence as to the number of immigrants from Italy and to the effect that 10% of those employed were unable to carry on a conversation in English, and other evidence from expert witnesses as to the "profile" of an average Italian immigrant of the 1950s and 1960s, the board ruled that the Commission had failed to establish that the respondent's requirements had a disproportionate effect on persons of Italian origin. Instead, the board characterized the requirement as having an adverse impact on persons who are functionally illiterate, a group not specifically protected by the *Code*. Disappointingly, this approach was upheld by the Divisional Court on appeal,[23] in a brief judgment.

It is submitted that this approach, in focussing on a characteristic that might be shared, for example, by persons identified by ancestry, place of origin, and handicap, fails to give sufficient weight to the purpose of the *Code*. It would appear to be a gross misconstruction of the purpose of section 11 to require the complainant to prove not that his or her group is disproportionately affected, but that it is the only group affected, before section 11 can provide redress.

Ethnic Origin

Definition

The *Concise Oxford Dictionary* defines ethnic as "pertaining to race," but the term is frequently used in a much broader sense to describe groups

---

21. *Ibid.*, at D/473.
22. (1987), 8 C.H.R.R. D/4347 (Ont. Bd. of Inquiry).
23. Affirmed (1988), 10 C.H.R.R. D/5807 (Ont. Div. Ct.).

characterized by specific social, cultural or religious practices, carried on in a largely traditional way. Professor Tarnopolsky[24] approves of the definitions given by the *International Encyclopedia of the Social Sciences*,[25]

> An ethnic group is a distinct category of the population in a larger society whose culture is usually different from its own. The members of such a group are, or feel themselves, or are thought to be, bound together by common ties of race or nationality or culture;

and by Hughes and Kallen in *The Anatomy of Racism: Canadian Dimensions*:[26]

> The concept *ethnicity*, as here defined, refers to any arbitrary classification of human populations utilizing the bio-cultural criterion of actual or assumed ancestry in conjunction with such socio-cultural criteria as actual or assumed nationality and religion.
>
> The most important criterion underlying the concept of ethnicity is that of common ancestry or peoplehood. Common ancestry, in turn, is a multi-faceted concept implying at least three criteria: biological descent from common ancestors, maintenance of a shared ancestral heritage (culture and social institutions), and attachment to an ancestral territory (homeland). These criteria provide the foundation for the actual or assumed distinctiveness of an ethnic category — a people classified as alike on the basis of ethnicity. The criterion of biological decent from common ancestors underlies actual or assumed physical distinctiveness. When this criterion of ethnicity is emphasized in classification, we may speak of a *racially-defined* ethnic category. The criterion of attachment to an ancestral territory or homeland underlies actual or assumed distinctiveness deriving from national origin. When this criterion of ethnicity is emphasized we may speak of a *nationally-defined* ethnic category. The criterion of maintenance of an ancestral heritage underlies actual or assumed socio-cultural distinctiveness. When this criterion is emphasized we may speak of a *culturally-defined* ethnic category. Frequently, the criterion of ancestral heritage emphasizes one socio-cultural phenomenon such as language or religion. When the aspect of culture selected for emphasis is language, we may speak of a *linguistically-defined* ethnic category; when it is religion, we may speak of a *religiously-defined* ethnic category.
>
> Although these distinctions are analytically useful, it is important to note that a given ethnic category may be arbitrarily classified on the basis of any one or any combination of these criteria of ethnicity.

There are no Ontario boards of inquiry that have defined "ethnic origin." Defining the term in construing the *Race Relations Act, 1976*, the House of Lords found that it included a group which was a segment of the population distinguished from others by a combination of shared customs, beliefs, traditions and characteristics drawn from a common past.[27]

---

24. *Discrimination and the Law* (1985).

25. Vol. 5 (1968), p. 167; quoted in Tarnopolsky, *ibid.*, p. 5-25.

26. (1974), pp. 83-4; quoted in Tarnopolsky, note 24, above, p. 5-25. Also, see R. Amand, "Ethnic Equality" in *Equality Rights and the Canadian Charter of Rights and Freedoms* (1985) Carswell.

27. *Mandla (Serva Singh) v. Dowell Lee* (1983), 2 A.C. 548.

Disparate Treatment

It is difficult to find cases in which ethnic origin is not coupled with ancestry, place of origin, etc. In *Romano v. North York (City) Board of Education*,[28] discussed above, the board's decision focused primarily on ethnic origin, although it is suggested that place of origin is more relevant to language questions.

It is difficult to suggest an example of discrimination on the basis of ethnicity that does not also involve religion, race, language, etc. Possibly the best example of a purely ethnic problem is discrimination against a person who is or appears to be a member of a particular group bound by religion, language, and/or custom, but who lacks a salient characteristic of that group, such as practising the religion or speaking the language. An example would be a "non-believing" Hutterite, Doukhobor or Mennonite who nevertheless retains outward signs of membership in the group, such as manner of dress, and is subjected to adverse treatment for this reason.

Constructive Discrimination

Clearly, aspects of a person's behaviour or appearance can be reasonably considered products of his or her ethnic origin. A requirement, qualification or consideration imposed without understanding that the same behaviour may carry different meanings in different cultures has the potential for disproportionate impact upon particular groups.

This type of situation was noted in *Malik v. Ontario (Minister of Government Services)*,[29] in which the complainant argued that his deference to persons perceived to be higher in rank was interpreted by a hiring board as a lack of initiative. The evidence in *Malik* was considered insufficient to establish a breach of the *Code*, but the board acknowledged that the problem could be a serious one. Certainly a decision to dismiss or a refusal to hire based on distaste for, or misinterpretation of, characteristics that are closely related to ethnicity could give rise to a section 11 complaint under the present *Code*.[30]

A board considering a complaint of sex discrimination in employment made some observations that may be of interest to a board faced with a section 11 complaint of constructive discrimination on the ground of ethnicity. In *Hendry v. Ontario (Liquor Control Board)*,[31] the board noted that, while the complainant was perceived as difficult to get along with, this was due in part to the fact that she tended to present herself in a way that clashed with her co-worker's expectations as to how a woman should behave and how a

---

28. *Ante*, note 22.
29. (1981), 2 C.H.R.R. D/374 (Ont. Bd. of Inquiry).
30. See discussion of constructive discrimination in Chapter 4.
31. (1980), 1 C.H.R.R. D/160 (Ont. Bd. of Inquiry).

woman in her position in the hierarchy should behave. Since she was in fact an excellent worker in regard to essential elements of her job, the board found that her failure to live up to these expectations did not constitute a reasonable cause for her employer's failure to grant her fulltime employment.[32] It is suggested that the clash of expectations noted by the board in *Hendry* has an analogy in the misunderstandings and misinterpretations that can arise in confrontations between people from different cultures.

Exceptions Relevant to Race, Colour, Ancestry, Place of Origin or Ethnic Origin

The statutory exceptions most likely to affect the right to freedom from discrimination on the ground of race, colour or ancestry, place of origin or ethnic origin are found in the following provisions:

1. section 14, which provides for "special programs";

2. section 18, which allows a religious, philanthropic, educational, fraternal or social institution or organization that is primarily engaged in serving the interests of persons protected by the Code to restrict membership or participation to persons similarly identified;

3. section 21(1), which allows discrimination on all grounds cited in section 2 in residential accommodation where
   (a) the owner or the owner's family resides in the accommodation, and
   (b) the occupant(s) are required to share a bathroom or kitchen with the owner or the owner's family; and

4. section 23(3), which allows questions to be asked concerning a prohibited ground of discrimination at an employment interview, where discrimination on that ground is otherwise permitted by the *Code*;

5. section 24(1)(a), which provides that,

   a religious, philanthropic, educational, fraternal or social institution or organization that is primarily engaged in serving the interests of persons identified by their race, ancestry, place of origin, colour, ethnic origin, creed, sex, age, marital status or handicap employs only, or gives preference in employment to, persons similarly identified if the qualification is a reasonable and *bona fide* qualification because of the nature of the employment;[33]

6. section 24(1)(c), which provides that section 5 is not breached where

   an individual person refuses to employ another for reasons of any prohibited ground of discrimination in section 5, where the primary duty of the employment is attending to the medical or personal needs of the person or of an ill child or an aged, infirm or ill spouse or other relative of the person.

---

32. *Hendry* is further discussed below in the section on discrimination on the ground of sex.
33. In relation to this exception, it is important to note that "reasonable and *bona fide*" imports a high standard of proof: see the discussion of ss. 24(1)(*a*) and (1)(*b*) in Chapter 6.

The exceptions are discussed in detail in Chapter 6.

CITIZENSHIP

Definition

While citizenship was a ground of discrimination new to the 1981 *Code*, complaints of discrimination on the ground of citizenship had been considered discrimination on the ground of nationality by more than one board of inquiry under the earlier legislation.[34] The source of this reasoning was *Ealing London Borough Council v. Race Relations Board*,[35] in which five Law Lords used the term nationality in the same sense that the term citizenship is used under the *Canadian Citizenship Act*. An example of a nationality case decided before the 1981 *Code* was enacted is *Snyker v. Fort Frances-Rainy River Board of Education*,[36] in which the issue was the implementation by the respondent board of redundancy guidelines in which Canadian citizenship was a primary consideration. The board in *Snyker* concluded:

> [T]he term "nationality" in the *Ontario Human Rights Code* is broad enough to prohibit discrimination on the basis of citizenship. While not in any way bound by it, I adopt the following discussion by Professor Ian Hunter as an accurate analysis of the relationship of these terms:
>
> > The terms "citizenship" and "nationality" refer to the status of the individual in his relationship to the state and are often used synonymously. The word "nationality," however, has a broader meaning than the word citizenship. Likewise the terms "citizen" and "national" are frequently used interchangeably. But here again the latter term is broader in its scope than the former. The term "citizen," in its general application is applicable only to a person who is endowed with the full political and civil rights in the body politic of the state. The term "national" includes a "citizen" and a person who, though not a citizen, owes permanent allegiance to the state and is entitled to its protection.
>
> Support for this interpretation can also be found in the Decision of Professor Tarnopolsky in the Complaint of Dr. M. Akram Rajput (dated May 12, 1976) and in the reasons of the majority of the House of Lords in *London Borough of Ealing v. Race Relations Board*, [1972] 1 All E.R. 105.[37]

Relying on *Snyker*, citizenship can be defined as membership in a state for the purpose of the relevant national and international law.[38]

---

34. See *Rajput v. Algoma University* (1976), unreported (Ont. Bd. of Inquiry); *Bone v. Hamilton Tiger Cats Football Club* (1979), unreported (Ont. Bd. of Inquiry); *Snyker v. Ft. Frances-Rainy River Board of Education* (1979), unreported (Ont. Bd. of Inquiry); *Barnard v. Canadian Corps. of Commissionaires* (1985), 6 C.H.R.R. D/2659.
35. [1972] A.C. 342 (H.L.).
36. *Ante*, note 34.
37. *Ibid.*, p. 5 (transcript).
38. See the discussion of the implications of the terms nationality and citizenship in Tarnopolsky, *Discrimination and the Law* (1982).

Disparate Treatment

In *Barnard v. Canadian Corps of Commissionaires*,[39] the complainant was rejected for membership (and therefore denied an employment opportunity) in the respondent organization due to the respondent's belief that certain qualities of character in its members could be assured by restriction by citizenship. The board of inquiry found this restriction to be discriminatory. A similar though more sophisticated argument by the Law Society of British Columbia was rejected by the Supreme Court of Canada.[40]

Constructive Discrimination

To date there have been no reported Ontario cases of constructive discrimination on the grounds of citizenship.

Other Issues

A concern periodically raised by commentators is the need for "Canadianization" in various sectors of the economy and in education.[41] Presumably, the Legislature was responding to such concerns in enacting section 16 of the *Code*, which allows a requirement of Canadian citizenship in certain circumstances. There has yet to be an Ontario board of inquiry in which section 16 has been considered.

Exceptions Relevant to Citizenship

The statutory exceptions most likely to affect the right to freedom from discrimination on the ground of citizenship[42] are found in the following provisions:

1. section 14, which provides for "special programs";

2. section 16(1), which provides an exemption for situations in which Canadian citizenship, as a requirement, qualification or consideration is imposed or authorized by law;

3. section 16(2), by which cultural, educational, trade union or athletic activities can be restricted to Canadian citizens and permanent residents;

---

39. *Ante*, note 34, confirmed in *Re Canadian Corps of Commissionaires* (1986), 55 O.R. (2d) 423 (Div. Ct.).

40. *Andrews v. Law Society of British Columbia* (1989), 1 S.C.R. 143.

41. See, for example, the remarks made by Professor Tarnopolsky sitting on a board of inquiry in *Rajput*, note 34, above, p. 21. I.A. Hunter: "Human Rights Legislation in Canada" (1976), 15 U. of W. Ont. L. Rev. 21 at 44, 45; J.I. Laskin "Proceedings under the Ontario Human Rights Code" (1980), 2 Advocates' Quarterly 280.

42. Sections 14, 18, 21(1) and 24(1)(c).

4. section 16(3), which provides an exemption for requirement respecting Canadian citizenship or domicile with the intention to obtain citizenship, when adopted by an organization or enterprise for the holder of senior executive positions;

5. section 18, which allows a religious, philanthropic, educational, fraternal or social institution or organization that is primarily engaged in serving the interests of persons protected by the Code to restrict membership or participation to persons similarly identified;

6. section 21(1), which allows discrimination on all grounds cited in section 2 in residential accommodation where
   (a) the owner or the owner's family resides in the accommodation, and
   (b) the occupant(s) are required to share a bathroom or kitchen with the owner or the owner's family; and

7. section 23(3), which allows questions to be asked concerning a prohibited ground of discrimination at an employment interview, where discrimination on that ground is otherwise permitted by the *Code*;

8. section 24(1)(c), which provides that section 5 is not breached where

   an individual person refuses to employ another for reasons of any prohibited ground of discrimination in section 5, where the primary duty of the employment is attending to the medical or personal needs of the person or of an ill child or an aged, infirm or ill spouse or other relative of the person.

The exceptions are discussed in detail in Chapter 6.

CREED

Definition

The principle of freedom of religion has been protected by Ontario legislation since the turn of the century.[43] However, neither religion nor creed has received statutory definition.

---

43. See, for example, the *Religious Freedom Act*, R.S.O. 1990, c. R.22, which can be set out conveniently in full:
"Whereas the recognition of legal equality among all religious denominations is an admitted principle of Provincial legislation; And whereas, in the state and condition of this Province, to which such principle is peculiarly applicable, it is desirable that the same should receive the sanction of direct legislative authority, recognizing and declaring the same as a fundamental principle of the civil policy of this Province:
   Therefore, Her Majesty, by and with the advice and consent of the Legislative Assembly of the Province of Ontario, enacts as follows: —
   1. The free exercise and enjoyment of religious profession and worship, without discrimination or preference, provided the same be not made an excuse for acts of licentiousness, or a justification of practices inconsistent with the peace and safety of the Province, is by the constitution and laws of this Province assured to all Her Majesty's subjects within the same."

In its 1977 report, *Life Together*, the Ontario Human Rights Commission raised two main issues in relation to creed: the imposition of ostensibly neutral requirements and the scope of the term.

On the first point, the inclusion in the 1990 *Code* of a provision against constructive discrimination has consolidated in the legislation a position taken by a number of boards of inquiry that the imposition of unnecessary requirements which conflict with religious observance can be discriminatory.

The definition of "creed" is a more complicated matter. It is settled law that differential treatment of persons professing established religions such as Protestantism, Catholicism or Judaism infringes the *Code*, unless the respondent qualifies for a statutory exception.[44] *Life Together* proposed a broader definition, one that would include not only the more recently established religious belief systems, but political beliefs. This is in line with a view that creed can encompass firmly held beliefs, particularly those founded in ethics or morals, whether or not focused upon a deity.

A comparison of the definitions provided by two major dictionaries illustrates different approaches. The *Oxford English Dictionary* defines creed as "an accepted or professed system of religious beliefs: the faith of a community or an individual, especially as expressed or capable of expression in a definite formula." As well as a duty-centered definition, *Webster's New Twentieth Century Dictionary* includes a broader definition: "a statement of belief, principles and opinion on any subject."

The *Religious Organizations' Lands Act* provides a fairly broad definition of religious organizations. The Act defines such organizations as:

[A]n association of persons

    (a)   that is charitable according to the law of Ontario,

    (b)   that is organized for the advancement of religion and for the conduct of religious worship, services or rites, and

    (c)   that is permanently established both as to the continuity of its existence and as to its religious beliefs, rituals and practices,

and includes an association of persons that is charitable according to the law of Ontario and that is organized for the advancement of and for the conduct of worship, services or rites of the Buddhist, Christian, Hindu, Islamic, Jewish, Baha'i, Longhouse Indian, Sikh, Unitarian or Zoroastrian faith, or a subdivision or denomination thereof.[45]

Courts in Canada, the United States and Great Britain have demonstrated a similarly catholic approach to the question of denomination.

---

44. Among the early Ontario decisions were: *Organ v. Fletcher* (1966), unreported (Ont. Bd. of Inquiry), which involved discrimination against Jews; *Gore v. Ottawa Separate School Board* (1971), unreported (Ont. Bd. of Inquiry), involving discrimination against a Protestant.

45. R.S.O. 1990, c. R.23, s. 1(1).

Overall, case law interpretations of the term creed are few and courts and other tribunals have tended to use the term interchangeably with "religion." It is perhaps because of this consideration of the two terms as synonymous that most decisions have indicated that belief in a deity is an integral part of a creed or religion.[46] Only occasionally has a more general definition been proposed. One example is found in an 1881 American decision, *Re Hinckley's Estate*.[47]

> The word "religion" in its primary sense . . . imports, as applied to moral questions, only a recognition of a conscious duty to obey restraining principles of conduct. In such sense we suppose there is no one who will admit that he is without religion.

One of the reasons for the courts' view of religion or creed as deity-centred has possibly been the fact that only rarely has a non-deistic belief been at issue. A recent decision by the English Court of Appeal provides a possible exception. In *R. v. Registrar General*,[48] the court was asked to consider whether the services of the Church of Scientology could be considered religious worship for the purpose of the *Places of Worship Registration Act, 1855*. The decision of Lord Denning, concurred in by Lords Winn and Buckley, was that the Scientology chapel could not be considered a place of religious worship. Lord Denning's rationale for this finding was expressed as follows:

> We have had much discussion on the meaning of the word "religion" and of the word "worship," taken separately, but I think we should take the combined phrase, "place of meeting for religious worship" as used in the statute of 1855. It connotes to my mind a place of which the principal use is as a place where people come together as a congregation or assembly to do reverence to God. It need not be the God which the Christians worship. It may be another God, or an unknown God, but it must be reverence to a deity. There may be exceptions. For instance, Buddhist temples are properly described as places of meeting for religious worship. But, apart from exceptional cases of that kind, it seems to me the governing idea behind the words "place of meeting for religious worship" is that it should be a place for the worship of God. I am sure that would be the meaning attached by those who framed this legislation of 1855.
>
> Turning to the creed of the Church of Scientology, I must say that it seems to me to be more a *philosophy* of the existence of man or of life, rather than a *religion*. Religious worship means reverence or veneration of God or of a Supreme Being. I do not find any such reverence or veneration in the creed of this church, or, indeed, in the affidavit of Mr. Segerdal. There is considerable stress on the spirit of man. The adherents of this phi-

---

46. See *Hammer v. State*, 89 N.E. 850 (1909); *R. v. Ontario (Labour Relations Board)* (1963), 39 D.L.R. (2d) 593 (Ont. H.C.); *Cummings v. Weinfeld*, 30 N.Y.S. 2d 36 (1941). These and other decisions are reviewed in Tarnopolsky, *Discrimination and the Law* (1982), pp. 180-223.

47. 58 Cal. 457 (1881); see also *Fulwood v. Clemmer*, 206 F. Supp. 370 (1962), where the court notes, in defining religion, that "It is sufficient here to say that *one concept of religion* calls for a belief in the existence of a supreme being controlling the destiny of man." (Emphasis added).

48. [1970] 2 Q.B. 697 (C.A.).

losophy believe that man's spirit is everlasting and moves from one human frame to another; but still, so far as I can see, it is the spirit of man and not of God. When I look through the ceremonies and the affidavits, I am left with the feeling that there is nothing in it of reverence for God or a deity, but simply instruction in a philosophy. There may be belief in a spirit of man, but there is no belief in a spirit of God.

This is borne out by the opening words of the book of ceremonies: It says, at p. 7:

> In a Scientology Church Service we do not use prayers, attitudes of piety, or threats of damnation. We use the facts, the truths, the understandings that have been discovered in the science of Scientology.

That seems to me to express the real attitude of this group. When Mr. Segerdal in his affidavit uses the word "prayer" he does not use it in its proper sense, that is, intercession to God. When the creed uses the word "God" (as it does in two places) it does not use it in any religious sense. There is nothing which carries with it any idea of reverence or veneration of God. The "sample sermon" has no word of God in it at all. It says that man has a body, mind and spirit. It emphasises man and not God. It seems to me that God does not come into their scheme of things at all.

I do not think this evidence is sufficient to bear out the contention that this is a place of meeting for religious worship.[49]

It is suggested that the narrow interpretation of the term religious expressed in the above-noted decision is not congruent with the approach taken by Canadian courts, which will be discussed below. Furthermore, Lord Denning's point of view as to religion was not completely supported in the concurring judgment of the other two Law Lords, who seemed to confine their decisions to a consideration of whether worship took place at the Scientology chapel.[50]

An interesting point about the *Segerdal* decision was that, while Lord Denning declined to consider Scientology a religion, he referred to the group's expressed philosophy as a "creed." Lord Buckley also used this

---

49. *Ibid.*, at 707.
50. Lord Winn stated, *ibid.*, at 708: "I am not concerned to dwell upon the question which necessarily was discussed in the course of this appeal, whether Scientology is or is not a religion. The answer to that specific question must depend so directly upon the meaning that one gives, for the particular purpose and in the particular context, to the chameleon word "religion" or "religious." . . . It seems to me, therefore, that while it may be right — or it may not be right — to call this philosophy (because that is what it is) a religion, when adherents to it come together in any building or other place for communing one with the other — since there is no suggestion that they commune with a deity — and discussion and instruction by sermon and otherwise, they do not, so far as the evidence reveals to my own mind, observe any form whatsoever of worship: by no "worship," if I am bound to define my terms, I mean to indicate that they do not humble themselves in reverence and recognition of the dominant power and control of any entity or being outside their own body and life."

characterization.[51]

No Ontario board has yet dealt with a case involving other than a relatively well-established, deistic religion. It is not remarkable, therefore, that the definition of creed ventured in two board decisions has relied on the *Oxford English Dictionary* and *Webster*'s primary definitions in which religious faith is central.[52]

Issues that may arise in future boards of inquiry are whether the protection of the *Code* extends to atheists and to members of recently-created religions. Unless boards of inquiry elect to view creed in its broadest sense, it is unlikely that membership in a political party will itself be seen as the profession of a creed, unless by extension of the case law that indicates that people may be protected from sanctions imposed in response to actions that are an expression of moral or ethical convictions.

In regard to the status of atheists, and as a general statement relevant to the status of the newer religions, a 1943 Australian High Court decision provides a useful view. In *Adelaide Company of Jehovah's Witnesses v. Commonwealth*,[53] Latham C.J. interpreted section 116 of the Constitution of the Commonwealth of Australia which provides that

> The Commonwealth shall not make any law for establishing any religion, or for imposing any religious observance, or for prohibiting the free exercise of any religion, and no religious test shall be required as a qualification for any office or public trust under the Commonwealth.

The Chief Justice's approach is demonstrated in the following remarks:

> It would be difficult, if not impossible, to devise a definition of religion which would satisfy the adherents of all the many and various religions which exist, or have existed, in the world. There are those who regard religion as consisting principally in a system of beliefs or statement of doctrine. So viewed religion may be either true or false. Others are more inclined to regard religion as prescribing a code of conduct. So viewed a religion may be good or bad. There are others who pay greater attention to religion as in-

---

51. Lord Buckley noted, *ibid.*, at 710, that "According to the evidence there are two creeds, one of which has already been mentioned by Lord Denning M.R. and one which is rather fuller in its terms and which does in fact contain more references to God than the creed which is set out in the book of ceremonies; but when one comes to read those creeds, they are not, in my judgment, documents which can in themselves be regarded as constituting acts or worship; they are affirmations of faith, but they do not, I think, partake of the character of worship. The fact that in other faiths the recital of a creed may very probably take place in the course of a religious service which is undoubtedly an act of worship does not mean that any creed used on any occasion will itself constitute an act of worship."

52. See *Singh v. Security & Investigation Services Ltd.* (1977), unreported (Ont. Bd. of Inquiry), pp. 13-14. The same definition was used in *Rand v. Sealy Eastern Ltd., Upholstery Division* (1982), 3 C.H.R.R. D/938 (Ont. Bd. of Inquiry). In that case, the board commented, after citing the Oxford English and Webster's dictionaries, that "clearly Judaism, as an established religion, is a creed under this definition."

53. (1943), 67 C.L.R. 116.

volving some prescribed form of ritual or religious observance. Many religious conflicts have been concerned with matters of ritual and observance. Section 116 must be regarded as operating in relation to all these aspects of religion, irrespective of varying opinions in the community as to the truth of particular religious doctrines, as to the goodness of conduct prescribed by a particular religion, or as to the propriety of any particular religious observance. What is religion to one is superstition to another. Some religions are regarded as morally evil by adherents of other creeds. . . .

It was suggested in argument that no system of beliefs or code of conduct or form of ritual could be protected under the section unless the general opinion of the present day regarded the belief or conduct or ritual as being really religious. It is true that in determining what is religious and what is not religious the current application of the word "religion" must necessarily be taken into account, but it should not be forgotten that such a provision as s. 116 is not required for the protection of the religion of a majority. *The religion of the majority of the people can look after itself. Section 116 is required to protect the religion (or absence of religion) of minorities, and, in particular, of unpopular minorities.* . . . Almost any matter may become an element in religious belief or religious conduct. . . . *It is not for a court, upon some a priori basis, to disqualify certain beliefs as incapable of being religious in character.* . . . The prohibition in section 116 operates not only to protect the freedom of religion, but also to protect the right of a man to have no religion. . . . Section 116 proclaims not only the principle of toleration of all religions, but also the principle of toleration of absence of religion. [Emphasis added.][54]

The Ontario Court of Appeal has also expressed the view that religion should be interpreted subjectively. In *Donald v. Hamilton (Board of Education)*[55] the question before the court was whether some pupils of the Jehovah's Witnesses faith could be excused from saluting the flag under a section of the *Public Schools Act* which allowed exemptions from "religious exercises." In response to an argument that an objection to saluting the flag could not be construed as a religious belief, Gillanders J.A. stated:

If I were permitted to be guided by my personal views, I would find it difficult to understand how any well disposed person could offer objection to joining in such a salute on religious or other grounds. . . . But . . . it would be misleading to proceed on any personal views on what such exercises might include or exclude. . . . The statute, while it absolves pupils from joining in exercises of devotion or religion to which they, or their parents, object, does not further define or specify what such exercises are or include or exclude. Had it done so, other considerations would apply. *For the Court to take to itself the right to say that the exercises here in question had no religious or devotional significance might well be for the Court to deny that very religious freedom which the statute is intended to provide.* [Emphasis added.][56]

Courts in the United States have exhibited a somewhat similar point of view when dealing with the religious practices of Black Muslims. *Holden v. Board of Education of the City of Elizabeth Union County*[57] involved a situation similar to that in *Donald*. In *Holden*, the exempting provision was for

---

54. *Ibid.*
55. [1945] 3 D.L.R. 424 (Ont. C.A.).
56. *Ibid.*, at 428-30.
57. 216 A. 2d 387 (1966).

"children who have conscientious scruples against" saluting the flag. In the words of the Supreme Court of New Jersey,

> Respondent argues that the exemption for conscientious scruples was never intended to be so broadly construed as to include petitioners' beliefs. Respondent sought to establish through cross-examination of petitioners that their beliefs were as much politically as religiously motivated, and were closely intertwined with their racial aspirations. In effect, respondent challenges petitioners' accuracy in labelling their objections to participation in the pledge of allegiance as "conscientious scruples."[58]

The Court cited a number of cases including a decision of the United States Supreme Court[59] to the effect that

> If there is any fixed star in our constitutional constellation, it is that no official, high or petty, can prescribe what shall be orthodox in politics, nationalism, religion, or other matters of opinion or force citizens to confess by word or act their faith therein.

The court refused to make a distinction between religious and political teachings in this instance.[60]

A second Black Muslim case was *Fulwood v. Clemmer*,[61] in which the petitioner, an inmate of a federal jail, claimed that he and other Black Muslims had been discriminated against in that they were denied the opportunity to hold religious services. The prison authorities had declined to extend publicly-funded religious privileges to the Black Muslim inmates on the ground that the Black Muslim faith "teaches racial hatred." To some extent, this was supported by evidence before the court.[62] However, the court found that the Black Muslim faith should be considered a religion:

> Under freedom of religion in this country a person has an absolute right to embrace the religious belief of his choice. The Constitution does not define "religion," and reference to standard sources of the meaning of words indicates that there is not complete agreement on even a definition of the term. Nor is it the function of the court to consider

---

58. *Ibid.*, at 389.
59. *West Virginia Bd. of Education v. Barnette*, 63 S. Ct. 1178.
60. *Holden, Ante*, note 53, at 391.
61. 206 F. Supp. 370 (1962).
62. *Ibid.*, at 390. The court notes that Clemmer's "belief that the Muslims teach racial hatred is not without support in the record. An expert called by petitioner testified: 'I don't know any other religion that teaches racial hatred as an essential part of the faith of the religion. There are many religions which have practiced racial hatred at various times, but this movement is the only movement that I know of which makes it a tenet of the faith that all white people should be hated.' The Muslims 'consider the white man as their natural enemy according to a handbook which a witness for petitioner regards as 'a standard and recognized text of religious denominations in the United States.' ·

> The spiritual leader of the Muslims is Elijah Muhammad. He describes himself as the messenger of Allah and such description is accepted by his followers. In his writings he portrays the white race as a race of total evil — a race of devils, murderers, thieves, robbers, scientists at tricks, world snoopers, meddlers, and liars. He declared that to survive, negroes and whites must be separated. He advocates the establishment of a separate Black State."

the merits or fallacies of a religion or to praise or condemn it, however excellent or fanatical or preposterous it may be. Whether one is right about his religion is not a subject of knowledge but only a matter of opinion.

It is sufficient here to say that one concept of religion calls for a belief in the existence of a supreme being controlling the destiny of man. That concept of religion is met by the Muslims in that they believe in Allah, as a supreme being and as the one true god. It follows, therefore, that the Muslim faith is a religion.[63]

Considering the evidence as to differential treatment, the court in *Fulwood* found that discrimination had, in fact, occurred.

It would seem reasonable, in the light of the above-noted decisions, to assume that members of the more recently established religions will be able to claim the protection of the *Code*. Protection will almost certainly extend to all deistic religions, and may possibly extend to atheistic or agnostic beliefs.

It is interesting to note that boards and courts have extended the protections accorded to religion or creed to actions that, while associated with the actor's religious belief, are not required by an established doctrine. This may take the form of "ultra-orthodoxy" (*i.e.*, scrupulously literal conformity to "the word" of religious teachings), or behaviour based on the individual's own interpretation of "the word".

Cases involving subjective interpretation of the demands of religion have arisen in the context of objections to joining trade unions. An example of this type of case is *Stel v. North York*,[64] a 1971 decision of the Ontario Labour Relations Board. *Stel* was one of the first cases decided under the present section 47 of the Ontario *Labour Relations Act*.[65] The applicant argued that he should not be required to continue as a member of the union, since he felt that it "did not have a Christian outlook."

The board extensively reviewed relevant case law as to the meaning of religion. In the course of the decision it dealt with the argument "that Stel's belief is not religious but rather a principle of social and ethical conduct," and that the belief was not in accordance with doctrine laid down by the synod of Stel's church. The board concluded:[66]

whether Stel was rightly informed or not on the position of the Christian Reformed Church with respect to neutral unions, whether or not he made the careful, conscious analysis urged by counsel for C.U.P.E. and despite his support for the C.L.A.C., the evidence leaves us in no doubt that Stel's objection to joining C.U.P.E. is because of his religious conviction or belief.

---

63. *Ibid.*, at 390.
64. [1971] O.L.R.B. Rep. 363.
65. R.S.O. 1990, c. L.2.
66. *Ante*, note 60 at 387.

The *Stel* approach has been used in a number of cases.[67] A test has developed in subsequent Ontario Labour Relations Board decisions in dealing with such cases. The questions addressed are:

1. Is the belief sincerely held?
2. Is it religious?
3. Is it the cause of the applicant's objection to paying dues?[68]

Since *Stel*, it would seem that the Labour Relations Board has placed somewhat greater emphasis on the second branch of this test, demanding somewhat clearer proof that the applicant's objection to the union is a necessary extension of his or her religion.[69] This approach is congruent with the purpose of the *Labour Relations Act* and the wording of section 47 thereof. Given that the Ontario *Human Rights Code* speaks of creed rather than religion, and given the purpose of the *Code*, it is possible that human rights boards of inquiry will take a different approach. It is suggested that a test appropriate to the *Code* is:

1. Is the belief sincerely held?
2. Is it an expression of the complainant's creed?
3. Did the complainant act or refuse to act as he or she did because of this belief?

It would appear that recent boards of inquiry are honouring the right of the individual to interpret the demands of his or her creed subjectively. In *Singh v. Workers' Compensation Board Hospital and Rehabilitation Centre*[70] and more recently in *Sehdev v. Bayview Glen Junior Schools Ltd.*,[71] the boards accepted that while there might be some debate among Sikhs as to the degree of necessity of, respectively, a kirpan of a particular size and long hair and a turban to the practicing Sikh, the point is that the practice is

---

67. See, for example: *Civil Service Assn. of Ontario v. Anderson* (1975), 9 O.R. (2d) 341 (Div. Ct.); *Funk v. Manitoba (Labour Board)*, [1976] 3 W.W.R. 209 (Man. C.A.); *Saggers v. British Railway Bd.*, [1977] 1 W.L.R. 1090 (Employment App. Trib.); *Burns v. Southern Pacific Transport Co.*, 589 F. 2d 403 (1978), *cert.* den. 439 U.S. 1072 (1979); *Brown v. Centennial College of Applied Arts*, [1979] O.L.R.B. Rep. 174; *Froese v. Pine Creek School Div. No. 30* (1978), unreported (Man. Bd. of Inquiry); *Singh v. Workmen's Compensation Board Hospital & Rehabilitation Centre* (1981), 2 C.H.R.R. D/459 (Ont. Bd. of Inquiry).

68. See, for example: *Wybenga v. University of Ottawa*, [1976] O.L.R.B. Rep. 422; *Amalgamated Meat Cutters and Butcher Workmen of North America v. Gordons Markets*, [1979] O.L.R.B. Rep. 1085; *Daub v. O.N.A.*, [1979] O.L.R.B. Rep. 538.

69. See especially, *Daub, ibid.*, and *Spellman v. University of Windsor*, [1979] O.L.R.B. Rep. 458.

70. *Ante*, note 67.

71. (1988), 9 C.H.R.R. D/4881 (Ont. Bd. of Inquiry).

"an inherent component of the complainant's religion *as he practices it*"[72] [emphasis added]. A similar approach was taken in respect of strict observance of a Sunday day of rest in *Janssen v. Ontario (Milk Marketing Board).*[73]

To summarize, it seems clear that members of relatively new and probably of non-deistic creeds will be afforded the protection of the *Code*. It is unlikely that the term creed will be extended to protect persons discriminated against on the ground of membership in a political party. However, depending on the circumstances and the board's perception of public policy in this area, it is possible that creed may be held to include behaviour based on person, ethical or moral convictions. If this prediction is correct, the protection of the *Code* may be applied to issues that might be considered political.

Disparate Treatment

There have been few recent Ontario cases involving differentiation because of creed. In *Morra v. Metropolitan Separate School Board,*[74] the respondent had refused to hire the complainant as a caretaker, despite his qualification for the position because, although he was eligible under the *Education Act* to elect that his tax payments go to support Catholic schools, he did not do so. The board found no discrimination, concluding that the School Board's policy not to employ persons who were eligible to support Catholic schools but did not do so was based on economic rather than religious grounds. With respect, it appears that the board in *Morra* paid undue attention to questions of motive, to the extent of virtually ignoring the effect of the respondent board's rule. Since only taxpayers identifying themselves as Roman Catholic were eligible to make the election required by the board, the board was effectively imposing an extra requirement for employment on Roman Catholic applicants only. Thus, of two equal applicants, both of whose taxes supported non-denominational schools, the Roman Catholic would be denied employment because he/she was Roman Catholic and therefore eligible to divert his/her taxes.

Since the decision of the Supreme Court of Canada in *O'Malley,*[75] with its definitive statement as to the narrow relevance of intent in cases of discrimination, it is unlikely that *Morra* would be decided similarly today.

---

72. *Ibid.*, p. D/4885. A more recent case is *Pandori v. Peel (Region) Bd. of Education* (1990), 12 C.H.R.R. D/364 (Ont. Bd. of Inquiry), confirmed by the Ontario Divisional Court (1991), 3 O.R. (3d) 531.
73. (1991), 13 C.H.R.R. D/397
74. (1981), 3 C.H.R.R. D/1034 (Ont. Bd. of Inquiry).
75. (1985), 7 C.H.R.R. D/3102 (S.C.C.).

Constructive Discrimination

Of the relatively few Ontario cases that have dealt with constructive discrimination, a significant number have addressed discrimination on the ground of creed. This was anticipated in the *Life Together* report, which raised, as an example of a predictable issue the dilemma faced by hospital personnel who feel obliged, because of their creed, not to participate in abortions. A general requirement that all nurses hired by a particular hospital be prepared to assist at abortions, for example, may constitute a breach of section 11 of the *Code*. On the other hand, the requirement may be considered reasonable and *bona fide* when applied to the hiring of nurses for the gynaecology department of a hospital.[76]

The earliest religious constructive discrimination cases in Ontario had to do with employers' dress codes, which essentially involved no more than a question of culture-bound esthetic expectations.[77] Regrettably, this continues to be an issue. In *Sehdev v. Bayview Glen Junior School*[78] the respondent school refused to allow a religious Sikh student to wear long hair confined in a turban with the school uniform, despite professed "respect for differences" among students. The board found that the rule did not meet the "reasonable and bona fide" test and was therefore not justified. Othe cases have raised more serious questions. In *O'Malley v Simpson-Sears*[79] the issue was the conflict between the requirements of practitioners of Sabbatarian religions and work schedules historically based on a Sunday day of rest. *O'Malley* reached the Supreme Court of Canada, but left unresolved many issues concerning work and religious requirements.[80] In *Pandori v. Peel Board of Education*,[81] the issue was the possible safety implications of the wearing of a kirpan by Sikh students.

Exceptions Relevant to Creed

The statutory exceptions most likely to affect the right to freedom from discrimination on the ground of creed are found in the following provisions:

76. This approach was taken in an arbitration decision involving interpretation of the previous *Code*. See *Peterborough Civic Hospital v. Wilson* (1981), unreported (Labour Arb. Bd.).
77. *Singh v. Security & Investigation Services Ltd.* (1977), unreported (Ont. Bd. of Inquiry).
78. *Ante*, note 71
79. (1980), 2 C.H.R.R. D/267 (Ont. Bd. of Inquiry).
80. For discussion of these issues, see Chapter 4. Recent cases include *Bhinder v. Canadian National Railway Co.*, [1985] 2 S.C.R. 561; *Central Okanagan School District No. 23 v. Renaud* (1989), 11 C.H.R.R. D/62 (B.C. C.A.); *Warford v. Carbonear General Hospital* (1988), 9 C.H.R.R. D/4947 (Nfld. Com. of Inquiry); *Pederson v. Canada (Canadian Armed Forces)* (1989), 10 C.H.R.R. D/5976 (Cdn. Human Rights Trib.).
81. *Ante*, note 72.

1. section 14, which provides for "special programs';

2. section 18, which allows a religious, philanthropic, educational, fraternal or social institution or organization that is primarily engaged in serving the interests of persons protected by the Code to restrict membership or participation to persons similarly identified;

3. section 19(1), which maintains those rights or privileges of separate schools and their supporters that are provided under the *British North America Act* and the *Educational Act*;

4. section 19(2), which provides that the *Code* does not affect "the application of the *Education Act* with respect to teachers";

5. section 21(1), which allows discrimination on all grounds cited in section 2 in residential accommodation where
    (a) the owner or the owner's family resides in the accommodation, and
    (b) the occupant(s) are required to share a bathroom or kitchen with the owner or the owner's family; and

6. section 23(3), which allows questions to be asked concerning a prohibited ground of discrimination at an employment interview, where discrimination on that ground is otherwise permitted by the *Code*;

7. section 24(1)(a), which provides that

    a religious, philanthropic, educational, fraternal or social institution or organization that is primarily engaged in serving the interests of persons identified by their race, ancestry, place of origin, colour, ethnic origin, creed, sex, age marital status or handicap employs only, or gives preference in employment to, persons similarly identified if the qualificaiton is a reasonable and *bona fide* qualification because of the nature of the employment;

8. section 24(1)(c), which provides that section 5 is not breached where

    an individual person refuses to employ another for reasons of any prohibited ground of discrimination in section 5, where the primary duty of the employment is attending to the medical or personal needs of the person or of an ill child or an aged, infirm or ill spouse or other relative of the person.

The exceptions are discussed in detail in Chapter 6.

SEX, PREGNANCY

Definition

Sex is defined by the *Oxford English Dictionary* as follows:

1. Either of the two divisions of organic beings distinguished as male and female respectively; the males or the females (of a species, etc., esp. of the human race) viewed collectively.

2. The distinction between male and female in general. In recent use often with more explicit notion: The sum of those differences in the structure and function of the reproductive organs on the ground of which beings are distinguished as male and female, and

of the other physiological differences consequent on those; the class of phenomena with which these differences are concerned.

Since sex as a ground of discrimination has usually been left without statutory definition, there has been considerable demand that courts and tribunals in Canada and other jurisdictions address whether sexual harassment or discrimination because of pregnancy or because of sexual orientation should be considered sex discrimination. For the most part, tribunals accepted sexual harassment as sex discrimination, but rejected pregnancy and sexual orientation in the definition of sex.[82]

The inclusion of a prohibition against sexual harassment in the 1981 *Code* consolidated in legislation the conclusions reached by Ontario boards of inquiry that sexual harassment constituted sex discrimination. Sexual harassment, and cases decided both prior to and in reference to a specific statutory prohibition thereof, will be discussed in Chapter 7.

In 1986, amendments to the 1981 *Code* included a provision that expanded "the right to equal treatment without discrimination because a woman is or may become pregnant." The 1986 amendments also added sexual orientation to the prohibited grounds of discrimination in all areas. Relevant case law concerning pregnancy and sexual orientation will be discussed below.

Sex

Disparate Treatment

There are a considerable number of Ontario decisions dealing with disparate treatment on the ground of sex. This is one of the few areas in Ontario human rights law in which there are sufficient decisions that trends and development of the law may be observed. Most cases involve discrimination against women, and it is probably fair to say that the cases both mirror some development in social attitudes and reflect some areas in which progress is minimal.

Early cases frequently involved admitted differentiation by sex which respondent sought to justify on the basis of stereotypic assumptions. Early Ontario boards held that concern on the part of an employer that a woman employee might be alone in the office late at night did not justify refusal to hire.[83] Boards have declined to consider as reasonable and *bona fide* em-

---

82. For a review of the law in this area, see Tarnopolsky and Pentney, *Discrimination and the Law*, at 8-2 to 8-42, and discussion below.
83. See *Shack v. London Drive-Ur-Self* (1974), unreported (Ont. Bd. of Inquiry). The board in *Shack* quoted (at 22) the American case of *Weeks v. Southern Bell Telephone and Telegraph*, 408 F. 2d 228 (1969), in finding "this type of romantic paternalism . . . unduly Victorian." See discussion of *Shack* in Chapter 6. Also see *Bruton v. M.H.G. International Ltd.* (1982), 83 C.L.L.C. 17,003 (Ont. Bd. of Inquiry).

ployers' concerns that there would be "rough language" or harassment from male co-workers.[84] Boards have also clearly rejected the notion that dirty or dangerous work is not for women,[85] along with the idea that men cannot perform delicate work.[86]

Boards have also dismissed contentions that a man should not be hired because women employees[87] or customers[88] might feel uncomfortable. It is clear that an employer's fear that hiring women might lead to attendance problems due to child-care responsibilities is not a valid reason for refusing to hire.[89]

In cases heard in the 1980s, there appears to be a shift in employment matters away from the facile assumptions noted above toward the position that differences in treatment between employees has to do with job function rather than with sex. This position is reminiscent of employers' arguments in respect of equal pay. Few equal pay cases have been the subject of boards of inquiry under the Ontario *Human Rights Code*, undoubtedly due to the fact that differences in pay based on sex were addressed in Ontario's *Employment Standards Act*[90] and its predecessor legislation, and more recently and effectively in the *Pay Equity Act*.[91] However, a recent case, which the Ontario Divisional Court considered appropriately dealt with under the *Code* despite the above noted legislation, is illustrative. In *Nishimura v. Ontario (Human Rights Commission)*[92] the workplace had two categories of advertising sales staff, distinguished as "inside" and "outside" advertising salespersons. The predominately female "inside" workers were paid less the than predominately male "outside" workers.

---

84. *Andersen v. Bianchet (Taro Painting & Decorating Div.)* (1986), 8 C.H.R.R. D/3871 (Ont. Bd. of Inquiry).
85. See *Robertson v. Metropolitan Investigation Security Ltd.* (1979), unreported (Ont. Bd. of Inquiry); *Adler v. Metropolitan Toronto Board of Commissioners of Police* (1979), unreported (Ont. Bd. of Inquiry); *Hartling v. Timmins Commissioners of Police* (1981), 2 C.H.R.R. D/487 (Ont. Bd. of Inquiry); *Cinkus v. Diamond Restaurant & Tavern* (1980), 2 C.H.R.R. D/339 (Ont. Bd. of Inquiry); *Bulger v. Branch No. 4, Royal Canadian Legion* (1978), unreported (N.B. Bd. of Inquiry); *Stairs v. Maritimes Co-op. Services* (1975), unreported (N.B. Bd. of Inquiry).
    British case law has shown a trend toward the views expressed by Ontario boards, after a slow start in *Peake v. Automotive Products*, [1978] 1 All E.R. 106 (C.A.), in which Lord Denning waxed eloquent on the need to preserve chivalry. Lord Denning specifically retracted this view in a later case, *Minister of Defence v. Jeremiah*, [1979] 3 All E.R. 833 (C.A.).
86. *Boyd v. Mar-Su Interior Decorators* (1978), unreported (Ont. Bd. of Inquiry).
87. *Segrave v. Zeller's* (1975), unreported (Ont. Bd. of Inquiry).
88. *Imberto v. Vic & Tony Coiffure* (1981), 2 C.H.R.R. D/392 (Ont. Bd. of Inquiry).
89. See cases discussed in section on family status.
90. R.S.O. 1990, c. E.14.
91. R.S.O. 1990, c. P.7.
92. (1989), 70 O.R. (2d) 347 (Div. Ct.).

The achievement of justice in pay equity issues requires acknowledgment of the existence of "job ghettoes" and a willingness to go behind job titles and minor differences in job descriptions. However, compared to other conditions of employment, the pay issue is simplified by a general appreciation of the fact that remuneration is an important issue.

The same does not appear to be true of the issue of dress "codes" in employment, and this has recently caused some blurring of the issues.

The first Canadian case to discuss sex discrimination via employment dress codes was *Doherty v. Lodger's International Limited.*[93] The complaint was based on section 3(1) of the New Brunswick *Human Rights Act*, which provides that no employer shall refuse to continue to employ any person because of sex, or discriminate against any person in respect of any term or condition of employment because of sex.

The complainants in *Doherty* were waitresses who were required to wear uniforms consisting of a tuxedo-style jacket, shorts and high-heeled shoes. Their difficulties with this uniform are expressed succinctly in the decision.[94]

> Their reasons for not wanting to wear the uniforms, as expressed by them, include; their assessment that the uniform is "hideous"; that the wearing of it made them feel "exploited, humiliated and degraded"; that they were no longer just serving drinks but had become some form of "entertainment"; that their customers reacted to them in a "different" (i.e. less pleasant) way such that they became the recipients of apparently mild, but nonetheless repugnant, verbal and physical sexual harassment.

The women discussed the situation with their manager, offering to replace the shorts with trousers, at their own expense. The discussion was not fruitful, and the complainants reported to work the next day in their own clothes. They were told that their continued employment was conditional on wearing the uniforms, whereupon they left the premises and did not return.

The board concluded that the uniforms in question could not be described as "sexually revealing" or exploitative. However, the chairman pointed out:

> the Complainants were called upon to accentuate their female sexuality and to draw attention to it by the wearing of the uniform, to a greater degree than had previously been required of them. I am satisfied that this was required of the Complainants primarily, if not exclusively, because of their sex — their gender — because they were women, in circumstances which contravened the *Human Rights Act*.[95]

The board considered that the absence of a uniform requirement for male employees was supportive of this conclusion, despite the fact that the men's jobs were not identical to those of the complainants. The chairman noted

---

93. (1981), 3 C.H.R.R. D/628 (N.B. Bd. of Inquiry).
94. *Ibid.*, at D/633.
95. *Ibid.*, at D/634.

also that if gender was only one proximate cause of the treatment complained of, this was sufficient for a finding that the Act had been breached.

Doherty is a cautious decision. The board emphasized its narrowness as follows:

> I must emphasize what this decision is *not*. It is not a finding that the *Human Rights Act* proscribes the imposition by an employer of uniform requirements on its employees, including uniform requirements which serve to accentuate the sexuality of those employees. But the employer must be prepared to demonstrate comparable treatment of both male and female employees and where comparable or similar treatment is not present, to demonstrate that the disparity is based on reasons which do not include the gender of the employees, and where employees of only one gender are present, to demonstrate that if employees of the other gender were present, they would probably receive similar or comparable treatment.[96]

Shortly after *Doherty* was decided, an Ontario board decided *Ballantyne v. Molly 'N Me Tavern*.[97] In *Ballantyne* the offer of employment as a waitress was made to the complainant on the condition that she perform the job naked from the waist up. Male waiters were not subject to the same condition of employment.

The Board in *Ballantyne* accepted that a dress requirement could be discriminatory on the ground of sex if imposed on a job category filled by only one sex:

> In summary, then, the legal framework within which the present problem must be considered is the following. In a case where male and female employees occupy the same position of employment and are subjected to disproportionately burdensome dress codes, a clear infringement of the *Code* is established. Secondly, in any case where although the job in question is held only by female employees, there are male employees doing essentially similar work who are not subjected to a similarly burdensome dress requirement, a contravention of the *Code* is also established. Thirdly, and perhaps more controversially, it appears to me that where a separate job category is set up for female employees only, an unusual dress code requirement would be defensible only if on an assessment of the essential characteristics of the job, it could be established that being a member of the female sex is a bfoq for the job in question. Otherwise, the employer would be able to lift itself outside the *Code* and deprive female employees of the protection of section 4(1)(*g*) [see now section 5] by committing acts of discrimination against potential male employees.[98]

Without going into great detail, the board in *Ballantyne* also had no problem with finding the requirement onerous. In finding for the complainant, the Board suggested that the "dress code" at issue essentially imposed on female serving staff an obligation to become "entertainers," which obligation was not imposed on their male counterparts.

In the most recent Ontario case on dress code, however, the board of inquiry appeared both to have difficulty in comparing treatment of male and

---

96. *Ibid.*, at D/635.
97. (1983), 4 C.H.R.R. D/1191 (Ont. Bd. of Inquiry).
98. *Ibid.*, at D/1196.

female staff across job categories and to believe that a great degree of hardship is necessary to a finding of discrimination. The test enunciated by the board in *Allan v. Riverside Lodge*[99] was as follows:

> Although I am here in judicially uncharted waters (at least in Canada) the circumstances which I believe would warrant a broader interpretation are these: (1) that males and females perform the same or roughly similar work for the employer; (2) that the employer has imposed a requirement of employees of one sex which is clearly more burdensome or exploitative than the requirement imposed on employees of the other sex; (3) that the requirement in question lacks justification in "commonly" accepted social norms"; and (4) that the requirement is not proved (by the employer) to be reasonably related to the employer's needs.

The major reason for the board's decision that the dress requirements imposed in *Allan* did not constitute sex discrimination appeared to be the view that the uniform at issue fell within "commonly accepted social norms." On appeal, two out three judges of the Divisional Court upheld the finding of the board.[100] However, Van Camp J. for the majority held that the board's criteria for finding discrimination were incorrect. Van Camp J. stated that a comparable group of male employees was not necessary for comparison purposes, in coming to a finding of discrimination, and that a uniform in accordance with commonly accepted social norms could amount to the discrimination in employment if the impact of the requirement were sufficiently adverse.

It is suggested that the board in *Allan*, in imposing an objective test of hardship in addition to requiring proof of disparate treatment based on sex, indulged in circular thinking. The very reason that an incident of disparate treatment of the sexes is "commonly accepted" or is not considered particularly serious may be the entrenchment of sexual discrimination within society. The Ontario *Code* provides a screening mechanism in the operation of the Ontario Human Rights Commission, which reduces the number of minor (and even, arguably, of novel cases) sent to boards of inquiry.[101] Boards and courts should not be providing a further screen. It is suggested that a *prima facie* case of sex discrimination though disparate treatment is made out in the establishment of an adverse consequence arising from different treatment of the two sexes, and that there is no harm in a subjective element in the establishment of whether a consequence is adverse. The appropriate time for a board to balance the degree of detriment to the employee against the employer's business necessity is after the employer has adduced evi-

---

99. (1985), 6 C.H.R.R. D/2978 at D/2986 (Ont. Bd. of Inquiry), affirmed (1987), 9 C.H.R.R. D/4516 (Div. Ct.).
100. (1987), 61 O.R. (2d) 460.
101. See the Commission's power to refuse to deal with a complaint which is "trivial, frivolous, etc." (s. 34(1)(*b*), and the board's power to award costs against the Commission (s. 41(6)).

dence that the requirements are "reasonable and bona fide because of the nature of the employment."[102] The matter of degree of adversity can also be addressed in an order made by the board of inquiry, if the requirement is found to be discriminatory.

Other Issues

As with other grounds of discrimination, cases of disparate treatment because of sex may not feature direct evidence. Ontario boards, while accepting circumstantial evidence, have treated it with caution. In *Offierski v. Peterborough Board of Education,*[103] the female complainant was clearly qualified for the disputed senior position with the respondent school board. However, the successful male candidate was also highly qualified.

The Board considered statistical evidence to the effect that the respondent board of education hired significantly more men than women for senior positions, but declined to regard this as establishing a *prima facie* case of discrimination due to corresponding evidence as to the relatively low rate of women applicants for these positions.[104] Without discussion of the possibility that low numbers of applicants can be as much a result of past discriminatory practices as a reason for low representation of a particular group, the board concluded that the actual reason for the respondent's failure to hire the appellant was concerns about how well she got along with colleagues.[105]

In two other cases, boards of inquiry declined to make findings of sex discrimination despite strong circumstantial evidence. In *Prestanski v. Windsor Western Hospital Center Inc.,*[106] the respondent maintained employment classifications including those of porter/janitor (held only be male staff) and maids (held only be female staff). The female appellant applied for a porter's job and was refused. After a lengthy hearing involving considerable evidence of the respondent's employment practices, the board found that the actual basis of the hiring decision was length of time employed by the respondent (all applicants had worked on a "casual" basis).[107]

The board concluded that, given the "basically unskilled nature of the job," the hiring date criterion was a fair basis for choice. The board noted its "discomfort with clearly sexist job labels such as maid and porter,"[108]

---

102. Ss. 24(*a*), (*b*).
103. (1980), 1 C.H.R.R. D/33 (Ont. Bd. of Inquiry).
104. Statistical evidence, and evidence generally, will be further discussed in Chapter 9.
105. Parenthetically, it should be noted that other assessments of the suitability of certain personality traits are often sex biased. See remarks by the board in *Hendry v. Ontario (Liquor Control Board)* (1980), 1 C.H.R.R. D/160 (Ont. Bd. of Inquiry).
106. (1986), 8 C.H.R.R. D/3919 at D/3923 (Ont. Bd. of Inquiry).
107. *Ibid.*
108. *Ibid.*

and pointed out that since the initiation of the complaint, "the maid classification has been retitled 'helper' and the evidence indicates that a small number of females have applied for and been hired as porter/janitors."[109]

In *Newman v. F.W. Woolworth Ltd.*[110] six women were the only employees out of a work force of 292 who were subjected to a wage freeze. Once again, the board heard extensive evidence as to the corporate structure and practices of the respondent, before concluding that the wage freezes had been implemented because of a decision to "red-circle" certain jobs selected by classification and location. Circumstances reviewed by the board included the fact that all of the complainants were senior employees and were the highest paid employees in the office, the fact that sixty-eight other women received raises in the same office, and that all women working in categories with men received identical raises.

While there are some differences in the circumstances of the cases, it is interesting to compare the approach of the boards in *Offierski, Pretanski* and *Newman* with the board in *Action Travail des Femmes v. Canadian National Railway Co.*[111]

In that case, there was clear evidence of hiring practices that included tests that disproportionately disadvantaged women, as well as evidence of discriminatory actions tolerated by management. However, it appears that, independent of these factors, the board was relatively more willing to infer discriminatory practices from the statistics that showed the scarcity of women employees, and more willing to draw negative inferences from inaction on the part of an employer who knew that it hired very few women.[112] Since the findings of the Tribunal in this respect remained undisturbed up to the Supreme Court of Canada, *Action Travail* may give tribunals more confidence in dealing with circumstantial evidence.

Constructive Discrimination on the Ground of Sex

A number of sex discrimination cases under the previous *Code* have involved employment requirements or other considerations that rendered it virtually impossible for a woman to be hired. In these situations, boards

---

109. *Ibid.*, at D/3919.

110. (1986), 7 C.H.R.R. D/3153 (Ont. Bd. of Inquiry).

111. (1984), 5 C.H.R.R. D/2327 (Cdn. Human Rights Trib.).

112. The Board in *Action Travail* stated that statistics showing a relatively low rate of hire of a protective group could provide prima facie evidence of discrimination. Remarking on C.N.'s knowledge of its position in hiring women, the board remarked disapprovingly on C.N.'s lack of effort to seek out prospective female candidates, maintenance of a walk-in application system, and failure to make special efforts to make its employment office more receptive.

have held that, for example, an absence of suitable accommodation[113] may not be relied upon as an excuse for not hiring women. Further, height and weight requirements[114] that were found not to be a *bona fide* occupational requirement have been held to contravene the *Code*. Under section 11, any requirement, qualification or consideration that operates to the detriment of one sex, or so as to confer a preference on one sex breaches the *Code* unless it can be shown to be either subject to an exception in the *Code* or "reasonable and *bona fide* in the circumstances."

Pregnancy or Potential for Pregnancy

Disparate Treatment

There has been a lengthy history of debate among human rights tribunals and courts as to whether disparate treatment because of pregnancy constitutes sex discrimination. Generally speaking, boards of inquiry considered themselves bound by the Supreme Court of Canada decision in *Bliss v. Canada (Attorney General)*,[115] to find that discrimination on the ground of pregnancy was something other than sex discrimination. Latterly, however, a line of cases beginning with *Canada (Treasury Board) v. Tellier-Cohen*[116] either distinguished *Bliss* or suggested that its reasoning was inappropriate in the context of human rights legislation.[117] The Supreme

---

113. See *Robertson v. Metro. Investigation Security Ltd.* (1979), unreported (Ont. Bd. of Inquiry). These concerns were raised by the respondent but ignored by the board in *Hartling v. Timmins (Municipality) Commissioners of Police* (1981), 2 C.H.R.R. D/487 (Ont. Bd. of Inquiry). Also see *Hermolle v. Government Communications Headquarters*, Gloucester Indust. Trib., case no. 24389/79, an unreported employment case under England's Sex Discrimination Act in which an Industrial Tribuanl held that employers could not refuse to hire a woman for a residential position because of inadequate accommodation where adequate accommodation could be arranged without undue fuss and expense. A similar result was reached in *Wallace v. Peninsular & Oriental Steam Navigation Ltd.*, London (Central) Indust. Trib., case no. 3100/79A (unreported).

114. See *Colfer v. Ottawa Bd. of Commrs. of Police* (1979), unreported (Ont. Bd. of Inquiry); *Hartling v. Timmins (Municipality) Commissioners of Police* (1981), 2 C.H.R.R. D/487 (Ont. Bd. of Inquiry), also see *Chapdelaine v. Air Canada* (1987), 9 CH.R.R. D/4449 (Can. Human Rights Review Trib.), varied (June 19, 1991), Doc. No. T.D. 8/91 (Cdn. Human Rights Review Trib.).

115. [1979] 1 S.C.R. 183.

116. (1982), 3 C.H.R.R. D/792 (Cdn. Human Rights Review Trib.), reversed in part (1982), 4 C.H.R.R. D/1169 (Cdn. Human Rights Review Trib.).

117. See *Holloway v. MacDonald* (1983), 4 C.H.R.R. D/1454 (B.C. Bd. of Inquiry); *Paton v. Brouwer & Co.* (1984), 5 C.H.R.R. D/1946 (B.C. Bd. of Inquiry); *Winterburn v. Lou's Place* (1984), 5 C.H.R.R. D/2052 (Ont. Bd. of Inquiry); *Riggio v. Sheppard Coiffures* (1987), 9 C.H.R.R. D/4520 (Ont. Bd. of Inquiry); *Stefanyshyn v. Four Seasons Management Ltd.* (1986), 8 C.H.R.R. D/3934 (B.C. Human Rights Council); *Pattison v. Fort Frances (Town) Commissioners of Police* (1987), 8 C.H.R.R. D/3884 (Ont. Bd. of Inquiry), affirmed (1988), 66 O.R. (2d) 714 (Ont. Div. Ct.).

Court of Canada finally confirmed their view, repudiating *Bliss* in 1989 when it decided *Dixon v. Canada Safeway Ltd.*[118]

Prior to the *Brooks* decision, the Ontario Legislature anticipated the Supreme Court of Canada's approach by enacting subsection 9(2) [now s. 10(2)], which reads as follows: "the right to equal treatment without discrimination because of sex includes the right to equal treatment without discrimination because a woman is or may become pregnant."

There have been no cases decided under this provision; however a case decided under subsection 4(1) [now 5(1)] of the 1981 *Code* addresses some important issues which arise in circumstances in which potential pregnancy is a reason for disparate treatment.

In *Wiens v. Inco Metals Co., Ont. Division*[119] the complainant was a woman of child-bearing age employed as a "hot metal operator" at a nickel refinery. She successfully completed training to work in a particular area of operators (the "IPC") the year before the employer promulgated a policy that women of child-bearing potential would be excluded from employment in that area. The reason for the policy was health hazards to unborn children both from nickel carbonyl and from medication that would be given to counteract exposure to nickel carbonyl.

The board heard extensive evidence, both as to the dangers of nickel carbonyl, and as to the degree of likelihood of exposure of workers employed at the IPC. The board also expressly considered the risks routinely undertaken by pregnant or potentially pregnant women every day, such as drinking and smoking; the need to balance the interests of individual women in the workforce with society's interests in the health of unborn children; and the interest of the employer in minimizing its potential civil liability. Finally, in finding for the complainant, the board summed up as follows:

> The legitimate concerns of the respondent with respect to fetal risk could be met by providing full information to female employees, recommending the use of a reliable method of birth control, advising against becoming pregnant while employed in the IPC workplace, and providing the option to transfer to a carbonyl-free area of the workplace upon intending to become pregnant, without disadvantage in terms of earnings, benefits and seniority. Inco made it clear in the testimony of its management that it would be quite willing to accommodate female employees in respect of alternative work being made available, upon an employee indicating she intended to become pregnant.
>
> Inco asserts that it should be able to adopt a very restrictive policy, out of abundant caution. Just as its safety engineering should minimize risk, Inco asserts its employment policies should minimize risk as much as humanly possible, even if the risk is minimal at the outset. Inco's position is that it should seek to preclude any possibility of risk.
>
> Much of the evidence went to the issue as to whether the scientific evidence supported the view that carbonyl gas constitutes a significant risk to the fetus, or supported

---

118. [1989] 1 S.C.R. 1219.
119. (1988), 9 C.H.R.R. D/4795 (Ont. Bd. of Inquiry).

the opposing view that only a relatively minor risk is present. This is a difficult question for scientists, let alone for a lay board of inquiry. My own assessment of the evidence is that the scientific opinions (Drs. Nieboer, Spielberg and Halton in particular) suggesting the risk is insignificant, are to be preferred. Having said that, I would add, however, that an employer in Inco's position could reasonably assert that on the basis of the scientific literature there is certainly a possibility of harm to a fetus from exposure to carbonyl gas.

However, in my opinion the resolution of this specific question (the potential for harm to a fetus by exposure to nickel carbonyl gas) is not really determinative of the larger issue, in any event. In my view, the risk of a female employee becoming pregnant while practising a reliable method of birth control is very minimal, and the risk of having an unintended pregnancy not yet realized and suffering an exposure to carbonyl gas (which in itself is very unlikely) during that short period of time, result in rendering the overall risk unsubstantial and minimal. When one then considers the further point, as I find on the evidence, that it is very uncertain that exposure to nickel carbonyl gas to a fetus would be harmful, then the already minimal risk is rendered even more insignificant.

This is a case of conflicting interests, claims and values. In my opinion, considering all the evidence "reasonableness" applied to the instant factual situation dictates a balancing of the interests between fetal protection and a female employee's right to equality of opportunity in employment, in favour of the complainant and not the employer.

It is more in keeping with equality objective to allow the individual the informed choice of accepting the very slight risk or rejecting the very slight risk in favour of alternative employment. In the instant situation, the Complainant testified she is using birth control and does not intend to become pregnant.

If such exclusionary rules of a discriminatory nature are considered warranted it is within the realm of the role of government to make such a policy decision, and to enact regulations as seen under the federal *Atomic Energy Control Act*, discussed above. In the absence of such regulations, it is sufficient for Inco to give full information regarding the potential risk to prospective female employees, require an assurance that a reasonable method of birth control is being used, and then allow the woman herself to decide whether to expose herself to the risk. The management of Inco testified that they would be able to accommodate a women who became, or stated she had an intention of becoming pregnant, through a transfer to an area out of the IPC.[120]

Constructive Discrimination

There have been no Ontario boards of inquiry dealing with constructive discrimination on the ground of pregnancy.

Exceptions Relevant to Sex, Pregnancy

The statutory exceptions most likely to affect the right to freedom from discrimination on the ground of sex or pregnancy are found in the following provisions:

1. section 14, which provides for "special programs";
2. section 18, which allows a religious, philanthropic, educational, frater-

---

120. *Ibid.*, at D/4819.

nal or social institution or organization that is primarily engaged in serving the interests of persons protected by the Code to restrict membership or participation to persons similarly identified;

3. section 20(1), which allows the restriction of services or facilities to "persons of the same sex on the ground of public decency";

4. section 20(3), which allows a "recreational club" to restrict or qualify "access to its services or facilities" or give "preferences with respect to membership dues and other fees because of age, sex, marital status or family status";

5. section 21(1), which allows discrimination on all grounds cited in section 2 in residential accommodation where
   (a) the owner or the owner's family resides in the accommodation, and
   (b) the occupant(s) are required to share a bathroom or kitchen with the owner or the owner's family; and

6. section 21(2), which allows discrimination on the ground of sex, "where the occupancy of all the residential accommodation in the building, other than the accommodation, if any, of the owner or family of the owner, is restricted to persons who are of the same sex";

7. section 22, which allows discrimination on the basis of age, sex, marital status, family status or handicap (where the discrimination is reasonable and *bona fide*) in a contract of automobile, life, accident, sickness or disability insurance, or a non-employment group life insurance contract, or a life annuity;

8. section 23(3), which allows questions to ba asked concerning a prohibited ground of discrimination at an employment interview, where discrimination on that gorund is otherwise permitted by the *Code*;

9. section 24(1)(a), which provides that,

   a religious, philanthropic, educational, fraternal or social institution or organization that is primarily engaged in serving the interests of persons identified by their race, ancestry, place of origin, colour, ethnic origin, creed, sex, age, marital status or handicap employs only, or gives preference in employment to, persons similarly identified if the qualification is a reasonable and *bona fide* qualification because of the nature of the employment;

10. section 24(1)(b) which allows discrimination that would otherwise breach section 5 where:

    the discrimination in employment is for reasons of age, sex, record of offences or marital status if the age, sex, record of offences or marital status of the applicant is a reasonable and *bond fide* qualification because of the nature of the employment;

11. section 24(1)(c), which provides that section 5 is not breached where

    an individual person refuses to employ another for reasons of any prohibited ground of discrimination in section 5, where the primary duty of the employment is attending to the medical or personal needs of the person or of an ill child or an aged, infirm or ill spouse or other relative of the person.

12. section 25(2) which provides that certain employment benefit plans may discriminate on the ground of age, sex, marital status or family status where such plans comply with the *Employment Standards Act* and Regulations. However, employment may not be denied because of failure to qualify in such a plan, nor made conditional on qualifying for inclusion.[121]

The exceptions are discussed in detail in Chapter 6.

SEXUAL ORIENTATION

Disparate Treatment

Sexual orientation as a prohibited ground of discrimination was added to the *Code* through a 1986 amendment.[122] In cases decided prior to this amendment, Canadian courts and tribunals had dismissed the idea that discrimination on the ground of sex could encompass discrimination on the ground of sexual orientation.[123] Recently, however, in a case decided under the federal *Human Rights Act*, a board decided that a provision for family bereavement leave in a collective agreement was discriminatory because it did not allow leave for a same-sex spouse, but this result was overturned on appeal.[124]

To date there have been no Ontario boards of inquiry dealing with discrimination on the ground of sexual orientation. A recent Divisional Court decision declined to find disparate treatment of non-heterosexual spouses in the provincial health insurance scheme discriminatory under section 15 of the *Charter of Rights and Freedoms*. The Court also denied the applicant a declaration that the *Code* prevails over and renders null and void provisions of the *Health Insurance Act* that preclude a partner of the same sex from being defined as a dependent for insurance purposes. However, the court specifically declined to consider the provisions of the *Code*, or to interpret rights under the *Code*.[125]

After the *Andrews* case, the Ontario government amended its contract to allow for insurance benefits to same-sex spouses of public servants.

---

121. Section 25(1); see Chapter 6.
122. S.O. 1986, c. 64.
123. See *University of Saskatchewan v. Saskatchewan (Human Rights Commission)* (1976), 66 D.L.R. (3d) 561 (Sask. Q.B.); and *Vogel v. Manitoba* (1983), 4 C.H.R.R. D/1654 (Man. Bd. of Adjud.).
124. *Mossop v. Canada (Secretary of State)* (1989), 10 C.H.R.R. D/6064, reversed (1990), 12 C.H.R.R. D/355.
125. *Andrews v. Ontario (Minister of Health)* (1988), 64 O.R. (2d) 258 (H.C.).

Constructive Discrimination

There have been no Ontario boards of inquiry dealing with constructive discrimination on the ground of sexual orientation to date.

Exceptions Relevant to Sexual Orientation

The statutory exceptions most likely to affect the right to freedom from discrimination on the ground of sexual orientation are found in the following provisions:

1. section 14, which provides for "special programs";

2. section 18, which allows a religious, philanthropic, educational, fraternal or social institution or organization that is primarily engaged in serving the interests of persons protected by the Code to restrict membership or participation to persons similarly identified;

3. section 21(1), which allows discrimination on all grounds cited in section 2 in residential accommodation where
    (a) the owner or the owner's family resides in the accommodation, and
    (b) the occupant(s) are required to share a bathroom or kitchen with the owner or the owner's family; and

4. section 23(3), which allows questions to be asked concerning a prohibited ground of discrimination at an employment interview, where discrimination on that ground is otherwise permitted by the *Code*;

5. section 24(1)(c), which provides that section 5 is not breached where

    an individual person refuses to employ another for reasons of any prohibited ground of discrimination in section 5, where the primary duty of the employment is attending to the medical or personal needs of the person or of an ill child or an aged, infirm or ill spouse or other relative of the person.

The exceptions are discussed in detail in Chapter 6.

AGE

Definition

In its 1977 report, *Life Together*, the Ontario Human Rights Commission addressed the fact that the previous *Code* had limited the protection afforded against discrimination on the ground of age to persons between forty and sixty-five.[126] There were two major concerns raised in the report: the rate of unemployment among young people, and the plight of those over the age of sixty-five who are forced to retire.[127] The 1981 *Code* responded to some extent to the former concern. The

---

126. See R.S.O. 1980, c. 340, s. 26(*a*).
127. See *Life Together*, (1977), pp. 64-68.

lower limit for protection from age discrimination was extended in 1981 to eighteen and remains at that age in respect of employment and most other areas covered by the *Code*. Pursuant to a 1987 amendment, persons aged sixteen or seventeen are also protected from age discrimination in the areas of occupancy of and contracts for accommodation, as long as such persons have withdrawn from parental control. The amendment specifically states that a contract for accommodation entered into by a person aged sixteen or seventeen who has withdrawn from parental control is enforceable against that person as if the person were eighteen years old.[128]

Neither the 1981 *Code* nor recent amendments responded to the latter concern raised in *Life Together*. The upper limit for protection from age discrimination in employment remains at age sixty-five.

The most recent amendment to the *Code* is an addition that reads as follows:

> the right under section 1 to equal treatment with respect to services, goods and facilities without discrimination because of age is not infringed by the provisions of the *Liquor Licence Act, 1990* and the regulations under it relating to providing for and enforcing a minimum drinking age of nineteen years.[129]

The restriction of protection in employment to persons under sixty-five, imposed by subsection 10(1), has been challenged, to date unsuccessfully, as discriminatory under section 15 of the Canadian *Charter of Rights and Freedoms*. At issue in *Bregzis v. University of Toronto*,[130] which was later joined with other applications before the Ontario Court of Appeal in *McKinney v. University of Guelph*[131] were the mandatory retirement policies of several Ontario universities. The court unanimously found that the restricted definition of age in subsection 9(1)(a) [now s. 10(1)] was contrary to section 15. The majority, however, found under section 1 of the *Charter* that subsection 9(1)(a) was a reasonable limit on the equality rights of applicants. With one dissent, the Court of Appeal found that: "the objectives of making it possible for parties to negotiate a mandatory retirement date in keeping with the tenure system, of preserving existing pension plans, and of facilitating faculty renewal, can reasonably be held to be objectives which are not trivial but are pressing and substantial. In the university context, they warrant overriding a constitutionally protected right."[132]

The dissent in *McKinney* declared that section 9(1)(a) failed to meet the section 1 test because it did not satisfy the requirement that the measure should impair the freedom in question as little as possible. The provision

---

128. S.O. 1986, c. 64, s. 18(4).

129. *Liquor Licence Act*, S.O. 1990 c. L.19, s. 65, which amends S.O. 1986, c. 64, s. 18.

130. (1986), 53 O.R. (2d) 348 (H.C.).

131. (1987), 9 C.H.R.R. D/4573 (Ont. C.A.).

132. *Ibid.*, at 9 C.H.R.R. D/4597.

denies protection against age discrimination after the age of 65; it did not merely limit or restrict it. Because of the absence of any qualification on section 10(1), the minority found it to be of no force or effect.

An appeal to the Supreme Court of Canada was dismissed without reasons.[133]

Compulsory retirement at age sixty-five where there is no statutory equivalent to subsection 10(1) has been found by the Supreme Court of Canada[134] to offend human rights legislation.

The lower limit of age discrimination protection afforded by the *Code* has also been challenged in Ontario in the context of "adults only" condominiums. In *Dudnik v. York Condominium Corp. No. 216*,[135] the matter at issue was a restriction on occupation of condominium units that barred persons under the ages of, respectively, sixteen and fourteen years. The respondent condominium corporations enforced the restrictions to prevent (and in one case to undo) the sale of condominium units to families with children under those ages. The prospective purchasers and vendors complained under the *Code* of discrimination on the ground of family status and age.

During the course of the Commission's investigation one respondent corporation commenced an action which would require one of the complainant families to offer their unit for sale to the Corporation. The complainants brought a motion to stay the action pending the completion of the Commission's investigation. In denying the motion, the court pointed to the lower age limit of *Code* protection as the reason the *Code* did not apply.[136]

At the same time, another respondent corporation applied to court for an injunction to prevent the sale of one complainant's unit. In granting the injunction, the court also stated that the statutory age limitation protected the corporation's rule.[137]

When the matter reached the board of inquiry, the board, having previously ruled itself a court of competent jurisdiction for the purpose of section 24 of the Canadian *Charter of Rights and Freedoms*,[138] ruled that the condominium's rule was discriminatory on the ground of both family status and age. The board went on to rule that the respondents could not rely on the lower age limit set out in subsection 10(1) of the *Code* since, in the cir-

---

133. (1990), 2 O.R. (3d) 319n (S.C.C.).
134. *Winnipeg School Division No. 1 v. Craton* (1985), 6 C.H.R.R. D/3014 (S.C.C.).
135. (1990), 12 C.H.R.R. D/325 (Ont. Bd. of Inquiry), reversed in part (1991), 14 C.H.R.R. D/406 (Ont. Div. Ct.).
136. *York Condominium Corp. No. 29 v. Cryderman* (1988), 10 C.H.R.R. D/5439 (Ont. Dist. Ct.).
137. *Metropolitan Toronto Condominium Corp. No. 624 v. Ramdial* (1988), 10 C.H.R.R. D/5440 (Ont. Dist. Ct.), appeal quashed (1988), 10 C.H.R.R. D/5442 (Ont. C.A.).
138. *Dudnik v. York Condominium Corp. No. 216* (1988), 9 C.H.R.R. D/5080.

cumstances of the case, the provision violated section 15 of the *Charter*, and was not saved by section 1.

> In our opinion, section 9(1)(*a*) [now section 10(1)] is unnecessarily broad in its sweeping language. Although it is reasonable to provide that a 14 year old who cannot enter into an enforceable contract to purchase or rent a condominium unit therefore does not have a complaint sustainable under sections 2(1) and (3) of the *Code* for a refusal by a landlord to rent to, or by an owner to sell to, it is a different situation with the infant complainants in this inquiry. None of the infant complainants are seeking to contract; nor is anyone seeking to contract with them. Contractual rights and obligations are not at issue where the child is seeking occupancy of accommodation through the contract which the child's adult parent is seeking to enforce. Accordingly, in our opinion, and we so find, section 9(1)(*a*) [now section 10(1)] is without force and effect in respect of the infant complainants' situations.[139]

This ruling was confirmed by the Divisional Court on appeal.

Disparate Treatment

The majority of cases in which age discrimination is alleged involve employment decisions or practices. Early cases under previous Codes dealt with relatively straightforward issues; for example, a refusal to hire a woman due to the employer's wish for an attractive "girl" secretary was pronounced discriminatory, as was an unsupported assumption that a stout, fifty-one year old women, who had that year successfully completed a welding course, could not tolerate "heavy" work.[140]

In a more recent case, *O'Brien v. Ontario Hydro*,[141] a 40-year-old man with a varied employment background applied for an apprenticeship, a six-year program, with Ontario Hydro. Considerable evidence was adduced before the board as to Hydro's hiring practices. It was noted that in fact Hydro had hired a number of persons in the forty to sixty-five age range, but not in the apprenticeship program. While the Board acknowledged that there may have been other reasons for the respondent's failure to hire O'Brien, such as overqualification and fears of instability due to a varied work background, the chairman concluded that age stereotyping by the employer was a proximate cause of the refusal and found for the complainant.

The respondent in *O'Brien* did not raise the defence that age might be a reasonable and *bona fide* occupational qualification for its apprenticeship program for reasons of economics.

The theory that the age of apprentices might have an impact on the return on expenses of training expected by the employer has been raised in few cases, but as yet it is difficult to discern principles that might guide a

---

139. *Ante*, note 135 at D/351.
140. See *Britnell v. Brent Personnel Placement Services* (1968), unreported (Ont. Bd. of Inquiry); and *Hawkes v. Brown's Iron Works* (1977), unreported (Ont. Bd. of Inquiry).
141. (1981), 2 C.H.R.R. D/504 (Ont. Bd. of Inquiry).

board's examination of this issue. In *obiter*, tribunals have suggested that clear and objectively reliable evidence as to cost and benefit would be required as to establish such a defense. In one board of inquiry, a projected period of fully trained service of only ten years was considered by the board to be sufficient.[142]

Constructive Discrimination

There are to date no Ontario decisions concerning constructive discrimination on the basis of age.

Other Issues

There have been a number of cases in which boards have considered factors considered by respondents to be linked to aging which might have an impact on ability to do a job safely or well. These will be reviewed in Chapter 6 in the section on "reasonable and bona fide" justifications for otherwise discriminatory actions.

Exceptions Relevant to Age

The statutory exceptions most likely to affect the right to freedom from discrimination on the ground of age are found in the following provisions:

1. section 14, which provides for "special programs";

2. section 15, which provides an exemption in respect of preferential treatment for those aged sixty-five and over;

3. section 18, which allows a religious, philanthropic, educational, fraternal or social institution or organization that is primarily engaged in serving the interests of persons protected by the Code to restrict membership or participation to persons similarly identified;

4. section 20(2), which allows for the enforcement of a minimum drinking age of nineteen years;

5. section 20(3), which allows a "recreational club" to restrict or qualify "access to its services of facilities" or give "preferences with respect to membership dues and other fees because of age, sex, marital status or family status";

6. section 21(1), which allows discrimination on all grounds cited in section 2 in residential accommodation where

---

142. *Arnison v. Pacific Pilotage Authority* (1980), 1 C.H.R.R. D/138 (Cdn. Human Rights Trib.); see general discussion in *Carson v. Air Canada*, (1984), 5 C.H.R.R. D/1857 (Cdn. Rev. Trib.).

(a) the owner or the owner's family resides in the accommodation, and (b) the occupant(s) are required to share a bathroom or kitchen with the owner or the owner's family; and

7. section 22, which allows discrimination on the basis of age, sex, marital status, family status or handicap (where the discrimination is reasonable and *bona fide*) in a contract of automobile, life, accident, sickness of disability insurance, or a non-employment group life insurance contract, or a life annuity;

8. section 23(3), which allows questions to be asked concerning a prohibited ground of discrimination at an employment interview, where discrimination on that ground is otherwise permitted by the *Code*;

9. section 24(1)(a), which provides that,

    a religious, philanthropic, educational, fraternal or social institution or organization that is primarily engaged in serving the interests of persons identified by their race, ancestry, place of origin, colour, ethnic origin, creed, sex, age, marital status or handicap employs only, or gives preference in employment to, persons similarly identified if the qualification is a reasonable and *bona fide* qualification because of the nature of the employment;

10. section 24(1)(b) which allows discrimination that would otherwise breach section 5 where:

    the discrimination in employment is for reasons of age, sex, record of offences or marital status if the age, sex, record of offences or marital status of the applicant is a reasonable and *bona fide* qualification because of the nature of the employment;

11. section 24(1)(c), which provides that section 5 is not breached where

    an individual person refuses to employ another for reasons of any prohibited ground of discrimination in section 5, where the primary duty of the employment is attending to the medical or personal needs of the person or of an ill child or an aged, infirm or ill spouse or other relative of the person;

12. section 25(2) which provides that certain employment benefit plans may discriminate on the ground of age, sex, marital status or family status where such plans comply with the *Employment Standards Act* and Regulations. However, employment may not be denied because of failure to qualify in such a plan, nor made conditional on qualifying for inclusion.

The exceptions are discussed in detail in Chapter 6.

MARITAL STATUS, FAMILY STATUS

Definition

Marital status was broadly defined in the 1981 Code by section 9(1)(a) [now s. 10(1)]:

"marital status" means the status of being married, single, widowed, divorced or separated and includes the status of living with a person of the opposite sex in a conjugal relationship outside marriage.

Marital status was included in the previous *Code*, but was not defined; an early board of inquiry demonstrated the need for a legislated definition.

In *Blatt v. Catholic Children's Aid Society of Metropolitan Toronto (Municipality)*,[143] the complainant had been hired as a childcare worker; however, he was discharged the same day he was hired when the respondent agency discovered, from information on Blatt's employment forms, that he was living with a woman in a common-law relationship. The board of inquiry dismissed Blatt's complaint, citing the *Oxford English Dictionary* to the effect that marital meant "pertaining to marriage." The board noted that the Ontario *Family Law Reform Act* provided certain rights to unmarried spouses, but declined to find that a "new form of marriage" was thereby created.

The narrow view taken by the board in *Blatt* seemed, in part, to result from the Chair's anxiety that the *Code* not be construed, in the absence of specific wording, to override the "freedom to differ about . . . moral issues."[144] The distinction was summed up as follows:

> The key to the Society's objection was not that Mr. Blatt was married nor that Mr. Blatt was single, by any legal definition of the terms, but that he was living with a woman other than his wife. In the Board's view this is an issue of "life style" or sexual morality, not an issue of marital status.[145]

Clearly, the legislature has provided a response to *Blatt*. However, one difficulty with the scope of the section may still arise. The present Ontario *Code*, unlike the Saskatchewan *Code*[146] which, by its regulation, includes "the state of being engaged to be married" in its definition of marital status, makes no mention of this interim state. The omission of protection for engaged persons constituted a serious difficulty in one English case,[147] in which the complainant's employment as a teacher in a girls' school was terminated when she announced her engagement. An industrial tribunal held that it did not have jurisdiction to make a finding in this case, as the complainant was not, at the time of the dismissal, a "married person." However, in a subsequent case, a tribunal saw no such difficulty in regard to engaged persons.[148]

While it would seem reasonable, on a "fair, large and liberal" reading of section 10(1) to include engaged persons, a board might feel precluded

---

143. (1980), 1 C.H.R.R. D/72 (Ont. Bd. of Inquiry).
144. *Ibid.*, p. D/73.
145. *Ibid..*
146. S.S. 1979, c. S-24.1.
147. *Bick v. Royal School for the Deaf*, [1976] I.R.L.R. 326 (Indust. Trib.).
148. See *Maclean v. Paris Travel Service*, [1976] I.R.L.R. 202 (Indust. Trib.).

from construing the section broadly because of the use of the phrase "the *status* of being married, etc."

The confinement of *Code* protection to opposite-sex couples has not yet been dealt with in a published Ontario board decision. However, the issue has been raised in other provinces and in regard to the federal legislation, where the term is undefined. In *Vogel v. Gov't of Manitoba*[149] a Board of Adjudication held that an employment dental plan that included common law spouses but excluded same-sex couples was not discriminatory on this ground. In *Mossop v. Canada (Secretary of State*[150] a board of inquiry held that a collective agreement which did not provide family bereavement leave to a member of a same-sex couple was discriminatory on the basis of family status. In coming to this conclusion, the board invoked s. 15 of the *Charter of Rights and Freedoms* as an aid to interpretation. *Mossop* was reversed on appeal,[151] the Federal Court of Appeal being of the opinion that the term "family" could be clearly defined and confined to blood or adoptive relationship, and that the term "status" with it is coupled limits the definition to relationships now recognised by law as giving rise to legal obligations. Further, the Court disagreed with the board's invocation of the *Charter* despite previous authority to the effect that sexual orientation could be a ground of discrimination under s. 15 of the *Charter*.

Family status is defined by subsection 10(1) as "the status of being in a parent and child relationship." Protection from discrimination on the ground of family status was introduced in the 1990 *Code*. A recent Ontario board decision in *obiter* further extended the definition as follows:

> Section 9(1)(*d*) [now 10(1)] says "family status means the status of being in a parent and child relationship." Obviously this includes both a biological and an adoptive parent . . . In our view, the definition looks to a "status" arising from being in a parent and child type of "relationship." That is, someone acting in the position of parent to a child is, in our view, embraced by this definition; for example, a legal guardian or even an adult functioning in fact as parent. Occasionally, for example, due to death or illness of a relative or friend, someone will step in and act as parent to a child of the deceased or incapacitated adult. Thus, if a nephew were to reside with an aunt for an indefinite period, in our view their relationship would fall within the meaning of "family status" in section 9(1)(*d*) [now 10(1)].[152]

Disparate Treatment

Cases involving discrimination on the ground of marital status often appear to stem from stereotypic assumptions about individuals based on their marital status.

---

149. (1983), 4 C.H.R.R. D/320.
150. (1989), 10 C.H.R.R. D/6064.
151. *Canada (Attorney General) v. Mossop* (1990), 12 C.H.R.R. D/355.
152. *Dudnik v. York Condominium Corp. No. 216, ante,* note 135, at D/348.

A classic example of such assumptions can be seen in the 1968 case of
Fortey v. Middlesex Creamery Ltd.,[153] in which an employer who made employment decisions based on the assumption that the male spouse would always be the major breadwinner was found to have discriminated. The
respondent admitted to maintaining separate rates of pay for two similar
categories of job. In one job all the employees were male; in the other they
were exclusively female. Further, the respondent admitted that the female
egg-grader was so classified largely because this position was soon to be
"phased out." The decision quotes from the transcript of the hearing as follows:

> THE CHAIRMAN: This is one of the problems of automation, but it also involves, it
> seems to me, assumptions that the legislation, modern legislation dealing with the place
> of women, was designed to overcome. Not your industry, but industry-wide and society
> wide.
> A. Well, I think if you wouldn't mind me say so, sir, the one reason that some of these
> jobs are being classified as female jobs is because there is no future. There will be no fu-
> ture in this . . . [job] that we are doing within a few years. Within a few years, it will be
> gone by the boards, so that is why — why should a man study and read up to become a
> professional egg grader when it's almost not a planned obsolescence, but it will be done
> away with. There is no question about it.
> THE CHAIRMAN: There can be no quarrel with this statement except for one assump-
> tion. I am sure if you asked the current Royal Commission on the Status of Women and
> all the people who were appearing before it, they would say your assumption is wrong,
> that it is a women's job because it will essentially disappear. Why should a woman not
> aspire to as such as a man?
> A. Well, a man has — you know, must prepare his future with his pension and insurance
> and so on and this is not up to me to say, but this type of — it is more a transient job,
> this egg grader, today than it was a few years ago. It was a profession. When Mrs.
> Fortey used to do it, it was a profession. Not to any of our planning, but it is just mecha-
> nization and modern equipment that has sort of done away with these jobs.[154]

A 1981 Ontario board dealt with the common assumption that a married person or, perhaps more specifically, a married woman, would be unwilling to undertake employment travel duties. The board in *Niedzwiecki v.
Beneficial Insurance System*[155] made it clear that, where the employer fails
to test the assumption by asking the individual about his or her willingness
to travel, a refusal to hire for this reason cannot be justified. *Niedzwiecki*
followed the approach already taken in other jurisdictions, including the
United States and England, where interested assumptions as to the undesir-

---

153. (1968), unreported (Ont. Bd. of Inquiry).
154. *Ibid.*, at p. 16 (transcript).
155. (1981), 3 C.H.R.R. D/1004 (Ont. Bd. of Inquiry).

ability of mothers as employees had been considered "sex-plus" discrimination.[156]

A recent Ontario board of inquiry took an approach consistent with *Niedzwiecki* when it found discrimination where an employer chose to lay off an employee on the basis of an assumption that as the mother of an infant, she would be less interested in her job than employees without children.[157]

Only one recent Ontario case seems to have departed from the general trend away from honoring unsupported assumptions. In *Geiger v. London Monenco Consultants Ltd.*[158] the board refused to find that an employer's practice of giving married employees a higher living allowance and company-paid return trips to their home city every three weeks, if they accepted an assignment to a Northern Ontario location, contravened the *Code*. These benefits were not provided to unmarried employees. The board made their

---

156. In *Phillips v. Martin Marietta Corp.*, 400 U.S. 542 (1971), a school had refused two female teachers with pre-school age children because it was of the opinion that mothers should be at home with young children. Male teachers with pre-school age children were not refused employment. The court said that an employer may not refuse to hrie women with pre-school age children while hiring men with such children unless it could show that such a rule was a *bona fide* occupational qualification. Marshall J., concurring, said that this could never be a *bona fide* occupational qualification.

In *Re Consolidated Pretrial Proceedings in the Airline Cases*, 582 F. 2d 1142 (1978), female flight attendants were required to take ground duties on becoming mothers while male flight attendants were permitted to remain in the air on becoming fathers. The court found that this fact situation was indistinguishable from the fact situation in *Phillips* and held that this rule constituted discrimination on the basis of sex. The airlines attempted to argue that mothers of young children would have unacceptably high rates of absenteeism but gave no evidence that this was in fact so. They also argued that mothers might be subject to overriding domestic concerns that would make them questionable risks for competent performance in times of crisis but presented no evidence either that this was so or that fathers would be any different. The court rejected these arguments as being based on stereotypical assumptions. Another argument adduced by the airlines was that mothers returning from maternity leaves of absence would require expensive retraining and that business necessarily precluded hireback. The court rejected this argument, noting that retraining women returning from leaves of absence would be less expensive than training their replacements.

In *Hurley v. Mustoe*, [1981] 1 R.L.R. 208 (Employment App. Trib.), a woman had been fired from her new job as a waitress when her employer discovered that she had four young children, despite the fact that the children were well cared for by their father while she was at work. It was the employer's policy not to hire women with young children because he believed them to be unreliable. He had no such policy against hiring men with young children. An employment appeal tribunal held that this was discrimination on the basis of sex.

157. While the Board in *Broere v. W.P. London and Associates Ltd.* (1987), 8 C.H.R.R. D/4189 (Ont. Bd. of Inquiry) found discrimination on the basis of marital status, the complaint as framed cited both marital status and family status.

158. (1987), 9 C.H.R.R. D/4543 (Ont. Bd. of Inquiry).

find on the basis that the employment benefits in question were "bona fide occupational requirements," despite the fact that the respondent employer apparently could bring no evidence to satisfy the objective requirement of the *Etobicoke* test. The view of the board in *Geiger* seems inconsistent with other authority and presumably is unlikely to be followed.

An obvious area of concern about discrimination on the ground of family status is restrictions relating to children in housing accommodation. In *Life Together: A Report on Human Rights in Ontario*, the Ontario Human Rights Commission noted the proliferation of "adult-only" apartment buildings in Ontario municipalities as rationales for including in the *Code* protection from discrimination on the basis of "family relationship." However, until 1986, a specific provision in the *Code* operated to allow the maintenance of "adult-only" apartment buildings. The former subsection 20(4) was repealed, effective December 18, 1986.[159]

In a recent case, condominium corporations that enforced rules against occupancy by persons under, respectively, fourteen and sixteen years old, were found to have discriminated on the basis of both age and family status.[160] In making its decision the board heard evidence as to demographics affecting housing supply, the impact of changes to the economy, the availability of rental housing, as well as survey evidence concerning preferences.[161] In *Fakhoury v. Las Brisas Ltd.*,[162] a landlord was found to have discriminated in maintaining a rule that required a single parent with three children to rent a more expensive three-bedroom apartment rather than a less expensive two-bedroom plus den unit. The respondent landlord did rent two-bedroom units to families of four, but did so only if two of the four family members were parents. In *Booker v. Floriri Village Investments Inc.*,[163] a board found discrimination where a single mother was rejected as a prospective tenant due to a preference for married couples.

Constructive Discrimination

To date, no cases of constructive discrimination on the ground of marital or family status have been decided under the Ontario *Code*. However, there is certainly scope for such cases, particularly in the area of employ-

---

159. S.O. 1986, c. 64. Remaining exceptions to the protection afforded by the *Code* are discussed further below.

160. *Dudnik v. York Condominium Corp. No. 216*, (1990), 12 C.H.R.R. D/325 (Ont. Bd. of Inquiry), revised in part (1991), 14 C.H.R.R. D/406 (Ont. Div. Ct.).

161. See also *Moxon v. Samax Investments* (1984), 5 C.H.R.R. D/2835, in which a Manitoba Board of Inquiry found that a landlord's refusal to rent to people with children, on the basis of an assumption that children create more noise than other tenants, was discriminatory.

162. (1987), 8 C.H.R.R. D/4028 (Ont. Bd. of Inquiry).

163. (1989), 11 C.H.R.R. D/44 (Ont. Bd. of Inquiry).

ment, and tribunals in other jurisdictions have recognized such complaints. In the English case of *Meeks v. National Union of Agricultural and Allied Workers*,[164] an industrial tribunal considered whether certain employment terms were constructively discriminatory. The complainant was employed as a part-time clerical worker. As a part-time employee she received a lower hourly rate of pay than full-time workers. She argued that fewer women than men could qualify for the higher rate of pay, since fewer women could manage full-time work in addition to their domestic responsibilities. While the tribunal dismissed the claim for reasons related to the terms of the English equal pay legislation, it was prepared to accept this argument.

A similar argument was adduced in a later case, *Price v. Civil Service Commission*.[165] Once again, constructive discrimination was involved; in this case, a rule that no applicant over twenty-eight years of age would be considered for employment. Price argued that this rule constructively discriminated against women, in that fewer women than men were available for full-time employment before age twenty-eight, due to child-bearing and the raising of young children. An employment appeal tribunal accepted this argument and remitted the case to an industrial tribunal with a suggestion that it consider statistical and other evidence on this issue. At the subsequent tribunal hearing, the respondent conceded that there was an adverse impact on women and the tribunal found in favour of the complainant.[166]

Other Issues

An important issue in this area is whether an impugned action taken because of a marriage or family relationship to a particular person (as opposed to because of reaction to the status itself) is discriminatory. Such cases arise, for example, when the spouse or child of an employee is in a position such that his or her relationship could cause problems to the employer.

It is fair to say that the law here is unsettled. Courts and tribunals in England and the United States have differed as to whether the broader interpretation is warranted.[167] Canadian jurisdictions other than Ontario have

---

164. [1976] I.R.L.R. 198 (Indus. Trib.)
165. [1977] 1 W.L.R. 1417 (Employment App. Trib.).
166. *Price v. Civil Service Commission (No. 2)*, [1978] I.R.L.R. 3 (Indust. Trib.).
167. *Coleman v. Skyrail Oceanic Ltd.*, [1981] I.C.R. 864 (C.A.); and *Maclean v. Paris Travel Service*, [1976] I.R.L.R. 202, represent the broader view taken by English tribunals. *Yukas v. Libbey-Owens Ford Co.*, 562 F (2d) 496 (1977) is an example of a case in which U.S. courts took the narrower view.

similarly contradicted each other.[168]

Cases to date in Ontario have also conflicted on this point. In *Bosi v. Michipicoten (Township),*[169] the complainant was refused a job as a clerk in a township office because, as a clerk, she would have had access to contract negotiation documents in which the complainant's husband, a police officer for the township, would have had an interest. The Board in *Bosi* found that the term "marital status" was not to be extended to encompass marriage to a particular individual. The board went on specifically to find that, assuming that marital status should properly be given a wider meaning, the restriction in the case was a "bona fide occupational qualification."

In *Mark v. Porcupine General Hospital*[170] the complainant was discharged when her employer realized that she was married to someone in the same department. The board in *Mark,* in finding for the complainant, specifically disagreed with the Board in *Bosi* as to the extension of "marital status" to fit the circumstances. Despite evidence that the husband of the complainant might occasionally be in a position to supervise her work on an "acting basis, the board ruled that there was no 'bona fide' occupational requirement" to justify the wife's dismissal in the circumstances.

In *Szabo v. Atlas Employees Welland Credit Union,*[171] the complainant was not considered for an advertised position because his father was an employee of the company to which the respondent credit union was attached, and was a member of the supervisory committee of the credit union. The board in *Szabo* accepted that the focus on the identity of the complainant's father did not prevent a finding of discrimination on the basis of family status. The board went on to consider whether the respondent credit union could claim the exception provided by subsection 24(*d*) of the *Code*:

> 24(1) The right under section 5 to equal treatment with respect to employment is not infringed where,
>
> . . . .
>
> (d) an employer grants or withholds employment or advancement in employment to a person who is the spouse, child or parent of the employer or an employee.

After considering the circumstances, the board found that neither the respondent's father, as a member of the credit union or as a member of the

---

168. See *Hanvold Expediting British Columbia Ltd. v. Fast* (1985), 6 C.H.R.R. D/2813 (N.W.T.S.C.) and *Murray v. Toope* (1991) 13 C.H.R.R. D/94; *Cashin v. Canadian Broadcasting Corp.* (1988), 9 C.H.R.R. D/5354 (Fed. C.A.), leave to appeal refused (1988), 97 N.R. 395 (note) (S.C.C.) as examples of the narrower interpretation. In *Monk v. C.D.E. Holdings Ltd.* (1983), 4 C.H.R.R. D/1391 (Man. Bd. of Adjud.), a Manitoba board favoured the broader interpretation, as did the tribunal in *Druken v. Canada (Employment & Immigration Commission)* (1987), 8 C.H.R.R. D/4379 (Cdn. Human Rights Trib.), affirmed [1989] 2 F.C. 24 (C.A.).
169. (1982), 4 C.H.R.R. D/1252 (Ont. Bd. of Inquiry).
170. (1985), 6 C.H.R.R. D/2538 (Ont. Bd. of Inquiry).
171. (1988), 9 C.H.R.R. D/4735 (Ont. Bd. of Inquiry).

supervisory committee, was put in to the position of acting as a potential employer to his son, nor was the father an employee of the credit union. Hence, the board found that subsection 24(*d*) did not apply.

To date, there has been no authoritative pronouncement from the Supreme Court of Canada, but there is some indication that the Court might be willing to extend the definition to situations in which the identity of the spouse or family member is at issue. In 1988, the Supreme Court of Canada denied leave to appeal the decision of the Federal Court of appeal in *Cashin v. Canadian Broadcasting Corp.*[172] That decision had restored the order of a board of inquiry which ruled that a woman who had been denied further employment because she was married to a prominent public figure had been discriminated against on the ground of marital status for the purpose of the *Canadian Human Rights Act*. A year later, in an *obiter* pronouncement in *Brossard (Town) v. Quebec (Comm. des droits de la personne)*, Beetz, J. said:

> . . . I am inclined . . . to think that in some circumstances the identity of a particular spouse might be included in marital or civil status.[173]

It is suggested that the wider interpretation of the terms marital and family status is the more appropriate, for several reasons. First, fair large and liberal interpretation of the *Code* is in accordance with both section 10 of the Ontario's *Interpretation Act* and with recent jurisprudence.[174] Secondly, section 12 of the *Code*, which specifically encompasses discrimination by association, signals the Legislature's intent to create a wide-ranging Code. Finally, it is suggested that, on a narrow reading of marital and family status, there would be little need for the specific exception set out in subsection 24(*d*).[175]

Exceptions Relevant to Marital or Family Status

The statutory exceptions most likely to affect the right to freedom from discrimination on the ground of marital or family status are found in the following provisions:

1. section 14, which provides for "special programs";

2. section 18, which allows a religious, philanthropic, educational, fraternal or social institution or organization that is primarily engaged in

---

172. *Ante,* note 168.
173. (1989), 53 D.L.R. (4th) 609, 10 C.H.R.R. D/5516 at 5526 (S.C.C.).
174. See R.S.O. 1990, c. I.11 and discussion in Chapter 1.
175. It is possible that subsection 24(*d*) does not go far as to exempt from the application of the *Code* an employer's decision to fire an employee because he or she "is a spouse, child or parent of the employer or employee" (see discussion in Chapter 6). However, the subsection clearly relates to the broader definition of marital or family status.

serving the interests of persons protected by the Code to restrict membership or participation to persons similarly identified;

3. section 19(1), which maintains those rights or privileges of separate schools and their supporters that are provided under the *British North America Act* and the *Education Act*;[176]

4. section 20(3), which allows a "recreational club" to restrict or qualify "access to its services or facilities" or give "preferences with respect to membership dues and other fees because of age, sex, marital status or family status";

5. section 21(1), which allows discrimination on all grounds cited in section 2 in residential accommodation where
    (a) the owner or the owner's family resides in the accommodation, and
    (b) the occupant(s) are required to share a bathroom or kitchen with the owner or the owner's family; and

6. section 22, which allows discrimination on the basis of age, sex, marital status or handicap (where the discrimination is reasonable and *bona fide*) in a contract of automobile, life, accident, sickness or disability insurance, or a non-employment group life insurance contract, or a life annuity;

7. section 23(3), which allows questions to be asked concerning a prohibited ground of discrimination at an employment interview, where discrimination on that ground is otherwise permitted by the *Code*;

8. section 24(1)(a), which provides that,

    a religious, philanthropic, educational, fraternal or social institution or organization that is primarily engaged in serving the interests of persons identified by their race, ancestry, place of origin, colour, ethnic origin, creed, sex, age, marital status or handicap employs only, or gives preference in employment to, persons similarly identified if the qualification is a reasonable and *bona fide* qualification because of the nature of the employment;

9. section 24(1)(b), which allows discrimination that would otherwise breach section 5 where:

    the discrimination in employment is for reasons of age, sex, record of offences or marital status if the age, sex, record of offences or marital status of the applicant is a reasonable and *bona fide* qualification because of the nature of the employment;

10. section 24(1)(c), which provides that section 5 is not breached where

    an individual person refuses to employ another for reasons of any prohibited ground of discrimination in section 5, where the primary duty of the employment is attending to

---

176. It would appear that separate schools are likely to be able to discriminate on the ground of marital or family status for reasons having to do with religion; see discussion of section 19 in Chapter 6.

the medical or personal needs of the person or of an ill child or an aged, infirm or ill spouse or other relative of the person;

11. section 24(1)(*d*), which provides that an employer may grant or withhold employment or advancement in employment to a person who is the spouse, child or parent of the employer of an employee;

12. section 25(2) which provides that certain employment benefit plans may discriminate on the ground of age, sex, marital status or family status, where such plans comply with the *Employment Standards Act* and Regulations. However, employment may not be denied because of failure to qualify in such a plan, nor made conditional on qualifying for inclusion.[177]

The exceptions are discussed in detail in Chapter 6.

HANDICAP

Definition

The protection offered by the *Code* against discrimination on the ground of handicap is offered to persons suffering virtually any handicap, past or present, real or perceived. Section 10(1) defines handicap as follows:

"because of handicap" means for the reason that the person *has or has had,. or is believed to have or have had,*

(a) any degree of physical disability, infirmity, malformation or disfigurement that is caused by bodily injury, birth defect or illness and, without limiting the generality of the foregoing, including diabetes mellitus, epilepsy, any degree of paralysis, amputation, lack of physical co-ordination, blindness or visual impediment, deafness or hearing impediment, muteness or speech impediment, or physical reliance on a dog guide or on a wheelchair or other remedial appliance or device,

(b) a condition of mental retardation or impairment,

(c) a learning disability, or a dysfunction in one or more of the processes involved in understanding or using symbols or spoken language,

(d) a mental disorder or,

(e) an injury or disability for which benefits were claimed or received under the *Workers' Compensation Act*. [Emphasis added].

It is quite clear that this definition is intended to encompass any handicap including those that exist only in the perceptions or imaginations of others.

Recent Ontario cases have dealt with allegations of discrimination

---

177. Subsection 25(1); see Chapter 6.

against people suffering from diabetes,[178] cerebral palsy,[179] malformation of fingers,[180] musculoskeletal injury[181] and developmental handicap,[182] all of which are clearly and specifically "handicaps" within the definition provided by the *Code*.

Recently, a board of inquiry under the Canadian *Human Rights Act* ruled that persons carrying the HIV virus come under the definition of "disability" in that Act, despite the fact that they may yet be without symptoms of Acquired Immune Difficiency Syndrome.[183]

The question of whether obesity is to be considered a handicap was raised in *Horton v. Niagara (Regional Municipality)*.[184] The board in that case found that the Commission had not discharged the onus on it to prove that the complainants obesity was caused by "bodily injury, birth defect or illness" since it had not adduced medical evidence to that effect. However, the board in *Horton* rejected the respondent's submission that hypertension and obesity should be "equated" and held that "both in common understanding and previous jurisprudence,[185] hypertension is considered an illness," and as such was included in the definition of handicap. The board explicitly declined to make a ruling as to whether obesity could be considered a handicap, although it can be inferred that it was prepared to entertain evidence as to the etiology of the obesity so as to make such a determination.[186]

It appears unlikely that temporary disability will be considered handicap. In *Nielson v. Sandiman Four Ltd.*,[187] a British Columbia case which concerned an employee who was dismissed because she missed eleven days

---

178. *Barnard v. Fort Frances (City)* (1986), 7 C.H.R.R D/3167 (Ont. Bd. of Inquiry).
179. *Kellerman v. Al's Restaurant and Tavern Ltd.* (1986), 8 C.H.R.R. D/3924 (Ont. Bd. of Inquiry).
180. *Cameron v. Nel-Gor Nursing Home* (1984), 5 C.H.R.R. D/2170 (Ont. Bd. of Inquiry).
181. *Belliveau v. Steel Co. of Canada* (1988), 9 C.H.R.R. D/5250 (Ont. Bd. of Inquiry).
182. *Hickling v. Lanark, Leeds and Grenville County Roman Catholic School Board* (1986), 7 C.H.R.R. D/3546 (Ont. Bd. of Inquiry), revised (1987), 8 C.H.R.R. D/4235 (Ont. Div. Ct.), affirmed (1989), 10 C.H.R.R. D/6336 (Ont. C.A.) and *Boehm v. National System of Baking* (1987), 8 C.H.R.R. D/4110 (Ont. Bd. of Inquiry).
183. *Fontaine v. Canadian Pacific Ltd.* (1989), 11 C.H.R.R. D/288 (Cdn. Human Rights Trib.), affirmed (1990), 91 C.L.L.C. 17,008 (Fed. C.A.).
184. (1987), 9 C.H.R.R. D/4611 (Ont. Bd. of Inquiry).
185. The Board cited *Wamboldt v. Canada (Department of National Defence)* (1983), 4 C.H.R.R. D/1479 (Cdn. Human Rights Trib.).
186. Quebec Tribunals have conflicted as to whether obesity fits the definition of handicap. See *Québec (Commission des Droits de la personne) c. Cote St. Luc (Cité)* (1982), 4 C.H.R.R. D/1287 (C.S. Qué.); and *Québec (Commission des Droits de la Personne) c. Héroux* (1981), 2 C.H.R.R. D/388. Also, see *Davison v. St. Paul Lutheran Home of Melville Saskatchewan* (1991), 91 CL.L.C. 17,017 (Sask. Bd. of Inquiry) (Human Rights).
187. (1986), 7 C.H.R.R. D/3329 (B.C. Human Rights Council).

work due to an injury, the board declined to find discrimination on the ground of physical disability. More recently, in *Ouimette v. Lily Cups Ltd.*,[188] an Ontario board ruled that influenza causing "few days illness" does not constitute handicap.

The *Ouimette* decision involved the unwritten employment practice of the respondent company that if a probationary employee missed more than two days of work for any reason, the employee was dismissed. The complainant, having missed two days due to influenza and one day to an allergic reaction, was dismissed. She claimed that her dismissal constituted discrimination on the ground of handicap. The board found that discrimination had not occurred.

Except for the above noted finding as to influenza not constituting handicap, the reasons for the board's finding are obscure. Clearly, the board accepted that the complainant suffered from an allergy, and apparently the board accepted allergies as handicap. It would appear that the board concluded that an allergic reaction was not proven to be the cause of the complainant's first absence. However, the board goes on to discuss at some length the concept of "reckless negligence" (in the context of the complainant having taken an analgesic without satisfying herself that it did not contain aspirin, to which she was allergic) as though to support a theory that handicap cannot exist where the individual plays some part in triggering or contributing to the handicap.

The board also discussed the concept of constructive discrimination, both in relation to persons who might be subject to influenza and to persons with allergies. The board appeared to dismiss the concept of constructive discrimination in relation to influenza because the group potentially affected was so large as to be unidentifiable and because influenza is not a handicap. However, it appeared to ignore the possibility that persons with allergies (surely an identifiable group for the purpose of section 11) might be adversely affected, more than the general population, by the dismissal rule at issue; the point is not addressed in the decision.

Disparate Treatment

An example of discrimination on the ground of handicap in employment is *Cameron v. Nel-Gor Castle Nursing Home*[189] in which an applicant for a nurse's aide position, one of whose hands had three fingers that were shorter than normal length, was refused the position on the basis that she could not do the required lifting. At the subsequent inquiry, the board pointed to evidence that established that the applicant could do the lifting, and would have been able to demonstrate her ability had she been given the chance.

---

188. (1990), 12 C.H.R.R. D/19 (Ont. Bd. of Inquiry).
189. *Ante*, note 80.

An example of discrimination in service provision arose in the case of *Hickling v. Lanark, Leeds and Grenville Co. Roman Catholic School Board*[190] which involved a refusal by the respondent school board to provide services locally to mentally handicapped children. The decision in favour of the complainant was successfully appealed on another ground.[191]

Constructive Discrimination

To date, there are no published Ontario decisions concerning constructive discrimination on the ground of handicap.[192] In the interim, the Commission has set out a number of written policy positions or guidelines[193] concerning certain "requirements, qualifications and factors," such as prospective employers requesting a driver's license number on application forms for employment, requiring medical examinations as part of the job application and conducting drug and alcoholic testing.

The Commission's interpretation of the *Code*, as implied in the guidelines, is that requiring a driver's license number on an application form would breach section 23(2)[194] of the *Code* and would "automatically exclude handicapped applicants who are otherwise qualified for the position." (Although the guideline does not refer to section 11, clearly if such exclusion were proven, a prima facie case of constructive discrimination would be made out.) In regard to pre-employment medicals, the Commission's position is that pre-employment medicals can only be considered "reasonable and bona fide" requirements if conducted

> after a written offer of employment, where the specific physical abilities required to perform the essential duties of a position have been identified, *i.e.*, the essence of the business would be undermined or the safe performance of duties threatened by persons who lack these specific physical abilities to have a certain physical condition, where the medical examination is limited to determining the person's ability to perform the essential duties of the position, (and where), reasonable accommodation for those failing to pass the test is included as part of the process.

A Saskatchewan Human Rights Commission exemption hearing[195] on pre-employment medicals resulted in a similar view being expressed by that

---

190. *Ante*, note 182.
191. (1987), 8 C.H.R.R. D/4235 (Ont. Div. Ct.), affirmed (1989), 10 C.H.R.R. D/6336 (Ont. C.A.).
192. There are few such decisions in other jurisdictions, either. One example is *Issac v. Tahsis Co.* (1984), 84 C.L.L.C. 17,007 (B.C. Bd. of Inquiry) in which a requirement that an applicant for a labouring job have finished grade 12 was held to be constructive discrimination against a learning-disabled complainant.
193. Guidelines issued by the Commission are interpretations by the Commission by provisions of the *Code*. They are further discussed in Chapter 8.
194. This provision is further discussed in Chapter 5.
195. "Exemption Orders" are considered upon request by the Saskatchewan Commission, pursuant to s. 48(1) of the Saskatchewan Human Rights Code, S.S. 1979, c. S-24.1.

Commission. After public hearings, the Commission decided that pre-employment medicals are too easily used to make decisions that operate to a handicapped applicant's disadvantage and are not job-related. Furthermore,

if employers solicit this information and incorporate it into their hiring decisions, a disabled applicant may receive a simple refusal of employment and have no knowledge as to the basis for the refusal. Without knowledge, that person then has little ability to assert his or her right to employment without discrimination.[196]

The Saskatchewan Commission concluded:

[I]t is our view that the rights of disabled persons can only be advanced by separating employment decisions and medical examinations into two distinct steps, with medical examinations conducted only after a job has been offered.

The employer maintains the ability, by this procedure, to refuse to employ a person who, upon examination, is found to have a job-related disability. Disabled persons will also know that they are protected, since they will know that there were found otherwise qualified, were hired, and were subsequently not placed in employment because, in the employer's view, they have a job-related disability. The disabled person may then, if he or she disagrees, challenge that decision. . . .[197]

The Ontario Human Rights Commission's published position on drug and alcohol testing in respect of prospective or current employees is that such testing may amount to constructive discrimination against persons whose use of alcohol or drugs has become an illness or is perceived by a prospective employer to be an illness. The Commission states that where such an prospective employee's testing is done it should be done only after a conditional offer of employment, and only where the need for testing is linked to the ability to perform essential duties or requirements of the job. The policy statement goes on to suggest that testing in respect of current employees should only be done where there is "objective basis to believe" that reduced job performance, absenteeism or safety concerns might result from alcohol or drug dependency. The policy statement also contains suggestions as to reasonable accommodation of employees with drug or alcohol dependency handicaps, and comments as to the need for testing to be done correctly and for the result of testing to be kept confidential.

Other possible sources of complaints of constructive discrimination include the practice by some employers of refusing job applications of persons who previously have made Worker's Compensation claims. A requirement that prospective employees be claim-free could not be maintained unless the employer could prove that:

(a) the requirement, qualification or factor is reasonable and bona fide in the circumstances; or

---

196. *Saskatchewan (Department of Labour, Occupational Health & Safety Branch) v. Voice of the Handicapped* (1980), 2 C.H.R.R. D/261 at 262 (Sask. Human Rights Comm.).
197. *Ibid.*

(b) it is declared in this Act, other than in section 17, that to discriminate because of such ground is not an infringement of a right.[198]

Subsection 11(2) of the *Code* goes on to require that:

> The Commission, a board of inquiry or a court shall not find that a requirement, qualification or factor is reasonable and *bona fide* in the circumstances unless it is satisfied that the needs of the group of which the person is a member cannot be accommodated without undue hardship on the person responsible for accommodating those needs, considering the cost, outside sources of funding, if any, and health and safety requirements, if any.

Other Issues

Handicap cases have given rise to development in the "reasonable and bona fide" and "reasonable accommodation" areas. These are discussed in Chapter 6.

Exceptions Relevant to Handicap

The statutory exceptions most likely to affect the right to freedom from discrimination on the ground of handicap are found in the following provisions:

1. section 14, which provides for "special programs";

2. section 17(1), which provides an exception when the sole reason for the facts giving rise to a complaint by a handicapped person is that the person is incapable of performing or fulfilling the essential duties or requirements attending the exercise of the right because of handicap;

3. section 18, which allows a religious, philanthropic, educational, fraternal or social institution or organization that is primarily engaged in serving the interests of persons protected by the Code to restrict membership or participation to persons similarly identified;

4. section 21(1), which allows discrimination on all grounds cited in section 2 in residential accommodation where
   (a) the owner or the owner's family resides in the accommodation, and
   (b) the occupant(s) are required to share a bathroom or kitchen with the owner or the owner's family; and

5. section 22, which allows discrimination on the basis of age, sex, marital status, family status or handicap (where the discrimination is reasonable and *bona fide*) in a contract of automobile, life, accident, sickness or disability insurance, or a non-employment group life insurance contract, or a life annuity;

---

198. Ss. 11(1)(*a*), (*b*).

6. section 23(3), which allows questions to be asked concerning a prohibited ground of discrimination at an employment interview, where discrimination on that ground is otherwise permitted by the *Code*;

7. section 24(1)(a), which provides that,

   a religious, philanthropic, educational, fraternal or social institution or organization that is primarily engaged in serving the interests of persons identified by their race, ancestry, place of origin, colour, ethnic origin, creed, sex, age, marital status or handicap employs only, or gives preference in employment to, persons similarly identified if the qualification is a reasonable and *bona fide* qualification because of the nature of the employment;

8. section 24(1)(c), which provides that section 5 is not breached where

   an individual person refuses to employ another for reasons of any prohibited ground of discrimination in section 5, where the primary duty of the employment is attending to the medical or personal needs of the person or of an ill child or an aged, infirm or ill spouse or other relative of the person;

9. section 25(3), which provides that certain employment benefit plans may discriminate on the ground of handicap where the distinction is reasonable and *bona fide*. Employment may not be made conditional on qualification in such plans, and an excluded employee must be compensated (sections 25(1) and 25(4)).

The exceptions are discussed in detail in Chapter 6.

RECEIPT OF PUBLIC ASSISTANCE

Definition

"Public assistance" is not defined in the *Code*, but presumably it includes any form of income supplement provided by the government. Discrimination and harassment because of receipt of public assistance is prohibited in regard to accommodation only. This ground of discrimination was added in the 1981 *Code*.

Disparate Treatment

To date there has been only one Ontario board of inquiry dealing with discrimination in this area. In *Willis v. David Anthony Phillips Properties*[199] a single mother on family benefits was first accepted as a tenant by one of the co-owners of the rental accommodation in question, and subsequently rejected by the other owner when he found out the complainant was a recipient of public assistance. The board held that the refusal was discriminatory.

---

199. (1987), 8 C.H.R.R. D/3847 (Ont. Bd. of Inquiry).

Constructive Discrimination

There have been as yet no reported Ontario decisions on constructive discrimination on the ground of receipt of public assistance.

Exceptions Relevant to Receipt of Public Assistance

The statutory exceptions most likely to affect the right to freedom from discrimination on the ground of receipt of public assistance are found in the following provisions:

1. section 14, which provides for "special programs";

2. section 18, which allows a religious, philanthropic, educational, fraternal or social institution or organization that is primarily engaged in serving the interests of persons protected by the Code to restrict membership or participation to persons similarly identified;

3. section 21(1), which allows discrimination on all grounds cited in section 2 in residential accommodation where
    (a) the owner or the owner's family resides in the accommodation, and
    (b) the occupant(s) are required to share a bathroom or kitchen with the owner or the owner's family.

The exceptions are discussed in detail in Chapter 6.

RECORD OF OFFENCES

In *Life Together*, the Ontario Human Rights Commission noted the high rate of recidivism of inmates in Ontario prisons. The Commission cited a number of presentations it had received to the effect that the lack of employment opportunity for ex-offenders was a significant contributing factor to this problem.

> Many companies use employment application forms which ask the question: "Do you have a past criminal record? Answer, Yes or No." If the question is answered in the affirmative, the application is often automatically rejected, and the applicant is given no opportunity to explain in an interview the circumstances and background surrounding his or her record. No further consideration is given to the qualifications and experience of the individual or to whether or not this past offence would affect in any way the applicant's ability to perform the duties required. The Commission has encountered examples of individuals who committed a minor offence years ago, often as young teenagers, who still face discrimination and repeated rejections in employment because of that criminal record, even though it has not been repeated.
>
> There is no desire on the part of the Commission to deny the right of employers to know the background of employees or of job applicants in order to determine their suitability for a particular position, particularly when that position is a sensitive and responsible one. However, the Commission believes that this background should be explored during an interview, not on the application form, and that it should be assessed fairly in terms of the individual's overall record and current ability to perform the job.
>
> The Commission, therefore, recommends that "criminal record" be added to the *Ontario Human Rights Code* as a ground on which discrimination is prohibited, with

provision for exemptions to be granted in cases where, in the Commission's view, criminal record may be a valid consideration.

The Commission also recommends that a special provision be added to the *Code* to allow employers during the course of an employment interview to raise oral questions about a person's past criminal record in order to understand the nature of the offence and whether it will affect a person's ability to perform the duties of the job being considered.[200]

Definition

The provisions requested by the Commission were enacted to only a limited extent, due to the restrictive definition of record of offences, as set out in section 10(1):

"record of offences" means a conviction for,

> (i)   an offence in respect of which a pardon has been granted under the *Criminal Records Act* (Canada) and has not been revoked, or

> (ii) an offence in respect of any provincial enactment.

Record of offences, as a ground of discrimination, applies only to employment. Its inclusion in Part I means that the provisions of the *Code* in regard to employment agencies, advertisements, application forms and interviews apply in respect of the applicant's pardoned criminal or provincial offence conviction.[201]

In fact that "record of offences means a conviction" raises the question whether an employer may discriminate on the ground of a person having been charged with an offence.

Three British Columbia cases have addressed this question. In *Dreidger v. Dalke*[202] the board held that someone discharged from employment due to being charged with a criminal offence had not been discriminated against. However, *Insurance Corporation of British Columbia v. Heerspink*[203] and subsequent appellate authority in that case appear to indicate, at least though a failure to rebut the proposition, that discrimination due to criminal charges should be treated as discrimination because of criminal conviction. *Heerspink* involved a complaint that insurance coverage had been refused the complainant because he had been charged with trafficking in marijuana. The first set of *Heerspink* decisions were concerned with the board's jurisdiction, but once that matter had been resolved, a board of inquiry found that the complainant had been discriminated against, based on a provision of the *Human Rights Code* of British Columbia which provided that "a conviction for a criminal or summary

---

200. (1977), p. 80.
201. See s. 25, discussed in Chapter 5.
202. (1977), unreported (Ont. Bd. of Inquiry).
203. (1977), 79 D.L.R. (3d) 638 (B.C. S.C.), affirmed (1978), 91 D.L.R. (3d) 520 (B.C. C.A.).

conviction charge" was not reasonable cause for discrimination except in certain statutory-defined circumstances. An appeal from this decision was allowed by the British Columbia Supreme Court because the Court found that British Columbia's *Insurance Act* took precedence over the *Code*. However, the court's judgment was revised by the Court of Appeal, and the reversal was further affirmed by the Supreme Court of Canada. The original appeal decision and subsequent decisions were concerned solely with the issues of whether the human rights legislation took precedence over other legislation and the proper scope of appellate review; presumably none of the higher courts took issue with the Board's finding that discrimination because a person had been charged with a criminal offence should be included within the ambit of discrimination because of a conviction.

Most recently, the British Columbia Human Rights Council affirmed that "conviction" encompasses a criminal charge. In *Dore v. Crown Tire Services Ltd.*,[204] the complainant's employment was terminated two days after he was charged with a criminal conviction.

The Council first cited *Insurance Corp. of British Columbia v. Heerspink*;[205] *Ontario (Human Rights Commission) v. Simpsons-Sears*;[206] and *Action Travail des femmes v. Canadian National Railway Co.*,[207] for the general proposition that human rights legislation is of a special nature which should be given a broad, purposive interpretation.

The Council then went through a number of arguments to show that person charged with an offence should have the protection of the Act.

The Council first stated that it would be an absurdity to give protection to those found guilty of a crime but to extend none to those who have merely been charged. The Council stated that this was not the intent of the legislation and it should not be interpreted this way given the nature of the human rights legislation.

Secondly the Council stated that to make such an interpretation — that a person charged with an offence is not protected — is against the fundamental principle of presumption of innocence and the general policy that a person shouldn't be presumed guilty before there has been an opportunity to present a defence. The Council also pointed out that this principle is upheld in 11(*d*) of the Canadian *Charter of Rights and Freedoms*.

The Council then looked at whether the interpretation of section 9 that the Council preferred was possible under the wording of section 9.

The Council used section 15 of the *Charter* as an aid in interpretation, indicating that, as a general rule of interpretation, if there are two interpre-

---

204. (1988), 10 C.H.R.R. D/5433 (B.C. Human Rights Council).
205. *Ante*, note 203.
206. [1985] 2 S.C.R. 536.
207. [1987] 1 S.C.R. 1114.

tations, one that is unconstitutional and one that is constitutional, the one that is constitutional is the interpretation that should be taken.

> The problem at hand seems to call for the application of this principle, for there is a significant risk that the right to equal benefit of the law would be violated if section 8(1) [now section 9] of the Act were interpreted as protecting persons found guilty but as denying protection to those found innocent or awaiting trial.[208]

The Council also stated that it could think of no factor that would "justify a distinction between two groups."

The Council then set out the argument that a perception that a person is a member of a protected group will fall under the Act (i.e., perceived disability). Therefore, the "charge leads to a perceived conviction" and thus the person charged falls under the protection of the Act.

Finally, the Council stated that a charge could be seen as an incident of conviction

> necessary incidents of being charged with a criminal charge must be linked with it in such a way as to merit the same protection for a criminal offence." "In summary, I find that a person who is terminated from his or her employment because of a criminal or summary conviction charge is protected under section 8(1) [now s. 9] of the Act.[209]

Disparate Treatment

In the sole case in which an Ontario board had dealt with discrimination on the ground of record of offences, the Board seemed to confuse the question of whether discrimination on the ground of record of offences had occurred with the issue of whether it was justified in the circumstances. In *Lancaster v. Zellers*[210] the complainant was discharged from employment pursuant to a rule that the employing company could not employ, or continue to employ, anyone who had been previously discharged for theft.

The complainant, while employed by Zellers at the age of 22, had been convicted of theft under $50, the theft being from his employer. He was discharged. Ten years after the incident, he was granted a pardon by the Governor General in Council. For the six years following his pardon, he worked as a Correctional Officer, Security Courier and Retail Store Investigator, and subsequently applied for the position of Loss Prevention Officer.

The respondent admitted that part of their employment application form contained questions that asked if the applicant had ever been convicted of a criminal offence[211] as well as whether he or she had ever been

---

208. *Ante*, note 200, at D/5437.
209. *Ibid*.
210. (1986), 10 C.C.E.L. 249 (Ont. Bd. of Inquiry).
211. No complaint had been made under section 23 of the *Code* and the Board, acknowledging this, refrained from further comment.

employed by Zellers. The complainant admitted that he had answered "no" to these questions, the first answer being given because he believed he was legally entitled to deny criminal conviction, having received a pardon.

The board in *Lancaster* found that, had the complainant answered the question as to previous criminal conviction in the affirmative, the respondent would not have employed him and allowed that such a refusal to employ in the circumstances would have breached section 5(1) of the *Code*. The board then discussed at some length a previous British Columbia decision which had explored the circumstances under which it could be reasonable to deny employment on the ground of a criminal conviction. However, the Board concluded that in this case, the complainant's employment had not been terminated because of the previous conviction "qua conviction," but rather because he had not disclosed his previous employment with Zellers and because the company had a policy not to employ anyone whom it had discharged for theft. As noted above, this somewhat puzzling conclusion appears to stem from a blurring of the distinction between find the existence of "reasonable and bona fide grounds"[212] to discharge, and acknowledging a *prima facie* case of discrimination.

Constructive Discrimination

There have been no Ontario decisions to date on constructive discrimination on the ground of record of offences.

Other Issues

Decisions involving discrimination on the ground of record of offences have contributed to the development of theories on how closely the offence in question must relate to job responsibilities to justify discrimination on that ground. This is further discussed in Chapter 7.

Exceptions Relevant to Record of Offence

The statutory exceptions most likely to affect the right to freedom from discrimination on the ground of record of offences are found in the following provisions:

1. section 14, which provides for "special programs";
2. section 18, which allows a religious, philanthropic, educational, fraternal or social institution or organization that is primarily engaged in serving the interests of persons protected by the Code to restrict membership or participation to persons similarly identified;

---

212. For the purpose of a defence under subsection 24(1)(*b*).

3. section 24(1)(b) which allows discrimination that would otherwise breach section 5 where:

    the discrimination in employment is for reasons of age, sex, record of offences or marital status if the age, sex, record of offences or marital status of the applicant is a reasonable and *bona fide* qualification because of the nature of the employment;

4. section 24(1)(c), which provides that section 5 is not breached where

    an individual person refuses to employ another for reasons of any prohibited ground of discrimination in section 5, where the primary duty of the employment is attending to the medical or personal needs of the person or of an ill child or an aged, infirm or ill spouse or other relative of the person.

The exceptions are discussed in detail in Chapter 6.

4

CONSTRUCTIVE (ADVERSE EFFECT) DISCRIMINATION: SECTION 11

A prohibition against constructive (also called adverse effect or disproportionate impact) discrimination was effected for the first time in the 1981
Code. Section 10 [now s. 11] holds out the possibility of an effective attack
on systemic discrimination. In enacting the provision, the legislature has
gone beyond the question of intent and focussed on the effect of certain
practices. In the absence of a statutory exception, a practice which has a
disproportionate effect upon a group protected by the *Code* may not be continued unless it can be justified as reasonable and *bona fide*.

INTENT v. EFFECT: THE GENESIS OF THE SECTION 11 APPROACH

Section 11 did not introduce a novel concept in human rights legislation and case law. In Canada, the United States and England, both statute
and common law developed to prohibit unintentional discrimination that results from the imposition of a seemingly neutral requirement that disproportionately affects a particular group.

The English and American Approach

Recognition of constructive discrimination has been present in English
human rights legislation for some time. The English *Sex Discrimination Act*
of 1975 defines discrimination as follows:

1.(1) A person discriminates against a woman in any circumstances relevant for the purposes of any provision of the Act if;

    (*a*) on the ground of her sex he treats her less favourably than he treats or would
treat a man; or

    (*b*) he applies to her a requirement or condition *which he applies or would apply
equally to a man; but*

        (i) which is such that *the proportion of women who can comply with it is
considerably smaller* than the proportion of men who can comply with it;
and

(ii) which he *cannot show to be justifiable* irrespective of the sex of the person to whom it is applied; and

(iii) which is to her detriment because she cannot comply with it.

(2) If a person treats or would treat a man differently according to the man's marital status, his treatment of a woman is for the purposes of subsection (1)(*a*) to be compared to his treatment of a man having the like marital status. [Emphasis added.]

The *Race Relations Act, 1976* has a similar provision.

It is, presumably, because the wording of the legislation is so clear that there is not a great deal of English case law on the subject of intent in regard to discriminatory acts.[1] By contrast, the law in regard to intent has developed, in the United States and Canada, through courts and other tribunals. American decisions dealing with the problem of intent in human rights cases were of considerable assistance to Ontario boards prior to the enactment of the present *Code*, since, like Ontario boards, American courts were dealing with legislation that did not specifically prohibit constructive discrimination. Indeed, the American legislation appeared to require that intent to discriminate be established. Section 706(*g*) of the 1964 *Civil Rights Act*[2] provided:

If the Court finds that the respondent had intentionally engaged in or is intentionally engaging in unlawful employment practice charged in the complaint, the court may enjoin the respondent from engaging in such unlawful employment practice.

Prior to the passage of the *Civil Rights Act*, American courts had defined discrimination as "acts causing economic harm . . . that are motivated by personal antipathy to the group of which . . . [the person discriminated against] . . . is a member."[3] After the Act was passed, the focus of the courts shifted from *animus* to the establishment of intent to treat differently; that is, deliberate differentiation on the ground of race, sex, etc. As the case law developed, this type of intent was held to be inferrable, in some circumstances, from the fact of differential treatment inflicted upon a member or members of a particular group, although the differential treatment alone was insufficient proof that discrimination occurred.[4]

A broader judicial interpretation of section 706(*g*) of the *Civil Rights Act*, and a quantum leap in the expansion of the concept of discrimination,

---

1. But see *Clay Cross (Quarry Services) v. Fletcher* (1978), [1979] 1 All E.R. 474 (C.A.); *Price v. Civil Service Comm.*, [1977] 1 W.L.R. 1417 (Employment App. Trib.); *Price v. Civil Service Comm. (No. 2)*, [1978] I.R.L.R. 3 (Indust. Trib.); *Grieg v. Community Indust.*, [1979] I.C.R. 356 (Employment Appl. Trib.); *Steel v. Union of Post Office Workers*, [1978] 1 W.L.R. 64 (Employment App. Trib.).

2. 42 U.S.C. 200-5(*g*) Pub. L. 88-352 78 Stat.

3. See A.W. Blumrosen "Strangers in Paradise: *Griggs v. Duke Power Company* and the Concept of Discrimination" (1972), Mich. Law Rev. 59 at 67.

4. See *Arlington Heights v. Metropolitan Housing Development Corp.*, 429 U.S. 252 at 265-6 (1977).

was initiated in *Griggs v. Duke Power Company*.[5] In *Griggs*, the defendant power company, prior to 1965, had reserved its skilled jobs for white employees. After that year, it had ostensibly opened such jobs to non-white workers, but had required applicants to obtain a particular score on two tests to qualify for the jobs. It was found that this requirement virtually excluded non-white applicants. The Supreme Court of the United States held that since the employment practice, although neutral on its face, had a disparate impact on black applicants, it was unlawful under Title VII of the *Civil Rights Act*, unless the employer could show that the practice was a business necessity.

Regarding the issue of intent, the court stated:

> good intent or absence of discriminatory intent does not redeem employment procedures or testing mechanisms that operate as "built-in headwinds" for minority groups and are unrelated to measuring job capability.[6]

The effect of *Griggs* was that American courts began to distinguish between types of discriminatory actions. Two types of discrimination were identified: disparate treatment and the imposition of qualifications or practices that have a disproportionate impact on a particular group or groups. The former requires evidence of an intent to treat differently.[7] In regard to the latter, intent is irrelevant; impact is the important factor. In the "disproportionate impact" cases, once it was proved that a deliberate (i.e., non-accidental)[8] action by the respondent affected most members of a minority group adversely, a *prima facie* case was made out.[9] The burden of proof then shifted to the respondent to prove that the practice or qualification was a business necessity.[10]

The Canadian Cases

A similar sequence of development can be observed in the human

---

5. 91 S. Ct. 849 (1971).

6. *Ibid.*, at 854.

7. See, for example, *International Brotherhood of Teamsters v. U.S.*, 431 U.S. 324 (1977).

8. *Rogers v. International Paper Co.*, 510 F. 2d 1340 (1975); *Kober v. Westinghouse*, 480 F. 2d 240 (C.A.-3) (1973).

9. The *Griggs* approach was followed in numerous cases, including: *Albermarle Paper Co. v. Moody*, 442 U.S. 407 (1975); *Dothard v. Rawlinson*, 433 U.S. 321 (1977). American jurisprudence is not without "disproportionate impact" cases in which the U.S. Supreme Court has considered evidence as to motive; an example of this is *Memphis v. Greene*, 101 S. Ct. 1584 (1981). *Cf. Palmer v. Thompson*, 403 U.S. 217 (1971). However, *Greene*, like most of the cases in which intent is considered, was a complaint that involved the interpretation of the American Constitution (13th and 14th Amendments), which has consistently received different treatment from Title VII cases. See "Racially Disproportionate Impact of Facially Neutral Practices" (1977), Duke L.J. 1267.

10. For a discussion of business necessity see the discussion of the "reasonable and *bona fide*" defence in Chapter 6.

rights case law in various Canadian provinces. While most early human rights statutes were so broadly worded as to admit almost any interpretation as to intent, it was acknowledged in a 1976 decision that discriminatory intent need not be inspired by antipathy toward the group affected. In *British Columbia (Human Rights Commission) v. British Columbia College of Physicians and Surgeons,*[11] the issue was whether a requirement by the respondent that newly-licensed non-Canadian doctors be required to practise in remote areas of British Columbia for a period of time was discriminatory. Despite a finding by the board of inquiry that the requirement was based on "high public purpose," the respondent was found to have breached the *Human Rights Code.* An Ontario case decided at about the same time included a similar finding. In *Jones v. Huber,*[12] a case in which landlords argued that their decision not to rent to a black person was motivated by fear that their other tenants would react unfavourably, Chairman S. N. Lederman stated:

> It matters not what the motivating factor for the racially discriminatory act is. Although motive may be an important factor with respect to the question of redress, it cannot justify the offensive behaviour. . . . [A]lthough Mr. Huber professes to bear no personal animosity or adverse feelings toward blacks and claims he was just responding to the wishes of his tenants, he has nevertheless been responsible for a contravention of the Code.[13]

The first Canadian human rights case to specifically address the issue of intent was *Alberta (Attorney General) v. Gares,*[14] an equal pay case under Alberta's *Individuals' Rights Protection Act.* In that decision, the Supreme Court of Alberta stated:[15]

> relief . . . should . . . be granted . . . even in the absence of present or past intent to discriminate on the ground of sex. It is the discriminatory result which is prohibited and not a discriminatory intent.

The first Ontario "adverse effect" case was *Singh v. Security and Investigation Services Limited.*[16] In *Singh* the complainant had been denied employment because, as an orthodox Sikh, he had refused to conform to a dress code that required him to be clean-shaven and wear a cap rather than a turban. Board Chairman Peter Cumming found that the respondent company bore no ill-will towards Sikhs, and had adopted its dress requirements because of its perceptions as to customer preferences. However, he also found that the policy would have the effect of excluding any practising Sikh from the job. After a thorough review of analogous legislation and relevant

---

11. (1976), unreported (B.C. Bd. of Inquiry).
12. (1976), unreported (Ont. Bd. of Inquiry).
13. *Ibid.*, p. 5 (transcript).
14. (1976), 67 D.L.R. (3d) 635 (Alta. T.D.).
15. *Ibid.*, at 695.
16. (1977), unreported (Ont. Bd. of Inquiry).

case law, including *Gares* and *Griggs*, he concluded that the imposition of a restriction that resulted in an employment disadvantage to a particular group might contravene the *Code*, despite the absence of any intent to discriminate.

The second issue discussed in *Singh* was whether such an ostensibly neutral requirement might be considered valid, despite its disproportionate impact. In deciding this issue in relation to the case at hand, Chairman Cumming began with the assumption that such a restriction was allowable if it was "in good faith and . . . reasonably necessary to the employer's business operations."[17] He characterized the methods of analysis to be used in balancing the interests of employer and employee in the following manner:

> First, one decides whether the employees' request is important and valid, i.e.: not trivial or arbitrary. Second, one determines the extent of the inconvenience that would be caused to the employer if the request were granted.[18]

In regard to the issue of employee inconvenience, Chairman Cumming considered the doctrine of reasonable accommodation. This doctrine, which originated in religious discrimination cases in the United States,[19] had been applied to Canadian labour arbitration cases.[20] As summed up in *Singh*, it provides that, where a seemingly neutral qualification has a disproportionately negative impact on a group, the onus is "upon the employer to demonstrate that he is unable to reasonably accommodate a prospective employee's religious observance or practice without undue hardship on the conduct of his business."[21] The major hardship demonstrated in *Singh* was the possibility that some clients might not like to have a Sikh as a security guard. The board concluded that this possibility did not constitute undue hardship, and found for the complainant.

Singh was succeeded by other Ontario "adverse effect" cases which

---

17. *Ibid.*, p. 16 (transcript).

18. *Ibid.*, p. 30.

19. Decisions cited included *Sherbert v. Verner*, 374 U.S. 398 (1963), which concerned the right of a Seventh-Day Adventist to receive unemployment compensation when she was discharged for refusing to work on Saturday. Chairman Cumming also considered and dismissed *Eastern Greyhound Lines v. New York State Div. of Human Rights*, 265 N.E. 2d 795 (1970), and *Dewey v. Reynolds Metals Co.*, 429 F. 2d 324 (1970), two decisions of U.S. Courts of Appeal which held that reasonable accommodation would not be imposed in the absence of proof of intent to discriminate. These cases were considered by Chairman Cumming to have been contradicted by the U.S. Supreme Court in *Griggs* and *Albermarle.*

20. See, for example, *Canada Valve v. I.M.A.W., Local 279* (1975), 9 L.A.C. (2d) 414 (Ont.); *Brunswick Hotel v. Bartenders' Union, Local 280* (1969), unreported; *Printing Specialties & Paper Products Union, Local 466 v. Grace Chemicals Ltd., Cryovac Division* (1972), 24 L.A.C. 127; *Dominion Stores Ltd. v. United Steelworkers* (Sept. 25 1975), unreported.

21. *Ante*, note 16, pp. 31-2 (transcript).

concerned, among other things, the application of height and weight requirements,[22] appearance requirements,[23] Saturday-Sabbath employment,[24] the implementation of a "designated import" rule by a football team[25] and a rule against the carrying of offensive weapons.[26]

The progression of decision-making in these cases differed because of disparities between provisions of the previous *Code* dealing with various grounds of discrimination. Because the "height and weight" cases were complaints of sex discrimination, the board could consider the application of a statutory exception, provided by the previous *Code*, which stated that employment discrimination was permissible where sex was a "reasonable and *bona fide* occupational qualification and requirement."[27]

There was no such exception in respect of creed. Where adverse effect on persons of a particular creed was claimed, therefore, Ontario boards, following *Singh*, adopted the doctrine of reasonable accommodation. Ontario boards applied the doctrine by first considering whether the religious practice at issue was important and valid. Once the validity was established, the respondent had the onus of proving that he or she had made reasonable attempts to accommodate the employee's religious practice, and that this could not be done without a degree of inconvenience sufficient to counterbalance the complainant's right to both the benefit denied and his or her "important and valid" practice.[28]

Ontario Courts and Adverse Effect

The first case of adverse effect discrimination to go before the Ontario courts was *O'Malley v. Simpson-Sears*,[29] which involved the issue of Sabbath employment. The complainant had become a Seventh-Day Adventist some three years after she had been hired as a full-time employee by the respondent. After her conversion. she requested that she be relieved

---

22. *Adler v. Metropolitan Toronto Bd. of Commissioners of Police* (1979), unreported (Ont. Bd. of Inquiry); *Hartling v. Timmins (Municipality) Commissioners of Police* (1981), 2 C.H.R.R. D/487 (Ont. Bd. of Inquiry).

23. *Khalsa v. Co-Op Cabs* (1980), 1 C.H.R.R. D/167 (Ont. Bd. of Inquiry).

24. *O'Malley v. Simpson-Sears* (1980), 2 C.H.R.R. D/267, affirmed (1982), 36 O.R. (2d) 59 (Div. Ct.), affirmed (1982), 38 O.R. (2d) 423 (C.A.), reversed [1985] 2 S.C.R. 536. (Both the divisional court and the court of appeal disagreed with the reasons given by the board.)

25. *Bone v. Hamilton Tiger Cats Football Club* (1979), unreported (Ont. Bd. of Inquiry). In *Bone*, intentional discrimination was also found. The case is discussed in Chapter 3.

26. *Singh v. Workmen's Compensation Board Hospital & Rehabilitation Centre* (1981), 2 C.H.R.R. D/459 (Ont. Bd. of Inquiry).

27. *Ante*, note 22.

28. *Singh v. Security & Investigation Services* (1977), unreported (Ont. Bd. of Inquiry); *ante*, note 26; *ante*, note 24.

29. *Ante*, note 24.

from the obligation to work Friday evenings and Saturdays, since her church observed its Sabbath from sunset Friday to sunset Saturday. Her employer refused to relax its rule that all full-time employees must work the disputed evening and day, and offered O'Malley a choice of accepting part-time work or resigning. She accepted the part-time work, at a considerable loss of pay and benefits, and complained of discrimination on the ground of creed.

Neither at the board of inquiry nor on appeal was it questioned that:

1. it was reasonably necessary that the respondent require Saturday work as a general rule;

2. the respondent had no malicious motive or intent to discriminate against Seventh-Day Adventists; and

3. the complainant's religious beliefs were held in good faith.

The first argument raised by the respondent was that malice, bigotry or bad faith must be shown before a finding of discrimination could be made. Chairman Ratushny appeared to hold that evidence of motive could be relevant where intent must be proved, but went on to find that intent need not always be proved. He cited *Gares, Singh*, the preamble of the *Code*, and section 10 of the *Interpretation Act* as support for the conclusion that the scope of the *Code* was broad enough to encompass cases in which an employer's requirement, although not intentionally discriminatory, had discriminatory results.

Chairman Ratushny acknowledged that the responsibility of the employer to avoid discriminatory results could not be absolute: "it would be ludicrous to suggest that a business which operated only on Saturdays could not insist that all of its employees work on that day."[30] Accordingly, he went on to consider how far the employer must go to relieve the discriminatory results, in order to avoid a contravention of the *Code*. In the absence of guidance from the legislation, he concluded that he should apply a very general standard as to "whether the employer acted reasonably in attempting to accommodate the employee in all of the circumstances of the case, as well as in the context of the general scope and objects of the *Code*."[31] Moreover, chairman Ratushny found that the onus was on the Commission to establish that the respondent's offer of alternate employment was not reasonable. In the absence of such evidence the chairman found that the respondent had acted reasonably and, therefore, concluded that the respondent had not contravened the *Code*.

On appeal by the complainant to the Divisional Court, Southey J., with whom Gray J. concurred, considered whether the question of intent was a

30. *Ante*, note 24, at D/268 (C.H.R.R.).
31. *Ibid.*, at D/269.

necessary part of a finding of discrimination. Southey J., approached the problem by first considering whether a duty of reasonable accommodation was imposed by the *Code*. He concluded that no such "saving provision" could be inferred from the words of the statute, and went on to find:

> The absence of a saving provision provides a strong reason for inferring that an intention to discriminate on a prohibited ground is essential to a contravention of s. 4(1)(*g*). If that were not so, the Legislature would have enacted a saving provision to fill the vacuum.[32]

Southey J. concluded:

> Although the language of s. 4(1)(*g*) is logically susceptible of the interpretation given to it by the learned Chairman, the construction of the words in their ordinary and natural meaning, in my judgment, results in an interpretation in which the intention to discriminate on a prohibited ground is essential to a contravention. The relevant portions of s. 4(1)(*g*) of the Code provide that no one shall discriminate against any employee with regard to any term or condition of employment *because of* creed (emphasis added). In my judgment, the words "because of" refer to the reason or reasons why the employer imposed the term or condition of employment that is in question.[33]

At no point in the decision did Southey J. discuss the nature of the intent he had in mind. Certainly he did not specifically subscribe to the "proof of malice, bigotry, etc." argument.

Smith J. agreed with the result reached by Southey and Gray JJ., but held that proof of intent to discriminate is not an essential element to a finding that the *Code* had been infringed. Smith J. stated that an overly simplistic approach to the question of intent to discriminate is inappropriate. He agreed with Chairman Ratushny's finding that a discriminatory result that offends the *Code* might exist "without any ill-will, or even knowledge on the part of the employer," but declined to subscribe

> to the board proposition that intent is irrelevant. The state of mind of the discriminator, whether it leads him directly to an intent to discriminate or simply makes him prefer the balance sheet, for instance, to the effects of his actions on a protected class, may well turn out to be the key as to whether a contravention has arisen in certain kinds of cases.[34]

Smith J. went on to note that both state of mind and causation may be relevant to a finding of discrimination, depending on the circumstances of the case and, in concluding, he proposed a sort of "middle ground" in regard to intent:

> What must be avoided is to place boards of inquiry and courts in straightjackets. If resort is had to intent in the sense of *mens rea*, the attack is only upon the more blatant cases and, if one makes use of *causation* without more, then the danger arises of doing an injustice to alleged discriminators.[35]

---

32. *Ontario (Human Rights Commission) v. Simpson-Sears* (1982), 36 O.R. (2d) 59 at 65 (Div. Ct.).
33. *Ibid.*, at 66.
34. *Ibid.*, at 73.
35. *Ibid.*, at 73.

The divisional court's essential conclusion that the definition of the term discrimination must be read to include intent was upheld by the Ontario Court of Appeal.[36] Lacourcière J.A. wrote for a unanimous bench of three. Without giving reasons, he held that neither the *Gares* decision nor English case law was helpful in the interpretation of the Ontario *Code*. He noted that the Supreme Court of Canada, in deciding *Ontario (Human Rights Commission) v. Etobicoke (Borough)*,[37] was dealing with a clear case of differential treatment based on age, but he did not refer to that court's remarks about the employer's motives before he dismissed the case from consideration.[38] Finally, he stated that only those American cases decided prior to a 1972 amendment to the American *Civil Rights Act*[39] were truly analogous to the case at issue. He cited with approval *Dewey v. Reynolds Metal Co.*[40] as authority for the proposition that

> there was no obligation on an employer to accommodate each of the varying religious beliefs and practices of his employees, and that discharge of an employee for refusal to perform certain specific work on Sundays did not constitute an unlawful employment practice as tending to discriminate against the employee because of his religious beliefs.[41]

The decisions of the board, the Ontario Divisional Court and the Court of Appeal were overturned when *O'Malley* reached the Supreme Court of Canada. Mr. Justice McIntyre, for the unanimous Court, based his reasoning not only on established rules of statutory construction, but on the "special nature, not quite constitutional but certainly more than ordinary"[42] of human rights law. In his decision, McIntyre J. put to rest the notion that discrimination requires intent, and at the same time made it clear that proof of "intent" for this purpose was not synonymous with proof of malice. He identified two types of discrimination, one including both actions inspired by malice and differential treatment for other reasons, and the other "adverse effect" discrimination, described as occurring:

> . . . where an employer for genuine business reasons adopts a rule or standard which is on its face neutral, and which will apply equally to all employees, but which has a discriminatory effect upon a prohibited ground on one employee or group of employees in that it imposes, because of some special characteristic of the employee or group, obliga-

---

36. *O.H.R.C. v. Simpson-Sears* (1982), 38 O.R. (2d) 423 (C.A.).
37. (1982), 40 N.R. 159 (S.C.C.).
38. *Ibid.*, at 166. The court, while upholding a finding of discrimination, stated that "there was no evidence to indicate that the motives of the employer were other than honest and in good faith in the sense described."
39. The effect of the 1972 amendment is discussed further below.
40. 429 F. 2d 324 (1970).
41. *Ante*, note 36, at p. 7.
42. *Ontario (Human Rights Commission) v. Simpsons-Sears Ltd.*, [1985] 2 S.C.R. 536.

tions, penalties or restrictive conditions not imposed on other members of the work force.[43]

Further, Mr. Justice McIntyre concluded that, once a prima facie case of adverse effect discrimination was made out, the onus was on the respondent to establish that reasonable steps had been taken to accommodate the complainant, short of undue hardship.

The *O'Malley* judgment was welcomed as a significant step in the task of defining the scope of the term discrimination. However, the Ontario Legislature had anticipated the Supreme Court of Canada in enacting a provision which specifically prohibits adverse-effect discrimination, effectively doing away with the debate as to whether such discrimination is prohibited by Ontario Law. An amendment of this provision established the same limit to the protection as that used by the Court in *O'Malley*.

SECTION 11 OF THE CODE

The first statutory provision explicitly directed toward prohibiting constructive discrimination in Ontario, section 10 of the 1981 Code, read as follows:

> (1) A right of a person under Part I is infringed where a requirement, qualification or consideration is imposed that is not discrimination on a prohibited ground but that would result in the exclusion, restriction or preference of a group of persons who are identified by a prohibited ground of discrimination and of whom the person is a member, except where,
>
> (a) the requirement, qualification or consideration is a reasonable and *bona fide* in the circumstances; or
>
> (b) it is declared in this Act that to discriminate because of such ground is not an infringement of a right.

Through the passage in 1986 of the *Equality Rights Statute Law Amendment Act*,[44] several words used in the former section 10 were changed and a new subsection was added which explicitly establishes the duty to accommodate to the point of undue hardship. The amended section 10 [now section 11] reads as follows:

> 10(1) A right of a person under Part I is infringed where a requirement, qualification or factor exists that is not discrimination on a prohibited ground but that results in the ex-

---

43. *Ibid.*, at D/3106. The Supreme Court's inclusion of intentional, adverse effects actions in the term discrimination was continued in *Bhinder v. Canadian National Railway Co.* (1985), 7 C.H.R.R. D/3093 (S.C.C.). La Forest J., in a subsequent decision, *Robichaud v. Brennan*, [1987] 2 S.C.R. 84, wrote that since the Act is essentially concerned with the removal of discrimination, as opposed to punishing anti-social behaviour, it follows that the motives or intention of those who discriminate are not central to its concerns. Rather, the Act is directed to redressing socially undesirable conditions, quite apart from the reasons for their existence.

44. S.O. 1986, c. 64.

clusion, restriction or preference of a group of persons who are identified by a prohibited ground of discrimination and of whom the person is a member, except where,

(a) the requirement, qualification or factor is reasonable and bona fide in the circumstances; or

(b) it is declared in this Act, other than in section 17, that to discriminate because of such ground is not an infringement of a right.

(2) The Commission, a Board of Inquiry, or a court shall not find that a requirement, qualification or factor is reasonable and bona fide in the circumstances unless it is satisfied that the needs of the group of which the person is a member cannot be accommodated without undue hardship on the person responsible for accommodating those needs, considering the cost, outside source of funding, if any, and health and safety requirement, if any.

(3) The Commission, a Board of Inquiry or a court shall consider any standards prescribed by the regulations for assessing what is undue hardship.

The Establishment of a Prima Facie Case

The *O'Malley* case discussed above provides an outline of what must be proven to establish a *prima facie* case of adverse effect discrimination, even before the Ontario Legislature had enacted section 11. McIntyre J. stated that, in the employment context, adverse effect discrimination arises

where an employer for genuine business reasons adopts a rule or standard which is on its face neutral, and which will apply equally to all employees, but which has a discriminatory effect upon a prohibited ground on one employee or group of employees in that it imposes, because of some special characteristic of the employee of group, obligations, penalties, or restrictive conditions not imposed on other members of the workforce.[45]

The establishment of the elements noted above, he continued, would be "sufficient to justify a verdict in the complainant's favour in the absence of an answer from the respondent."[46]

It is suggested that the elements of a *prima facie* case are changed only in relatively minor ways by the statutory provision. The element first mentioned by McIntyre J., the "genuine business reasons" supporting the "rule or standard," has always, along with "facial neutrality," been a *sine qua non* of entering into consideration of constructive discrimination in any event. (If a "requirement, qualification, or factor" stipulates a prohibited ground of discrimination, it is direct differential treatment. The same is true if it is proven that the reasons given for the existence of facially neutral "requirement, qualification or factor" are not genuine business reasons but rather an excuse for deliberate discrimination.) The words of section 11 make it clear (*O'Malley* had raised doubts on this score) that constructive discrimination is prohibited not only in employment but in all the areas covered by the

---

45. *Ante*, 42, 23 D.L.R. (4th) 321 at 332.
46. *Ibid.*, at 338.

Code. The substitution in 1986 of the term "exists" for "is imposed" removes any doubt that the respondent is responsible for "unwritten rules," *ad hoc* managerial decisions and agreements that evolve into entrenched customs, without the requirement that a "controlling mind" has formally imposed them. Finally, the substitution for "factor" for "consideration" and "restriction" for "qualification" appears to have been done from a preference for more appropriate use of language than from any legislative motivation toward substantive change.

The elements of a *prima facie* case under section 11, as amended, appear to be the following:

- proof that a requirement, qualification or factor that in itself is not discrimination on a prohibited ground exists;

- proof that the existence of the requirement, qualification or factor results in the exclusion, restriction or preference of a group of persons identified by a prohibited ground of discrimination; and

- proof that a person who is a member of the group allegedly affected by the requirement, qualification or factor has been excluded, restricted or preferred as a result of the existence of the requirement, qualification or factor.

The elements will be briefly examined in turn.

"Requirement, Qualification or Factor . . . Exists"

The *Oxford English Dictionary* defines "requirement" as

to order . . . demand or ask . . . especially as of right, to lay down as imperative." "Qualification" is defined as a "restricting or limiting circumstance . . . quality or accomplishment fitting person or thing (for post, etc.) . . . condition that must be filled before right can be acquired or office held," and "factor" is defined as a "circumstance, effect or influence, contributing to a result.

Under the previous wording of section 10 and prior to its enactment, constructive discrimination has been found to have occurred in respect of "requirements" such as dress codes or uniforms that forbid beards, turbans, or the wearing of certain religious symbols,[47] and work schedules too rigid to allow for religious observances.[48] Due to the substitution of the word "exists" for "is imposed" in the former version, there will be less need for debate as to the liability of a respondent in respect of unwritten rules, ad

---

47. See: *Singh v. Security and Investigation Services Ltd.* (1977), unreported (Ont. Bd. of Inquiry); *Singh v. Workmen's Compensation Board Hospital and Rehabilitation Centre* (1981), 2 C.H.R.R. D/459 (Ont. Bd. of Inquiry); *Sehdev v. Bayview Glen Junior Schools Ltd.* (1988), 9 C.H.R.R. D/4881 (Ont. Bd. of Inquiry).
48. See: *O'Malley v. Simpson-Sears, ante*, note 42; *Gohm v. Domtar Inc.* (1990), 12 C.H.R.R. D/161 (Ont. Bd. of Inquiry).

hoc managerial decisions, and "shop-floor understandings" that effectively discriminate.[49]

Requirements, Qualifications and Considerations that may Pose Special Problems

Employment Testing

Pre-employment or pre-promotion testing is useful to employers for various reasons. A valid test may be a good predictor of successful performance of the job in question. Even when the test is less than valid, testing gives an appearance of "scientific" objectivity to employment decisions, reduces the number of applicants who must be seen by top management, and generally relieves some of the pressure on decision-makers to make a good choice. However, research in both Canada and the United States has shown that some tests are either poor predictors of job success or are improperly used; that is, they are used to test for qualities that they are not suited to assess. Furthermore, some tests have been discredited because of culture-specificity; the test problems are "geared" to people coming from a specific cultural background, and only people from that background are apt to do well on them.[50] The potential for constructive discrimination is obvious.

One of the first cases to deal with discriminatory impact in employment testing was *Griggs v. Duke Power Company*.[51] In *Griggs*, the plaintiff challenged the use of the Wonderlic Aptitude Test and the Bennett Mechanical Test. The United States Supreme Court was required to interpret a 1972 amendment to the 1964 *Civil Rights Act*, which amendment[52] provided that the use of a "professionally developed ability test" is not an unlawful employment practice, "provided that such test, its administration or action upon the results is not designed, intended or used to discriminate

---

49. See remarks in Chapter 9 on corporate liability.
50. See E. Ghiselli, *The Validity of Occupational Aptitude Tests*, (1966); Cooper and Sobol, "Seniority and Testing under Fair Employment Law: A General Approach to Objective Criteria of Hiring and Promotion" (1969), 82 Harv. L. Rev. 1598.

    Reliable methods of test-validation are available. The U.S. Equal Employment Opportunities Commission has issued guidelines (29 C.F.R., s. 1607, 1978) on employment test use; these might prove useful in informally evaluating the practice of Canadian employers. A demonstration of these standards in practice can be seen in *Contreras v. City of Los Angeles*, 656 F. 2d 1267 (1980); *Craig v. County of Los Angeles*, 626 F. 2d 659, *cert.* den. 101 S. Ct. 1364 (1980); *Ensley Branch of the N.A.A.C.P. v. Seibels*, 616 F. 2d 812, *cert.* den. 101 S. Ct. 783 (1980). Also see *Metropolitan Toronto Licensing Commission v. Canadian Union of Public Employees Local 79* (March 28, 1982), unreported (Ont. Arb. Bd.). This decision canvasses exhaustively the issue of the validity of psychological tests used in assessing candidates for promotion in employment, and illustrates and evaluates the various methods of establishing test validity.
51. 91 S. Ct. 849 (1971), discussed above.
52. 42 U.S.C. 2000e-2(*n*).

because of race, color, sex, or national origin." The United States Supreme Court held that this section was breached where it could be shown that the test barred a disproportionately large number[53] of minority group candidates, unless the employer could prove that use of the test was a business necessity.

The court did not specify what might constitute a business necessity in this situation, but noted that neither test challenged in *Griggs* bore

> a demonstrable relationship to successful performance of the jobs . . . . [T]esting requirements that take into account capability for the next succeeding position or related future promotion might be utilized upon a showing that such long-range requirements fulfill a genuine business need.[54]

Four years later, the United States Supreme Court again considered the question of standardized aptitude tests that effectively screened out minority group applicants. In *Albermarle Paper Company v. Moody*,[55] the lower courts had found that the tests used by the appellant company had been validated only haphazardly or not at all. Specifically, the court found that Albermarle's efforts to validate its tests had been inadequate in four respects:

1. Statistically significant correlations were obtained only for some of the tests, and not on all lines of progression.

2. The judgments made by supervisors in "ranking" candidates were based on vague standards.

3. The validation study concentrated on the more senior jobs, not those at entry level.

4. The validation study tests were given to older and more experienced workers, whereas the job applicants who complained were younger and less experienced.

The court, in its decision, quoted guidelines issued by the Equal Employment Opportunities Commission and noted that:

> The message of these Guidelines is the same as that of the *Griggs* case — that discriminatory tests are impermissible unless shown, by professionally acceptable methods, to be predictive of or significantly correlated with important elements of work behaviour which comprise or are relevant to the job or jobs for which candidates are being evaluated.[56]

---

53. In *Griggs* it was found that fifty-eight percent of whites passed the test while only six percent of black applicants passed. As discussed above, there is no reason that Ontario complainants should have to demonstrate that any particular percentage of their groups is affected, although it will be necessary to demonstrate that it is not merely a personal idiosyncrasy that causes the complainant to fail the test.

54. *Ante*, note 51, at 853-4.

55. 442 U.S. 407 (1975).

56. *Ibid.*, at 431.

Since the employer's tests had not been shown to possess this degree of validity, the court concluded that the tests did not satisfy the *Griggs* standard of job-relatedness.

In *Albermarle* the court laid down some guidelines in respect of the evidentiary process in cases involving employment testing. First, it said the complainant must show "that the tests in question select applicants for hire or promotion in a racial pattern significantly different from that of the pool of applicants." Secondly, the employer must meet the burden of proving that its tests are job-related and, if the employer is successful,

> it remains open to the complaining party to show that other tests or selection devices, without a similarly undesirable racial effect, would also serve the employer's interest in "efficient and trustworthy workmanship." Such a showing would be evidence that the employer was using the tests merely as a "pretext" for discrimination.[57]

While the evidentiary progression described above is obviously reflective of those situations in which the employer is shielding a discriminatory attitude, a similar, less pejorative approach has been used in the only Ontario case that has yet considered employment testing. In *Malik v. Ontario (Minister of Government Services)*,[58] however, board Chairman Mary Eberts appeared to impose the responsibility on the respondent to consider, as well as the complainant to suggest, alternatives. More than once in the decision, Chairman Eberts indicated that the respondent must have considered other methods before he or she could establish the business necessity of an employment test:

> once disproportionate impact is established, the employer must show not only that the impugned device produces employees with the job related qualities required, but that it is *the only way* of selecting such employees[59] [emphasis added].
>
> . . . .
>
> Had there been a showing of disproportionate impact, the Respondent Ministry would have been, in my view, unable to satisfy its burden of showing the interview to be a business necessity, performing functions which would not be done in any other way.[60]
>
> . . . .
>
> It is up to the Complainant to show that the requirement in question has a disproportionate impact on members of the group to which he belongs. That group must, to be sure, be one that is protected by the *Human Rights Code*. Once the Complainant has established the disproportionate impact on his group of a seemingly neutral requirement, the burden shifts to the employer to show that use of the offending test or criterion is a business necessity. The employer must show that certain employee traits are necessary for, say, greater efficiency or safety and also that the impugned practice or criterion is actually successful in measuring or predicting these qualities. If the employer succeeds

---

57. *Ibid.*, at 425.
58. (1981), 2 C.H.R.R. D/374 (Ont. Bd. of Inquiry).
59. *Ibid.*, at D/376.
60. *Ibid.*, at D/381.

at that, then the employee may still show that other selection devices without similar discriminatory effect would also serve the employer's legitimate business interests.[61]

Seniority Systems and Section 11

Seniority systems are a fact of life in unionized employment, and are often used, in an informal sense, in non-union workplaces. Such systems are beneficial to both workers and management. However, there are two aspects of seniority systems that may come under consideration in section 11 complaints: accruing benefits[62] and employee ranking as it relates to promotion and job security.

The essence of the problem is the existence of past discrimination, which has given non-minority workers a head start over other employees. This may be due to the employer's previously having hired no minority-group employees, or to the existence of job ghettos that involve separate lines of progression, with the minority group channelled into those jobs that are likely to be made obsolete by advancing technology.

Seniority undoubtedly fits section 11's criteria: it is a facially neutral requirement, qualification or consideration in many employment decisions. The employee who, because of past discriminatory practices, is about to be laid off or declared redundant is obviously being excluded. The main questions before the board will therefore be whether the system is reasonable and *bona fide* in the circumstances.

The focus of the attack on a seniority system will probably be the job-relatedness of the system. Indeed, this is the system's most vulnerable point, if promotion is not closely related to ability in the particular case. However, the respondent might be in a position to point to each stage in the employment ladder as requiring skills learned in the past. Furthermore, the "reasonableness" of a seniority system may lie as well in its smoothing of industrial relations by providing an objective framework for employment decisions, and its tendency to discourage rapid turnover of employees. Thus the proof required by section 11(1)(*a*) might be met.

Where the respondent does not meet the "reasonable and *bona fide*" test, the question of how far to interfere with the system will arise. The approach taken by the board to such awards may vary according to the circumstances of the case. In the situation in which the complainant has been ghettoized and therefore lacks the benefits accrued by employees in the main stream, the board might well make an order integrating the employee in the main stream of job progression at a point indicated by the employee's number of years with the employer. The problem of the last-hired em-

---

61. *Ibid.*, at D/376. A similar approach is demonstrated in *Contreras v. City of Los Angeles*, 656 F. 2d 1267 (1980).
62. *I.e.*, longer vacations, pension benefits. parking privileges, etc.

ployee, who is last-hired only because of previous discriminatory practice, and is now facing lay-off, is more thorny. Are other employees to be "bumped" because of a discriminatory situation that existed in the past and was likely not of their doing?

The United States Supreme Court grappled with these views in some early cases. In *Franks v. Bowman Transportation Company*,[63] the court divided over a class action on behalf of black employees who had applied for promotion to a particular job category, but had been denied the promotion because of discrimination built in to the seniority system. A majority of the court held that the applicants were entitled to priority consideration in respect of job vacancies in the category. The court also held that, if hired, the applicants had the right to full seniority benefits, retroactive to the time they had first applied. The court based this decision on the theory that anti-discrimination legislation should be used to "make whole" the victim of discrimination.[64]

Chief Justice Burger and Justice Powell, in dissent, agreed that some seniority relief would be appropriate, but drew a distinction between the award of "accrued benefits" seniority and competitive seniority.[65] They argued that an award of benefits seniority would properly penalize the employer, whereas an award of competitive seniority would frustrate the legitimate expectations of innocent third parties, thus punishing the wrong party.[66]

Obviously, the view taken by Ontario tribunals on the issue of competitive seniority will be of vital interest to unions and employers, as well as to the affected worker. The legitimate expectations of all parties will present a consideration challenge to a board's creativity.[67]

"That Results in the Exclusion, Restriction or Preference"

The *Oxford English Dictionary* defines exclusion as "shutting out," restrictions as "limitation placed on action" and preference as "liking of or for one thing better than (to or over) another."

"Preference" is an interesting inclusion in human-rights legislation, since discrimination is usually thought of as the imposition of adversity of some sort. Presumably, a requirement, qualification or factor that results in a group being "preferred" might include the sort of paternalistic or patron-

---

63. 96 S. Ct. 1251 (1976).
64. *Ibid.*, at 1264.
65. *I.e.*, priority for recall and impunity from lay-off.
66. *Ante*, note 63, at 1272.
67. For further arguments on this issue, see "Employment Discrimination and Title VII of the *Civil Rights Act* of 1964" (1971), 84 Harv. L.R. 1109 at 1155-64; P. Brest "In Defense of the Antidiscrimination Principle" (1976), 90 Harv. L. Rev. 1 at 36-9; and "Past Discrimination and Present Violations of Title VII" (1979), 92 Harv. L. Rev. 757.

izing actions which, while they might benefit a group in the short term, would have collateral or long-term effects that are detrimental.

"Of a Group of Persons . . . Of Whom The Person is a Member"

The overall purpose of the *Code* is to encourage treatment of individuals based on characteristics actually possessed or demonstrated by the individual, not treatment based on some characteristic that is attributed to the individual solely because of his or her membership in a group. This emphasis on the characteristics of the individual gives way, in a section 11 complaint, to a focus on the characteristics of a particular group. In a section 11 complaint, the complainant points to the existence of a group characteristic and alleges that, when a particular requirement, qualification or preference is applied, his or her group is excluded, restricted or preferred because of the existence of that characteristic.

This argument requires:

1. demonstration of the existence of the characteristic among the group in question, to an extent not found among the general population; and,

2. evidence that the requirement, qualification or factor does have, or would be likely to have, the effect claimed.

The Existence of the Characteristic within the Group

The types of characteristics considered in complaints of constructive discrimination have not been limited to intrinsic characteristics such as height, colour or ability to become pregnant, but have been extended to differences that are to some degree a question of choice, such as religious practice, social custom and so on. The characteristic in question might be as simple and obvious as the wearing of a beard and turban, or as subtle as a culturally-based way of speaking or manner of presenting oneself in relation to a perceived superior. The less obvious characteristic presents unique problems in proving a *prima facie* case, as was demonstrated in an Ontario complaint of constructive discrimination. *Malik v. Ontario (Minister of Government Services)*[68] involved a complaint that the interview/assessment procedure used by the respondents had a disproportionate impact on people of Pakistani-Muslim ethnic origin. The complainant had been unsuccessful in obtaining a permanent job with the respondent, although he had been employed on a contract basis, in the same position, for almost four years.

The assessment procedure in question rated the candidate's education, experience, expression, initiative, etc., by assigning a numerical value to phrases descriptive of these qualities. The assessors were required to pick the phrases that best described each applicant.

---

68. (1981), 2 C.H.R.R. D/374 (Ont. Bd. of Inquiry).

The Commission argued that people of the complainant's ethnic background were likely to score lower than other candidates in those areas which measured assertiveness, initiative, expression and similar attributes. The Commission offered the expert evidence of an anthropologist to the effect that the Pakistani-Muslim society is one of the most stratified in the world, and that persons of that background, when interviewed by anyone representing authority, are likely to demonstrate respect and loyalty by a deferential, low-key, non-assertive manner.

Malik's marks in these areas had, in fact, been low. Although there was evidence that two other East Asians had scored highly on the test, the Commission's expert witness noted that these candidates were of different religion and nationality than the complainant, and that one of them had a university education.

Board Chairman Mary Eberts commented upon the difficulties inherent in cases where an alleged group characteristic is less than obvious. She noted that the Commission had adduced no statistical evidence to show that the respondent had a disproportionately high rate of rejection of Muslim-Pakistani applicants. Nor was there any statistical evidence that persons of the complainant's ethnic group might do disproportionately badly at this type of interview. She pointed out, however, that statistical evidence is unlikely to be available in all cases. Indeed, in some cases, the collection of relevant evidence will be barred by *Human Rights Code*'s prohibitions against soliciting, in employment applications, information about race, national origin or religion. She concluded that:

> In the circumstances, it would not be helpful or realistic to impose a flat bar against the use, in a proper case, of expert opinion evidence to establish the disproportionate impact of a particular requirement. However, it must be remembered that that evidence must still enable the plaintiff to make out a *prima facie* case of disproportionate impact on the members of a protected group. Even Mr. Justice Stewart in *Dothard* stated that there was no need for the plaintiff to exhaust every possible source of evidence if the evidence presented "on its face *actually* demonstrates" a requirement's disproportionate impact.[69]

Malik was eventually decided against the complainant, based on the Commission's failure to establish a *prima facie* case:

> Although the Commission tried to deal somewhat generally, through Dr. Henry's evidence, what its submission really amounted to was that Mr. Malik was a group of one — with certain characteristics — and that the interview method was unfairly hard on this group. One must show something more than this in order to show indirect discrimination arising from a superficially neutral requirement.[70]

---

69. *Ibid.*, at D/378. The chairman was alluding to the American case of *Dothard v. Rawlinson*, 433 U.S. 321 (1977).

70. *Ante*, note 68, at D/378.

The Prevalence of the Characteristic within the Group

It would seem reasonable to assume that the complainant should establish, where it is not obvious,[71] that a significant proportion of the group of which he or she is a member shares the characteristic in question.[72] A related issue is whether the complainant displays a group characteristic to an unusual degree. This would be the case where, for example, the complainant is ultra-orthodox and unusually rigid in religious observance. To date, ultra-orthodoxy has not been a factor that has barred relief for the complainant, nor has the practice of individual beliefs consistent with the holder's creed but not mandated by that creed.[73] This has been consistent with the fairly broad interpretation of religion taken by both Canadian and American tribunals. This result is also logically consistent with the wording and purpose of section 11. For example, it would be reasonable for the complainant to argue that the requirement, qualification or consideration that has the effect of completely excluding the religiously very orthodox person will at least make access to the benefit difficult for the less orthodox.

---

71. Presumably, judicial notice may be taken of some types of characteristics, such as the fact that most women between certain ages are capable of becoming pregnant. On the subject of judicial notice, see *Phipson on Evidence*, 12th ed., (1976), paras. 46-60. Otherwise on this issue, see *Price v. Civil Service Commission*, [1977] 1 W.L.R. 1417 (Employment App. Trib.); *Price v. Civil Service Commission (No. 2)*, [1978] I.R.L.R. 3 (Indust. Trib.); *Phipson on Evidence*, ante, note 67.

72. Boards of Inquiry have not demanded that it be proved that all members of a group share a characteristic. See *Sehdev v. Bayview Glen Junior School* (1988), 9 C.H.R.R. D/4881 (Ont. Bd. of Inquiry).

73. In *Singh v. Workmen's Compensation Board Hospital & Rehabilitation Centre* (1981), 2 C.H.R.R. D/459 (Ont. Bd. of Inquiry), the board upheld the complainant's right to wear an eight-inch sacred dagger on his person, rather than the "small, symbolic" dagger worn by some less orthodox members of his faith.

   In *Donald v. Hamilton (Board of Education)*, [1945] 3 D.L.R. 424 (Ont. C.A.), the Ontario Court of Appeal considered whether the expulsion from school of two children of the Jehovah's Witnesses faith, for refusing to salute the flag, etc., was a denial of religious freedom. Although the court did not agree that saluting the flag was of religious significance, it held, in finding for the appellants, that the important factor was whether the appellants considered the salute to have religious significance. See the discussion of this case in Chapter 3.

   Similar views of the meaning of religious freedom were taken by the U.S. courts in *Lewis v. Califano*, 616 F. 2d 73 (1980), which involved a belief in faith-healing; *Edwards v. School Bd. of Norton, Virginia*, 21 F.E.P. Cases 1375 (1980), in regard to the complainant's extreme view of the length of a religious holy-day period; *Redmond v. GAF Corp.*, 574 F. 2d 897 (1978). For views as to the proper limitation of religious rights, see *R. v. Harrold*, [1971] 3 W.W.R. 365 (B.C. C.A.); Paul Marcus, "The Forum of Conscience: Applying Standards Under the Free Exercise Clause" (1973), Duke L.J. 1217.

   The most recent Ontario case raising this point are *Sehdev, ante*, note; *Bhadauria v. Toronto (City) Board of Education* (1990), 12 C.H.R.R. D/105 (Ont. Bd. of Inquiry); *Quereshi v. Central High School of Commerce (No. 3)* (1991), 42 O.A.C. 258 (Div. Ct.).

The Onus Shift and Defences to a Section 11 Complaint

Once a *prima facie* case of constructive discrimination has been made out, the burden of proof in establishing a defence under subsection 11(1)(*a*) or 11(1)(*b*) shifts to the respondent.[74] Subsections 11(1)(*a*) and (*b*) read as follows:

> (a) the requirement, qualification or factor is reasonable and *bona fide* in the circumstances; or

> (b) it is declared in this Act, other than in section 11, that to discriminate because of such ground is not an infringement of a right.

The exceptions that would establish a defence under subsection 11(1)(*b*) are discussed in some detail in Chapter 6. Obviously, if a respondent can establish that such an exception applies, a defence to a section 11 complaint is made out.

The establishment of a defence under subsection 11(1)(*a*) is considerably more complicated, involving as it does both the standards set to date in the interpretation of the term "reasonable and *bona fide*", and the application of a newly-specified duty to accommodate short of undue hardship.

"Reasonable and Bona Fide in the Circumstances"

In a number of specific exceptions, the *Code* allows discriminatory actions or results where the respondent can prove that the differentiation or the effect complained of was "reasonable and *bona fide* in the circumstances." This standard was introduced in the 1981 *Code*; its predecessor was the "*bona fide* occupational qualification" considered by the Supreme Court of Canada in *Ontario (Human Rights Commission) v. Etobicoke (Borough)*.[75]

Etobicoke established finally that to be considered *bona fide* under human rights legislation, an impugned requirement, qualification or factor must be not only imposed in good faith but reasonable from an objective point of view:

> To be a *bona fide* occupational qualification and requirement a limitation, such as a mandatory retirement at a fixed age, must be imposed honestly, in good faith, and in the sincerely held belief that such limitation is imposed in the interests of the adequate performance of the work involved with all reasonable dispatch, safety and economy, and not for ulterior or extraneous reasons aimed at objectives which could defeat the purpose of the *Code*. In addition it must be related in an objective sense to the performance of the employment concerned, in that it is reasonably necessary to assure the efficient and eco-

---

74. This rule was clearly established in *Ontario (Human Rights Commission) v. Simpsons-Sears Ltd.*, [1985] 2 S.C.R. 536, and was followed in *Gohm v. Domtar Inc.* (1990), 12 C.H.R.R. D/161 (Ont. Bd. of Inquiry).
75. [1982] 1 S.C.R. 202.

nomical performance of the job without endangering the employee, his fellow employees and the general public.[76]

In regard to the weight of the respondent's evidentiary burden in establishing objectively the necessity of the impugned action, McIntyre J. in *Etobicoke* distinguished between cases in which economics are the main concern and those in which public safety might be at issue. This issue is further discussed in the general discussion of the reasonable and *bona fide* standard in Chapter 6. In respect of this discussion of subsection 11(1)(*a*), it should be noted that something in the nature of an objectively discernable necessity must be proven by the respondent to fulfill the requirement of the "reasonable and *bona fide*" test. Clearly, if a requirement, qualification or factor is not, as described by McIntyre J. in *Etobicoke* "rationally related to the performance of the job" (or other activity), it is unnecessary to go on to a consideration of reasonable accommodation.[77]

"Accommodation without Undue Hardship"

Subsection 11(2) states that the Commission, a board of inquiry or a court shall not find that a requirement is reasonable and *bona fide* in the circumstances unless it is satisfied that the needs of the group of which the person is a member cannot be accommodated without undue hardship on the person responsible for accommodating those needs, considering the cost, outside sources of funding, if any, and health and safety.

The inclusion in the *Code* of subsection 11(2) may be a result of a rather confusing Supreme Court of Canada judgment interpreting the federal *Human Rights Act*. In *Bhinder v. Canadian National Railway Co.*[78] the majority of the Court ruled that under, the Federal Act, if an employer can establish that the impugned requirement is a "*bona fide* occupational quali-

---

76. *Ibid.*, at 208 and 3 C.H.R.R. D/781 at D/783.

77. It is possible that the distinction between the "business necessity/objectively verifiable" part of the "reasonable and *bona fide*" test and the element of reasonable accommodation has been blurred in the past. This is likely due to the fact that the requirement at issue in most cases was fairly clearly a business necessity (an example can be seen in *O'Malley* — the requirement was that a retail store be staffed on Saturdays). The area in which a distinction might usefully be made between "reasonable and *bona fide*" and "duty to accommodate" is in such relatively hard to justify requirements as dress codes, or aspects thereof. However, there appears to be some evidence of a shift in approach by Boards of Inquiry in this respect. In *Singh v. Security and Investigation Services* (1977), unreported (Ont. Bd. of Inquiry), the case in which reasonable accommodation was introduced to Ontario case law, the Board did not address the business necessity for a requirement that security officers be clean-shaven and wear caps instead of turbans. By contrast, in *Sehdev v. Bayview Glen Secondary School, ante*, note 72, the board specifically concluded that the respondent school's "preference for a strict uniform policy is not a relevant reason for compromising the complainant's religion" (at D/4886).

78. (1985), 23 D.L.R. (4th) 481 (S.C.C.).

fication," he or she need not go on to prove that reasonable accommodation had been made.

The inclusion of subsection 11(2) makes it clear both that reasonable accommodation is a part of the Ontario *Code*[79] and that, rather than being superseded by the "reasonable and bona fide" defense, it is a necessary part of establishing this defence.

A number of cases dealt with the concepts of "reasonable accommodation" or "accommodation short of undue hardship"; prior to the 1986 amendments of the Ontario *Code*.

1. In *Singh v. Security and Investigation Services Limited*,[80] the board held that a relaxation of dress regulations to allow the wearing of a turban did not impose undue hardship.

2. In *Froese v. Pine Creek School Division No. 30*,[81] the board characterized nine days' absence from employment, without pay, to fulfill religious obligations, as reasonable.

3. In *O'Malley v. Simpsons-Sears*,[82] the employer offered a full-time employee the option of working "on a contingent basis," which would have reduced her hours of employment to little more than half of what she had been receiving formerly. The board considered this effort reasonable, but note that the board did not hear evidence as to undue hardship. At the Supreme Court of Canada, the complainant was compensated for the difference between part-time and full-time employment, but, again, on the basis of no evidence as to undue hardship.

4. In *Singh v. Workmen's Compensation Board Hospital*,[83] the issue was a hospital regulation against offensive weapons that had been forced against a Sikh patient wearing a kirpan (a small dagger worn as a religious observance). The board held that it would have been reasonable for the respondent hospital to have educated its staff about the symbolic nature of the dagger and to have made an effort to calm the apprehensions, if any, of other patients. Essentially, the board's opinion was that the respondent should have been able to accommodate the patient's wearing a five-inch or eight-inch dagger.

---

79. Debate on this subject was renewed before the board in a preliminary decision in *Roosma v. Ford Motor Co. of Canada* (1987), 9 C.H.R.R. D/4743 (Ont. Bd. of Inquiry) despite the fact that the decision of the Supreme Court of Canada in *O'Malley* had already been made. The Board in *Roosma* ruled that, even in the absence of specific provision in the statute, the 1981 [now 1990] *Code* did impose a duty of reasonable accommodation.

80. (1977), unreported (Ont. Bd. of Inquiry).

81. (1978), unreported (Man. Bd. of Inquiry). See the extensive discussion of this case in Tarnopolsky, *Discrimination and the Law* (1982).

82. [1985] 2 S.C.R. 536.

83. (1981), 2 C.H.R.R. D/459 (Ont. Bd. of Inquiry).

5. In *Sehdev. v. Bayview Glen Junior Schools*,[84] the board found that the relaxation of a school uniform rule to allow Sikh students to wear turbans and kirpans would be a reasonable accommodation.

6. In *Gohm v. Domtar Inc.*,[85] the Board of Inquiry found that it would have been reasonable for the respondent employer and union to have arranged for an employee who was a member of a Sabbatarian religion to have worked on Sundays rather than Saturdays, even if that had necessitated paying her overtime for the Sunday employment.

Of the cases noted above, only *Sehdev* and *Gohm* were decided after the Supreme Court's decision in *O'Malley*, and only in *Gohm* did the Board have occasion to comment on how *O'Malley* might properly be applied. In particular, the Board addressed the argument that a minimal effort by the respondent should be considered to meet the responsibility to accommodate, a rule established by the U.S. Supreme Court in *Trans-World Airlines v. Hardison*:[86]

> I find that the duty to accommodate short of undue hardship imposes a duty on employers (and, as will be discussed later, trade unions) to take substantial or meaningful steps to accommodate the requirements of the complainant. This duty defies generalization, because each case will involve unique circumstances, but as a general matter I find that the law requires more than a *de minimus* effort or expenditure on the part of the respondent. As counsel for the Commission pointed out, the very term "undue" hardship itself indicates that there is some hardship which is "due," and it is only hardship which goes beyond this minimum that can be relied upon by a respondent as a defence. It would be inconsistent with the purpose of human rights laws to prohibit adverse effect discrimination and at the same time to interpret the defence of reasonable accommodation short of undue hardship in such a manner that virtually any desultory effort to meet the complainant's needs, or any minimal expense, would be sufficient to justify the challenged rule or practice.
>
> The *de minimus* rule was urged upon me by counsel for the company, on the basis that the Supreme Court in *O'Malley* incorporated the concepts of reasonable accommodation and undue hardship from American law, and in doing so it adopted this standard, as enunciated in the leading case of *Trans-World Airlines v. Hardison*, 97 S. Ct. 2264 (1977). Counsel for the Commission argued that the *Hardison* standard is inconsistent with the general approach to Canadian human rights law, and that it was decided on the basis of a statute and in the context of a Constitution which has no parallel in Canada.
>
> A close examination of the *O'Malley* decision indicates that while McIntyre J. referred to American authorities on the issues of adverse effect discrimination and reasonable accommodation short of undue hardship he did not specifically adopt them, and indeed he equally referred to Canadian authorities on these issues. Thus, while it is true that Justice McIntyre referred to *Hardison*, at p. 333, of this decision, he did not discuss it in detail, nor did he specifically adopt its standard. In my view, this reference in equivocal, and the matter must be approached from a reading of the decision as a whole. At each state of the analysis in this decision McIntyre J. was careful to point out that while these concepts may have originated in the United States, they have been incorporated

---

84. (1988), 9 C.H.R.R. D/4881 (Ont. Bd. of Inquiry).

85. (1990), 12 C.H.R.R. D/161 (Ont. Bd. of Inquiry).

86. 97 S. Ct. 2264 (1977).

into Canadian law by previous board of inquiry and court decisions. (See pp. 329-30 [D/3106; and 332 [D/3107]). The standards of reasonable accommodation and undue hardship set out in these Canadian decisions, I would suggest, are as relevant if not more so than that which is contained in American law.

As well, the Supreme Court has adopted a uniquely Canadian approach to the interpretation of human rights laws in the line of cases I referred to earlier. In recent decisions the Court has indicated that American authorities are not to be taken as binding, or to be incorporated into Canadian law without reference to the unique — almost constitutional — nature of Canadian human rights law: see *Brooks v. Canada Safeway Ltd.* (1989), 10 C.H.R.R. D/6183; *Janzen v. Platy Enterprises* (1989), 10 C.H.R.R. D/6205. In particular, in *Brooks*, Dickson C.J.C rejected American authorities on the point in issue, because (D/6197): "In my view, the reasoning in those two cases does not fit well within the Canadian approach to issues of discrimination."

A close examination of the majority decision in *Hardison*, in my view, leads to the conclusion that it cannot be directly applied to Canadian human rights law. In *Hardison*, the Court held that TWA had made reasonable efforts to accommodate the plaintiff, in that it had attempted to meet his needs without breaching the seniority system set out in the collective agreement and without incurring extra expense. The Court ruled that since the relevant law included a specific provision which accorded *bona fide* seniority provisions a special protection (s. 703(h) of Title VII), *TWA* could not reasonably be required to exempt *Hardison* from the seniority system, or the shift preferences that resulted from it. The Court also held that to accord such special treatment to *Hardison* would amount to unequal treatment of other employees on the basis of religion, by denying them their shift preferences in order to accommodate his religious needs. Finally, the Court ruled at p. 2277 that to "require *TWA* to bear more than a de minimus cost in order to give *Hardison* Saturdays off is an undue hardship."

The essence of the majority's reasoning is encapsulated in the following passage (p. 2277): "In the absence of clear statutory language or legislative history to the contrary, we will not readily construe the statute to require an employer to discriminate against some employees in order to enable others to observe their Sabbath."

In my view the *Hardison* decision can be distinguished on the basis that it relates to a statutory scheme which is significantly different that the *Ontario Human Rights Code*, and it does not fit well with the Canadian approach to issues of discrimination. In particular, the *Code* contains no parallel to the exemption in respect of *bona fide* seniority systems in Title VII, and indeed under Canadian law a collective agreement provides no defence to an allegation of discrimination: see *Etobicoke*, supra. As well, Canadian law is not restricted by the doctrine of separation of Church and State which prevails in the United States, and which may have influenced the majority's approach to this issue in that to adopt a stronger standard of undue hardship may have amounted to favouring one religion over another: see the dissent by Marshall J., at pp. 2279-80.

Finally, it is my view that *Hardison* proceeds upon the basis of an unduly restrictive notion of discrimination, which finds no support in current Canadian law. Indeed, the Supreme Court of Canada has stated that sometimes equality will require different treatment to accommodate special needs: *Regina v. Big M. Drug Mart*, [1985] 1 S.C.R. 295, and furthermore it has sanctioned a purposive approach to discrimination which seeks to interpret human rights law so as to eliminate discrimination and to provide relief for the victims of discrimination: see *O'Malley*. These considerations lead me to conclude that the *Hardison* standard of undue hardship, that is the *de minimus* standard, should not be adopted for the purposes of this decisions.[87]

---

87. *Ante*, note 5, at D/175-176.

Only two published decisions of Ontario boards of inquiry have considered the 1986 amendment to section 10, and neither have differed discernably from those of boards dealing with the section prior to its amendment. In *Janssen v Ontario (Milk Marketing Board)*,[88] the issue was a rule of the respondent that assessed special transportation charges to farmers who did not wish to ship milk on Sundays. The complainant successfully established that this constituted constructive discrimination on the basis of creed. In a brief decision, the board considered the effect of sharing the costs of no Sunday shipping among all dairy farmers, as opposed to levying a special fee on those who declined to ship on Sundays. Finding that sharing costs would work out to between one and two cents per hectolitre, the board concluded that such a hardship would not be "undue".

In *Pandori and Ontario Human Rights Commission v. Peel Board of Education*,[89] the matter at issue was the right of teachers and students who are baptised Sikhs to wear kirpans. The respondent Board had a policy that forbade the wearing of weapons on school grounds, and it defined the kirpan as a weapon. After a lengthy review of the requirements of the Sikh religion and of the kirpan in particular, the board concluded that the rule created adverse consequences for Sikhs, and turned to the issue of undue hardship.

At particular issue was the question of safety. There being no evidence of misuse of the kirpan by the Sikh teachers and students, the respondent argued that the availability of the kirpan might be an incitement to violence by others.

The board considered both evidence offered by the Commission as to an absence of incidents of violence involving kirpans in schools which did not restrict the wearing of kirpans, and a line of cases in which attempts to restrict the wearing of kirpans had not been upheld. The board allowed that if a school had in fact experienced incidents of violence, some restriction might be allowed, but concluded that no need for restrictions had been established. In conclusion, the board ordered that kirpans of a reasonable size might be worn by baptised Sikh teachers and students, subject to a right of school principals to suspend the right to wear a kirpan if it were misused, and to effect policy changes if misuse were widespread. The extremely cautious nature of the board's order appears somewhat surprising, given the evidence set forth in the decision as to the virtual absence of risk. However, the safeguards were mentioned with approval by the Ontario Divisional Court,[90] which dismissed the respondent's appeal.

---

88. (1990), 13 C.H.R.R. D/397.
89. (1990), 12 C.H.R.R. D/364.
90. *Peel (Region) Board of Education v. Ontario (Human Rights Commission)* (1991), 3 O.R. (3d) 531 (Div. Ct.).

Subsection 11(2) lists three considerations common to the determination of undue hardship, these being "cost, outside sources of funding, if any, and health and safety requirement, if any." It is arguable that this list is meant to be conclusive, since a phrase such as "among other circumstances" has not been included in the statutory provision. However, even a narrow interpretation does not preclude the board of inquiry or court from considering the balancing of financial, health and safety considerations, in the words of Mr. Justice McIntyre, "in the interest of preserving a social structure in which each right may receive protection without undue interference with others." As Professor Pentney points out[91] "the question of whether a measure of reasonable accommodation will impose an undue hardship upon an employer or service provider cannot be resolved by focussing solely upon the expense or inconvenience associated with the change." In the *O'Malley* case, Mr. Justice McIntyre emphasized that this involves a balancing of rights "in the interest of preserving a social structure in which each right may receive protection without undue interference with others. The hardship (in the sense of expense or inconvenience) caused by an accommodative change therefore must be measured in the light of the benefits gained by the complainant, and others who are similar situated, in order to determine whether the particular accommodation imposed an undue burden on the respondent."[92]

Is there any obligation for the complainant to accept accommodation that does not fully meet his or her needs? Mr. Justice McIntyre in *O'Malley* alluded to this possibility, suggesting that if reasonable steps were taken to accommodate the complainant, the complainant might be expected to take "some accommodating steps on his own part."[93]

While there may be some obligation on the complainant to compromise in accepting accommodation that does not fill all of his or her needs, there is no reason to suppose that there is any obligation on the complainant to suggest the form which accommodation might take, although this might well happen in the course of negotiations with the respondent.[94]

---

91. In *Discrimination and the Law*, Richard De Boo, 1985, cumulative supplement, September 1989, page 25.

92. *Ibid*, at 335.

93. *Ontario (Human Rights Commission) v. Simpson-Sears* (1985), 23 D.L.R. (4th) 321 at 335 (S.C.C.). There is an interesting discussion to accept reasonable accommodation in *Rand v. Sealy Eastern Ltd., Upholstery Division* (1982), 3 C.H.R.R. D/938 (Ont. Bd. of Inquiry).

94. The Board of Inquiry in *O'Malley* and *Malik* made suggestions as to such an obligation, but this point of view was part of an interpretation of the onus of proof since contradicted by the Supreme Court of Canada in *O'Malley*.

5

SPECIFIC DISCRIMINATORY ACTIONS

This chapter will review sections 12, 13, 23 and 25(1), which proscribe certain specific actions.

DISCRIMINATION BECAUSE OF ASSOCIATION: SECTION 12

Section 12 reads:

A right under Part I is infringed where the discrimination is because of relationship, association or dealings with a person or persons identified by a prohibited ground of discrimination.

While there was no similar provision in the *Code* prior to 1981, discrimination because of association was recognized by two boards of inquiry prior to the enactment of the 1981 *Code*. In *Cooper v. Belmont Property Management*,[1] one of the two complainants claimed to have been fired because she was married to a black man. Although the board eventually concluded that the complaints were unfounded, the chairman found that he had jurisdiction under the *Code* to deal with a complaint of discrimination because of association, on a "fair, large, and liberal" interpretation of section 4(1)(*b*) of the former *Code*.[2]

In *Jahn v. Johnstone*[3] the complainant was a white tenant who had brought a black friend home for dinner. The presence of this guest upset the respondent landlord, who visited the complainant, and later telephoned her, charged her with "disgracing" his property and told her that she would have to leave in a month. The board of inquiry found that the landlord's actions had breached the convenant of quiet enjoyment of the premises. In finding that the landlord's conduct amounted to "discrimination in a term and condition of occupancy,"[4] the board considered whether the landlord's action

---

1. (1973), unreported (Ont. Bd. of Inquiry).
2. *Ibid.*, pp. 6 and 11 (transcript).
3. (1977), unreported (Ont. Bd. of Inquiry).
4. The relevant section of the former *Code* was s. 3(1), which stated that:
   "No person, directly or indirectly, alone or with another, by himself or by the interposition of another shall,

could be said to amount to differential treatment. The chairman reasoned that, in effect, the landlord was offering the complainant tenant a convenant for quiet enjoyment that was available "for all usual purposes *except* the offering of hospitality to blacks" and that the complainant was therefore put in a worse position than other Ontario tenants, for reasons of race.[5]

In *Tabar v. Scott*[6] a board of inquiry dealt with a complainant in which the complainant had been refused permission to assign a lease to persons of East Indian or Pakistani origin. This case too was decided under the 1981 *Code*, and the board relied in *Jahn* in ruling that discrimination against the complainants, as well as against others as a class, had occurred. This part of the decision was confirmed by the Divisional Court.[7]

To date, the section case of discrimination because of association under the 1981 *Code* has been *Kafato v. Halton Condominium Corp. No. 4*.[8] In that case, the board ruled that the corporate complainant, being identified with handicapped persons, could be a complainant, and that the actions of the respondent corporation in denying occupancy of condominium accommodation to the complainant could constitute discrimination under section 11 [now section 12].

It is arguable that Part I rights are worded so broadly that section 12 is unnecessary. Throughout Part I, equal treatment is mandated "with regard to" services, accommodation, employment, etc. This broad wording would probably enable section 3, for example, to cover the situation in which a contractor's tender is refused because of the race, sex, etc., of his or her employees, as it would a refusal of tender because of the contractor's own race or sex. Be that as it may, it is clear that in any of the areas listed in Part I, discrimination because of association breaches the *Code*.

It should be noted that section 12 contains no excepting provisions such as the familiar "*bona fide* and reasonable." Furthermore, section 12 can be construed as being unaffected by any of the exceptions contained in Part II of the *Code*. The section speaks of a "right under Part I," rather than "a right under this Act." Presumably, therefore, section 11 refers to Part I rights in their "pure" form, unaffected by the excepting provisions that are found in Part II. By contrast, section 11, which also speaks of "a right . . .

     (*a*)   deny to any person or class of persons occupancy of any commercial unit or any housing accommodation; or

     (*b*)   discriminate against any person or class of persons with respect to any term or condition of occupancy of any commercial unit or any housing accommodation,

because of race, creed, colour, sex, nationality, ancestry or place of origin of such person or class of persons or of any other person or class of persons."

5. Note 3, pp. 16-17.

6. (1984), 6 C.H.R.R. D/2471 (Ont. Div. Ct.), reversed in part (1986), 9 C.H.R.R. D/4537 (Div. Ct.), reversed in part (1989), 10 C.H.R.R. D/6491 (Ont. C.A.).

7. *Ibid.*

8. (1991), 14 C.H.R.R. D/154.

under Part I," clearly indicates that the right to freedom from constructive discrimination is affected by the Part II excepting provisions; subsection 11(1)(*b*) states that the right applies where "it is declared in this Act . . . that to discriminate because of such ground is not an infringement of a right."

There are strong public policy reasons for supporting the interpretation of section 12 as an unqualified right. For example, suppose the landlord of the type of accommodation that is subject to a broad exception from the provisions of the *Code*, under section 21(1),[9] were to threaten a tenant with eviction, or impose a "no visitors" rule, because the tenant had a black visitor. It is reasonable to assume that the legislature did not intend section 21(1) to be interpreted as to allow the landlord to discriminate this extensively.[10]

It is unlikely that this interpretation would cause any particular difficulties in application, as the sections that provide exceptions are unlikely to conflict with an unqualified right to freedom from discrimination by association. Only section 21(1) presents any difficulties, due to the unusual breadth of the exceptions, and even then direct conflicts are unlikely to arise. For example, if a section 21(1) landlord, exercising the right to discriminate because of family status, were to refuse accommodation to a woman because she has a child, the refusal may well be "because of relationship," but the relationship is not "with a person . . . identified by a prohibited ground of discrimination."

PUBLICATION OF SIGNS, SYMBOLS, ETC.: SECTION 13

Section 13 reads:

(1) A right under Part I is infringed by a person who publishes or displays before the public or causes the publication or display before the public of any notice, sign, symbol, emblem, or other similar representation that indicates the intention of the person to infringe a right under Part I or that is intended by the person to incite the infringement of a right under Part I.

(2) Subsection (1) shall not interfere with freedom of expression of opinion.

In Ontario, legislative prohibition against the display or publication of discriminatory notices, signs, symbols, etc., dates back to 1944.[11] The previ-

---

9. Section 20(1) states:

"The right under section 2 to equal treatment with respect to occupancy of residential accommodation without discrimination is not infringed by discrimination where the residential accommodation is in a dwelling in which the owner or his or her family reside if the occupancy or occupants of the residential accommodation are required to share a bathroom or kitchen facility with the owner or family of the owner."

10. It is settled law that exceptions to the *Code* are to be construed narrowly. See the discussion of this point in Chapter 6.

11. See the *Racial Discrimination Act*, S.O. 1944, c. 51, s. 1 [rep. S.O. 1954, c. 28, s. 9].

ous *Human Rights Code* contained a provision similar to the current section 13.[12]

Preliminary Jurisdictional Issues

Before the substance of section 13 is examined, it is appropriate to discuss briefly the issue of provincial jurisdiction, contemplated by section 13; over the expression of ideas and the media.

Jurisdiction over the Message

An obvious primary issue, in the consideration of a provision that can be said to limit freedom of expression, is whether it is *ultra vires* a provincial legislature. On this issue of jurisdiction, Professor Tarnopolsky sums up recent case law as follows.[13]

> In considering the constitutional validity of the provincial prohibitions against discriminatory messages, one could start with the majority judgment of Mr. Justice Beetz in *Attorney General of Canada v. Dupond* where he had asserted:
>
> > None of these freedoms (speech, assembly and association) is a single matter coming within exclusive federal or provincial competence. Each of them is an aggregate of several matters which, depending on the aspect, come within federal or provincial competence.
> >
> > Therefore . . . insofar as a message relates to employment, provision of goods, services, facilities or public accommodation, or the selling or leasing of real property, whether for private or commercial purposes, legislative jurisdiction with respect to the message will be determined by the legislative jurisdiction with respect to the person, thing or activity. Furthermore, it would appear that as long as the provincial prohibition applies to the message, the medium by which it is transmitted will not alter jurisdiction.

Questions of federal or provincial jurisdiction aside, the substance of section 13 may well be challenged under the *Charter of Rights* on the issue of whether the section represents a "reasonable limit . . ., [such as] can be demonstrably justified in a free and democratic society," on freedom of expression. Given the remedial nature of the legislation and the qualification of its application expressed by section 13(2), a successful challenge would

---

12. See R.S.O. 1980, c. 340, s. 1.
13. Tarnopolsky, *Discrimination and The Law in Canada* (1985), p. 10-13. In his thorough discussion of jurisdiction, Professor Tarnopolsky reviews *Canada (Attorney General) v. Dupond* (1978), 84 D.L.R. (3d) 420 (S.C.C.); *Quebec (Attorney General) v. Kellogg's Co.* (1978), 83 D.L.R. (3d) 314 (S.C.C.); *Jabour v. Law Society of British Columbia* (1980), 115 D.L.R. (3d) 549 (B.C. C.A.); *Reference Regulation and Control of Radio Communication in Canada*, [1932] A.C. 304 (P.C.); *C.F.R.B. Ltd. v. Canada (Attorney General) (No. 2)* (1973), 38 D.L.R. (3d) 335 (Ont. C.A.); *Dionne v. Quebec (Public Service Board)* (1977), 83 D.L.R. (3d) 178 (S.C.C.); *Capital Cities Communications Inc. v. Canada (Canadian Radio-Television & Telecommunications Commission)* (1977), 81 D.L.R. (3d) 609 (S.C.C.); *McKay v. R.*, [1965] S.C.R. 798. Also see *McNeil v. Nova Scotia (Board of Censors)*, [1978] 2 S.C.R. 662.

seem unlikely. The freedom of speech issue, insofar as boards have commented upon it to date, is referred to further below, in the discussion of the substance of section 13.

Jurisdiction over the Medium

The wording of section 13 indicates that it is concerned with the more concrete forms of communication, such as written or printed material and design. Cases have involved the use of sign,[14] a publicly-displayed letter,[15] and a button bearing a photograph and slogan.[16]

A point of contention arises over whether material in newspapers is included. In *Linklater v. Winnipeg Sun* the complainant was concerned with a series of newspaper articles, and a complaint was made under the Manitoba *Human Rights Code*, which contains terms identical to the Ontario *Code*. The Board found for the complainant, but, on appeal, the Manitoba Court of Queen's Bench and the Court of Appeal ruled that "other representation" should be interpreted in reference to "notice, sign and symbol," and that it therefore could not include such complex works as newspaper articles or editorials.[17] Arguably, such items as advertisements placed in newspapers can come within section 13, even with application of the *eusdem generis* rule.

It is reasonably clear that the section does not contemplate any regulation of the content of radio or television broadcasts.

The Substance of the Section

The Intention of the Person to Infringe a Part I Right

Clearly, the concept of intent is central to section 13. For this reason, case law from other jurisdictions should be used with caution. Other provincial human rights legislation prohibits such actions as the "indication" of discrimination[18] or the publication or display of any representation that "affronts the dignity"[19] of a group protected by the legislation. By contrast, section 13 forbids only two relatively more clearly defined actions: the publication or display, or the causation thereof, of a representation that

---

14. See *Lam v. McCaw* (1977), unreported (Ont. Bd. of Inquiry); *Singer v. Iwasyk* (1976), unreported (Sask. Bd. of Inquiry), reversed *(sub nom. Iwasyk v. Sask. Human Rights Comm.)*, [1977] 6 W.W.R. 699 (Sask. Q.B.), reversed [1978] 5 W.W.R. 499 (Sask. C.A.).
15. See *McKinlay v. Dial Agencies* (1980), 1 C.H.R.R. D/246 (Sask. Bd. of Inquiry).
16. See *Rasheed v. Bramhill* (1980), 2 C.H.R.R. D/249 (N.S. Bd. of Inquiry).
17. (1984), 5 C.H.R.R. D/2098 (Man. Bd. of Adjud.). Also see *Saskatchewan (Human Rights Commission) v. Engineering Students' Society* (1989), 10 C.H.R.R. D/5636 (Sask. C.A.), leave to appeal to S.C.C. refused (1989), 102 N.R. 320 (note) (S.C.C.).
18. See, for example, the Nova Scotia *Human Rights Act*, S.N.S. 1969, c. 11, s. 12(1).
19. See the Saskatchewan *Human Rights Code*, SS. 1979, c. S-24.1, s. 14.

either *indicates an intention to infringe* a Part I right or is *intended to incite* such an infringement. Because they do not deal with intent as a central issue, the very few Canadian human rights cases dealing with publications, signs, etc., are of little value as precedents in the interpretation of section 13, except insofar as they comment on free expression of opinion, which will be discussed below.[20]

A classic example of a representation indicating an intention to discriminate is a sign, displayed by a landlord, that says "whites only."[21] In view of the broad exceptions found in section 21, this example raises the issue discussed above in regard to section 12: what is the effect of section 13 in those situations in which the *Code* provides exceptions?

In the one Ontario case to date that has considered section 12 of the 1981 *Code*, the board considered a real estate listing that contained a requirement that the purchaser be of "German extraction or speaking." In that case, *Gregory v. Donauschwaben Park Waldheim*,[22] the board had found against the complainant in regard to the actual conditions of the sale, ruling that a defence under section 17 [now 18] of the *Code* applied. The board also dismissed the related complaint against the real estate agency, holding that "if I am correct in holding that the section 17 [now 18] defence is available to the respondent, (this complaint is) unfounded and must also be dismissed."[23]

The decision contains no indication of any argument against the availability of the section 17 defence. Presumably, the board's logic was where an activity is permissible by law, the setting out of a notice describing that activity is also permissible. However, it is suggested that consideration might be given to other arguments. As with section 12, there is no specific indication in section 13 that the exceptions in Part II of the *Code* apply to diminish the rights protected by section 13.

Furthermore, there is a strong public policy argument against allowing

20. The cases on the display or publication of discriminatory material include: *Singer v. Iwasyk, ante,* note 14, an unreported 1976 decision under Saskatchewan's *Fair Accommodation Practices Act* . In this case the board found that a caricature "indicated discrimination" in that it disclosed a discriminatory predilection, belief or attitude; *McKinlay v. Dial Agencies, ante,* note 15. In this Saskatchewan case the question was whether a publicly-displayed letter "ridiculed, belittled, or otherwise affronted the dignity of any person or class of persons because of . . . physical disability (at D/247)"; *Rasheed v. Bramhill, ante,* note 16. In this Nova Scotia case the board considered whether a button "indicated discrimination."

21. Those who believe that the use of discriminatory signs in Ontario is antique will be surprised to know that a case involving a landlord who posted a sign advertising an apartment to let to "Caucasian Adults Only" was decided in 1977. See *Lam v. McCaw, ante,* note 14.

22. (1990), 13 C.H.R.R. D/505 (Ont. Bd. of Inquiry).

23. Supra, at 48.

the kind of public affront that would result from the example noted above.

In a given case, counsel for the respondent would undoubtedly point to section 23 as support for the argument that section 13 must be read in conjunction with the exemptions provided by the *Code*. Section 23 indicates that the right under section 4 to equality in employment is infringed by discriminatory advertising and applications. It will undoubtedly be argued that this section would be made redundant by the operation of section 13, if section 13 were unaffected by the exception sections. To state the position another way, it will be argued that a special prohibition against discriminatory employment advertising would only be necessary if section 13 were affected by the many exceptions to which employment rights are subject. This argument would be valid only if there were no essential differences between the two sections. However, it is suggested that there are significant differences.

First, a purposive approach to the *Code* would support the view that section 23 is phrased in the way it is because the legislature perceived a need to provide guidance as to the application of section 13 in the complicated area of employment recruitment. The *Code* therefore sets out a three-step process that guides the employer who wishes to take advantage of an employment exemption in the procedure he or she must follow to avoid breaching section 13.

A more telling argument is that section 23 deals with a broader subject matter than section 13. While an employer might well advertise via a "notice, sign, symbol, emblem or other similar representation," he or she might also advertise via oral announcement on radio or television." Such announcements appear to be within the ambit of section 23, whereas it is clear that section 13 does not extend so far.[24] Since section 23 cannot be seen as a mere repetition of section 13, its inclusion does not support any inference as to whether section 13 is affected by the *Code*'s exempting sections.

Does the interpretation of section 13 as an independent provision create any significant problems in its application? Some theoretical examples of situations that involve both exemptions provided by the *Code* and possible section 13 implications illustrate that no logical inconsistencies need arise, provided that section 13's emphasis on intention receives due recognition.

The first example is a "Ukranian Canadian Club" sign posted over the

---

24. The term publish is used in both s. 13 and s. 23; publishing can include making information public by verbal as well as written communications. See, generally, *Gatley on Libel and Slander*, 7th ed. (1974); Williams, *The Law of Defamation in Canada* (1976). However, the wording of s. 13 ("any notice, sign, symbol, emblem or other *similar* representation," my emphasis) obviously excludes verbal "publication" from the subject matter addressed by the section. In regard to the issue of jurisdiction over radio and television broadcasts, see the discussion of s. 23, below.

door of a social organization that may, because of the operation of section 18, limit its membership to the ethnic group noted on the sign. The second example is a silhouette of a figure wearing a skirt, displayed over the door of a women's washroom. Both of these facilities are the subject of exemptions under the *Code*.[25] However, it is not necessary to invoke the exemption sections in order to spare the proprietors of both facilities from liability under section 13.

The key element, of course, is intention. While both signs unmistakably suggest that usage by a particular group is intended, they do not expressly bar anyone else. The Ukranian Canadian Club may or may not bar membership to people of Polish origin; one would have to inquire within to find out for sure. Furthermore, the women's washroom may well be used by men on occasion; the sign alone does not indicate that measures will be taken to repel invaders of the opposite sex.[26]

Compare these signs with ones saying "Whites Only" or "No Jews Allowed." Clearly, the latter indicate an intention to deny admission to a specific group and, as clearly, these signs contravene section 13 when used in respect of services, facilities, etc.

It may well be argued that not all signs, symbols, etc. will be so unambiguous as the examples noted above, and that some will convey a meaning that results from the relevant social milieu. For example, what is one to make of a sign above a washroom door that says "white ladies"? In response to this argument, it should first be noted that Ontario society is beyond the stage where racially segregated washrooms would be tolerated, so this is a somewhat far-fetched example. However, in the unlikely event that such a sign were posted, it would be reasonable for a board to take judicial notice of the surrounding circumstances that would lead it to conclude that, in fact, the sign could give rise to a reasonable inference of intention to discriminate. Human rights legislation is, after all, designed to deal with just such nebulous and socially-charged situations.

Intent to Incite

Before considering intent to incite, it is necessary to define incitement. The *Oxford English Dictionary* defines incite as "to urge or to spur on, to stir up, to instigate, to stimulate." The term has, of course, a criminal-law

---

25. Public lavatories are affected by s. 30(1).

26. As a practical point, it should be noted that a complaint of this nature would be unlikely ever to reach a board of inquiry. Under s. 34(1)(*b*) the Commission has the power to refuse to deal with a complaint that is "trivial, frivolous, vexatious, or made in bad faith." The Commission is thus empowered to dismiss at an early stage complaints which cannot fairly be said to reflect the problems properly addressed by the *Code*.

meaning as well. V.G. Rose[27] reviews the common-law and *Criminal Code*[28] development of the offence of incitement.[29] Considerations relevant to section 13 include the following:

1. In an incitement, the offence counselled is not committed. If the offence counselled is committed, the person who incited the commission is properly charged with being a party to the offence rather than with incitement.[30]

2. The incitement need not be explicitly directed at any particular person, and can be directed at any or all members of a group, although "there must be a completed communication, from the counsellor, received by the person(s) counselled.[31]

3. The solicitation in question may incite, although it is ambiguous, if "it is understood and intended to be understood as an incitement by the person to whom it is addressed.[32]

4. While the communication must be shown to have reached an audience intended, "it is not necessary that the person to whom it is directed be in any way influenced by it.[33]

5. Incitement may include advising another to commit an offence some time in the future "even if the facts were such that at the time the incitement was made the offence counselled could not have been committed."[34]

6. The incitor need not originate the idea that the offence should be committed: it is no defence that one is responding to a request for a perceived need.[35]

There are, to date, no Canadian cases dealing with the "incitement" of discrimination or harassment. However, there was an English decision

---

27. *Parties to an Offence* (1982), pp. 101-22.

28. The section in question is s. 422.

29. While it may be argued that criminal law standards are inappropriate to the interpretation of civil legislation, it is suggested that the safeguards offered the accused in the interpretation of criminal legislation are not too protective when freedom of expression is at stake.

30. See, generally, Rose, *Ante*, note 27, pp. 108-22.

31. *Ibid.*, pp. 110-11. Cases cited as authority for this proposition include: *R. v. Krause* (1902), 66 J.P. 121; *R. v. McLeod* (1970), 12 C.R.N.S. 193 (B.C. C.A.); *R. v. Most* (1881), 7 Q.B.D. 244 (C.C.R.).

32. Rose, *ante*, note 27, at p. 112; *R. v. Cope* (1921), 16 Cr. App. R. 77 (C.C.A.); *R. v. Miskell*, [1954] 1 W.L.R. 438 (Ct. Martial Appl. Ct.).

33. Rose, *ante*, note 27, at p. 114; *R. v. McLeod*, *ante*, note 31; *R. v. Krause*, *ante*, note 31; *R. v. Quail* (1866), 4 F. & F. 1076.

34. Rose, at p. 120; *R. v. Shephard* (1919), 14 Cr. App. R. 26 (C.C.A.).

35. Rose, at p. 121; *R. v. Crichton*, [1915] S.A.L.R. 1 (Aust. C.C.R.); *R. v. Quail*, *ante*, note 33; *R. v. Glubisz (No. 2)* (1979), 9 C.R. (3d) 300 (B.C. C.A.).

based in part on section 12 of the *Race Relations Act* of 1968, which section provided:

> Any person who deliberately aids, induces or incites another person to do an act which is unlawful by virtue of any provision of this Part of this Act shall be treated for the purposes of this Act as doing that act.[36]

In *Race Relations Board v. Applin*[37] the respondent had brought pressure on a couple who had provided foster care for children of various races, in order to persuade them to foster only white children. The means used were the circulation, to the couple's neighbours, of a leaflet containing disparaging remarks about the couple and the calling of a public meeting at which exerpts from the leaflet were read aloud. The Race Relations Board lost its case at trial, but was successful on appeal. On the issue of what constitutes incitement Lord Denning opined that "a person may 'incite' another to do an act by threatening or by pressure as well as by persuasion."[38]

Freedom of Expression of Opinion

As mentioned above, there has been recent case law to the effect that freedom of speech is neither a federal nor a provincial matter exclusively.[39] Provincial legislation that is, in pith and substance, *intra vires* provincial power may still affect freedom of speech without being struck down as unconstitutional. Section 13(2) appears to be a legislative recognition of this potential for provincial interference with freedom of speech; the section provides boards and courts with some guidance in regard to the interests that must be balanced when applying section 13(1). Clearly, when a notice, sign, symbol, emblem "or other similar representation" can be fairly considered a pure expression of opinion, no matter how adverse, about persons protected by the *Code*, the expression of that opinion is not to be held as an infringement of the *Code*.

The result is less clear when the expression of opinion can also fairly be described as the expression of an intention to discriminate, or to incite discrimination. Take, for example, a button that says "A Woman's Place is in the Home — Not in our Police Force." While this may seem a fairly harmless expression of opinion, circumstances, such as its distribution during a town council's deliberations on police staffing, may render it an incitement. The issue here will be whether boards and courts interpret section 13(2) as indicating that any "opinion" content in a representation renders the whole immune from the provisions of section 13(1).

---

36. The current version of this provision is found in the *Race Relations Act, 1976*, s. 31. The term "incite" is replaced by "induce."
37. [1973] 1 Q.B. 815, affirmed [1975] A.C. 259 (H.L.).
38. [1973] 1 Q.B. 815 at 825.
39. *Canada (Attorney General) v. Dupond* (1978), 84 D.L.R. (3d) 420 (S.C.C.).

It is suggested that section 13(2) does not demand this interpretation. A balancing of the rights protected in section 13(1) with the right to free expression of opinion is surely in order. Further to this approach, the board has the power to make orders that are in keeping with specific situations.[40] For example, a respondent might be ordered to obliterate only that part of a sign which is *not* an expression of his or her opinion, or might be enjoined from distributing a button in a particular situation in which its display might amount to incitement. Clearly, these "mixed content" cases will require fine judgment and, in some cases, creativity in fashioning remedies. However, it is suggested that such is the task imposed by section 13(2).[41]

Just as clearly, the issue of freedom of expression is so situation-specific that it is difficult to make more than a general comment upon the probable approach of future boards of inquiry under section 13. The remarks of the Nova Scotia board in *Rasheed v. Bramhill*[42] are illustrative of the most probable approach. Chairman Charles suggested that:[43]

> In particular cases, the right of free speech may have to give way to other human rights, such as the right not to be discriminated against, so that although the law infringes the right to freedom of speech, it does not inviolate it and it is, therefore, not unconstitutional. . . . Section 12(2) [now 13(2)] should not be read as imposing an absolute limit upon Section 12(1) [now 13(1)] but, rather, in the context of a right of expression that is not absolute and which must, in some circumstances, give way or be curtailed in order to make other rights effective. It could be interpreted as a declaration that the Provincial Legislature did not intend, by virtue of Section 12(1) [now 13(1)] to go beyond the bounds of what is necessary in order to prevent discrimination by signs, symbols, etc.

Liability under Section 13

It is probable that, where a "notice sign, symbol or emblem" that breaches section 13 is made public through, for example, its reproduction in a newspaper, both the author of the representation and the owner of the medium involved are properly named as respondents.

Dual liability certainly applies in the law of defamation.[44] It is suggested that the law of defamation is closely comparable to those sections of the *Code* that deal with the dissemination of material that incites or indicates an intention to discriminate, since such material, by implication, af-

---

40. A board of inquiry may "direct the party to do anything that, in the opinion of the board, the party ought to do to achieve compliance with this Act, both in respect of the complaint and in respect of future practices." See s. 41.

41. This is the approach advocated by the N.S. board of inquiry in *Rasheed v. Bramhill* (1980), 2 C.H.R.R. D/249 at para. 2168 (N.S. Bd. of Inquiry), when interpreting a similar clause of the Nova Scotia *Human Rights Act*.

42. *Ibid.*

43. *Ibid.*, at D/252.

44. *Ante*, note 24; *Thomson v. Lambert*, [1938] S.C.R. 253; *Vizetelly v. Mudie's Select Library*, [1900] 2 Q.B. 170 (C.A.); *Allan v. Bushnell T.V. Co.*, [1969] 2 O.R. 6 (C.A.).

fects the public's perception of the target group. Respondent newspaper owners may point to the wording of the section, and argue that it seems to speak only of one person.[45] However, an equally reasonable interpretation is that, depending on the circumstances, a board might reasonably infer that the newspaper that publishes a notice that contravenes section 13 intends itself to discriminate or to incite discrimination. In such circumstances, it would be up to the newspaper to rebut the inference.

Publishers would also be well advised to note that there is a power to prosecute for alleged violations of the *Code*.[46] In egregious circumstances, such as the publication of a series of blatantly racist messages, a prosecution might be undertaken,[47] and a publisher could be found guilty as an aider or abettor.

EMPLOYMENT ADVERTISING, APPLICATIONS AND INTERVIEWS: SECTION 23(1), (2) AND (3)

Sections 23(1), (2), (3) read as follows:

(1) The right under section 5 to equal treatment with respect to employment is infringed where an invitation to apply for employment or an advertisement in connection with employment is published or displayed that directly or indirectly classifies or indicates qualifications by a prohibited ground of discrimination.

(2) The right under section 5 to equal treatment with respect to employment is infringed where a form of application for employment is used or a written or oral inquiry is made of an applicant that directly or indirectly classifies or indicates qualifications by a prohibited ground of discrimination.

(3) Nothing in subsection (2) precludes the asking of questions at a personal employment interview concerning a prohibited ground of discrimination where discrimination on such ground is permitted under this Act.

Section 23 does not deal with all aspects of pre-employment practice. Methods of recruitment other than advertisements or the use of employment agencies are presumably covered by section 5. However, in the first 4 subsections, section 23 provides a guide to recruitment by advertisement, the use of applications, and the manner in which an employer or employment agency who chooses to take advantage of the numerous employment exemptions in the *Code* may screen applicants.

Advertising Media Addressed by the Section

The predecessors of section 23(1) were sections 4(2), (3) and (4) of the

---

45. "A right . . . is infringed by a person who publishes . . . any notice . . . that indicates the intention *of the person*." (My emphasis).

46. See s. 44.

47. A publisher might be prosecuted directly, or as a party to the offence; see the *Provincial Offences Act*, R.S.O. 1990, c. P.33, s. 77.

previous *Code*. These provisions specifically proscribed the broadcast, publication, circulation or display of discriminatory words, symbols or other representations, by way of employment advertisements. By contrast, it might appear *prima facie* that section 23 does not prohibit oral dissemination of discriminatory job advertisements, such as radio "job market" broadcasts. However, it would surely be contrary to the spirit of the legislation to allow discriminatory verbal advertisements where written ones are barred. The more reasonable interpretation is probably that "published" is intended to cover spoken advertisements or invitations to apply for employment where these are in any way made public. This interpretation is supported by the *Shorter Oxford English Dictionary*'s definition of publication, which includes, "The action of publishing; . . . the action of making public by known; public notification or announcement; promulgation."

The law of defamation, in which the issue of "publication" is essential, includes numerous cases in which verbal communications have been said to be "published"; more recent cases extend to radio and television broadcasting.[48]

Can provincial human rights legislation be applied to radio and televisions broadcasts? As discussed above in the review of section 13, there is authority to suggest that it can, insofar as it relates to a matter properly under provincial jurisdiction. As noted above, the law of defamation has been applied to television broadcasts. The Supreme Court of Canada has upheld provincially-legislated prohibitions of the use of cartoons in advertising for children.[49] In *Canada (Attorney General) v. Montreal (City)*,[50] Mr. Justice Beetz held:

> None of those freedoms (speech, assembly and association) is a single matter coming within exclusive federal or provincial competence. Each of them is an aggregate of several matters which, depending on the aspect, come within federal or provincial competence.[51]

The Supreme Court of Canada has upheld the validity of provincial legislation authorizing the Benchers of British Columbia's Law Society to ban advertising by lawyers.[52]

---

48. *Arnott v. College of Physicians and Surgeons (Saskatchewan)* (1953), 10 W.W.R. 446 (Sask. C.A.), affirmed [1954] S.C.R. 538; *Allan v. Bushnell T.V. Co., ante*, note 44; see, generally, *Gatley on Libel and Slander*, 7th ed. (1974); Williams, *The Law of Defamation in Canada* (1976).
49. *Quebec (Attorney General) v. Kellogg's Co.* (1978), 83 D.L.R. (3d) 314 (S.C.C.).
50. [1978] 2 S.C.R. 770.
51. *Ibid.*, at 796-7.
52. See *Canada (Attorney General) v. Law Society of British Columbia*, [1982] 5 W.W.R. 289 (S.C.C.).

The Liability of Publishers

It seems clear that section 23(1) allows for complaints against both the employer who arranges for the publication of a discriminatory advertisement and the newspaper, radio station, etc. that undertakes to assist in its publication. While the previous *Code* provided separate clauses dealing with advertisements by the employer and advertisements "on behalf of" an employer,[53] the description of the prohibited activity in section 23(1) would seem to apply in respect of both. Certainly, the subsection cannot reasonably be seen to narrow the range of possible respondents.

There have been, to date, no Ontario cases against publishers, but in *Alberta (Human Rights Commission) v. Whitecourt Star*[54] and *Hope v. Gray-Grant*[55] board have issued cease-and-desist orders. In the latter case, the board also ordered a publisher to include in its classified advertisements section a notice that British Columbia human rights legislation prohibits discriminatory advertising.

The Substance of the Advertisement

It would appear from the wording of the legislation that under no circumstances, not even in respect of employment that might qualify for an exception, may employers directly or indirectly classify employment or indicated qualifications by a prohibited ground of discrimination. This is a change from the previous *Code*. Under that *Code* all clauses related to employment, including advertisements, were listed under section 4. The final clause, section 4(6) said:

> The provisions of this section relating to any discrimination, limitation, specification or preference for a position or employment based on age, sex or marital status do not apply where age, sex, or marital status is a *bona fide* occupational qualification and requirement for the position or employment.

Clearly, under the former *Code*, employment that qualified for an exception under section 4(6) could be advertised in a way which suggested that the employer would hire only someone of the appropriate age group, sex or marital status. Equally clearly, section 23(1) of the new *Code* does not provide for such exceptions. Section 23 states that neither advertisements nor application forms may be drafted so as to suggest qualification by a prohibited ground of discrimination. Where an area of employment qualifies for an exception the employer may screen his or her candidates, but only at the personal interview stage.

The broad wording of section 23(1) suggests that employers would be well-advised to give some thought to the wording of advertisements. Gone

---

53. R.S.O. 1980, c. 340, ss. 4(2) and (3).
54. (1976), unreported (Alta. Bd. of Inquiry).
55. (1980), 2 C.H.R.R. D/256 (B.C. Bd. of Inquiry).

are the days when an employer could with impunity post a requirement for a "healthy young man." The appropriate course of action is, of course, to focus the advertisement on a description of the job and its requirements. This practice will result in a certain amount of self-selection among the pool of prospective applicants. If a person who seems at first glance to be obviously unsuitable does apply, the message of the *Code* is clear: the person must be given the same chance as other similarly-qualified applicants to convince the employer that he or she can meet the job requirements.

Prior to the passage of the present *Code*, the Ontario Human Rights Commission had developed an informal screening function, at the request of employers who believed that they qualified for an exemption under section 4(6) of the former *Code*, and who wished to advertise in a way that indicated that they were seeking applicants of a particular age group, sex or marital status. The Commission would review the nature of the employment, decide whether age, sex, etc., appeared to be a *bona fide* occupational qualification in this instance and send the employer a written response, approving or disapproving the draft advertisement. In approving an advertisement, the Commission undertook only to refrain from initiating a complaint itself. It specifically declined to bind its own discretion in respect of a complaint by anyone else.

Given the wording of the 1981 *Code*, it would appear that the Commission has no jurisdiction to continue this limited practice, as it seems clear that under no circumstances may an employer advertise in a manner prohibited by section 23(1).

Screening by Application Form and Interview

Sections 23(2) and (3) regulate the screening of applicants. In essence, oral or written inquiries that could give rise to an inference that the employer's attitude is discriminatory are prohibited. There is an exception only in respect of oral inquiries relating to a ground of discrimination that the employer, by virtue of an exception in the *Code* is permitted.

There have been few Ontario boards of inquiry specifically concerned with application forms. The most recent is *Taylor v. Via Security Systems*,[56] in which a board found that an application form that included questions as to nationality, place of birth, and complexion contravened subsection 23(2).

The prohibitions relating to applications obviously represent the legislature's attempt to prevent an employer from screening out an applicant, sight unseen, because of race, sex, religion, etc. The broad wording of section 23(2) clearly represents an effort to discourage employers from eliciting information that could be used to discriminate. Clearly, a question

---

56. (1986), 8 C.H.R.R. D/3925 (Ont. Bd. of Inquiry). For a similar case, see *Lomer v. Ottawa* (1964), unreported (Ont. Bd. of Inquiry).

about marital status on an application form must not be used. It would also be unlawful to try to obtain this information indirectly, for example, by asking "Is there a second income in your family?" "Do you live alone?", or "Does your husband mind if you work?"

As with advertising, it is obviously wise for employers to give some thought to the drafting of application forms. If the real reason an employer is unwilling to hire a married woman is a fear that a married woman would be reluctant to travel, it is surely appropriate simply to ask the candidate if she is willing to travel. This question elicits information that is legitimately required, without breaching the *Code*.

Obviously, the more closely the form directs itself to the requirements of the job, as opposed to data about the applicant that is not strictly related to job performance, the less likely it will be that the use of the form breaches section 23(2). While data such as marital status, number of dependents, and state of health may be relevant to a company benefits plan, such data need not be elicited until the applicant is actually hired and, of course, after hiring the eliciting of such data is permissible.

Employment interviews have been the subject of considerable comment in several recent Ontario boards of inquiry. As noted above, oral inquiries relating to a ground of discrimination are permitted only where an exception to the *Code* allows discrimination on that ground. Inquiries related to the applicant's race amounted to circumstantial evidence of racial discrimination in *Suchit v. Sisters of St. Joseph.*[57] In that case, the interviewer asked a candidate for a position of director of a detoxification centre, who was of East Indian origin, a number of questions concerning his attitude to racism that were not asked of non-minority candidates.

Four Ontario boards of inquiry have raised the question as to whether certain hiring criteria and interview questions might adversely affect candidates of other ethnic backgrounds than the interviewers.[58] No complaint of this nature has yet been successful, but boards have accepted the idea that, if a facially neutral criterion or question could be proven to disproportionately disadvantage a group protected by the *Code*, such a practice would breach section 11. Forward-thinking employers would be well-advised to implement cultural sensitivity training in their human resources departments.

---

57. (1983), 4 C.H.R.R. D/1329 (Ont. Bd. of Inquiry).
58. See *Malik v. Ontario (Minister of Government Services)* (1981), 2 C.H.R.R. D/374 (Ont. Bd. of Inquiry), *Quereshi v. Central High School of Commerce (No. 3)* (1989), 12 C.H.R.R. D/394 (Ont. Bd. of Inquiry), reversed (1991), 42 O.A.C. 258 (Div. Ct.); *Romano v. North York (City) Board of Education* (1987), 8 C.H.R.R. D/4347 (Ont. Bd. of Inquiry), affirmed (1988), 10 C.H.R.R. D/5887 (Ont. Div. Ct.) and *Bhadauria v. Toronto Board of Education* (1990), 12 C.H.R.R. D/105 (Ont. Bd. of Inquiry). These cases are further discussed in Chapter 3.

Finally, it is clear that an employment interview process that is not logically planned and directed toward selecting candidates with qualifications that fit defined job requirements can both give rise to unnecessary complaints of discrimination, and leave the respondent with little evidence to support his or her choice later. In *Bhadauria v. Board of Education, City of Toronto*,[59] evidence before the board of inquiry revealed a process that relied on many vaguely-defined criteria, not all of which were consistently applied. While the board found no discrimination, the Chair commented that the process was "so seriously flawed in so many aspects that it is no wonder that a complaint of this nature has come forward."[60]

In *Underwood v. Board of Commissioners of Police (Smiths Falls)*[61] the hiring process revealed no fixed criteria for choice and no reference checks, as well as a lack of structure for soliciting the views of senior officers. There was circumstantial evidence that the complainant was not hired because of his age, and there was no evidence of any legitimate reason for his refusal. The board found for the complainant.

EMPLOYMENT AGENCIES: SECTION 23(4)

Section 23(4) reads:

(4) The right under section 4 to equal treatment with respect to employment is infringed where an employment agency discriminates against a person because of a prohibited ground of discrimination in receiving, classifying, disposing of or otherwise acting upon applications for its services or in referring an applicant or applicants to an employer or agent of an employer.

Section 23(4) is an almost verbatim repetition of a 1972 amendment of the previous *Code*.[62] There are no board decisions under the employment agencies clause in the previous *Code*. The most recent case on the subject was a 1968 decision of a board of inquiry under the 1966 *Age Discrimination Act*.[63] In *Britnell v. Brent Personnel Placement Services*,[64] the respondent had published a newspaper advertisement for a secretarial position. The advertisement listed a requirement for a "girl, age 25-35." The complainant, a qualified secretary, aged 46, applied for the position, but the agency refused to refer her to the employer because of her age. The board found for the complainant.

While no other employment agency cases have gone to boards in Ontario, it cannot be concluded that section 23(4) is unnecessary. An em-

---

59. *Ibid.*
60. *Ibid.*, at D/139.
61. (1986), 7 C.H.R.R. D/3176 (Ont. Bd. of Inquiry).
62. See the Ontario *Human Rights Code*, R.S.O. 1980, c. 340, s. 4(5).
63. See R.S.O. 1970, c. 7 [rep. S.O. 1972, c. 119, s. 15].
64. (1968), unreported (Ont. Bd. of Inquiry).

ployment agency, like any other business, must remain competitive; there is an obvious potential for conflict between the agency's duty under the *Code* and its desire to retain employers' business. On 28 October 1975, the Canadian Civil Liberties Association published in the *Globe and Mail* the results of a survey of fifteen employment agencies in Metro Toronto. This survey involved, in each case, a telephone call to the agency in which the caller posed as the representative of a company. Without placing an order, the telephone caller asked the agency whether it would agree to refer only white applicants for employment interviews. The report noted that two agencies refused outright to screen applicants, two expressed some disapproval, and eleven undertook to co-operate with the request.

Discouragingly, similar results resulted from a similar survey by the CCLA, conducted in 1990.

An obvious problem in the enforcement of section 23(4) is that often an applicant will not know how, or if, his or her application has been processed. Therefore, for the most part, it will be left to the employees of the agency itself to complain. The only method of effectively policing the agencies would seem to be by an amendment to the regulations under the *Employment Agencies Act* that would require agencies to keep records as to the sex, colour, race, etc. of their applicants[65] and to provide for the regular monitoring of such records by an outside agency such as the Ontario Human Rights Commission. However, such a provision would in itself be controversial, to say the least, in view of the fact that one of the reasons behind the Code's prohibition of certain questions on employment applications was that employers should not be provided in advance with information on which a discriminatory decision could be based. In the alternative it is possible that the Commission could effectively police the agencies by periodic random testing similar to that done by the Canadian Civil Liberties Association.

In regard to appropriate remedies where complaints against employment agencies are substantiated, it should be noted that the Commission could request that the board make a recommendation, to the supervisor of employment agencies, that the agency lost its licence. Section 6 of the *Employment Agencies Act*[66] indicates that such a recommendation may carry considerable weight.[67]

---

65. Agencies are presently required (by Ont. Reg. 280, s. 18) to keep certain records. However, in respect of the application, these records must contain only name, address and qualifications.

66. R.S.O. 1990, c. E.13.

67. S. 6 of the Act provides:
    "Subject to section 8, the supervisor may refuse to issue a licence to an applicant who otherwise has complied with the requirements of section 3 if in his opinion,
    (*a*) the past conduct of the applicant affords reasonable grounds for belief that he

HIRING AND BENEFIT PLANS: SECTION 25(1)

This section is mentioned here for completeness only, as it would appear to be relatively straightforward. Section 25(1) provides that the right under section 5 to equal treatment with respect to employment is infringed where a term or condition of employment requires enrolment in an employee benefit, pension or superannuation plan or fund or a contract of group insurance between an insurer and an employer, that makes a distinction, preference or exclusion on a prohibited ground of discrimination, and where employment is denied, or made conditional, because of that term or condition. In other words, the section appears to forbid denying employment because the applicant does not qualify for a discriminatory benefit plan, or making an employment offer conditional upon the applicant's qualifying for a discriminatory pension plan.

Discriminatory pension plans are discussed in Chapter 6.

---

will not carry on the employment agency in accordance with law and with honesty and integrity; or

(*b*) having regard to his financial position, the applicant cannot reasonably be expected to be financially responsible in the carrying on of the employment agency; or

(*c*) where the applicant is a corporation,

    (i)   the past conduct of its officers or directors affords reasonable grounds for belief that the employment agency will not be carried on by it in accordance with law or with honesty and integrity, or

    (ii) having regard to its financial position, it cannot reasonably be expected to be financially responsible in the carrying on of the employment agency."

6

EXCEPTIONS TO THE RIGHTS DECLARED IN PART I OF THE CODE

INTERPRETATION OF EXCEPTIONS

Section 10 of the *Interpretation Act*[1] provides:

> Every Act shall be deemed to be remedial, whether its immediate purport is to direct the doing of any thing that the Legislature deems to be for the public good or to prevent or punish the doing of any thing that it deems to be contrary to the public good, and shall accordingly receive such fair, large and liberal construction and interpretation as will best ensure the attainment of the object of the Act according to its true intent, meaning and spirit.

The rule of fair, large and liberal interpretation has often been cited by human rights boards of inquiry, and is fundamental to the protection of basic rights.

A corollary to this rule is that those exceptions to remedial legislation that restrict declared rights are to be construed narrowly. This principle has been discussed and applied in numerous boards of inquiry[2] and has received support from recent pronouncements of the Supreme Court of Canada. In *Ontario (Human Rights Commission) v. Etobicoke (Borough)*,[3] McIntyre J. suggested that "It will be seen at once that under the *Code* non-discrimination is the rule of general application, and discrimination, where permitted, is the exception."[4] Since *Etobicoke*, the Supreme Court of Canada has continued to interpret human rights legislation liberally, specifically rejecting

---

1. R.S.O. 1990, c. I.11.
2. See, for example, *Shack v. London Drive-Ur-Self* (1974), unreported (Ont. Bd. of Inquiry); *Hadley v. Mississauga* (1976), unreported (Ont. Bd. of Inquiry); *Adler v. Metro. Toronto Bd. of Commrs. of Police* (1979), unreported (Ont. Bd. of Inquiry); *Robertson v. Metro. Investigation Security Ltd.* (1979), unreported (Ont. Bd. of Inquiry); *Barnard v. Canadian Corps of Commissionaires (Toronto & Region)* (1985), 6 C.H.R.R. D/2659 (Ont. Bd. of Inquiry), affirmed (1986) 9 C.H.R.R. D/4829 (Ont. Div. Ct.).
3. (1982), 132 D.L.R. (3d) 14 (S.C.C.).
4. *Ibid.*, at 19.

attempts to use strict grammatical interpretation to limit rights conferred by the legislation.[5] Liberal construction appears likely to continue to prevail when minority rights are pitted against those of the majority, since protection of these rights is so clearly the purpose of the legislation.

A problem which has been addressed only in part by the Supreme Court (and has rarely been addressed by human rights tribunals) arises in those instances when the rights and interests of minority groups protected by the legislation conflict. Instances of such conflict are relatively rare compared to the bulk of human rights complaints; however they can arise, for example, when a "special program" designed to ameliorate disadvantage to a particular group excludes others who are just as (or more) disadvantaged.

In the Ontario *Code*, there are four exceptions which are clearly intended to promote the rights of groups protected by the *Code*. They deal with "special programs" [s. 14], the rights of separate schools [s. 19], and the rights of organizations "primarily engaged in serving the interests" of a group protected by the *Code* to restrict services [s. 18] or give preference in employment [s. 24(a)] to persons "similarly identified". Only the last-mentioned further qualifies the exception by stating that the qualification imposed must be "reasonable and *bona fide*".

The approach that is most clearly in line with the little available authority is probably to subject to rigorous scrutiny the claim of the respondent that the program, school or organization fits within the definition set out in the exception. However, once that hurdle is passed, it may be that balancing of interests is not required,[6] except in regard to subsection 24(a),

---

5. See, for example, the remarks of Mr. Justice Dickson for a unanimous Court in *Canadian National Railway Co. v. Canada (Canadian Human Rights Commission)* (1987), 8 C.H.R.R. D/4210 at D/4223, as well as other judgments cited in this chapter.

6. As yet, the Supreme Court of Canada has decided only one case that required the Court to rule upon the appropriate interpretative approach to competing interests protected by human rights legislation. In *Caldwell v. Stuart* (1984), 6 C.H.R.R. D/2643, the Court indicated (at D/2650) that a statutory provision similar to s. 22(a) was not to be construed "merely as a limiting section deserving of a narrow construction". However, in that case, there was no argument that the respondent separate school was not the type of organization contemplated by the provision.

 In *Brossard (Town) v. Quebec (Commission des droits de la personne)* (1989), 10 C.H.R.R. D/5515 at D/5545, Mr. Justice Beetz, construing another provision similar to s. 22(a), held that

> Rather than adopting a liberal or a restrictive interpretation . . . , I shall therefore endeavour to give the expressions "non-profit institution" and "political nature" their ordinary meaning, using the traditional rules of statutory interpretation.

 In that case, however, the Court adopted a purposive interpretation to conclude that the respondent city could not be defined as a "non-profit institution" of a "political nature" so as to fit within the exception provided by s. 20 of Quebec's *Charter of Rights and Freedoms*.

which carries the further requirement that the reason for preference be "reasonable and *bona fide*". The interpretation of exceptions under the *Code* in these situations will clearly be a major challenge, as boards attempt to do justice as between competing and legitimate interests, while promoting the purpose of the legislation.

"Affirmative Action" and other Special Programs: Section 14(1)

Section 14(1) exempts from the provisions of the *Code* any

> special program designed to relieve hardship or economic disadvantage or to assist disadvantaged persons or groups to achieve or attempt to achieve equal opportunity or that is likely to contribute to the elimination of the infringement of rights under Part I.

It is possible that, but for this type of provision, the implementation of a program designed to eliminate or reduce the disadvantages caused by discrimination would be forbidden by the *Code*,[7] except by order of a board of inquiry after a finding of discrimination.

Section 14 represents an expansion and elaboration of a provision of the predecessor *Code* which allowed the Commission to approve programs designed to increase employment among various classes of persons. Sections 14 and 26[8] represent a more positive legislative commitment to the active promotion of equality than had been seen in previous *Codes*. Thus, section 14, while technically an exception to the *Code*, is in fact clearly in-

---

7. The issue is in some doubt because of two cases on this point that have been heard under the Alberta *Individual's Rights Protection Act*, R.S.A. 1980, c. I-2. In the first, *Bloedel v. University of Calgary* (1980), 1 C.H.R.R. D/25, an Alberta board of inquiry considered whether a special program which facilitated the admission of native students to university studies offended the Act. A majority of the three-person board concluded that it did. However, in a second case, the Supreme Court of Canada made comments that suggest a different interpretation. In *Athabasca Tribal Council v. Alsands* (1979), unreported (Alta. Energy Resources Conservation Bd.), a decision under the *Individual's Rights Protection Act*, S.A. 1972, c. 2 [now R.S.A. 1980, c. I-2], involved an "affirmative action" program proposed by Alberta Energy Resources Conservation Board. The board had intended to prescribe as a condition of project approval that special measures be taken to employ native people. The proposal was appealed to the Alberta Court of Appeal where it was dismissed: *Athabasca Tribal Council v. Amoco Can. Petroleum Co.* (1980), 1 C.H.R.R. D/174. A major issue in the appeal was the E.R.C.B.'s jurisdiction to impose such a program. The majority of the court held that it had no such authority. The majority also ruled that the proposed program offended the *Individual's Rights Protection Act*.

    Athabasca was appealed to the Supreme Court of Canada, [1981] 6 W.W.R. 342. The court unanimously concluded that the proposed action by the E.C.R.B. was *ultra vires* the board's power. Four members of the court concluded that this decision made it unnecessary to consider whether the program could have conflicted with the *Individual's Rights Protection Act*. However, Laskin C.J.C. and Ritchie, Dickson and McIntyre JJ. ruled that there was no conflict between the Act and the proposed program (see discussion below).

8. S. 26 is the "contract compliance" section discussed in Chapter 2.

tended to allow enhancement of the rights of the groups protected by the legislation.

The definition of a special program may not be wide enough to encompass such long-established government programs as Family Benefits, which differentiates among its recipients on the grounds of sex and marital status.[9] However, section 14 is clearly directed at "affirmative action" programs that are aimed at redressing imbalances caused by past and present discrimination. Since the private sector, as well as the government, is likely to be subject to strong public pressure to initiate affirmative action, and since boards may be asked to make orders that programs be initiated,[10] it is appropriate to consider the effect of section 14 on such programs.

Although section 14 applies to programs affecting any area, affirmative action is most commonly directed at access to education and employment opportunities. The rationale of affirmative action is probably, at this date, too obvious to require explanation. Shelagh Day, in an article on the subject,[11] summarized the important issues:[12]

> Canadian human rights legislation has not had a significant impact on the patterns of disadvantage experienced by native people, women, the disabled, and other groups in terms of their access to education and work opportunities.
>
> Until recently, human rights legislation has dealt only with individual complaints, and interpreters of the legislation have defined discrimination as those overt acts which are motivated by bigotry and prejudice. This statutory structure and this interpretation have failed to touch the most pervasive forms of discrimination which are embedded in the normal functionings of our employment and education systems. . . .
>
> For . . . disadvantaged groups there are two problems. The first is for those who meet the realistic requirements for better and different opportunities but who are often barred from them by systemic practices which, while they may look neutral, have discriminatory effects. . . .
>
> The second problem for disadvantaged groups is that, because of the effects of historical patterns of discrimination and disadvantage, some members of these groups have not had the opportunity to qualify for better and different opportunities. Even if systemic barriers are removed, this group will remain significantly behind the other groups in the population unless special assistance is provided to them.

Action directed at these problems is being proposed and undertaken in most Canadian jurisdictions, including the federal sphere.[13]

---

9. Welfare and family benefits programs have been held not to be protected by section 15(2) of the *Canadian Charter of Rights and Freedoms* (see *Reference re Family Benefits Act (N.S.), Section 5* (1986), 75 N.S.R. (2d) 338, 26 C.R.R. 336 (C.A.)).
10. See Chapter 9 re "special program" orders.
11. "Affirmation Action: The Distribution of Well-Being" (1980), 1 C.H.R.R. C/13.
12. *Ibid.*, at C/13-14.
13. Planning and Research Executive Council of Saskatchewan, "Data Sheet on Saskatchewan Natives" (1976) at 11-12; Employment and Immigration Canada, *The Development of an Employment Policy for Indian, Inuit and Metis People* (1978); Joan Brown, *A Hit and Miss Affair: Policies for Disabled People*, Canadian Council on Social Development (1977), pp. 195-290; Coalition of Provincial Organizations for the

The methods of affirmative action vary with the circumstances and the goals sought to be achieved. A good general definition was included in an unpublished paper prepared by Employment and Immigration Canada for a 1980 conference of federal and provincial ministers responsible for human rights:

> Affirmative Action includes changing systems to ensure equality of opportunity, but it means considerably more. It means implementing a comprehensive plan to achieve definite, measurable results according to goals and timetables established and reviewed in the same manner as any other business objective. The major aim of Affirmative Action is to change the existing distribution of employment. Changes can be tracked statistically, in the same way the original work force was analyzed. Goals and timetables are developed in short, intermediate and long term focus. Actual results are compared with the stated goals at appropriate times and, if necessary, adjustments to the plan are made to improve "production."

Affirmative action programs aimed at increasing the representation of a target group in a particular sector of the economy generally involve the implementation of one or more of the following strategies:

1. Criteria for the position are reviewed and, where the maintenance of relatively unimportant criterion would bar most members of a specific group, that criterion is dropped or relaxed.

2. The employer or institution actively recruits within the minority group population through advertisements in ethnic newspapers, appropriately worded general advertisements, etc.

3. The employer or institution initiates or supports special training programs designed to "upgrade" the qualifications of a specified group.

4. "Goals and timetables" are imposed so that, through the use of the above four or other strategies, the employer or institution, by a specific date, might achieve the employment or enrolment of a number of minority group people equal to their representation in the population.

The mention of goals and time tables is guaranteed to give rise to negative reaction among employers and educators. However, it should be noted that

---

Handicapped, *Follow-up Report to the National Conference on Employment* (June, 1978); Economic Council of Canada, "A Time for Reason" (1978), 15 Annual Review at 92-3. Also see Policy Statements of the Canadian Human Rights Commission; e.g.: "Aboriginal Employment Preferences," and the 1984 *Report of the Royal Commission on Equality in Employment*.

The Canadian *Charter of Rights and Freedoms*, s. 15(2), specifically allows for ameliorative laws and programs. Corresponding legislative provisions to accommodate "special programs" are in force in the federal *Human Rights Act* and in human rights legislation in all the provinces except Alberta and British Columbia, the Northwest Territories and the Yukon. In 1986, the federal *Employment Equity Act* (S.C. 1984-85-86, c. 31) was proclaimed. The Act requires the provision of data that will show employment practices relating to women, aboriginal peoples, members of visible minorities and disabled people in Crown and federally-regulated places of employment.

nowhere in the literature of affirmative action has there ever been a serious recommendation that opportunities for employment or higher education be extended to unqualified persons, nor has there ever been an affirmative action program ordered by a court[14] that suggested that unqualified persons be hired.

Challenges to Affirmative Action Programs

A type of quota system was the subject of a lawsuit in *Regents of the University of California v. Bakke.*[15] The case concerned a special admissions program directed at "or educationally disadvantaged" candidates for a medical school. Bakke challenged the program as contrary to both the Constitution of California and the federal *Civil Rights Act.*

The split decision of the United States Supreme Court in *Bakke* is thoroughly analyzed by Professor Tarnopolsky in *Discrimination and The Law.*[16] Briefly, four of the nine justices who decided *Bakke* based their decision that the program was invalid solely on a section of the *Civil Rights Act* that forbids exclusion because of race from any program receiving federal financial assistance. Five justices based their decisions on the equal protection clause of the California Constitution. Of these, only one found the admissions program to violate the clause. Five justices held that the adoption of racial classifications in admissions decisions was not discriminatory when used to redress the effects of past discrimination, to increase the number of minority professionals, to obtain a "diverse" student body or to remedy discrimination practised in the past by the particular institution.[17]

A year later, the same court decided *United Steelworkers of America v. Weber.*[18] *Weber* was a challenge, under the *Civil Rights Act*, to the legality of a collectively-bargained affirmative action plan that reserved fifty percent of the openings in a craft training program for black applicants "until the percentage of black craft workers in the plant is commensurate with the percentage of blacks in the local labour force."[19] For the majority, Justice Brennan held that race-conscious affirmative action was not discriminatory, in that the purpose of the plan was to forward the policy of the *Civil Rights Act*, the plan was temporary, and it did not require the discharge of white workers, nor absolutely bar their advancement.

---

14. The courts referred to here are in the United States, where such orders are not uncommon. To date, the major no court-affirmed "special program" is described in *Action Travail des Femmes v. C.N. Railway* (1984), 5 C.H.R.R. D/2327, reversed in part (1985), 6 C.H.R.R. D/2908 (Fed. C.A.), reversed (1987), 8 C.H.R.R. D/4210. The case is further discussed in Chapter 9.
15. 98 S. Ct. 2733 (1978).
16. (1982), pp. 127-43; revision, Pentney (1985) at p 4-56 to 4-80.
17. *Ante*, note 15, at 2785-94. The last condition was assumed not to apply in *Bakke*.
18. 99 S. Ct. 2721 (1979).
19. *Ibid.*, at 2724.

It should be noted that the *Bakke* and *Weber* decisions are very much a product of the American legislation considered in each case. Of the two, however, the statutory provisions considered in *Weber* are more similar to the Ontario *Code*.[20]

Since *Bakke* and *Weber*, the U.S. Supreme Court has continued to consider the appropriate boundaries for affirmative action programs. To date, U.S. Supreme Court decisions have affirmed that:

- affirmative action programs are an acceptable remedy for discrimination as long as they are justified by a "compelling state interest" and are narrowly tailored to meet their goals;[21]

- there is no requirement that a court or other body make a finding of discrimination for such a program to be valid; however, the entity to seeking to implement the plan must have a firm basis for believing that remedial action is required;[22]

- plans agreed to by parties (e.g., in a collective agreement) may go beyond legislative requirements for such plans;[23] and

- a court may impose goals and timetables for improved employment practices on employers guilty of discrimination in the past, even though the actual victims of the discrimination are not benefited thereby.[24]

There have been fewer challenges to affirmative action programs in Canada to date.

In *Athabasca Tribal Council v. Amoco Canada Petroleum Company*,[25] the Supreme Court of Canada considered two issues. The first was whether Alberta's Energy Resources Conservation Board had jurisdiction to prescribe, as a condition of granting approval on a proposed bitumen-recovery project, an affirmative action program giving preference in employment and business opportunities to native people in the area. The second issue was whether an affirmative action program based on race would infringe Alberta's *Individual's Rights Protection Act*.

The Supreme Court of Canada found that the Energy Resources Conservation Board did not have the jurisdiction to impose the program as a condition of approval. However, in regard to the question of whether a

---

20. For a detailed discussion of the effect of these decisions in the Canadian context see Tarnopolsky, *Discrimination and The Law* (1982), pp. 143-54.

21. *Wygant v. Jackson Board of Education* (1986), May, U.S.S.C.

22. *Ibid.*

23. *Local 93, International Assoc. of Firefighters, AFL-CIO, CLC v. City of Cleveland* (1986), July U.S.S.C.

24. *Local 28, Sheetmetal Workers' Ind. Assoc. Local 28 Joint Apprenticeship Committee v. E.E.O.C.* (1986), July U.S.S.C.

25. [1981] 6 W.W.R. 342 (S.C.C.).

special training program for native people breached Alberta's *Individual's Rights Protection Act*, Ritchie J., speaking for Laskin C.J. and Dickson and McIntyre JJ., stated:[26]

> I can see no reason why the measures proposed by the "affirmative action" programs . . . should be construed as "discriminating against" other inhabitants. The purpose of the plan, as I understand it, is not to displace non-Indians from their employment, but rather to advance the lot of the Indians so that they may be in a competitive position to obtain employment.

In light of the fact that the *Individual's Rights Protection Act* had, at the time, no clause similar to section 14 of the Ontario *Code*, this statement augered well for the reception of any *bona fide* affirmative action program under section 14. Further, its applicability to the Ontario legislation is enhanced by the fact that it focuses, as does section 14, on the purpose of the program.

There has been one Canadian case in which an affirmative action program has been ruled discriminatory. In *Bloedel v. University of Calgary*[27] the issue was "Special Support Services" offered by the respondent to native students only. It should be noted, however, that *Bloedel* is distinguishable from cases under section 14, since the Alberta Act, under which *Bloedel* was decided, had no provision similar to section 14. Moreover, *Bloedel* preceded *Athabasca* and can probably be said to have been overruled by it.

There has been one case in which the Supreme Court of Canada has considered an order imposing an affirmative action program (including goals and timetables) in the light of a legislative provision similar to section 13 of the Ontario *Code*. In *Action Travail des Femmes v. Canadian National Railway Co.*,[28] considering subsection 14(2)(*a*) of the Canadian *Human Rights Act*, the Court rejected an argument to the effect that a statutory provision for special programs "to prevent (discriminatory practices) occurring in the future" could not be used to rectify past wrongs. The Court's broad, purposive analysis confirms the validity of affirmative action programs as remedies in cases of systemic discrimination, and allow for the full scope of such programs.[29]

Chief Justice Dickson in *Action Travail* set out three reasons for affirmative action, described in that case as employment equity:

> An employment equity program thus is designed to work in three ways. First, by countering the cumulative effects of systemic discrimination, such a programme renders further discrimination pointless. To the extent that some intentional discrimination may

---

26. At 352.
27. (1980), 1 C.H.R.R. D/25 (Alta. Bd. of Inquiry).
28. (1987), 8 C.H.R.R. D/4210 (S.C.C.).
29. See further discussion of *Action Travail* in Chapter 9.

be present, for example in the case of a foreman who controls hiring and who simply does not want women in the unit, a mandatory employment equity scheme places women in the unit despite the discriminatory intent of the foreman. His battle is lost.

Secondly, by placing members of the group that had previously been excluded into the heart of the work place and by allowing them to prove ability on the job, the employment equity scheme addresses the attitudinal problem of stereotyping. For example, if women are seen to be doing the job of "brakeman" or heavy cleaner or signaller at Canadian National, it is no longer possible to see women as capable of fulfilling only certain traditional occupational roles. It will become more and more difficult to ascribe characteristics to an individual by reference to the stereotypical characteristics ascribed to all women.

Thirdly, an employment equity program helps to create what has been termed a "critical mass" of the previously excluded group in the work place. This "critical mass" has important effects. The presence of a significant number of individuals from the targeted group eliminates the problems of "tokenism"; it is no longer the case that one or two women, for example, will be seen to "represent" all women. See Carol Agocs, "Affirmative Action, Canadian Style" (1986), 12 *Can. Pub. Policy* 148 at p. 149. Moreover, women will not be so easily placed on the periphery of management concern. The "critical mass" also effectively remedies systemic inequities in the process of hiring:

> There is evidence that when sufficient minorities/women are employed in a given establishment, the informal processes of economic life, for example, the tendency to refer friend and relatives for employment, will help to produce a significant minority [or female] applicant flow.
>
> (A. Blumrosen, "Quotas, Common Sense and Law in Labour Relations: Three Dimensions of Equal Opportunity" in W. S. Tarnopolsky, ed. *Some Civil Liberties Issues of the Seventies* (1975), Toronto: Osgoode Hall Law School/York University, 5, at p. 15).

If increasing numbers of women apply for non-traditional jobs, the desire to work in blue collar occupations will be less stigmatized. Personnel offices will be forced to treat women's applications for non-traditional jobs more seriously. In other words, once a "critical mass" of the previously excluded group has been created in the work force, there is a significant chance for the continuing self-correction of the system.[30]

Use of Section 14 as a Defence:

Two Ontario boards of inquiry have discussed the former section 13 [now s. 14] as a defence to otherwise discriminatory activity. In *Blainey v. Ontario Hockey Association*,[31] the board considered a hockey program, administered by the Ontario Women's Hockey Association, available only to female players. The board found on the evidence that female hockey players operated at a disadvantage relative to male players, and ruled that the program qualified for section 13 protection. However, the board rejected an argument that would extend section 13 protection to hockey programs restricted to male players, since male players did not suffer from similar disadvantages.

---

30. *Ante*, note 26 at D/4230-4231.
31. (1987), 9 C.H.R.R. D/4549 (Ont. Bd. of Inquiry).

In *Roberts v. Ontario (Ministry of Health)*[32] the complainant, who had severe visual impairment, applied to the Assistant Devices Program of the respondent for funding for the purchase of a visual aid. He was informed that funding was restricted to persons 22 years old and younger, and he complained of discrimination in respect of handicap and age.

While conceding that *prima facie* the program did discriminate because of age, the board went on to find that the differentiation was justified under section 13.

The *Roberts* case is illustrative of a major source of concern in the interpretation of section 14. On one hand, a person who was in need of the assistance the program could provide was refused because of a restriction otherwise prohibited under the *Code*. On the other, the provider of the program could point to legitimate concerns about allocation of often scarce resources. In the light of this, it is worthwhile reviewing *Roberts* in some detail.

The board first reviewed the four-part disjunctive standard for special programs:

1. designed to relieve hardship

2. designed to relieve economic hardship.

3. designed to assist economic disadvantaged persons or groups to achieve or attempt to achieve equal opportunity.

4. likely to contribute to the elimination of the infringement of rights under Part I of the *Code*.

In reviewing the respondent's counsel's arguments for the inclusion of the program under the first three points noted above. the board rejected the idea that it was part of the board of inquiry's function to evaluate the efficacy of affirmative action measures. The board interpreted the use of the term "designed to" relieve or assist as importing a subjective test, such that, while respondents seeking the protection of section 14 must establish that they had a *bona fide* belief that the program was intended to relieve disadvantage, "the goals may indeed exceed the reach of the program."[33] The board specifically rejected an interpretation that section 14 requires "that the program be reasonably likely to achieve its objectives."[34]

The board in *Roberts* clearly contemplated only two grounds for challenge of a section 14 program; an argument that the beneficiaries of the program are not disadvantaged, and an argument as to the *bona fides* of the respondent in establishing the program. Equally explicitly, the decision states that a section 14 program need not benefit all disadvantaged groups equally.

---

32. (1989), 10 C.H.R.R. D/6353 (Ont. Bd. of Inquiry).

33. *Ibid,* at D/6374.

34. (1989), 10 C.H.R.R. D/6353 at D/6373-75.

The decision by the board in *Roberts* to refrain from any examination of the efficacy of a program, or the relationship of an exclusionary measure to the ostensible aims of a program, seems unfortunate. It would appear that a major reason for the board's position was its view that section 14 should be interpreted broadly, as befits a position which creates or promotes rights, rather than narrowly, as befits an exception to such provisions. As section 14 can be said to be both, it would appear at least within the realm of possibility to take a situation-specific approach to its construction.

The decision of the board in *Roberts* was appealed to Divisional Court. In view of the complexity of the issues, the Court's confirmation of the board's decision is disappointingly brief:

> This appeal must be dismissed. We agree with the Board of Inquiry that the age restriction built into the Assistive Devices Program which on its face appears to violate s. 1 of the *Code* is protected by s. 13(1) of the *Code*.
>
> Programs, such as that in issue in this case, will, by their very nature, create differences in treatment on many and varied grounds. The only issue in this case is whether or not the program is a "special program" designed to relieve hardship or economic disadvantage. It is agreed that this program was developed and implemented in order to assist its beneficiaries to achieve greater equality of opportunity. While the constitutionality of s. 13(1) was not challenged, the appellants submitted that the age criteria applied in the program removed the program from the protection of s. 13.
>
> In our view, the wording of s. 13(1) is plain, clear and can admit of no doubt. It is not possible to read into that section the qualificaiton suggested by the appellants when the legislature has not itself seen fit to impose such a limitation. Generally speaking, courts should not lightly second guess clear legislative judgments, particularly when dealing with programs designed to proceed to greater equality of opportunity for disadvantaged persons. In our view, the age limitation in the program is protected by s. 13 and the appeal must be dismissed.
>
> In the circumstances there will be no order as to costs.[35]

Leave to appeal has been granted by the Court of Appeal

The Commission's functions in regard to special programs are discussed in Chapter 8.

Preferential Treatment for Persons Aged Sixty-Five and Over: Section 15

Section 15 provides:

> A right under Part I to non-discrimination because of age is not infringed where an age of sixty-five or over is a requirement, qualification or consideration for preferential treatment.

The section is probably necessary to protect special benefits for those aged sixty-five and over. It might be argued that section 14 provides all the pro-

---

35. (1990), 14 C.H.R.R. D/1.

tection necessary for such programs as the Ontario Property Tax Rebate system and reduced senior rates for public transit. However, section 14 probably would not exempt a cinema offering cut-price senior citizen tickets, as such programs are frequently limited to hours when business is slack, and the primary motive behind them would seem to be the attraction of customers for those times. Be that as it may, section 15 is clear enough to resolve any doubts on the issue of true preferential treatment.

There have been no board decisions on this section.

Canadian Citizenship: Section 16

The question of giving preference to job applicants who are Canadian citizens has received some public attention during the 1980s, particularly in regard to teaching positions from high school to university level.

As noted above in Chapter 3, citizenship was not specified as a ground of discrimination under the previous *Code*, but differentiation based on citizenship had been held to constitute discrimination on the ground of nationality or national origin. In the light of past decisions, section 15 [now s. 16] of the 1981 *Code* can be seen as an unprecedentedly broad protection of "Canada-first" initiatives.[36]

Section 16(1) of the *Code* provides:

> A right under Part I to non-discrimination because of citizenship is not infringed where Canadian citizenship is a requirement, qualification or consideration imposed or authorized by law.

An obvious example of a situation contemplated by this section is the right of the Law Society of Upper Canada to restrict admission to "Canadian citizens or permanent residents of[37] Canada".

Regulations dealing with teacher qualifications were considered in *Snyker v. Fort Frances-Rainy River Board of Education*,[38] an Ontario board decision which, as noted in Chapter 2, held that "nationality" as a ground of discrimination was broad enough to include citizenship. In that case, a teacher who was not a Canadian citizen was dismissed pursuant to a school board policy on redundancy. The policy indicated that teachers who were not Canadian citizens were to be among the first declared redundant. The school board had argued that, since it was required to employ only persons qualified according to the regulations, it was required by law to discriminate on the basis of citizenship. The board of inquiry rejected this argument, holding that the school board's policy was not necessitated by the regulation and that, therefore, there was no conflict between the *Code* and

---

36. No Canadian human rights legislation contains any provision similar to scope and effect to s. 16.
37. The *Law Society Act*, R.S.O. 1990, c. L.8, s. 28(*c*).
38. (1979), unreported (Ont. Bd. of Inquiry).

the *Education Act* and its regulations.

It is unlikely that *Snyker* would be decided differently today, since the school board was not acting in obedience to the Act or its regulations. However, where a permanent teaching certificate is denied by the Deputy Minister of Education on the basis of citizenship, section 16(1) would appear to exempt denial from the provisions of the *Code*.

Section 16(2) is an extraordinarily broadly worded section which provides that Canadian citizenship or lawful admission to Canada for permanent residence" may be "a requirement, qualification or consideration" in, it would seem, any decision, as long as the requirement, qualification or consideration is

> adopted for the purpose of fostering and developing participation in cultural, educational, trade union or athletic activities by Canadian citizens or persons lawfully admitted to Canada for permanent residence.

The political genesis of section 16(2) is obvious: from the activities of the "Committee for An Independent Canada" to the question of Canadian content in Ontario universities,[39] the issue has been well publicized. Two Ontario cases dealing with the sort of issues raised by the section are *Bone v. Hamilton Tiger Cats Football Club*,[40] and *Rajput v. Algoma University*.[41]

The *Bone* decision illustrates that the predecessor *Code* provided ample protection against discrimination suffered because of Canadian citizenship. The complainant, a Canadian citizen, alleged that he had been denied a chance to try out for a quarterback position on the respondent football team because of the existence of a "Designated Import Rule." The complainant argued that the rule, while actually limiting the number of non-Canadian players one team, in fact encouraged the team to appoint American quarterbacks. Board Chairman McCamus did not find that the rule itself offered a rational basis for preferring American "import" players for the quarterback position. However, he concluded that the respondent had indirectly discriminated against Canadians by using the term "imports" in an attempt to avoid the impact of human rights legislation. In addition, the board found that the head coach had made full use of this rule because of the general belief that American football players were better than Canadian ones.

If *Bone* demonstrated that Canadians were to be protected from discrimination, *Rajput* made it clear that a "Canadianization" effect could not

---

39. On which issue, see I.A. Hunter, "The Development of the Ontario Human Rights Code: A Decade in Retrospect" (1972), 22 U.T.L.J. 237 at 241-3, and, by the same author, "Human Rights Legislation in Canada: Its Origin, Development and Interpretation" (1976), 15 U. of W. Ont. L. Rev. 21.

40. (1979), unreported (Ont. Bd. of Inquiry).

41. (1976), unreported (Ont. Bd. of Inquiry).

be allowed, under the former *Code*, to result in discrimination against persons of non-Canadian origin. In *Rajput*, the complainant was an applicant who was denied a lecturer's position at the respondent college. One of the concerns of the person in charge of appointments was evidently the "Canadianization" of the department; specifically, his decision was influenced by the number of persons of other than Canadian origin already holding teaching positions. In finding for the complainant, board Chairman Tarnopolsky noted that:

> A great deal of time, both in evidence, and in argument, was spent discussing the matter of "Canadianization" of universities in Ontario. In another capacity, I could express my views as to the desirability of such a policy. Clearly, the C.A.U.T., the A.U.C.C., and the Report of the Special Commission appointed by the A.U.C.C. to study the problem, suggest that there is a problem here to be considered. It seems to me that all academic bodies agree, that if the problem exists, it is probably most acute in the various Departments of Sociology. However, as a Chairman of a Board of Inquiry under the Ontario Human Rights Code, it is not my prerogative to express here my views regarding the desirability or otherwise of a certain policy. My duty is to construe and apply the legislation as it exists.[42]

The Ontario Legislature has obviously decided that the protection afforded by the previous *Code*, as demonstrated in *Bone*, is not sufficient and that active promotion of "Canadianization" is necessary. Obviously, special funding or grant programs in the arts or athletics can apparently be limited to Canadian citizens and permanent residents without offending the *Code*. If "participation . . . in . . . educational . . . activities" is to be construed as including teaching, the "Canadianization" of universities may proceed without being impeded by the operation of the *Code*. The exemption may also facilitate the development of Canadian-controlled trade unions.

Notable by its absence is any requisite that the requirement, qualification or consideration be reasonable or *bona fide*. The respondent must prove only that the requirement, etc., was adopted for the allowed purpose. The Commission, in deciding whether to request a board of inquiry, will confine itself to considering only the organization's stated purpose in applying the requirement, or its application, will be assessed in the light of its stated purpose, at least to the extent necessary to establish that "fostering and developing" Canadian "participation" is in fact its *raison d'être*. It is obvious that a complaint might go to a board where, for example, the requirement, etc., is not applied consistently, thus raising an inference as to the *bona fides* of the requirement.

Section 16(3) provides:

> A right under Part I to non-discrimination because of citizenship is not infringed where Canadian citizenship or domicile in Canada with the intention to obtain Canadian

---

42. *Ibid.*, p. 21 (transcript).

citizenship is a requirement, qualification or consideration adopted by an organization or enterprise for the holder of chief or senior executive positions.

This subsection evidently springs from the same political considerations as the rest of section 16, and would appear to be self-explanatory.

There have been no board decisions in respect of section 16.

The Major Exception in Respect of Handicap: Section 17

The 1981 Code's prohibition on discrimination because of handicap was subject to an exception provision specifically related to handicap. Section 16 of the *Code* provided that:

(1) A right of a person under this Act is not infringed for the reason only,

(*a*) that the person does not have access to premises, services, goods, facilities or accommodation because of handicap, or that the premises, services, goods, facilities or accommodation lack the amenities that are appropriate for the person because of handicap; or

(*b*) that the person is incapable of performing or fulfilling the essential duties or requirements attending the exercise of the right because of handicap.

The limitation of the rights of handicapped persons imposed by subsection 16(1)(*a*) was a significant one, the more so because of rapid advances in the availability of technology directed to ameliorating handicap. Ontario's *Equality Rights Statute Law Amendment Act*,[43] which received Royal Assent on December 18, 1986, and was proclaimed on April 18, 1988, repealed the previous section 16 and substituted the following [now 1990, s. 17]:

17.-(1) A right of a person under this Act is not infringed for the reason only that the person is incapable of performing or fulfilling the essential duties or requirements attending the exercise of the right because of handicap.

(2) The Commission, a board of inquiry or a court shall not find a person incapable unless it is satisfied that the needs of the person cannot be accommodated without undue hardship on the person responsible for accommodating those needs, considering the cost, outside sources of funding, if any, and health and safety requirements, if any.

(3) The Commission, a board of inquiry or a court shall consider any standards prescribed by the regulations for assessing what is undue hardship.

The removal of the exception concerning access and amenities brings rights for handicapped persons in line with those accorded after groups protected by the *Code*.

The exception contained in section 16 is the major exception to the general prohibition against handicap discrimination in the *Code*.[44]

A number of issues arise from the wording of the new section 17(1).

---

43. S.O. 1986, c. 64.

44. The other sections containing such restrictions are ss. 22 and 25(3), discussed below.

There have been no cases decided under the new provision; however, some of the authority based on similar provisions may be helpful.

"Incapable of Performing or Fulfilling"

The onus of proof of incapacity clearly lies on the respondent.[45] A major issue is how the respondent comes to the opinion that the complainant is incapable. *Cameron v. Nel-gor Nursing Home*[46] illustrates a common approach. In *Cameron*, a young woman applied for employment as a nurse's aide. The respondent refused the position, assuming that, due to the fact that three fingers of Cameron's hand were shorter than normal, she would be unable to do the lifting required by the job. At the board of inquiry, evidence was brought to establish that Cameron could in fact perform the tasks that the respondent had assumed, without inquiring or testing, were beyond her competence.

After establishing that the complainant had been refused a job due to her handicap, the board considered the respondent's reliance on subsection 16(1)(*b*) of the 1981 *Code* which, as set out above, is worded almost identically to the present section 17. The board noted that the individual respondent was an experienced nurse who had made a good-faith assumption as to incapacity, based on her experience and judgment. The board also took into account that the safety of the patients might be affected by a nurse's aide who was unable to lift them effectively. However, in the circumstances, the board found that, in order to rely on the exception provided by the *Code*, the respondent should have tested the complainant's lifting abilities.

In a more recent case, *Chamberlin v. Stirling Honda*,[47] a board found the respondent to have discriminated on the ground of handicap, despite the fact that the board found it unlikely that the complainant could have performed the job, because the employer failed to assess the complainant's ability:

> In the *Beliveau* case it was held that the employer was required to objectively assess whether an individual with an injured shoulder was capable of returning to work and performing the essential functions of the job before it reached the conclusion that he could not do so. I adopt that reasoning with respect to the instant case. Given the structure and purpose of the *Code*, I find that in order to rely on the provisions of Section 16(1)(*b*) Stirling Honda was required to fairly and accurately assess Mr. Chamberlin's ability to perform the business manager position at the time he returned to work on June 17, 1985. In order to enable the dealership to properly do so, it would have been open for the respondents to require that Mr. Chamberlin provide a medical certificate indicat-

---

45. See *Cameron v. Nel-gor Nursing Home* (1984), 5 C.H.R.R. D/2170 (Ont. Bd. of Inquiry); *Belliveau v. Steel Co. of Canada* (1988), 9 C.H.R.R. D/5250 (Ont. Bd. of Inquiry); *Morgoch v. Ottawa (City)* (1989), 11 C.H.R.R. D/80 (Ont. Bd. of Inquiry).
46. *Ante*, note 45.
47. (1989), unreported (Ont. Bd. of Inquiry).

ing that he was capable of returning to work in his former position. If the respondents had reasonable grounds to doubt the correctness of such a certificate, or the adequacy of the information provided by Mr. Chamberlin to the doctor who prepared the certificate, they could have required that Mr. Chamberlin secure additional medical certification or, in the circumstances, even require that he undergo a medical examination by a specialist in mental disorders.[48]

Clearly, it is a rare situation in which it can be said that the bare fact that a person suffers from a particular handicap guarantees that he or she cannot perform a particular function. This is true both because of the variable nature of any handicap and its effect on the particular individual, and because of the growing technology in ameliorative devices, which clearly must be taken into account under subsection 17(1) and (2). Thus the best course of action on the part of the potential respondent to a complaint is to test the individual about whose capacity there is some doubt, or to allow that individual an opportunity to try.

In handicap cases decided under the federal *Human Rights Act*, the individual test has been found to be a requirement.[49] In other cases, an absence of individual assessment has clearly been the basis for a board's finding that discrimination had occurred.[50] In *Belliveau v. Steel Co. of Canada*, the board stated:

> A respondent cannot rely upon mere impressionistic evidence that a person cannot perform the essential functions of a job. In some situations, it will be very obvious that a person is not able to perform the essential requirements. However, where the handicap does not, in itself, suggest that there is a reasonable certainty of his being unable to do the task, the logical route for the employer is to put the person to either the test of the job itself, or to the test of a simulated equivalent.[51]

The view was reiterated in *Morgoch v. City of Ottawa*,[52] a case in which the complainant was refused an opportunity to be hired as a firefighter because of allergies. The board held that the city had a duty to assess the complainant himself in light of the the actual requirements of the job.

It is not yet clear whether the best available evidence of capability, the individual test, will be required in all cases. Exceptions may be made where an actual trial of an activity could potentially endanger others and where

---

48. *Ibid*, at 27.

49. *Villeneuve v. Bell Canada* (1985), 6 C.H.R.R. D/2988, reversed for other reasons (1986), 7 C.H.R.R. D/3519.

50. See *Lindahl v. Auld-Phillips Ltd.* (1986), 7 C.H.R.R. D/3396 (B.C. Human Rights Council); *Kellerman v. Al's Restaurant and Tavern Ltd.* (1986), 8 C.H.R.R. D/3924 (Ont. Bd. of Inquiry); *Ward v. Canadian National Express* (1982), 3 C.H.R.R. D/689 (Cdn. Human Rights Trib.).

51. *Ante*, note 45 at D/5252.

52. *Ante*, note 45.

there is no satisfactory surrogate of an actual trial.[53]

If boards, in construing the new provisions, follow the view of past tribunals dealing with "reasonable and *bona fide*" defence and allow for the maintenance of a group exclusion in circumstances in which safety is at issue and individual assessment not practical, there will be an issue as to what kind of evidence will be needed to support a group assessment. Cases from other jurisdictions in which exclusion on the ground of handicap was justified as "reasonable and *bona fide*" give some guidance as to dealing with medical evidence and other expert evidence, but they conflict on some important points. For example, some boards of inquiry have indicated that the respondent is entitled to rely on his or her own medical advisor, especially where medical opinion is not settled.[54] Others have disagreed with this opinion.[55]

As noted above, cases based on the previous wording of the *Code* and cases from other jurisdictions must be regarded with caution since they are based on the "reasonable and *bona fide*" standard, which arguably encompasses more considerations than the test now used in section 17. Even with the wider test of "reasonable and *bona fide*," boards have found the following actions unjustified:

- refusal to allow a stable diabetic a job as a "trackman."[56]

---

53. See cases discussed in regard to s. 24(*b*), later in this chapter.

54. The Supreme Court of Canada in *Ontario (Human Rights Commission) v. Etobicoke (Borough)*, [1982] 1 S.C.R. 202, did not touch on this specific question. The court stated generally that it would be unwise to create fixed rules as to the nature and sufficiency of evidence relating to capability in the context of mandatory retirement decisions. However, the court held that

> it would seem to be essential that the evidence should cover the detailed nature of the duties to be performed, the conditions existing in the work place, and the effect of such conditions upon employees, particularly upon those at or near the retirement age sought to be supported. . . . Where a limitation upon continued employment must depend for its validity on proof of a danger to public safety by the continuation in employment of people over a certain age, it would appear to be necessary in order to discharge the burden of proof resting upon the employer to adduce evidence upon this subject . . . in cases such as this, statistical and medical evidence based upon observation and research on the question of aging, if not in all cases absolutely necessary, will certainly be more persuasive than the testimony of persons, albeit with great experience in firefighting, to the effect that firefighting is "a young man's game." (at 212)

55. See *Andruchiw v. Burnaby* (1981), 3 C.H.R.R. D/663 (B.C. Bd. of Inquiry), affirmed (1982), 4 C.H.R.R. D/1182 (B.C. S.C.); *Vitcoe v. Dominion Life Insurance Co.* (1984), 5 C.H.R.R. D/2029 (B.C. Bd. of Inquiry); *Forseille v. United Grain Growers Ltd.* (1985), 6 C.H.R.R. D/3051 (Cdn. Human Rights Comm.). The board in *Morgoch* also apparently held the view that the employer was not entitled to rely on its own medical expert. A useful discussion of the advantages of reliance on medical evidence is set out in Vizkelety, *Proving Discrimination in Canada*, pp. 210-211.

56. *Mahon v. Canadian Pacific* (1986), 7 C.H.R.R. D/3278 (S.C.C.).

- disqualification of candidate pilots for malformation of the spine.[57]
- refusal of jobs as "warehousemen"[58] or nurses' aide[59] to candidates with less than the usual number of fingers.
- refusal of jobs as serving staff on trains because of lack of vision in one eye.[60]
- refusal of job at telephone answering service because of occasional epileptic seizures.[61]

Willingness by the complainant to take on more than he or she can reasonably do, or to undertake risk of injury, is unlikely to prevent a board from finding that he or she is "incapable." This was confirmed by the board in *Belliveau v. Stelco Steel Co. of Canada.*[62]

"The Essential Duties or Requirements"

In *Cameron*, the board addressed the meaning of the above-noted phrase, pointing out that not every component of a job can be considered an "essential duty or requirement."

> What do the words of paragraph 16(1)(*b*) mean? "Essential" means that which is "needed to make a thing what it is; very important; necessary" — The World Book Dictionary, Vol. 1, *supra*, p. 727. Synonyms are "indispensable, requisite, vital." Thus, peripheral or incidental, non-core or non-essential aspects of a job, are not pertinent to a determination under paragraph 16(1)(*b*). For example, if a handicapped person used a pencil to write with in her work as a nurse's aide, and had no difficulties with any aspect of her work, but could not sharpen pencils by herself because of her handicap, the employer could not bring herself within the exception of paragraph 16(1)(*B*) as pencil-sharpening would simply be an incidental, non-essential, aspect of the job (which could easily be done by someone else, without any real inconvenience for the employer). Therefore, paragraph 16(1)(*b*) builds in an aspect of reasonable accommodation being required of an employer.
>
> "Duty" is defined in the *World Book Dictionary*, Vol. I, *supra*, at p. 655, as meaning:
>
>> "1. a thing that is right to do; what a person ought to do; obligation – 2. the thing that a person has to do in doing his work; function; business; office (with a suggested synonym being "responsibility."

57. *Labelle v. Air Canada* (1983), 4 C.H.R.R. D/311 (Cdn. Human Rights Trib.).
58. *Ward v. Canadian National Express* (1982), 3 C.H.R.R. D/689 (Cdn. Human Rights Trib.).
59. *Cameron v. Nel-gor Nursing Home* (1984), 5 C.H.R.R. D/2170 (Ont. Bd. of Inquiry).
60. *Foreman v. Via Rail Canada Inc.* (1980), 1 C.H.R.R. D/233 (Cdn. Transport Comm.).
61. *Sandiford v. Base Communications Ltd.* (1984), 5 C.H.R.R. D/2237 (Sask. Bd. of Inquiry).
62. (1988), 9 C.H.R.R. D/5250 (Ont. Bd. of Inquiry); see also *Loveday v. Baker Manufacturing Ltd.* (1984), 7 C.H.R.R. D/3145 (Man. Q.B.); and *Chamberlin*, op. cit. note 47.

"Duty" is discussed in *Black's Law Dictionary*, 5th ed., West Publishing: St. Paul, Minn., 1979 at 453:

> Duty: A human action which is exactly conformable to the laws which require us to obey them. Legal or moral obligation. Obligatory conduct or serve. Mandatory obligation to perform.
>
> . . .
>
> A thing due; that which is due from a person; that which a person owes to another. An obligation to do a thing. A word of more extensive signification that "debt," although both are expressed by the same Latin word "debitum."

Sometimes, however, the term is used synonymously with debt.

"Requirement" is defined in the *World Book Dictionary*, Vol. 2, at p. 1775, as meaning:

> "1. a need; thing needed (with the suggested synonym being "essential"). 2. a demand; thing demanded".

With respect to "requirements," *Stroud's Judicial Dictionary, supra*, says at 2565:

> 3. Requirements as meaning "needs": see *Kier & Co. v. Whitehead Iron & Steel Co.*, 168 L.T. 228.[63]

Clearly, evidence as to precisely what "duties or requirements" of doing a job or of availing oneself of a service, facility, etc. are "essential" will be an important feature of any case in which the respondent claims incapability on the part of the complainant.

There is no Ontario case to date in which the essential nature of a duty or requirement has been contested. The closest analogous authority can be found in cases in which a requirement has been analyzed in terms of whether it can stand as a "reasonable and *bona fide*" bar to employment affecting persons with various handicaps.[64]

---

63. *Ante*, note 59, at D/2192-2193.

64. Because cases from other jurisdictions do not tend to focus on individual analysis of person and situation. it is difficult to pinpoint what may have been considered "essential" elements by a particular tribunal. The following list of essentials can be inferred from previous cases: "normal" reflexes and alertness, without unforeseeable lapses in manual jobs such as grain handling (*Forseille v. United Grain Growers Ltd.* (1985), 6 C.H.R.R. D/3051 (Cdn. Human Rights Comm.)) and "trackman" duties (*Mahon v. Canadian Pacific Ltd.* (1985), 7 C.H.R.R. D/3278 (S.C.C.)) and in police officers' work (*Barnard v. Fort Frances (Town) Commissioners of Police* (1986), 7 C.H.R.R. D/3167 (Ont. Bd. of Inquiry)); ability to drive a car in police officers (*Barnard*); the ability to grip in jobs such as warehouseman (*Ward v. Canadian National Express* (1982), 3 C.H.R.R. D/689 (Cdn. Human Rights Trib.)) and nurse's aide (*Cameron, ante*, note 59); ability to distinguish colours in airline pilots (*Bicknell v. Air Canada* (1984), 5 C.H.R.R. D/1992 (Cdn. Human Rights Comm.)).

"Undue Hardship"

As noted above, a board may not find a person "incapable" unless it is satisfied that the needs of the person cannot be accommodated without undue hardship.[65] The term "undue hardship," which developed and was to some extent defined in case law under the previous *Code* and in other jurisdictions, has been given additional statutory definition by the specific inclusion of considerations of cost, outside sources of funding and health and safety requirements. There is provision for further definition of the term by regulation,[66] but none has yet been passed. Existing authority concerning undue hardship is discussed in Chapter 4 and in this chapter in respect of exceptions that use the term. For the purpose of this section, it should be noted that with rapid advances in prosthetic and other ameliorative devices, as well as design features that render buildings and machinery accessible and usable, undue hardship is likely to be increasingly difficult to establish.

The General Effect of the 1988 Amendments

To date, no cases have been decided under the 1988 amendments to the *Code*. It is suggested that, in dealing with the new provisions embodied in section 17, boards of inquiry should treat previous Ontario authority and case law from other jurisdictions with some caution, since all such cases have been dealt with in the context of whether a denial of opportunity was "reasonable and *bona fide*" rather than the higher "essential" standards. The Board in *Cameron* addressed this point in *obiter*:

> [I]n Bill 188, both the subjective and objective components of the exemption were present, in respect of handicap situations. However, in Bill 209, 1980, the mixed subjective/objective components of the "reasonable and *bona fide*" exception were dropped in respect of the ground of "handicap," the subjective component being removed through the adoption of the language now seen in the paragraph 16(1)(*b*) [now 17(2)] exception. In my opinion, paragraph 16(1)(*b*) [now 17(3)] expresses, in itself, simply an objective requirement. A respondent must establish by a preponderance of evidence on an objective basis that the handicap of the complainant renders her incapable of performing or fulfilling the essential duties or requirements relating to the employment position. The subjective component is not present in paragraph 16(1)(*b*) [now 17(3)]. The respondent's state of mind or *bona fides* seems irrelevant (except when it comes to the issue of an award.[67]

A further point is that the new provisions suggest an order of considerations to be dealt with by the tribunal. Clearly, a *prima facie* case of discrimination must first be established. A succinct summary of the *prima facie* case in the context of an allegation of discrimination in employment

---

65. S. 17(2).
66. S. 17(3).
67. *Cameron v. Nel-gor Nursing Home* (1984), 5 C.H.R.R. D/2170 (Ont. Bd. of Inquiry), at D/2191-2192.

on the ground of handicap was given by the board in *Warner v. Connell*[68] as follows: "the evidence must show that not only was (the complainant) not hired for the position that was later given to someone else, but that he was rejected despite the fact that he had the requisite qualifications, and that one basis for his rejection was a prohibited ground pursuant to the *Human Rights Code.*"

Once the *prima facie* case has been established, the respondent must either prove a defence under one of the situation-specific exemptions under the *Code*, or establish that the complainant was incapable of performing the essential duties and requirements. This, it is suggested, demands a finding as to whether the area in which the respondent claims incapability is in fact essential. It is only after the respondent has proved that the area cited was an essential duty or requirement that the tribunal should move on to consider reasonable accommodation in the performance of that duty or requirement.

Special Interest Organizations: Sections 18 and 24(1)(*a*)

The *Code* provides two special exemptions for "religious, philanthropic, educational, fraternal or social institutions or organizations."[69] The relevant sections are 18 and 24(1)(*a*); the exemptions provided differ somewhat, as will be noted below. The exemptions are broader than those provided by section 4(7) of the 1980 *Code*, particularly since the present *Code* no longer restricts special interest organizations to those that are non-profit and public. The areas covered are employment and membership or participation.

Membership or Participation

Section 18 allows a special interest organization that is "primarily engaged in serving the interests of persons identified by a prohibited ground of discrimination" to restrict membership or participation "to persons who are similarly identified."

There have been three cases in which section 18 has been raised as a defence before an Ontario board. To date, the section has been narrowly construed.

In *Barnard v. Canadian Corps of Commissionaires*,[70] an organization that acted primarily as an employer to its "members" was unable to maintain a requirement that they be Canadian citizens. In *Sehdev v. Bayview*

---

68. (1980), unreported (Ont. Bd. of Inquiry), at page 15 (transcript).
69. Hereinafter referred to as special interest organizations.
70. (1985), 6 C.H.R.R. D/2659 (Ont. Bd. of Inquiry), affirmed (1986), 55 O.R. (2d) 423 (Div. Ct.).

Glen Junior School[71] the board considered the position of a school that constructively discriminated by not allowing a Sikh to maintain his turban, due to uniform requirements. The board ruled that the school could not be said to be an institution "primarily engaged in serving the interests of persons identified" by one or more creeds.

Gregory v. Donauschwaben Park Waldheim[72] concerned an organization which was the registered owner of a parcel of land on which a number of permanent and semi-permanent residences had been enacted by members of the organization. A member listed her cottage for sale and the complainant made an offer, only to find his offer rejected because his purchase had not been approved by the Park Committee of the organization. The approval had been withheld because the complainant was not of German origin.

At issue before board was the extent to which the respondent organization was engaged in the delivery of "services or facilities with accommodation" rather than being essentially a residential subdivision restricted by place of origin.

The board acknowledged that the fundamental difficulty in applying section 18 is that it appears to run counter to the egalitarian objectives of the *Code*. The board rationalized the inconsistency as follows:

> No doubt, the *Code* permits the creation of exclusive organizations and institutions in order to permit the fostering of certain other objectives, be they, for example, religious, educational or cultural, whose attainment is not considered to be, broadly speaking, inconsistent with the attainment of the objectives of the *Code*. Thus, if the *Code* envisages a non-discriminatory market place for employment and goods and services, for example, it also envisages that the promotion of religious belief through the creation of institutions whose exclusivity is protected by section 17 [now section 18] is not inconsistent with that objective.[73]

However, the board also acknowledged the danger of sham "special interest organizations" being set up to effect segregated neighbourhoods. Thus, while failing to accept the proposition that, to qualify under section 18, accommodation can only be a minimal part of the "benefits package" offered by the organization, the board concluded that the services and facilities cannot be "peripheral or insubstantial" or lack legitimate connection to the accommodation. In finding that section 18 applied, the board took into account that, with few exceptions, members were not in residence year-round, that a broad range of cultural and social activities were carried out on the site, and that meetings and activities were carried on off-site during the winter.

---

71. (1988), 9 C.H.R.R. D/4881 (Ont. Bd. of Inquiry).
72. (1990), 13 C.H.R.R. D/505 (Ont. Bd. of Inquiry).
73. *Ibid.*, at D/512.

Employment

Section 24(1)(*a*) allows a special interest organization

that is primarily engaged in serving the interests of persons identified by their race, ancestry, place of origin, colour, ethnic origin, creed, sex, age, marital status or handicap [to employ] only, or [give] preference in employment to, persons similarly identified if the qualification is a reasonable and *bona fide* qualification because of the nature of the employment.

There have been no cases under this section.

The effect of section 10 of the *Interpretation Act*, as well as abundant case law on the subject of exemptions to remedial legislation, is likely to restrict the application of section 24(1)(*a*), as will the requirement that any qualification be reasonable and *bona fide*.[74] The organization will have a reasonably heavy burden of proof to establish the legitimacy of a discriminatory qualification. On the strength of the aforementioned case law, it is unlikely that, for example, a Filipino social club could deny employment as a cook to a non-Filipino who was expert in Filipino cuisine. Certainly, it is unlikely that a special organization that is religious in nature could deny employment as a secretary or a janitor to a person of another faith.[75]

Separate Schools and the Education Act: Section 19

Section 19(1), which has no precedent in the previous *Code*, provides:

This Act shall not be construed to adversely affect any right or privilege respecting separate schools enjoyed by separate school boards or their supporters under the *Constitution Act, 1867* and the *Education Act*.

The term "separate school" is applicable, for historical reasons,[76] only

---

74. The effect of this term will be discussed further below.

75. In *Gore v. Ottawa Separate School Board* (1971), unreported (Ont. Bd. of Inquiry), Chairman Tarnopolsky considered an argument by the respondent that all employees, including secretaries, must be Catholic because of the need to provide a "Catholic atmosphere." The board rejected this argument: "I think it would be reasonable for the Separate School Board to refuse to hire a secretary who is hostile to the Catholic faith or to the aims of the Separate School system, regardless of her religious upbringing, but I cannot see how a secretary can be expected to provide an example for the children. This is surely the responsibility of the teachers, and the religious aspect is the responsibility of the ecclesiastics as well as most of the teachers. The secretary performs secretarial and clerical functions. . . . It is reasonable to expect the Secretary to be prepared to learn what is required to meet her duties in answering telephones, compiling questionaires, etc. It is reasonable to expect that she be prepared to help the Principal, the teachers, the pupils, and their parents within the bounds of her duties, *in a co-operative spirit*, whether she herself be a Roman Catholic or not, as a child, in the past, or in the present."

76. Although the term "separate school" is not expressly defined in the *Education Act*, R.S.O. 1990, c. E.2, the limitation may be inferred through the wording of s. 93 of the *Constitution Act, 1867*, and by reference to the definitions of "elementary school," "rural separate school," "separate school supporter," and "separate school zone": *Education Act*, s. 1(1), and Pt. V of the Act.

to Roman Catholic[77] and Protestant schools in Ontario. The reference to rights under the *British North America Act, 1867*[78] is to the provisions of section 93 of that Act. Of especial importance to human rights law is section 93(1), which provides that, while the provinces may exclusively legislate in relation to education, "Nothing in any such Law shall prejudicially affect any Right or Privilege with respect to Denominational Schools which any Class of Persons have by Law in the Province at the Union." The effect of section 93 will be discussed further below.

Neither the *Constitution Act, 1867* nor the *Education Act* specifically grant a separate school board, or, for that matter, a public school board, the authority to hire or fire teachers or other employees on the ground of religion.[79] However, the wording of section 93 of the *Constitution Act* has been so broadly interpreted by the courts that it is likely that most hiring and firing decisions based on religion will be immune from the effect of the *Code*. It is to be expected that this will be one of the major issues in the interpretation of section 19(1). Specifically, boards of inquiry are likely to be faced with deciding whether a board of education is in breach of the *Code* if it:

1. refuses to hire or promote a teacher or another category of employee, such as a secretary or janitor, on the ground that the applicant is not a member of the religion in question; or

2. refuses to hire, fires or demotes a teacher or another category of employee who has breached a rule of the religion in question.

Refusal to Hire or Promote a Non-Member of the Religion

A complaint by a teacher of failure to hire or failure to promote on the ground of religion has never been considered by an Ontario board of inquiry, as the Commission has never recommended that a board of inquiry be appointed in respect of such a matter.

The Commission has, however, recommended a board in response to a complaint of refusal to hire an applicant for a non-teaching position. In *Gore v. Ottawa Separate School Board*,[80] a non-Catholic applicant for a

---

77. Defined in the *Education Act*, s. 1(1) as including "a Catholic of the Greek or Ukrainian Rite in union with the See of Rome."

78. Renamed the *Constitution Act, 1867*, as amended by the *Constitution Act, 1982*, s. 53(1) and Schedule item 1.

79. It may be noted, however, that pursuant to an amendment enacted in 1986, the *Education Act* specifically provides for employment rights given under the *Code* to be extended to "designated" public school employees who are transferred to a Roman Catholic school board (ss. 135(28) and 136(2)), which might imply that such employees' rights would otherwise not be as extensive as those employed by other school boards. Parenthetically, s. 136(1) provides that teachers so hired, agree, after ten years, to "respect the philosophy and traditions of Roman Catholic separate schools in the performance of their duties".

80. *Ante*, note 75.

secretarial position was refused employment by the respondent school board. Board of inquiry Chairman Tarnopolsky, after reviewing the duties involved in the position, concluded that a requirement that the applicant be Roman Catholic was unreasonable. He also rejected the argument that the respondent board was obliged to impose the requirement "because their tax supporters would not like it otherwise."

The chairman then considered the constitutional issue. Basing its argument on the judgment of the Judicial Committee of the Privy Council in *Winnipeg v. Barrett*,[81] the school board argued that section 93 of the *Constitution Act, 1867* had the effect of preserving pre-Constitutional rights and privileges held by separate schools, and that the freedom to hire on the basis of religion was one of these privileges. The response of the board of inquiry to this argument is best summed up by quoting Chairman Tarnopolsky's own subsequent comments[82] on *Gore*:

> In considering the decision of the Board of Inquiry in the *Gore* case it is important to keep in mind that the very wording of section 93(1) of the *B.N.A. Act* (and its counterparts in the three Prairie Provinces and Newfoundland), protects the rights and privileges *as they were at the time of Confederation* and therefore they may very well, and in fact do, vary from province to province. . . .
>
> Thus, the Chairman initially pointed out that section 22 of the *Manitoba Act*, which was the legislation dealt with in the *Barrett* case, is different from section 93(1) of the *B.N.A. Act*. The reference in the *Manitoba Act* as to the right or privilege which is protected, is to such as "any class of persons have by law *or practice*" at the time of Confederation. He made reference to the leading work on this constitutional issue, to point out that the words "or practice" made the *Manitoba Act* wider in scope. This distinction, he remarked, was specifically referred to in the *Barrett* case by Lord Macnaghten. It was subsequently reaffirmed by Lord Buckmaster in the case of *Trustees of the Roman Catholic Schools for the City of Ottawa*.
>
> . . . [I]t has been decided by this Board that the right or privilege reserved in the provision is a legal right or privilege, and does not include any practice, instruction, or privilege of a voluntary character which at the date of the passing of the Act might be in operation: *City of Winnipeg v. Barrett*.
>
> The Chairman went on to point out that in any case no evidence was submitted of what the practice was with respect to employment of personnel in 1867. He suggested that the "Act to Restore to Roman Catholics in Upper Canada certain rights in respect to Separate Schools", enacted in 1863 and applicable in 1867, contained no provision restricting the right of employment in separate schools to Roman Catholics. There were restrictions, such as section 3, which provided that only Roman Catholics could participate in election of trustees, and section 7, which confined the power to levy school taxes to those persons who subscribed towards the support of such schools, but otherwise nothing confined employment to separate school supporters and, in fact, section 9 provided that the trustees should perform "the same duties and be subject to the same penalties as trustees of Common Schools; and teachers of Separate Schools shall be liable to the same obligations and penalties as teachers of Common Schools". The current *Separate Schools Act*, he added, did not indicate any change on this matter.

---

81. [1892] A.C. 445.
82. In *Discrimination and The Law* (1982), pp. 212-14.

The Chairman suggested that the most that could be said concerning hiring practices was that in 1867 there was no prohibition at common law against discriminating. The initial provisions in the *Ontario Human Rights Code* prohibiting discrimination on grounds of, *inter alia*, religion, he noted, specifically exempted educational institutions from the Code but it was only subsequently that this exemption was restricted to cases where there was "a reasonable occupational qualification".

He went on to point out that as early as 1878, in the case of *Board of Trustees of the Roman Catholic Separate Schools of Belleville v. Grainger et al.*, it was asserted that section 93(1) of the *B.N.A. Act* was not intended to preclude all legislation. To this same effect, he quoted from the description of section 93(1) by the Judicial Committee in *City of Toronto Corp. v. Trustees of the Roman Catholic Separate Schools of Toronto*:

> It is a restriction upon the power of the Province to make laws in relation to education, but does not prevent the provisions of the Municipal Act with reference to building, and other matters relating to building, and other matters relating to the health and convenience of the population, from applying to denominational schools as well as to other buildings.

He also referred to the Judicial Committee decision in *Roman Catholic Separate Schools Trustees for Tiny et al. v. The King* where it was asserted that while the settlement between Catholics and Protestants was to be maintained, the province retained the power "to mould the educational system in the interests of the public at large, as distinguished from any section of it, however important". For this purpose, the Judicial Committee pointed out that the province retained power of overall regulation "in the full sense" — it possessed "full power of regulation".

Based upon these authorities, the Chairman concluded that (p. 14):

> Section 93(1) could not have been intended, therefore, to prevent the legislature from enacting any law which affects the rights and powers of Separate School Boards. It must have been contemplated that the province could, for the sake of health, or morals, or for public policy reasons, enact laws or regulations with respect to schools.

As a further illustration he pointed to the present *Schools Administration Act* for a number of provisions, not in existence in 1867, which now apply both to separate and public schools such as section 6, providing for compulsory attendance from age six to 16, and section 16, requiring certain conditions with respect to salaries, sick pay, etc., which must apply to every contract between teachers and school boards, whether separate or public. Similarly, he pointed out that it could not be argued that collective bargaining or trade union legislation not in existence in 1867 could not apply to separate schools today. On this point the stated (p. 14):

> If recognition of trade unions or teachers' associations can now be made applicable to school boards, despite the fact that there could be an argument that the school boards were free to ignore such associations in 1867, then surely the province could decide to apply the Ontario Human Rights Code to schools unless the discrimination practised by the school board is such as can be described as being a "reasonable occupational qualification".

Under the circumstances, therefore, the Chairman decided that there was discrimination, that the "reasonable occupational qualification" provision was not a defence, and that the prohibition of discrimination was not *ultra vires*.

In a more recent case, a board of inquiry failed to find discrimination on the basis of creed when a Catholic school refused to hire a janitor who, although eligible to divert his taxes to the support of separate schools, elected not to do so.[83]

Firing, Demoting or Refusing to Hire Persons who have Breached a Rule of the Religion in Question

The Ontario Court of Appeal has upheld a separate school board's decision to dismiss two teachers who had contracted civil marriages to divorced non-Catholics. Although the case did not involve the application of the Ontario *Human Rights Code*, it is analogous in that the operation of a provincial statute vis-à-vis section 93 of the *Constitution Act, 1867* was the central issue. In *Re Essex (Roman Catholic Separate School Board) v. Porter*,[84] the School Board brought an application for judicial review to set aside an order of a board of reference, under the Schools Administration Act,[85] that the contracts of the teachers be continued.

Both the Divisional Court and the Court of Appeal held that section 93 protected a right of separate schools to dismiss for "denominational reasons," the reasoning being that separate schools had enjoyed this right prior to Confederation.

In the Divisional Court, Weatherston J., for the majority, referred to the *Act to Restore to Roman Catholics in Upper Canada Certain Rights in Respect to Separate Schools*,[86] and the *Upper Canada Common School Act*.[87] The former contains provisions stating that separate school trustees and teachers were subject to the same duties and penalties as trustees and teachers of common schools, while the latter authorizes trustees to hire teachers and to set the terms and conditions of their employment. After a brief review of early Privy Council cases on section 93, Weatherston J. observed that it was "clear from these authorities that the right or privilege preserved by s. 93 must be a right or privilege which, if lost, would impair the integrity of the separate schools."[88] He did not define the "denominational reasons" that might constitute cause for dismissal, nor did he explain the nature of the type of right that, if lost, would impair a separate school's "integrity."

In dissent, Steele J. reviewed the provisions of the *Upper Canada Common School Act* and the *Act to Restore to Roman Catholics in Upper Canada Certain Rights in Respect of Separate Schools*, concluding that nei-

83. *Morra v. Metropolitan Separate School Board* (1981), 3 C.H.R.R. D/1034 (Ont. Bd. of Inquiry) is further discussed in Chapter 3. Also see *Black v. Metropolitan Separate School Board* (1988), 65 O.R. (2d) 598 (Div. Ct.).

84. (1977), 16 O.R. (2d) 433 (Div. Ct.), affirmed (1978), 21 O.R. (2d) 255 (C.A.).

85. R.S.O. 1970, c. 424, s. 229(1) [rep. S.O. 1974, c. 109, s. 272].

86. S.C. 1863 (2nd Sess.), c. 5.

87. C.S.U.C. 1859, c. 64.

88. 16 O.R. (2d) 433 at 438.

ther Act provided separate school trustees with employment rights other than those enjoyed by common school trustees. He then proceeded to quote from *Winnipeg v. Barrett*:[89]

> "It is agreed that there was no law or regulation or ordinance with respect to education in force at the time. There were, therefore, no rights or privileges with respect to denominational schools existing by law."[90]

He concluded:[91]

> Even if there had been a practice by the trustees of Roman Catholic separate schools at the time of union to dismiss teachers that entered into civil marriages (and it may be that there was limited or no authority for civil marriages at that time) or marriage outside the Roman Catholic Church, I am of the opinion that there was no such right or privilege in law.

The court of appeal later briefly confirmed the majority decision in *Essex*. Zuber J.A., writing for the court, stated the law as follows:[92]

> It is apparent that the staring point must be an inquiry into the rights and privileges with respect to separate schools in Ontario as of 1867. Section 7 of "An Act to restore to Roman Catholics in Upper Canada certain rights in respect to Separate Schools", 1863 (Can.) (2nd Sess.), c. 5, provided that the trustees of separate schools should have the same powers in respect of separate schools that the trustees of common schools had with respect to common schools. As employers, the trustees of common schools had the power to hire and dismiss teachers. I find nothing in the *Upper Canada Common Schools Act*, U.C.C.S. 1859, c. 64, which takes away or diminishes the trustees' common law rights as employer. If authority is needed to support this proposition, it can be found in *Raymond v. School Trustees of Village of Cardinal* (1887), 14 O.A.R. 562. I take it to be obvious, that if a school board can dismiss for cause, then in the case of a denominational school cause must include denominational cause. Serious departures from denominational standards by a teacher cannot be isolated from his or her teaching duties since within the denominational school religious instruction, influence and example form an important part of the educational process: *cf. Tiny Separate School Trustees v. The King*, [1928] 3 D.L.R. 753 at p. 773, [1928] A.C. 363 at p. 390, [1928] 2 W.W.R. 641. I therefore conclude that as of 1867, separate school trustees in Ontario possessed the power to dismiss teachers for denominational cause. In my view, it follows that the power of the trustees to dismiss for denominational cause is a "right or privilege with respect to denominational schools" possessed by separate school supporters and by virtue of s. 93 of the *British North America Act, 1867*, nothing in the legislation of the Province of Ontario can prejudicially affect this right.

Although the reasoning in *Essex* is sparsely developed, it is difficult to argue with the conclusion. Given the broad powers presumably enjoyed by all employers prior to the advent of modern employment legislation, it would seem reasonable to assume that separate school boards were within their rights in hiring or firing teachers for "denominational reasons."

---

89. *Ante*, note 80.
90. 16 O.R. (2d) 433 at 444.
91. *Ibid.*, at 445.
92. 21 O.R. (2d) at 457-8.

Section 93 of the *Constitution Act, 1867* has been carried forward in the *Charter of Rights.*[93]

Further, a 1984 decision of the Supreme Court of Canada confirms that a requirement based on denominational reasons can be considered "reasonable and *bona fide*" for the purpose of human rights legislation in respect of the employment of teachers in a Catholic school. In *Caldwell v. Stuart*[94] the court upheld the decision of a Roman Catholic school not to renew the contract of a teacher who had married a divorced man as related, in an objective sense, to the performance of the job.

To summarize the scope of section 19, in the light of *Caldwell*, and of *Essex* and the case law reviewed therein, it would seem that teachers will continue to be considered peculiarly essential to the maintenance of the religious "integrity" or ambience of separate schools. Thus, employment decisions made for denominational reasons will probably be exempted from the effect of the *Code* where they affect teachers. In regard to non-teaching employees the situation may be different. Since such legal rights in Ontario as are "frozen" by section 93 of the *Constitution Act, 1867* do not appear to extend to non-teachers, it is probable that section 19 does not affect their employment.[95] The only exception that may be applicable, if this view is accepted, is section 24(1)(*a*), the "special interest organization" employment exception discussed above. In that case, the test for a board would be whether the employment decision is reasonable and *bona fide*, and the analysis by Chairman Tarnopolsky in *Gore* would be the appropriate approach.

Duties of Teachers

Section 19(2) provides that the *Code* "does not apply to affect the application of the *Education Act* with respect to the duties of teachers."

The duties of teachers are enumerated under section 264 of the *Education Act*. Those presumably most likely to become the subject of a human rights complaint, and to bring into question section 19(2), are found in sections 264(1)(*c*) and (*f*) which provide:

---

93. The *Constitution Act, 1982*, includes "freedom of conscience and religion; freedom of thought, belief, opinion and expression" among the "fundamental freedoms" set out in s. 2. Furthermore, the "equality rights" set out in s. 15 include the right to the equal protection and equal benefit of the law without discrimination based on religion. However, s. 29 of the Act provides that "Nothing in this Charter abrogates or derogates from any rights or privileges guaranteed by or under the Constitution of Canada in respect of denominational, separate or dissentient schools," and s. 26 states that "The guarantee in this Charter of certain rights and freedoms shall not be construed as denying the existence of any other rights or freedoms that exist in Canada."

94. [1984] 2 S.C.R. 603.

95. Subsections 135(28) and 136(2) of the *Education Act (ante*, note 78) refer to all employees, but s. 136(1) singles out teachers as the employees from whom respect for philosophy and tradition is expected.

235(1) It is the duty of a teacher,

. . . . .

(*c*) to inculcate by precept and example respect for religion and the principles of Judaeo-Christian morality and the highest regard for truth, justice, loyalty, love of country, humanity, benevolence, sobriety, industry, frugality, purity, temperance and all other virtues;

. . . . .

(*f*) in instruction and in all communications with the pupils in regard to discipline and the management of the school,

(i) to use the English language, except where it is impractical to do so by reason of the pupil not understanding English, and except in respect of instruction in language other than English when such other language is being taught as one of the subjects in the course of study, or

(ii) to use the French language in schools or classes in which French is the language of instruction except where it is impractical to do so by reason of the pupil not understanding French, and except in respect of instruction in a language other than French when such other language is being taught as one of the subjects in the course of study.

To date there have been no Ontario board decisions dealing with the above-noted provisions.

EXCEPTIONS APPLICABLE TO GOODS, SERVICES AND FACILITIES

Public Decency: Section 20(1)

Section 20(1) continues an exemption contained in section 2(2) in the 1980 *Code*. It provides that:

The right under section 1 to equal treatment with respect to services and facilities without discrimination because of sex is not infringed where the use of the services or facilities is restricted to persons of the same sex on the ground of public decency.

There have been no cases dealing with the predecessor section; however, a "public decency" argument was addressed by Wilson J.A., as she then was, in *Ontario (Human Rights Commission) v. Ontario Rural Softball Association*,[96] a case in which the Ontario Court of Appeal, in a split decision, upheld the right of a boys' softball association to refuse a girl player the right to participate. The response of Wilson J.A. implies that where "decency" can be maintained in a situation it will not be an issue:[97]

[A] word must be said on the submission of counsel for the respondent that s-s. (2) of s. 2 applies to take segregated softball out of the operation of s-s. (1). The board found as a fact that the "public decency" criterion did not apply to the O.R.S.A. playoffs

---

96. (1979), 26 O.R. (2d) 134 (C.A.), leave to appeal to S.C.C. denied (1979), 31 N.R. 171 (note) (S.C.C.).

97. *Ibid.*, 26 O.R. (2d) 134 at 147.

> for children under 11 years of age since the children invariably changed at home and were driven to and from their homes in their baseball attire. I do not think that finding can be interfered with on appeal.

In a British Columbia case, a human rights board of inquiry considered and rejected a decency argument in deciding that a male teacher had been discriminated against when he was not considered for a position as a girls' physical education instructor. The evidence established that there was no necessity for constant supervision of changing-rooms, and that a female teacher could be called upon to assist should such a need arise.[98] However, a Saskatchewan board was not persuaded to "remove" an exemption which allowed a men's correctional facility to limit its employment of female staff, holding that such duties as "skin frisks" should be performed by staff of the same sex as inmates.[99]

Athletics and Recreation: Sections 20(1), (2) and (3)

Subsection 19(2) of the 1981 *Code*, which allowed sex discrimination in athletic organizations and activities, was successfully challenged under section 15 of the *Charter* in *Blainey v. Ontario Hockey Association*.[100] In 1986, it was repealed.

Briefs opposing sex segregation in sports had been submitted to the Standing Committee on Resource Development, before the 1981 *Code* received third reading, by, among others, representatives of the School of Physical and Health Education of the University of Toronto. The Committee was reminded of the UNESCO-sponsored International Charter for Physical Education and Sport,[101] which prescribes equality of access to sports and athletics. In the light of these efforts, section 19(2) of the 1981 *Code* was obviously a firm legislative policy in support of sex-segregated athletics in Ontario.

This policy is also visible in section 20(3), which provides:

> The right under section 1 to equal treatment with respect to services and facilities is not infringed where a recreational club restricts or qualifies access to its services or facilities or gives preferences with respect to membership dues and other fees because of age, sex, marital status or family status.

---

98. *Rossi v. School District No. 57* (1985), 7 C.H.R.R. D/3237 (B.C. Human Rights Council).
99. *Saskatchewan (Social Services Corrections Branch) v. Saskatchewan Government Employees' Union* (1983), 4 C.H.R.R. D/1236 (Sask. Human Rights Comm.).
100. (1986), 54 O.R. (2d) 513 (C.A.), leave to appeal to S.C.C. refused (1986), 58 O.R. (2d) 274 (headnote) (S.C.C.).
101. Ottawa, Canadian Commission for UNESCO (1980), cited in R.B. Beamish and B. Kidd. "A Brief to the Standing Committee on Resource Development, Legislature of Ontario," School of Physical and Health Education, University of Toronto (Sept. 1980).

This provision exempts from the provisions of the *Code* any recreational club that:

1. restricts services or facilities on the ground of age, sex, marital status or family status;[102] or

2. gives preferences in respect of dues and other fees on these grounds.[103]

The "drinking age" in Ontario was the subject of a 1986 amendment; subsection 20(2) provides:

> (2) The right under section 1 to equal treatment with respect to services, goods and facilities without discrimination because of age is not infringed by the provisions of the *Liquor Licence Act* and the regulations under it relating to providing for and enforcing a minimum drinking age of nineteen years.

To date, no Ontario boards have interpreted these subsections.

EXCEPTIONS APPLICABLE TO RESIDENTIAL ACCOMMODATION: SECTION 21

Section 21(1) reads:

> The right under section 2 to equal treatment with respect to the occupancy of residential accommodation without discrimination is not infringed by discrimination where the residential accommodation is in a dwelling in which the owner or his or her family reside if the occupant or occupants of the residential accommodation are required to share a bathroom or kitchen facility with the owner or family of the owner.

This exemption for housing and accommodation in which "the owner or his or her family reside" and "share a bathroom or kitchen facility" with the tenant seems to be firmly entrenched as an irreducible minimum in the eyes of the Ontario Legislature.[104] It should be noted that rooms in houses and other types of shared accommodation, as the cheapest type of accommodation in many situations, are the types most likely to be needed by just those groups that the *Code* is designed to protect — the economically disadvantaged, single parents with children, and immigrants who have yet to become financially established in this country. Nonetheless, the exemption is a blanket one; discrimination on all grounds is allowed.

Section 21(2) reads:

---

102. Thus, it would seem, for example, that "ladies' hours" that are restricted to times inconvenient for employed persons are not to be considered discriminatory.

103. "Family memberships" are preserved, for example, and it appears that clubs may restrict eligibility for family membership to married couples and their children, if they so choose.

104. The type of accommodation that qualifies for the exemption has been progressively narrowed since the earliest Ontario legislation on the subject exempted buildings having six or fewer residential units. See I.A. Hunter, "The Development of the Ontario Human Rights Code: A Decade in Retrospect" (1972), 22 U.T.L.J. 237 at 239-40.

> The right under section 2 to equal treatment with respect to the occupancy of residential accommodation without discrimination because of sex is not infringed by discrimination on that ground where the occupancy of all the residential accommodation in the building, other than the accommodation, if any, of the owner or family of the owner, is restricted to persons who are of the same sex.

This section is also a continuation of a provision of the predecessor *Code*, but it has been broadened somewhat. Section 3(2) of the 1980 *Code* restricted the exemption to buildings in which the owner or the owner's family lived. Section 20(2) has no requirement for residency by the owner or his or her family. The subsection thus operates to exempt non-coed university residences, men's and women's hostels, and the like.

Subsections 20(3) and (4) of the 1981 *Code*, which dealt with exceptions in respect of marital status and family status, were repealed in 1986.

Section 21 exemptions relate only to the right to equal treatment without discrimination. If the exemption is to be read in a properly restrictive manner, "discrimination" will be construed in its most common and, therefore, most restrictive sense, allowing landlords only the freedom to deny or limit accommodation to people belonging to those groups specified in the section.

The following points flow from a restrictive interpretation of section 21:

1. A landlord or agent who discriminates for two reasons, one allowed under section 21, and one forbidden by the *Code*, may be found to have breached the *Code*.[105]

2. A landlord will not be able to claim the protection of section 21 if the landlord, his or her agent, or other tenant harasses a tenant on any of the grounds covered by sections 2(2) or 7(2) (that is, where a landlord has accepted a tenant when he or she might have rejected the tenant under, say, section 21(1), the landlord cannot later change his or her mind and try to get rid of the tenant by harassing him or her).

3. A landlord, agent, etc., "covered" by section 21 may not with impunity breach section 12, by taking any discriminatory action against the tenant because he or she disapproves of the tenant's friends.[106]

4. It is probable that the section 13 prohibition against the publication or display of a notice, sign, etc., indicating an intention to discriminate applies to landlords protected by section 21. If so, it means that such landlords may not, in advertising accommodation for rent, be specific as to which groups they wish to exclude.[107]

To date, no Ontario boards have dealt with these exceptions.

---

105. See discussion of "mixed motive" cases (the *Bushnell* line of cases) in Chapter 9.
106. See discussion of this point in Chapter 5.
107. See discussion of this point in Chapter 5.

EXCEPTIONS APPLICABLE TO INSURANCE CONTRACTS: SECTION 22

Section 22 reads:

> The right under sections 1 and 3 to equal treatment with respect to services and to contract on equal terms, without discrimination because of age, sex, marital status, family status or handicap, is not infringed where a contract of automobile, life, accident or sickness or disability insurance or a contract of group insurance between an insurer and an association or person other than an employer, or a life annuity, differentiates or makes a distinction, exclusion or preference on reasonable and *bona fide* grounds because of age, sex, marital status, family status or handicap.

"Group insurance" is defined by section 10:

> "group insurance" means insurance whereby the lives or well-being or the lives and well-being of a number of persons are insured severally under a single contract between an insurer and an association or an employer or other person.

A provision dealing with insurance contracts other than those relating to employment is unprecedented in Ontario human rights legislation and was obviously included in response to section 3 of the *Code*. The extent to which the section allows an insurance company to derogate from the overall policy of the *Code* by treating the customer as a member of a class rather than as an individual depends on the type of evidence that boards and courts require to establish reasonable and *bona fide* grounds and, thus, rebut a *prima facie* case of discrimination.

The essence of a section 22 complaint would be a challenge by the complainant to the reasonableness of factors used by the respondent in generating actuarial data. The reasonableness of differences based on sex, age, marital status, family status and handicap has been analyzed in considerable detail in reports by the Alberta and Saskatchewan Human Rights Commissions.[108] Both reports point out that mortality tables based on such distinctions are frequently inaccurate, that classifications are arbitrary and misleading, and that risk is far more accurately predicted on the basis of such factors as amount of exercise taken, smoking, weight, stress and geographic location. There have also been three reports by a Select Committee of the Ontario Legislature: two on the subject of auto insurance[109] and one on insurance generally.[110] In regard to automobile insurance the Committee recommended the elimination of age, sex and marital status as criteria for use in determining insurance premiums. In regard to life insurance, dis-

---

108. Alberta Human Rights Commission, *Discrimination in the Insurance Industry in Alberta* (1981); Saskatchewan Human Rights Commission, *Human Rights and Benefits in the '80's* (1981).

109. Select Commission on Company Law, *First Report on Automobile Insurance* (1977); *Second Report on Automobile Insurance* (1978).

110. Select Committee on Company Law, *Report on General Insurance* (1979).

cussed in the general insurance report, the findings in respect of age, handicap and marital status are somewhat ambiguous. However, the Committee discussed sex-based classifications in the light of existing human rights legislation. It concluded that sex-based classification was "actuarially sound and not inherently unfair," but "could be questioned on social grounds as a discriminatory practice."[111]

To date, there have been two Ontario cases that discussed automobile insurance. In *Hope v. Royal Insurance Co.*,[112] the complainant claimed a violation of section 3 of the *Code* on the ground of family status in respect of the rates for occasional driver coverage for his unmarried son, which were higher than those for a married person or a daughter. The board upheld the complaint, but the Divisional Court quashed the decision of the board.[113] The major reason for the decision of the court was that the date of the insurance contract preceded the proclamation of the 1981 *Code* in 1982. However, the court also rejected the ruling that a complaint of discrimination on the ground of family status could be maintained.

In *Bates v. Zurich Insurance Co. of Canada*,[114] the complainant was an unmarried male driver under the age of 25, who claimed discrimination in view of the fact that his premiums were higher than those of people over 25, married men and women. Section 21 was squarely in issue. The board reviewed extensive evidence concerning the manner in which auto insurance rates were set. The board found that the company had failed to demonstrate that its classifications were reasonably necessary. In doing so, the board relied on the decision of the Supreme Court of Canada in *Etobicoke*[115] and on United States jurisprudence to hold that, in order to establish a section 22 defence, the respondent would have to show that the very existence of its business would be undermined if it could no longer rely on its discriminatory rate classification system.

On appeal, the Ontario Divisional Court ruled that the board had erred in using the *Etobicoke* standard to interpret "reasonable and *bona fide*," as there were sufficient differences between an employment situation and insurance contracts. The court went on to conclude that the current classification system, while not ideal, satisfied the section 22 test, since its distinctions were supported by reasonable, actuarily verified statistics.[116] This decision was briefly confirmed by the Court of Appeal.[117]

---

111. *Ibid.*, pp. 235-6.
112. (1985), 51 C.R. (2d) 797 (Div. Ct.).
113. *Ibid.*
114. (1985), 6 C.H.R.R. D/2948 (Ont. Bd. of Inquiry).
115. (1982), 132 D.L.R. (3d) 14 (S.C.C.).
116. (1987), 8 C.H.R.R. D/4069 (Div. Ct.).
117. (1989), 70 O.R. (2d) 639 (C.A.), leave to appeal granted (1990), 39 O.A.C. 102 (note) (S.C.C.).

It is arguable that the decision of the Divisional Court does not go far enough, in the light of recent developments in the *Etobicoke* standards[118] and leaves a number of questions concerning the objective validity of insurance classification systems to be explored in future cases.

A review of the cases on sex discrimination in regard to employment benefit plans also yields some comments on reasonableness.

A major issue in regard to sex discrimination in insurance benefits is the smaller periodic payments made to women, as opposed to men, under money-purchase pension plans, annuities or other insured schemes.

The ubiquitous sex-based mortality tables as applied to pension plans have been challenged successfully in the United States. In *City of Los Angeles Department of Water and Power v. Manhart*[119] the respondent employer required women employees to make larger contributions to a pension plan than men. The employer, a self-insurer, argued the validity of the practice on the basis of mortality tables that showed that the cost of a pension for the average female employee was greater than that of her male counterpart. The United States Supreme Court held that the practice constituted sex discrimination. In response to the employer's "fairness" argument, the court stated:[120]

> The basic policy of the statute requires that we focus on fairness to individuals rather than fairness to classes. Practices which classify employees in terms of religion, race, or sex tend to preserve traditional assumptions about groups rather than thoughtful scrutiny of individuals. The generalization involved in this case illustrates the point. Separate mortality tables are easily interpreted as reflecting innate differences between the sexes; but a significant part of the longevity differential may be explained by the social fact that men are heavier smokers than women.
>
> Finally, there is no reason to believe that Congress intended a special definition of discrimination in the context of employee group insurance coverage. It is true that insurance is concerned with events that are individually unpredictable, but that is characteristic of many employment decisions. Individual risks, like individual performance, may not be predicted by resort to classifications proscribed by Title VII. Indeed, the fact that this case involves a group insurance program highlights a basic flaw in the department's fairness argument. For when insurance risks are grouped, the better risks always subsidize the poorer risks. Healthy persons subsidize medical benefits for the less healthy; unmarried workers subsidize pensions of married workers; persons who eat, drink or smoke to excess may subsidize pension benefits for persons whose habits are more temperate. Treating different classes of risks as though they were the same for purposes of group insurance is a common practice which has never been considered inherently unfair. To insure the flabby and the fit as though they were equivalent risks may be more common than treating men and women alike; but nothing more than habit makes one subsidy seem less fair than the other.

---

118. See discussion, *infra* of "reasonable and *bona fide*."
119. 435 U.S. 702 (1978).
120. *Ibid.*, at 709-10.

This individual-based approach has been followed in a number of subsequent American cases[121] that have dealt with smaller monthly benefits to women who have made contributions equal to, or greater than, those made by men.

These issues are further discussed in the section on employee benefit plans, *infra*.

PERSONAL EMPLOYMENT INTERVIEWS: SECTION 23(3)

Section 23(3) allows employers to question applicants, at a personal employment interview, "concerning a prohibited ground of discrimination." This may be done only where discrimination on that ground is permitted by the *Code*. This provision is obviously necessitated by the restrictions on employment advertising, applications and oral inquiries set out in section 23(1) and (2). These restrictions are discussed in Chapter 5.

"REASONABLE AND BONA FIDE" QUALIFICATIONS FOR DISCRIMINATION IN EMPLOYMENT: SECTION 24(1)(*b*)

Section 24(1)(*b*) allows discrimination in employment on the basis of age, sex, record of offences or marital status where any of these "is a reasonable and *bona fide* qualification because of the nature of the employment."[122] As a result, the "realities of the workplace" have, in some circumstances, been allowed to counteract the sweeping protections promised in Part I of the *Code*.

Before commencing a discussion of this subsection, it should be noted that the phrase "reasonable and *bona fide*" is used in the following *Code* provisions:

Section 22: in respect of age, sex, marital status, family status or handicap discrimination in specified contracts of insurance;

---

121. *Henderson v. Oregon*, 405 F. Supp. 1271 (1975), preceded *Manhart* but displayed a similar approach. Post-*Manhart* cases include *Equal Employment Opportunity Comm. v. Colby College*, 589 F. 2d 139 (1978); *Peters v. Wayne State University*, 476 F. Supp. 1343 (1979); *Norris v. Arizona Governing Council*, 486 F. Supp. 645 (1980). This approach is evident even in cases complicated by issues as to the supremacy of state legislation affecting insurance: see *Spirt v. Teachers' Ins. & Annuity Assn.*, 475 F. Supp. 1298 (1979); and *Women in City Govt. United v. City of New York*, 515 F. Supp. 295 (1981). For comment on the issues raised by *Manhart*, see Kistler and Healy, "Sex Discrimination in Pension Plans Since *Manhart*" (1981), Labour Law J. 229, and a section of the Commentary on the Supreme Court 1977 Term, [1978] 92 Harv. L. J. 299.

122. Note that race, ancestry, place of origin, colour, ethnic origin, creed and handicap cannot be adduced as *bona fide* requirements for hiring, except by a special organization as described in s. 24(1)(*a*). Citizenship and family status can never be adduced as *bona fide* requirements, but see ss. 16 and 24(1)(*d*).

Section 24(1)(*a*): in respect of race, ancestry, place of origin, colour, ethnic origin, creed, sex, age, marital status or handicap discrimination in employment by "special interest" organizations.

Section 24(1)(*b*): as described above.

Sections 25(3)(*a*) and (*b*): in respect of discrimination because of pre-existing handicaps in certain employment disability and pension plans.

Section 11(1)(*a*): as a defence to an allegation of constructive discrimination in any area, on any ground.

Although there might properly be reasons for variation in the test imposed by the phrase "reasonable and *bona fide*" depending on the situation, it is suggested that lack of consistency should be considered exceptional and reasons for departure from consistent interpretation should be express. This section deals with subsection 24(1)(*b*) and discussion will therefore largely focus on the way in which "reasonable and *bona fide*" and its predecessor clause "*bona fide* occupational qualification and requirement" has been used in the context of employment. However, there may be obvious extensions of the principles developed in the employment context to other situations in which these terms are used.

"Bona Fide"

The term "*bona fide*" has often been discussed in connection with the term "reasonable," with little differentiation between the two terms. However, the Supreme Court of Canada has confirmed that the term "*bona fide*" denotes both an honest subjective belief that an impugned requirement is appropriate, and a substantial element of objective reasonableness.[123] While the later element may now be considered redundant in the light of the addition of the term "reasonable" to the test for establishing a defense under subsection 24(1)(*b*),[124] it should be noted that, it would be difficult to find a requirement *bona fide* where it is patently unreasonable.

In most cases decided subsequent to *Etobicoke*, there have been little discussion concerning the subjective branch of the test. In *Large v Stratford (City) Police Dept.*, however, the board had some doubt that the subjective branch of the test had been met in respect of a policy of mandatory retirement at age 60. Factors which raised the doubt included the postponement of implementation of the policy by the respondent until some officers over the age of 60 had retired, and the exemption of the chief and deputy chief from the policy despite an argument that, on a small force, all officers had to be available for any duties. The board made the following observations:

---

123. In *Ontario (Human Rights Commission) v. Etobicoke* (1982), 3 C.H.R.R. D/781 (S.C.C.).
124. The *Etobicoke* decision construed "*bona fide* occupational requirement," the term used under the previous *Code*.

On question of legal interpretation arises with respect to the subjective branch of the test, that is, whether the elements of honesty, good faith and sincerely held belief, on the one hand, and absence of ulterior or extraneous reasons, on the other hand, are identical or separate. There was no evidence that the respondents had any ulterior motive in adopting the age 60 mandatory rule. If these two elements are identical, therefore, the absence of ulterior motivation might be sufficient to satisfy the good faith requirement.

While there is no doubt a considerable overlap between these two elements of the subjective branch, I am not persuaded that an absence of ulterior or extraneous reasons is sufficient. A sincerely held belief in the need for a policy can hardly exist if a respondent has simply not addressed its mind to the issue, although it may be hard to show that this involved any ulterior motivation. There was, therefore, an onus on the respondents to show that they actually had some rational basis for the policy.[125]

"Reasonable"

The narrowness with which boards and courts have interpreted reasonableness, as an element of *"bona fide"* or as a specific requirement, has varied both among grounds of discrimination and in respect of the basis on which an employer has sought to defend a rule or action as "reasonable." Those bases can be roughly organized as stereotypes and business related reasons.

Stereotypes

For the most part, reasons based on stereotypes have not convinced tribunals that a decision or rule is reasonable. An early example of such a case is *Shack v. London Drive-Ur-Self.*[126] In *Shack*, the complainant had been denied employment partly due to the employer's belief that a woman would be unable to lift heavy truck equipment, and partly due to his concern about a woman employee being left in the office alone from time to time. In finding for the complainant, Chairman Lederman relied on American cases[127] arising from section 703 of the *Equal Employment Opportunity Act* of 1972.[128] In commenting on the employer's reasons, Professor Lederman quoted from a decision of a United States Court of Appeal:[129]

Title 7 rejects just this type of romantic paternalism as unduly Victorian and instead vests individual women with the power to decide whether or not to take on unromantic

---

125. (1991), 14 C.H.R.R. D/138 at D/142.
126. (1974), unreported (Ont. Bd. of Inquiry).
127. *Weeks v. Southern Bell Telephone & Telegraph Co.*, 408 F. 2d 228 (1969); *Diaz v. Pan Am World Airways Inc.*, 442 F. 2d 385 (1971), *cert.* den. 404 U.S. 950 (1971); *Phillips v. Martin Marietta Corp.*, 400 U.S. 542 (1970).
128. That section's exemption provision reads, in part, "Notwithstanding any other provision of this sub-chapter , it shall not be an unlawful employment practice for an employer to hire and employ employees . . . where . . . sex . . . is a *bona fide* occupational qualification reasonably necessary to the normal operation of that particular business or enterprise."
129. *Weeks, ante,* note 127, at 236.

tasks. Men have always had the right to determine whether the incremental increase in remuneration for strenuous, dangerous, obnoxious, boring or unromantic tasks is worth the candle. The promise of Title 7 is that women are now to be on equal footing. We cannot conclude that by including the *bona fide* occupational qualification exception Congress intended to renege on that promise.

Since the *Shack* decision, several more boards of inquiry have rejected an employer's automatic assumption as to the suitability of women employees for heavy, dirty or dangerous work, or men for delicate work.[130]

In *Niedzwieki v. Beneficial Insurance System*,[131] an employer's decision, based on an interested assumption that a married woman would be unwilling to transfer to another office was ruled discriminatory.

In regard to age, the employer's view that firefighting is "a young man's game" was held insufficient to support mandatory retirement at age 60 in *Ontario (Human Rights Commission) v. Etobicoke*.[132]

Business Reasons

Influenced by United States case law (discussed below), Ontario boards of inquiry early raised the issue of nexus between an impugned decision and the requirements of the job.

In a number of early decisions, employers concerned with establishing

---

130. See, *Hartling v. Timmins (Municipality) Commissioners of Police* (1981), 2 C.H.R.R. D/487 (Ont. Bd. of Inquiry); *Cinkus v. Diamond Restaurant & Tavern,* (1980), 2 C.H.R.R. D/339 (Ont. Bd. of Inquiry); *Robertson v. Metro. Investigation Security Ltd.* (1979), unreported (Ont. Bd. of Inquiry); *Bruton v. M.H.G. International Ltd.* (1982), 4 C.H.R.R. D/1173 (Ont. Bd. of Inquiry); *Boyd v. Mar-Su Interior Decorators* (1978), unreported (Ont. Bd. of Inquiry); *Shack v. London Drive-Ur-Self* (1974), unreported (Ont. Bd. of Inquiry) (concern by an employer that a female employee might be alone in office late at night not barring employee from deciding for herself whether she wished to run that risk); *Segrave v. Zeller's* (1975), unreported (Ont. Bd. of Inquiry); *Imberto v. Vic & Tony Coiffure* (1981), 2 C.H.R.R. D/392 (Ont. Bd. of Inquiry) (board rejecting notion that man should not be hired because women employees or customers might feel uncomfortable in his presence); *Boyd v. Mar-Su Interior Decorators* (1978), unreported (Ont. Bd. of Inquiry) (insubstantial assumptions that men cannot do delicate work rejected along with notion that dirty or dangerous work is not for women); see *Robertson v. Metro. Investigation Security Ltd.* (1979), unreported (Ont. Bd. of Inquiry); *Adler v. Metro. Torotno Bd. of Commrs. of Police* (1979), unreported (Ont. Bd. of Inquiry); *Hartling v. Timmins (Municipality Commissioners of Police)* (1981), 2 C.H.R.R. D/487 (Ont. Bd. of Inquiry); *Cinkus v. Diamond Restaurant & Tavern* (1980), 2 C.H.R.R. D/339 (Ont. Bd. of Inquiry); *Bulger v. Branch No. 4, Royal Cdn. Legion* (1978), unreported (N.B. Bd. of Inquiry); *Stairs v. Maritimes Co-op. Services* (1975), unreported (N.B. Bd. of Inquiry); *Fortey v. Middlesex Creamery Ltd.,* (court dealing with assumption that male spouse should always be sole or major breadwinner).

131. (1982), 3 C.H.R.R. D/1004 (Ont. Bd. of Inquiry); see also *Broere v. W.P. London and Assoc.* (1987), 87 C.L.L.C. 17,026 (Ont. Bd. of Inquiry).

132. *Ante*, note 22; see also remarks of the board in *Hawkes v. Brown's Iron Works* (1977), unreported (Ont. Bd. of Inquiry).

bona fide occupational qualifications raised views attributed both to themselves and customers that, for example, women should not be employed as serving staff in the more elegant restaurants, or that a man does not have the requisite "care, taste and delicacy" to install drapes.[133] These beliefs, no matter how honestly held, have not sufficed to support an exception.

A landlord's assertion that he or she would not employ[134] people of a particular group because the other tenants might not like it has been declared unacceptable by Ontario boards.

Another variation on the theme of discrimination because others discriminate is that of an employer claiming that customers and/or other employees would object to the employment of a person of a particular sex. One of the earliest of these cases was one in which a man was refused employment in personnel management because the personnel he would be managing were women, and "a female [sic] would not come to a male personnel manager with personal problems."[135] Another case involved the owners of a hairdressing salon who refused to hire a male hairdresser because they believed that both staff and customers would dislike having a male hairdresser around.[136] In neither of these cases did the board accept the respondent's reviews as reasonable.

Parenthetically, recent cases involving different uniform or dress requirements for male and female employees may be seen as the latest in the line of differences made on the basis of sex due to perceived customer preferences. To date boards of inquiry have not dealt with these cases in the context of the "reasonable and *bona fide*" defence, as there has been considerable difficulty to date in establishing such differentiations as discrimination, for others.[137]

One area of "customer preference" presents some complicated issues that may take time to resolve. That area is the matter of privacy which arises in hospitals and prisons and results in attempts to restrict the hiring of nurses, attendants and guards by sex.

No Ontario board has yet grappled with this issue. In the United States, in cases involving prison guards, such as *Dothard v. Rawlinson*,[138] there has been a much criticized emphasis on safety issues (such as women

---

133. See *Dubniczky v. J.L.K. Kiriakopoulos Co.* (1981), 2 C.H.R.R. D/485 (Ont. Bd. of Inquiry); and *Boyd v. Mar-Su Interior Decorators* (1978), unreported (Ont. Bd. of Inquiry).
134. *Cooper v. Belmont Property Management* (1973), unreported (Ont. Bd. of Inquiry).
135. *Segrave v. Zeller's* (1975), unreported (Ont. Bd. of Inquiry).
136. *Imberto v. Vic & Tony Coiffure* (1981), 2 C.H.R.R. D/392 (Ont. Bd. of Inquiry). See also *Singh v. Security & Investigation Services Ltd.* (1977), unreported (Ont. Bd. of Inquiry), in regard to customers' dress preferences.
137. See discussion under "sex discrimination," Chapter 3.
138. 433 U.S. 321 (1977).

guards being unable to maintain control among male prisoners) which is debatable on the facts and impugns the ability of women to perform a particular job. Much more difficult to criticize is the approach taken by recent Canadian boards of inquiry. In *McKale v. Lamont Auxiliary Hospital*,[139] the board, upheld on appeal by the Alberta Court of Queen's Bench, ruled that an employer had brought sufficient evidence to establish a *bona fide* occupational qualification to justify the hiring of a male nursing assistant, by adducing evidence as to the privacy and dignity concerns of male patients concerning intimate care. The same approach was taken in *Stanley v. Royal Canadian Mounted Police*[140] in regard to the hiring of male guards to supervise male prisoners in a lock-up.

Obviously, in such cases, a careful balancing of interests is called for, a thorough review of the actual requirements of particular jobs must be made, and exclusions should be as limited as is consistent with privacy and dignity interests. Boards should be wary of any attempt to disguise concern as to capability with insubstantial "privacy and dignity" concerns.

Efficiency and Safety

Clearly, there are interests to be balanced where the accusation of a discriminatory practice would seriously threaten the operation or the safe operation of a business. Early U.S. case law addressed this point.

Weeks v. Southern Bell Telephone & Telegraph Co.,[141] a leading U.S. case referred to in a number of boards of inquiry, was the first confirmation by the U.S. Supreme Court that "bfoq" was to be interpreted very narrowly, and linked to ability to perform the job.

Weeks concerned the refusal of Southern Bell to consider women as applicants for the position of switchmen. Southern Bell had based its restriction on state labour code rules that had been repealed before Weeks's application. Since the issue of protective legislation had been done away with, Southern Bell relied on the exemption to the United States *Civil Rights Act* of 1964 provided by section 703(*e*)(1), which states that:

> it shall not be an unlawful employment practice for an employer to hire and employ employees . . . on the basis of . . . sex . . . in those certain instances where . . . sex . . . is a *bona fide* occupational qualification reasonably necessary to the normal operation of that particular business or enterprise.

Southern Bell succeeded at trial, but the trial court's decision was reversed by a court of appeal decision. The appeal court held that:[142]

---

139. [1987] 3 W.W.R. 748 (Alta. Q.B.).
140. (1987), 8 C.H.R.R. D/3799 (Cdn. Human Rights Trib.).
141. 408 F. 2d 228 (1969).
142. *Ibid.*, at 235.

in order to rely on the *bona fide* occupational qualification exception an employer has the burden of proving that he had reasonable cause to believe, that is, a factual basis for believing, that all or substantially all women would be unable to perform safely and efficiently the duties of the job involved.

The court held that Southern Bell's argument must fail because it had introduced no evidence as to the ability of women to accomplish the tasks in question.

A further development of the doctrine of business necessity was found in *Diaz v. Pan Am World Airways.*[143] In that case, a United States Court of Appeals considered the issue of when customer preference might properly be taken into account as a basis for imposing a rule that certain types of jobs be open to female applicants only. The plaintiff, a man, had applied for a job as a flight attendant. The defendant sought to bring its restrictions of applications under section 703(*e*) of the 1964 *Civil Rights Act.* Pan Am brought forward considerable empirical evidence at trial, including the testimony of a psychiatrist as to passengers' psychological needs, to show that female flight attendants tended to be superior in the performance of "non-mechanical tasks" to male attendants, and that passengers preferred to deal with women attendants.[144]

The "*bona fide* occupational qualification" defence succeeded at trial, but *Diaz* was reversed on appeal. The court of appeals prefaced its decision by noting the remedial purpose of the legislation, and concluding that exceptions must be narrowly construed. The court first considered whether "non-mechanical" flight attendant tasks were reasonably necessary to the normal operation of the business, and concluded that they were not.[145] The court held that, even if Pan Am had established that all or substantially all male applicants were inferior to female applicants in certain tasks, it could not impose a qualification as to sex where those tasks were not essential.

As to the customer preference, the court found that it might be taken into account "only when it is based on the company's inability to perform the primary function or service it offers."[146] Even in those cases, the *Diaz* decision suggests that customer preference might be taken into account only when:

1. it could be established that all, or substantially all of the class in question could not perform the job adequately (the *Weeks* test), and

2. it was impracticable to develop a screening system to identify those members of the class who could perform adequately, and

---

143. 442 F. 2d 385 (1971), *cert.* den. 404 U.S. 950 (1971).
144. 311 F. Supp. 559, reversed, note 143.
145. "The primary function of an airline is to transport passengers safely from one point to another." 442 F. 2d at 388.
146. *Ibid.*, at 389.

3. the customer preference is based on an informed judgment rather than mere stereotyped thinking.

Group Standard v. Individual Assessment: Safety

It is probably fair to say that *Weeks, Diaz* and similar cases underlined the necessity, in cases where an employer wished to impose a sex-based requirement, that the employer adduce clear and convincing evidence that all or substantially all members of that sex are unable to perform the job. Otherwise the employee must confine him – or herself to job-related requirements, which tend to require individual testing on other means to ensure that the candidate can perform the job. It was inevitable that employers would object to such a requirement where safety was concerned, particularly in cases in which it is difficult or impossible to devise a surrogate for on-the-job testing of individual ability. This appears to be one of the reasons for the much-criticized decision of the U.S. Supreme Court in the case *Dothard v. Rawlinson*,[147] in which the court upheld regulations excluding women as guards in men's prisons.

Safety was also at issue in *Hodgeson v. Greyhound Lines Inc.*[148] In that case, the respondent bus line had imposed a maximum hiring age of 35 years. In support of this restriction, Greyhound argued that new drivers, because of lack of seniority, had little choice of routes and would therefore be assigned primarily to the more arduous strips. Greyhound also adduced evidence as to the nature of the work on those trips, empirical evidence as to physical degeneration beginning in the late thirties, and statistical evidence as to a correlation between accident rates and the more arduous routes. Greyhound also produced evidence as to the lack of reliability of available medical technology in detecting degenerative changes.

Considering this evidence, the court in *Hodgeson* supported Greyhound's requirement as a *bona fide* occupational qualification:

> (A) public transportation carrier, such as Greyhound, entrusted with the lives and well-being of passengers, must continually strive to employ the most highly qualified persons available for the position of inter-city bus driver for the paramount goal of a bus driver is safety. Due to such compelling concerns for safety, it is not necessary that Greyhound show that all or substantially all bus driver applications over forty could not perform safely. Greyhound need only demonstrate, however, a minimal increase in harm for it is enough to show that elimination of the hiring policy might jeopardize the life of one more person than might otherwise occur under the present hiring practice.[149]

Shortly after *Hodgeson* a competing view was expressed in *Usery v. Tamiami Trail Tours Inc.*[150]

---

147. *Ante*, note 138; see discussion in *Discrimination and the Law* p. 8-62-63.
148. 499 F. 2d 859 (1974), *cert.* den 419 U.S. 1112 (1975).
149. *Ante*, at 863.
150. (1976), 531 F. 2d 224 (U.S.C.A. 5th).

In *Tamiami*, a tour operator sought to defend a minimum age for hiring bus drivers. The rationale for the practice was that seniority rules in the workplace had the effect of requiring new employees to spend approximately ten years on "extra board" service, which meant that they would be on 24-hour call and would frequently be required to go, on short notice, on early morning inter-city runs.

The employer took the view that such service was particularly demanding and better done by younger employees. The hiring practice was defended on the basis of public safety concerns with respect to the performance of drivers over forty during their first ten years of service.

The District Court and Court of Appeal accepted the employer's position that older bus drivers could compensate for their decline in physical attributes as they aged by choosing day shifts and shorter routes, and that there were no available tests that could accurately identify those drivers not yet affected by age-related, accident-causing impairments such as loss of stamina. In doing so, the Court of Appeal found that the employer "had reasonable cause, that is, a factual basis, for believing that all or substantially all persons over 40 would be unable to perform safely and efficiently the duties of the job involved, or whether it is impossible *or* impractical to deal with persons over forty on an individualized basis."[151]

More recently, in *Western Airlines v. Criswell*,[152] a 1985 case involving pilots denied reassignments as flight engineers at the age of 60, the United States Supreme Court adopted the *Tamiami* standard as the appropriate standard for assessing a *"bona fide"* occupational qualification.

In Ontario, the leading case on age limits as a reasonable qualification in employment, and the first Supreme Court of Canada case to deal with the nexus between the impugned requirement and ability to do the job, was *Ontario (Human Rights Commission) v. Etobicoke (Borough)*.[153] This case concerned the complaint of two firefighters who had been compulsorily retired at age 60. The Divisional Court and Court of Appeal of Ontario had overturned a board of inquiry's finding that opinion evidence, tendered by officers of the employer and the union, to the effect that firefighting was a "young man's game" was insufficient to establish that early retirement was a *bona fide* requirement. The Supreme Court of Canada restored the decision of the board that the rights of the complainants had been infringed.

Mr. Justice McIntyre, for a unanimous court, prefaced his decision with an acknowledgment that "under the *Code* non-discrimination is the rule of general application and discrimination, where permitted, is the exception."[154]

---

151. *Ibid.*, p. 236.
152. 105 S. Ct. 2743 (1985).
153. (1982), 132 D.L.R. (3d) 14 (S.C.C.).
154. *Ibid.*, at 19.

He followed this assertion with some general remarks as to the nature of a *bona fide* occupational qualification:

> To be a *bona fide* occupational qualification and requirement a limitation, such as mandatory retirement at a fixed age, must be imposed honestly, in good faith, and in the sincerely held belief that such limitation is imposed in the interests of the adequate performance of the work involved with all reasonable dispatch, safety and economy, and not for ulterior or extraneous reasons aimed at objectives which could defeat the purpose of the *Code.* In addition it must be related in an objective sense to the performance of the employment concerned, in that it is reasonably necessary to assure the efficient and economical performance of the job without endangering the employee, his fellow employees and the general public.[155]

He then proceeded to differentiate between situations in which the main concern is productivity, and those in which public safety is at issue:

> In cases where concern for the employee's capacity is largely economic, that is where the employer's concern is one of productivity, and the circumstances of employment require no special skills that may diminish significantly with aging, or involve any unusual dangers to employees or the pubic that may be compounded by aging, it may be difficult, if not impossible, to demonstrate that a mandatory retirement at a fixed age, without regard to individual capacity, may be validly imposed under the *Code.* In such employment, as capacity fails, and as such failure becomes evident, individuals may be discharged or retired for cause.
>
> Faced with the uncertainty of the aging process an employer has, it seems to me, two alternatives. He may establish a retirement age at 65 or over, in which case he would escape the charge of discrimination on the basis of age under the *Code.* On the other hand, he may, in certain types of employment, particularly in those affecting public safety such as that of airline pilots, train and bus drivers, police and firemen, consider the risk of unpredictable individual human failure involved in continuing all employees to age 65 may be such that an arbitrary retirement age be justified for application to all employees. In the case at bar it may be said that the employment falls into the category. While it is no doubt true that some below the age of 60 may become unfit for fire-fighting and many above that age may remain fit, recognition of this proposition affords no assistance in resolving the second question. In an occupation where, as in the case at bar, the employer seeks to justify the retirement in the interests of public safety, to decide whether a *bona fide* occupational qualification and requirement has been shown the board of inquiry and the court must consider whether the evidence adduced justifies the conclusion that there is sufficient risk of employee failure in those over the mandatory retirement age to warrant the early retirement in the interests of safety of the employee, his fellow employees and the public at large."[156]

McIntyre J. went on to find that the "impressionistic" evidence adduced before the board was insufficient. While he declined to lay down a rule that "scientific" evidence would be necessary in all cases, or, indeed, "any fixed rule" covering the nature and sufficiency of the evidence required to justify a mandatory retirement, he suggested:

---

155. *Ibid.*, at 19-20.
156. *Ibid.*, at pp. 20-21.

> It would seem that evidence as to the duties to be performed and the relationship between the aging process and the safe, efficient performance of those duties would be imperative. Many factors would be involved and it would seem to be essential that the evidence should cover the detailed nature of the duties to be performed, the conditions existing in the work place, and the effect of such conditions upon employees, particularly upon those at or near the retirement age sought to be supported.[157]

Boards of inquiry subsequent to *Etobicoke* that have dealt age categories and safety issues have, for the most part, declined to read McIntyre J.'s remarks concerning "sufficient risk" as importing the test used in *Hodgeson*. Tribunals under the federal *Human Rights Act* have followed the *Tamiami* test in declining to support a hiring policy for pilots because the airline company had not established that all or substantially all persons hired over the age of 27 would not be able to perform pilot duties safely, or that individual testing would be impracticable,[158] and in confirming that a bus company had to establish a maximum hiring age of 35 as a *bona fide* occupational qualification.[159]

The most recent Ontario board to deal with the issue of group standards as opposed to individual testing where safety is an issue was *Hope v. St. Catherine's (City)*.[160] In that case a policy of mandatory retirement for firefighters was unsuccessfully challenged. In *Hope*, Chairman McCamus stressed that there exists first of all an obligation to establish the need for age-based employment restrictions as objectively reasonable grounds. Once that test has been met, and

> the employer's qualifications are established as being appropriate in light of public safety concerns, the analysis then turns to the second issue, that is whether a mandatory retirement scheme is a defensible means of achieving the objective of ensuring that employees have this qualification. In *Criswell*, the Supreme Court adopted the view that the mandatory retirement age would be defensible if either "all or substantially all" employees no longer possessed the qualifications at the age in question or, alternatively, even if this were not the case, it would be "impossible or highly impractical" to identify the deficient employees through other means. The second branch of the test would be satisfied, presumably, by demonstrating that there was no feasible means of testing employees on an individual basis for the attributes in question.
>
> I find this to be an illuminating analysis of the factors that would lead one to conclude that a particular mandatory retirement age was or was not a bfoq. Assuming that the qualifications insisted upon by the employer were reasonable in the light of public safety concerns, the question surely is simply whether age alone is a satisfactory proxy for determining the absence of the attribute (as it would be if "all or substantially all" of the employees at this age lack the attribute in question) and, if not, whether there is some satisfactory means of identifying the deficient employees. If there is no such

---

157. *Ibid.*, at p. 22.
158. *Carson v. Air Canada* (1984), 5 C.H.R.R. D/1857 (Cdn. Rev. Trib.), affirmed (1985), 5 C.H.R.R. D/2848 (Fed. C.A.).
159. *McCreary v. Greyhound Lines of Canada Ltd.* (1986), 7 C.H.R.R. D/3250 (Cdn. Human Rights Trib.), affirmed (1987), 8 C.H.R.R. D/4184 (Fed. C.A.).
160. (1986), 9 C.H.R.R. D/4635 (Ont. Bd. of Inquiry).

method, the employer is permitted to fall back on the no less unsatisfactory method of simply having a retirement age. Surely it would not be open to the employer to demonstrate that even though a substantial number of employees are capable of discharging their responsibilities beyond the retirement age and even though there is a satisfactory means of testing the capacities of these employees, the employer chooses not to do so because there is some element of public safety involved. It is this that is precluded by the *Criswell* analysis and it appears to me to be perfectly consistent with the analysis in *Etobicoke* that employers would not be able to defend such an approach under the Ontario *Code*. The preference of the *Code* is for individualized treatment, even in cases of occupations with a public safety dimension, where this is a practical alternative to an arbitrary mandatory retirement age.[161]

However, Chairman McCamus offered one caveat:

Although *Criswell* does suggest that there is a clear bifurcation between the first step in the analysis, within which the public safety element becomes relevant, and the second step in which the particular age qualification is measured against the two prongs of the *Tamiami* test, it may well be that so strict a division is not desirable. Thus, it may well be that in determining whether or not it is "practical" to engage in individualized testing of employee capacities, the accuracy of these tests themselves may become an issue. Indeed, it may be that there are very few contexts within which absolutely accurate testing is possible. In determining whether a particular testing arrangement is satisfactory for the employer's purposes, it may well be appropriate to require a higher level of accuracy in testing where defective performance by an employee creates a substantial risk to public safety. Subject to this one possible gloss, however, I am persuaded that the analysis adopted by the Supreme Court in *Criswell* offers a useful analytical framework within which to apply the test set forth in the *Etobicoke* decision by the Supreme Court of Canada.[162]

In conclusion, Chairman McCamus set out the following guidelines for the interpretation of the "reasonable and *bona fide* occupational qualification" provision of the *Code*:

1. The respondent must satisfy both the subjective and objective branches of the *Etobicoke* test, i.e., that the mandatory retirement is imposed honestly and in good faith and is related in an objective sense to the performance of the employment concerned (in that it is reasonably necessary to assure the efficient and economical performance of the job without endangering the employee, his fellow employees or the general public). (p. 20, D/783)

2. Where, as in the present case, there is a public safety dimension to the occupation, the adjudicator must determine whether there is sufficient risk of employee failure in those over the mandatory retirement age to warrant the early retirement in the interests of safety of the employee, his fellow employees and the public at large. (p. 21, D/784)

3. In making the determination indicated in item 2, it is appropriate to first determine whether the qualification imposed by the employer is reasonably necessary in light of the public safety implications of the occupation in question and secondly, to determine whether all or substantially all of the employees at the mandatory retirement age would not be able to meet the qualification in question or, alternatively, whether the

---

161. *Ante*, p. D/4644.
162. *Ibid.*, at p. D/4645.

qualification is such that it is impossible or impractical to make individualized assessments of employees.

The adjudicator must consider evidence relating to the duties to be performed by the employee, the conditions existing in the workplace and the effect of such conditions upon employees at or near the retirement age sought to be supported. As well, evidence concerning the relationship between the aging process and the safe, efficient performance of the duties would be required and in this regard, "statistical and medical evidence based upon observation and research on the question of aging, if not in all cases absolutely necessary, would certainly be more persuasive" than anecdotal evidence of individuals familiar with the workplace environment in question. (at p. 23, D/784)[163]

In actually applying the test enunciated to the evidence in *Hope*, the board concluded that the respondent had met the obligation of establishing that it would be impractical to undertake individualized testing due to the fact that diagnostic tests suggested as applicable to the situation were unreliable.

Previously in the decision, the board had also found that the respondent had made "rather good progress" toward establishing that "all or substantially all" 60-year-old firefighters do not have the necessary level of physical fitness to properly discharge their responsibilities.

The most recent pronouncement from the Supreme Court of Canada arises from two related Saskatchewan cases, *Day v. Moose Jaw (City)*,[164] and *Craig v. City of Saskatoon*,[165] both of which concerned mandatory retirement of firefighters. In these cases the court upheld the proposition that if individualized testing is feasible, a group standard discriminating rule cannot be maintained as "reasonable and *bona fide*":

While it is not an absolute requirement that employees be individually tested, that employer may not satisfy the burden of proof of establishing the reasonableness of the requirement if he fails to deal satisfactorily with the question as to why it was not possible to deal with employees on an individual basis, by *inter alia*, individual testing. If there is a practical alternative to the adoption of a discriminatory rule, this may lead to a determination that the employer did not act reasonably in not adopting it.[166]

Presumably the ruling of the Supreme Court in the *Craig* and *Day* cases overrules the view expressed in *obiter* in *Hope* to the effect that if an employer can prove that "all or substantially all employees over the mandatory age in question cannot perform the necessary functions of the job, it need not also prove that there is no practical means of measuring on an individual basis, unless the Commission can demonstrate that group assessment is discriminatory to the complainant."[167]

---

163. *Ibid.*, p. D/4645.
164. (1983), 4 C.H.R.R. D/1805 (Sask. Bd. of Inquiry), reversed (1987), 8 C.H.R.R. D/4201 (Sask. C.A.), reversed (1989), 11 C.H.R.R. D/217 (S.C.C.).
165. (1984), 5 C.H.R.R. D/2209 (Sask. Bd. of Inquiry), reversed (1987), 8 C.H.R.R. D/4201 (Sask. C.A.), reversed (1989), 11 C.H.R.R. D/204 (S.C.C.).
166. *Ibid.*, at D/215.
167. *Hope*, note 160 at pp. 87-91.

It should be noted that cases involving age discrimination and individual assessment are closely analogous on their issues to arguments in defense of restrictions based on handicap — see discussion of section 17, earlier in this chapter.

Objectively Verifiable Evidence, Linked to Job Requirements

The Supreme Court of Canada in *Etobicoke* was firm in its rejection of impressionistic evidence; clearly, that case also supports the principle that discriminatory requirements unsupported by objectively verifiable data will be accepted as "reasonable and *bona fide*" only in cases in which public safety might otherwise be jeopardized. Pursuant to the decision in *Craig v. City of Saskatoon*, it is also clear that individual assessment, where possible, is required, and that this route is the alternative available to the employer who lacks objective evidence to support a group standard.

It is also clear that the evidence as to capability must be linked to the actual job. In *Action Travail des Femmes*,[168] the Supreme Court of Canada upheld a board of inquiry which had, *inter alia*, found certain pre-employment tests to be both sex-discriminatory and insufficiently related to actual job requirements. In *Ogelski v. Winnipeg (City)*,[169] a board of inquiry, eventually supported by the Manitoba Queen's Bench and Court of Appeal, rejected the idea that an employer could impose a retirement age of 60 on all ranks of police officers, regardless of the differing requirements of employment at a various ranks.

In respect of record of offences, there is no Ontario authority that deals squarely with when it would be "reasonable and *bona fide*" to discriminate in employment. In *McCartney v. Woodward Stores Ltd.*,[170] a British Columbia board of inquiry set out a three-part test designed to assist in assessing whether a refusal to employ or to continue to employ because of a previous criminal conviction was reasonable:

1. Does the behaviour for which the charge was laid, if repeated, pose any threat to the employer's ability to carry on its business safely and efficiently?
2. What were the circumstances of the charge and the particulars of the offence involved? For example, how old was the individual when the events in question occurred,

---

168. *Action Travail des Femmes v. Canadian National Railway Co.*, [1985] 1 F.C. 96 (Fed. C.A.).

169. (1985), 6 C.H.R.R. D/2664 (Man. Bd. of Adjud.), affirmed (1985), 6 C.H.R.R. D/3079 (Man. Q.B.), affirmed (1986), 7 C.H.R.R. D/3570 (C.A.).

   This approach accorded with that affirmed by Manitoba Court of Appeal in an earlier case, *Finlayson v. Winnipeg Police Department* (1983), 4 C.H.R.R. D/1255 (Man. C.A.) in which compulsory retirement at age sixty was ruled non-discriminatory in the case of staff inspectors, with the *caveat* that the ruling could not be applied in respect of other ranks of police officers.

170. (1982), 3 C.H.R.R. D/113 (B.C. Bd. of Inquiry), affirmed (1983), 4 C.H.R.R. D/1325 (B.C. S.C.).

were there any extenuating circumstances?

3. How much time has elapsed between the charge and the employment decision? What has the individual done during that period of time? Has he shown any tendencies to repeat the kind of behaviour for which he was charged? Has he shown a firm intention to rehabilitate himself?[171]

Economic Justification

There have as yet been no Ontario decisions in which a tribunal has considered the argument that an age-based requirement is necessary for economic reasons.

The decision of the tribunal in *Carson*[172] heard arguments from the airline company as to the costs of the lengthy training period for pilots vis-a-vis the trained pilots' expected number of years of active service. The tribunal accepted that economics might form the basis for a *bona fide* occupational qualification, but stressed that economic considerations must be "serious," and rejected such factors as customer preference. The tribunal rejected the airline's claim because it had failed to prove that its hiring costs justified the impugned age limitation, or that it needed the limitation so that employees could progress through the ranks to the most senior position.[173]

Duty to Accommodate and the "Reasonable and Bona Fide" Defence

In a number of cases, tribunals have acknowledged the existence of a *bona fide* occupational requirement, but have gone on to impose on the employer a duty to accommodate the individual complainant, short of undue hardship to the employer.[174] However, in *Bhinder v. CNR*,[175] the Supreme Court of Canada, considering provisions of the federal *Human Rights Act*, ruled that there is no duty to accommodate once a *bona fide* occupational qualification is proven to exist.

Due to the statutory amendments to sections 11 and 17 of the Ontario

---

171. *McCartney* was relied on in *Iwanchuk v. British Columbia (Ministry of Human Resources)* (1987), 9 C.H.R.R. D/4670 (B.C. Human Rights Council); *Griffiths v. Coquitlam* (1988), 10 C.H.R.R. D/5852 (B.C. Human Rights Council); *Salter v. Peace River South School (District)* (1989), 10 C.H.R.R. D/6150 (B.C. Human Rights Council); *Thompson v. Granny's Fried Chicken Ltd.* (1989), 11 C.H.R.R. D/477 (B.C. Human Rights Council).

172. *Carson v. Air Canada* (1985), 6 C.H.R.R. D/2848 (Fed. C.A.).

173. Professor Pentney in *Discrimination and the Law in Canada*, has suggested that economic considerations are relevant to the reasonable and *bona fide* determination only if there is a duty to accommodate, but see remarks on the topic later in this chapter.

174. This has occurred seemingly exclusively in cases of constructive discrimination; see, for example, *Singh v. Security & Investigation Services* (1977), unreported (Ont. Bd. of Inquiry); *Adler v. Metropolitan Toronto Board of Commissioners of Police* (1979), unreported (Ont. Bd. of Inquiry).

175. (1985), 63 N.R. 185 (S.C.C.).

Code, the *Bhinder* decision will not affect the duty to accommodate in constructive discrimination and discrimination because of handicap, arguably the cases in which duty to accommodate is most needed. However, if the effect of *Bhinder* is as described by most analysts,[176] the duty to accommodate will not attach to employers who establish a "reasonable and *bona fide*" defence pursuant to provisions of other sections of the *Code*.

EXCEPTIONS IN REGARD TO SPECIFIC EMPLOYMENT SITUATIONS: SECTIONS 24(1)(*c*) AND (*d*)

Section 24(1)(*c*) is all that is left of a former blanket exemption[177] that effectively denied the protection of the *Human Rights Code* to people in domestic employment. This exemption has now been replaced by one limited to situations in which "the primary duty of employment is attending to the medical or personal needs of [the employer] or of an ill child or an aged, infirm or ill spouse or other relative of [the employer]." An appropriately narrow construction of this clause would confine the type of employment qualifying for this exemption to such occupations as nurse or personal attendant.

It should be noted that the employer addressed by section 24(1)(*c*) is an "individual person," not an agency. The effect of this subsection, combined with section 23(4), which forbids discriminatory referrals by employment agencies, it would appear to be that even when an employer has enlisted the aid of an agency in his or her attempt to find a personal attendant, any screening must be done by the employer. This obviously poses a problem for the agency, which will be caught between the provisions of the *Code* and the demands of the employer who wants a preliminary weeding out of applicants. The agency may also have to deal with disgruntled applicants who go to the trouble of attending an interview when there is no chance that they will be hired. On the other hand, there would seem to be nothing in the *Code* to prohibit the agency from warning the applicant as to the employer's probable requirements, as long as this is in the nature of a warning rather than a refusal to arrange the interview.

It would also appear that an employer who wishes to impose such restrictions as are contemplated by section 24(1)(*c*) will be unable to advertise such restrictions without running afoul of section 23(1).[178]

The effect of these legislatively-imposed inconveniences is not incongruent with the overall purpose of the *Code*. It is possible that an employer who is limited to the personal interview as a means of screening on prohibited grounds may be willing to drop a discrimination requirement on actu-

---

176. See detailed discussion by Professor Pentney, *ante*, note 173.
177. See s. 4(8) of the predecessor *Code*.
178. See the discussion of this point in Chapter 5.

ally meeting the applicant. The necessity of a personal interview may encourage assessment of individuals, as opposed to pre-judgment based on the individual's membership in a group.

A final note on the "personal attendant" subsection is that, given that only refusal to employ is allowed, harassment is prohibited in the type of employment contemplated by section 24(1)(c), as well as in other types of employment.

To date, no board decisions have discussed subsection 24(1)(c).

Section 24(1)(d) is the section that excepts both the "family firm" and anti-nepotism rules. The section protects the employer who "grants or withholds employment or advancement in employment to a person who is the spouse, child or parent of the employer or an employee." Thus, where the employer wishes to favour his or her spouse,[179] child or parent, or the spouse, child or parent of an employee, the relative can be hired in preference to another applicant, or promoted in preference to another equally qualified employee. It remains to be seen whether "advancement" in employment would be confined to promotion, or whether the employer would be justified in merely paying the relative more for performing the same job as other workers. It is debatable whether an employer's practice of allowing different terms and conditions of employment, such as longer lunches, etc., to a relative who is otherwise doing the same job as other employees would constitute the granting of advancement.

Section 24(1)(d) speaks only of *withholding* employment or advancement, rather than terminating employment, withholding further employment, or demoting. Thus, it would seem that the exception does not apply to action taken against someone who is already an employee, for example, where two employees marry or when the relationship only becomes known to the employer after hiring the spouse, child or parent. However, this is not to say that an employer may not take such action in certain situations where a "spousal" relationship is at issue; section 24(1)(b) states that discrimination in employment on the ground of marital status[180] is permissible where reasonable and *bona fide*.

Only one board of inquiry decision to date has been concerned with subsection 24(1)(d). In *Szabo v. Atlas Employees Welland Credit Union*,[181] a credit union refused to hire as an officer the son of one of its supervisory

---

179. Spouse is defined, in s. 10, as "the person to whom a person of the opposite sex is married or with whom the person is living in a conjugal relationship outside marriage."

180. Marital status is defined by s. 10 as "the status of being married, single, widowed, divorced or separated and includes the status of living with a person of the opposite sex in a conjugal relationship outside marriage." The term "spouse" is somewhat narrower (see note 179), and would definitely fit within the scope of marital status. Employment decisions made because of an employee's marriage are discussed in Chapter 3.

181. (1988), 9 C.H.R.R. D/4375 (Ont. Bd. of Inquiry).

committee members. The board decided on the facts that a member of the supervisory committee was neither the employer nor the employee of the respondent and that therefore subsection 24(1)(*d*) was unavailable as a defence.

EMPLOYEE PENSION, DISABILITY INSURANCE PLANS: SECTION 25

Special exempting provisions are made for employee pension or superannuation funds and benefit or insurance plans. The employer may not deny employment because a prospective employee does not qualify for such a plan, nor may he or she make employment conditional on the applicant qualifying.[182] However, depending on the type of plan, exemptions are allowed by sections 25(2) and (3) for discriminatory conditions based on various grounds. The exemptions relating to each plan will be briefly examined in turn.

Employee Superannuation or Pension Funds, or Employment Group Insurance Plans: Section 25(2)

Superannuation or pension funds and employee group insurance plans may have discriminatory conditions based on age, sex, marital status or family status without offending the *Code*, as long as they are in compliance with the *Employment Standards Act* and its regulations. The relevant provision of the *Employment Standards Act*[183] is section 33, which identifies the plans affected as follows:

33.(1) This Part applies to a fund, plan or arrangement provided, furnished or offered or to be provided, furnished or offered by an employer to the employees,

(*a*) under a term or condition of employment; or

(*b*) in which an employee may elect to participate or not and to which the employer contributes or does not contribute,

that directly or indirectly provides benefits to the employees, their beneficiaries, survivors or dependents, whether payable periodically or not, for superannuation, retirement, unemployment, income replacement, death, disability, sickness, accident, or medical, hospital, nursing or dental expenses, or other similar benefits or benefits under a deferred profit sharing plan in which employees participate in profits of the employer where the profits accumulated under the plan are permitted to be withdrawn or distributed upon death or retirement or upon contingencies other than death or retirement.

The Act goes on, in section 33(2), to forbid an employer or anyone acting on the employer's behalf to offer any plan that "differentiates or makes any distinction, exclusion or preference between employees or a class or classes of employees or their beneficiaries, survivors or dependents

---

182. See s. 25(1).
183. R.S.O. 1990, c. E.14.

because of the age, sex or marital status of the employees," except as provided in the regulations.

The regulation in question is Ontario Regulation 282,[184] which defines age as "any age of eighteen years or more and less than sixty-five years." It defines sex in the following unusual way:[185]

> (*l*) "sex" includes a distinction between employees in a plan, fund or arrangement provided, furnished or offered by an employer to his employees that excludes an employee from a benefit thereunder or gives an employee a preference to a benefit thereunder because the employee is or is not a head of household, principal or primary wage earner or other similar condition, and further includes a distinction between employees in such a plan, fund or arrangement because of the pregnancy of a female employee.

Marital status is defined as follows:[186]

> (*i*) "marital status" includes the condition of being an unmarried person who is supporting in whole or in part a dependent child or children, and includes a "common law" status of husband and wife as defined in the pension, life insurance, disability insurance or benefit, or health insurance or benefit plan, fund or arrangement provided, furnished or offered by an employer to an employee.

The regulation goes on to provide a lengthy list[187] of situations in which the differentiations, qualifications or exclusions defined above shall not be held to breach section 33(2) of the *Employment Standards Act*. Some involve straight exemptions;[188] others provide an exemption as long as the differentiation, exclusion or qualification has been "determined upon an actuarial basis." Actuarial basis is defined as follows:[189]

> (*a*) "actuarial basis" means the assumptions and methods generally accepted and used by a Fellow of the Canadian Institute of Actuaries to establish the costs of pension benefits, life insurance, disability insurance, health insurance or any other similar benefits including the actuarial equivalents of such benefits which costs depend upon the contingencies of human life, such as death, accident, sickness and disease.

The probable combined effect of the wording of section 25(2) of the *Code*, and the provisions under the *Employment Standards Act* and Regulation 282 is that there is no need for a respondent to prove that the criteria used by an insurance company to generate its actuarial tables were reasonable.[190] The *Code* therefore appears to impose no changes on the *status quo* in employment benefit plans.

---

184. R.R.O. 1980, Reg. 282, s. 1(*b*). These provisions were affected by 1988 amendments to the Regulation (O. Reg. 443/88). *Inter alia* the amendments removed a reference to the cessation of surviving-spouse benefits on remarriage.
185. *Ibid.*, s. 1(*l*).
186. *Ibid.*, s. 1(*i*).
187. *Ibid.*, ss. 3-9, as amended.
188. *Ibid.*, ss. 3(*a*) to (*c*), 4(*a*) to (*f*), 6(*a*) to (*c*), 8(*c*), and 9(*c*) and (*d*).
189. *Ibid.*, s. 1(*a*).
190. Except insofar as required by the stipulation that they be "generally accepted and used by a Fellow of the Canadian Institute of Actuaries," etc.

Regulation 282 as amended also refers to the *Pension Benefits Act*,[191] provisions of which are deemed by Regulation to constitute further qualification of s. 33(2) of the *Employment Standards Act*.

Given the breadth of the exemption provided by Regulation 282, the two restrictions on discrimination imposed therein bear mentioning. Unless the employer has denied employment because the applicant does not qualify, or made employment conditional on the applicant qualifying for the plan, these would seem to provide the only grounds for complaint under section 25(2) of the *Code*:

1. Where a plan[192] to which Part X applies allows an employee on leave of absence to continue to participate, an employee whose leave of absence is due to pregnancy may not be excluded from that privilege.[193]

2. An exclusion that was valid before section 33 of the *Employment Standards Act* came into effect may not be maintained past the date on which the plan in question became subject to section 33.[194]

Employee Disability Plans or Benefits; Employee Life Insurance Plans or Benefits: Section 25(3)(*a*)

Employee disability or life insurance plans or benefits may contain "a reasonable and *bona fide* distinction, exclusion or preference" on the ground of a "pre-existing handicap that substantially increases the risk." It is worth stressing that the types of plan included under section 25(3)(*a*) must meet a two-part test in order to qualify for the exemption. The differentiation must be because of a pre-existing handicap that substantially increases the risk and it must be reasonable and *bona fide*. It is suggested that the effect of the latter part of the test will be that distinctions, exclusions or preferences will be disallowed where unsupported by acceptable evidence as to risk, and that the evidence adduced to support any such assumptions must be objectively reasonable.

The Saskatchewan Human Rights Commission, in its 1981 report,[195] mentioned several practices that are unlikely to meet this test:[196]

> The Manitoba Human Rights Commission recently settled a complaint in which a blind person alleged that he was refused coverage under an accidental death and dis-

---

191. R.S.O. 1990, c. P.8. Provisions of particular interest in this context include s. 47, which deals with the remarriage of a surviving spouse, s. 49, which allows for variations of payments in respect of disabled persons, and s. 52, which deals with sex discrimination.

192. "Plan" will hereafter be used to denote "superannuation or pension fund or employee insurance plan."

193. R.R.O. 1980, Reg. 282, s. 10.

194. *Ibid.*, s. 11.

195. *Human Rights and Benefits in the '80's* (1981).

196. *Ibid.*, pp. 35-6.

memberment plan. The investigation revealed that all blind persons were excluded from coverage on the assumption that blind persons as a group represent a higher risk under such policies. The Manitoba Commission found that there was no evidence to support this assumption.

The Alberta Human Rights Commission also reports that a member of the Alberta Commission "has on several occasions effectively been denied life insurance coverage by prohibitively high rates only because he does not have the use of his legs, notwithstanding the fact that there is no valid evidence which indicates his life expectancy is shorter because of his disability."

Additionally, the Alberta Commission reports that it "has been approached by two persons suffering from epilepsy who were denied life insurance coverage through their employment groups, again notwithstanding the fact that there is no valid evidence indicating epilepsy shortens life expectancy."

In discussing these practices, the Commission acknowledged "the pervasiveness of the notions that persons with physical disabilities are, by definition, ill, more likely to be ill, more likely to die early," but concluded that "no such simple equation can or should be made. The condition of each person's health is individual and the presence or absence of a specific disability may or may not affect an individual's health.[197]

Employee-Pay-All Benefits in Pension Funds or Insurance Plans; Plans Offered by Employers with Fewer than Twenty-five Employees: Section 25(3)(*b*)

In respect of employee- or participant-pay-all benefits in an employee benefit, pension or superannuation fund, and employee insurance plans or policies as well as plans, funds or policies offered by employers employing fewer than twenty-five persons, a distinction, exclusion or preference may be made on the ground of a pre-existing handicap. Unlike section 25(3)(*a*), there is no requirement that the handicap "substantially increase the risk." However, the differentiation must be reasonable and *bona fide*; therefore the remarks made above apply here.

The most recent case in which the Supreme Court of Canada reviewed a benefit plan in the light of human rights legislation was *Brooks v. Canada Safeway Ltd.*[198] In that case, the Court found that a benefit plan that denied pregnant employees disability benefits during a 17-week period contravened Manitoba's *Human Rights Act*. At the relevant time, the Manitoba legislation had no exempting provisions similar to s. 25; however, the decision is interesting in that it once again demonstrates the purposive approach taken by the Supreme Court to human rights legislation.

To date, there have been no published Ontario board decisions that have dealt with benefit plans. A number of issues involving discrimination

---

197. *Ibid.*, p. 37.
198. (1989) 10 C.H.R.R. D/6183 (S.C.C.).

on the grounds of sex, age, sexual orientation and handicap remain to be litigated, and these cases will inevitably involve challenges to the relevant legislative provisions under the *Canadian Charter of Rights and Freedoms.*

7

HARASSMENT AND SEXUAL HARASSMENT

HARASSMENT, SEXUAL SOLICITATION, REPRISAL

The *Code*'s provisions dealing with harassment addresses two different manifestations of discrimination. The first is "vexatious comments or conduct" directed at a person because of his or her race, ancestry, place of origin, citizenship, creed, age, marital status, family status, handicap, the receipt of public assistance (in accommodation), or record of offences (in employment).[1] The second is any unwelcome sexual solicitation or advance by someone who is in a position of power *vis-à-vis* the victim, with or without threats or actual reprisals for the rejection of such advances. The former type of harassment is addressed in subsections 2(2), 5(2), 7(1) and 7(2); the latter, in subsections 7(3)(*a*) and (*b*). The two types of harassment will be dealt with separately below.

Although harassment was not explicitly prohibited under the legislation previous to the 1981 *Code*, insulting, intimidating or annoying behaviour directed at employees of a particular race or sex had, in a few cases, been found to breach section 4(1)(*g*) of that *Code*.[2] Section 4(1)(*g*) forbade any employer to "discriminate against any employee with regard to any term or condition of employment, because of race, creed, colour, age, sex, marital status, nationality, ancestry of place or origin of such person or employee."

The rationale in bringing harassment under the former *Code* was that racial slurs, name-calling and other offensive behaviour created a hostile working environment constituted a term or condition of employment, inflicted on the target employee(s), that was different from other employees' terms and conditions of employment, and hence discriminatory.

Since only employers could be held liable for discrimination under section 4(1)(*g*), boards of inquiry invariably held, in cases in which the

---

1. Sexual orientation as a ground is not specifically included in the harassment provisions. This omission is further discussed below at note 31.

2. See R.S.O. 1980, c. 340 [now R.S.O. 1990, c. H.19].

harasser was not the employer, that there must be evidence that the employer knew about the offensive behaviour of the harassing employee, and that he or she had done nothing to stop it. Not surprisingly, boards held from the beginning that a single offensive incident was insufficient to establish a breach of the *Code*. The boards of inquiry in *Simms v. Ford Motor Company*[3] summed up all of these points as follows:[4]

> to permit, even passively, a black employee in a plant where the majority of employees are white to be humiliated repeatedly by insulting language, relating to his colour, by other employees, even, I would go so far as to say, by non-supervisory employees, would be to require the black employee to work under favourable working conditions which do not apply to white employees. In such circumstances the employer has an obligation, imposed by section 4(1), to remove the cause of the discriminatory working conditions and police the prohibition against the humiliating conduct or language. But where the employer had no reason to anticipate that an isolated insulting act would occur, it cannot be said that, if and when it does, the mere occurrence immediately puts the employer in violation of section 4(1). Finally, where, on such an isolated occurrence, the employer does not, but does not *in good faith*, believe that such conduct on the part of one of its supervisory personnel has occurred, and, as a result of such disbelief, does not discipline the offender, there is again, in my view, no violation of section 4(1) on the part of the employer. I need hardly add that a finding of bad faith might well change the result.

Harassment cases decided under the provisions of the 1980 *Code* must be applied with caution. In the current *Code* the areas in which harassment is prohibited have been broadened to include accommodation and employment. Further, where the alleged harasser is a fellow employee or co-tenant, he or she may now be named as a respondent. Finally, the issue of employer or, more generally, top level management responsibility is now very different.

"A Course of Vexatious Comment or Conduct"

Subsections 2(2), 5(2) and 7(1) and (2) prohibit harassment in the following terms:

> 2(2) Every person who occupies accommodation has a right to freedom from harassment by the landlord or agent of the landlord or by an occupant of the same building because of race, ancestry, place of origin, colour, ethnic origin, citizenship, creed, age, marital status, family status, handicap or the receipt of public assistance.
> 5(2) Every person who is an employee has a right to freedom from harassment in the workplace by the employer or agent of the employer or by another employee because of race, ancestry, place of origin, colour, ethnic origin, citizenship, creed, age, record of offences, marital status, family status or handicap.
> 7(1) Every person who occupies accommodation has a right to freedom from harassment because of sex by the landlord or agent of the landlord or by an occupant of the same building.

---

3. *Simms v. Ford Motor Co.* (1970), unreported (Ont. Bd. of Inquiry).
4. *Ibid.*, pp. 18-19.

(2) Every person who is an employee has a right to freedom from harassment in the workplace because of sex by his or her employer or agent of the employer or by another employee.

The reluctance, expressed by the board in *Simms*, to impose liability in respect of a single offensive incident has been carried over into the present *Code*. The definition of "harassment" as found in section 10 is "engaging in *a course of* vexatious comment or conduct that is known or ought reasonably to be known to be unwelcome" (emphasis added).

The view that more than one event is necessary to establish sexual harassment under subsection 7(2) was expressed by the first board to consider that provision, *Cuff v. Gypsy Restaurant.*[5] In a case decided after *Cuff, Purdy v. Marwick Manufacturing Co.*,[6] the board found (without comment) that section 6(2) had been breached as a result of a single incident. Most cases, however, have involved at least one repetition of "vexatious" behaviour, and it is suggested that *Cuff* represents the correct approach.

What type of conduct might give rise to a complaint of harassment? The Concise Oxford Dictionary defines vexatious as "annoying" or "distressing." The conduct at issue could range from physical contact[7] to relentless racist jokes[8]: any conduct, in fact, that is known or reasonably ought to be known by the respondent to be embarassing, intimidating or frightening to the complainant. The term vexatious clearly invokes a subjective assessment;[9] that is was *this complainant* frightened, annoyed, embarrassed, etc.? This element of subjectivity is balanced by a certain degree of subjectivity in favour of the respondent, since the complainant must prove, as part of the *prima facie* case, that the respondent knew, or reasonably ought to have known, that his or her behaviour was unwelcome. (This is further discussed below.)

The use of racial slurs has clearly been identified by boards of inquiry as constituting discrimination.[10] However, in three cases, despite proof of

---

5. (1987), 8 C.H.R.R. D/3972 (Ont. Bd. of Inquiry).

6. (1987), 9 C.H.R.R. D/4840 (Ont. Bd. of Inquiry).

7. *Cox v. Jagbritte Inc.* (1981), 2 C.H.R.R. D/609 (Ont. Bd. of Inquiry); *Coutrubis v. Sklavos Printing* (1981), 2 C.H.R.R. D/457 (Ont. Bd. of Inquiry); *Torres v. Royalty Kitchenware Ltd.* (1982), 3 C.H.R.R. D/858 (Ont. Bd. of Inquiry); *Sharp v. Seasons Restaurant* (1987), 8 C.H.R.R. D/4133 (Ont. Bd. of Inquiry); *Morano v. Nuttall* (1988), 9 C.H.R.R. D/4876 (Ont. Bd. of Inquiry); *Hall (Furlotte) v. Sonap Canada* (1989), 10 C.H.R.R. D/6126 (Ont. Bd. of Inquiry).

8. *Wei Fu v. Ontario Government Protective Service* (1985), 6 C.H.R.R. D/2797 (Ont. Bd. of Inquiry).

9. This point as acknowledged by the Board in *Cuff* (*ante*, note 5).

10. *Simms, ante*, note 3. *Dhillon v. F.W. Woolworth Co.* (1982), 3 C.H.R.R. D/743 (Ont. Bd. of Inquiry). In *Dhillon* board Chairman Peter Cummings responded to the argument that racial slurs are no more than the "rough talk" common in many work situations (at D/759-60):

racial slurs, the board did not find that the complainants had been discriminated against. In *Watson v. Highway Trailers of Canada Ltd.*,[11] *Wei Fu v. Ontario Government Protective Service*[12] and *Nimako v. Canadian National Hotels*,[13] the complaints were that dismissal or employment discipline of the complainant was undertaken for discriminatory reasons. In each case, the board accepted evidence as to the use of racial slurs by supervisory personnel.

It would appear that, in respect of the boards that were called under the 1980 *Code*, (*Watson* and *Nimako*), the use of racial slurs was not considered sufficiently frequent or widespread as to give rise to the inference of intent to discriminate on the part of the respondent was outweighed by

---

"Undoubtedly, the ambiance of a warehouse in Toronto, bringing together many men of very diverse backgrounds doing physical labour, is not going to be the equivalent of a Sunday School picnic. It will be common to have profanity or 'rough talk' as one might call it, as an ordinary part of the conversation, and whatever one's views as to the niceties of such an environment, one cannot ignore reality.

I am sure that the Respondent's warehouse was not exceptional in this regard, but rather is typical. However, the 'rough talk' in the Respondent's warehouse contained racial epithets and insults, that is, verbal harassment of a racial nature and on a regular basis. Occasionally this verbal harassment was coupled with mild physical harassment (for example, the ruffling of hair incidents in respect of Malkit Singh Pabla). Whether the truck-pushing incident involving Mr. Dhillon was truly intentional or not, the actions of those who bumped him after the fact (laughing at him and not apologizing, or not seeming to be sincere in apologizing, for the accident) together with the general warehouse climate left Mr. Dhillon with the not unreasonable inference that he was being abused in that incident because he was an East Indian.

The overall impression given by the evidence on the preponderance of evidence is that the warehouse was not just a 'rough' place in which to work, with demanding physical labour for men at the lower end of society's income scale, coupled with swearing and rough language, but that the internal 'pecking-order' within the warehouse placed the East Indian workers at the bottom of the informal, internal status for warehousemen. They were the butt of many of their co-workers' aggressiveness and hostility, because of their race. I do not want to generalize — undoubtedly the majority of the white workers were friendly, or at least tolerant, towards the East Indians. However, there was a solid number, if an overall relatively small minority, of white workers who would insult the East Indian workers on a racial basis. No doubt, the word 'wop' was heard as often as 'Paki' within the warehouse. (*Evidence*, vol. III, p. 100). However, the fact of racial insults toward one group does not justify racial insults toward another. As well, the fact that other groups, as new Canadians, experienced racial prejudice historically with legal impunity to those who discriminated, and the receivers of the insults simply had to tough it out, does not excuse racial discrimination now prohibited by the *Code* in the contemporary work environment". Also see *Singh v. Domglas Ltd.* (1980), 2 C.H.R.R. D/285 (Ont. Bd. of Inquiry); *Fuller v. Candur Plastics* (1981), 2 C.H.R.R. D/419 (Ont. Bd. of Inquiry); *Ahluwalia v. Metropolitan Toronto (Municipality) Commissioners of Police* (1983), 4 C.H.R.R. D/1757 (Ont. Bd. of Inquiry); *Lee v. T.J. Applebee's Food Conglomeration* (1987), 9 C.H.R.R. D/4781 (Ont. Bd. of Inquiry).

11. (1983), 4 C.H.R.R. D/1621 (Ont. Bd. of Inquiry).
12. *Ante*, note 8.
13. (1987), 8 C.H.R.R. D/3985 (Ont. Bd. of Inquiry).

other evidence. This also appears to be the rationale in *Wei Fu*, which was decided under the 1981 *Code*. As well, the board in *Wei Fu* did not consider the behaviour at issue to be harassment because the racial slurs had not been directed at the complainant. This latter point does not appear to be a major factor in the board's rationale; it should also be noted that,

(a) A board under the 1981 *Code* has found an employer liable under subsections 4(1) and 8 [now 5(1) and 9] of the *Code* when racial slurs directed at others were a major reason for the complainant leaving her employment.[14]

(b) A board has found sexual harassment to include *inter alia*, sexual remarks aimed at women other than the complainant.[15]

Just as the motivation of a person who engages in sexual harassment may have nothing to do with sexual attraction, the motivation of a person who engages in racial harassment may not be purely racist. In *Persaud v. Consumers Distributing*, the board pointed out that racial harassment by the respondent employee was simply one manifestation of a generally aggressive, bullying approach to others:

> Mr. Dassy is a very volatile individual who retaliates quickly and forcefully against anyone who crosses his path. He is a short-tempered, aggressive bully who will retaliate verbally, and even physically, against anyone, whether white or non-white who challenges him. The totality of the evidence indicates that Mr. Dassy would get into disputes with other employees, but as often with caucasian as with non-white employees. When he thinks he is being challenged or criticized, or crossed in any way, then he retaliates—often physically and violently. His motivation in his fights with fellow employees when he was employed at Consumers was not one of racism; rather the fights would be triggered by specific issues arising that were work-related. But his expressions in such fights would include derogatory racial epithets and name-calling as one means of belittling and humiliating the opposition when the opponent was a member of a visible minority . . .

> While Mr. Dassy's motive for his actions and words was not racially-based, his words and actions clearly had an active racial component. One operative factor in Mr. Dassy's treatment of Mr. Bhardwaj was Mr. Bhardwaj's race, colour, ancestry and place of origin. Racial harassment is present when one person verbally insults another person on the basis of his race, colour, ancestry and place of origin, irrespective of the underlying events that trigger the outburst. Such harassment is contrary to s. 4(2) of the *Code* and Mr. Dassy is in breach of that provision.[16]

---

14. *Lee v. T.J. Applebee's Food Conglomeration, ante*, note 10.
15. See *ante*, note 5. In *Cuff*, the board approvingly cited *Rogers v. Equal Employment Opportunity Commission*, 454 F. (2d) 234 (1971), *cert.* den. 406 U.S. 957 (1972) in which the complainant was an employee of Hispanic origin, whose employer, an optometrist, regularly segregated his Hispanic patients, treated them in a discrimatory way and spoke of them in an offensive manner. The court held that, despite the fact that the employer's discriminatory conduct had not been directed at the employee, it had adversely affected her working environment. See also *Waters v. Herblein Inc.*, 547 F. (2d) 466 (1977) in which a non-black employee successfully brought an action against her employer in regard to verbal abuse of black co-workers.
16. (1991), 14 C.H.R.R. D/23 at D/27.

In regard to other sorts of behaviour that can be considered harassment, the board in *Wei Fu* made the following general remark:

> Clearly, racial jokes, insults, slurs or other "comment" such as false and embarrassing accusations of misbehaviour could amount to "harassment" as defined, and "conduct" would include discriminatory treatment with respect to posting, transfers, hours of work, or other working conditions. Simply picking-on an employee because of his race could constitute harassment.

An example of such ill treatment is seen in *Boehm v. National System of Baking*,[17] in which a supervisor singled out a developmentally handicapped employee, yelling at him, referring to him as a "dummy" or a "retard" and repeatedly telling him that if he could not handle the work "we'll get someone that can."

In *Dufour v. J. Roger Deschamps Comptable Agréé*,[18] harassment because of creed was found where an evangelical Christian employer put up religious posters and stickers both in common areas and individual employee stations, made explicitly derogatory remarks about Catholicism, proselytized coercively on her own initiative to employees, and pressed employees to contribute financially to a particular church charity.

Harassment because of sex has been found in respect of unwanted "compliments" on appearance, persistent initiation of discussion of sexual matters, and sexually-oriented comments about others.[19] Harassment because of sex can also comprise "more subtle conduct such as gender-based insults and taunting."[20]

By including the above noted phrase in the definition of harassment, the legislature has clearly imported some degree of objectivity as to when "vexatious comment or conduct" breaches the *Code*. However, the standard is not completely objective. The comments of the *Cuff* board of inquiry are instructive.

> Comment or conduct "that is known or ought reasonably be known to be unwelcome" imports an objective element into the definition of harassment. The fact that this particular complainant found the behaviour vexatious is not sufficient. Respondents either must

---

17. (1987), 8 C.H.R.R. D/4110 (Ont. Bd. of Inquiry).
18. (1989), 10 C.H.R.R. D/6153 (Ont. Bd. of Inquiry).
19. See *Torres v. Royalty Kitchenware Ltd.* (1982), 3 C.H.R.R. D/858 (Ont. Bd. of Inquiry); *Cuff v. Gypsy Restaurant* (1987), 87 C.L.L.C. 17,015 (Ont. Bd. of Inquiry); *Giouvanoudis v. Golden Fleece Restaurant* (1984), 5 C.H.R.R. D/1967 (Ont. Bd. of Inquiry); *Graesser v. Porto* (1983), 4 C.H.R.R. D/1569 (Ont. Bd. of Inquiry); *Bishop v. Hardy* (1986), 86 C.L.L.C. 17,022 (Ont. Bd. of Inquiry); *Mitchell v. Traveller Inn (Sudbury) Ltd.* (1981), 2 C.H.R.R. D/590 (Ont. Bd. of Inquiry); *Cox v. Jagbritte Inc.* (1981), 2 C.H.R.R. D/609 (Ont. Bd. of Inquiry); *McPherson v. Mary's Donuts* (1982), 3 C.H.R.R. D/961 (Ont. Bd. of Inquiry); and *Aragona v. Elegant Lamp Co.* (1982), 3 C.H.R.R. D/1109 (Ont. Bd. of Inquiry).
20. *Bell v. Ladas* (1980), 1 C.H.R.R. D/155 at D/156 (Ont. Bd. of Inquiry). Also see *Shaw v. Levac Supply Ltd* (1990), 14 C.H.R.R. D/36 (Ont. Bd. of Inquiry), further discussed below.

have known, or they ought reasonably to have known, the behaviour to be unwelcome. Nevertheless, there are outstanding issues of interpretation raised by this phrase which are unnecessary to decide in this case. For example, from whose perspective is the reasonableness requirement to be framed? Can it be framed in terms of a reasonable victim, or in other words, a reasonable person having the perspective of the complainant? It will be particularly important to define the standard of reasonableness where the employer admits engaging in the course of conduct but denies that he could reasonably have known of the response.

A complainant who clearly indicates to the respondent that his actions were unwelcome will more likely be able to satisfy the condition that the respondent knew the behaviour was unwelcome. A complainant who did not clearly make it known to the respondent that his behaviour was unwelcome will have to show the respondent ought to have known it was unwelcome. In the latter case, attempts to let the respondent know that his behaviour was unwelcome, albeit perhaps indirect or weak, will go towards establishing whether or not the respondent ought to have known his behaviour was unwelcome. But in addition, the "ought to have known" alternative recognizes that the responsibility for appreciating the offensiveness of certain behaviour does not rest entirely with the complainant. Boards of inquiry under the previous *Code* had a similar understanding of the nature of sexual harassment. In *Bell & Korczak v. Ladas and the Flaming Steer Steak House, supra,* at D/157 the Board stated: "[t]he willingness to work is of no moment because persons in need of employment may be prepared to endure certain humiliations because of their financial need." Failure to terminate employment or a willingness to ensure the situation similarly did not inhibit a finding of sexual harassment in *Torres v. Royalty Kitchenware Ltd. & Guercio* (1982), 3 C.H.R.R. D/858 at D/860 (Ont. Board of Inquiry). The American case of *Bundy v. Jackson* 641 F. 2nd 934(1981) at 946 states some of the policy considerations behind this stance:

> It may even be pointless to require the employee to prove that she "resisted" the harassment at all. So long as the employer never literally forces sexual relations on the employee, "resistance" may be a meaningless alternative for her. If the employer demands no response to his verbal or physical gestures other than good-natured tolerance, the woman has no means of communicating her rejection. She neither accepts nor rejects the advances; she simply endures them. She might be able to contrive proof of rejection by objecting to the employer's advances in some very visible and dramatic way, but she would do so only at the risk of making her life on the job even more miserable.

> In general, the legislative enunciation of the right to be free from sexual harassment and advances indicates a public awareness of the unacceptable nature of this behaviour and carries with it an expectation that this understanding is shared by the members of the community.[21]

In *Cuff*, the employee was found to clearly have communicated to the respondent that his remarks were unwelcome when she stated that he was embarassing her, threatened to tell his wife of his behaviour and refused his requests to kiss him or to "make love" to him.

---

21. *Ante*, note 5, at D/3981-2. For another case in which a board declined to accept that the complainant's willingness to continue employment should be considered in assessing whether the respondent should have known his or her conduct to be unwelcome, see *Sharp v. Seasons Restaurant, ante*, note 7.

In *Boehm v. National System of Baking Ltd.*, the board noted that the developmentally handicapped complainant tended to smile as a nervous reaction when under strain or pressure in front of others. However, the board clearly felt that the level of verbal abuse suffered by the complainant was such that anyone would have known it was unwelcome. Further, the board noted that:

> where a disabled person is an employee there is an obligation upon the supervisor not to use even relatively innocuous conversation which might not offend non disabled persons, if such conversation can be reasonably perceived to be hurtful to the disabled employee. That is, the sensitivity of the disabled employee must be reasonably accommodated . . . (the Code imposes) a subjective as well as an objective analysis to the behaviour of the Respondent. Ignorance or insensitivity are not defences under this test.[22]

Boards have noted that the circumstances of each case must be carefully weighed, insofar as standards of formality in workplaces can differ, and it is possible that the respondent's behaviour, in context, did not depart significantly from what had been acceptable. In *Purdy v. Marwick Manufacturing Co.*,[23] the complainant had shown magazines with pictures of naked men and women to the respondents, approaching them in their area of work to do so. The board held that this might be seen as "initiating" the subsequent incident in which the respondent exposed his genitals to the complainant. However, this did not render the incident any less a matter of harassment; rather, the board considered it in the issue of damages. In another case, *Hall (Furlotte) v. Sonap Canada*,[24] the board accepted that standards of behaviour might differ in various communities and cultures.[25] However, the board maintained that, in any event, management has a responsibility that arises from the inequality of the relationship with employees, to behave with discretion.

It is likely that boards will continue to weigh whether, and how, the complainant made an effort to indicate his or her feelings to the respondent, as evidence that will go both to whether the respondent "knew," and whether he or she "should have known." However, it is suggested that boards of inquiry are too cognizant of personal and cultural differences to expect evidence of a clear, blunt rebuff in all cases. Undeniably, some complainants will be so influenced by particularly hierarchical, soft-spoken or polite cultural backgrounds as to be virtually incapable of firm and clear discouragement. The complainant may also be influenced by a conscious-

---

22. *Ante*, note 17 at D/4122-4123.
23. (1987), 9 C.H.R.R. D/4840 (Ont. Bd. of Inquiry).
24. (1989), 10 C.H.R.R. D/6126 (Ont. Bd. of Inquiry).
25. Also see *Dufour, ante*, note 18, in which a claim of religious harassment was not upheld in regard to one employee because, due to the employee's previous friendship with the employer, it may not have been clear to the employer that her remarks about religion were unwelcome.

ness of the respondent's relative power. Even though the respondent may be a co-worker, a complainant who is outnumbered by members of the respondent's group may consider it imprudent to "cause trouble." On a personal level, the complainant may simply be a "quiet type."

On the other hand, the respondent, for reasons that may also reflect his or her cultural background, or simply because of insensitivity, may be genuinely unaware that his or her actions are bothersome.

It is suggested that, where the respondent's degree of knowledge is not clear, boards will continue to weigh all the circumstances of the case. Certainly the complainant's response will be an important factor, but so will the sophistication of the respondent.[26] Other issues to be weighed include the reaction of people other than the complainant,[27] and whether the nature of the conduct gives rise to an inference that the respondent's state of mind was other than innocent. Lastly, if there has been a Commission investigation or board of inquiry in respect of harassment by the respondent in the past, he or she would find it difficult to account successfully for insensitivity on a second occasion.

"Because of" Race, Ancestry, etc.

Another aspect of harassment is the demonstration of a causal connection between the "vexatious comment or conduct" and the race, creed, colour, etc., of the complainant. In past cases involving harassment, the causal connection between the act in question and the ground of discrimination alleged has been reasonably clear, as the conduct involved has usually included insults and racial slurs that clearly suggest the reason for the harassment.

In a recent case, the reason for the abuse was less clear. In *Shaw v. Levac Supply Ltd.*[28] the complainant, a large woman who held a clerical and administrative position with the respondent company, was the target of actions and comment by the respondent office manager, some of which was clearly intended to be insulting and some of which , while unpleasant, were ambiguous. The respondent would whistle "Slow Down, You Move Too Fast," apparently to imply that the complainant was working too slowly. He also referred to her, to others, as a "fat cow." According to one witness,

---

26. Sophistication used in this sense might include such issues as whether the respondent appreciates that a black and/or female employee, for example, might perceive the respondent's behaviour differently from the way a white male employee might perceive it, *i.e.*, as another distressing incident of discrimination. It would also include the degree to which the respondent, who is more senior than the complainant in a company's hierarchy, is aware that his or her actions carry clout.

27. *I.e.*, did co-workers protest between one incident and another; did management speak to the respondent?

28. *Ante*, note 20.

. . . . there seemed to be quite a bit of tension in the general office and Herb was always making derogatory remarks. . . . One thing he did quite a bit was — Carol's desk was in front of him and he was always snickering. He was always watching Carol when he did it. And he'd snicker and go "Yea, Yea" or, when Carol left the office, quite often when she just — in front of her desk there was a little spot to hang coats and when she got out behind it he would say out loud "horse, horse," "Neigh, neigh." [The witness did not say the word "neigh," but made a neighing sound.] And at other times, when he was going out of the office, when he got past, just outside the door, or Carol did, he'd always yell "insecurity, insecurity." [To the question "could Carol hear what he was saying? he replied, "oh, yes." And when asked how many times he remembered such incidents he replied "I'd say just about every day there would be something.]²⁹

As the complainant walked around the office, the respondent would remark "waddle, waddle" or "swish, swish" to no one in particular. Despite the fact that the respondent was not the complainant's supervisor, he would time her phone calls and follow her when she left the office. There was also some evidence that the respondent made critical remarks about the complainant's relationship with her children, and that he had expressed some bias against working women.

In addressing the question as to whether the respondent's conduct was "because of sex," the board considered and dismissed theories that it might have been occasioned by "professional jealousy," personal animosity, or a misplaced notion of managerial responsibility.

In finding that the respondent's actions amounted to sexual harassment, the board asserted that, although most harassment cases are concerned with unwanted sexual advances, actions or words to the effect that the complainant is sexually unattractive can also be harassment because of sex for the purpose of subsections 7(1) and (2). The board also discussed the effect of evidence that, while he indulged in degrading remarks to other female co-workers, the respondent treated them less badly than he did the complainant. In respect of this point, the board made these remarks:

> While similar conduct towards other women would lend support to a finding of gender bias, I reject any suggestion that there can be no finding that the complainant was mistreated because she is a woman unless the respondent similarly mistreated all women. The *Torres* and *Janzen* cases also indicate that conduct does not have to be directed to all the members of a given class in order to be gender discriminatory. Nor is it reasonable in my view to suggest that gender bias cannot be found unless such mistreatment of the complainant manifested itself virtually from their initial meeting. In any case, evidence of a tendency to mistreat other women has been reviewed, and in this regard the following observation made in *Re Canada Post Corp. and Canadian Union of Postal Workers (Gibson)* (1988), 34 L.A.C. (3rd) 27 seems apt: [A] second form of sexual harassment is harassment aimed not at an employee's sexuality, but at the employee's gender itself. This may be harassment because the employee is of a particular gender, or harassment amounting to degradation of persons of that gender. (At pp. 43-44)³⁰

---

29. *Ibid.*, at D/39.
30. *Ibid.*, at D/58.

The *Shaw* case also contains a review of the evidence given by one witness, on whose testimony the board did not rely, who was qualified as an expert on the range and patterns of behaviour exhibited by men in workplaces who hold biased attitudes toward women co-workers.

The *Shaw* decision is an illustration of a board's willingness to acknowledge that, as with discrimination generally, harassment can manifest itself in indirect or ambiguous actions intended to discourage or drive away the victim without drawing attention to bias on the part of the harasser.[31]

---

31. An example of a similar case is seen in *Kyriazi v. Western Electric Co.*, 461 F. Supp. 894 (1978). The complainant, who was quite obese, was singled out as the target of the office "jokers." Kyriazi's co-workers made derogatory remarks concerning her marital status, and speculations concerning her virginity. They would tease her by deliberately blocking per path as she tried to move in the aisle. Her co-workers also created a cartoon designed to embarass and humiliate her, and placed it on her desk. The court found that these acts constituted sex discrimination in Kyriazi's conditions of employment.

A board also addressed the question of the cause of the harassment in *Aquilina v. Pokoj* (1991), 14 C.H.R.R. D/230. in that case a landlord had accepted the complainant as a tenant having been informed that she had a handicap, but without a clear idea of the nature of the handicap. The complainant had cerebral palsy which caused both cognitive and motor disfunction. The board determined that the respondent's harassment, which included frequent complaints about the complainant's use of heat and light, banging on the ceiling, issuing an illegal eviction notice accompanied by a highly insulting note and referring to the complainant as retarded, began when the complainant demonstrated a wish to lead an independent life without undue influence and control from her landlord. The board also found that the complainant's handicap affected both the nature and the intensity of the harassment.

Some of the remarks of the board in *Shaw (ante,* note 20) give rise to speculation as to whether the concept of sexual harassment, as developed to date, might extend to situations in which harassment in employment or accommodation is inflicted because of the sexual orientation or perceived sexual orientation, of the victim. Central to this argument is the understanding that, at base people are harassed because of their sexual orientation because the harasser does not think the victim behaves sexually as a man or woman ought to behave. The review in *Shaw* of the Supreme Court of Canada's decision in *Janzen v. Platy Enterprises Ltd.* (1989), 10 C.H.R.R. D/6205 illustrated that Court's reluctance to maintain a narrow definition of behaviour that is "sexual in nature", its refusal to deny protection because only one of the same-sex group is singled out, and its road and purposive focus on eliminating the poisoning of the work environment for discriminatory reasons. As noted by the board in *Shaw* (at D/53):

> . . . Chief Justice Dickson set out the following guidelines established by the American Equal Employment Opportunity Commission, which he points out "have been quoted with approval by courts and human rights tribunals in both the United States and Canada" (D/6225, para. 44445):

>> Unwelcome sexual advances, requests for sexual favors, and other *verbal* or physical *conduct of a sexual nature constitute sexual harassment, when* (1) submission to such conduct is made either explicitly or implicitly a term or condition of employment, (2) submission to or rejection of such conduct by an individual is used as the basis for employment decisions affecting such individual, or (3) *such conduct has the* purpose or *effect of* unreasonably interfering

Direct or Indirect Harassment

Harassment may be conducted through the offices of another person. For example, an employer who instructs a supervisor to institute actions that amount to harassment will be directly liable under section 9.[32] There may also be some responsibility on employers to take steps to assist employees who are harassed by customers or clients, when the matter is brought to their attention. In a recent British Columbia case, remarks to this effect were made by a Board of inquiry in a case in which the employer fired an employee who, on being racially harassed a second time by a customer, told him rudely to take his business elsewhere.[33]

Sexual Solicitation, Reprisal

Subsection 7(3) states as follows:

(3) Every person has a right to be free from

(a) a sexual solicitation or advance made by a person in a position to confer, grant or deny a benefit or advancement to the person where the person making the solicitation or advance knows or ought reasonably to know that it is unwelcome; or

(b) a reprisal or a threat of reprisal for the rejection of a sexual solicitation or advance where the reprisal is made or threatened by a person in a position to confer, grant or deny a benefit or advancement to the person.

The *Concise Oxford Dictionary* defines solicit as "invite, request or importune." The definition of advance includes "personal approach; overture." Thus it would seem reasonable to assume that the legislature intended solicitation and advance to be read disjunctively. On this reading it is clear that section 7(3)(*a*) covers both requests or demands for sexual "favours" or

---

with an individual's work performance or *creating an* intimidating, hostile, or *offensive working environment*. [Emphasis added.]

The Chief Justice went on to make the following observation (D/6226, para. 44447):

Emerging from these various legislative proscriptions is the notion that *sexual harassment may take a variety of forms*. Sexual harassment is not limited to demands for sexual favours made under threats of adverse job consequences should the employee refuse to comply with the demands . . . *Sexual harassment also encompasses* situations in which sexual demands are foisted upon unwilling employees or in which employees must endure sexual groping, propositions, and *inappropriate comments*, but where no tangible economic rewards are attached to involvement in the behaviour. [Emphasis added.]

[126] What seems to be the common thread running through all of this is that sexual harassment has to do with sexual activity, whether effected, proposed or *referred to*.

32. S. 9 states that: "No person shall infringe or do, directly or *indirectly*, anything that infringes a right under this Part" (emphasis added).

33. *Mohammad v. Mariposa Stores* (1991), 14 C.H.R.R. D/215.

co-operation in sexual acts, and the more forcible type of approach to sexual gratification. Boards of inquiry dealing with sexual harassment complaints under the former *Code* have described both types of behaviour as sexual harassment.

In *Cuff v. Gypsy Restaurant*[34] the board, in outlining the differences between the 1980 *Code* and the *Code* enacted in 1981, pointed out that the specific wording of the sexual harassment provisions make it clear that the *Code* is intended to address all types of unwelcome behaviour related to sex, and that such harassment can be manifested in other ways than by sexual solicitation or advances. The demands of making out a case under subsections 2(2), 5(2) and 7(1) and (2) are also different from those under 7(3), since only one sexual solicitation or advance need be proved, as opposed to "a course of vexatious comment or conduct."

"A Person in a Position to Confer, Grant, or Deny a Benefit or Advancement"

The above definition would seem to embrace a fairly wide range of respondents: landlords, employers, teachers and professors will obviously be included, as would persons with whom an apprentice student is placed for a work term, or a social worker whose adverse report may disqualify a welfare recipient.

An issue may arise as to whether the complainant's perception of the respondent as a person who could "confer a benefit" must be objectively true. For example, an employee may feel forced to submit to the advances of someone in middle management because of a threat that the manager will get him or her fired. If, in fact, the manager has no such power, it may be argued that the board has no jurisdiction. The Commission may approach this argument in at least two ways. The first is that to refuse the protection of the *Code* to a complainant who sincerely believed that the respondent had such power is contrary to the spirit of the legislation. The second is that there is a benefit that the respondent in this example can in fact deny, and that is the complainant's right to go about his or her work unmolested.

The Person Making the Solicitation or Advance Knows or Ought Reasonably to Know that it is Unwelcome

It is clear that Ontario boards of inquiry have accepted sexual harassment as an "evil to be avoided" even before the enactment of the present *Code*. The first board of inquiry under the previous *Code* put the issue this way:

> The forms of prohibited conduct that, in my view, are discriminatory run the gamut from overt gender based activity, such as coerced intercourse to unsolicited physical contact to persistent propositions to more subtle conduct such as gender based insults and taunting,

---

34. (1987), 8 C.H.R.R. D/3972 (Ont. Bd. of Inquiry).

which may reasonably be perceived to create a negative psychological and emotional work environment. There is no reason why the law, which reaches into the work-place so as to protect the work environment from the physical or chemical pollution or extremes of temperature, ought not to protect employees as well from negative, psychological and mental effects where adverse and gender directed conduct emanating from a management hierarchy may reasonably be construed to be a condition of employment.[35]

It is also clear that boards have been mindful of the argument that "normal social conduct" should not be prohibited. The same board of inquiry addressed this argument:

> The prohibition of such conduct is not without its dangers. One must be cautious that the law not inhibit normal social contact between management and employees or normal discussion between management and employees. It is not abnormal, nor should it be prohibited, activity for a supervisor to become socially involved with an employee. An invitation to dinner is not an invitation to a complaint. The danger or the evil that is to be avoided is coerced or compelled social contact where the employee's refusal to participate may result in a loss of employment benefits.[36]

In most cases decided prior to the 1981 *Code* and since its passage, there has, on the evidence, been no possibility of ambiguity, or confusion of the actions complained of with normal social interaction.[37] In the few cases in which the respondent might have made this argument, boards have appeared generally to understand the essential feature of the problem, that is, the inequality between parties.

The board in *Giouvanoudis v. Golden Fleece Restaurant* described the approach of another board to an ambiguous situation as follows:

> In *Kim Fullerton v. Davey C's Tavern, Glen Relph, and Zantav Limited* (Aug. 3, 1983: Ont. — F.H. Zemans), the Complainant, age 24, was employed as a waitress at a newly opened Toronto restaurant by the assistant manager, Mr. Relph. After two weeks work, the Complainant and Mr. Relph had dinner together and went dancing, but "nothing unusual took place" and it was "an innocent occasion" (p. 6). The Complainant alleged that after this occasion the assistant manager would ask her out, and on occasion put his arm around her and attempted to kiss her. He denied any sexual intent. She felt she had been directly sexually propositioned on one occasion after about a month of working, but the assistant manager respondent claimed that if he had suggested anything, it was obviously in jest. The Chairman felt that Mr. Relph "may very well have been testing the waters" with the complainant (at p.12). Shortly thereafter the complainant was transferred to a less lucrative part of the restaurant facilities, and then she was dismissed, and she inferred that her demotion and dismissal were related to her rejection of what she perceived to be sexual advances by the assistant manager. However, the evidence of the owner of the business was that he, quite independently, had observed the complainant's

---

35. *Bell v. Ladas* (1980), 1 C.H.R.R. D/155 at 156 (Ont. Bd. of Inquiry).
36. *Ibid.*, at D/156. Also see *Torres v. Royalty Kitchenware Ltd.* (1982), 3 C.H.R.R. D/858 (Ont. Bd. of Inquiry).
37. See, for example, *Torres ibid.*, *Sharp v. Seasons Restaurant* (1987), 8 C.H.R.R. D/4133 (Ont. Bd. of Inquiry); *Green v. Safieh* (1987), 9 C.H.R.R. D/4749 (Ont. Bd. of Inquiry); *Noffke v. McClaskin Hot House* (1989), 11 C.H.R.R. D/407 (Ont. Bd. of Inquiry); *Morano v. Nuttall* (1988), 9 C.H.R.R. D/4876 (Ont. Bd. of Inquiry).

dress and demeanor as a waitress over a period of time, and he found them to be unsatisfactory, and noticed on an occasion that she seemed to be lacking in personal hygiene as she had an unpleasant body odour, so that he instructed the general manager to terminate her employment forthwith. Other witnesses confirmed these observations in respect of the complainant.

The Chairman concluded there was not sufficient evidence to indicate that the assistant manager had treated the complainant "in a fashion that went beyond that of a reasonable involvement" (at p. 25) and therefore dismissed the complaint because there was not sexual harassment in the workplace, prohibited by paragraph 4(1)(*g*) of the *Code*, and found further that she was not dismissed from her employment because of any refusal of sexual advances, prohibited by paragraph 4(1)(*b*) of the *Code*.[38]

However, boards have distinguished between consensual social activity and voluntary continued contact which arises out of need or even out of convenience. In *Sharp v. Seasons Restaurant*[39] the harassment took the form of the respondent restaurant owner repeatedly grabbing his employee, the complainant, touching her breasts, and, when she placed a bar order, grabbing his own groin and making remarks such as "I will give you my cock instead." The evidence also showed that the complainant had driven the respondent home late at night after the restaurant closed, continued an arrangement in which she left her child for day care with the respondent's mother, and returned to employment with the respondent on two occasions, after having quit. The board appeared to accept that the complainant needed employment (and day care) and that, given that the evidence had established the conduct of the respondent and clear verbal indication from the complainant that the conduct was unwelcome, harassment was proven.[40]

As noted above in the discussion of "vexatious comment or conduct," boards have taken note of the "culture" of a particular workplace in deciding what standard of behaviour might properly be expected. While clearly such evidence is relevant, a board will presumably confine the consideration of such evidence to situations in which the complainant does not clearly object to the impugned action, or appears by his or her own behaviour to condone it.

Evidentiary Issues Related to Sexual Harassment

Boards of inquiry in human rights cases have frequently commented on the fact that discrimination can be a subtle phenomenon, and that frequently the board must rely on circumstantial evidence, drawing inferences

---

38. *Giouvanoudis v. Golden Fleece Restaurant* (1983), 5 C.H.R.R. D/1967 at D/1976-1977 (Ont. Bd. of Inquiry).

39. *Ante*, note 37.

40. Several boards have pointed out that willingness to continue in employment cannot be equated with accepting an employer's harassment. See *Bell v. Ladas, ante*, note 35; *Noffke v. McClaskin Hot House, ante*, note 37.

from conduct.[41] Nowhere are evidentiary difficulties more likely than in sexual harassment cases.

As Professor Backhouse points out, in a 1982 article,[42]

> Resolution of evidentiary matters will always be critical in sexual harassment cases, since corroborative witnesses are rarely available. Furthermore, our legal system is imbued with deep-rooted fears about unfounded claims of sexual abuse. In most cases of sexual harassment it is to be expected that the complainant will be the sole witness for her side, and the alleged sexual harasser will deny all of the allegations. As a result, the trier of fact will be hard-pressed to determine which side to believe.

Professor Backhouse strongly criticizes the approach of the board in *Bell v. Flaming Steer Steak House*, the first sexual harassment case to go to a board in Canada, and the only one to discuss witness credibility at any length. The complainant's grievances were found to be unsubstantiated. Professor Backhouse points out that the board drew negative inferences from certain behaviour of the complainants that is characteristic of victims of sexual harassment,[43] and the board was overly conservative in its exclu-

---

41. For comments as to this issue see *Ruest v. International Brotherhood of Electrical Workers* (1968), unreported (Ont. Bd. of Inquiry); *Kennedy v. Mohawk College* (1973), unreported (Ont. Bd. of Inquiry); *Britnell v. Brent Personnel Placement Services* (1968), unreported (Ont. Bd. of Inquiry); *Mitchell v. O'Brien* (1968), unreported (Ont. Bd. of Inquiry); *Massey v. Castlefield Apts.* (1969), unreported (Ont. Bd. of Inquiry); *Morgan v. Toronto General Hospital* (1977), unreported (Ont. Bd. of Inquiry); *Ingram v. National Footwear* (1980), 1 C.H.R.R. D/59 (Ont. Bd. of Inquiry). Also see discussion of evidence before boards in Chapter 9.

42. See C. Backhouse, *"Bell v. The Flaming Steer Steak House Tavern: Canada's First Sexual Harassment Decision"* (1981) U.W.O.L. Rev. 141.

43. "[I]n the case of Cherie Bell, the Board concluded that Bell's evidence was less than completely candid and rejected her complaint. [Board Chairman] Shime noted that Bell had telephoned her employer after the alleged sexual harassment had taken place to find out her hours of work for the following week. This was the point at which she learned she had been dismissed. Yet she alleged in her complaint that the psychological trauma of the sexual harassment incapacited her from work for seven months following the incidents. When she filed her complaint she had been inaccurate about the dates on which she alleged the sexual harassment had occurred. Her specific testimony during the hearing differed slightly from the details of her complaint made to the Commission in the first instance.

It is understandable that a board which is forced to choose between the credibility of conflicting witnesses will seize on these evidentiary problems as indications of exaggeration and inaccuracy. However, there are two problems with Shime's judgment. Firstly, he seemed to be insensitive to the trauma which surrounds sexual harassment. Victims of sexual harassment (as well as victims of other traumatic events) are not going to escape the incident emotionally unscathed. As yet there is little empirical or medical evidence on the impact of sexual harassment. But one group, the Alliance Against Sexual Coercion (a non-profit centre which counsels victims of sexual harassment throughout the United States) has suggested that women experiencing the stress of sexual harassment may undergo a level of tension which can cause them to ramble, lose focus, and become confused in their descriptions of sexual incidents. To disbelieve sexual harassment complainants

sion of certain similar fact evidence.[44]

It is difficult to predict whether boards of inquiry dealing with complaints of sexual harassment that lack witnesses will continue to manifest the difficulties commented upon by Professor Backhouse, since there have been few such cases; however, there is cause to believe that they will not. In a number of cases, boards have found that sexual harassment occurred, despite an absence of direct witnesses, although usually there was evidence that the complainant had told someone else of the events shortly after they occurred.[45]

---

because they do not appear objective, rational, and collected may be unfair. While the Board's response to inconsistencies in Bell's testimony is understandable, its approach may well deny a legal remedy to a large number of *bona fide* sexual harassment complainants." Backhouse, *ante*, note 42 at 148.

44. "Shime refused to admit the similar fact evidence in this case on the ground that the alleged sexual approaches differed in nature and tone and thus did not indicate a pattern. Focusing on the differing features of the alleged sexual approach, the Board stated that in one case Ladas was alleged to have slapped Korczak on the rear, whereas no physical contact of this sort was suggested in the other complaint. Approaches made to one of the women allegedly involved invitations for drinks and to a hotel room, whereas the complainant in the other case made no mention of this type of behaviour. The Board concluded that it was 'not prepared to find that the alleged sexual overtures made to the two complainants were so unusual, or bore such a striking similarity, that the evidence of each of the complaints should be treated as similar fact evidence having some probative value in the other's complaint.' The degree of similarity which the Board required here was too onerous. Making sexual overtures to two subordinate female employees in the work setting and then firing each of them for failing to comply constitutes, where proved, a pattern of conduct in itself. Similarity exists in that this man chooses to make sexual advances to a female person in his employ, the approach is made on the job, and both employees suffer similar ramifications for failing to comply with the advances. Requiring a 'striking similarity' in sexual approach before utilizing one complainant's testimony as probative evidence for another complaint is likely to eliminate the usefulness of this legal doctrine in sexual harassment cases.

In English law the discretion exists for judges to exclude any evidence where the probative value is outweighed by the prejudicial effect. In Canada the discretion exists only where, in the opinion of the trial judge, the evidence is gravely prejudicial to the accused and is of trifling probative force in relation to the main issue. Shime refused to admit the similar fact evidence, concluding that the 'prejudicial value [of the evidence] outweigh[ed] its probative value.' Given the obvious proof problems faced by most sexual harassment complainants, who lack witnesses or tangible evidence, testimony from other employees who have experienced sexual harassment from the same defendant will be compellingly probative. In this context, tribunals will repeatedly have to struggle to draw the difficult balance between the essential need to admit the evidence in order to enforce the legislation and the potentially prejudicial effect upon the defendant." Backhouse, *ante*, note 42 at 147.

45. There have been over 20 board decisions in cases of sexual harassment since *Bell*, most of which had evidence of witnesses to consider. It is notable that nine cases in which there were no witnesses to the harassment, the board found for the complainant in eight. In *Graesser v. Porto* (1983), 4 C.H.R.R. D/1569 (Ont. Bd. of Inquiry); *Giouvanoudis v.*

On the issue of "similar fact" evidence, the board in *Graesser v. Porto* put the situation clearly:

> When dealing with matters involving sexual harassment . . . one rarely encounters the situation where the offence or alleged offence takes place in the open, and therefore can be proven through eye witness testimony. That is, rarely will one sexually harass another in full public view. Rather, these events usually take place behind closed doors with no witnesses. Such being the case, if similar fact evidence were excluded, the trier of fact would be faced with having to decide an issue based solely on the evidence of the parties before him.[46]

Similar fact evidence has frequently been accepted by boards of inquiry in cases of sexual harassment, and for the most part, boards have not confined themselves to the more restrictive interpretation of similar fact evidence used by the board in *Bell*. In *Graesser v. Porto*, the board accepted similar fact evidence of actions somewhat less similar than the degree of identity that seemed to be expected by the board in *Bell*. The board in *Graesser* cited recent Supreme Court of Canada authority, and went on to indicate that in the case at hand, there was no issue of identity to which the similar fact evidence must relate. Although the board did not elaborate, it would seem that this was a reference to the point that a requirement of striking similarity would appear to be relevant only when it is sought to prove the identity of a harasser, for example, by establishing a *modus operendi*. The identity of a harasser has not to date been at issue before a board.

Similar fact evidence is further discussed in Chapter 9.

Another evidentiary problem, particularly in subsection 7(3), arises from the fact that people are often not particularly explicit in making sexual advances.

Given that the language people use when dealing with sex is often euphemistic and suggestive rather than direct or clinical in nature, it is probable that a board at some time will be faced with a respondent's argument that he or she did not intend to solicit sexual activity, and that the complainant misunderstood. A board may be required to decide what inference

---

Golden Fleece Restaurant (1984), 5 C.H.R.R. D/1967 (Ont. Bd. of Inquiry); *Purdy v. Marwick Manufacturing Co.* (1987), 9 C.H.R.R. D/4840 (Ont. Bd. of Inquiry); *Morano v. Nuttall* (1988), 9 C.H.R.R. D/4876 (Ont. Bd. of Inquiry); and *Noffke v. McClaskin Hot House* (1989), 11 C.H.R.R. D/407 (Ont. Bd. of Inquiry) in all of which the board found for the complainant, there were no witnesses but the complainants told someone else of the incidents soon after they occurred. In *Robinson v. The Company Farm Ltd.* (1984); *Piazza v. Airport Taxi Assoc* (1986), 7 C.H.R.R. D/3196 (Ont. Bd. of Inquiry) and *Cuff v. Gypsy Restaurant* (1987), 8 C.H.R.R. D/3972 (Ont. Bd. of Inquiry), in all of which the board found for the complainant, there were neither witnesses nor confiding in others by complainants. In these latter cases, the board admitted "similar fact" evidence, although in *Robinson*, the Board did not appear to find the incident sufficiently similar to be probative.

46. *Ante*, note 45, at D/1572.

should be drawn, for example, from a respondent's practice of subjecting a complainant to tales of his or her sexual exploits with others.[47] Is this behaviour alone a solicitation, or advance, or is it merely the type of "vexatious comment or conduct" prohibited by section 7(1) and (2)? This issue may be important when the complaint is made in respect of a situation other than accommodation or employment, since if it were decided that the behaviour is harassment as defined in section 10 the board would have no jurisdiction to proceed.

An example of a case in which a board drew an inference from suggestive language is *Mitchell v. Traveller Inn (Sudbury)*. The complainant reported for a new job early one morning. In the words of the board:[48]

> There were no customers in the coffee shop adjacent to the office at this hour, however, the complainant asked what she should do, and Mr. Czaikowski, according to her testimony, asked to go to the backroom with him. She interpreted this request as having a sexual connotation and declined. He advised her that, if she did not, she would not have a job. He also offered to drive her home, suggesting it might be fun.

In making a finding of sexual harassment, the board characterized the respondent's second suggestion as "nearly explicit," but acknowledged that the situation had been far from unambiguous. However, the board concluded that "harassment does not have to be explicit to be contrary to the *Human Rights Code*."

In *Morano v. The Company Garden Center*, the solicitation took the form of an invitation to a conference:

> [The complainant] testified that the [respondent] stated that it was a conference of nursery people and that individuals from nurseries, garden centers and greenhouses got together for a weekend to have fun. She asked how much it would cost her and Mr. Nuttall indicated that if she was interested, it would be all expenses paid. He further stated that they would fly there in his plane and indicated: "You go there and he says you sleep with who you want, when you want. And he says when you come back to work you don't say anything about what went on.[49]

The board concluded that harassment had occurred.

Reprisal or Threat of Reprisal for the Rejection of a Sexual Solicitation or Advance: Section 7(3)(*b*):

Section 7(3)(*b*) reads:

> (3) Every person has the right to be free from,

---

47. A case in which the respondent subjected the complainant to unwelcome monologues about his sexual exploits is *Torres v. Royalty Kitchenware* (1982), 3 C.H.R.R. D/858 (Ont. Bd. of Inquiry). In that case the board clearly understood this behaviour to be either part of an attempt to convince the complainant to engage in sexual activity, or a source of sexual gratification in itself. Also see remarks by board in *Shaw, ante* note 20, at D/53.

48. (1981), 2 C.H.R.R. D/590 at D/591 (Ont. Bd. of Inquiry).

49. *Morano, ante*, note 45 at D/4878.

(b) a reprisal or a threat of reprisal for the rejection of a sexual solicitation or advance where the reprisal is made or threatened by person in a position to confer, grant or deny a benefit or advancement to the person.

In respect of a complaint under section 7(3)(*b*), it is clear that one solicitation or advance, followed by a reprisal (or threat thereof) for rejection is sufficient to attract liability.

An example of a case in which a board found a breach of subsection 7(3)(*b*) is *Bishop v. Hardy*.[50] In that case, the complainant had worked for the respondent for some five weeks. On occasion, they had a drink together after work on the business premises, and as the complainant often worked until 10:00 p.m. the respondent normally drove her home. On one evening, the complainant and respondent had the following interview:

> Mr. Hardy said that he would like to have a person in the shop whom he could trust and who would make sure that the work was getting done. She stated that Mr. Hardy then said: "He'd really have to get to know this person . . . inside and out, go to bed with them sort of thing, and I could be that person if I wanted to be." When Ms. Bishop said no, she did not want that, he started to compare her work with that of another woman, saying their work was the same, but since the other worker had four children he would keep her on the job. Again, according to Ms. Bishop, Mr. Hardy then added: "If I still wanted the job I could go to bed with him and I could still keep my job." She said no again, and asked whether she was "officially fired." He said that she was, but called to her as she left that if she changed her mind he would always be there.[51]

The act or threat of reprisal might comprise almost any unpleasant consequence. As with the issue of when a person is to be considered capable of conferring a benefit, a board may be faced with deciding whether a "threat of reprisal" is objectively realistic. As with the complainant's perception of whether the respondent could "confer a benefit," it is suggested that the test should be whether the complainant sincerely believes in the respondent's ability to carry out his or her threat.

Responsibility for Stopping or Preventing Harassment; Corporate Liability

As noted above, the issue of the employer's responsibility for harassment by his or her employees was central to cases under the former *Code*. In several cases, principles of liability were discussed by boards.[52]

---

50. (1986), 8 C.H.R.R. D/3868 (Ont. Bd. of Inquiry).
51. *Ibid.*, at D/3868. For other examples of reprisal see *Hughes v. Dollar Snack Bar* (1981), 3 C.H.R.R. D/1014, and *Noffke v. McClaskin Hot House, ante*, note 4, the latter decided under the present *Code*.
52. See, for example, *Simms v. Ford Motor Co.* (1970), unreported (Ont. Bd. of Inquiry); *Dhillon v. F.W. Woolworth Co.* (1982), 3 C.H.R.R. D/743 (Ont. Bd. of Inquiry); *Olarte v. Commodore Business Machines Ltd.* (1983), 4 C.H.R.R. D/1705 (Ont. Bd. of Inquiry), affirmed (1984), 16 C.H.R.R. D/2833 (Ont. Div. Ct.).

The 1981 *Code* contained a section [now s. 45(1)] which specifically dealt with liability on the part of a "corporation, trade union, trade or occupational association, unincorporated association or employers' organization" for the acts of employees, officers, etc. The provisions of the *Code* ✳ that deal with harassment were not included in the section, which led to questions concerning, for example, the liability of employers for harassment of employees by other employees. Ontario boards of inquiry dealt with that issue by maintaining in the context of the 1981 *Code* the "organic theory of corporate responsibility" developed under the previous *Code* when dealing with harassment.[53]

In *Wei Fu v. Ontario Government Protective Service*, the board indicated that the existence of subsection 41(4) should not be taken to eliminate corporate liability, and proceeded to summarize situations in which, on theories developed to date, corporate liability might arise from harassment by an employee:

> It seems arguable that the purpose of subsection 40(4) [now 41(2)] is simply to expand upon the ordinary remedies and better prevent a "repetition" of harassment by stating that a board of inquiry "shall remain seized of the matter" and be able to make a further, directing order if there is a repetition. The purpose of the new *Code* is to expand upon the then existing human rights and remedies at the time of its enactment, not detract from them. Subsection 40(4) [now 41(2)] should not be interpreted, in the absence of explicit language, as meaning that there cannot be an infringement of sections 4 and 8, and an order given under subsection 40(1), against an artificial entity employer on the basis of the organic theory of corporate responsibility.
>
> From my review of the law, it seems an employer would be personally in breach of the *Code* in the following types of situations:
>
> (1) Where the individual employer himself, by his own personal action, directly or indirectly, intentionally infringes a protected right, under section 4 [now s. 5], then he has, of course, contravened sections 4 and 8 [now s. 9] of the *Code*.
>
> (2) Where the individual employer does not intend to discriminate, but there is a constructive discrimination, then the employer is in contravention of sections 10 and 8 [now ss. 11 and 9] of the *Code*. That is, the employer has personally breached the *Code*.
>
> (3) Where the individual employer himself takes no direct action of discrimination, but authorizes, condones, adopts or ratifies an employee's discrimination, then the employer is himself personally liable for contravening the *Code* (whether on a basis of contravening section 8 [now s. 9], or section 10 [now s. 11] coupled with section 8) as it is the employer himself you had infringed or done, directly or indirectly, an act, "that infringes a right under this Part" (section 8). Section 8 [now s. 9] of the *Code* says "no person shall infringe or do . . . anything that infringes a right . . ." The employer is infringing or doing something by its mere passive inaction of allowing an infringement of a right in the workplace when the employer could rectify the situation. To do nothing can be, in the circumstances, to "do" something that "infringes a right" within the meaning of section 8.

---

53. See, for example, *Olarte v. Commodore Business Machines Ltd.*, *ante*, note 52, and other cases noted in Chapter 9 under "Vicarious, corporate liability."

(4) Where the employer is a corporate entity, and an employee is in contravention of the *Code*, and that employee is part of the "directing mind" of the corporation, then the employer corporation is itself personally in contravention. The act of the employee becomes the act of the corporate entity itself, in accordance with the organic theory of corporate responsibility. See *Edilma Olarte et al v. Rafael Deflippis and Commodore Business Machines Ltd.*, (1983) 4 C.H.R.R. D/1705 at D/1746. For example, in *Cowell and Cox v. Gadhoke and Super Great Submarine et al* (1982) 3 C.H.R.R. D/609, (Ont. P.A. Cumming) under the former legislation, the Ontario Human Rights Code, R.S.O. 1980, c. 340 as amended, where the sole managerial employee was guilty of sexual harassment, then the employer corporation was itself personally committing the act of sexual harassment. While they were not necessary facts to the result, in that case the individual respondent was not only the sole manager, but also was the owner (shareholder), a corporate officer, and corporate director. Any one of these factors, coupled with the improper act coming in the course of carrying on the corporation's business, would have rendered the corporation in personal contravention of sections 4 and 8 [now ss. 5 and 9] of the *Code*.

For example, in another case under the former legislation, *Dhillon v. F. W. Woolworth Co. Ltd.* (1982), 3 C.H.R.R. D/206 (Ont. P.A. Cumming) where the management in a warehouse "knew, or should as reasonable men acting in management have known, that there was regular, and significant verbal racial harassment" and "did not take reasonable steps to put an end, or at least minimize, the racial abuse" the Respondent corporation was held to be in breach of the *Code*.

5. The difficulty in applying the organic theory of corporate responsibility (as referred to in #4) comes in the factual determination as to whether the employee in question is part of the "directing mind." *Gadhoke* illustrates the obvious case — the individual respondent was the sole manager, the owner, corporate officer and corporate director. Other situations are not as easy. Generally speaking, whenever an employee provides some functions of management, he is then part of the "directing mind." Once an employee is part of the directing mind, and the contravention of the *Code* comes in his performing his corporate function, the corporation is itself also personally in breach of the *Code*.

6. Where an employee unlawfully (*i.e.*, in contravention of the *Code*) causes the breach of a contract between his employer (the employee-agent's principal) and a complainant, then the employer is liable for a contravention of the *Code* under the common law in respect of agency, for the act of the employee-agent is the act of the employer principal so far as the third party complainant is concerned.

7. If the employee is a mere servant (not part of the "directing mind," and there is not a contract between the employer and a third party that the servant-agent is causing a breach of) then the employer is still liable for certain contraventions of the *Code* by the employee in the course of his employment, even though there is no personal contravention of the *Code* by the employer, under subsection 44(1) [now 45(1)]. . . . It is only in the #7 situation that an employer is not liable for the harassment by an employee.[54]

More recently, in *Robichaud v. Brennan*[55], the Supreme Court of Canada considered whether a corporate respondent should be liable for unauthorized harassment by a supervisory employee under the *Canadian Human Rights Act*, which at the time of the original decision contained no specific provision allowing for corporate liability.

---

54. (1985), 6 C.H.R.R. D/2797 at D/2800-1 (Ont. Bd. of Inquiry).
55. (1987), 8 C.H.R.R. D/4326 (S.C.C.).

Mr. Justice LaForest, for a unanimous court, held that the employer was liable. In doing so, he specifically rejected theories of liability developed in a context of criminal or quasi-criminal conduct, or even in tort. Instead, he based his rationale on the line of Supreme Court judgments that maintain that human rights legislation is concerned with effect rather than intent, with removing discrimination rather than punishing anti-social behaviour.

Mr. Justice LaForest also pointed to the broad remedial powers under the Canadian Act (analogous to those under the *Code*), which allow such remedies as reinstatement, as further proof of legislative intent that the employer is liable for discriminatory working conditions.

The decision of the Supreme Court in *Robichaud* goes even farther than the organic theory of corporate liability developed in Ontario case law to date, which was recognised by the board of inquiry in *Persaud v. Consumers Distributing Ltd.*[56] In that case, the board found that an employee was racially harassed by another employee, one who had no supervisory responsibilities. The board found no evidence that the employer had known of the incidents of harassment. In deciding the issue of employer liability for harassment by an employee, the board reviewed the *Robichaud* judgment and concluded that *Persaud* could be distinguished. The Board acknowledged that the *Robichaud* judgment "would seem to mean that employers are always liable for unlawful discrimination by their employees, even where those acts of discrimination are committed by mere servants".[57] The Chair went on to point out that in the *Robichaud* judgment, LaForest J. had quoted with approval remarks from a judgment of the United States Supreme Court that "seem(ed) limited to supervising personnel".[58] The board then noted that s. 44(1) of the Ontario *Code*, which has no counterpart in the federal legislation considered in *Robichaud*, expressly excepts sections 2(2), 4(2), and 6 from the imposition of vicarious liability. The board concluded that the organic theory of corporate responsibility, as set out in cases such as *Wei Fu*,[59] applied in harassment situations, and that, accordingly, the employer in *Persaud* was not responsible for harassment.

The board in *Persaud* sets out a reasonable explanation for the failure of the legislature to include those sections of the *Code* which deal with harassment in the section on vicarious liability. Further, the board's declining to read s. 44(1) as totally excluding employer liability for harassment is consistent with the purposive interpretation to human rights legislation urged by the Supreme Court of Canada. however, it is arguable that the jux-

---

56. (1991), 14 C.H.R.R. D/23.
57. *Supra*, at D/28.
58. *Supra*.
59. *Ante*, note 8.

taposition of *Robichaud* and *Persaud* lends itself to another interpretation. If it is correct that, absent the effect of *Robichaud*, principles borrowed from tort such as the organic theory of liability should be applied, it is possible that the *Robichaud* judgment sweeps away any reliance on tort principles, and substitutes a preventive approach that essentially effects vicarious liability despite the wording of the statute.

Awards in Harassment Cases

Awards are discussed in some detail in Chapter 9. For the purpose of this chapter it should be noted that the general award power in subsection 41(1)(*a*) has been used by boards to fashion awards especially appropriate to harassment situations, such as a requirement that a male employer found to have sexually harassed employees notify the Commission every time a female employee left his employ,[60] for a period of two years.

An Alberta board of inquiry, on a finding of harassment, awarded the complainant $500 toward the cost of psychological counselling.[61] It remains to be seen whether Ontario boards will consider this type of award to be in the nature of the restitution contemplated by section 41(1)(*a*).

Where a respondent has engaged in harassment, he or she is particularly liable to an award of damages for mental anguish under subsection 41(1)(*b*), since harassment by nature usually comprises actions "engaged in wilfully and recklessly."[62]

Subsection 41(2), which specifically relates to harassment that is repeated after a board has found liability, allows for a particular type of order after a somewhat complicated process. If a complaint goes to a board, anyone, who, "in the opinion of the board, knew or was in possession of facts from which he or she ought reasonably to have known of the conduct and who had authority to penalize or prevent the conduct,"[63] can be added as a party "at any state of the proceeding."[64] If the board finds that harassment has occurred, it may then proceed to make a finding as to whether the person added as a party:

(a) knew or was in possession of knowledge from which he ought to have known of the infringement; and

(b) had the authority by reasonably available means to penalize or prevent the conduct and failed to use it.

If such a finding is made, the board must remain seized of the matter.

---

60. See *Sharp v. Seasons Restaurant* (1987), 8 C.H.R.R. D/4133, discussed in Chapter 9.
61. See *Deisting v. Dollar Pizza* (1982), 3 C.H.R.R. D/898 (Alta. Bd. of Inquiry).
62. See discussion of factors considered as listed by the board in *Graesser v. Porto* (1983), 4 C.H.R.R. D/1569 (Ont. Bd. of Inquiry) discussed in Chapter 9.
63. S. 38(2)(*e*).
64. S. 38(3).

If there is another complaint of harassment, the Commission may, after investigation, request the board to reconvene. Once again the board must consider whether the employer, landlord or other person in authority:

(c) knew or was in possession of knowledge from which he or she ought to have known of the repetition of infringement; and

(d) had the authority by reasonably available means to penalize or prevent the continuation or repetition of the conduct and failed to use it.

On such a finding being made, "the board may make an order requiring the person to take whatever sanctions or steps are reasonably available to prevent any further continuation or repetition of the infringement of the right."[65]

Such an order could conceivably be quite comprehensive. "Sanctions or steps" that are "reasonably available" could conceivably include the firing, demotion or transfer of harassing employees, the eviction of harassing tenants,[66] the formulation and posting of an anti-harassment policy, the establishment of complaints procedure in respect of harassment, the establishment of middle-management or employee training programs related to cultural differences and race relations, and so on. One board of inquiry under the previous *Code* ordered the respondent to constitute a Management–Employee Race Relations Committee. The Committee was to include as an *ex officio* member, an officer of the Ontario Human Rights Commission, and was to meet regularly, on company time, for four months, in order to formulate effective anti-harassment measures for the respondent company.[67]

---

65. S. 41(2).

66. The *Landlord and Tenant Act*, R.S.O. 1990, c. L.7 at ss. 107(1)(c) and (d) permits a tenant to be evicted where "the conduct of the tenant or a person permitted in the residential premises . . . is such that it substantially interferes with the reasonable enjoyment of the premises for all usual purposes by the landlord and the other tenants", or where "the safety or other lawful right, privilege or interest of any other tenant in the residential premises is or has been seriously impaired by an act or omission of the tenant or a person permitted in the residential premises by the tenant where such an act or omission occurs in the residential premises or its environs".

67. See discussion in Chapter 9.

8

THE COMMISSION AND ITS FUNCTIONS

The Ontario Human Rights Commission is composed of at least seven persons appointed by Cabinet.[1] The Chief Commissioner holds a full-time position; the rest of the Commissioners hold office on a part-time basis.

According to subsection 28(1) of the Act, "the Lieutenant Governor in Council shall designate at least three members of the Commission to constitute a race relations division of the Commission and shall designate one member of the race relations division as Commissioner for Race Relations." However, since approximately 1985, there has been no such designation by Cabinet. The former Race Relations Division of the Human Rights Commission was transferred from the Ministry of Labour to the Ministry of Citizenship, where its functions, personnel and name have undergone changes. Currently, the Ministry of Citizenship has an Anti-Racism Secretariat, which undertakes responsibilities similar to those formerly undertaken by the Race Relations Division.

The Commission is charged with the administration of the *Code*.[2] Executive functions are largely delegated to staff appointed under the *Public Service Act*.[3] Senior staff currently include Directors of Legal Services, Policy and Research, Systemic Investigations, Case Management, Regional Services, and Communications and Education.

The investigation of complaints is carried out by the Commission staff, herein referred to as officers. None of the staff are members of the Commission.

The Commission's functions are set out in section 29 of the *Code*:

> It is the function of the Commission,
> (*a*) to forward the policy that the dignity and worth of every person be recognized and that equal rights and opportunities be provided without discrimination that is contrary to law;
> (*b*) to promote an understanding and acceptance of and compliance with this Act;

---

1. See s. 27(1) of the *Code*. At present, an All-Party Committee approves the appointments.
2. See s. 27(2).
3. See s. 27(4).

(c)   to recommend for consideration a special plan or program designed to meet the requirements of subsection 14(1), subject to the right of a person aggrieved by the implementation of the plan or program to request the Commission to reconsider its recommendations and section 37 applies with necessary modifications;

(d)   to develop and conduct programs of public information and education and undertake, direct and encourage research designed to eliminate discriminatory practices that infringe rights under this Act.;

(e)   to examine and review any statute or regulation, and any program or policy made by or under a statute and make recommendations on any provision, program, or policy, that in its opinion is inconsistent with the intent of this Act;

(f)   to inquire into incidents of and conditions leading or tending to lead to tension or conflict based upon identification by a prohibited ground of discrimination and take appropriate action to eliminate the source of tension or conflict;

(g)   to initiate investigations into problems based upon identification by a prohibited ground of discrimination that may arise in a community, and encourage and coordinate plans, programs and activities to reduce or prevent such problems;

(h)   to promote, assist and encourage public, municipal or private agencies, organizations, groups or persons to engage in programs to alleviate tensions and conflicts based upon identification by a prohibited ground of discrimination;

(i)   to enforce this Act and orders of boards of inquiry; and

(j)   to perform the functions assigned to it by this or any other Act.

It is beyond the scope of this book to discuss the Commission's research and education functions. However, there will be a discussion of some of the implications of sections 29(c), (g), (i), and (j). The chapter will deal with only actions taken by the Commission itself. Proceedings before boards of inquiry will be discussed in Chapter 9.

SPECIAL PROGRAMS: SECTION 29(c)

Two separate Commission functions will be discussed here. The first is a recommendation by the Commission that a special program be undertaken. The second is review by the Commission of actual or proposed special programs.

Section 28(c) provides the Commission with jurisdiction, and, to some extent, mandates Commission activity in recommending special plans or programs "designed to meet the requirements of subsection 14(1)."

A special program is defined by section 14(1) as a program "designed to relieve hardship or economic disadvantage or to assist disadvantaged persons or groups to achieve or attempt to achieve equal opportunity or that is likely to contribute to the elimination of the infringement of rights under Part I."

Section 14 has several aspects: it declares that a "special program" as defined does not breach the *Code*; it provides for review of proposed or existing programs by the Commission; it sets out a procedure by which the Commission may make a declaratory order as to the validity of a program, with or without modification; and it allows a "person aggrieved" by such an order to have the Commission reconsider its order.[4]

---

4. S. 14 will be discussed further in Chapter 6.

Nowhere in section 14 is there any mention of the Commission recommending special programs — the section appears to deal solely with methods for ascertaining whether an existing or proposed program qualifies for a section 14 exemption, or what changes it needs to qualify for such an exemption. Therefore, it would seem that the legislature is providing for an additional function in section 29(*c*): that is, the active *recommendation* by the Commission of special programs in areas where they have not been voluntarily undertaken.[5]

Apart from its powers to recommend special programs, the Commission has powers and responsibilities in regard to existing or proposed programs.[6]

> (2) The Commission may,
>> (*a*) upon its own initiative;
>> (*b*) upon application by a person seeking to implement a special program under the protection of subsection (1); or
>> (*c*) upon a complaint in respect of which the protection of subsection (1) is claimed,
>
> inquire into the special program[7] and, in the discretion of the Commission, may by order declare,
>> (*d*) that the special program, as defined in the order, does not satisfy the requirements of subsection (1), or
>> (*e*) that the special program as defined in the order, with such modifications, if any, as the Commission considers advisable, satisfies the requirements of subsection(1).

It should be noted that when the Commission is investigating upon its own initiative, the *Code* does not appear to grant the same powers it has when investigating a complaint.[8] However, the person or company implementing the program under scrutiny runs the risk of an adverse declaratory order where there is no co-operation with the investigation.

The declaratory order contemplated by sections 14(2)(*d*) and (*e*) obviously would have no immediate effect on the program at issue. However, if there is a complaint of discrimination arising out of the operation of the program the following consequences are possible:

1. If an adverse order has been made under section 14(2)(*d*), or where an order has been made declaring that the program would qualify with

---

5. Although the Commission has power only to "recommend," its intercession could be seen as a useful addition to pressure from individuals and groups on the target corporation. However, it would appear that there has been little activity in this area, outside of the context of complaints, in the years since the 1990 *Code* was proclaimed.

6. S. 14(2).

7. Other than those "implemented by the Crown or an agency of the Crown": s. 14(5).

8. S. 37, which sets out these powers, speaks only of the investigation "of a complaint," therefore, unless the Commission were investigating pursuant to a complaint (see s. 14(2)(*c*)), these powers are seemingly not applicable.

certain modifications, and those modifications have not been made, the way is clear for the Commission to appoint a board of inquiry in respect of the complainant. The findings of the investigation would certainly be adduced as evidence for the Commission at that board.

2. If there is a finding that the program qualifies for an exemption under section 14(1), or if there is an order that it would so qualify with certain modifications, and those modifications are made, the Commission would probably refuse to deal with any subsequent complaint, unless substantial time has elapsed and/or there has been a change in circumstances.[9]

Anyone "aggrieved" by the making of an order under section 14(2) may request that Commission reconsider its decision.[10] Pursuant to section 14(3), the provisions of section 37 are imported *mutatis mutandis* to the reconsideration. Thus, the time limit for filing an application for reconsideration is fifteen days after the date of the mailing of the order "or such longer period as the Commission may for special reasons allow."[11] If there is another party to be notified, as in the case where the program has been investigated because of the filing of a complaint, the Commission must notify that party that the order is being reconsidered, and the party may make written submissions.[12] The written decision of the Commission, with reasons, must be "promptly communicated to the complainant and the person complained against," or, presumably, solely to the person whose program has been reviewed if he or she is the only "person aggrieved." The decision on reconsideration is final.[13]

In July, 1990, the Commission published a guideline on special programs in "working document" form. The guideline sets out suggestions for designing a special program and remarks on the legitimacy of suitable advertising for an employment equity program. It also reiterates the Commission's authority to inquire into special programs and to make orders. The guideline concludes with a description of a procedure for applying for an order in respect of a special program.

To date, the Commission has not published orders in respect of special programs. However, the Saskatchewan Human Rights Commission, which

---

9. See s. 34(1)(*c*). In *Roberts v. Ontario (Ministry of Health)* (1989), 10 C.H.R.R. D/6353 (Ont. Bd. of Inquiry), the board commented in *obiter* that a declaration by the Commission that a special program "satisfies" the requirements of subsection 13(1) [now s. 14] might not be a complete defence to further attack on that program by way of a complaint, which position seems in accord with the relevant provisions of the *Code*.

10. S. 14(3).

11. S. 37(1).

12. S. 37(2).

13. S. 37(3).

has in its governing legislation a provision similar to section 14,[14] has published several decisions approving or disapproving special programs.[15] The Saskatchewan Commission's evaluation of special programs is influenced by its regulations governing the acceptability of such programs. As the factors considered by the Ontario Commission may be different, the Saskatchewan decisions will not be discussed here.

In *Ontario Women's Hockey Assn. v. Blainey*,[16] the Divisional Court of Ontario found that the Commission need not rule on the validity of an alleged special program under subsection 13(2) before appointing a board of inquiry in which the respondents plan to use section 13 as a defence.

DEALING WITH COMPLAINTS: SECTIONS 29(g) AND (i)

The procedures by which the Commission fulfils its enforcement responsibilities will be divided into six areas: investigation of complaints; decisions not to deal with complaints; conciliation; recommendation of a board of inquiry; requests that a board of inquiry reconvene; and prosecutions by the Commission.

Investigation of Complaints

Anyone may file a written complaint on a belief that the *Code* has been breached in a way that affects his or her rights.[17] The Commission may also make a complaint "by itself or at the request of any person."[18]

There are no time limits for complaints specified by the *Code*. This was recently confirmed on appeal to the Court of Appeal of Ontario in *West End Construction Ltd. v. Ontario (Human Rights Commission)*.[19] In that

---

14. See the Saskatchewan *Human Rights Code*, S.S. 1979, c. S-24.1, s. 47.

15. *Re Saskatchewan Pipe Fitting Industry Joint Training Board v. Assn. of Metis and Non-Status Indians of Saskatchewan* (1981), 2 C.H.R.R. D/452 (Sask. Bd. of Inquiry); *Re Can. Employment & Immigration Comm.* (1981), 2 C.H.R.R. D/595 (Sask. Human Rights Comm.); *Re Regina Plains Community College* (1981), 2 C.H.R.R. D/605 (Sask. Human Rights Comm.); *Re Saskatchewan Power Corp.* (1981), 3 C.H.R.R. D/673 (Sask. Human Rights Comm.).

16. (1987), 8 C.H.R.R. D/4180 (Ont. Div. Ct.).

17. S. 32(1).

18. S. 32(2). It would seem that this provision represents a narrowing of the ability of a third party to bring a complaint under the *Code*. The previous *Code* provided for complaints by "any person who has reasonable grounds for believing that any person has contravened a provision of this Act." (R.S.O. 1980, c. 340, ss. 13(1) and (2).) Thus it was possible for the coach of a children's softball team to bring an action on behalf of one of his players in *Bannerman v. Ont. Rural Softball Assn.* (1977), unreported (Ont. Bd. of Inquiry). Presumably, any third party wishing to lodge a complaint must now persuade the Commission to act for him or her. Note, though, that in a complaint under s. 12, the "third party" is properly the complainant.

19. (1989), 70 O.R. (2d) 133 (C.A.).

case, the Divisional Court upheld an appeal in part, that part being in respect of a complaint brought in 1979 but based on events that had occurred
in 1976. The Court held that the complaint was barred by subsection
45(1)(*h*) of the *Limitations Act*.[20] That section provides for a two-year limitation period for "an action for a penalty, damages or sum of money given
by any statute."

In allowing the appeal, the Court of Appeal found that the filing of a
complaint under the *Code* was not the institution of an action within the
meaning of the *Judicature Act*.

The Commission can, in certain circumstances, refuse to deal with a
complaint that is over six months old; this will be further discussed below.

The *Code* provides[21] that investigation of a complaint can be carried
out by a member of the Commission. However, this function is routinely
undertaken by an employee[22] of the Commission.

Overview of the Investigation Process

In some cases, a complaint of discrimination appears straightforward
and the officer may try to handle it by phone (this process is referred to the
Commission as Priority Case Handling). This process may fail or may not
be attempted. In that case the more ordinary course of investigation proceeds. That process is summarized by Mary Eberts as follows:

> . . . . Firstly, the respondent is asked to complete a questionnaire setting out its response
> to the items in the complaint. Then, the parties are asked to attend a fact-finding confer-
> ence (FFC) chaired by Commission staff, usually the officer in charge of the case and
> his or her supervisor. The allegations and answers are canvassed with a view to finding
> whether there is any common ground. No witnesses other than the parties are present at
> the FFC, and all questions and comments notionally are routed through the chair. Thus it
> is very difficult to use the FFC to test the credibility of the other party, or the strength of
> its case. At the end of the proceedings, there will be a formal break, after which the so-
> called conciliation phase will be embarked upon. The officers will try to discover
> whether a settlement is possible. Sometimes, they will play a real mediating role, going
> back and forth between the parties. Other times, they will be quite passive.
>
> During the FFC, statements made by the parties will be recorded by Commission
> staff, and can form part of the record of investigation. At the start of conciliation, how-
> ever, it is made clear that statements made in that phase are privileged.
>
> If the FFC produces no settlement, then the case enters the extended investigation
> phase. The officer will interview witnesses suggested by the complainant and respondent
> as well as others believed to have knowledge of the events complained of.
>
> At the conclusion of the interviews a report is prepared, containing a summary of
> the evidence and analysis of investigation findings. Whereas formerly only the gist of
> that report was shared with the parties, now they have a copy of it, and an opportunity to
> make submissions in writing on it to the Commissioners when they consider the case.

---

20. R.S.O. 1990, c. L.15.
21. At s. 33(2).
22. Hereinafter referred to as an officer.

Usually, the officer will meet once more with the parties at the end of the investigation to review the findings and attempt a settlement. If this effort is unsuccessful, the report of the case any submissions by the parties are placed before the Commissioners at their next meeting.[23]

Powers of the Investigator

To date, most Commission investigations have been carried out without use by the officers of the coercive powers granted by the 1981 *Code*. Most respondents, seemingly, have recognized the value of having an opportunity either to persuade the officer that the *Code* has not been breached, or to settle the complaint without recourse to a board of inquiry.[24]

Although it appears that the present *Code* allows the investigator much less independent authority than its predecessor,[25] the Commission as a whole has been given a number of effective methods of dealing with uncooperative respondents.

Section 33(3) provides that the investigator may:

(*a*) enter any place, other than a place that is being used as a dwelling, at any reasonable time, for the purpose of investigating the complaint;

(*b*) request the production for inspection and examination of documents or things that are or may be relevant to the investigation;

(*c*) upon giving a receipt therefor, remove from a place documents produced in response to a request under clause (*b*) for the purpose of making copies thereof or extracts therefrom and shall promptly return them to the person who produced or furnished them; and

(*d*) question a person on matters that are or may be relevant to the complaint subject to the person's right to have counsel or a personal representative present during such questioning, and may exclude from the questioning any person who may be adverse in interest to the complainant.

In regard to section 33(3)(*a*), when the place is "being used as a dwelling," the investigator must get permission of the occupier[26] to enter. If

---

23. M. Eberts, "Ontario Human Rights Commission" in *Recent Developments v. Administrative Law*, Carswell; this article contains *inter alia* a very useful guide to counsel dealing with the Commission's investigation and settlement process.

24. It is, obviously, to encourage such voluntary co-operation that the *Code* provides that both Commissioners and staff may invoke a privilege, in respect of information obtained in the course of an investigation, in any civil suit or other proceedings. S. 30 provides:

"(1) No person who is a member of the Commission shall be required to give testimony in a civil suit or any proceedings as to information obtained in the course of an investigation under this Act.

(2) No person who is employed in the administration of this Act shall be required to give testimony in a civil suit or any proceeding other than a proceeding under this Act as to information obtained in the course of an investigation under this Act."

25. See R.S.O. 1980, c. 340, s. 16.

26. In regard to rented premises, a question may arise as to who is the "occupier" from whom permission must be obtained. The *Occupiers, Liability Act*, R.S.O. 1990, c. 0.2, s. 1(*a*), defines "occupier" as

such permission is not given, the officer must go through the procedure for obtaining a warrant to enter.[27]

If a person who is or may be a party to a complaint denies entry to a place that is not used as a dwelling, or impedes or prevents an investigation therein, the Commission has two options. It may request the appointment of a board of inquiry,[28] or it may authorize the investigator "to apply to a justice of the peace for a warrant to enter." The procedure for obtaining a warrant is set out in section 33(8). The warrant is effective for fifteen days and must be executed "at reasonable times as specified in the warrant."[29]

In regard to section 33(3)(*b*) and (*c*), where the officer is refused permission to examine the relevant documents and things, or to make copies,[30] the Commission may either request a board of inquiry or authorize the investigator to apply for a search warrant under section 33(7). That subsection provides:

> Where a justice of the peace is satisfied on evidence upon oath that there are in a place documents that there is reasonable ground to believe will afford evidence relevant to the complaint, he or she may issue a warrant in the prescribed form authorizing a person named in the warrant to search a place for any such documents, and to remove them for the purposes of making copies thereof or extracts therefrom, and the documents shall be returned promptly to the place from which they were removed.

Provisions as to reasonable time of execution and expiry date are the same as with a warrant for entry.

Finally, an officer may, under section 33(3)(*d*),

"(i) a person who is in physical possession of premises, or
(ii) a person who has responsibility for and control over the condition of premises or the activities there carried on, or control over persons allowed to enter the premises,

notwithstanding that there is more than one occupier of the same premises."
However, the *Oxford English Dictionary* gives a more simple definition of "occupier" as "the person who holds or is in actual possession of a piece of property." If this definition is used, the tenant's permission is sufficient for the purposes of the investigation; the landlord need not be applied to.

27. This procedure is discussed below.
28. In *Ryckman v. Board of Commissioners of Police* (1987), 8 C.H.R.R. D/4138 (Ont. Bd. of Inquiry), the board held that, when met with resistance to its investigation, the Commission may request the appointment of a Board of Inquiry, and in that case, need not take steps to complete its investigation or "endeavour to effect a settlement," as otherwise required by subsection 33(1). At the board of inquiry, the Commission can apply for a *subpoena duces tecum* and request an adjournment to review documents thereby obtained.
29. Ss. 33(9) and (10).
30. S. 33(13) states that "Copies of, or extracts from, documents removed from premises under clause 3(*c*) or subsection (7) certified as being true copies of the originals by the person who made them, are admissible in evidence to the same extent as, and have the same evidentiary value as, the documents of which they are copies or extracts."

question a person on matters that are or may be relevant to the complaint subject to the person's right to have counsel or a personal representative present during such questioning, and may exclude from the questioning any person who may be adverse in interest to the complainant.

While it is true that Commission investigators have lost the independent power to require entry and production of documents, it should be noted that, in a practical sense, the Commission's power to recommend an immediate board of inquiry where respondents deny the investigator's requests carries considerable persuasive weight. A respondent would be well advised to consider whether denying access is worth the publicity and expense attendant on a public hearing, and the loss of any opportunity either to persuade the investigator or the Commission that there is no case, or to settle at the conciliation stage.[31]

The Commission has another power that should be noted here. Anyone may be charged with an offence, should he or she "hinder, obstruct or interfere with a person in the execution of a warrant or otherwise impede an investigation under this Act" other than by refusing documents.[32]

The investigative powers of administrative tribunals have been subject to challenge under the *Canadian Charter of Rights and Freedoms*. To date, however, the courts have distinguished between civil and criminal investigative processes for the purpose of *Charter* review. Two cases in which government officials were empowered to enter the premises and require the production of documents on other things illustrate this point: *Bertram S. Miller Ltd. v. R.*[33] involved inspections under the *Plant Quarantine Act*, and *Belgoma Transportation Ltd. (Belgoma) v. Ontario (Director of Employment Standards)*[34] dealt with the powers of an officer under the *Employment Standards Act*. These cases, involving as they do the power of an officer to enter and demand production without a warrant, impose far more of a potential threat to *Charter* rights than does the current investigative power of officers under the *Code*, involving as it does the application to a justice of the peace for a warrant. While the test established by subsection 33(7) for the issuance of a warrant does not meet the standards set out by the Supreme Court of Canada in *Hunter v. Southam Inc.*,[35] it would appear unlikely that the courts would hold investigative proceedings in re-

---

31. Where the Commission requested certain documents during investigation but was denied them, the Chair of the subsequent board of inquiry was sympathetic to the Commission's request for a *subpoena duces tecum* at the hearing. See *Youmans v Lily Cups, Inc.* (1990), 13 C.H.R.R. D/395.
32. See ss. 33(11) and 44(1).
33. [1986] 3 F.C. 291 at 324 (Fed. C.A.), leave to appeal refused (1986), 75 N.R. 158 (note) (S.C.C.).
34. (1984), 47 O.R. (2d) 309 (Div. Ct.), affirmed (1985), 51 O.R. (2d) 509 (C.A.).
35. (1984), 11 D.L.R. (4th) 641 (S.C.C.).

spect of the *Code* to the same standards as those imposed in respect of the *Combines Investigation Act.*[36]

REFUSAL TO DEAL WITH A COMPLAINT: SECTION 34

The inclusion of section 34 was presumably intended to prevent the waste of time involved in giving a dubious complaint the full investigation that would be necessary before the Commission could properly decide whether or not to recommend a board of inquiry. The Commission may decide not to deal with a complaint

(1) Where it appears to the Commission that,

    (*a*) the complaint is one that could or should be more appropriately dealt with under an Act other than this Act;

    (*b*) the subject-matter of the complaint is trivial, frivolous, vexatious or made in bad faith;

    (*c*) the complaint is not within the jurisdiction of the Commission; or

    (*d*) the facts upon which the complaint is based occurred more than six months before the complaint was filed, unless the Commission is satisfied that the delay was incurred in good faith and no substantial prejudice will result to any person affected by the delay.

Under section 34(1)(*a*), the Commission may decide not to deal with complaints that could more properly be dealt with under an Act other than the *Code*. In such cases, the Commission would presumably refer the complainant to the more appropriate route.

Section 34(1)(*b*) provides that the Commission may choose not to deal with complaints that are "trivial, frivolous, vexatious or made in bad faith."

Black's Law Dictionary[37] defines "trivial" as "trifling, inconsiderable; of small worth or importance," and "frivolous" as "of little weight or importance." It adds that a "proceeding" is "frivolous when it is clearly insufficient on its face . . . and is presumably interposed for mere purposes of delay or to embarrass the opponent." It is suggested that an adherence to these definitions would assist the Commission in separating intrinsically worthless or absurd complaints from those that are merely novel.

"Vexatious" is defined in *Black's Law Dictionary* as:

without reasonable or probable cause or excuse. When the party bringing the proceeding is not acting *bona fide* and merely wishes to annoy or embarrass his opponent, or when it is not calculated to lead to any practical result, such a proceeding is often described as "frivolous and vexatious" and the court may dismiss it on that ground.

---

36. For useful reviews of the law in this area, see Neil Finkelstein, "Constitutional Rights and Investigative Powers" in N. Finkelstein and B. Rogers (eds.), *Recent Developments in Administrative Law* (1987) Carswell Ltd. at 127-168, and "Charter Limits on Investigative Powers" in Finkelstein and Rogers (eds.), *Administrative Tribunals and the Charter* (1990) Carswell Ltd.

37. 5th ed. (1970).

It may also be "vexatious" to being a complaint under the *Code* in regard to facts that have been litigated in another forum.[38]

"Bad faith" is defined in *Black*'s as:

> The opposite of "good faith," generally implying or involving actual or constructive fraud, or a design to mislead or deceive another, or a neglect or refusal to fulfill some duty or some contractual obligation, not prompted by an honest mistake as to one's right or duties, but by some interested or sinister motive. The term "bad faith" is not simply judgment or negligence, but rather it implies the conscious doing of a wrong because of dishonest purpose or moral obliquity; it is different from the negative idea of negligence in that it contemplates a state of mind affirmatively operating with furtive design or ill mind.

Section 34(1)(*c*) provides that the Commission may refuse to deal with a complaint that is outside its jurisdiction. As a practical matter, complainants with issues that are clearly within the jurisdiction of, for example, the Canadian Human Rights Commission or the Employment Standards Division of the Ontario Minister of Labour are often referred directly when they approach the Commission to lay a complaint. By contrast, refusal to deal pursuant to section 34(1)(*c*) will usually occur when, after a certain amount of investigation and a review by the Commission, it is concluded that the respondent has a clear defence under one of the exception sections of the *Code*.

Finally, section 34(1)(*d*) empowers the Commission to refuse to deal with a complaint that is based on facts that occurred more than six months prior to the filing of the complaint unless the Commission finds that the delay was incurred in good faith and with no substantial prejudice to the person concerned. It should be noted that this section in no way imposes a time limit. In order to refuse to deal with the complaint, the Commission must be satisfied not only that the facts occurred more than six months before filing, but that they delay was not incurred in good faith, and that the proceeding with the complaint will result in prejudice to "any person affected by the delay." Even so, the provision is discretionary; the Commission may proceed with the complaint.

Where the Commission decides not to deal with a complaint, it must inform the complainant, in writing, of its decision and the reasons therefore, and must inform the complainant as to how to apply for reconsideration.[39]

---

38. See *Wightman v. Coffin* (1914), 6 O.W.N. 112 (H.C.), in which the court said. "'An action is considered frivolous, vexatious and an abuse of the process of the court' and liable to be dismissed if its effect is to re-litigate a case disposed of in a former action." Note, however, that human rights boards of inquiry have heard cases that were the subject of contemporaneous or previous grievance proceedings in employment matters (see the discussion of *res judicata* and issue estoppel in Chapter 9). Thus, the Commission may consider it appropriate to have a board appointed when there is doubt that the matter is a re-litigation in all respects.

39. S. 34(2).

The procedure for reconsideration is the same as that outlined above in the discussion on review and recommendation of section 14 programs.[40]

CONCILIATION

The Commission is charged, under section 33, with the responsibility to attempt to settle every complaint.[41] In fact, the majority of complaints are settled.

In regard to the handling of complaints, Professor Tarnopolsky, in *Discrimination and The Law*,[42] stresses the importance of the clear separation of the investigation and conciliation processes. He concludes:[43]

> it is most important that investigations and settlement be conducted by different individuals, if at all possible, and this has been provided for in subsection 37(2) of the Canadian Act. If this is not possible because of lack of personnel, or because the respondent and the place where the pertinent events occurred are too distant from a Human Rights Commission office, then, at the least, the human rights officer should leave the respondent after completing the investigation in order to assess the evidence. Only after concluding that there is probable cause should such officer return to attempt settlement. . .

In Ontario, the practice is for the same officer to have carriage of the complaint through both the investigation and conciliation stages. However, as Professor Tarnopolsky note,[44]

> The investigating officer indicates in the file the date he begins his conciliation function. This ensures that the officer takes stock of the results of his investigation since he will not be able to give evidence he has garnered after this date.

The officer clearly defines the time at which the investigation has been completed and the conciliation is to begin. When the parties are convened at a conciliation meeting they are advised that conciliation is commencing and that everything they say at this stage is privileged. No evidence discovered in the course of conciliation is ever led before a board.

It would appear from the language of the *Code* that the duty to attempt to reach a settlement in each case is mandatory. The Board of Inquiry in *McMinn v. Sault Ste. Marie Professional Firefighters' Association*[45] appears

---

40. See pp. 215-18 above. The Federal Court of Appeal has ruled that in making analogous decisions, the federal Human Rights Commission must act in accordance with the rules of natural justice. See *Latif v. Canada (Canadian Human Rights Commission)* (1979), 105 D.L.R. (3d) 609 (C.A.).

41. This responsibility is explicitly made subject to the right of the Commission to refuse to deal with a complaint; see s. 33(1).

42. (1985) at 15-8 to 15-10.

43. *Ibid.*, p. 15-9.

44. *Ibid.*, p. 15-9.

45. (1986), 7 C.H.R.R. D/3458 (Ont. Bd. of Inquiry). See also *Alberta v. Pro Western Plastics Ltd.*, [1983] 5 W.W.R. 730 (Alta. C.A.), mentioned with approval in *F.W.T.A.O. v. Ontario (Human Rights Commission)* (1988), 67 O.R. (2d) 492 (Div. Ct.)

to have taken this view. In addition, it would appear that the obligation to attempt to achieve settlement arises even where the Commission is unlikely to appoint a board of inquiry; subsection 33(1) explicitly makes the obligation to investigate and conciliate subject only to section 34 (the section that allows the Commission to refuse to deal with a complaint).

There may be an exception to this obligation where the respondent refuses to cooperate with the investigation. In *Ryckman v. Board of Commissioners of Police (Kenora)*[46] the Board indicated that, in such circumstances, the Commission need not take steps to complete its investigation or endeavour to effect settlement.

There are indications that, as long as conciliation efforts have been undertaken, the timing of the officer's attempt to conciliate is not a matter of major importance. The board in *McMinn*[47] declined to rule that conciliation must be the last step in the investigation. Nor did the Divisional Court in *Re F.W.T.A.O. v. Ontario (Human Rights Commission)*[48] require the Commission to formally include an affiliate of the respondent in all of its conciliation efforts, when that affiliate had only intervenor status, and where it was clear the respondent and affiliate took the same position.

Another issue in relation to conciliation is what will happen if the complainant and the Commission disagree as to what constitutes a reasonable offer of settlement. Where this stalemate occurs before a board has been appointed, the Commission is clearly free to decide not to request a board. Where an offer of settlement is made after the appointment of a board, however, the complainant may have the right to a hearing despite the Commission's view that the settlement is appropriate.[49]

Where a written settlement is signed by the parties and approved by the Commission, it is binding upon the parties. A breach of the settlement is a ground for a complaint.[50]

The Commission is under no obligation to ratify a settlement. In *Consumer's Distributing Co. Ltd. v. Ontario (Human Rights Commission)*[51] a complainant was represented by a lawyer in agreeing to a settlement. He then contacted the Commission, stating that he had signed the agreement under duress and requesting that the Commission not ratify the agreement. Ultimately, the Commission did not ratify the agreement. The respondent applied for judicial review, arguing that, absent proof of duress, the Commission was under the same duty as a court to apply the common law to enforcement of settlements between parties, and that the Commission

---

46. (1987) 8 C.H.R.R. D/4138 (Ont. Bd. of Inquiry).
47. *Ante*, note 45.
48. *Ante*, note 45.
49. See the discussion of this issue in Chapter 9.
50. S. 43.
51. (1987), 24 Admin. L.R. 1 (Ont. Div. Ct.).

should hold a *viva voce* hearing to determine whether the complainant had settled under duress.

The Divisional Court refused the respondent's application. The Court's reasons were summed up as follows:

> It is our opinion that the Commission is under no obligation to approve of a settlement, such as that in issue in this application. Section 28 [now s. 29] of the *Code* imposes on the Commission a broad, complex and subtle statutory mandate. That mandate as augmented by ss. 32(1) and 35(1) [now ss. 33(1) and 36(1)] includes the necessity, if possible, to seek "to effect" a settlement of a complaint.
>
> Any settlement, even if the result of the active intervention of the Commission, would at the end of the day, have to be in consonance with what the Commission judged to promote the policy ends of the statute, as particularly noted in s. 28. To say the least, those policy ends are much broader in scope than would be engaged by the mere resolution of the simple issue of whether the complainant was under duress when he signed the agreement of January 18, 1985.
>
> Among the appropriate concerns of the Commission in that regard would be all of the matters specified in s. 28. Not the least among the Commission's concerns, is that noted in para. (*f*) of s. 28:
>
> (*f*) to inquire into incidents of and conditions leading or tending to lead to tension or conflict based upon identification by a prohibited ground of discrimination and take appropriate action to eliminate the source of tension or conflict;
>
> Within the purview of the Commission's duty under s. 28(*f*), would be a consideration of whether the agreement was procured by duress; however, a decision on that score, one way or the other, would not fulfil the Commission's obligations under s. 28(*f*). To merely find that a settlement, negotiated without the active intervention and participation of officers of the Commission, was not a product of duress would not relieve the Commission of its duty under s. 28(*f*) to "take appropriate action to eliminate the source of tension or conflict." To take such appropriate action, the Commission would indeed have to delve further into the facts than is involved in an ascertainment of whether the agreement was procured by duress.
>
> Its decision whether to ratify the agreement, or rather as s. 42 [now s. 43] states, to "approve" of the agreement, requires the Commission to take into account the promotion of the policy ends of the *Code* stated to be pursued as a "function" of the Commission under s. 28. Those policy ends seem to be essentially administrative in nature. Even if the Commission were to have factually determined that the agreement was not a product of duress, it could very well be of the opinion that in ratifying the agreement it was not taking "appropriate action to eliminate the source of tension or conflict."[52]

DETERMINATION AS TO WHETHER TO APPOINT A BOARD OF INQUIRY

Section 36(1) provides:

> Where the Commission fails to effect a settlement of the complaint and it appears to the Commission that the procedure is appropriate and the evidence warrants an inquiry, the Commission may request the Minister to appoint a board of inquiry and refer the subject-matter of the complaint to the board.

---

52. *Ante*, at 8-9.

If settlement is not achieved after the conciliation meeting, the Human Rights officer drafts a recommendation as to whether a board of inquiry should be called. The officer sends the recommendation, along with a summary of the evidence in support of the recommendation, to the parties for written comments. The recommendation and the parties' responses are sent with the file to the Commission for review.

The right of the parties to be informed of the evidence and to be given an opportunity to have their comments thereon considered by the Commission was established in *Cashin v. C.B.C.*,[53] a case under the federal human rights legislation. In *Cashin*, the Federal Court of Appeal went so far as to state that the complainant was entitled to test the credibility of adverse witnesses, thus clearly contemplating something in the nature of a *viva voce* hearing at the stage at which the Commission decides whether to appoint a board of inquiry. Subsequent cases have not affirmed the right to procedural fairness carried to this extent, although they have confirmed that the complainant is entitled to at least the substance of the investigator's report, and an opportunity to respond in writing.[54] In the most recent Ontario case, *F.W.T.A.O. v. OHRC*,[55] the Divisional Court declined to rule that the Commission must allow the parties access to its files, but held that there is a duty to provide a fair summary of the evidence.

The court in *F.W.T.A.O.* went on to distinguish between the duty owed where the Commission's decision is to appoint a board of inquiry and the situation in which the decision is to discuss the complaint, since the latter decision cuts off the complainant's right to pursue the complaint:

> The law is clear that a party must know the substance of the case against it and be allowed to respond. The Commission was not disposing of the complaint by requesting the Minister appoint a board of inquiry. The standard of justice is different if the Commission decided to dismiss the complaints since the complainants would have had no further rights to pursue this matter. A full hearing is offered to all who allegedly infringed any rights at the board of inquiry.[56]

No Ontario cases have explored the standard by which the Commission should evaluate evidence. Authority from other jurisdictions suggest that a board should be appointed when there is evidence on which a reasonable board could find discrimination on a balance of probabilities,[57] or

---

53. (1984), 8 Admin L.R. 161 (Fed. C.A.)
54. *Re Dagg v. Ontario (Human Rights Commission)* (1979), 102 D.L.R. (3d) 155 (Div. Ct.); *Radulesco v. Canada (Canadian Human Rights Commission)* (1984), 2 S.C.R. 407; *Assad v. Canada Correctional Service* (1987), unreported (Fed. C.A.). *Labelle v. Canada (Treasury Board)* (1987), 25 Admin. L.R. 10 (Fed. C.A.).
55. *Ante*, note 45.
56. *Ante*, note 45, at 510.
57. *Cook v. British Columbia Council of Human Rights)* (1988), 9 C.H.R.R. D/4967 (B.C. S.C.).

which lifts the case for the complainant out of the realm of conjecture.[58]

As noted above, a board may be appointed after the completion of the investigation and conciliation process, or where the investigation has been obstructed by reason of refusal of entry or refusal to comply with a request for production of documents.[59] In most cases, the completed file, with the detailed account of investigation and conciliation, and a legal opinion by counsel to the Commission, is reviewed by the commissioners prior to the decision being made.

Reconsideration

If the Commission declines to request a board of inquiry, it must send both complainant and respondent its written decision with reasons therefor. It must also advise the complainant as to his or her right to reconsideration. The procedure for reconsideration is the same as that outlined in the discussion above of recommendation and review of section 14 programs.

In *Commercial Union Assurance v. Ontario (Human Rights Commission)*[60] the Ontario Divisional Court held that the parties have a right to review and respond to the material before the Commission on a reconsideration decision, just as they do on the initial decision whether to appoint a board.

Appointment

Where the Commission suggests a board of inquiry, the Minister must appoint one or more persons to form the panel. The Minister must then inform the parties who has been chosen.[61]

Challenges to the validity of a board's appointment have been made, but to date boards have found that they lack jurisdiction to rule on the technical validity of the appointment.[62]

An application before the Ontario Divisional Court, which argued that the Commission did not have jurisdiction to appoint a board before consid-

---

58. *Onischak v. British Columbia (Council of Human Rights)* (1989), 10 C.H.R.R. D/6290 (B.C. S.C.).

59. See ss. 33(5) and (6).

60. (1987), 59 O.R. (2d) 481 (Div. Ct.), affirmed (1988), 63 O.R. (2d) 112 (C.A.), leave to appeal to S.C.C. refused (1988), 65 O.R. (2d) x (note) (S.C.C.)

61. S. 36(2). As of this writing, there are plans to institute a panel system for boards of inquiry.

62. See *Barnard v. Fort Frances (Town) Commissioners of Police* (1986), 7 C.H.R.R. D/3167 (Ont. Bd. of Inquiry), in which the Board cited *Canada (Canadian Human Rights Commission) v. British American Bank Note Co.* (1980), 116 D.L.R. (3d) 178 (Fed. C.A.) and *Whitehead v. Servodyne Canada Ltd.* (1986), 8 C.H.R.R. D/3874 (Ont. Bd. of Inquiry), in which the board, while agreeing on this point, added that it would be appropriate for a board to refer the matter back to the Minister if there should be "cogent evidence of an egregious error that substantially prejudiced the respondent."

ering the validity of a defence under subsection 14(2), was refused.[63]

When a board of inquiry is, for any reasons, unable to hold a hearing or make a finding or order, the Commission may request the minister to appoint a new board.[64]

REQUESTS THAT A BOARD RECONVENE

As noted above in the chapter on harassment, a board may make a finding in harassment situations as to the responsibility of a person in authority in that situation. When this finding is made, the board remains seized of the matter. Upon a complaint of continuation or repetition of the harassment, the Commission, after investigation, may request the board to reconvene.[65]

PROSECUTION BY THE COMMISSION

Section 44 provides that the infringement of a right contrary to section 9, the obstruction of an investigation contrary to section 33(11), and the contravention of an order of a board of inquiry are provincial offences carrying a possible penalty of a $25,000 fine. Anyone, including the Commission, could conceivably seek to commence proceedings but no prosecution can be instituted without the written consent of the Attorney General.[66]

To date there have been few prosecutions for contravention of an order of a board of inquiry, and the preferred method of dealing with breaches of the *Code* has obviously been through the board of inquiry.

---

63. Re *Ontario Women's Hockey Association v. Human Rights Commission (Ontario)* (1987), 8 C.H.R.R. D/4180 (Ont. H.C.).

64. S. 41(3).

65. S. 41(2). Where the board cannot reconvene, the Commission "may request the Minister to appoint a new board of inquiry in its place" (s. 41(3)).

66. S. 44(2).

9

BOARDS OF INQUIRY

INTRODUCTION

This chapter will discuss a number of issues relating to the conduct of boards of inquiry, including jurisdiction, procedural and evidentiary matters, and award powers.

Board as Sole Forum for Human Rights Litigation

It is probably correct to say that a board of inquiry is the only means by which an action based solely on rights granted by the *Code* may be litigated. The Supreme Court of Canada in *Seneca College of Applied Arts and Technology v. Bhadauria*[1] made a ruling in 1981 to this effect. In *Bhadauria*, the plaintiff issued a writ in the Supreme Court of Ontario against Seneca College for damages for refusing to interview her for an opening on its teaching staff. The plaintiff claimed that the college, in refusing her an interview, discriminated against her on the ground of her ethnic origin.

The defendant made an application under Ontario Rule 126 to have the plaintiff's statement of claim struck out as disclosing no reasonable cause of action. Callaghan J. allowed the application, holding that the plaintiff had no cause of action at common law for discrimination. That decision was reversed by a unanimous Ontario Court of Appeal[2] which recognized a tort of discrimination and, therefore, found it unnecessary to decide whether a breach of the *Code* gave rise to a civil cause of action. However, the Supreme Court of Canada unanimously rejected the judgment of the Court of Appeal and restored the judgment of Callaghan J. Laskin C.J.C. held for the court that "not only does the (Ontario Human Rights) *Code* foreclose any civil action based directly upon a breach thereof but it also excludes any common law action based on an invocation of the public policy expressed in the *Code*."[3]

---

1. (1981), 124 D.L.R. (3d) 193 (S.C.C.).
2. (1980), 27 O.R. (2d) 142 (C.A.).
3. *Ante*, note 1, at 203. The *Bhadauria* decision is critically examined by I.B. McKenna in a

The application of *Bhadauria* has been somewhat uneven. It has been applied to strike out a statement of claim in a wrongful dismissal action, *Tenning v. Manitoba*,[4] to deny an interim injunction to prevent a mandatory retirement, (*Lamont v. Air Canada*),[5] and to deny an application for a declaration that a dismissal from employment breached British Columbia's *Human Rights Act, Moore v. the Queen*.[6] However, other approaches have been taken by the courts, and there is direct conflict on the part of the Manitoba and British Columbia Courts of Appeal. The Manitoba Court of Appeal in *Parkinson v. Health Sciences Centre*[7] had no difficulty in distinguishing an application for declaratory relief from a bylaw that imposed mandatory retirement from the situation in *Bhadauria*. (The *Moore* decision did not refer to *Parkinson*). Further, while the Ontario High Court in *Ghosh v. Domglas Inc.*[8] stayed proceedings pending the outcome of a board of inquiry on the same matter, the Court seemed to contemplate the continuation of a wrongful dismissal action based on an allegation of discrimination.

The most recent pronouncement on the subject from Ontario's Court of Appeal is contained in *Canada Trust Co. v. Ontario (Human Rights Commission)*.[9] The application, from the trustee of a discriminatory scholarship fund, was made under s. 60 of the *Trustee Act* R.S.O. 1989, c. T.23 and under the Rules of Civil Procedure. The trustee requested the advice, opinion and direction of the court concerning the administration of the trust. In *Canada Trust*, two of a panel of three judges (Robbins and Osler, J.J.A.) decided that certain provisions of the trust could be struck out as

---

casenote at [1982] 60 C.B.R. 122. *Bhadauria* has been applied to strike out a statement of claim in a wrongful dismissal action: *Tenning v. Manitoba* (1983), 4 C.H.R.R. D/1612 (Man. Q.B.), reversed in part (1983), 25 Man. R. (2d) 179 (C.A.), to deny an interim injunction to prevent a mandatory retirement: *Lamont v. Air Canada* (1981), 3 C.H.R.R. D/1128 (Ont. H.C.), and to deny an application for a declaration that a dismissal from employment constituted a breach of British Columbia's *Human Rights Act*: *Moore v. British Columbia* (1988), 50 D.L.R. (4th) 29 (B.C. C.A.), leave to appeal to S.C.C. refused (1988), 50 D.L.R. (4th) vii (note) (S.C.C.). However, in regard to the last noted example, it should be noted that the Manitoba Court of Appeal took a different view; in *Parkinson v. Health Sciences Centre* (1982), 3 C.H.R.R. D/724 (Man. C.A.), leave to appeal to S.C.C. refused (1982), 18 Man. R. (2d) 31 (S.C.C.) it held that an application for a declaration that a mandatory retirement scheme was contrary to the *Human Rights Act* could be distinguished from the type of "civil action" contemplated in *Bhadauria*. Further, while the Ontario High Court in *Ghosh v. Domglas Inc.* (1986), 9 C.H.R.R. D/4833 (Ont. H.C.) stayed proceedings pending the outcome of a board of inquiry, it seemed to contemplate the continuation of a wrongful dismissal action based on an allegation of discrimination.

4. (1983), 4 C.H.R.R. D/1612 (Man. Q.B.).
5. (1981), 3 C.H.R.R. D/1128 (Ont. H.C.).
6. (1988), 50 D.L.R. (4th) 29 (B.C. C.A.).
7. (1982), 3 C.H.R.R. D/724 (Man. C.A.).
8. (1986), 9 C.H.R.R. D4833 (Ont. H.C.).
9. (1990), 74 O.R. (2d) 481 (C.A.).

contrary to public policy without reference to the *Ontario Human Rights Code*. Tarnopolsky, J.A. concurred in the result, but distinguished *Bhadauria* in order to find the trust instrument contrary to the *Code*. He relied on four points of difference from *Bhadauria:*

1. that there was no need to apply the law of tort to support a ruling on the trust

2. that this was not a typical proceeding involving an allegation of discrimination, such as is dealt with under the *Code*, and that had it been so, settlement, a major feature of the statutory scheme, would have been impossible, as the trustee had no power to settle.

3. that a board of inquiry would not have had the power to alter the terms of a trust or to declare it void.

4. that there was no need in this case for a fact finding function such as is exercised by the Commission and boards of inquiry; no facts were in dispute and only a question of law was involved.

A closer examination of the rationale used by the Manitoba Court of Appeal in *Parkinson (supra)* shows that Freedman, C.J.M., and Matas, J., distinguished *Bhadauria* on two bases:

1. the plaintiff was asking for a declaration under Manitoba's Queen's Bench Rules, which read in part:

> Where the rights of any person depend on the construction of any statute, by-law . . . or other instrument, he may apply by way of originating motive . . . to have his rights declared and determined.

and that therefore the court had discretion to grant such an order.

2. Manitoba's human rights legislation specifically referred to the right of anyone to bring an application to the Queen's Bench for an injunction against anyone responsible for a violation of the legislation.

Justices Monin and Huband confined their approach to focussing on the conclusion of the Laskin judgment in *Bhadauria* that the *Code* forcloses any "civil action based directly upon a breach thereof". They simply concluded that the Chief Justice had not intended to prohibit the courts from granting declaratory relief under proper circumstances.

Constitutional Validity

The validity of boards of inquiry under section 96 of the *Constitution Act* has been tested unsuccessfully in Ontario and in other jurisdictions.[10]

Jurisdiction of Boards To Undertake Charter Scrutiny

As with all administrative tribunals, there is a question as to whether boards of inquiry under the *Code* are to be considered "courts of competent

---

10. *Olarte v. Ontario (Minister of Labour)* (1984), 49 O.R. (2d) 17 (Div. Ct.); *Janzen v. Platy Enterprises*, [1987] 1 W.W.R. 385 (Man. C.A.); *Scowby v. Glendinning*, [1986] 2 S.C.R. 226.

jurisdiction" under section 24 of the *Canadian Charter of Rights and Freedoms*, and a separate question as to whether a board may make a ruling, under section 52(1) of the *Charter*, that a provision of its enabling legislation is "of no force and effect". To date, neither a board nor a court has ruled upon the section 24 question in respect of boards of inquiry, although a 1988 board of inquiry, *Dudnik* and *Cryderman*, indicated in *obiter* that a board could be a court of competent jurisdiction "within the limits of its jurisdiction as defined by the statute creating it.".[11]

The board in *Dudnik* did rule that it had jurisdiction under section 52(1) of the *Charter* to find that a *Code* provision which limited the right to protection from age discrimination in housing was without force and effect,[12] and did so find.[13] This finding was not disturbed on appeal to the Divisional Court,[14] but this was because the court decided that the point did not need to be addressed.

The matter of section 52 jurisdiction might be raised again, because *Dudnik* was decided before the second and third of a trilogy of decisions recently handed down by the Supreme Court of Canada: *Douglas College v. Douglas/Kwantlen Faculty Association*,[15] *Cuddy Chicks v. Ontario (Labour Relations Board)*,[16] and *Canada (Employment and Immigration Commission) v. Tétreault-Gadoury*.[17]

In *Douglas College* the Court was called upon to determine the jurisdiction of a labour arbitrator to apply the *Charter*. Mr. Justice LaForest (writing for the majority on this point) stated that where a tribunal was engaged in performing what it by law was empowered to do,

> . . . it was entitled not only to construe the relevant legislation but to determine whether that legislation was validly enacted. Section 52(1) of the *Constitution Act, 1982* provides that any law that is inconsistent with the provisions of the Constitution of Canada—the supreme law of the land—is, to the extent of the inconsistency, of no force or effect. A tribunal must respect the Constitution so that if it finds invalid a law it is called upon to apply, it is bound to treat it as having no force or effect.[18]

---

11. (1988), 9 C.H.R.R. D/5080 at 5082. As of this writing, there has been no ruling from the Supreme Court of Canada as to whether, or under what circumstances, an administrative tribunal is a "court of competent jurisdiction". The Pay Equity Tribunal will shortly be deciding whether it falls under s. 24 for the purpose of effectively amending legislation by order; *Ontario Nurses Association v. Women's Christian Assoc. of London, Parkwood Hospital* Pay Equity Hearings Tribunal File #0188-91.

12. *Supra.*

13. (1990), 12 C.H.R.R. D/325

14. *York Condominium Corp. #216 v. Dudnik* (1991), 3 O.R. (3d) 360

15. (1990), 77 D.L.R. (4th) 94 (S.C.C.)

16. (1991) 81 D.L.R. (4th) 121 (S.C.C.).

17. (1991) 81 D.L.R. (4th) 358 (S.C.C.).

18. *Ante*, note 15, at 117.

In coming to this conclusion, LaForest, J. conceded that there are disadvantages to allowing administrative tribunals to exercise *Charter* jurisdiction. Among these were the slowing effect on tribunal proceedings, the fact that tribunals vary in degree of legal expertise and independence, the possible unavailability of evidence, resulting in an inadequate record, and the lack of the automatic mechanism in court proceedings for obtaining the participation of the Attorney General. However, he also noted the advantages, which include generally facilitating the assertion of constitutional rights, ensuring that constitutional issues are raised early in proceedings, providing a relatively speedy and inexpensive forum, and both ensuring that administrative tribunals incorporate constitutional values and bringing their specialized expertise to bear on the issue.

In *Cuddy Chicks Ltd.* the Supreme Court of Canada considered the jurisdiction of the Ontario Labour Relations Board to determine whether s. 2(b) of the *Labour Relations Act*, which excludes persons employed in agriculture from the Act, contravened the *Charter*. Mr. Justice LaForest (for the majority) reiterated the Court's holding in *Douglas College* stating

> . . . this Court articulated the basic principle that an administrative tribunal which has been conferred the power to interpret law holds a concomitant power to determine whether that law is constitutionally valid.

> . . . s. 52(1) does not specify which bodies may consider and rule on Charter questions, and cannot be said to confer jurisdiction on an administrative tribunal. Rather, jurisdiction must have expressly or impliedly been conferred on the tribunal by its enabling statute or otherwise. This fundamental principle holds true regardless of the nature of the issue before the administrative body. Thus, a tribunal prepared to address a Charter issue must already have jurisdiction over the whole of the matter before it, namely, the parties, subject matter and remedy sought.[19]

Mr. Justice LaForest held that the Labour Board had jurisdiction over the employer and the union (the parties). However, the subject matter and the remedy were premised on the application of the *Charter*, and, as such, the authority to apply the *Charter* had to be found in the Labour Board's enabling statute. After noting that the Board's enabling statute conferred authority on the Board to decide points of law, he stated (at p. 10):

> It is clear to me that a Charter issue must constitute a question of law; indeed, the Charter is part of the supreme law of Canada. This comports with the view expressed in *Douglas College* that the statutory authority of the arbitrator in that case to interpret any "Act" must include the authority to interpret the Charter.[20]

Mr. Justice LaForest made two very important caveats to his reasoning in *Cuddy Chicks*. The first was that no curial deference would be displayed to a tribunal with respect to its constitutional decisions. The second was that a tribunal could not give a formal declaration of invalidity. Instead the tribunal

---

19. *Ante*, note 16, at 127-128.
20. *Supra*, at 128-129.

> . . . simply treats any impugned provision as invalid for the purposes of the matter before it. Given that this is not tantamount to a formal declaration of invalidity, a remedy only exercisable by the superior courts, the ruling of the Board on a Charter issue does not constitute a binding legal precedent, but is limited in its applicability to the matter in which it arises.[21]

An obvious distinction between the OLRB's position and that of boards of inquiry lies in the fact that, unlike the OLRB, boards have no express statutory authority to decide all questions of fact and law that come before them. To date, the Supreme Court of Canada has not ruled upon this situation, but its decision in *Tétreault-Gadoury* gives some indication of the view of the Court may take.

In *Tétreault-Gadoury* the respondent had lost her job shortly after turing 65 years of age. She had applied for benefits under the *Unemployment Insurance Act* but, because the Act at that time prohibited the payment of benefits to persons over the age of 65, she had been denied. She appealed this decision to the Board of Referees arguing that the section of the Act which prohibited the payment of such benefits violated her equality right under the *Charter*. The Board of Referees upheld the decision but did not make a decision on the constitutional question. The respondent elected to challenge this decision directly in the Federal Court of Appeal rather than appealing to an umpire. The Court of Appeal found that the Act did violate the *Charter* and that the Board of Referees had erred in not considering the constitutional arguments. The Employment and Immigration Commission appealed the Court's decision to the Supreme Court of Canada. The preliminary issue before the Supreme Court was whether the Board of Referees had jurisdiction to consider the constitutional validity of a section of the Act.

In *Tétreault-Gadoury* the Court for the first time was faced with deciding whether an administrative tribunal which had not been expressly provided with the power to decide all relevant questions of law could undertake constitutional review. As section 52(1) had been held not to specifically confer jurisdiction to make *Charter* findings, the Court was obliged to examine the mandate given to the Board of Referees by the legislature in order to determine whether the Board had the power to determine a legislative provision to be unconstitutional. Mr. Justice LaForest, writing again for the majority, noted that administrative tribunals are created by the state, and the state had the ability to confer or restrict the authority of the tribunal to consider constitutional matters. If the state had conferred the power, then that would be the end of the issue. If not then the Court would be obliged to consider "other factors" in order to make its determination.

The Court began its analysis by examining the Act, and LaForest J. observed that the power to consider all relevant law, including the power to

---

21. *Supra*, at 130.

declare a provision of the Act or Regulations *ultra vires*, had been expressly conferred, not upon the Board but upon the umpire. He found it significant that the Board of Referees had not been provided with this power and he concluded that it had not been an oversight on the part of the legislature. While noting that the Board of Referees was not without the practical capability to consider *Charter* issues, LaForest J. held that the scheme of the Act "contemplates that the constitutional question should more appropriately have been presented to the umpire, on appeal, rather than to the Board itself".[22] Therefore, applying the test outlined in *Douglas College* and *Cuddy Chicks* he found that while the Board had jurisdiction over the parties, it did not have jurisdiction over the subject matter (the determination of the respondent's eligibility for benefits and the constitutionality of the section of the Act) nor the remedy (which would have required the Board to ignore the section of the Act which it had found unconstitutional, a determination it had no jurisdiction to make).

Mr. Justice LaForest also considered some of the practical advantages which he had canvassed in *Douglas College* and *Cuddy Chicks*. He felt that many of these advantages were still present in the Unemployment Insurance context, since his decision left the applicant able to appeal to the umpire, who possessed the requisite jurisdiction. An applicant was not required to seek redress in the regular court process; a constitutional challenge could still be made within a relatively accessible and inexpensive administrative proceeding. As such, the advantage of having the constitutional issue dealt with within the administrative process was preserved. LaForest J. also noted that the Unemployment insurance scheme still allowed for the specialized expertise of the administrative tribunal to be reflected in the consideration of *Charter* issues. The umpire's broad experience with the legislation would provide valuable insight to the determination of the *Charter* issue. As well, the fact that the umpire was further up the administrative decision-making ladder (and whose functions were more adjudicative in nature than the Commission's) would render him or her in a better position to resolve difficult constitutional questions.

The judgment of Mr Justice LaForest in *Tétreault-Gadoury* does not seem to shut the door to section 52(1) jurisdiction in situations in which the statute provides no express authorization to decide all questions of fact and law. Indeed, he recognises the practical reasons why, in some legislative schemes, the power to undertake *Charter* review is necessary. It would appear that the statutory scheme established by the *Code*, taken as a whole, would fit within his remarks as to rationale for section 52(1) jurisdiction. It might also be noted that boards under the previous *Code* did have express

---

22. *Ante*, note 17 at 365.

authority to decide all questions of fact and law.[23] The disappearance of that provision from the present *Code* cannot be taken as a rethinking by the legislature; section 18 of the *Interpretation Act*[24] provides:

> The amendment of an Act shall be deemed not to be or to involve a declaration that the law under the Act was or was considered by the Legislature to have been different from the law as it has become under the Act as so amended.

As long as the remedy requested is a ruling that a limiting provision of the *Code* is of no force and effect in the circumstances of a particular case, it appears likely that boards of inquiry would be found to have section 52(1) jurisdiction, even without a specific legislative provision to that effect.

NATURE OF HEARING

A board of inquiry under the *Code* is an adversarial proceeding, but also has elements of a public inquiry. The Commission, which has a statutory mandate to educate the public[25] as well as to enforce the Act, is a party to and has carriage of the complaint.[26] The hybrid nature of the hearing has an effect on various aspects of procedure, which will be further discussed below, and is particularly evident where the interests of Commission and complainant diverge, or where questions as to the public nature of the hearing arise.

That the hearing is subject to the rules of natural justice has been established in more than one case.[27] More specifically, the board of inquiry is governed by the *Statutory Powers Procedure Act*.[28]

APPOINTMENT OF THE BOARD

Where a complaint appears to be substantiated but cannot be settled, the Commission may request the appropriate minister[29] to appoint a board of inquiry.[30] Under the previous Code, the minister had discretion to refuse

---

23. R.S.O. 1980, c. 340, s. 18(6).
24. R.S.O. 1990, c. I-11.
25. S. 29 is discussed in Chapter 8.
26. S. 39(2).
27. See *Bell v. Ontario (Human Rights Commission)*, [1971] S.C.R. 756; *Morgan v. Toronto General Hospital* (1977), unreported (Ont. Bd. of Inquiry), pp. 7-13 (transcript).
28. R.S.O. 1990, c. S.22.
29. At this writing, the Minister of Citizenship.
30. Ss. 36(1) and 46 are referred to here. S. 36(1) states that "Where the Commission fails to effect a settlement of the complaint and it appears to the Commission that the procedure is appropriate and the evidence warrants an inquiry, the Commission may request the Minister to appoint a board of inquiry and refer the subject-matter of the complaint to the board." S. 46 states that "In this Act . . . 'Minister' means the member of the Executive Council to whom the powers and duties of the Minister under this Act are assigned by the Lieutenant Governor in Council."

the Commission's request;[31] however, this is no longer the case.[32]

The minister must appoint a panel of persons to act as members of boards of inquiry.[33] Typically, the members of this panel have been professors of law who have no connection with the Ontario Human Rights Commission; the *Code* contains an express prohibition against any member of a board having "taken part in any investigation or consideration of the subject-matter of the inquiry before the hearing."[34]

When the minister has appointed the board from the panel, he or she must "communicate the names of the persons forming the board to the parties to the inquiry."[35] Typically, a board consists of only one person. As cases get more complex, the minister will presumably consider whether a tripartite board, for example, may be appropriate.

It would appear that the board of inquiry has no jurisdiction to consider arguments as to the technical validity of its appointment; the *Code* appears to limit the issues to be heard to those relating to the complaint.[36] An argument as to "reasonable apprehension of bias" concerning the appointment process has, however, been considered initially at boards of inquiry. "Reasonable apprehension of bias" will be discussed below in the section on preliminary objections.

---

31. See R.S.O. 1980, c. 340, s. 17(1).

32. See s. 38(1) of the current *Code*.

33. S. 35(1).

34. S. 38(2).

35. S. 38(1).

36. See s. 39(1); *Garnett v. Kompleat Janitorial Services* (1978), unreported (B.C. Bd. of Inquiry). Also see *Barnard v. Fort Frances (Town) Commissioners of Police* (1986), 7 C.H.R.R. D/3167 (Ont. Bd. of Inquiry). In *Whitehead v. Servodyne Canada Ltd.* (1986), 8 C.H.R.R. D/3874 (Ont. Bd. of Inquiry) the board took this view, but added that it could "refer the matter back to the Minister for review" if there should be cogent evidence of a serious error prejudicial to the respondent. One question that may arise is whether the board shall proceed in cases where the Commission successfully seeks to amend the complaint, but the appointment is made out in the same style as the complaint. There are no cases on this point, but it is suggested that no problem of jurisdiction arises here since the board is charged with its responsibility primarily with reference to the complaint, and in such broad terms as to suggest that, where amendment of the complaint can properly be made, the wording of the appointment will not raise a problem. S. 39(1) states:
    "(1) The board of inquiry shall hold a hearing,
    > (*a*) to determine whether a right of the complainant under this Act has been infringed;
    > (*b*) to determine who infringed the right; and
    > (*c*) to decide upon an appropriate order under section 41,
    and the hearing shall be commenced within thirty days after the date on which the members were appointed." A board has also declined to review alleged procedural irregularities in the investigation of the complaint; see *Sinclair v. Peel Non-Profit Housing Corp.* (1989), 11 C.H.R.R. D/341 (Ont. Bd. of Inquiry)

SETTING A DATE FOR THE HEARING

As noted above, the minister must inform the parties that the board has been appointed. The board has a duty to commence the hearing within thirty days after the date of its appointment,[37] although presumably adjournments will be arranged where the parties are not prepared to proceed at that time. Where the board does not commence within the thirty day period, it would seem to lack jurisdiction to proceed after that time. However, the Commission may "request the Minister to appoint a new board of inquiry in its place."[38]

Notice of the Hearing

Parties must be given reasonable notice of the hearing. The notice must include the time, place and purpose of the hearing, a reference to the Ontario *Human Rights Code* and a statement that, if the notified party does not attend, the board may proceed in his or her absence without further notice.[39]

Notice in the sense of information as to the particulars of the case to be met, and the effect of the non-attendance of parties, will be discussed later in this chapter. Service on the respondent of notice of hearing by means of an advertisement in a newspaper may be sufficient.[40]

PRELIMINARY MATTERS

Questions of Procedure Generally

A board of inquiry under the Ontario *Human Rights Code* may adopt such procedures as seem proper in the circumstances of the case before it.[41]

---

37. S. 39(1).
38. S. 41(5).
39. *Statutory Powers Procedure Act*, R.S.O. 1990, c. S.22, ss. 6,7.
40. *Williams v. Ouellette* (1973), unreported (Ont. Bd. of Inquiry).
41. *Nimako v. Canadian National Hotels* (1985), 6 C.H.R.R. D/2894 (Ont. Bd. of Inquiry). As authority for this proposition, the board in *Nimako* cited *Cedarvale Tree Services Ltd. v. L.I.U.N.A., Local 183* (1971), 22 D.L.R. (3d) 40 (Ont. C.A.). Although that decision was in respect of the capacity of the Ontario Labour Relations Board to determine its own procedures, the board noted: "as to the appropriateness of the analogy between the Ontario Labour Relations Board and a board of inquiry under the Ontario Human Rights Code, it may be observed that Mr. Justice Arnup held applicable to the former the decision of the Supreme Court of Canada made in relation to the latter in *Bell v. Ontario Human Rights Comm.* (1971), 18 D.L.C. (3d) 1. Finally, in *Re Toronto Police Commissioners and Ontario Human Rights Commission* (1979), 27 O.R. (2d) 48 (Div. Ct.), Labrose J., speaking for the Division Court of Ontario in relation to a board of inquiry under the Code stated at p. 5 that the board has exclusive jurisdiction over the conduct of its procedure and the exercise of its discretion to grant the adjournment is not reviewable by this Court, provided, that the board has not violated recognized principles of fairness. . ."

Reasonable Apprehension of Bias

The statutory procedure governing the role of the Commission in the appointment has been challenged on the ground of reasonable apprehension of bias; however, such challenges have been unsuccessful.[42] Various personal and professional attributes of board members have also been made the subject of applications, without success.[43] There has been no finding of actual bias in regard to an Ontario board of inquiry.[44]

In one case, a board invoked subsection 40(5) in order to withdraw from hearing a complaint. The board was to approve a settlement of a related complaint against the same respondent. While Chairman Hubbard had not seen the settlement, and was therefore unable to form an opinion as to the reasonableness of any apprehension of bias, he decided to declare himself "unable" to continue as a board in respect of the related complaints.[45]

The Effect of other Proceedings that Relate to the Complaint

Where the facts of a complaint could be, have been, or are about to be, the subject of other proceedings, such as labour arbitration, a grievance proceeding, or civil action, three issues may be raised before the board:

1. Does the board have jurisdiction over the subject-matter?

2. Should the board hearing be suspended pending the outcome of the other proceedings?

---

42. *Olarte v. Ontario (Minister of Labour)* (1984), 49 O.R. (2d) 17 (Div. Ct.); a similar application was dismissed by the Div. Ct., referred to in *West End Construction Ltd. v. Ontario (Minister of Labour)* (1986), 57 O.R. (2d) 391 (Div. Ct.), reversed on another point (1989), 70 O.R. (2d) 133 (C.A.). Also see *Piazza v. Airport Taxi Cab (Malton) Assn.* (1987), 24 Admin. L.R. 149 (Ont. Div. Ct.), reversed on another point (1989), 69 O.R. (2d) 281 (C.A.).

43. *Rajput v. Algoma University* (1976) unreported (Ont. Bd. of Inquiry) (complaint concerning non-appointment of complainant to university faculty position; respondent alleging board chairman's status as university professor creating reasonable apprehension of bias; chairman distinguishing human rights complaint from one involving wrongful dismissal of interpretation of contract of employment; respondent withdrawing objection); *Jorgensen v. British Columbia Ice & Cold Storage Ltd.* (1981), 2 C.H.R.R. D/289 (B.C. Bd of Inquiry) (board denying that participation by one of its members, fifteen years earlier, as employer nominee in arbitration between respondent union and another company, gave rise to reasonable apprehension of bias).

44. An argument as to bias, in the context of s. 1 of the *Charter of Rights and Freedoms*, was raised and dismissed by the Divisional Court without reasons in *West End Construction v. Ontario (Minister of Labour)*, *ante*, note 42. In another jurisdiction, an argument was made that the positive public stance taken by a tribunal member in favour of the enforcement of human rights law disqualified that person as an adjudicator. This argument was dismissed by the tribunal: *Campbell v. Hudson Bay Mining & Smelting* (1984), 5 C.H.R.R. D/2268 (Cdn. Human Rights Trib.).

45. *Gohm v. Domtar Inc.* (January 20, 1988), Doc. No. 331 (Ont. Bd. of Inquiry).

3.   If the other hearing has been completed, can the defences of *res judi-cata* or issue estoppel be raised?

Jurisdiction over the Subject Matter

It is clear that the mere existence of a collective agreement or other means of dispute resolution will not oust the jurisdiction of a human rights board of inquiry.

In two Ontario cases, the respondents argued that the board lacked jurisdiction to deal with a dispute between a firefighter and his union and employer. In *Hall v. International Firefighters' Association*[46] the respondents pointed to the *Fire Departments Act*[47], which provided for arbitration of disputes with respect to the collective agreement. The respondents argued that the complainant should have resorted to the grievance procedures and arbitration rather than to the human rights procedure. The board disagreed, saying.[48]

> [T]he matter is not just a private dispute between parties to a collective agreement. It raises an issue of public importance and general concern provided for by statute, and the right of individuals to complain, and of the Commission to inquire, cannot be restricted by a collective agreement and is not limited by s. 7(5) of the *Fire Departments Act*.

A similar finding was made by the board in *Hadley v. Mississauga*.[49]

In *Hall*, the board also noted that the provisions of a contract could not be held to exclude the effect of the *Code*.[50] This finding was specifically affirmed when *Hall* was appealed to the Supreme Court of Canada. For a unanimous Court, McIntyre J. found that:[51]

> Although the *Code* contains no explicit restriction on such contracting out, it is nevertheless a public statute and it constitutes public policy in Ontario as appears from a reading of the Statute itself and as declared in the preamble. It is clear from the authorities, both in Canada and in England, that parties are not competent to contract themselves out of the provisions of such enactments and that contracts having such effect are void, as contrary to public policy.

The Ontario Divisional Court has also taken the position that the fact that disciplinary action has been undertaken by a vocational association does not deprive a board of inquiry of the right to hear evidence on the same matter, where the complainant alleges that the disciplinary action was discriminatory.[52]

---

46. (1977), unreported (Ont. Bd. of Inquiry), reversed (1980), 26 O.R. (2d) 208, affirmed (1980), 29 O.R. (2d) 499, reversed (1982), 40 N.R. 159 (S.C.C.).

47. R.S.O. 1970, c. 169, s. 7(5) [now R.S.O. 1990, c. F.15, s. 7(5)].

48. Note 46 above, pp. 2-3 (transcript).

49. (1976), unreported (Ont. Bd. of Inquiry).

50. Note 46 above, p. 10 (transcript).

51. (1982), 40 N.R. 159 at 170.

52. *Joseph v. College of Nurses (Ontario)* (1985), 51 O.R. (2d) 155 (Div. Ct.).

There may also be room for complaints under the Ontario *Human Rights Code* despite the existence of other legislative avenues directed toward the same ends. In *Nishimura v. Ontario (Human Rights Commission)*[53] the applicants had filed complaints of sex discrimination under the *Code*, pertaining to an employment classification system in which one class of salespersons, mostly male, was paid more than another, mostly female, class of salespersons. The complaints were filed in 1984, and in 1987 the Commission declined to appoint a board of inquiry, taking the position that the legislature had not intended to give effect to the principle of equal work for equal value under the *Code*. The applicants applied for judicial review of the Commission's decision, in the course of which the Commission changed its position.

The court acknowledged that the principle of equal pay for work of equal value had not been specifically addressed in the legislation until the *Pay Equity Act* was passed in 1987, and that therefore the applicant's only recourse for their 1984 complaint was under the *Human Rights Code*. Referring to the endorsement of a broad and liberal construction of human rights legislation recently made by the Supreme Court of Canada, the court concluded that a complaint of sex discrimination arising from circumstances of unequal pay for work of equal value is within the jurisdiction of the Ontario Human Rights Commission. This decision may well open the way for complaints of unequal pay for work of equal value from employees who do not qualify for the protection of the *Pay Equity Act*.

Commencing 15 June 1984, the Code had primacy over all other Ontario Acts and regulations, unless there is an express provision to the contrary. Thus, any provision in a statute or regulation that purports to require or authorize a contravention of the *Code* is rendered inoperative,[54] absent a specific saving provision.

Stay Pending the Outcome of another Proceeding

In respect of a complaint in an employment matter where there is union representation, a respondent might argue that grievance proceedings should be exhausted before a complaint is heard before a human rights board. While human rights boards have not been unanimous on this issue, it is unlikely that an argument that proceedings under a human rights board of inquiry should be stayed will be successful in Ontario.

In *Mitton v. Parent*,[55] a Canadian human rights tribunal opined that internal dispute resolution procedures should be exhausted before a com-

---

53. (1989), 70 O.R. (2d) 347 (Div. Ct.).
54. See s. 47(2). For a discussion of the issue of conflict with other statutes see W. Tarnopolsky, *Discrimination and The Law* (1982), pp. 476-82.
55. (1981), 2 C.H.R.R. D/334 (Cdn. Human Rights Trib.).

plaint went to a human rights board of inquiry. However, in *Hadley v. Mississauga*,[56] the board of inquiry refused to stay the proceedings to await the outcome of grievance proceedings that were under way at the same time.

The major reason for the refusal of the board in *Hadley* to suspend the hearing appears to be that the board did not share the respondent's view that the question of early retirement was, in fact, arbitrable under the collective agreement in question. However, Chairman Lederman also gave a general opinion that, if one board were to defer to the other, the arbitration board ought to defer to the board of inquiry. The chairman provided several reasons in support of this opinion.

First, the grievance and arbitration procedures are controlled by the employer and the union. As union policy tends to reflect the interests of the majority of its members, unions may fail to protect adequately individuals with interests contrary to those of the majority. Most union members are relatively young, and an early retirement age ensures them greater employment. Second, it is the union that argues the grievor's case at the hearing. Because the union has a duty to provide fair representation, it is difficult for a grievor to show that this was not done, and the courts are reluctant to interfere with the union's discretion in handling its grievances. Third, the arbitration board only has authority to interpret the collective agreement, not an external statute such as the *Code*. Fourth, labour arbitration is a private proceeding between contracting parties. The board of inquiry proceeding is public and the parties are granted the protections of the *Statutory Powers Procedure Act*. There is a public interest in preventing discrimination, and such issues should not be submerged in private labour arbitration. Fifth, the legislature, aware of the arbitration process, gave ultimate responsibility with respect to issues of discrimination to the board of inquiry. Finally, the *Code* provides for much broader rights of appeal than does the decision of an arbitrator.

An action for stay of proceedings may also be made because of pending litigation concerned with the same matter as the complaint.

In *Metropolitan Toronto Board of Commissioners of Police v. Ontario Human Rights Commission*,[57] the complainant had commenced both an application for judicial review of the Police Board decision and a civil action for defamation against one of the personal respondents to his complaint under the *Code*. Labrosse J. found no error

> in the decision of the board of inquiry in refusing to stay the proceedings. In so far as our discretion to stay the proceedings before the board of inquiry is concerned, we are of the view that it should not be exercised. The proceedings before the board are ready to

---

56. *Ante*, note 49.
57. (1979), 27 O.R. (2d) 48 (Div. Ct.).

proceed; the respondent Ahluwalia will receive the benefit of a full investigation; the board of inquiry has wider powers than the Courts; the reliefs under the Code are unique; and lastly, different remedies are requested in other proceedings.[58]

In *F.W.T.A.O.* v. *Ontario (Human Rights Commission)*,[59] a board of inquiry had been appointed in respect of a by-law of the Association. The decision of the Divisional Court is largely concerned with a challenge to the process by which the Commission came to its decision, but the court also addresses a request that further proceedings under the *Code* be stayed pending civil proceedings, challenging the by-law as being *ultra vires* the Ontario Teachers' Federation, and breaching the *Canadian Charter of Rights and Freedoms*. (A hearing of the civil matter before the Court of Appeal was scheduled.)

In deciding not to grant a stay, the Divisional Court took into account the public interest in the resolution of the complaint under the *Code*.

A court dealing with a civil matter associated with a complaint may grant a stay of its own proceedings to allow a human rights board of inquiry to proceed first. In *Ghosh* v. *Domglas Inc.*,[60] the court considered a previous decision to stay proceedings, made by the Ontario Divisional Court in *Benet* v. *G.E.C. Canada Ltd.*[61] The Benet decision, which as based on a previous version of the *Code*, was interpreted by the court in *Ghosh* as having been made because of a clause in the previous *Code* that gave the boards of inquiry exclusive jurisdiction to determine any question of fact or law relating to whether the *Code* had been contravened. Since the clause was eliminated from the 1981 *Code* the court considered whether it should differ in approach from the court in *Benet*. In deciding to grant a stay, the court in *Ghosh* placed emphasis on the remedial powers of a board of inquiry, which are broader than those of a court. The court also expressed concern about the possibility of differing findings of fact or double recovery under some heads of compensation.

A final note on the subject of stay of proceedings is that the *Statutory Powers Procedure Act* provides that the board of inquiry proceedings are to be stayed when an appeal of its decision is taken to the Divisional Court pursuant to the appeal procedure set out in the *Code*.[62] However, a board of inquiry proceeding need not be stayed pending the outcome of an applica-

---

58. *Ibid.*, at 52.
59. (1988), 67 O.R. (2d) 492 (Div. Ct.).
60. (1986), 57 O.R. (2d) 710 (H.C.).
61. (1980), 31 O.R. (2d) 49 (H.C.).
62. S. 25(1) of that Act states that "Unless it is expressly provided to the contrary in the Act under which the proceeding arises an appeal from a decision of a tribunal to a court or other appellate tribunal operates as a stay in the matter except where the tribunal or the court or other body to which the appeal is taken otherwise orders."

tion for judicial review,[63] unless there is a court order to the contrary.

Res Judicata and Issue Estoppel

Human rights tribunals have dealt with the issues of *res judicata* and issue estoppel where labour arbitration and grievance boards have considered, to one extent or another, the matter at issue.

One of the earliest cases, *Derksen v. Flyer Industries*,[64] involved a complaint under the Manitoba *Human Rights Act*.[65] The complainant had followed the grievance procedure pursuant to a collective agreement and had lost his case before the arbitration board.

The respondent argued:

1. The issues were *res judicata* because substantially the same issues, between the same parties, had been decided at a prior proceeding.

2. There was a defence of issue estoppel since the issue as to whether there had been a contravention of the *Human Rights Act* had already been decided in a prior proceeding and that that decision was binding on the parties.

3. There was a defence of issue estoppel by election in that the complainant, having had a choice as to which procedure to follow in vindicating his claim, elected to follow one procedure and, having been unsuccessful, was now pursuing another course.

The board concluded that *res judicata* was not a true issue, on the test quoted by Sopinka and Lederman in *The Law of Evidence in Civil Cases:*[66]

> The constituent elements of estoppel by res judicata were enumerated by Aikens J. in *Re Bullen:*
> (i) that the alleged judicial decision was what in law is deemed as such;
> (ii) that the particular judicial decision relied upon was in fact pronounced, as alleged;
> (iii) that the judicial tribunal pronouncing the decision had competent jurisdiction in that behalf;
> (iv) that the judicial decision was final;
> (v) that the judicial decision was, or involved, a determination of the same question as that sought to be controverted in the litigation in which the estoppel is raised;

---

63. S. 25(2) provides that "An application for judicial review under the *Judicial Review Procedure Act*, or the bringing of proceedings specified in subsection 2(1) of that Act is not an appeal within the meaning of subsection (1)." Also see *Cedarvale Tree Services Ltd. v. L.I.U.N.A., Local 183*, [1971] 3 O.R. 832 (C.A.) and *Roosma v. Ford Motor Co.* (1988), 66 O.R. (2d) 18 (Div. Ct.).
64. (1977), unreported (Man. Bd. of Inquiry).
65. S.M. 1970, c. 104 [amended 1975, c. 42, s. 26; 1976, c. 48; 1977, c. 46; 1978, c. 43].
66. The case cited in the quotation used by the board is *Re Bullen* (1971), 21 D.L.R. (3d) 628 at 631 (B.C. S.C.).

(vi) that the parties to the judicial decision, or their privies, were the same persons as the parties to the proceeding in which the estoppel is raised, or their privies, or that the decision was conclusive in rem.[67]

In regard to issue estoppel, the board quoted Lord Denning in *Fidelitas Shipping Company v. V/O Exportchleb:*[68]

Within one cause of action, there may be several issues raised which are necessary for the determination of the whole case. The rule then is that, once an issue has been raised and distinctly determined between the parties, then, as a general rule, neither party can be allowed to fight that issue all over again.

The board in *Derksen* concluded that neither of the above-quoted tests had been met. It first pointed out that the proceedings under the *Human Rights Act* differed from a grievance arbitration in that the latter was essentially a dispute between parties, while the former involved protection of public interests. In support of this proposition, the board noted that a complaint under the *Human Rights Act* might be initiated by a third party or by the Commission itself, as well as by the complainant, and that, where the Commission initiated a complaint, the consent of the complainant was unnecessary. Furthermore, it noted that only the Commission might request a board of inquiry, and that it had done so because it had reason to believe that the Act was being violated.

Secondly, the board observed that the Commission has carriage of the complaint and must be a party to the board of inquiry proceedings. The Commission was not a party, and probably could not have joined as a party, to the proceedings before the board of arbitration, yet it was a necessary party to any proceeding wherein rights are determined under the *Human Rights Act*. Therefore, the parties to the two proceedings were not the same.

Thirdly, the board of inquiry found that the issues decided by the two proceedings were different. The board of arbitration was appointed to interpret and enforce the collective agreement while the board of inquiry was appointed to interpret and enforce the *Human Rights Act*.

Finally, the remedies available to the respective boards were different, those available to the board of inquiry being much broader in scope.

In *Abihsira v. Arvin Automotive of Canada Limited*,[69] an Ontario case, a grievance with respect to the events involved in the complaint had been decided against the complainant by an arbitration board. The arbitration board had based its decision on the interpretation of an anti-discrimination clause in the collective agreement which was almost identical to the comparable *Code* provisions. The respondent argued that the board of inquiry had no jurisdiction to hear the case. The board considered two arguments:

---

67. *Ante*, note 64, p. 28 (transcript).

68. [1966] 1 Q.B. 630 at 640 (C.A.).

69. (1980), 2 C.H.R.R. D/271 (Ont. Bd. of Inquiry).

whether section 37(1) of the *Labour Relations Act* precluded the board's jurisdiction, and whether the doctrine of *res judicata* applied.

The section 37(1) argument was directed to three points:

1. Section 37(1) of the *Ontario Labour Relations Act*[70] provides for "a final and binding settlement by arbitration . . . of all differences between the parties."

2. A finding by a human rights board of inquiry might produce different findings and an inconsistent decision.

3. The hearing would require the human rights board of inquiry to interpret the collection agreement which, it was argued, was the sole prerogative of an arbitration board.

    In regard to the first point, the board of inquiry concluded that[71]

> "Final and binding" in section 37(1) of the *Labour Relations Act* can only mean final and binding for the purposes of that Act, not for all legal purposes. For example, if an employee is discharged in an offensive or insulting manner, he would not forfeit his right of access to the court for defamation simply because an arbitration board had dismissed his grievance. Of course, a board of inquiry is a quasi-judicial tribunal, not a court, and it might be argued that the presumption of statutory interpretation against depriving a subject of his right of access to the courts has less force; nevertheless, the Board of Inquiry is the tribunal empowered by the Ontario legislature to hear and decide alleged contraventions of the Ontario Human Rights Code and the subject cannot, in my opinion, be deprived of his right of access to that tribunal simply because of a pre-existing arbitration award concerning the same incident. An alleged breach of the Ontario Human Rights Code is not, in short, ". . . a difference . . . between the parties relating to the interpretation, application or administration of an agreement."

Further, the board noted that the Act and the *Code* have different purposes, as reflected in their preambles, and that they have different remedial provisions reflecting their different purposes, the *Code*'s remedial provisions being much more extensive. The board conceded that the same facts and issues may arise in arbitration and before a board of inquiry, and that some issues might be heard twice. However:[72]

> Had the legislature intended to bar an employee from having a second chance, it could easily have done so. . . . Some commentators have gone so far as to presume that the lack of such a statutory bar suggests ". . . that the legislature at least in part enacted the *Ontario Human Rights Code* because it believed the grievance-arbitration machinery was not adequate to protect employees from discrimination."

The board in *Abihsira* also suggested that a board of inquiry might not have jurisdiction to decline to hear a complaint, simply because there might

---

70. R.S.O. 1970, c. 232, s. 37(1) [now R.S.O. 1990, c. L.2, s. 45(1)].

71. *Ante*, note 69 at D/272.

72. *Ibid.*, at D/273.

be another forum in which the complaint might be heard.[73] The board of inquiry also decided that it had authority to interpret the collective agreement if it found it necessary to do so. The board found this authority in a clause of the previous *Code* which granted a human rights board exclusive jurisdiction to determine any question of law or fact or both that must be decided in order to reach a decision under the *Code*.[74]

The *res judicata* argument arose in *Abihsira* because the collective agreement interpreted by the arbitration board contained a clause similar in wording to the relevant section of the Ontario *Human Rights Code*.

In considering whether *res judicata* applied, the board of inquiry in *Abihsira* used the test in *Re Bullen* as cited by the board in *Derksen*.[75] The board concluded that the test did not apply, and would not apply even if the clause in the collective agreement were identical to the wording of the *Code*, because the question determined by the arbitration board was not the same as the question before the human rights board, and the parties in the two proceedings were not the same, the Ontario Human Rights Commission not having been a party to the grievance arbitration.

In support of these conclusions, the board in *Abihsira* pointed to the decision in *Hall v. International Firefighters' Association* in which[76]

> The Board chairman wrote: ". . . the matter is not just a private dispute between parties to a collective agreement. It raises an issue of public importance and general concern provided for by statute, and the right of individuals to complain, and of the Commission to inquire, cannot be restricted by a collective agreement."[77]

---

73. In support of this, the board cited s. 19(*a*) of the previous *Code*. It would appear that the comparable section of the present *Code*, s. 39(1), likewise does not include any specified jurisdiction to decline to proceed for this reason.

74. The clause of the previous *Code* was s. 18(6) which provided that "Subject to appeal under section 20, the board of inquiry has exclusive jurisdiction and authority to determine any question of fact or law or both required to be decided in reaching a decision as to whether or not any person has contravened this Act or for the making of any order pursuant to such decision." There is no similar clause in the present *Code*; therefore it is likely that the issue will be raised again, as Ontario arbitration boards have been granted exclusive jurisdiction by the *Labour Relations Act*, R.S.O. 1990, c. L.2, s. 45, with respect to the interpretation of collective agreements. However, it is possible that the same conclusion will be reached since, in addition to its reliance on the subsection quoted above, the board in *Abihsira* relied on the differences in purpose between the two types of hearings: "An arbitration board under section 37(1) of the *Labour Relations Act* has authority to interpret the collective agreement for the purpose of resolving differences between the parties relating to or arising from the collective agreement; if it became necessary, I would be examining and interpreting the collective agreement for a quite different purpose — namely, to hear and decide whether or not Arvin Automotive have contravened section 4(1)(b) or (g) of the *Ontario Human Rights Code*" (at D/273).

75. *Ante*, note 64.

76. (1977), unreported (Ont. Bd. of Inquiry), reversed (1980), 26 O.R. (2d) 308, affirmed (1980), 29 O.R. (2d) 499, reversed (1982), 40 N.R. 159 (S.C.C.).

77. 2 C.H.R.R. D/271 at D/273.

The board in *Abihsira* also quoted from an American decision, *Alexander v. Gardner-Denver*,[78] in which

the U.S. Supreme Court held that an employee's statutory rights under Title VII of the *Civil Rights Act* are not foreclosed by prior submission of his claim to final arbitration under the non-discrimination clause of a collective agreement. Mr. Justice Powell, writing for the Supreme Court, indicated the policy grounds underlying the Court's decision:

> Title VII was designed to supplement, rather than supplant existing laws and institutions relating to employment discrimination. In sum, Title VII purpose and procedures strongly suggest that an individual does not forfeit his private cause of action if he first pursues his grievance to final arbitration under the non-discrimination clause of a collective agreement (page 1020)
>
> . . . rights are conferred on employees collectively to foster the processes of bargaining and properly may be exercised or relinquished by the Union as collective bargaining agent to obtain economic benefits for union members. Title VII, on the other hand, stands on plainly different grounds; it concerns not majoritarian processes, but an individual's right to equal employment opportunities (page 1021)
>
> . . . a contractual right to submit a claim to arbitration is not displaced simply because Congress has also provided a statutory right against discrimination. Both rights have legally independent origins and are equally available to the aggrieved employee . . . (page 1022)
>
> . . . in instituting an action under Title VII, the employee is not seeking review of the arbitrator's decision. Rather, he is asserting a statutory right independent of the arbitration process. An employer does not have "two strings to his bow" with respect to an arbitral decision for the simple reason that Title VII does not provide employers with a cause of action against employees. An employer cannot be the victim of discriminatory employment practices (page 1022-3).[79]

A different approach to the *res judicata* issue was taken by the Ontario board of inquiry in *Singh v. Domglas Limited*.[80] In *Singh*, as in *Abihsira*, a grievance arbitration had previously dealt with the complainant's dismissal *vis-à-vis* an anti-discrimination clause in the collective agreement. However, in *Singh* the board concluded that, in the circumstances, *res judicata* was an evidentiary rather than a jurisdictional issue:[81]

> While normally this is an issue which it is expedient to deal with on a preliminary motion, I concluded that I should not do so in this case for several reasons. First, since there did not appear to be a prior ruling on the effect of a prior arbitration award on proceedings before a human rights tribunal in Ontario or Canada; the issue was one of first impression and should, therefore, only be ruled upon after full consideration, and in light of the entire case. Secondly, since the arbitration award did not on its face deal with the issue of discrimination, I would not be in a position to discharge the obligation in section 14c(*a*) of the *Code* to decide whether there was a contravention of the Act unless I heard further evidence. Thirdly, since the complainant was ready to proceed with his evidence, and the matter had already been long delayed, it would be more convenient to

---

78. 94 S.Ct. 1011 (1974).
79. *Ante*, note 77, at D/274.
80. (1980), 2 C.H.R.R. D/285 (Ont. Bd. of Inquiry).
81. *Ibid.*, at D/285.

proceed with the taking of evidence, rather than adjourn pending a decision on the preliminary motion. While the third consideration ceased to operate at the conclusion of the first three days of the hearing, I decided that, particularly in light of the first consideration, I should continue to reserve my decision until the end of the case.

The board in *Singh* also took a different view of the importance of the Commission as a separate party, where *res judicata* is raised. It held that "the Commission's status in the matter derives from the complaint," and that

> [I]f the party filing the complaint has no basis for the complaint because of an arbitration award, then I do not see how the presence of the Commission as a party can add anything to the matter. The Commission has, of course, the option of initiating a complaint under section 13(3) of the *Code*, and it should do so if it does not wish to be bound by the rights between particular complainants and respondents.
>
> Even if I am wrong in holding that the Commission is bound in this way by the origin of the complaint, the courts of Ontario have recognized a broader principle that one party who identifies its interest with that of another, as the Commission does by proceeding on the complaint of the complainant, is bound by an estoppel as to issues already adjudicated between that other person and parties opposed in interest: *Nigro v. Agnew-Surpass Shoe Stores* (1977), 18 O.R. (2d) 215 (H.C.), affd., (1977), 18 O.R. 714 (C.A.). Whether the Commission is bound by the award for the purposes of a complaint under the Code, or merely stopped, the effect is the same.

The board maintained that *res judicata* could not be raised where the rights dealt with in an arbitration award were different from those dealt with by a human rights board of inquiry. However, Chairman Kerr raised certain "policy considerations" that the board should consider in "deciding whether these rights should in law be treated as distinct."[82] The considerations raised included:

1. the undesirability of conflicting decisions on a single situation;

2. the fact that labour arbitrations are mandated by law in Ontario and that, therefore, their decisions should be accorded greater respect than those of arbitration boards in the United States, where arbitration is a voluntary procedure;

3. that the greater appeal rights under the *Code*, as opposed to the *Labour Relations Act*, give rise to an inference that the rights involved are different.

The chairman in *Singh* also seemed to consider an arbitration board the more suitable tribunal to adjudicate issues relating to dismissal.[83]

> Another consideration is the general policy of avoiding excessive legal proceedings which underlies the rules of res judicata and issue estoppel. It has been established that discrimination can vitiate a claim of cause for dismissal: *MacDonald v. 283076 Ontario Inc.* (1979), 26 O.R. (2d) 1 (C.A.). Since a board of inquiry has no jurisdiction to

---

82. *Ibid.*, at D/285-6.
83. *Ibid.*, at D/286.

enforce rights other than those arising from unlawful discrimination, it would appear that an arbitration board is in a better position to dispose of an entire dispute than is a board of inquiry. This argues in favour of giving the widest possible weight to an arbitral award in order to encourage the full litigation of such issued before arbitrators, and to avoid the less complete adjudication of a board of inquiry.

In summing up, the chairman suggested that the appropriate position for Ontario human rights boards, *vis-à-vis* arbitration decisions, is similar to that taken by the United States National Labor Relations Board on private arbitration in that country.[84]

Under this approach, the Board may, in its discretion, defer to an arbitral award if it is satisfied that the arbitration procedure was fair and regular, all parties are bound, and the decision is not clearly repugnant to the purposes and policies of the statute. In relation to the last factor, one concern is whether or not the award has actually dealt with the principal issues raised by the statute. If it does, the Board is inclined to defer: *National Radio Co.*, 205 N.L.R.B. 1179 (1973).

Such an approach accommodates public interest in enforcement of the statute with appropriate respect for the private relationship of the parties through the exercise of the tribunal's discretion. If statutory rights have been ignored, the tribunal is free to intervene. On the other hand, the tribunal can avoid unnecessary relitigation of issues by reviewing on a preliminary motion whether it will defer to the arbitral award. While this does not prevent the complainant-grievant from commencing multiple proceedings, there is a substantial disadvantage in doing so. One only has a real chance at two hearings by splitting one's case, that is, taking proceedings under the *Code* with respect to the discrimination issue and under the collective agreement with respect to other issues. To split one's case in this manner is to weaken it and increase the risk of losing in both forums.

While the control of the union over proceedings under the collective agreement may undermine the ability of the grievant to obtain a hearing of the discrimination issues through arbitration, the individual's opportunity to get a full hearing in that process is protected by the duty of fair representation under section 60 of the *Labour Relations Act* and the ultimate right of individuals directly affected by an arbitration award to appear on their own behalf: *Hoogendoorn v. Greening Metal Products & Screening Equipment Co.*, (1968) S.C.R. 30. These are better protections than absolute refusal by boards of inquiry to respect arbitration awards. Indeed under the approach suggested the board of inquiry would not respect the award if it concluded that the grievant did not have a fair hearing. It may be noted that this also accords with the rule of res judicata which does not apply in a case where the party presently claiming contrary rights was represented by another party in the previous proceedings and such representation was not fair: Sopinka and Lederman, *The Law of Evidence in Civil Cases* (1974), at 375.

Since this approach recognizes that the rights being enforced in arbitration are legally separate from those under the statute, the dilemma created by the different relationship between the courts on the one hand and the arbitrator or the board of inquiry on the other is avoided. It is only the statutory rights, not the rights under the collective agreement, that are subject to ordinary appeal to the courts. While the possibility of practically conflicting results does occur, the object of deferral to the arbitral ruling is to limit such conflicts to cases where the arbitration award is unacceptable in light of the statutory rights involved.

---

84. *Ibid.*, at D/286.

In regard to the matter at issue in *Singh* the board found that[85]

> [O]n the face of the arbitration award in this case, there was no consideration of the question of discrimination which is the only issue under the *Code*. In such a case, it is not appropriate for a board of inquiry to give deference to the arbitration award with respect to the statutory issues.

The views expressed by the board in *Singh* were not shared by the board in *Hyman v. Southam Murray Printing Division*,[86] another Ontario case in which a previous arbitration award had canvassed the issue of discrimination in a dismissal. The board in *Hyman* found the *Singh* approach to be at odds with the intent of the *Human Rights Code*.[87]

> The [United States] Supreme Court in the *Gardner-Denver* case was at great pains to indicate that it was not their intention to undermine the strong public policy favouring labour arbitration by refusing to defer to labour arbitration decisions in Title VII cases. Accordingly, I am not inclined to share Professor Kerr's view that a sharp distinction can be drawn between American and Canadian experience on this basis. Further, when one examines the discretion to defer which Professor Kerr favours, it appears to operate in a manner very similar to that of the *res judicata* rules. If essentially the same issue has been litigated before the grievance arbitration in a fair and regular manner, the National Labor Relations Board will defer. In such circumstances, traditional *res judicata* or *issue estoppel* principles would similarly command deferral. For the reasons elaborated above, it is my view that a principle of deferral of this kind is inconsistent with the legislative intent evidenced in the provisions of the Ontario *Human Rights Code*.

The board in *Hyman* held that, despite the respondent's interest in avoiding, in effect, being sued twice, and the public interest in "bringing an end to the litigation of disputes between parties and in avoiding the prospect of inconsistent decisions being reached with respect to the same dispute by different tribunals," there were two reasons why the board should proceed. The first was that

> the effect of permitting previous grievance arbitration awards to engage the principles of *res judicata* would undermine the objectives of the Ontario *Human Rights Code* and, at the same time, would provide an undesirable disincentive to the use of grievance arbitration as a means for resolving employment related disputes which involve, perhaps amongst other factors, allegations of discriminatory treatment.[88]

The board's reasons for this conclusion, though lengthy, are worth setting out in full:

> A comparison of these two institutional devices for dispute resolution indicate that there are a number of advantageous features to the remedial scheme set out in the Ontario *Human Rights Code* which have no parallel in the grievance arbitration process. A complaint lodged under the Ontario *Human Rights Code* is taken to a public body, the Ontario Human Rights Commission, whose exclusive mandate is to investigate such

---

85. *Ibid.*, at D/287.
86. (1981), 3 C.H.R.R. D/617 (Ont. Bd. of Inquiry).
87. *Ibid.*, at D/625.
88. *Ibid.*, at D/623.

complaints and seek their resolution. Prosecution of the complaint by the Commission is uncomplicated by any ongoing relationship between the Commission and the respondent in a particular case. In the grievance arbitration context, however, the parties to the arbitration are, of course, the employer and the union. It is established labour relations law that the union has control over the carriage of the grievance and thus, for example, is permitted to settle or withdraw the grievance at any time without the consent of the individual grievor. To be sure, the union could not refuse to process a grievance on discriminatory grounds without exposing itself to redress under Section 60 of the Ontario *Labour Relations Act*, R.S.O. 1970, c. 232. But the union may have other legitimate reasons for not pursuing the grievance as aggressively as the grievor might wish. As the Ontario Labour Relations Board noted in a decision dealing with Section 60, "we think it clear that the union's obligation to administer the collective agreement gives it the right to settle grievances. An employee does not have an absolute right to have his grievances arbitrated . . .". See *Gebbie v. UAW and Ford Motor Co.*, [1973] O.L.R.B. 519 at p. 526. Again, the Commission is unencumbered by considerations of this kind in determining whether or not to vigorously pursue the rights of an individual who has lodged a complaint under the *Code*.

Secondly, it is to be noted that the rights of appeal are different in the two contexts. The parties to a hearing before a Board of Inquiry is [*sic*] entitled to a full hearing *de novo* on questions of law or fact or both on an appeal to the Supreme Court of Ontario under Section 14d of the *Code*. The standard of judicial review of labour arbitration decisions is much more limited in its scope. A third difference between the two schemes may be found in the remedial powers of an arbitrator as opposed to a Board of Inquiry. Although it is true that arbitrators possess broad powers to reinstate dismissed employees and award appropriate compensation or, under Section 37(8) of the *Labour Relations Act* "substitute such other penalty for the discharge or discipline as to the arbitrator or arbitration board seems just and reasonable in all the circumstances," the remedial powers conferred on a Board of Inquiry under Section 14c of the *Code* appear to be much more extensive. In fashioning remedies pursuant to those powers, Boards of Inquiry have typically attempted to achieve not only the immediate objective of compensation for the injury sustained but also preventive measures designed to prevent their recurrence.

Further, it should be noted that the remedies available to an aggrieved union member, under Section 60 of the *Labour Relations Act*, who complains of a failure of adequate representation in a grievance process are less accessible to the aggrieved individual than are the remedies afforded by the Ontario *Human Rights Code*. The prosecution of a complaint under the *Code* will be undertaken by the Commission at public expense and thus will represent what is for the most part cost-free adjudication of the dispute as far as the complainant is concerned. The aggrieved party pursuing a complaint under Section 60 of the *Labour Relations Act* would, however, face substantial cost disincentives to proceeding against the union.

Finally, it must be noted that the nature of the investigation which may be undertaken by the Human Rights Commission may be of a significantly different quality than that undertaken in preparation for the arbitration of a grievance. The Commission has been assigned extensive powers of investigation under Section 14 of the *Code*. Moreover, the Commission is no doubt intended by the legislation to be a body which develops expertise in the investigation and conciliation of human rights disputes. It may be hoped that the Commission will develop a sensitivity to the kinds of evidence which might be useful in substantiating a claim of discrimination which may not be shared by those who only occasionally engage in the investigation of this kind of dispute.

More generally, when one examines the scheme set forth in the Ontario *Human Rights Code*, it becomes evident that the legislature has developed a comprehensive and accessible scheme for the enforcement of human rights. I would be reluctant to accede to an application of *res judicata* principles which would render that scheme less accessible to members of trade unions, or at least, to those members of trade unions who take the quite reasonable course of first pursuing the remedial scheme most familiar and immediately available to them, i.e. grievance arbitration under the collective agreement.

In addition to this policy of favouring recognition of rights of access to the remedial scheme of the *Code* for aggrieved individuals, the provisions of the *Code* also manifest the presence of a public interest in the investigation and resolution of discriminatory conduct which stands apart from the immediate interests of the individual complainant. Thus, for example, under Section 13(3) of the *Code*, the Commission is empowered to initiate a complaint on its own motion. Even in the absence, then, of an individual prepared to lodge a complaint and seek its resolution, the Commission has a mandate to see fulfillment of the broad principles of public policy set out in the preamble to the *Code* on its own motion.

An examination of the role assigned to the Commission by the *Code* also indicates that the problem of inconsistent verdicts or decisions cannot be swept away through the operation of *res judicata* principles. If one of the arguments supporting the application of *res judicata* is that respect for the administration of justice will be decreased by the phenomenon of inconsistent verdicts, it must be noted that in the human rights context, it appears to be inevitable in cases of this kind that there will be a sense in which inconsistent verdicts have been pronounced by the time a Board of Inquiry has been appointed to hear and decide the complaint. Under Section 14(1) of the *Code*, where a complaint has been filed with the Commission, the Commission must make an inquiry into the complaint and attempt to achieve a settlement. Where it appears that the complaint cannot be settled, the Commission may recommend to the Minister that a Board of Inquiry be appointed. The complainant has no direct access, then, to the Board of Inquiry mechanism. The evident purpose of the statute is that a screening function of some kind be performed by the Commission at this stage of the investigation of the complaint. The frustrations of an individual who perceived himself to be the victim of racial discrimination would be seriously intensified if, after his complaint has been investigated and subjected to this screening process by the Commission, a Board of Inquiry were to conclude that it was precluded from investigating the matter as a result of a prior and unsuccessful grievance arbitration. Although the individual's complaint was unsuccessful in the grievance process, a public body charged with the investigation and enforcement of human rights in the province has come to the conclusion that further litigation of the dispute is worthy of public support through the mechanism established in the *Code*.

In summary, the comprehensiveness and the accessibility of the enforcement mechanisms established by the *Code*, together with the specific role assigned to the Commission by the *Code* strongly suggest a legislative intention which is inconsistent with the idea that boards of inquiry would be precluded from conducting an investigation, once appointed, by the result of a previous grievance arbitration. These factors, together with the absence of any explicit direction on this point in the *Code* itself, lead me to the conclusion that any rights which may be conferred on an individual through a collective bargaining regime to seek resolution of complaints of discrimination in the workplace must be considered to restrict the accessibility of the remedial scheme of the *Code* to individuals covered by such schemes.

I would also draw some support from this conclusion from the implications which, in my view, can be drawn from the public policy evidenced in the Ontario *Labour Relations Act* of encouraging the use of labour arbitration as a device for the resolution of disputes in the workplace. Section 37(1) of that act requires that "every collective agreement shall provide for the final and binding settlement by arbitration . . . of all differences between the parties arising from the interpretation, application, administration or alleged violation of the agreement . . ..." I would be reluctant to adopt an application of the *res judicata* rules which would have the effect of providing a disincentive for the use of this mechanism. Were I to hold, however, that individuals whose human rights complaints were dismissed through the grievance arbitration process could not then invoke the remedial scheme of the *Human Rights Code*, I would provide an incentive for thoughtful victims to bypass the arbitration process completely and seek directly to invoke the more comprehensive and advantageous remedial provisions of the *Code*. If, on the other hand, a negative decision in the grievance arbitration process carries no risk for the victim of discrimination, there will be no reason to resist using this more accessible and informal process to seek a resolution of the dispute. Labour relations policy thus appears to provide an additional ground for treating rights conferred under collective agreements as additional to those conferred by the *Human Rights Code*.[89]

Notably, the board held that *res judicata* did not apply even though it disagreed with the finding of the board in *Abihsira* that the issues decided by an arbitration board, and those decided by a board of inquiry, were necessarily different.

The second reason for proceeding was based on "considerations specific to the present case which suggest that even if *res judicata* should have some sweep in this context, they ought not [to] preclude further proceedings relating to the matters before the present Board of Inquiry."[90] One of the allegations made was against the respondent union for lack of proper representation during the grievance arbitration. In the board's view, the raising of this issue disposed of the *res judicata* argument.

In a later case discussing *res judicata*, the board reviewed the decisions in *Abihsira, Singh* and *Hyman*, concluding that the views expressed in *Hyman* and *Abihsira* were more persuasive. In *Fleming v. Byron Jackson Division, Borg-Warner (Canada) Ltd.*,[91] the board discussed the differences between arbitration proceedings and human rights boards of inquiry, first quoting the different objectives stated in the preambles of the two Acts. The board expressed the view that[92]

> The addition of the Human Rights Commission as a party is not a mere formality which has no effect on the Inquiry. The duties and obligations of the Commission to these complainants in particular and the residents of Ontario in general is [*sic*] very much a fundamental aspect of the administration of the *Code*.

The board summarized the differences as follows.[93]

> Upon review of the provisions of the Ontario *Human Rights Code*, I am convinced that the Ontario legislature has created a unique and highly comprehensive process for dealing with human rights cases. I do not accept the submission that the respondent has been prejudiced by being subjected to two hearings or that *res judicata* is an applicable doctrine. I rather perceive the legislation as protecting both employers and employees

---

89. *Ibid.*, at D/623-4.
90. *Ibid.*, at D/623.
91. (1982), 3 C.H.R.R. D/765 (Ont. Bd. of Inquiry).
92. *Ibid.*, at D/766.
93. *Ibid.*, at D/767.

from frivolous complaints and potentially vexatious employees. The Commission has an obligation to investigate and to attempt to settle as well as to assess the legitimacy of the complaint. The Commissions may choose not to proceed with a human rights complaint in cases where it feels that an arbitration hearing has adequately dealt with the discrimination issue. Similarly, s. 14(a)(1) specifically grants to the Minister of Labour discretion to appoint a Board of Inquiry. In my opinion this is another significant distinction from the labour arbitration situation and a further protection against vexatious proceedings.

The board also cited *Seneca College of Applied Arts and Technology v. Bhadauria*[94] in support of its view that an individual cannot be precluded from seeking the protections afforded by the *Code* because of prior resort to grievance arbitration.

The most recent Ontario case to consider *res judicata*, *Dennis v. Family and Children's Services*,[95] focused on items 3, 5 and 6 of the test in *Re Bullen*; that is, the jurisdiction of the tribunal that had dealt with the matter, the "same question" issue, and the question as to whether the parties had been the same. At issue was an arbitration hearing, dealing with an alleged unjust termination of employment due to pregnancy. The board of arbitration dismissed the grievance because the grievor's probationary status excluded her from a grievance under the clause in the collective agreement that prohibited discrimination. The board of arbitration had nonetheless been invited to consider the documentation arising from the grievor's complaint under the *Human Rights Code*, and counsel for the complainant had been given the opportunity to call evidence relating to the complaint, and had invited the arbitration board to rule on the complaint.

The board ruled that the doctrine of *res judicata* did not apply. The finding of the board focused on the issues of identity of question and of parties. In regard to the former, the board took note that the arbitration board, while quoting extensively from the collective agreement, had not reiterated relevant provisions of the *Code*; nor had it referred to decisions made under the *Code*. Further, the arbitration board's decision linked the finding of no discrimination to the grievor's probationary status; thus the board concluded that the same question had not been determined.

In regard to the parties, the board concluded that, despite the submission by counsel for the respondent that the Commission had been aware of the arbitration proceedings and had not been prevented from attempting to join, the board ruled that the absence of the commission from the arbitration was "fatal" to the *res judicata*" argument.

After summing up its views on the *res judicata* argument, the board added that, "even if all the elements [in the *Bullen* test] had been present,

---

94. [1981] 2 S.C.R. 181.

95. *Dennis v. Family and Children's Services of London and Middlesex* (1990), 12 C.H.R.R. D/285 (Ont. Bd. of Inquiry).

this doctrine ought not to be utilized to stay human rights proceedings on the basis of prior arbitration rulings. The systems differ dramatically in their function, purpose and process. A ruling in one should not preclude or bar a proceeding in the other."[96]

Issue estoppel was also raised in *Fleming*; however, the board dismissed the argument for the same reasons that it had addressed in discussing *res judicata*.

A final point in *Fleming* was the discussion as to whether the arbitration award could be admitted in evidence. Despite a previously expressed difficulty in determining exactly which issues, of those to be decided by the board of inquiry, were decided by the arbitration board,[97] the board held that the award might be admitted. However, the board ruled that little weight should be given to the award because there was no way of assessing the procedural fairness of the arbitration hearing or the extent to which the issues of discrimination were considered.

Discovery and Motions for Particulars

The *Code* sets out no formal discovery process. However, the procedures followed in the investigation of a complaint are such that many of the facts on which the Commission will rely at a board are made known to the respondent.

The complaint that the respondent receives is made out "in a form approved by the Commission."[98] Typically, that form provides the information that recently was pronounced essential by a Canadian Human Rights Act board of inquiry in *Canada (Human Rights Commission) v. Bell Canada.*[99]

> (i) Identification of the Complainant, whether it is an individual person, a class, or the . . . Commission itself;
> (ii) Identification of the victim or of the class being discriminated against as the class may be;
> (iii) The time during which the violation of the Act took place;
> (iv) The location of the alleged violation;
> (v) The nature of the discriminatory practice;
> (vi) The section and subsection upon which the discriminatory practice is based; and finally,
> (vii) An affirmation by the Complainant and/or the Commission that they have reasonable grounds to believe that the conduct constituted a discriminatory practice in violation of the . . . Act.

---

96. *Ibid.*, at D/288.
97. The transcript from the arbitration board's proceedings was not before the board of inquiry.
98. S. 32(1).
99. (1981), 2 C.H.R.R. D/265 (Cdn. Human Rights Trib.).

The complaint is usually phrased in an informal manner and generally the allegation noted above does not include the term "reasonable grounds."

Neither in the Ontario *Code* nor the *Statutory Powers Procedure Act*[100] are there specific provisions about what information must be included in the complaint. However, section 8 of the latter provides:

> Where the good character, propriety of conduct or competence of a party is an issue in a proceeding, the party is entitled to be furnished prior to the hearing with reasonable information of any allegations with respect thereto.

A board of inquiry has held that the complaint must contain all the "essential elements" including identification of the complainant and the victim or the class being discriminated.[101] However, the Divisional Court has held that section 8 was not intended to preclude evidence being adduced that arose out of issues raised by an opposing party at a hearing, and therefore refused to quash a complaint that did not contain those issues.[102]

Typically, before a complaint reaches a board of inquiry, there is a conciliation conference at which the findings of the Commission's investigation are presented to the respondent in an effort to reach a settlement.[103]

At the board of inquiry stage, the issue of the entitlement of any party to knowledge of facts relevant to the other party's case has revolved around applications for particulars made under sections 6 and 8 of the SPPA, and arguments against the issuance of *subpoena duces tecum* under section 12 of the SPPA.

In the context of the section 8 cases, Ontario boards have expressed the view that full and frank disclosure before a hearing is desirable.[104] However, boards have also consistently maintained that neither the *Code* nor the *Statutory Powers Procedures Act* provide for discovery in the sense that is usual with civil litigation. The most recent comment to this effect was made in *Bhadauria v. Toronto Bd. of Education*.[105] In an interim decision, the board granted part of an application for particulars, but said:

> . . . the civil procedure concept of furnishing "particulars" is analogous but not identical to the requirements of the *Statutory Powers Procedures Act*. The Legislature could easi-

---

100. R.S.O. 1990, c. S.22.
101. In *Ontario (Human Rights Commission) v. Ontario (Ministry of Education)* (1986), 9 C.H.R.R. D/4535 (Ont. Bd. of Inquiry), Chairman Zemans denied a request for particulars of the names of persons who were affected by a challenge to a policy of the respondent that had been initiated by the Commission itself.
102. *Olarte v. Ontario (Minister of Labour)* (1984), 49 O.R. (2d) 17 (Div. Ct.).
103. See discussion in Chapter 8.
104. See *Niedzwieki v. Beneficial Insurance System* (1982), 3 C.H.R.R. D/1004 (Ont. Bd. of Inquiry); *Joseph v. North York General Hospital* (1982), 3 C.H.R.R. D/854 (Ont. Bd. of Inquiry).
105. (1987), 9 C.H.R.R. D/4501 (Ont. Bd. of Inquiry).

ly have drafted section 8 of the *Statutory Powers Procedure Act* to require that particulars of allegations be furnished to the respondents in hearings such as these. This would have imported the jurisprudence which identifies particulars and eventually leads to discovery of the opponent's case. But section 8 puts a different onus on the parties. It simply requires that reasonable information be given of any allegation with respect to a claim impugning character or conduct. "Reasonable information" is not as rigid a requirement as the furnishing of particulars. It only requires that the respondent has sufficient information about the allegations to prepare itself to answer the allegations.[106]

The requirements of section 8 of the *Statutory Powers Procedure Act* have been interpreted by a number of boards. In *Nembhard v. Caneurop Manufacturing Ltd.*, the board opined that

[P]rior to the hearing, a respondent is entitled to receive sufficient information about the allegations to enable him to prepare his answer to them. This section does not, however, refer to advance notice of documentary evidence but merely to reasonable particularity of allegations.[107]

In *Morgan v. Toronto General Hospital*,[108] another Ontario board agreed with the decision in *Nembard* and refused to order disclosure of the Commission's file to the respondent.

Both the rule of natural justice on this point, as elaborated by the courts, and s. 8, merely require that the other party be given full particulars as to the case which is required to be met. Although there is no pre-trial discovery in the case of a complaint which comes before a Board of Inquiry under the Ontario *Human Rights Code*, it should be remembered that the *Code* does require a proceeding unlike that in any civil or criminal proceeding, and that is that an attempt be made at conciliation towards achieving a settlement. It is hardly conceivable that in the course of such negotiations with the Respondent, (and there was evidence at the hearing both of such meetings and other communications), the Respondent would not be extensively aware of the case that is required to be met.

Therefore, as I decided at the time at the hearing, there is no need either statutorily, or in accordance with any rule of fairness, that the notes and reports made or obtained by the investigating officers be produced at that time or prior thereto. At the appropriate time during the course of the hearing, when these are referred to by the witness who prepared them, copies of them should be and in this hearing were, made available to counsel for the Respondent.[109]

The board noted that the file contained, as well as notes with respect to the investigation, notes and correspondence regarding attempts at settlement that would not be admissible as evidence at the hearing. However, the board held that any notes or documents referred to by witnesses on the stand should be made available to the respondent.

In *Dubajic v. Walbar Machine Products of Canada Limited*,[110] the

---

106. *Ibid.*, at D/4502.
107. (1976), unreported (Ont. Bd. of Inquiry), at p. 22 (transcript).
108. (1977), unreported (Ont. Bd. of Inquiry), at p. 11 (transcript).
109. See further discussion of privileged evidence, later in this chapter.
110. (1980), 1 C.H.R.R. D/228 (Ont. Bd. of Inquiry).

respondent argued that section 8 of the *Statutory Powers Procedure Act* entitled him to be informed, not only of the material facts relating to the allegations, but also of the evidence by which those facts were to be proven together with the production of any documents concerning the allegations. The board refused to accede to this argument.[111]

> My interpretation of s. 8 is that is is concerned with the furnishing of "reasonable information of . . . allegations . . ." and not with the means whereby those allegations will be proved. It is concerned with particulars to know a case and not with evidence as to how the case will be proved. It is concerned with the case intended to be made and not with the information allegedly favourable or unfavourable to the case. Furthermore, it is not concerned with facts which might assist the party, against whom the claim is being made, to discover evidence in support of its defence, as contrasted with information of the case to be met, although I would expect that the Commission would, at the hearing, adduce evidence arguably favourable as well as unfavourable to Walbar.

The board noted that:[112]

> Hearings before the Board of Inquiry, under the *Code*, are adversarial in nature. Each party remains responsible for the preparation of its case and, as in the case of an action brought in the Supreme Court, in the absence of statutory authority, each party cannot be compelled to disclose the evidence which it may use at the hearing on the merits in support of a claim or defence. I would repeat my earlier conclusion that such a radical change in the previous law would only be effected by more specific language.
>
> Even if s. 8 could be interpreted as encompassing documents and statements of evidence within the meaning of "reasonable information" the furnishing of such information would only be necessary where it was required by a party, to either know the issues or to be able to prepare its answer to the allegations. That is, unlike discovery in the Supreme Court, the information does not include facts or documents which may assist a party in leading to a train of inquiry which might, in turn, result in the obtaining of evidence which could assist in making the party's case.

The respondent in *Dubajic* specifically requested information as to the identity of persons from whom the Commission had obtained information. The board rejected as invalid the Commission's contention that the disclosure of these persons' names might lead to an order that they be joined as parties. The board accepted the Commission's argument that the disclosure of these persons' names would amount to a disclosure of evidence, but stated that this would not always be the case. Rather, on some occasions, the name of an informant would be a material fact that the respondent would be entitled to know. The board set out the criteria on which a decision to order disclosure of the names of informants ought to be based:[113]

> In ruling on the right to disclosure of the names of persons unnamed but referred to in the Complaints I will consider:

---

111. *Ibid.*, at D/230.
112. *Ibid.*, at D/230.
113. *Ibid.*, at D/229.

(a) If the disclosure will result in identifying Commission witnesses whose identity does not "form a substantial part of the facts material to the issues." . . .

(b) Whether knowledge of the names of the persons referred to is reasonably necessary in order that Walbar may have sufficient information about the allegations relating to its good character or propriety of conduct, so as to enable it to prepare to meet such allegations.

The board then commented on the purpose of section 8 of the *Statutory Powers Procedure Act*:

> My view of s. 8 of the Act is that it was introduced to regulate one aspect of procedural natural justice which must be followed by certain tribunals including a Board of Inquiry appointed pursuant to s. 14(a)(1) of the *Code*. Whatever the scope of the information which must be furnished, its purpose is to define the issues and thereby prevent surprise by enabling the party against whom the allegations are made to prepare for the hearing. At the very least, s. 8 of the Act in order to fulfill this purpose would require that Walbar be furnished with a written statement of the material facts upon which the Commission intends to rely in support of the allegations with respect to the issues involving Walbar's good character or the propriety of its conduct. Such material facts should include when and where the alleged acts, which raised the issues, occurred, as well as the names of such persons who are referred to in the allegations, subject to the exceptions above noted.[114]

The board noted that, if its rulings resulted in the respondent being surprised by an issue or fact raised for the first time at the hearing, the board has the power to grant an adjournment to give the respondent a chance to prepare to meet the issue.

In *Bezeau v. Ontario Institute for Studies in Education*,[115] the respondent argued that it was entitled to receive a statement of all the material facts on which the Commission intended to rely in proof of its allegations as to denial of tenure to Canadian professors. However, the Commission submitted that the tenure review process of the respondent was so secretive that the only particulars the Commission could provide were the facts that, of five professors eligible for tenure, the three non-Canadians were granted tenure while the two Canadians whose qualifications were allegedly superior were denied tenure. The respondent wanted more particulars with respect to who was responsible for the denial of tenure and their discriminatory intent. The board, in denying the request, cited *Walbar* with approval.[116]

> The word "reasonable" in section 8 must be interpreted in the context of the proceedings which are involved. In hearings under the *Ontario Human Rights Code*, there is often a total absence of any specific, overt misconduct which, in itself, would establish discrimination.

---

114. *Ibid.*, at D/229.
115. (1982), 3 C.H.R.R. D/874 (Ont. Bd. of Inquiry).
116. *Ibid.*, at D/876.

In *Joseph v. North York General Hospital*,[117] the Commission had responded to a request by the respondent for particulars. At a preliminary hearing, the respondent argued that the particulars furnished were inadequate. The board noted that the complaint involved a long list of specific incidents which were alleged to amount to a "campaign of harassment" of the complainant by the employer. In the original complaint form not all of the incidents had been sufficiently described for the employer to identify them. However, the Commission had described each incident in more detail in its "Response to Request for Particulars" and the board, as a result, found that the respondent had sufficient information to defend itself. The test used by the board was the one used in *Fairbairn v. Sage*.[118]

> Particulars are, I think, ordered for several purposes:
> (1) to define the issue;
> (2) to prevent surprise;
> (3) to enable the parties to prepare for trial;
> (4) to facilitate the hearing.

Section 12 of the *Statutory Powers Procedure Act* allows for the issuance of a *subpoena duces tecum*:

> 12.(1) A tribunal may require any person, including a party, by summons . . .
> (b) to produce in evidence at a hearing documents and things specified by the tribunal,
>
> relevant to the subject matter of the proceedings and admissible at a hearing.

It is clear that, where a board considers that its subpoena power under section 12 of the *Statutory Powers Procedure Act* is being used to obtain discovery, it will refuse to issue, or will quash a *subpoena duces tecum*.

In *Guru v. McMaster University*,[119] for example, both parties applied to have each other's *subpoena duces tecum* set aside. Both parties acknowledged that the purpose of the subpoena was to obtain discovery. The chairman asserted that the power of a tribunal, under section 12, was intended to obtain documents to be produced in evidence, not for the mere purpose of obtaining discovery. He also noted that the Commission had powers under the *Code* to "require the production of documents" in the course of an investigation but that the board of inquiry had no similar power. Therefore, he ordered the subpoena set aside.

A similar view as to both the effect of section 12, and the responsibility of the Commission to use its investigatory power to require production, was expressed by the board in an interim decision in *Niedzwiecki v. Beneficial Finance*.[120] In that case, the respondent was asked to produce

---

117. (1982), 3 C.H.R.R. D/854 (Ont. Bd. of Inquiry).
118. (1925), 56 O.L.R. 462 at 470 (C.A.).
119. (1980), 2 C.H.R.R. D/253 (Ont. Bd. of Inquiry).
120. (1982), 3 C.H.R.R. D/1004 (Ont. Bd. of Inquiry).

(a) All documents, records, notes and/or writings pertaining to the matter of the complaint of Helen Niedzwiecki against the Beneficial Finance System. . . .

(b) Records reflecting the number, sex and marital status of cashiers, customer representatives, loan officers and assistant managers of the respondent from 1979 to the present;

(c) All records reflecting the hiring policy and the formulation of the hiring policy of the respondent, including transferability, from 1979 to the present;

(d) The originals of all documents previously given to the Commission.

The chairman in *Niedzwiecki* applied the test enunciated in *Dalgleish v. Basu*[121] as to the acceptability of a *subpoena duces tecum*:

(1) The witness must be fairly informed in advance what he is to produce. He must be asked to produce documents rather than to make discovery of documents.

(2) Greater latitude will be permitted in describing the documents where there is no prior compulsory discovery of documents and where voluntary disclosure has been refused.

(3) Greater latitude will also be permitted where the witness in question is a party or agent and can be taken to know the issues reasonably well.

(4) The issues involved in the proceedings must be considered. The broader the scope of the hearing, "the greater should be the permissible breadth of a *subpoena duces tecum*."

Using this test, the chairman disallowed the request for the documents denoted "(a)" above, but allowed the others, with a stipulation that the "(d)" group be specified in a list.

In *Joseph v. North York General Hospital*,[122] the respondent brought a motion requesting the board to set aside two *subpoena duces tecum* ordering its director of medical records and its personnel manager to produce certain documents. The board set aside the subpoenas with the observation that the documents could be subpoenaed at a later stage, if it became clear that they were necessary to be produced in evidence.[123]

The board in *Joseph* placed heavy emphasis on the power of the Commission, under the previous *Code*, to "require the production for inspection or examination of [documents] . . . that are or may be relevant to the investigation of the complaint." The board noted:[124]

Moreover, the legislation prohibits a respondent from failing to comply with a proper request for production in the course of investigation, or withholding documentation relevant to the investigation (s. 16(5)), and makes contravention a summary conviction offence (s. 21).

The board quoted from the decision of the Ontario Divisional Court in *Ontario (Human Rights Commission) v. Simpson-Sears*:[125]

The wide powers given to the Commission under s. 16 of the *Code* to enter private premises, seize documents, and question persons *in the course of inquiries into com-*

---

121. (1974), 51 D.L.R. (3d) 309 (Sask. Q.B.).
122. *Ante*, note 117.
123. *Ibid.*, at D/857.
124. *Ibid.*, at D/856.
125. (1982), 3 C.H.R.R. D/796 at D/800 (Ont. Div. Ct.).

plaints make it difficult, in my view, for an employer to conceal successfully an intentional discrimination. [Emphasis added.]

It drew the conclusion that the power of the Commission to require production of documents was limited to the investigative stage of a complaint, and that this power came to an end after the board was appointed. This view was also taken by the board in *Benet v. G.E.C. Canada Limited*.[126]

In *Bezeau v. Ontario Institute for Studies in Education*,[127] a more realistic view of the power of the Commission, under the previous *Code*, to obtain disclosure was taken by the board. The board noted that, although failure to comply with the Commission's request for disclosure during the investigation might result in prosecution, the minister's consent was required for such a prosecution. Counsel for the Commission argued that prosecution, as a method of obtaining documents, was too "heavy handed" in human rights cases. The only alternative was to obtain a search warrant which, as it requires a specific description of the object to be seized, is limited as a discovery device, and which the board also regarded as "heavy handed."[128] The board further noted that a heavy-handed approach might jeopardize settlement, which is the primary objective of the investigative stage of complaint. The board concluded that, from a practical standpoint, the investigative provisions of the *Code* are "restricted in scope to what is necessary to effect a settlement."[129]

In the event, the board in *Bezeau* set aside the requests for "any and all documents relating to the matters in issue," but permitted requests for all tenure files and papers of every kind, all the respondent's policy and procedure papers with respect to tenure review, and two service lists of all faculty members, because they were relevant tot he complainant's allegation of differential treatment in the granting of tenure.

A potential for serious difficulty in investigation has arisen pursuant to changes in the 1981 *Code*, coupled with boards' interpretation that section 12 of the *Statutory Powers Procedure Act* is not to be used for discovery. Unlike the *Code* at issue in the *Joseph* case, the present *Code* no longer empowers the Commission to require production of documents, or to prosecute when documents are withheld. The only options available to the Commission where the respondent refuses to produce documents are to apply for a search warrant, or to request the Minister to appoint a board of inquiry. In cases in which the most cogent evidence, or the largest part of the evidence, is likely to be found in documentary form, the Commission may have difficulty in either obtaining a search warrant or in appointing a board.[130]

---

126. (1981), unreported (Ont. Bd. of Inquiry).
127. (1982), 3 C.H.R.R. D/874 (Ont. Bd. of Inquiry).
128. *Ibid.*, at D/877.
129. *Ibid.*
130. The Commission may request a board when "the evidence warrants an inquiry": s. 36(1).

To date, two boards considering the *Code* have maintained that section 12 is not to be used for discovery purposes. Both have apparently contemplated the appointment of a board of inquiry at an early stage of the investigation if permission to view documents is refused. In *Ryckman v. Board of Commissioners of Police (Kenora)*,[131] the board noted that in cases of this type, the Commission need not take steps to complete its investigation nor to "endeavor to effect a settlement" as required by subsection 33(1) of the *Code*. Nor would it be necessary that it appear to the Commission that "the evidence warrants an inquiry," before it may require the minister to appoint a board.

In *Johnson v. East York (Board of Education)*[132] the board, while approving *Ryckman*, did not address the implications of proceeding with a board of inquiry when the investigation of the complaint is not complete. The board was not willing to require a witness to produce documents that had been subpoenaed by the Commission at a hearing preliminary to the presentation of the Commission's case. The board based its decision on the phrase "in evidence at the hearing" as used in section 12 of the SPPA, and on the fact that "no factual basis for the introduction of these documents has been established at this stage."[133]

The *Johnson* decision does not specify how much of the Commission's case would have to be presented to support an application for a *subpoena duces tecum*, nor address the difficulty that will arise for the Commission, in some cases, in identifying the appropriate person to be subpoenaed, without having seen the documents in question.[134] Nor does it address the appropriate approach to be taken by a board in determining whether the subpoena describes the documents too broadly. On this latter point, presumably the board would have regard to the second and fourth points of the test in *Dalgliesh v. Basu*.[135]

> "Greater latitude will be permitted in describing the documents *where there is no prior compulsory discovery of documents and where voluntary disclosure has been refused.* The issues involved in the proceedings must be considered. The broader the scope of the hearing, "the greater should be the permissible breadth of the subpoena duces tecum." [Emphasis added]

Presumably, the board in *Johnson* contemplated a necessarily brief and possibly incomplete introduction of the facts sought to be proved by the Commission, followed by an adjournment, pursuant to subsection 39(4) of the *Code*, to review the documents:

---

131. (1987), 8 C.H.R.R. D/4138 (Ont. Bd. of Inquiry).

132. (1988), 9 C.H.R.R. D/4791 (Ont. Bd. of Inquiry).

133. *Ibid.*, at D/4792.

134. The Board in *Johnson*, in *obiter* also departed from the position taken by the board in *Olarte v. Commodore Machines Ltd.* (1983), 4 C.H.R.R. D/1705 in taking the view that a person can be required to produce a document without giving oral testimony.

135. (1974), [1975] 2 W.W.R. 326 (Sask. Q.B.).

. . . As pointed out by counsel for the Commission, this may very well result in the need for an adjournment at the hearing so that Commission counsel can review the documents. In order to avoid the consequent delay, counsel frequently divulge the documents in advance of the hearing on the merits once the summons is issued. In this way the party who obtained the summons has an opportunity to study the documents and prepare its case accordingly. This is, however, a matter of volition since the Board has no power to order production of the documents in advance of the hearing on the merits.[136]

In a recent case in which the Commission requested a subpoena pursuant to section 12 of the SPPA, the respondent asserted that such a subpoena would breach sections 7, 8, 9, 11 and 15 of the *Canadian Charter of Rights and Freedoms*. This claim was dismissed by the board.[137]

Addition of other Grounds to the Complaint

Neither the *Code* nor the *Statutory Powers Procedure Act* specifically allow amendment of a complaint to add new grounds. However, the prescribed duty of the board in respect of hearing the complaint may be viewed as broadly-worded enough to allow the board to hear and decide an additional ground of complaint.[138] Presumably, the provisions of the *Statutory Powers Procedure Act* as to reasonable notice would apply.

In the only two Ontario cases in which the board of inquiry has discussed the addition of a new ground to the complaint, the board took the above-mentioned view as to its power to hear such an addition. In *Cousens v. Nurses' Association (Canada)*,[139] the complainant had alleged that he had been dismissed from his job because of his ancestry. At the outset of the hearing the Commission sought to add the further grounds of nationality and place of origin. The board of inquiry held that it had a duty to decide the complaints between the parties on all grounds, whether they were raised initially or not until the hearing, to determine whether there has been a contravention of the *Code*. The board said:[140]

> In ruling on this objection, the Board recognized the validity of the contention that prejudice could result. However, it was pointed out that section 14c of the *Code* suggests that the mandate of a board of inquiry might well extend beyond the specific ground of contravention alleged in the complaint:
> 14c. The board after hearing a complaint,
> (a) shall decide whether or not any party *has contravened this Act.* . . .
> In other words, the board is required not merely to decide upon the specific ground of discrimination which has been alleged, but to hear the circumstances of the complaint as

---

136. *Ante*, 113, at D/4793
137. *Dudnik v. York Condominium Corp. No. 216* (1990), 12 R.P.R. (2d) 1 (Ont. Bd. of Inquiry), reversed in part (1991), 16 R.P.R. (2d) 177 (Ont. Div. Ct.). .
138. S. 39(1)(*a*) provides that "The board of inquiry shall hold a hearing, to determine whether *a right* of the complainant under this Act has been infringed" (emphasis added).
139. (1980), 2 C.H.R.R. D/365 (Ont. Bd. of Inquiry).
140. *Ibid.*, at D/365-6.

presented by the parties and decide whether or not any party has "contravened this Act." The written complaint is not, therefore, in the nature of an information or indictment in a criminal case. Rather, it serves as general notice to a party in an administrative hearing. . . .

The wording of sections 14b(6) and 14(c)(a) are sufficiently broad to bear the practical interpretation that a board of inquiry has jurisdiction to amend the alleged grounds of contravention specified in a complaint. Surely, it was not intended that the Minister of Labour should have to make an additional appointment simply because, in preparation for the hearing, another possible ground of contravention has become apparent. It is clearly in the interests of all of the parties and the citizens of Ontario that the substantial complaint be dealt with at one hearing taking into account all of the possible ways in which any party may have "contravened this Act."

The board noted that the respondent must be given adequate notice of any new grounds and is entitled to an adjournment to prepare its defence.

The board of inquiry in the interim decision in *Tabar v. Scott*,[141] approved the reasoning of the board in *Cousens*.

Boards of inquiry in other jurisdictions have also been willing to allow such amendments. In *Bill v. Young*,[142] an additional ground of complaint had been added in the notice of hearing. The complainant had, in the complaint, alleged that she was denied rental of a trailer because she was a "Native Indian." The additional ground added by the director of the Commission was that the complainant was denied the rental because she was living in a common-law relationship. The respondent argued that, as the board of inquiry was appointed only to hear the first complaint, it did not have jurisdiction to hear the additional complaint. The board held that, when new grounds are added to a complaint, the respondent is entitled to particulars and to adequate time to prepare his or her defence.

In *Bremer v. Board of School Trustees, School District 62*,[143] the complainant had alleged that she was denied a teaching position because of her husband's political difficulties. At the hearing, she sought to add age as a further ground for the denial. The board of inquiry permitted the amendment:[144]

With regard to whether a complaint of a contravention of the *Code* is confined to particulars given prior to a Board of Inquiry hearing, it is apparent at the outset that such a restriction is entirely inconsistent with the principles upon which the onus may shift to the respondent in human rights proceedings. To confine a complaint in this manner would be to place upon the complainant the burden of establishing the cause for the impugned conduct, the very burden from which the complainant is relieved by establishing a prima facie case. Second, if complaints under the *Code* could be narrowed in this fashion, the result would be that an allegation of race discrimination could be successfully defended by proof that it was in reality sex discrimination.

---

141. (1982), 3 C.H.R.R. D/1073 (Ont. Bd. of Inquiry).
142. (1977), unreported (B.C. Bd. of Inquiry).
143. (1977), unreported (B.C. Bd. of Inquiry).
144. *Ibid.*, pp. 33-4 (transcript).

There is certainly no doubt that these proceedings are bound by the principles of natural justice and thus respondents are entitled to be made aware of the nature of the complaint and respondents are entitled to a full opportunity to prepare a case in reply. Where, during a hearing, a new but potentially prohibited consideration emerges in the evidence for the first time, the Board is of the view that such an event should be treated like any other situation in which the respondent may not have obtained sufficient details of a complaint to adequately present its case. In the *Oram [Oram v. Pho*, B.C. Human Rights Comm. Bd. of Inquiry, Wood (1975) (unreported)] decision, the Board of Inquiry said that in such circumstances the respondent would be entitled to an immediate adjournment. Such an adjournment would provide the respondent with an opportunity to prepare its case to answer any allegation which might have taken the respondent by surprise. The Respondents in these proceedings did have the benefit of adjournments including a particularly long one just prior to the presentation of the Respondent's case.

The board noted that the omission of the ground of age in the complaint was not through any fault of the complainant. She had been unaware that her age had been a factor in the respondent's decision until two officers of the respondent gave evidence at the hearing.

Finally, in *Jorgensen v. British Columbia Ice and Cold Storage Ltd.*,[145] board member Lynn Smith, dissenting on other grounds, rejected the respondent's argument that the board could only decide with respect to the allegation investigated by the Commission, reported to the minister, and referred to the board, finding that the allegation of discrimination in dismissal was sufficiently broad to include all grounds of discrimination that were argued before the board. She said that if the respondent suffered any prejudice, it would have been entitled to, at most, further particulars.

Boards of inquiry have also been willing to add (or to remove) parties from the complaint, as is further discussed below.

One Ontario board has drawn a distinction between adding parties and adding alleged incidents of discrimination. In *Gohm v. Domtar Inc.*[146] the Commission sought to add, to a complaint of discriminatory dismissal, two paragraphs containing allegations in regard to an application for another job with the respondent. The board struck out the amendments on the basis that they constituted a fresh complaint.

An issue that has recently arisen is whether amendment of a complaint is necessary to support a finding that a particular type of discrimination, namely constructive discrimination, has occurred. In *Velenosi v. Dominion Management*[147] Chairman Hubbard indicated that the Commission need not have specifically included an allegation of constructive discrimination along with a complaint of discrimination on the ground of age, concluding that constructive discrimination can be understood as part of a complaint of discrimination. However, the majority of a three-judge Divisional Court

---

145. (1981), 2 C.H.R.R. D/289 (B.C. Bd. of Inquiry).
146. (January 20, 1988), Doc. No. 331 (Ont. Bd. of Inquiry).
147. (1989), 10 C.H.R.R. D/6413 (Ont. Bd. of Inquiry).

panel did not take this view. In *Toronto (City) Board of Education*,[148] O'Leary J. (joined by Montgomery J.) quashed a finding of constructive discrimination in employment made by a board of inquiry, because the Commission had not cited section 10 [now s. 11] of the *Code*, as well as subsection 4(1), in the complaint. The rationale for this decision appeared to turn on the respondent school board not having been informed fully as to the case it had to meet.

The dissent of Archie Campbell J. in *Re OHRC and Quereshi* was prefaced with remarks as to the rationale behind the policy of curial deference — the fact that the reviewing court had not seen nor heard the witnesses and lacked the specialized knowledge and expertise of the tribunal reviewed. Campbell J. went on to point out that section 8 [now s. 9] of the *Code* prohibits both direct and indirect discrimination, and to opine that what the board had found in this case was the latter. Campbell J. clearly took the view that the effecting of discriminatory results could be addressed through section 9 as well as section 11. The point about the need to specifically cite section 11, if it was to be relied upon, as a matter of procedural fairness was not addressed by Campbell J.

It is clear that the *Quereshi* decision casts some doubt on the validity of the view expressed in *Velenosi*.

Parties

Section 5 of the *Statutory Powers Procedure Act*[149] states:

> The parties to any proceedings shall be the person specified as parties by or under the statute under which the proceedings arise or, if not so specified, persons entitled by law to be parties to the proceedings.

The *Code* does, in fact, specify who may be a party. Section 39(2) states:

> (2) The parties to a proceeding before a board of inquiry are,
>   (*a*) the Commission, which shall have the carriage of the complaint;
>   (*b*) the complainant;
>   (*c*) any person who the Commission alleges has infringed the right;
>   (*d*) any person appearing to the board of inquiry to have infringed the right;
>   (*e*) where the complaint is of alleged conduct constituting harassment under subsection 2(2) or subsection 5(2) or of alleged conduct under section 7, any person who, in the opinion of the board, knew or was in possession of facts from which he or she ought reasonably to have known of the conduct and who had authority to penalize or prevent the conduct.

The *Code* further specifies, in section 46, that the "person" noted above,

---

148. (1991), 42 O.A.C. 258 (Div. Ct.).
149. R.S.O. 1980, c. 484.

in addition to the extended meaning given it by the *Interpretation Act*, includes an employment agency, an employers' organization, an unincorporated association, a trade or occupational association, a trade union, a partnership, a municipality, a board of police commissioners established under the *Police Act*, being Chapter 381 of the Revised Statutes of Ontario, 1980, and a police services board established under the *Police Services Act*.

The "extended meaning" provided by the *Interpretation Act* is found in section 29(1) of the Act:[150]

"person" includes a corporation and the heirs, executors, administrators or other legal representatives of a person to whom the context can apply according to law.

The inclusion of section 46 in the present *Code* was obviously a response to the difficulties that arose in cases in which unincorporated associations were alleged to have maintained discriminatory practices. One example is found in *Cummings v. Ontario Minor Hockey Association*,[151] in which the Ontario Court of Appeal found that the Association's unincorporated status disqualified it from being considered a "person" for the purposes of the *Code*, despite the fact that the Association had agreed to be so considered.[152]

Recent Ontario boards of inquiry have dealt with questions arising when a charitable foundation operating a private school and a board of directors of a condominium were included as respondents. In *Sehdev v. Bayview Glen Junior Schools*,[153] the board had no difficulty in deciding that a corporate entity, even if run for charitable purposes, is properly a "person."

The condominium issue was more complicated. In *Dudnik v. York Condominium Co*,[154] the Commission had named individual condominium corporations "and (their) board of directors" rather than naming the directors individually. The board found that a board of directors is not legally a person, and ordered that part of the complaint deleted.

Complainants

The previous *Code* included as parties "the person named in the complaint as the complainant" and "any person named in the complaint and

---

150. Interpretation Act, R.S.O. 1990, c. I.11, s. 29(1), para. 26.
151. (1979), 26 O.R. (2d) 7 (C.A.).
152. By contrast, the Ontario Divisional Court, in *Metropolitan Toronto Bd. of Commissioners of Police v. Ontario Human Rights Commission* (1979), 27 O.R. (2d) 48 (Div. Ct.) had no difficulty in finding that the respondent Board of Commissioners was properly considered a "person," finding that the *Code*, as remedial legislation, should be broadly interpreted. However, the issue has been settled by the inclusion of "a board of police commissioners" in s. 46(c).
153. (1988), 9 C.H.R.R. D/4881 (Ont. Bd. of Inquiry). Also see *Rawala v. DeVry Institute of Technology* (1982), 3 C.H.R.R. D/1057 (Ont. Bd. of Inquiry).
154. (1988), 9 C.H.R.R. D/5080 (Ont. Bd. of Inquiry).

alleged to have been dealt with contrary to the provisions of this Act."[155] The present *Code* however, mentions only "the complainant." Presumably, this additional clause was considered redundant with the inclusion of section 12, which prohibits discrimination because of association.

Not all complaints under the *Code* provide that the complainant must have suffered direct injury. For example, section 11 prohibits requirements, qualifications or considerations that *would result* in specified consequences.[156] Neither section 13, which deals with notices, signs, symbols, etc., nor section 23, which deals with employment advertising, applications and agencies, appear to require that a complainant be personally injured or disadvantaged. Rather, these sections deal equally with actual and potential discrimination.[157] Further, in regard to the alleged breach of any section of the *Code*, the Commission may in fact be the complainant, "by itself or at the request of any person."[158]

Class Actions: The previous *Code* prohibited discrimination against any class of persons in several areas.[159] By contrast, the phrase, "a class of person" is nowhere to be found in the present *Code*. Interpreting the previous legislation, the board in *Tabar v. Scott*[160] found that a complaint could be filed on behalf of a class of persons without the members of the class being named. The rationale for this finding appears mainly to be the rule under the *Interpretation Act* that the singular includes the plural unless contrary intention appears, and that therefore, a "person" filing a complaint may complain on behalf of others. The board also pointed to the fact that the 1980 *Code* prohibited discrimination against a "class of persons." This, the board found, was sufficient to override the respondent's arguments that only the Commission could bring a complaint on behalf of a group of people.

There have been several cases on this point in other jurisdictions, most of which ruled against the possibility of a class action. However, in these cases, the legislation at issue provided standing as a complainant only for those "personally aggrieved by an action" and, as noted by the board in *Tabar*, this may be the rationale for the narrow interpretation.[161]

It is probably fair to say that, under the present *Code*, an individual does have the power to bring a class action. While the phrase "a class of persons" does not appear in the present *Code*, neither does a previously-included provision, considered by the board in *Tabar*, that said:

---

155. R.S.O. 1980, c. 340, s. 18(1).
156. See discussion of s. 11 in Chapter 4.
157. These sections are discussed in Chapter 5.
158. S. 32(2).
159. See R.S.O. 1980, c. 340, ss. 1, 2 and 3.
160. (1982), 3 C.H.R.R. D/1073 (Ont. Bd. of Inquiry).
161. See review of cases in *Tabar ibid.*

where a complaint is made by a person other than the person whom it is alleged was dealt with contrary to the provisions of this Act, the Commission may refuse to file the complaint unless the person alleged to be offended against consents thereto.[162]

The omission of this provision may signal a legislative intention to allow that discrimination be addressed by anyone with an interest in the matter, rather than an insistence on relying on the directly-affected victim, who may be ignorant of discrimination having taking place, or too intimated to come forward.

Where there are a number of related complaints, the Commission may combine them. By virtue of section 32(3), the Commission may combine two or more complaints where they

(*a*) bring into question a practice of infringement engaged in by the same person; or

(*b*) have questions of law or fact in common.

This provision will allow the Commission some flexibility in joining complaints. Furthermore, section 32(3)(*a*) is obviously especially designed for the efficacious enforcement of the *Code*, since it will be effective in dealing with such matters as a large corporation's hiring policies. While it is obvious that "class action" human rights complaints cannot be launched by individuals under the present *Code*, this is in keeping with the obvious "public interest" policy whereby the Commission bears the responsibility for *Code* enforcement.

The limits to the Commission's power to maintain the joinder of complaints will be discussed below in the section on joinder.

Respondents

As noted above, section 39(2)(*c*) of the *Code* provides that "any person who the Commission alleges has infringed the right" is a party to the proceedings. Section 39(2)(*d*) further provides that "any person appearing to the board of inquiry to have infringed the right" be a party to the proceeding. Where harassment is alleged, section 39(2)(*e*) provides that:

. . . any person who, in the opinion of the board, knew or was in possession of facts from which the person ought reasonably to have known of the conduct and who had authority to penalize or prevent the conduct

is also a party.

In *McMinn v. Sault Ste. Marie Professional Firefighters' Association*,[163] one respondent's name was omitted from the appointment and since the Notice of Hearing was wrongly addressed, the respondent, the Firefighters' Association, did not receive it. Counsel for the Association raised the issue of whether the Association should continue as a party. In

---

162. R.S.O. 1980, 340 s. 15(2).

163. (1986), 7 C.H.R.R. D/3458 (Ont. Bd. of Inquiry).

deciding that, despite the omission, the Association remained a party, the board took into account both the wording of subsection 39(2)(*c*) and the circumstances. The Association had notice of the complaint, participated in the investigation and fact-finding conference, had never been informed that the complaint against it was discontinued, and was represented by counsel throughout the proceedings.

Several Ontario decisions have addressed the question of misnomer of respondents. In *Matthew v. Seven City Development Co.*,[164] the complaint had originally been laid against "Seven City Developments Limited." The board allowed the respondent's name to be amended. Chairman Tarnopolsky found that the corporate respondent had been in no way prejudiced by the misnomer because it had referred to itself as "Seven City Developments" in its newspaper ads and correspondence.

In *Rawala v. DeVry Institute of Technology*,[165] the respondent argued that, subsequent to the complaint, it had amalgamated with another corporation, and that, at that time, the larger corporation had registered "DeVry Institute of Technology" as a trade name. The board cited

> two reasons which, in my view, are equally compelling for dismissing this objection. First, it is clearly established Canadian law that an incorporated entity which is amalgamated into another corporate entity does not cease to exist for all purposes and in particular, may be said to continue to exist for procedural purposes. Thus, a reference to a corporate entity by the name by which it was known prior to the amalgamation may be taken to refer to an entity which continues its existence as part of a larger entity now known by another name. In *Witco Chemical Co. Canada Ltd. v. The Corporation of the Town of Oakville*, [1975] 1 S.C.R. 273, the plaintiff issued a writ in the name by which it was known prior to its amalgamation with another corporation. By the time the plaintiff became aware of the error, the period of limitations had expired and it was argued by the defendant that no amendment to the pleadings should be allowed. The Supreme Court of Canada held that an amendment was appropriate inasmuch as the error was *bona fide* and of a minor and technical nature. Moreover, it was the Court's view that the amalgamation did not extinguish the previously existing corporate entities but rather continued their existence as one person. While the metaphysics underlying this rule may be thought to be somewhat obscure, it is evident that a procedural objection based on the premise that reference to a party by the name which it held prior to a corporate amalgamation was a reference to a nonentity would be unavailing. On this basis, the present objection should be dismissed. DeVry Institute of Technology is not a nonexistent person but rather a corporate person whose existence has continued under the name of Bell & Howell Ltd. Thus, these proceedings do not suffer from the fatal defect identified in the Cummings case. The named respondent is a corporate person continuing its existence as part of Bell & Howell Ltd.
>
> A second and distinct basis for dismissing this objection is that the naming of a respondent by its trade name constitutes, in my view, an adequate naming of the respondent for the purpose of instituting and conducting proceedings, provided that the use of the trade name is such as to clearly indicate to the corporate entity carrying on business

---

164. (1973), unreported (Ont. Bd. of Inquiry).
165. (1982), 3 C.H.R.R. D/1057 (Ont. Bd. of Inquiry).

under the trade name that it is the intended respondent in the proceedings. Use of the trade name to identify the respondent constitutes the use of a misnomer rather than reference to a non-existent entity. Thus, in civil proceedings, a plaintiff may bring action against a person, identifying that person by the name under which it carries on business and indeed, any order granted in the action may be enforced by execution against the property of the person so sued which is used or employed by the person in or in connection with the business in question. In Ontario, this rule is stated as Rule 110 of the Ontario Rules of Practice, R.R.O. 1980, Reg. 540, as amended. In the absence of any guidance on this point in the Ontario *Human Rights Code*, it would seem appropriate for a Board of Inquiry to conduct its proceedings in accord with this principle. Accordingly, it is my view that reference to a respondent by a trade name under which it carries on business is an adequate reference to a respondent for the purpose of proceedings under the Ontario *Human Rights Code*, and I would see this as merely one instance of the application of a more general principle that the erroneous use of a misnomer in an appointment or a complaint would not render proceedings initiated thereby a nullity.[166]

The board in *Rawala* found that amendment of the appointment that constituted the board of inquiry would be beyond the power of a board. The chairman also opined that amendment of the complaint would be both inappropriate and unnecessary.[167]

> Amendment of the Appointment itself, a ministerial order, would appear to be beyond the powers of a Board of Inquiry constituted thereby. Amendment to the Complaint would appear to be inappropriate inasmuch as a complaint under the *Code* does not appear to function as a pleading which might be amended from time to time by the party issuing it. It is consistent with this view, I would suggest, that the *Code* makes no provision for amending complaints and, further, that parties may be added to the proceeding (often, no doubt, pursuant to evidence which is introduced during the course of the proceedings) without the issuance of a further complaint.

However, the chairman ordered both the complaint and the appointment amended in case this view was erroneous.

In *Tabar v. Scott*,[168] the change from "West End Construction Co." to "West End Construction Ltd." was allowed on the ground that no possible prejudice could thereby result to the respondent.

Intervenors

Neither the previous nor the present *Code* specifically provides for the appearance of intervenors at a hearing. However, one boards have allowed entities who were not parties to make representations.

In *Simms v. Ford Motor Co.*,[169] the union sought to intervene, arguing that it had an interest in any allegations of racial discrimination by the employer towards the employees for whom the union was the sole bargaining agent. The board noted that, under the *Code* then in force, the parties to

---

166. *Ibid.*, at D/1065 (transcript).
167. *Ibid.*, at D/1065.
168. *Ante*, note 158.
169. (1970), unreported (Ont. Bd. of Inquiry).

the proceeding were the "parties to the complaint." In this case, they were the complainant, the Commission and the respondent employer. The board stated that this did not preclude it from permitting intervenors to appear.[170]

> This conclusion, however, means only that no one other than these three parties may participate in the proceedings *as of right*. It does not, in my respectful opinion, preclude the Board from exercising a discretion, in appropriate cases, to permit others to be involved. It is unnecessary, and indeed it would be unwise, to express any opinion as to the kind of case that might be said to be appropriate in advance. Each case should be decided on its own merits.

The board decided to deny the union status as an intervenor because it wished to avoid being involved in the collective bargaining process or having the hearing turned into a grievance proceeding. It also based its decision on that fact that all the relevant evidence was adduced at the hearing and that none was overlooked due to the union's absence. Although the union was denied the opportunity to adduce evidence or cross-examine witnesses, it was permitted to make representations at the end of the hearing.

In *Bhinder v. Canadian National Railways*,[171] a case under the Canadian *Human Rights Act*, the issue was whether a Sikh could be required to remove his turban and wear a hardhat. Because of the interest in the Sikh community, the Sri Guru Singh Sabha organization sought to be added as a party. The Canadian *Human Rights Act* gives the tribunal discretion to add any interested party.[172] The tribunal in this case chose not to add this organization as a party because its presence was not necessary to ensure that all relevant evidence was before the tribunal.

In *Tomen v. Ontario Teacher's Federation*,[173] the board provided an outline of considerations to guide the decision to allow participation by intervenor.

In *Sinclair v. Peel Non-Profit Housing Corp.*,[174] the board discussed the difference between intervenors being added as parties, and as *amicus curiae*.

Absence of Complainant or Respondent

Section 6 of the *Statutory Powers Procedure Act* requires that parties be given reasonable notice of the hearing and that such notice include: the time, place and purpose of the hearing; a reference to the Ontario *Human Rights Code*, under which the hearing is to be held; and a statement that, if the notified party does not attend, the board may proceed in his or her

---

170. *Ibid.*, p. 3 (transcript).
171. (1981), 2 C.H.R.R. D/456 (Human Rights Trib.), reversed for other reasons 4 C.H.R.R. D/1404 (Ont. C.A.), affirmed [1985] 2 S.C.R. 561.
172. S.C. 1976-77, c. 33, s. 40(1).
173. (1989), 11 C.H.R.R. D/104 (Ont. Bd. of Inquiry).
174. (1989), 11 C.H.R.R. D/341.

absence without further notice.[175] Section 7 of the Act goes on to provide that

> Where notice of a hearing has been given to a party to a proceeding in accordance with this Act and the party does not attend at the hearing, the tribunal may proceed in the absence of the party and the party is not entitled to any further notice in the proceeding.

At one Ontario board of inquiry a complainant was the absent party. In *Peterson v. Canadian Rubber Dealers & Brokers Limited*,[176] one of the complainants failed to attend. In her absence, the grievance of the other complainant was dealt with. As counsel for the Commission was unable to proceed in the first complainant's absence, she requested an adjournment. The board considered the request with reference to section 21 of the *Statutory Powers Procedure Act*, which allows a tribunal to grant an adjournment "of its own motion or where it is shown to the satisfaction of the tribunal that an adjournment is required to permit an adequate hearing to be held." The board concluded that:

> Given Mrs. Peterson's apparent lack of interest in the complaint, as evidenced by her failure to respond to the Notice of Hearing, to written, telephonic or telegram attempts to reach her and her failure to contact the Commission, I cannot conclude, in these circumstances, that an adjournment should be granted. An adjournment would have put the respondent to considerable inconvenience and the additional expense of at least an extra day of hearing; four witnesses for the respondent would have been similarly inconvenienced. Had I granted the adjournment this inconvenience would have occurred in the absence of any explanation of Mrs. Peterson's failure to attend on October 3, 1980 and in the absence of any statutory authority in the *Code* which would allow the Board of Inquiry to redress the respondent's inconvenience and added expense by way of costs.
>
> The granting of an adjournment is at the discretion of the Board, a discretion not to be exercised arbitrarily, but fairly and equitably, having regard to the balance of convenience to both parties. Speaking of the Ontario Labour Relations Board, Robins J. recently wrote: "In the case of a request for an adjournment, it [*i.e.*, the Board] is manifestly in the best position to decide whether, having regard to the nature of the substantive application before it, the adjournment should be granted or whether the interests of the employer, the employees or the union who, as the case may be, oppose the adjourn-

---

175. S. 6 states:

> "(1) The parties to a proceeding shall be given reasonable notice of the hearing by the tribunal.
>
> (2) A notice of a hearing shall include,
>> (*a*) a statement of the time, place and purpose of the hearing;
>> (*b*) a reference to the statutory authority under which the hearing will be held; and
>> (*c*) a statement that if the party notified does not attend the hearing, the tribunal may proceed in the absence of the party and the party will not be entitled to any further notice in the proceedings."

One Ontario has ruled that parties may waive this notice: *Dubniczky v. J.L.K. Kiriakopoulos* (1981), 2 C.H.R.R. D/485.

176. (1980), 2 C.H.R.R. D/257 (Ont. Bd. of Inquiry).

ment should prevail over the party seeking it. As a matter of jurisdiction it is for the Board to decide whether it should adjourn proceedings before it and in what circumstances." *Re Flamboro Downs Holding Limited and Teamsters Local 879* (1980), 99 D.L.R. (3d) 165 at 168.

It was not shown to my satisfaction that an adjournment should be granted in these circumstances. Accordingly, Mrs. Peterson's complaint is dismissed.[177]

The board in *Peterson* did not specifically address the issue of whether the adjournment was "required to permit an adequate hearing to be held." However, it should be noted that both complaints in *Peterson* were against the same respondent and both concerned age discrimination; presumably, the board found that an adequate hearing had been held in respect of age discrimination by that employer. However, this will obviously not be the case in all complaints. Given that the Commission has carriage of the complaint, it may wish to apply for a summons, under section 12 of the *Statutory Powers Procedure Act*, where the complainant fails to appear. That section also sets out a procedure whereby a person who persistently refused to attend may be compelled to do so.

There are, not surprisingly, more decisions dealing with the failure of a respondent to appear. In *Brown v. Blake*,[178] the board found that the respondent was absent because he was "deliberately seeking to avoid appearing before the board."[179] After hearing the complainant's case the board adjourned to give the respondent one last chance to appear. The board went so far as to endorse a warrant for the respondent's arrest, in case this was necessary to obtain his attendance. The board said:[180]

Although a Board Chairman is empowered to do so it is understandably an extreme step and I did so with considerable reluctance and only because I was satisfied that such an attitude on the part of Mr. Blake and others similary inclined could only frustrate and nullify the work of boards of inquiry and circumvent the Code itself. Instances of invoking the power to arrest to enforce the process of the Board will, I trust, be very rare indeed and should only be resorted to in cases of a systematic abuse of the process by a respondent.

The hearing in *Williams v. Ouellette*[181] was held just after the enactment of the *Statutory Powers Procedure Act*. At the commencement of the hearing the respondent was noted absent and it became apparent that he had not been served notice of the proceedings in the manner prescribed by the Act. He had been notified by the Commission of the time, date and place of the hearing and he had been served with a summons to attend as a witness. However, the Act required that the board send out notices of the hearing.

---

177. *Ibid.*, at D/258.
178. Memorandum from appointed Ont. Bd. of Inquiry (1971), unreported.
179. *Ibid.*, p. 1 (transcript).
180. *Ibid.*, p. 2 (transcript).
181. (1973), unreported (Ont. Bd. of Inquiry).

The board then sent out the required notices by registered mail to all the parties, and adjourned the hearing. When the hearing reconvened the respondent again did not appear. It was found that the respondent had been informed that there was a registered letter awaiting him at the post office but that, as he had not collected it, he was not aware of its contents. The board again adjourned and enlisted the assistance of the police to serve the respondent with notice, but he could not be located. The board then effected service by publishing an advertisement in the local newspaper of the city where the respondent was believed to be residing.[182] After all of these attempts to notify the respondent and a total delay of six months, the board decided that the respondent had been given adequate notice and that his failure to appear "was the result of a conscious decision to absent himself from the hearing."[183] The board then proceeded, but with caution. Chairman Krever noted that he "took pains to ask the witnesses more questions that [he] would normally [have done] and to consider the evidence very carefully."[184]

In *Murray and Landrum v. Anchor Wheel Inn*[185] the board took pains to ascertain that personal service upon the respondent of both complaint form and notice of hearing had been effected. In addition, the board had before it a letter from the respondent that stated, without reasons, that the respondent would be available only at certain months of the year. The board proceeded in the respondent's absence.

Although obviously the tribunal will proceed with care in the absence of a party, there is no doubt that, once notice to the party is proved, it can proceed.[186] Section 7 of the *Statutory Powers Procedure Act* provides that:

> Where notice of a hearing has been given to a party to a proceeding in accordance with this Act and the party does not attend at the hearing, the tribunal may proceed the absence of the party and the party is not entitled to any further notice in the proceeding.

---

182. The *Statutory Powers Procedure Act*, R.S.O. 1990, c. S.22, s. 24, permits the board to serve notice by public advertisement or other means in certain situations:
> "24.—(1) Where a tribunal is of opinion that because the parties to any proceeding before it are so numerous or for any other reason, it is impracticable,
>   (a) to give notice of the hearing;
>   . . .
> to all or any of the parties individually, the tribunal may, instead of doing so, cause reasonable notice of the hearing or of its decision to be given to such parties by public advertisement or otherwise as the tribunal may direct."

183. *Ante*, note 181, p. 4 (transcript).
184. *Ibid.*, p. 5.
185.
186. On the issue of sufficiency of notice in these circumstances, see the preliminary decision of the board in *Hughes v. Dollar Snack Bar* (1981), 3 C.H.R.R. D/1014 (Ont. Bd. of Inquiry), and *Murray and Landrum op cit.* fn. 176.

Joinder

The previous *Code* permitted the board of inquiry to join any persons as a party, with certain provisos.[187] The present *Code* specifically permits only the joinder of respondents by the board.[188] Joinder of complainants is left to the Commission.

Joinder of Complaints

Section 32(3) of the *Code* provides:

> (3) Where two or more complaints,
>   (*a*) bring into question a practice of infringement engaged in by the same person; or
>   (*b*) have questions of law or fact in common,
>   the Commission may combine the complaints and deal with them in the same proceeding.

Where the Commission has joined complaints, it is possible that a respondent may wish to apply to the board for severance of the complaints. It is unclear whether a board has jurisdiction to make such an order, except possibly under section 23(1) of the *Statutory Powers Procedure Act*, which provides that "A tribunal may make such orders or give such directions in proceedings before it as it considers proper to prevent abuse of its processes."

Obviously, the respondent will have to establish a substantial degree of embarrassment or oppression in order to satisfy the test in section 23(1). Therefore, it may be useful to examine two decisions in which Ontario boards have discussed the combination of complaints.[189]

In *Morgan v. Toronto General Hospital*[190] the board had been appointed to hear two complaints of alleged discriminatory hiring practices of the respondent hospital. At the outset of the hearing the respondent objected to the joinder of these two complaints in the same proceedings. The board discussed joinder in civil actions, citing the Ontario Rules of Practice:

> It would appear quite clearly that the judicial process attempts to avoid multiplicity of proceedings if related matters can be dealt with in one proceeding. Thus, although the Rules of Practice of the Supreme Court of Ontario are not binding upon administrative tribunals, nevertheless reference can be made to rule 66 thereof as an indication of the balance between fairness to the parties and the public convenience of avoiding multiplicity of proceedings. Rule 66 states:
>> All persons may be joined in an action as plaintiffs in whom any right to relief in respect of or arising out of the same transaction or occurrence, or series of transac-

---

187. R.S.O. 1980, c. 340, s. 18(1)(*e*).
188. See s. 39(2) of the current *Code*.
189. While there was no provision similar to s. 32(3) in the previous *Code*, boards have on several occasions heard two or more complaints in the same proceedings.
190. (1977), unreported (Ont. Bd. of Inquiry).

tions or occurrences, is alleged to exist, whether jointly, severally or in the alternative, where if such persons brought separate actions any common question of law would arise. . . .

The rule goes on to allow the court to order separate trials upon the application of the defendant "if it appears that such joinder (of plaintiffs) may embarrass or delay the trial of the action." In *Canadian Steel Corporation Limited v. Standard Lithographic Company Limited*, [1933] O.R. 624, Fisher J.A. described the purpose of the rule as follows:

> The object of this rule is to avoid, if possible, the expense and delay of two actions, if relief without inconvenience, expense or embarrassment can be given in one action.

In this particular instance, as counsel for the Commission submitted, the evidence of each of the Complainants would have been led in a hearing of the complaint of the other. Much of the evidence that was led would have applied to either complaint. It is difficult to see how joinder of the complaints could have caused "embarrassment" to the Respondent. Certainly, for all parties, the "inconvenience" and "expense" would have been far greater if the complaints had been heard separately rather than jointly.[191]

The board then cited several other human rights cases where complaints had been joined.[192]

In *Hyman v. Southam Murray Printing Division, Southam Murray Printing Limited*,[193] the board had been appointed to hear separate complaints by the same complainant against two different respondents, his employer and his union. The complainant alleged that he had received discriminatory treatment from his employee in a series of incidents that resulted in his dismissals. His allegations with respect to the union concerned his dissatisfaction with its responses to his request for assistance in obtaining redress for these incidents.

The board had received separate appointments on the same day with respect to both complaints. Prior to the hearing, the board decided that, as proof of the allegations in both complaints would require the same evidence and the same witnesses testifying to the same events, the complaints were to be. heard at the same time. The chairman sent notices to the parties to this effect.

At the commencement of the hearing, the respondent employer objected to the joinder of the two complaints. The respondent's first argument was to emphasize the fact that the word "complaint" was used in the singular form in the *Code*. The employer also argued that it would be prejudiced by the joinder of the two complaints:[194]

---

191. *Ibid.*, pp. 13-14 (transcript).
192. *Gares v. Bd. of Governors of Royal Alexandra Hospital*, (1974), unreported (Alta. Bd. of Inquiry); *Lopetrone v. Juan de Fuca Hospital Society* (1976), unreported (B.C. Bd. of Inquiry).
193. (1981), 3 C.H.R.R. D/617 (Ont. Bd. of Inquiry).
194. *Ibid.*, at D/625.

[T]he employer might be placed in the invidious position of having to defend itself against allegations made by the complainant and the Commission on the one hand and by the respondent union on the other. Counsel for the employer hypothesized that the respondent union may wish to take the position that certain actions ascribed to the union by the Commission might be argued by the union to the the responsibility of the employer. To be placed in a position where one must, as it were, defend oneself on both sides, it was argued, creates a situation of prejudice for the employer. Although it was conceded that there may be some convenience to be achieved in hearing all of the complaints together, it was argued that the possible prejudice to the employer was sufficiently grave as to outweigh considerations of mere convenience or expense.

The board commenced by noting that the *Code* under which it was appointed did not expressly permit the board to join complaints:[195]

The Ontario *Human Rights Code* does not deal expressly with this point. No express power is conferred upon Boards of Inquiry to consolidate complaints or otherwise hear them together. I am of the view, however, that the ability to hear complaints together must be considered to be a power conferred upon a Board of Inquiry by necessary implication from the provisions of the *Code*. The very establishment of Boards of Inquiry with certain powers under the *Code* suggests that they must have the power to control their own procedures, subject, of course, to over-riding principles of law such as those expressed in the Ontario *Statutory Powers Procedure Act*, and, presumably, general principles of fairness. With respect to the question of whether or not complaints should be heard together, the element of fairness would require a balancing of any prejudice sustained or potentially sustained by any of the parties against the public interest in avoiding a multiplicity of proceedings.

The board then turned to the Ontario Rules of Practice for guidance, noting the difference in the type of joinder contemplated here and joinder in a civil action. The Rules provide for joinder where the same event gives the plaintiff several causes of action against the same defendant or where the plaintiff is in doubt as to who, of several parties, is liable for the harm the plaintiff has uttered. In this case, the same events gave rise to different complaints against different respondents. The board dealt with this situation as follows:[196]

It is to be noted that two different kinds of circumstances are described in Rule 67 as setting up a basis for the joinder of defendants: first, different claims arising out of the same series of occurrences and second, a situation in which the plaintiff is in doubt as the the person from whom he is entitled to redress. Both of these circumstances appear to be present in the series of complaints brought against the respondent employer and the respondent union. Certainly, the series of occurrences which would form the subject matter of the evidence would be substantially the same for both respondents. Further, the possibility suggested by the employer to be prejudicial, that argument may be made by the respondent union to the effect that some actions alleged to be those of the union may more properly be ascribed to the employer, suggests that there may be some difficulty in the present case in determining which of the two respondents properly bear responsibility, if any, for alleged conduct. Far from creating prejudice, this circumstance is suggested in Rule 67 as being the kind of situation in which joinder is proper.

---

195. *Ibid.*, at D/626.
196. *Ibid.*, at D/626.

The board found that the interest in avoiding the expense and inconvenience of multiplicity of proceedings far outweighed the potential prejudice to the respondent employer.

The board in *Hyman* buttressed its decision that it had the power to direct that the complaints be heard together with a reference to the power, granted to a board by the previous *Code*, to add parties to the proceeding:

> Where there is more than one potential respondent to a complaint, the most open and fair way of proceeding against the additional respondent would be to make an additional complaint against that person rather than to wait until the appointment of a Board of Inquiry and, at that time, seek to join the additional respondent as a party to the proceeding. Since the *Code* explicitly gives power to a Board of Inquiry to adopt this less attractive mechanism for conducting proceedings relating to the conduct of more than one respondent, the *Code* should in my view be interpreted as permitting a Board to adopt the expeditious practice of hearing at the same time complaints brought against different respondents where, in the circumstances of the case, the advantages in so doing outweigh the potential prejudice to any party. I do not suggest that this is a case of the greater power including the lesser. Rather, the existence of the express power adds, in my view, support for the conclusion that the power to hear complaints together should be considered to have been implicitly conferred upon Boards of Inquiry by the *Code*.[197]

As noted above, the present *Code* confers upon the Commission the power to join complaints. Presumably the Commission will take into account the considerations expressed by boards in making its decisions.

Joinder of Respondents

The previous *Code* gave the board the power to join respondents, provided the respondents were given notice and an opportunity to argue against joinder.[198] Under section 39(2) of the present *Code* the board is permitted to add "any person appearing to the board of inquiry to have infringed the right" and, in a harassment complaint, any person who was aware of the harassment, and had authority to do something about it. These parties may be added at any stage of the proceeding and upon whatever terms the board considers appropriate.[199] While the provision as to notice is no longer explicit, the board's duty to ensure that reasonable notice is given is maintained by sections 6 and 8 of the *Statutory Powers Procedure Act*. Therefore, cases under the previous *Code* on this issue remain relevant.

In *Matthew v. Seven City Development Company*,[200] the board, at the commencement of the hearing, joined three officers of the respondent corporation. The board noted that:

---

197. *Ibid.*, at D/626-7.

198. R.S.O. 1980, c. 340, s. 18(1)(*e*).

199. S. 39(3).

200. (1973) unreported (Ont. Bd. of Inquiry); see also *Cooper v. Belmont Property Management* (1973) unreported (Ont. Bd. of Inquiry).

As far as the personal Respondents were concerned, it was quite clear that all three were involved either in the events concerning the attempted rental of an apartment by Mr. Matthew, or in the subsequent correspondence or discussions with the Ontario Human Rights Commission. All three personal Respondents had been subpoenaed some time before the Hearing, and were at the Hearing, and did not present any arguments which would seem to indicate that they were in any way prejudiced by being added as parties respondent at the Hearing.[201]

In *Nawagesic v. Rauman*,[202] the rental property about which the complaint was concerned was held by Mr. and Mrs. Rauman as joint tenants. The complaint had been filed against Mrs. Rauman alone. At the commencement of the hearing, the Commission sought to add Mr. Rauman as a respondent. The board noted that:

Generally, the preferred course of action when the Commission wishes to add a new party to a proceeding would be to give as much notice to the person affected as possible of the intended application before the Board of Inquiry, or even seek to apply to the Board for the person to be added as a party, well in advance of the actual hearing.[203]

In this case, however, the board found that there was no prejudice to Mr. Rauman in adding him as a party at the commencement of the proceedings. He was fully familiar with the matter. He was offered a chance to speak against his joinder and he was offered an adjournment of the hearing, which his counsel declined. The same counsel represented both Mr. and Mrs. Rauman and was prepared to proceed without an adjournment.

In a Manitoba Case, *Finlayson v. Winnipeg (City)*,[204] the complainant, who had been forced to retire from the police force at the age of sixty, laid a complaint against the Winnipeg Police Senior Officers' Association, believing that the Association was responsible. At the hearing before the board of inquiry, it became apparent that the Police Department and the City of Winnipeg bore responsibility for the retirement policy. The Police Department objected to being added as a respondent on the grounds that section 19(1) of the Manitoba *Human Rights Act* requires that a complaint be filed within six months of the alleged contravention of the Act. The Police Commission argued that no parties could be added after the six month period had passed. The board rejected the Police Commission's arguments, noting that section 19(1) only required that a complaint be filed within six months, and holding that did not preclude the board from adding more parties. In order to avoid "any potential denial of natural justice," the board offered the Department the opportunity to cross-examine witnesses "and/or to make submissions on any matters raised to date."[205]

---

201. *Matthew*, note 200, p. 2 (transcript).
202. (1978), unreported (Ont. Bd. of Inquiry).
203. *Ibid.*, p. 3 (transcript).
204. (1981), 2 C.H.R.R. D/429 (Man. Bd. of Adjud.).
205. *Ibid.*, at D/431.

In *Tabar v. Scott*[206] the board reiterated that prejudice to the respondent is the salient consideration in deciding whether to add a respondent. In that case, the principal of a corporation was added, with the board noting that the individual respondent had notice of the particulars of the complaint from its inception. In *Morano v. Nuttall*,[207] one of the corporate names of the employer had been left out of the complaint form and the appointment. The board noted that, on employment-termination forms submitted in evidence, the respondent had identified itself as the Company Farm Limited rather than as the Company Garden Centre. The board added the former entity as a respondent without further comment.

Representation of Parties

The *Code* makes no provision in respect of the representation of parties. The *Statutory Powers Procedure Act* contains only two references to representation: section 10(*a*), which provides that a party may be represented by counsel or an agent, and section 23(3) which provides:

> A tribunal may exclude from a hearing anyone, other than a barrister and solicitor qualified to practise in Ontario, appearing as an agent on behalf of a party or as an adviser to a witness if it finds that such person is not competent properly to represent or to advise the party or witness or does not understand and comply at the hearing with the duties and responsibilities of an advocate or adviser.

A motion by the respondent to limit the participation of counsel for the complainant was denied in *Gohm v. Domtar Inc.*[208] The board pointed out that, by virtue of subsection 39(3) of the *Code*, the complainant is a party, and the fact that the Commission has carriage of the complaint does not diminish the complainant's right to independent representation. Counsel for the complainant had undertaken not to duplicate the evidence, arguments or submissions of counsel for the Commission, and, in any event, the board pointed to its powers under sections 9(2) and 23 of the SPPA as sufficient to ensure that the hearing was orderly, fair and expeditious.

Complainants generally elect not to be separately represented, although this may cause difficulties should the interests of Commission and complainant diverge.[209] In this event, the board would presumably grant an adjournment, where requested to do so, to enable the complainant to obtain counsel.

In communicating notice of the complaint, the Commission invariably advises the respondent to obtain counsel. Where the respondent has

---

206. (1982), 3 C.H.R.R. D/1073 (Ont. Bd. of Inquiry).
207. (1988), 9 C.H.R.R. D/4876 (Ont. Bd. of Inquiry).
208. (January 20, 1988), Doc. No. 331 (Ont. Bd. of Inquiry).
209. See remarks of board in *Tomen v. Ontario Teachers' Federation* (1989), 11 C.H.R.R. D/104 (Ont. Bd. of Inquiry), and section, below, an offer to settle.

declined representation, boards have generally exhibited a willingness to allow the respondent considerable scope in the presentation of his or her case. The expressed attitude of the board in *Copenace v. West* is typical:[210]

> The hearing was delayed for some weeks while attempts were made to ascertain who would be representing Mrs. West at the hearing. In early August, I learned that Mrs. West intended to represent herself in this matter. By letter dated August 9th, I informed Mrs. West and counsel for the Commission that the hearing would be held in Kenora on September 20th. In addition to complying with the requirements of the *Statutory Powers Procedure Act*, the letter outlined the procedure which would be followed at the hearing. Mrs. West was also invited to call me by telephone if she had any problems with the date in question.
>
> On August 20th, I received a telephone call from Mrs. West, informing me that she had planned to attend a convention in Toronto during the week in question. She also informed me that she was 68 years of age and wanted her daughter to be present to assist her at the hearing. She added that her daughter resided in Winnipeg and could only attend on a Tuesday or Wednesday. Subsequently, both Mrs. West and counsel for the Commission, Mr. Ewart, agreed to the hearing being held on Tuesday, October 9th. In fact, it commenced and was completed on that day.
>
> I do wish to commend Mr. Ewart for his understanding and co-operation in both the selection of a hearing date and the conduct of the hearing, where a number of concessions were made to Mrs. West, taking into account that she was not represented by counsel. The testimony was frequently contradictory and, understandably, not always clearly presented because of the absence of counsel for the respondent. I, therefore, consider it important to provide a detailed, written analysis of the facts.

However, when the hearing is convened and at that point is presented with the respondent's request for adjournment while he or she obtains counsel, the attitude of the board has been less patient. An eleventh-hour request for an adjournment was refused in *Cinkus v. Diamond Restaurant & Tavern*,[211] and in *Styres v. Paikin*.[212] In both cases, the board noted that the respondent had had ample opportunity to retain counsel. In the latter case, the board noted that, shortly after arriving late for the hearing, the respondent

> announced that he was leaving at 12:00 noon to attend a meeting in Toronto. I treated this announcement as a request for an adjournment which in view of (a) the balance of convenience; that is, Mr. Jacobsen who had come from Toronto, the complainant who had come from St. Catharines, and myself who had come from London; and (b) the fact that Mr. Paiken had known well in advance of the hearing date and could have arranged his schedule accordingly; and (c) the relative importance of proceedings under the Ontario *Human Rights Code* versus a private business meeting, I declined to grant.
>
> Mr. Jacobsen then called his witness and completed the case for the Commission before noon. Mr. Paiken then gave evidence and was cross-examined by Mr. Jacobsen. Mrs. Paiken then gave evidence and was cross-examined. Mr. Paiken indicated he had no other witnesses present that he was intending to call unless I, as Board chairman,

---

210. (1979), unreported (Ont. Bd. of Inquiry), pp. 1-2 (transcript).
211. (1980), 2 C.H.R.R. D/339 (Ont. Bd. of Inquiry).
212. (1982), 3 C.H.R.R. D/926 (Ont. Bd. of Inquiry).

directed him to do so. I explained that he must decide what witnesses he intended to call on his own. Mr. Paiken then indicated he was calling no further evidence. At this time (approximately 12:10 p.m.) Mr. Paiken again announced that he was leaving the hearing to go to Toronto despite the fact that arguments and submissions had not yet been made. At this point, Mr. Jacobsen very fairly offered to yield his prerogative to make first submissions to the Board in order to assist Mr. Paiken. Mr. Paiken then made submissions on his own behalf for approximately thirty minutes. As soon as he had concluded, he began to leave. I again cautioned him that I was not granting an adjournment and that Mr. Jacobsen would be given an opportunity to make arguments and submissions and that he should remain to hear these. Mr. Paiken refused, however, and announced that "you should put me in jail if you want to but I'm not staying." He then left the hearing room. In Mr. Paiken's absence, Mr. Jacobsen made oral submissions to the Board and filed with the Board three previous Board of Inquiry decisions to which he referred in argument. No oral evidence was heard in Mr. Paiken's absence. At the conclusion of Mr. Jacobsen's submission the Board adjourned.

I have set out the conduct of the proceedings in some detail because Mr. Paiken was not represented by counsel. (At the outset of the hearing, I read to Mr. Paiken s. 19 of the *Code*, which sets out the responsibilities of the Board of Inquiry, and I invited him to reconsider whether he wished to have legal representation, an offer he declined).

This fact, combined with his attitude toward the proceedings and his determination that they be concluded between 10:20 a.m. and noon, made the hearing somewhat difficult to conduct. As I have said, Mr. Jacobsen went well beyond the call of duty in accommodating Mr. Paiken by expediting his examination and cross-examination and by deferring to Mr. Paiken in making submissions to the Board. As is evident from reading the transcript, Mr. Paiken regarded the proceedings as a nuisance and was adamant that they be arranged to suit his own schedule. A Board of Inquiry under the Ontario *Human Rights Code* is a procedure fashioned by the legislature of Ontario to determine a serious issue: an allegation of discrimination. In the discharge of its statutory obligation a Board cannot allow its conduct to be dictated by the whim of either party.[213]

In *Torres. v. Royalty Kitchenware Ltd.*,[214] the board noted that the respondent had had considerable notice of the hearing, and pointed out that section 7 of the *Statutory Powers Procedure Act* provides that, where a party who has been notified does not attend, the hearing may proceed in his or her absence. The board pointed out that the notice given the party must contain this information, by virtue of section 6 of the Act, and went on to say:[215]

> If the party has been given reasonable notice, including a statement that the tribunal may proceed even in the party's absence, it is implicit that the party has also been advised that if he or she attends the proceedings without counsel then the hearing may proceed notwithstanding the absence of representation. At no time did the Respondent assert that the notice did not so advise him, or that the notice was otherwise unreasonable. In any event, the Notice of Hearing . . . complies fully with the *Statutory Powers Procedure Act*. The individual Respondent admitted he had received the notice, both by registered mail and by way of personal service. . . .

---

213. *Ibid.*, at D/926.
214. (1982), 3 C.H.R.R. D/858 (Ont. Bd. of Inquiry).
215. *Ibid.*, at D/858-9.

In summary then, it is neither mandatory that a party be represented by counsel, nor that a party himself be present, so long as the party has received proper notice under the *Statutory Powers Procedure Act*.

Change of Venue

Neither the *Code* nor the *Statutory Powers Procedure Act* provide guidance as to when (or, indeed, whether) an application for change of venue might be granted. However, two Ontario boards have commented on the issue.

In *Tompkins v. Kyryliuk*,[216] the hearing was originally scheduled to take place at Geraldton, Ontario, where the events had occurred. On receipt of a letter from the respondents, stating that they had moved to Thunder Bay and were unable to attend at Geraldton, the board decided to hold a hearing at Thunder Bay to entertain an application for change of venue. The reason advanced by the respondents for the change was that they were elderly and in poor health and, therefore, unable to make the journey to Geraldton from their home in Thunder Bay. The board noted that it was more convenient for the Commission, the board and the court reporter for the hearing to be held in Thunder Bay. However, as the alleged discrimination in rental concerned property of the respondents that was located in Geraldton and as most of the witnesses resided in Geraldton, the board decided that the balance of convenience weighed in favour of holding the hearing in Geraldton. The board directed the Commission to provide transportation and overnight accommodation for the respondents if they desired it.

In *Younge v. Abraham*,[217] the hearing was convened in Sudbury. The complainant requested, by letter, that the hearing be held in Toronto, where she presently resided because "Sudbury was a racist city" and because she was unable to travel, due to ill health. Change of venue was not granted. The board cited two Ontario practice cases which stated that a change of venue will only be granted where there is an overwhelming preponderance of convenience. The board noted that the interests of not only the complainant, but also the respondent must be considered. Without a medical certificate to support the complainant's assertion of ill-health, strong reasons for change of venue had not been raised. Furthermore, the fact that the alleged discriminatory act took place in Sudbury weighted the scale in favour of holding the hearing in Sudbury for several reasons. First, the determination as to whether the rental premises were a "self-contained dwelling unit" might require the board to visit the premises which were located in Sudbury. Secondly, the educational purpose of the *Code* would be better served if the hearing were held in the community where the

216. (1971), unreported (Ont. Bd. of Inquiry).
217. (1972), unreported (Ont. Bd. of Inquiry).

alleged act of discrimination took place. Thirdly, the respondents and the witnesses resided in Sudbury. Finally, as the complainant had alleged that the whole community of Sudbury was racist, it would only be fair to the community that the hearing be held within it.

Motion to Dismiss for Delay

In a number of cases, Ontario boards have been asked to dismiss a complaint because of excessive time taken in bringing the matter before a board of inquiry. Over time, boards have considered the question of delay in the context of section 24 of the SPPA, of Rule 24 of the Rules of Civil Procedure, and of sections 11 and 7 of the *Charter of Rights and Freedoms.*

A preliminary question is how delay is to be measured. In *Morin v. Noranda Inc.,*[218] the board indicated that the time should be measured from the date of the practices alleged to be discriminatory as set forth in the complaint. Generally, this appears to be the measurement used in most cases.

Another preliminary question is the board's jurisdiction to dismiss the complaint because of delay. In *Hyman v. Southam Murray Printing,*[219] the board expressed some doubt on the point:

> Under section 14 [now s. 15] of the *Code* the Minister is given a discretion to appoint a Board of Inquiry to hear and decide a particular complaint. One of the facts that will be evident to the Minister on the face of the complaint is the amount of time which has passed between the alleged incidents and the initiation of a formal complaint. Once the Minister has appointed a Board of Inquiry to "hear and decide the complaint," it would be a surprising interpretation of the mandate conferred on the Board of Inquiry that would permit it to dismiss the complaint without making a decision as to its merits on the basis of the facts which must have been apparent to the Minister at the time of making the appointment. I note that the U.S. Supreme Court has, for different reasons, come to a similar conclusion with respect to the applicability of limitations rules to the operation of analogous provisions of Title VII of the *Human Rights Act* of 1964. See *Occidental Life Ins. Co. of California v. E.E.O.C.* (1977), 97S Ct. 2447, 432 U.S. 355.[220]

However, subsequent boards have indicated that section 23 of the *Statutory Powers Procedure Act* gives a board the jurisdiction to dismiss where delay constitutes an abuse of process.[221]

Boards have taken the position that section 23 of the *Statutory Powers Procedure Act* demands a careful scrutiny of the actual disadvantages caused by delay, even where delay is in excess of six years and the

---

218. (1988), 9 C.H.R.R. D/5245 (Ont. Bd. of Inquiry).

219. (1981), 3 C.H.R.R. D/617 (Ont. Bd. of Inquiry).

220. *Ibid.,* at D/621. This interpretation of the board's position was not accepted in a subsequent board: see *Gohm v. Domtar Inc.* (January 20, 1988), Doc. No. 331 (Ont. Bd. of Inquiry).

221. *Ibid. McMinn v. Sault Ste. Marie Professional Firefighters' Association* (1986), 7 C.H.R.R. D/3458 (Ont. Bd. of Inquiry).

Commission is unable to give good reasons for the lapse of time.[222] The board in *Gohm v. Domtar Inc.*[223] dismissed an argument that delay can be presumed to prejudice the position of the respondents. To date, boards have declined to order a complaint dismissed, despite such situations as material witnesses having left the employ of the respondent, died or moved away.[224]

Boards have also noted that it would be unfair to penalize the complainant, who has no other avenue in a complaint of discrimination, for the actions of the Commission.[225]

Motions for dismissal based on Rule 24 of Ontario's Rules of Civil Procedure have been made based on a ruling of the Divisional Court to the effect that boards of inquiry under the *Code* can be considered "actions" for some purposes.[226] As with a motion under the SPPA, boards have held that significant prejudice must be established before a complaint will be dismissed under Rule 24.[227]

In a number of cases, counsel for respondents dealing with delay have argued that section 11 of the *Charter of Rights and Freedoms* applies to proceedings under the *Code*. In almost all cases boards have concluded that section 11 does not apply since an inquiry under the *Code* is a purely civil, compensatory proceeding.[228]

In *McMinn v. Sault Ste. Marie Firefighters Assoc.*,[229] the board considered the application of section 11, reasoning that the *Code* does contain a provision allowing for prosecution for *inter alia*, a discriminatory action,[230] and that it is premature, at a board of inquiry, to assume that the provision would not be used. The *McMinn* case was decided prior to the decision of

---

222. See *Ante*, note 219; *Shepherd v. Bama Artisans Inc.* (1988), 9 C.H.R.R. D/5049 (Ont. Bd. of Inquiry).
223. *Ante*, note 220.
224. *Dennis v. Family & Children's Services of London and Middlesex* (1990), 12 C.H.R.R. D/285 (Ont. Bd. of Inquiry); *Mears v. Ontario Hydro* (1983), 5 C.H.R.R. D/1927 (Ont. Bd. of Inquiry); *Hyman, ante*, note 2; but see *Re Commercial Union Assurance v. Ontario (Human Rights Commission)* (1987), 59 O.R. (2d) 481 (Div. Ct.), affirmed (1988), 63 O.R. (2d) 112 (C.A.), leave to appeal to S.C.C. refused (1988), 65 O.R. (2d) x (note) (S.C.C.), in which the Divisional Court quashed a Commission consideration to appoint a board where a key witness had died.
225. See *McMinn, ante*, note 221, and *Gohm, ante*, note 220, in which part of a delay of over six years was due to a decision by the Commission to hold complaints in abeyance for 38 months pending the outcome of an appeal of a leading case.
226. *West End Construction Ltd. v. Ontario (Ministry of Labour)* (1986), 57 O.R. (2d) 391 (Div. Ct.).
227. See *Quereshi v. Central High School of Commerce* (1987), 9 C.H.R.R. D/4527 (Ont. Bd. of Inquiry).
228. See *Shepherd, ante*, note 222; *Dennis, ante*, note 224; *Gohm, ante*, note 225; and *Quereshi, ibid.*
229. *Ante*, note 221.
230. S. 43(1).

the Supreme Court of Canada in *Wiggleworth v. R.* in which the court found that a person charged with a disciplinary offence under the *Police Act* was not "charged with an offence" for the purpose of section 11 of the *Charter*, and in the light of *Wigglesworth* it appears probable that section 11 might not even apply in respect of a hearing under the *Code*.[231]

In three Ontario boards of inquiry respondents have argued that section 7 of the *Charter* should be applied to human rights boards of inquiry, and that complaints should be dismissed when delay prevents a respondent from presenting a full answer and defense to the complaint. The argument was based on a decision of the Saskatchewan Court of Queen's Bench in *Kodellas v. Saskatchewan (Human Rights Commission).*[232] In that case, the court applied section 7 to prevent a board from proceeding in a case that contained allegations of sexual assault, a delay of two and a half years before the hearing and no reason for the delay. On appeal the Saskatchewan Court of Appeal confirmed the application of section 7 to the circumstances of the individual (not the corporate) respondent, but clearly confined the ruling to allegations of such serious misconduct against an individual as to cause "stigmatization, loss of privacy, stress and anxiety . . . including possible disruption of family, social life and work . . ."[233]

Ontario boards considering the decision in *Kodellas* have taken seriously the stricture that each case must be examined individually. One, *Dennis v. Family & Children's Services of London & Middlesex,*[234] also cited *MacBain v. Canada (Canadian Human Rights Commission),*[235] another case of alleged sexual harassment in which the Federal court declined to find that "life, liberty and security of a person includes interference with one's good name, reputation or integrity."[236] In any event, none have dismissed a complaint for delay under section 7 of the *Charter*.[237]

A number of boards have noted that, in proceeding, it may be appropriate to weigh any prejudice or unfairness caused a party by the passage of time in making findings of fact or in refusing a remedy.[238]

---

231. (1988), 37 C.C.C. (3d) 385 (S.C.C.). See remarks by the Board in *Quereshi, ante,* note 227.
232. (1987), 8 C.H.R.R. D/3712 (Sask. Q.B.).
233. (1989), 10 C.H.R.R. D/6305 (Sask. C.A.).
234. (1990), 12 C.H.R.R. D/285 (Ont. Bd. of Inquiry).
235. (1984), 5 C.H.R.R. D/2214.
236. supra, at D/2219.
237. See *Dennis, ante,* note 234; *Quereshi* (1987), *ante,* note 227; and *Morin v. Noranda Inc., ante,* note 218.
238. *Hyman v. Southam Murray Printing* (1981), 3 C.H.R.R. D/617 (Ont. Bd. of Inquiry), noted with approval in *Quereshi, ibid., Shepherd, ante,* note 222, and *Gohm, ante,* note 225.

THE HEARING OF THE COMPLAINT

This section will discuss matters arising during the hearing process, including the issue of settlement offers, applications for a hearing *in camera*, the publicity attendant on the hearing, bifurcation of proceedings, and matters relating to evidence. It will also discuss the orders that may be made by a board, and the enforcement of such orders.

Offers of Settlement after the Appointment of a Board

In the course of several Ontario boards of inquiry, a settlement offer has been made after the board has been appointed. This inevitably raises the issue of whether the hearing ought to continue, particularly where the settlement offered is acceptable to only one of the Commission or the complainant.

Section 39(1) of the *Code* provides that the board "shall hold a hearing." However, section 4 of the *Statutory Powers Procedure Act* states:

> Despite anything in this Act and unless otherwise provided in the Act under which a proceeding arises, or the tribunal otherwise directs, a proceeding may be disposed of by,
>
> (*a*) agreement
> (*b*) consent order; or
> (*c*) a decision of the tribunal given,
>   (i)   without a hearing, or
>   (ii) without compliance with any other requirement of this Act,
> where the parties have waived such hearing or compliance.

Thus, it would seem that where all parties have agreed to waive "such hearing or compliance" the board may approve a settlement.[239] It seems clear from the above-noted provision that the board may approve the settlement via a consent order. This would appear to be the route that would best safeguard the interests of the Commission and the complainant, as an order of a board may be enforced via section 19 of the *Statutory Powers Procedure*

---

239. In *Smith v. Ralph Milrod Metal Products Ltd.* (1978), unreported (Ont. Bd. of Inquiry), a settlement was reached the morning the hearing was to commence. The board approved the settlement saying: "Although it has been held that once a Board of Inquiry has been appointed, any settlement agreed upon between the parties is subject to the approval of such a Board (see *Amber*. . .), it is quite clear by section 14(1) of the *Code* that settlement of the matter complained of is always an important alternative to the conduct of the hearing. Even though, with the appointment of a Board, it is important that the Board have final supervision in order to see that the terms are fair, it is only very rarely that a Board should contemplate proceeding with all the attendant strain on all parties, as well as the monetary cost to the parties and the taxpayers of Ontario. It is more important for Complainants to be satisfied with the resolution of the issue than it is for Respondents to be publicly condemned. And if the result is the forwarding of the overall protections of the Code, the Commission's role is fulfilled as well. Therefore, public policy would clearly seem to favour approval of a settlement mutually agreed upon."

Act or under section 43 of the *Code*.[240] In the absence of an order the settlement should conform to the provisions of section 42 of the *Code*.[241]

Where only the Commission or the complainant is willing to accept the settlement, an issue may be raised as to whether the board should proceed. Remarks made by one Ontario board of inquiry outline the issues.

In *Ruest v. International Brotherhood of Electrical Workers*,[242] a settlement had been reached on the day the hearing opened. However, the following day, for reasons unknown to the board, the Commission revoked the settlement and requested the board to re-open the hearing. The board did as requested but made a few comments on the relationship between settlements and the inquiry:

> The root of the problem is that the Act embodies a series of policy paradoxes. On the one hand, public respect for the policies embodied in the statute is enhanced by publicity, yet at the same time the opportunity to preserve confidentiality and anonymity, and to avoid stigma, is an inducement to a respondent to agree to a settlement. Second, because there is an individual complainant on whose behalf the proceedings are instituted, a premium is properly placed upon obtaining effective relief for him. Moreover, the hazards of litigation generate pressures for both sides to compromise their differences with the result that the complainant may forego some degree of vindication. Yet, to the extent that the complainant abandons his claim, the Commission's objectives remain unfulfilled. To this extent, pursuing the private interests of the complainant may be inimical to the full achievement of public purposes.[243]

In *Amber v. Leder*,[244] the respondents had offered a settlement that the Commission thought reasonable. However, the complainant refused to accept it, insisting that the case be heard by a board of inquiry. The Commission argued that, because it had decided that the offer was reasonable and ought to be accepted, the board of inquiry should not proceed. It argued that the public policy of the *Code* was best served by conciliation and settlement rather than by retribution. The complainant argued that the purpose of the *Code* was not served by enabling "the discriminator to buy off the dignity of the discriminatee,"[245] and that the educational purpose of the *Code* required that a public inquiry be held.

The board held that the attempts of the Commission to settle the matter were a function of its duty under the *Code* but that, once a board of inquiry

---

240. Enforcement is further discussed below.
241. S. 42 states that "Where a settlement of a complaint is agreed to in writing, signed by the parties and approved by the Commission, the settlement is binding upon the parties, and a breach of the settlement is grounds for a complaint under section 31, and this Part applies to the complaint in the same manner as if the breach of the settlement were an infringement of a right under this Act."
242. (1968), unreported (Ont. Bd. of Inquiry).
243. *Ibid.*, p. 24 (transcript).
244. (1970), unreported (Ont. Bd. of Inquiry).
245. *Ibid.*, p. 5 (transcript).

was appointed, it could not be terminated by a decision of the Commission alone. Nor could the Commission alone impose terms of settlement upon the parties. The board can impose terms of settlement on the parties, but only after giving each party a full opportunity to present evidence and make submissions. The hearing was continued.

It is suggested that section 4 of the *Statutory Powers Procedure Act*, which was enacted after the decisions in *Ruest* and *Amber*, settles the issue. Unless all parties waive their right to a hearing, the hearing must be held. Where the Commission favours settlement, it is free not to call evidence, and, presumably, to make submissions as the the suitability of the terms of settlement offered.

Obviously, there is value in settlements being final. However, in *Abary v. North York Branson Hospital*,[246] where a complainant withdrew his consent to a settlement and applied to the board to continue the hearing the board conceded, taking into account that the complainant was not represented.

Application for a Hearing In Camera and Publicity about the Hearing

Section 9 of the *Statutory Powers Procedure Act* states:

> (1) A hearing shall be open to the public except where the tribunal is of the opinion that,
>> (a) matters involving public security may be disclosed; or
>> (b) intimate financial or personal matters or other matters may be disclosed at the hearing of such a nature, having regard to the circumstances, that the desirability of avoiding disclosure thereof in the interests of any person affected or in the public interest outweighs the desirability of adhering to the principle that hearings be open to the public,
> in which case the tribunal may hold the hearing in the absence of the public.

Thus far, no request for an *in camera* hearing has been granted by an Ontario board, despite the fact that the only applications to date were made in cases that pre-dated the enactment of the *Statutory Powers Procedure Act*.

In *Amber v. Leder*,[247] the board said that, by opening the hearing to the public, the educative purpose of the *Code* was furthered.

In *Clarke v. Camelot Steak House & Tavern*,[248] the respondent argued that board of inquiry proceedings should generally be held *in camera* and, only in exceptional cases, conducted in public. The respondent cited in support of this argument the possible adverse effect on the respondent's business because of the appearance that he was an accused in a criminal prosecution. The board summarized the respondent's arguments as follows:[249]

---

246. (1987), 8 C.H.R.R. D/4156 (Ont. Bd. of Inquiry).
247. *Ante*, note 225.
248. (1971), unreported (Ont. Bd. of Inquiry).
249. *Ibid.*, pp. 6-9 (transcript).

It is, of course, trite to say that a Board of Inquiry constituted under the Ontario *Human Rights Code* is not a trial, much less a prosecution. All that the Board is empowered to do is to make recommendations, or make no recommendations at all. Nevertheless it is also true that a complaint or allegation of racial discrimination carries a moral obloquy which is more serious than a great many charges of criminal offences and an investigation under the Ontario *Human Rights Code* is only too likely to convey the impression that the person against whom the complaint is made is being tried as an accused. This wrong impression is given further credibility by the formal trappings and procedures which necessarily surround such an investigation. Thus the hearings are generally held in court rooms and court house, legal counsel are employed, witnesses are subpoenaed and testify under oath in an adversary atmosphere of examination, cross examination and re-examination, court reporters are present, etc. In short, in the public mind, appearances, are very much against a respondent, and unfounded allegations and testimony may cause very considerable damage to him, particularly if the allegations relate to a business or enterprise depending upon public good will and acceptance. Of course, because an investigation under the *Human Rights Code* is not a trial, whatever the appearances, the respondent does not have the rights and defences which are the concomitants of a trial.

. . . . .

From the point of view of a respondent I can sympathize with this argument, and it is an argument which can be validly addressed to the Legislature. However it is also of fundamental importance that hearings of allegations of racial discrimination, as contemplated by the *Human Rights Code*, be open to public scrutiny. This has a salutary effect upon complainants and respondents alike. In addition, those in our midst who are subject to discrimination, because they are "different," are the most vulnerable and the most suspicious. It is vitally important that the public and the individual complainant see and appreciate that fairness and justice is [sic] objectively sought. And this is not achieved behind closed doors. It has been rightfully said that "Justice is not a cloistered virtue: she must be allowed to suffer the scrutiny and respectful, even though outspoken, comments of ordinary men." (*Ambard v. Attorney General for Trinidad and Tobago*, [1936] A.C. 322, 355.)

In support of its decision, the board in *Clarke* cited the McRuer Report,[250] which recommended that hearings should be held in public unless "public security is involved" or "intimate financial or personal circumstances have to be disclosed."[251] This recommendation was enacted in section 9 of the *Statutory Powers Procedure Act*.

A request for an *in camera* hearing was allowed in the British Columbia case of *D.D. v. R.*[252] The complainant alleged he had been refused employment because of his criminal record. The complainant requested that the hearing be held *in camera* and that his name be concealed. The board granted the request stating that the respondent would be in no way prejudiced in the presentation of its case.

Obviously the issue of the publicity surrounding a hearing may raise somewhat different issues than those arising in an application for an *in camera* hearing.

---

250. *Royal Commission Inquiry into Civil Rights* (McRuer Report) (1968).
251. *Ibid.*, report I, vol. I, p. 214.
252. (1976), unreported (B.C. Bd. of Inquiry).

In *H. W. v. Kroff*,[253] the complainant alleged that she was dismissed from her position as a reservations clerk because she was pregnant. She requested that her identity be concealed for personal reasons. The board noted that by permitting the Commission to file a complaint without a personal complaint, the Code implicitly recognized "that some persons will be reluctant to bring forward a case and that there may be good reason for such cases to be heard."[254]

The board in *Kroff* also acceded to the respondent's request that the case not be reported until the decision was rendered by the board:

> This latter request violates the principle that human rights hearings should be publicly conducted. Secret hearings are anomalies in our judicial system. There is a public policy reason for public decisions in human rights cases, namely that under our governmental system in which some minor part is played by precedent, a decision in an individual case instructs the public generally as to appropriateness of conduct and is a method of advancing the legislative purpose to protect the human rights of society generally. Another reason for a public hearing is that in our history we have found that freedom of the press and freedom of speech are often two of the most useful and strongest weapons in advancing civil liberties and civil rights.[255]

The hearing was still held in public but all present were ordered not to disclose the name of the complainant and the press were subject to a "gag order" until the decision of the board was rendered.

In *Naugler v. New Brunswick Liquor Corp.*,[256] the respondent argued that it was prejudiced by a press release that was issued by the Commission before the hearing and published in a local newspaper. The board noted that it was not illegal for the Commission to make such press releases but stated that such practices were "undesirable."[257] The board said:

> Up until the Board of Inquiry is appointed, the Commission's primary role is that of a conciliator. To do anything to encourage or assist public criticism of one party at this stage would seem incompatible with the role of conciliator.
>
> Once the Board is appointed, it would seem preferable that the Commission should reserve the publication of any information it may have until it is presented as evidence before the Board. Publication may have the effect of making it difficult to ensure a fair and impartial hearing by the Board. While nothing restrains the parties from attempting to pre-try the case in the media, it would seem a wise policy for the Commission and its employees to exercise such restraint upon themselves.[258]

The board concluded that no actual prejudice had resulted from the publication of the press release as it was board policy not to read any materials relating to the case before it. The board also noted that these com-

---

253. (1976), unreported (B.C. Bd. of Inquiry).
254. *Ibid.*, p. 10 (transcript).
255. *Ibid.*, p. 11.
256. (1976), unreported (N.B. Bd. of Inquiry).
257. *Ibid.*, p. 6 (transcript).
258. *Ibid.*

ments were not intended to discourage the Commission from notifying the media that a board of inquiry had been appointed, the time and place of the hearing, and the nature of the complaint.

In *Morgan v. Toronto General Hospital*,[259] the Commission had issued a press release concerning the case on the morning the hearings had commenced. The board had not read it and the respondent did not attempt to argue that the board might be prejudiced. The respondent argued that the public might be prejudiced. The press release stated, basically, what was in the complaints, referring to the issues of the case as "allegations of racial discrimination." The board observed that, "even a Chairman conducting a hearing into a complaint for the first time must have sufficient training and common sense to realize that these are *allegations*."[260] As the respondent did not ask the board for a ruling on the press release it gave none.

Bifurcation of the Hearing

The bifurcation of a hearing into two parts, one dealing with the merits and the other with relief, if any, is not uncommon in labour arbitration.[261] There is no specific power, under the *Code* or the *Statutory Powers Procedure Act*, to divide a hearing in this manner, nor was there such an explicit power in the previous *Code*; however, hearings are often so divided.

In *Hyman v. Southam Murray Printing*,[262] the respondents requested that the proceedings be bifurcated so that one set of hearings could be held to deal exclusively with questions of liability. Then, if liability were established, another set of hearings would determine the remedial issues if the parties were unable to settle. The board considered whether, under the previous *Code*, it had the capacity to divide its hearing process. The board decided that, except where specific procedural requirements are mandated by the *Code*, the *Statutory Powers Procedure Act* and natural justice, the board has an inherent power to determine its own procedure. The board balanced the interests of minimizing expense and of minimizing delay in deciding whether to bifurcate the proceedings.

> In determining its procedures, a Board of Inquiry must obviously keep in mind the basic objectives of the statutory scheme under which it operates and should not adopt procedures which would have the effect of frustrating any of these objectives. It has been argued on behalf of the complainant that bifurcation of the proceedings would likely result in delayed justice to the complainant, assuming the complaint to

259. *Ibid.*, p. 16 (transcript).
260. *Ibid.*
261. See, for example, *Consumers' Gas Co. v. I.C.W., Local 161* (1974), 6 L.A.C. (2d) 61 (Ont.); *Beach Foundry Ltd. v. United Auto Workers* (1974), 7 L.A.C. (2d) 61; *Yardley of London (Can.) Ltd. v. International Chemical Workers, Local 351* (1973), 4 L.A.C. (2d) 75 (Ont.).
262. (1981), 3 C.H.R.R. D/680 (Ont. Bd. of Inquiry).

be well founded, and that it would therefore subvert the objective of securing appropriate redress to the complainant at the earliest possible opportunity. I am not persuaded, however, that this constitutes a sufficient reason for holding that a Board of Inquiry has no jurisdiction to restrict its initial hearings to liability issues with a view to reconvening to conduct hearings on remedial questions. In the first place, it is not evident to me that bifurcation of the proceedings will necessarily result in delay although delay is, of course, a distinct possibility. More importantly, however, the obvious advantages to restricting the initial set of hearings are, when balanced against the risk of delay, of sufficient weight to lead me to the conclusion that the exercise of such a jurisdiction would not be inconsistent with the fundamental objectives of the *Code*.

The conduct of inquiries under the *Human Rights Code* is an expensive process. The process is an expensive one for respondents who must bear the expense of litigation whether or not the complaint in question is successful. The process is also one which involves a significant expenditure of public funds both in furnishing the adjudicative mechanism and in bearing the best of carriage of the complaint. Bifurcation of the proceedings will ensure that the original hearings are less costly to the parties and, indeed where the complaint is held to be unfounded, the entire process will be less burdensome to the parties. Moreover, even in a case where the complaint is justified, it may often be the case that the parties will be bale to agree to the appropriate level of compensation for injuries sustained and further hearings may therefore be unnecessary. There is, then, a public interest in the abbreviation of the hearing process where this can be done in such a way as to not inhibit in any way the full exercise of the complainant's rights under the *Code*. This public interest in expedition of the proceedings would be furthered by bifurcation of the proceedings in appropriate cases and I am therefore of the view that Boards of Inquiry have the capacity to proceed in this manner in an appropriate case.[263]

The board decided that where, as in this case, the hearings with respect to compensation and mitigation were expected to be quite lengthy, the balance of convenience weighed in favour of bifurcating the proceedings.

The board cited, in support of its decision, *Hall v. International Firefighters' Association*,[264] where the board decided the substantive issues and then left it up to the parties to agree on the amount of damages, stating that if they could not agree the board would be prepared to reconvene to consider the matter.

Evidentiary Matters

The minimum rules of evidence before a board are set out in the *Statutory Powers Procedure Act*. Section 22 provides:

A member of a tribunal has power to administer oaths and affirmations for the purpose of any of its proceedings and the tribunal may require evidence before it to be given under oath or affirmation.

---

263. *Ibid.*, at p. D/681.
264. (1977), unreported (Ont. Bd. of Inquiry), reversed (*sub nom. Re Etobicoke v. Ontario Human Rights Commission*) (1980), 26 O.R. (2d) 308, affirmed (1980), 29 O.R. (2d) 499, reversed (1982), 40 N.R. 159 (S.C.C.).

Section 15(1) of the Act states:

> (1) Subject to subsections (2) and (3), a tribunal may admit as evidence at a hearing, whether or not given or proven under oath or affirmation or admissible as evidence in a court,
>   (*a*) any oral testimony; and
>   (*b*) any document or other thing,
> relevant to the subject-matter of the proceedings and may act on such evidence, but the tribunal may exclude anything unduly repetitious.

Section 16 provides:

> A tribunal may, in making its decision in any proceeding,
>   (*a*) take notice of facts that may be judicially noticed; and
>   (*b*) take notice of any generally recognized scientific or technical facts, information, or opinions within its scientific or specialized knowledge.

As with most administrative tribunals, a hearing before a human rights board of inquiry is informal. The manner in which the evidence is heard, the type of evidence that is considered relevant and the onus of proof are functions of the specific statute. An attempt will be made here to set out the general issues before raising specific points relating to evidence.

Burden of proof, onus of proof, and shifts in onus have occasioned extensive comment in human rights case law, as specific provisions relating to these issues are found in neither the previous nor the present *Code*. These issues, which have been touched on in the foregoing chapters, are intrinsic to every idea of human rights law, and are briefly summarized below.

Burden of Proof

Numerous boards of inquiry and, recently, the Supreme Court of Canada, have confirmed that the burden of proof in human rights cases is "the ordinary civil standard . . . upon a balance of probabilities."[265]

To support an allegation as to the breach of most sections of the *Code*, advertence must be proved,[266] in the sense that, where discriminatory treatment is due to a mistake, the respondent would not be found liable. However, malice toward, or dislike of, the group in question, need not be established.[267] A breach of the *Code* may be found where discrimination is one of several reasons for the action complained of.[268] In respect of a com-

---

265. *Ibid.*
266. See discussion of *Ontario (Human Rights Commission) v. Simpson-Sears* (1982), 36 O.R. (2d) 59 (Div. Ct.), affirmed (1982), 38 O.R. (2d) 423 (C.A.), reversed [1985] 2 S.C.R. 536 in Chapters 1 and 4.
267. In *Etobicoke v. Ontario Human Rights Commission* (1982), 40 N.R. 159 at 166 McIntyre J. stated that "there was no evidence to indicate that the motives of the employer were other than honest and in good faith," but upheld a finding that the *Code* had been breached.
268. See the section, below, on "mixed motives.."

plaint of constructive discrimination under section 10 of the *Code*, the legislation clearly establishes that it is not necessary to prove that the respondent intended or contemplated the discriminatory result at issue.

Onus of Proof and Prima Facie Case

The Commission has carriage of the case[269] and, together with the complainant, bears the onus of establishing a *prima facie* case of discrimination
or harassment.

The Supreme Court of Canada in *Ontario (Human Rights Commission)
v. Simpsons-Sears Ltd.*[270] defined a *prima facie* case under human rights law
as follows:

> A *prima facie* case in this context is one which covers allegations made and which, if
> they are believed, is complete and sufficient to justify a verdict in the complainant's
> favour in the absence of an answer from the respondent employer.[271]

The facts that must be proved are obviously closely tied to the wording
of the provisions of the *Code*[272] on which the complainant relies. One element that remains a vexed question is what proof would "justify a verdict in
the complainant's favour in the absence of an answer from the respondent."
Béatrice Vizkelety, in a detailed study of this area of the law,[273] has summarized cases across Canada as follows, in regard to "direct" discrimination:

> 1. In making out a *prima face* case, the complainant need not prove the discrimina-
> tory basis of the decision under attack; at this stage of the proceedings this fact is pre-
> sumed;
> 2. As a result of this *prima facie* case, the evidential or secondary burden shifts to
> the burden of proving discrimination remains with the complainant throughout;
> 3. In order to rebut the *prima facie* case, the respondent must provide an explana-
> tion which is credible or on all the evidence;
> 4. If the respondent is successful in this rebuttal it is still open to the complainant to
> show pretext.[274]

Ontario boards have differed in the way they have characterized the shift
of evidentiary burden; not all have expressed the caveat in item 3, above, *i.e.*,
that the burden remains with the complainant throughout.[275] However, it is

---

269. S. 39(2)(*a*).
270. (1985), 7 C.H.R.R. D/3102 (S.C.C.).
271. *Ibid.*, at D/3108.
272. For an example of a motive of a *prima facie* case in the context of discriminatory hiring
    practices, see the *McDonnel Douglas* test enunciated in *Almeida v. Chubb* (1984), 5
    C.H.R.R. D/2104 (Ont. Bd. of Inquiry).
273. B. Vizkelety, "Proving Discrimination in Canada" (1987), Carswell Co. Ltd.
274. *Ibid.*, at p. 128.
275. In *Etobicoke, ante*, note 267, McIntyre J. stated (at 165) that "Once a complainant has
    established before a board of inquiry a *prima facie* case of discrimination, in this case
    proof of a mandatory retirement at age sixty as a condition of employment, he is entitled
    to relief in the absence of justification by the employer. The only justification which can

clear that, for reasons that may have to do with a recognition of the logical difficulty of a requirement that the complainant prove the reason for the respondent's conduct, boards have been willing to accept circumstantial evidence as sufficient to shift a requirement for explanation to the respondent.

In regard to constructive discrimination, Maître Vizkelety defines the *prima facie* case as establishing that a standard, rule or requirement is more onerous for protected group members than for the majority.[276] It may be added that the complainant may have to establish the existence of a definable group, as well as his or her membership in it.[277]

Circumstantial Evidence; Inferences

It is a fact of life that, in most cases, discriminatory actions are not manifested openly before appropriate witnesses. Boards of inquiry have acknowledged the purpose of the legislation in accepting and drawing inferences from appropriate circumstantial evidence. One early case addressed the issue in some detail. In *Kennedy v. Mohawk College*,[278] the board noted:

> Discrimination on the grounds of race or colour are [sic] frequently practised in a very subtle manner. Overt discrimination on these grounds is not present in every discriminatory situation or occurrence. In a case where direct evidence of discrimination is absent, it becomes necessary for the Board to infer discrimination from the conduct of the individual or individuals whose conduct is in issue. This is not always an easy task to carry out. The conduct alleged to be discriminatory must be carefully analysed and scrutinized in the context of the situation in which it arises. In my view, such conduct to be found discriminatory must be consistent with the allegation of discrimination and inconsistent with any other rational explanation. This, of course, places an onus on the person or persons whose conduct is complained of as discriminatory to explain the nature and purpose of such conduct. It should also be added that the Board must view the conduct complained of in an objective manner and not from the subjective viewpoint of the person alleging discrimination whose interpretation of the impugned conduct may well be distorted because of innate personality characteristics, such as a high degree of sensitivity or defensiveness.[279]

---

avail the employer in the case at bar, is the proof, the burden of which lies upon him, that such compulsory retirement is a *bona fide* occupational qualification and requirement for the employment concerned."

This approach has been taken in numerous decisions. See, for example, *Hadley v. Mississauga* (1976), unreported (Ont. Bd. of Inquiry); *Singh v. Security & Investigation Services* (1977), unreported (Ont. Bd. of Inquiry); *Singh v. Workmen's Compensation Board Hospital & Rehabilitation Centre* (1981), 2 C.H.R.R. D/459 (Ont. Bd. of Inquiry); *Robertson v. Metro. Investigation Security* (1979), unreported (Ont. Bd. of Inquiry); *Offierski, Re* (1980), 1 C.H.R.R. D/33 (Ont. Bd. of Inquiry); *Ingram v. Natural Footwear Ltd.* (1980), 1 C.H.R.R. D/59 (Ont. Bd. of Inquiry); *Cox v. Jaqbritte Inc.* (1982), 3 C.H.R.R. D/609 (Ont. Bd. of Inquiry).

276. *Ante*, note 273, at p. 131.
277. See discussion of, *Inter alia*, *Bhadauria v. Toronto Bd. of Education* (1990), 12 C.H.R.R. D/105 (Ont. Bd. of Inquiry), in Chapters 3 and 4.
278. (1973) unreported (Ont. Bd. of Inquiry).
279. *Ibid.*, pp. 4-5 (transcript).

The necessity, in many cases, for boards of inquiry to draw inferences from circumstantial evidence has been acknowledged in a number of other boards of inquiry.[280]

The remarks of the board of inquiry in *Rawala v. DeVry Institute of Technology*[281] illustrate a fairly typical approach as to the relevance and probative weight of ambiguous evidence. In *Rawala*, the two complainants, who were visible members of a minority group, were students at the respondent Institute. Along with a "caucasian" fellow student they were caught cheating on an exam. The two complainants were suspended for a term and made to repeat the course. The white student was required only to write a supplemental exam, and was allowed to graduate from the program.

A principal element of the respondents' defence was that the school, in dealing with cheating, imposed punishments that differed according to whether the cheater had given or received information. At the hearing, it was acknowledged by all three of the students that each had both given and received answers; however the respondents maintained that the school officials had not known this at the time of the incident. It was argued by all parties that the complainants had confessed to both copying and sharing answers, but that the white student, Roy, had truthfully claimed only to have shared answers. However, the complainant Souza told officials at the time that Roy had copied answers as well.

The board of inquiry directed its attention to the manner in which the school officials had concluded that, despite one of the respondent's allegations, only the respondents had copied information.

> Mr. Greaves, in his testimony, conceded that after his interviews with the three students he had reached the conclusion that Messrs. Souza and Rawala had copied information from Mr. Roy but that Mr. Roy had not copied information from the others. In coming to this conclusion, it is evident that Mr. Greaves must have concluded that Mr. Roy was telling the truth and that Mr. Souza's allegations concerning Roy's participation was a lie. It must be asked, then, what possible basis there might be for concluding that Mr. Souza had been untruthful. Mr. Lehtila's observations, of course, related only to Mr. Roy's showing of his examination to the others and there was therefore independent evidence of the transfer of information in this direction. With respect to the transfer in the other direction, Mr. Greaves was confronted simply with Souza's allegation and Roy's denial. Considered from the perspective of assessing the incentives for deception in this context, it is evident that Mr. Roy would have very good reason to deceive and thus min-

---

280. See, for example, *Ruest v. International Brotherhood of Electrical Workers* (1968), unreported (Ont. Bd. of Inquiry); *Britnell v. Brent Personnel Placement Services* (1968), unreported (Ont. Bd. of Inquiry); *Ingram*, note 275 above; *Cousens v. Nurses' Association (Canada)* (1981), 2 C.H.R.R. D/365 (Ont. Bd. of Inquiry); *Morgan v. Toronto General Hospital* (1977), unreported (Ont. Bd. of Inquiry); *Scott v. Foster Wheeler Ltd.* (1985), 6 C.H.R.R. D/2885 (Ont. Bd. of Inquiry), additional reasons at (1985), 7 C.H.R.R. D/3193 (Ont. Bd. of Inquiry), varied (1987), 8 C.H.R.R. D/4179 (Ont. Div. Ct.).

281. (1982), 3 C.H.R.R. D/1057 (Ont. Bd. of Inquiry).

imize his role in the affair. It is less obvious that Mr. Souza had reason to deceive (except, as one witness suggested, on a "strength in numbers" theory) and it therefore seems less likely that Mr. Souza's allegation would be false. When confronted with this evidence, surely a rational response would be to suspend judgment on the matter unless some other basis for assessing the creditability [*sic*] of the individuals was present. Thus, Mr. Charran indicated that he did not either believe or disbelieve Mr. Roy's statements but simply suspended judgment with respect to his role in the cheating episode. Mr. Greaves, on the other hand, chose to believe Mr. Roy and disbelieve Mr. Souza, without any apparent reason for so doing. Indeed, when confronted with this point in cross examination . . . Greaves denied that he had disbelieved Mr. Souza and then ultimately conceded that indeed he must have done so. Mr. Greaves did not attempt to explain his willingness to believe Mr. Roy as against Mr. Souza on some rational basis, such as that he found Mr. Souza's manner to be such as to lead him to believe that Souza might be insincere. Rather, he simply seems to have discounted Mr. Souza's allegation once it was denied by Mr. Roy. Although there is some difficulty in reaching a finding with respect to a matter of this kind, it would appear that Mr. Greaves never consciously articulated his reasons for believing Mr. Roy and disbelieving Mr. Souza. In the absence of any apparent rational basis for preferring the creditability of one over the other and in the absence of any explanation from Mr. Greaves as to why he formed this conclusion, I am driven to conclude on a balance of probabilities that, whether consciously or not, some bias related to colour, race, or national origin must have played a part in Mr. Greaves' assessment of their respective creditability [*sic*]. Although Mr. Greaves has vehemently denied this allegation, and I believe that his protestation may well be sincere on this part, there simply is no other difference between Mr. Souza and Mr. Roy other than race, colour and national origin, which has been suggested to this Board of Inquiry as the basis for believing one to be truthful and the other not.[282]

Having drawn the above inference, the board concluded that the evidence was not probative of the allegation against the school, in the circumstances, since it was a committee, not Greaves, who had made the ultimate decision as to penalty.[283]

The board went on to consider the way in which the Committee had

---

282. *Ibid.*, pp. 40-43 (transcript).

283. The board found as follows (pp. 42-3 of the transcript): "It is my view, however, that this finding is not of any assistance to the complainants. Whatever Mr. Greaves' views or tentative conclusions concerning the respective roles of the three participants, his disposition in each case was the same. Each individual was at least advised of the normal penalty with respect to matters of this kind and was informed that they were, in some sense, suspended. Leaving aside the question of whether Mr. Souza was specifically advised of the necessity of a Committee meeting, I am satisfied that Mr. Greaves believed that a Committee meeting was necessary and that pending such meeting all three students were suspended. Further, I do not believe that Mr. Greaves' conclusions, tentative or otherwise, had any material impact on the decision-making processes of the Committee. It was, in my view, the Committee that effectively decided the fate of the three individuals. In short, whatever Mr. Greaves' opinions may have been on January 30, his actions with respect to the three participants were even-handed and the ultimate decision to impose differential sanctions on the three was not materially effected by those opinions. It is these deliberations of the Committee, therefore, to which attention must be directed."

arrived at its conclusions. The board noted[284] that evidence as to the nature of the Committee's deliberations would be relevant had this evidence pointed to bias on the part of the Committee.

In an attempt to determine whether Roy had copied answers, the Committee inspected the exams. The board noted:

> This comparative examination of the answer papers was a remarkably ill-conceived exercise. Each member of the Committee was cross-examined at length by Mr. Marshall with respect to the inferences drawn in the course of this comparison with the result that the deficiencies in this process were more than adequately revealed. Although members of the Committee were of the view that various signals of the direction of copying were to be found in the examination papers, Mr. Marshall's cross-examination of them demonstrated the frailty of those inferences. The underlying premise of Mr. Marshall's attack was simply that the fact that the same or similar notations might appear on two answer papers does not offer convincing evidence of either the existence or the direction of a copier. None of the explanations offered by members of the Committee undermine the obvious common sense of this proposition.[285]

However, the board found on the evidence that

> The Committee's deliberations, however inept they appear in retrospect, did amount to a genuine attempt on the part of members of the Committee to seek independent evidence of the existence and direction of copying in the AIE examination.[286]

Hence, in the circumstances, the methods used did not support an inference as to a discriminatory intent behind the preferential treatment.

Béatrice Vizkelety, in her book *Proving Discrimination in Canada*,[287] provides a useful discussion of circumstantial evidence, including a critique of a tendency in human rights boards of inquiry to incorrectly apply the standard used in criminal cases rather than keeping to the appropriate civil burden of proof.[288] She also proposes a way to formulate the test of rele-

---

While Greaves reported to the Committee, and may have suggested (evidence inconclusive) his conclusion that Roy had not copied, the board concluded: "This is not, in my view, a material fact . . . in as much as the evidence clearly establishes that the Committee did not in any sense accept this conclusion at an early point in the meeting but rather went on to conduct its own independent investigation with a view to testing the hypothesis that Mr. Roy might have copied from the others."

284. *Ibid.*, p. 47.
285. *Ibid.*, pp. 44-5.
286. *Ibid.*, p. 47.
287. *Ante*, note 273.
288. Maître Vizkelety cites the board in *Kennedy v. Mohawk College* (*ante*, note 278) as having mistakenly required circumstantial evidence of discrimination to be "consistent with the allegation of discrimination and inconsistent with any other rational explanation." The latter phrase, she argues, imports criminal standards to a civil matter. This standard was specifically rejected in *Fuller v. Candur Plastics Ltd.* (1981), 2 C.H.R.R. D/419 (Ont. Bd. of Inquiry). Also see *Johal v. Lake Cowichan* (1987), 8 C.H.R.R. D/3643 and *Challenger v. GMC Truck Centre* (1989), 11 C.H.R.R. D/141 (Ont. Bd. of Inquiry), which confirm this view.

vance and admissibility; that is, "to ask, does the evidence offered render the desired inference more probably than it would be without evidence."[289]

Circumstantial evidence from which a board has inferred that a particular action amounted to discrimination has included negative remarks about the group of which the complainant is a member,[290] tolerance of racial slurs in the workplace,[291] and racially-focussed questions at an employment interview, which were not directed at non-minority candidates.[292]

"Similar Fact" Evidence

The introduction of evidence of similar previous misconduct has a considerable history,mostly in the area of criminal law, in the context of an exception to the rule against the admission of evidence as to character. The rationale for the admission of similar fact evidence, and the rules concerning its admission, have been stated in complex and often confusing ways.[293]

Similar fact evidence has been admitted by boards of inquiry[294] for much the same reason that other circumstantial evidence is admitted — that is, because human rights violations by nature tend to be perpetrated privately, and the actions complained of are sometimes ambiguous. Sexual harassment cases frequently feature similar fact evidence. In *Bell v. Ladas*, the board said:

> In the context of sexual cases very close thought should be given to admitting similar acts. Apart from evidence tending to show particular peculiarities, careful consideration should be given to the statement of Lord Cross of Chelsea in *Boardman v. Director of Public Prosecutions*, [1975] A.C. 421, (1974), 3 All E.R. 887 where discussing similar fact evidence he said,
>
> > In such circumstances the first question which arises is obviously whether his accusers may not have put their heads together to concoct false evidence and if there is any real chance of this having occurred the similar fact evidence must be excluded. In *Reg. v. Kilbourne*, [1983] A.C. 729, it was only allowed to be given by boys of a different group from the boy an alleged offence against whom was being considered. But even if collaboration is out of the way it remains possible that the charge made by the complainant is false and that it is simply a coincidence that others should be making or should have made independently allegations of a similar

---

289. *Ante*, note 273, at page 143.
290. See *Cinkus v. Diamond Restaurant & Tavern* (1980), 2 C.H.R.R. D/339 (Ont. Bd. of Inquiry); *Willis v. David Anthony Phillips Properties* (1987), 8 C.H.R.R. D/3847 (Ont. Bd. of Inquiry); *Ingram v. Natural Footwear Ltd.* (1980), 1 C.H.R.R. D/59 (Ont. Bd. of Inquiry).
291. *Lee v. T.J. Applebee's Food Conglomeration* (1987), 9 C.H.R.R. D/4781 (Ont. Bd. of Inquiry).
292. *Suchit v. Sisters of St. Joseph* (1983), 4 C.H.R.R. D/1329 (Ont. Bd. of Inquiry).
293. See generally, Piragoff, *Similar Fact Evidence* (1981) Carswell, and Walt, "Similar Fact Evidence: A Re-examination" (1982), 21 C.R. (3d) 116.
294. Its admissibility was confirmed by the Divisional Court in *Olarte v. Ontario (Minister of Labour)* (1984), 49 O.R. (2d) 17 (Div. Ct.).

character against the accused. The likelihood of such a coincidence obviously becomes less and less the more people there are who make similar allegations and the more striking are the similarities in the various stories. In the end, as I have said, it is a question of degree.[295]

Despite the relaxed rules of evidence applicable to boards of inquiry under the *Statutory Powers Procedure Act*, similar fact evidence has been treated with much the same caution that characterizes its admission in civil litigation and criminal prosecutions. Indeed, the board of inquiry in *Bell v. Ladas* has been criticized by one commentator for requiring "striking similarity" between allegations in order for them to be treated as admissible similar facts.[296]

Shortly after the board's decision in *Bell* the Supreme Court of Canada in *Sweitzer v. The Queen*[297] came out clearly against rigid categorization of situations in which similar fact evidence may be admitted.

In *Olarte v. Commodore Business Machines*,[298] a case in which six employees complained about sexual harassment by a foreman, the board admitted evidence of eight other employees concerning similar events occurring prior to, within and subsequent to the timeframe referred to in the complaint was admitted, on the basis that it was relevant to a pattern or system of conduct toward female employees. In *Robinson v. The Company Farm Ltd.*,[299] evidence as to a sexual proposition made by the respondent to female employees other than the complainant was admitted.

In a case of alleged racial discrimination, the board discussed whether the fact that one complainant was discriminated against could be used to corroborate another complainant's allegations of discrimination. The board said:

> . . . the correct approach to similar fact evidence is that outlined by D.K. Piragoff's *Similar Fact Evidence* (Toronto: Carswell, 1981). As with all evidence, the primary test of admissibility is one of relevance, but similar fact evidence creates a danger of unduly prejudicing the mind of the fact-finder. In light of this, similar fact evidence should be excluded where the risk of undue prejudice outweighs the real probative value of the evidence as assessed in terms of its relevancy.
>
> Insofar as the evidence of the second incident might be used as probative in Mr. Wan's case, the main relevance of this evidence would be that it may show a proclivity on the Respondent's part to engage in some form of discrimination. Where the relevance of evidence is to show proclivity to engage in certain activity, it is generally recognized that the prejudicial effect greatly outweighs the real probative value. Indeed in the courts this realization has given rise to what might be called a "rule of evidence" excluding such similar fact evidence. While I am not bound by such rules, the policy behind the

---

295. (1980), 1 C.H.R.R. D/155, at D/156-157.
296. See discussion of this point in Chapter 7.
297. *R. v. Sweitzer* (1982), 68 C.C.C. (2d) 193 at 196-7 (C.A.), reversed [1982] 5 W.W.R. 555 (S.C.C.).
298. *Ante*, note 294.
299. (1984), Ont. Bd.

rule is sound and I would decline to accept the evidence of the second incident for this purpose in relation to Mr. Wan's complaint.

The main other possible relevancy of this similar fact evidence would be to rebut some defence such as misunderstanding by reason of the unlikelihood that such circumstances could have happened repeatedly if it were a mere case of misunderstanding. While such a defence was raised in this case, and therefore the similar fact evidence would be relevant, care must be used in accepting similar fact evidence for this purpose to ensure that there is not some other explanation for the similarity in the facts. Particular concern is shown in cases where the parties who allege the similar facts have discussed their respective situations prior to giving evidence.[300]

In that case, the evidence of one complainant as to the discriminatory treatment was accepted as relevant to the allegations of other complainants, since the occurrence he complained of was discreet and he had not discussed his evidence with the other complainants.

Boards have refused to admit similar fact evidence where witnesses had discussed their evidence with each other,[301] where the similar fact evidence was also hearsay evidence,[302] and when the incidents complained of were not sufficiently similar.[303]

No board of inquiry since *Bell* has addressed the degree of similarity necessary before "similar fact" evidence can be considered admissible. In *R. v. McNamara*,[304] the Ontario Court of Appeal confined the "striking simi-

---

300. *Wan v. Greygo Gardens Ltd.* (1982), 3 C.H.R.R. D/812 at D/813 (Ont. Bd. of Inquiry).

301. *Ibid.*

302. *Bishop v. Hardy* (1986), 8 C.H.R.R. D/3868 (Ont. Bd. of Inquiry).

303. *Bell v. Ladas* (1980), 1 C.H.R.R. D/155 (Ont. Bd. of Inquiry); *Mitchell v. Traveller Inn (Sudbury) Ltd.* (1981), 2 C.H.R.R. D/590 (Ont. Bd. of Inquiry).

304. In *R v. McNamara (No. 1)* (1981), 56 C.C.C. (2d) 193 (Ont. C.A.). At 287-88, the Ontario Court of Appeal said: "Although it may be questionable if it could be said that the acts were strikingly similar, there was undoubtedly an underlying unity which manifested a general scheme and which in these circumstances made them admissible as similar acts. Moreover, we do not think it is necessary to find "striking similarity" in order for the evidence to be admissible.

As Cleary, *McCormick's Handbook of the Law of Evidence*, 2nd ed. (1972), p. 452, points out, the courts are stricter in applying standards of relevancy when similar acts are tendered to prove identity or the doing of the criminal act than they are when similar acts are tendered on the issue of knowledge, intent or state of mind. In *Boardman v. Director of Public Prosecutions*, [1975] A.C. 421, [1974] 3 All E.R. 887 (P.C.), the similar act evidence was tendered to prove the commission of the offence by the accused. "In these circumstances, the strikingly similar test is properly applied as a condition precedent to admissibility. Here, however, the evidence was tendered to prove state of mind, knowledge, intent, authority and system. In these circumstances, we do not think that the strikingly similar test should be applied as a condition precedent to admissibility." In *Regina v. Carpenter (No. 2)* (1982), 1 C.C.C. (3d) 149 (Ont. C.A.). At 156, the Court of Appeal cited McNamara for the following: "There is no authority for the proposition that for purposes of refuting the defence of accident, the evidence of the similar facts must be 'strikingly similar'. That test has been applied when the Crown seeks to prove identity, but the test is less stringent where the evidence is adduced to show knowledge, intent, or state of mind or as here, to refute the defence of accident."

larity" requirement to situations in which identity is at issue.

This rather "cut and dried" view is not the current approach of the Supreme Court of Canada, as will be noted below, but it is useful as a reminder of one area in which similar fact evidence is distinctly relevant and has been admitted. The proof of a *modus operandi* that will tie an individual to the Commission of a particular action, where the identity of the perpetrator of that action is at issue, requires close similarity in the actions alleged.

The most recent pronouncements of the Supreme Court of Canada on similar fact evidence are more general. As with *McNamara* they arise in criminal cases, which, as noted by the Court, means that they import the highest standard of evidence in law, in contrast to the relaxed rules of evidence that govern administrative tribunals.

In *M.H.C. v. Her Majesty the Queen*,[305] the issue which gave rise to discussion of similar fact evidence was the conviction of an accused for indecent assault of his ex-wife (the Court of Appeal substituted a conviction for gross indecency). The complainant alleged that the accused had forced her to have sexual intercourse with a dog. The trial judge admitted the evidence of the accused's subsequent spouse in regard to:

1. evidence of requests that the subsequent spouse submit to intercourse with a dog;

2. a remark relating to intercourse with a bull; and

3. requests that the spouse engage in sexual conduct involving a cucumber and body oils and foams.

The Supreme Court of Canada (Madame Justice McLauchlin for the unanimous bench of five) pointed out that item 3 on the above list has "no probative force taking it out of the realm of mere evidence of disposition."[306] Madam Justice McLauchlin did, however, allow that

> the other evidence is more problematic, involving as it does requests (or in the case of the bull, a rather fantastic suggestion) that the appellant's subsequent spouse submit to sexual intercourse with an animal. It can be argued that the suggestion that one spouse should participate in such unnatural acts is so remarkable that the separate incidents might be viewed as highly similar, giving the evidence sufficient probative force to take it out of the category of mere "evidence of disposition."

In deciding to send the case back for a new trial, Madam Justice McLauchlin said as follows:

> Evidence as to disposition, which shows only that the accused is the type of person likely to have committed the evidence in question, is generally inadmissible. Such evidence is likely to have a severe prejudicial effect by inducing the jury to think of the accused as a "bad" person. At the same time it possesses little relevance to the real issue, namely,

---

305. Unreported, S.C.C. 18 April, 1991.
306. *Supra* at p. 8.

whether the accused committed the particular offence with which he stands charged. There will be occasions, however, where the similar act evidence will go to more than disposition, and will be considered to have real protective value. That probative value usually arises from the fact that the acts compared are so unusual and strikingly similar that their similarities cannot be contributed to coincidence. Only where the probative force clearly outweighs the prejudice, or the danger that the jury may convict for non-logical reasons, should such evidence be received.[307]

Madam Justice McLauchlin cited as authority for this proposition a recent Supreme Court of Canada decision in *R. v. B. (C.R.)*[308] That case contains remarks that give general guidance in regard to similar fact evidence.

R. v. B. (C.R.) is a criminal case — the accused was convicted of sexual offences against his 11-year-old daughter. The trial judge admitted evidence from a stepdaughter of the accused of incidents of sexual abuse that were very similar. The trial judge specifically stated that the appropriate test for the probative effect of the evidence was "whether the similarities are sufficient to show that the accused had common characteristics in the methods he used in the sexual acts with (the two girls) and it is likely that they are one and the same man.".

Both the Court of Appeal and the Supreme Court of Canada agreed that the evidence was admissible and pointed out that, in demanding the standard of similarity he did, the trial judge was in error.

The Supreme Court of Canada stated that the degree of similarity required by the trial judge was necessary only when the identity was at issue, which it had not been in the trial. The Supreme Court of Canada endorsed the view of the Court of Appeal that "the admissibility of the evidence of M.H.S. (the stepdaughter) depended on whether its probative value with respect to the credibility of (the complainant) outweighed its prejudicial effect."

The judgment begins with a review of the rationales in the *Makin* and *Boardman* cases. Among other things, it makes the point that the majority decided that evidence of propensity, while generally inadmissible, may be admitted where the probative value of the evidence in relation to the issue in question is so high that it outweighs possible prejudice. As Madam Justice McLauchlin put it, "it is no longer necessary to hang the evidence tendered on the peg of some issue other than disposition."[309]

Madam Justice McLauchlin listed the interpretations that emerge from recent Canadian jurisprudence;

1. Evidence of propensity, while generally inadmissible, may exceptionally be admitted where the probative value of the evidence in relation to an issue in question is so high that it displaces the heavy prejudice

---

307. *Ibid.*, p. 7-8.
308. (1990), 107 N.R. 243 (S.C.C.).
309. *Ibid.*, at 254.

which will inevitably inure to the accused where evidence of prior immoral or illegal acts is presented to the jury.

2. *Boardman* is a rejection of the category approach in favour of one of general principle.

3. Canadian courts have tended to accord a high degree of respect to the decision of the trial judge, who is charged with the delicate process of balancing the probative value of the evidence against its prejudicial effect.

4. The effect of the similar fact evidence must be considered in the context of other evidence in the case.

5. The analysis of whether the evidence in question is admissible must begin with the recognition of the general exclusionary rule against evidence going to disposition. Evidence which is adduced solely to show that the accused is the sort of person likely to have committed an offence is, as a rule, inadmissible.

6. The judge must consider factors as the degree of distinctiveness or uniqueness between the similar fact evidence and the offences alleged against the accused, as well as the connection, if any, of the evidence to issues other than propensity, to the end of determining whether, in the context of the case before him or her, the probative value of the evidence outweighs its potential prejudice and justifies its reception.

It is suggested that, for the purpose of human rights boards of inquiry, the actions complained of need not be identical. It is clear that what must be kept in mind is what is sought to be proved; for example, if what is sought to be proved is that the employer has a tendency to harass racial minorities, evidence of rudeness may be as relevant to that point as evidence of assault. Further, if what is sought to be proved is that the complainant is to be believed, evidence of complaints by other complainants is likely to be relevant. In short, the major focus should be whether the evidence speaks to a point relevant to the appeal, not whether it establishes that the respondent always acts in precisely the same way when dealing with racial minorities.

Another point to be borne in mind is the fact that a board of inquiry is a civil matter rather than a criminal matter with its necessarily high standards of evidence. This point is touched upon in *R. v. B. (C.R.)*:

> The second point emerging from *Boardman* is the proposition that to be admissible, the probative force of the evidence must outweigh its potential prejudice in all the circumstances of the case. This introduces the idea of a sliding scale of admissibility. The degree of probative value required to establish the admissibility of similar fact evidence will generally be high where the evidence is Crown evidence suggesting serious criminality or immorality as was the case in *Boardman*; hence their Lordship's assistance on such phrases as "striking similarity," the potential of the evidence to negate all "coincidence," "exceptional circumstances" and a "strong degree of probative force." Yet the possibility is left open that in other cases, where there is less prejudice to overcome (for

example, in similar fact evidence presented by the defence or *evidence of habits or business practices in civil cases*) the degree of probative value required for admission may be lower.[310] [emphasis added]

Proof of Relevant Past Practice: Statistics as Circumstantial Evidence

Statistics can be relevant and are admissible before boards of inquiry.[311] Whether the evidence is circumstantial or demonstrative in nature depends upon the nature of the case. In section 11 complaints (of constructive or adverse-effect discrimination), statistics can provide, for example, demonstrative evidence that a particular group is underrepresented in a workplace.[312] In section 8 complaints, which focus on the treatment of a particular individual at a particular time, statistics in respect of the group represented by the individual may be offered as circumstantial evidence.

In the context of considering statistics as circumstantial evidence, boards have taken the following positions:

- a *prima facie* case can be established by statistical evidence[313]

- statistics that support an inference that one minority group is treated fairly do not establish that a respondent does not discriminate against others.[314]

- statistics concerning past practices need not be dealt with as similar-fact evidence[315]

- in the face of statistical evidence of disadvantage to a particular group it is open to the respondent to establish that discrimination was not operative in a specific incident involving a particular member of that group.[316]

---

310. *Ibid.*, at 255.

311. See, for example, *Singh v. Domglas* (1980), 2 C.H.R.R. D/285 (Ont. Bd. of Inquiry); *Fuller v. Candur Plastics* (1981), 2 C.H.R.R. D/419 (Ont. Bd. of Inquiry); *Ingram v. Natural Footwear Ltd.* (1980), 1 C.H.R.R. D/59 (Ont. Bd. of Inquiry); *Hendry v. Ontario (Liquor Control Board)* (1980), 1 C.H.R.R. D/160 (Ont. Bd. of Inquiry).

312. Clearly, as long as the "requirement, qualification, or consideration" at issue in a section 11 complaint is proven, statistics that prove exclusion, restriction or preference of a group conclusively prove a s. 11 case.

313. *Blake v. Ontario (Minister of Correctional Services)* (1984), 5 C.H.R.R. D/2417 (Ont. Bd. of Inquiry).

314. *Massey v. Castlefield Apartments* (1969), unreported (Ont. Bd. of Inquiry); *Gabidon v. Golas* (1973), unreported (Ont. Bd. of Inquiry); *O'Brien v. Ontario Hydro* (1981), 2 C.H.R.R. D/504 (Ont. Bd. of Inquiry).

315. *Windsor (Board of Education) v. Federation of Women Teachers' Assn. of Ontario* (1982), 3 L.A.C. (3d) 426 (Ont.); and see *Blake, ante*, note 313.

316. *Offierski, Re* (1980), 1 C.H.R.R. D/33 (Ont. Bd. of Inquiry); *Bhadauria v. Toronto (City) Board of Education* (1990), 12 C.H.R.R. D/105 (Ont. Bd. of Inquiry); *Quereshi v. Central High School of Commerce* (1991), 42 O.A.C. 258 (Div. Ct.).

Evidence Derived from Test Cases

In view of the difficulty of gathering direct evidence of discrimination, it might seem remarkable that the Ontario Human Rights Commission has not conducted test cases more frequently than it has. There are two reported cases involving testing. In the first, the board took a dim view of the complainant's tactics, thereby, it is suggested, failing to draw an appropriate distinction between a test case and entrapment. In the second case, the appropriate distinction was drawn.

In *Davis v. Pleasant View Camp*,[317] the respondent had been suspected of discriminating against blacks in the rental of her cottages. To test whether she in fact did so, two couples approached her, first a black couple and then a white couple, requesting accommodation. Neither couple had any intention of actually renting a cottage. The black couple were told by the respondent that there were no vacancies. When, fifteen minutes later, the white couple inquired about renting a cottage, they were told that some were still available. Both these couples had conducted this test case in cooperation with the Commission. The board said that little weight should be given to their testimony.

> [T]here was resort to pretence and false statements for the purpose of inducing the respondent to act as she did. The Board in making this Report has not, therefore, overlooked the principle that where, because of zeal in pursuing a certain cause, persons have been led to resort to pretence and subterfuge in securing evidence their testimony must be weighted carefully lest the same motives may have a tendency to colour their evidence.[318]

However, despite this caveat, the board found that the respondent had denied accommodation on the basis of colour.

> The Board is entitled to act upon a preponderance of credible evidence in an inquiry of this nature which is merely for the purpose of making recommendations and is neither a criminal or quasi criminal proceeding. Taking the evidence as a whole, and having had the opportunity of observing the witnesses carefully and without overlooking the necessity of scrutinizing the evidence of the complainants most carefully for reasons already stated, the Board is of the opinion that Mrs. Doris Frankowski denied the Davis request for accommodation because they were coloured.[319]

The board disbelieved the justifications put forward by the respondent as to why she denied the complainants accommodation. The board pointed out inconsistencies in the respondent's evidence and explanations to justify its decision.

The board was lenient in making its recommendations, stating that:

> [I]t would appear that nothing could be less likely to foster the climate of understanding and mutual respect among people envisaged by the Ontario *Human Rights Code* than

---

317. (1962), unreported (Ont. Bd. of Inquiry).
318. *Ibid.*, p. 3 (transcript).
319. *Ibid.*, p. 5.

these so-called surveys or general tests for discrimination which are not founded on legitimate requests for accommodation.[320]

The respondent was ordered to apologize and to undertake not to discriminate in the future.

In *Harris v. Bouzide*,[321] a black couple, suspecting that the reason they were denied rental accommodation was not the reason given by the landlord but rather was because of their colour, complained to the Commission. The Commission then enlisted the aid of a white woman to contact the landlord on the pretense that she was interested in renting the apartment. The board made some comments on this practice:

> On other occasions, questions have been raised about the reliability of witnesses who have been engaged in helping the Commission and the Complainant to prove or disprove discriminatory intent by asking for the same accommodation. I would like to emphasize that I find the conduct of such witnesses to be not only courageous, but also exemplary in accordance with the duty imposed upon everyone in Ontario by the proclamation in the preamble of the Ontario *Human Rights Code* that,
>
> > It is public policy in Ontario that every person is free and equal in dignity and rights without regard to race, creed, colour, nationality, ancestry or place or origin.
>
> . . . . .
>
> Initially I want to emphasize the distinction between the actions of Mrs. Osborne and the "entrapment" which accompanies such police actions as those involving the obtaining of evidence of the illicit sale of either liquor or drugs. In the first place, in the case of entrapment with respect to the sale of drugs or alcohol, the police witness is involved in the actual illegal transaction. If the witness does not induce the act of illegality, at least he participates in it. With respect to an act of discrimination in accommodation, on the other hand, the act of discrimination is in the refusal of accommodation to the person who is the Complainant, and not the act of agreeing to give the accommodation to the other person who is attempting to help the Commission establish whether an act of discrimination occurred. I emphasize again, the unlawful act under the Ontario *Human Rights Code* is not the act of agreeing to let to the person who comes along subsequently, but the act of refusing to let to the Complainant who comes beforehand, *and* because this refusal is based upon those characteristics of the Complainant which are specifically listed at the end of section 3 of the Ontario *Human Rights Code*
>
> . . . . .
>
> Furthermore, a person who conducts a "test" for the Ontario Human Rights Commission is acting not only in the interests of the whole community, as recognized in the preamble to the Ontario *Human Rights Code*, but such person is also acting in the interests of those Respondents who have *not* committed an act contrary to the *Human Rights Code*. In other words, it is sometimes possible that a person conducting a "test," such as Mrs. Osborne did in this case, could actually provide proof that the Respondent did not offend the provisions of section 3. Thus, in order to aid the Commission to get sufficient evidence to see whether an act of discrimination occurred or not, the person conducting the test is acting in the ultimate best interests of both the Complainant and the Respondent, and the community at large.[322]

---

320. *Ibid.*, p. 8.

321. (1971), unreported (Ont. Bd. of Inquiry).

322. *Ibid.*, pp. 12-14 (transcript).

Statistical Evidence

As noted above in the discussion of statistics as circumstantial evidence, statistics can provide *prima facie* evidence of discrimination, or can be used in rebuttal. In the latter context, the Supreme Court of Canada has expressed a preference that respondents adduce statistical and scientific data in attempting to establish the "reasonable and *bona fide*" defence.[323]

An extensive discussion of the use of statistics in human rights cases can be found in *Blake v. Ontario (Minister of Correctional Services)*.[324] In *Blake*, the Board emphasized that parties adducing statistical evidence should have formulated a clear rationale as to the relevance of the evidence, and be aware of the strengths and weaknesses of statistics as proof.

In *Blake*, Chairman Cumming also ruled that appropriate methods of presenting statistical evidence vary according to the type of evidence. The Chairman did not accept a submission by the respondent that statistical evidence must be submitted via expert testimony by the person who collected the statistics. (The statistics sought to be adduced were the success rates of women and non-Europeans in obtaining job interviews, and, ultimately, employment with the respondent.) Chairman Cumming ruled that such data were different from, for example, the results of public opinion polls (in which bias or lack of expertise on the part of the surveyor may influence the outcome) and from information that is essentially analysis of statistical data. In respect of analytical material, the board made the following cautionary remarks:

> . . . when data is evaluated with interpretive judgments expressed before being utilized in a statistical way, the person or persons doing such should certainly be available as witnesses. Every step in physically transmitting the data should be addressable by those involved, as witnesses. Of even greater importance, every step in evaluating the data through making interpretive judgments and through categorizing the data, should be addressed by those involved, as witnesses. Data can be misunderstood and misconstrued, but cannot, of course, be cross-examined. The reliability of the statistical evidence at the end of the process depends upon the sanctity of the underpining, original raw data being preserved at every step and stage thereof.[325]

Further examination of issues in relation to statistical evidence can be found in *Proving Discrimination in Canada*, by Béatrice Vizkelety.[326]

Hearsay Evidence

Section 15(1) of the *Statutory Powers Procedure Act* clearly permits a

---

323. *Ontario (Human Rights Commission) v. Etobicoke (Borough)* (1982), 3 C.H.R.R. D/781 at D/784 (S.C.C.).
324. *Ante*, note 313.
325. *Ibid.*, at D/2431.
326. (1987), Carswell Co. Ltd.

board to admit hearsay evidence at its discretion.[327] Such evidence has been admitted, on occasion, by human rights boards of inquiry, with the caution warranted by the unavailability for cross-examination of the originator of the statement.

In *Warren v. Becket*,[328] the complainant had testified that the respondent Becket had told her that the manager of the company's Vancouver office had told him of a company policy of paying married men with family responsibilities at a higher rate than other employees. She testified that Becket had also told her that she had no chance of advancing within the company because she was a woman. Becket did not attend the hearing. The other respondents objected to this evidence on the ground that it was hearsay. The board classified this evidence as hearsay, but noted:

> While hearsay evidence is not always considered the most reliable, we believe that of the complainant has merit for the following reasons: the operation of larger enterprises is such that instructions or remarks from different persons in management are mostly passed on by word of mouth rather than written memos, and it is reasonable, in our opinion, to give some credence to this type of hearsay evidence than would normally be the case.[329]

The board emphasized that these statements came from the complainant's superiors and were not rebutted by them. They noted that, had these statements instead been made by a co-worker, very little weight would be given them.

In *Bremer v. Board of School Trustees, School District 62*,[330] the board held that it would not incorporate into board of inquiry proceedings the evidentiary principles of formal court proceedings with respect to hearsay. The board said that, due to "the inherently subtle character of the evidence which may establish a contravention of the *Code*," often the board must base its decision on hearsay and circumstantial evidence.[331] The evidence that the complainant had adduced to prove that the respondent had based its decision not to hire her on a prohibited ground was all hearsay. The board decided to admit the evidence, but the chairman quoted two rules:[332]

(a) uncorroborated hearsay evidence should not be preferred to direct sworn testimony; and
(b) hearsay evidence alone should not be admitted to establish the crucial and central question.

---

327. The Board's entitlement to admit hearsay has been confirmed in *Olarte v. Commodore Business Machines* (1984), 49 O.R. (2d) 17 (Div. Ct.).
328. (1976), unreported (B.C. Bd. of Inquiry).
329. *Ibid.*, p. 1 (transcript).
330. (1977), unreported (B.C. Bd. of Inquiry).
331. *Ibid.*, p. 37 (transcript).
332. *Ibid.*, p. 38 *Board of School Trustees of School District No. 68 (Nanaimo) v. Canadian Union of Public Employees, Local 606*, (7 October 1976) unreported (B.C. L.R.B.).

In *Underwood v. Board of Commissioners of Police (Smiths Falls)*[333] an Ontario board commented upon the weakness of hearsay evidence used as a defence to a claim of discrimination.

Evidence of Mixed Motives

Where there are a number of reasons for a discriminatory action, only one of which is a prohibited ground, the presence of that reason is sufficient to create a breach of the *Code*.

In *R. v. Bushnell Communications Ltd.*,[334] an employee was dismissed partly because of his inability to get along with his fellow workers and partly because of his union membership. Hughes J. said:

> If the evidence satisfies it beyond a reasonable doubt that membership in a trade union was present to the mind of the employer in his decision to dismiss, either as a main reason or one incidental to it, or as one of the many reasons regardless of priority, s. 110(3) of the *Canada Labour Code* has been transgressed.[335]

On appeal, Evans J.A. upheld the decision of Hughes J., saying that "to create an offence under s. 110(3) of the *Canada Labour Code*, R.S.C. 1970, c. L-1, union membership must be a proximate cause for dismissal, but it may be present with other proximate causes."

Numerous Ontario boards have also applied *Bushnell*.[336] Typical comments were made by the board in *O'Brien v. Ontario Hydro*.[337] In *O'Brien*, Hydro's reasons for failing to hire the complainant had included his "overqualification" and unstable work history, as well as his age. The board canvassed the Canadian and American law on age discrimination and said:

---

333. (1986), 7 C.H.R.R. D/3176 (Ont. Bd. of Inquiry).
334. (1973), 1 O.R. (2d) 442 (H.C.), affirmed (1974), 4 O.R. (2d) 288 (C.A.).
335. *Ibid.*, at 1 O.R. (2d) 447.
336. *Segrave v. Zeller's* (1975), unreported (Ont. Bd. of Inquiry); *Jones v. Huber* (1976), unreported (Ont. Bd. of Inquiry); *Hawkes v. Brown's Iron Works* (1977), unreported (Ont. Bd. of Inquiry); *Hendry v. Ontario (Liquor Control Bd.)* (1980), 1 C.H.R.R. D/160 (Ont. Bd. of Inquiry); *Reid v. Russelsteel* (1980), 2 C.H.R.R. D/400 (Ont. Bd. of Inquiry); *Mitchell v. Nobilium Products Ltd.* (1981), 3 C.H.R.R. D/641 (Ont. Bd. of Inquiry); *Dhaliwal v. British Columbia Timber Ltd.* (1983), 4 C.H.R.R. D/1520 (B.C. Bd. of Inquiry), additional reasons at (1984), 6 C.H.R.R. D/2532 (B.C. Bd. of Inquiry); *Watson v. Highway Trailers of Canada Ltd.* (1983), 4 C.H.R.R. D/1621 (Ont. Bd. of Inquiry); *Iancu v. Simcoe County (Bd. of Education)* (1983), 4 C.H.R.R. D/1203 (Ont. Bd. of Inquiry); *Underwood v. Bd. of Commissioners of Police (Smith Falls)* (1986), 7 C.H.R.R. D/3176 (Ont. Bd. of Inquiry); *Randhawa v. Lido Industrial Products Ltd.* (1985), 6 C.H.R.R. D/3005 (Ont. Bd. of Inquiry); *Almeida v. Chubb Fire Security* (1984), 5 C.H.R.R. D/2104 (Ont. Bd. of Inquiry); *Cameron v. Nel-Gor Castle Nursing Home* (1984), 5 C.H.R.R. D/2170 (Ont. Bd. of Inquiry); *Broere v. W.P. London & Associates Ltd.* (1987), 87 C.L.L.C. 17,026 (Ont. Bd. of Inquiry); *Engell v. Mount Sinai Hospital* (1989), 11 C.H.R.R. D/68 (Ont. Bd. of Inquiry).
337. (1981), 2 C.H.R.R. D/504 (Ont. Bd. of Inquiry).

If one were to summarize the Canadian decisions on age discrimination, it could be fairly said that if a board of inquiry finds that a respondent allowed a complainant's age to influence whatsoever his or her treatment of the complainant, notwithstanding any other factors, then discrimination has, in fact, occurred.

The essential issue, in considering the evidence in an inquiry such as this, is to determine whether "age" is or is not an operative factor by itself in the refusal to employ.[338]

Witnesses and Credibility

Under section 12(1)(*a*) of the *Statutory Powers Procedure Act*, the board may require any person, including any party, to give evidence at the hearing, provided that that evidence is relevant and admissible.[339] A witness is entitled to be advised by counsel, but that counsel may not take part in the hearing; if the hearing is held *in camera* the witness's counsel may only be present while that witness is giving evidence.[340] Witnesses are deemed to have objected to any questions the answers to which may tend to incriminate them or establish their liability in civil proceedings, and the board is obligated to inform witnesses of their right to object to any question under section 5 of the *Canada Evidence Act*.[341] The board may require that evi-

---

338. *Ibid.*, at D/508.
339. R.S.O. 1990, c. S.22, s. 12(1) reads:

> "12.—(1) A tribunal may require any person, including a party, by summons,
> (*a*) to give evidence on oath or affirmation at a hearing;
>
> . . .
>
> relevant to the subjectmatter of the proceedings and admissible at a hearing."

Among the witnesses, invariably, is the human rights officer who investigated the complaint. He or she may be compelled to testify, unlike the Commissioners themselves, S. 30 of the *Code* provides:

> "(1) No person who is a member of the Commission shall be required to give testimony in a civil suit or any proceeding as to information obtained in the course of an investigation under this Act.
>
> (2) No person *who is employed in the administration of this Act* shall be required to give testimony in a civil suit or any proceeding *other than a proceeding under this Act* as to information obtained in the course of an investigation under this Act. [Emphasis added.]"

340. R.S.O. 1990, c. S.22, s. 11 reads:

> "11.—(1) A witness at a hearing is entitled to be advised by counsel or an agent as to his or her rights but such counsel or agent may take no other part in the hearing without leave of the tribunal.
>
> (2) Where a hearing is closed to the public, the counsel or agent for a witness is not entitled to be present except when that witness is giving evidence."

341. R.S.C. 1985, c. C-5. S. 14 of the *Statutory Powers Procedure Act*, *ibid.*, provides:

> "(1) A witness at a hearing shall be deemed to have objected to answer any question asked him or her upon the ground that the answer may tend to criminate him or her or may tend to establish his or her liability to civil proceedings at the instance of the Crown, or of any person, and no answer given by a witness at a hearing shall be used or

dence be given under oath or affirmation, which it has the power to administer.[342]

Section 10 of the *Statutory Powers Procedure Act* permits a party to the proceedings to be represented by counsel, to call and examine witnesses and present his or her arguments and submissions, and to "conduct cross-examination of witnesses at a hearing reasonably required for a full and fair disclosure of the facts in relation to which they have given evidence." The right to cross-examine is not unlimited. Section 23(*a*) of the *Statutory Powers Procedure Act* authorizes the board to "limit further cross-examination where it is satisfied that the cross-examination of the witness has been sufficient to disclose fully and fairly the facts in relation to which he has given evidence."

Where a witness fails to attend on a summons, refuses to take an oath or affirmation as required, produce a document as required, answer a legitimate question, etc., the board may state a case to the Divisional Court. After a hearing, that court may deal with the matter as contempt of court.[343] A board may draw an adverse inference from a party's failure to call a crucial witness once a *prima facie* case has been proved.[344]

---

be receivable in evidence against the witness in any trial or other proceeding against him or her thereafter taking place, other than a prosecution for perjury in giving such evidence.

(2) A witness shall be informed by the tribunal of the right to object to answer any question under section 5 of the *Canada Evidence Act*."

342. S. 22 of the *Statutory Powers Procedure Act, ibid.*, provides: "A member of a tribunal has power to administer oaths and affirmations for the purpose of any of its proceedings and the tribunal may require evidence before it to be given under oath or affirmation."

343. S. 13 of the *Statutory Powers Procedure Act, ibid.*, provides:

"13. Where any person without lawful excuse,

(*a*) on being duly summoned under section 12 as a witness at a hearing makes default in attending at the hearing; or

(*b*) being in attendance as a witness at a hearing, refuses to take an oath or to make an affirmation legally required by the tribunal to be taken or made, or to produce any document or thing in his or her power or control legally required by the tribunal to be produced by him or her or to answer any question to which the tribunal may legally require an answer; or

(*c*) does any other thing that would, if the tribunal had been a court of law having power to commit for contempt, have been contempt of that court,

the tribunal may, of its own motion or on the motion of a party to the proceeding, state a case to the Divisional Court setting out the facts and that court may inquire into the matter and, after hearing any witnesses who may be produced against or on behalf of that person and after hearing any statement that may be offered in defence, punish or take steps for the punishment of that person in like manner as if he or she had been guilty of contempt of the court."

344. *Newman v. F. W. Woolworth* (1986), 7 C.H.R.R. D/3153 (Ont. Bd. of Inquiry); *Stairs v. Maritime Co-Op Services Ltd.* (1975), unreported (N.B. Bd. of Inquiry); *Sandison v. Rybiak* (1973), 1 O.R. (2d) 74 (Co. Ct.).

Only rarely have human rights boards of inquiry commented on the issue of witness credibility, other than in the case of complaints relating to sexual harassment.[345] However, one Ontario board has set out some considerations. In *Van Der Linde v. J. A. Wilson Display Limited*,[346] a complaint of age discrimination, a vital issue was what had been said at an employment interview. The complainant and respondent offered conflicting accounts.

The board set out its reasons for preferring the complainant's testimony:

Is the respondent's explanation credible? I have concluded that it is not for the following reasons:

(a) *Conflicting versions:* Mr. Wilson testified that when he first received the application form and resumé from Mr. Hunt, he perused it quickly and decided that Mr. Van Der Linde was totally unqualified. In fact, he was shocked that Mr. Hunt apparently regarded Mr. Van Der Linde as particularly well qualified . . . and he wrote "none" on the application form to diminish Mr. Hunt's ardour and then gave the application form back to him. He wanted Mr. Hunt to tell Mr. Van Der Linde that there was no job for him; Mr. Wilson thought Mr. Van Der Linde was still waiting in the lobby. Mr. Wilson testified that he then kept the resumé on his desk to look at later and only subsequently noticed Mr. Van Der Linde's age. Precisely when this occurred, Mr. Wilson is not sure.

Mr. Hunt, however, testifies that he was not particularly impressed by Van Der Linde's qualifications. He admitted that he had relevant work experience and was qualified, but stated that left to his own devices he would not have hired the complainant. Also, in Mr. Hunt's version he and Mr. Wilson had virtually no conversation at the time when the application form and resumé were first given to Mr. Wilson. It was only some time later that he discussed the matter with Mr. Wilson and the latter indicated that Van Der Linde was unsuitable for the job.

(b) *Inherent improbability:* Mr. Van Der Linde's qualifications, as outlined in his resumé, are impressive. Mr. Hunt, who had interviewed Van Der Linde, testified that he was certainly qualified. Mr. Wilson's production supervisor had just brought in an impressive resumé from a clearly qualified applicant, Mr. Hunt, according to Mr. Wilson, was extremely impressed with the applicant's qualifications. I regard it as inherently improbable that Mr. Wilson would simply reject such an applicant, sight unseen, and write none across his application form.

(c) *Internal inconsistency:* If Mr. Wilson's explanation is believed, Van Der Linde's application was rejected because he lacked relevant qualifications. Not only do I find this contrary to the evidence (in particular Van Der Linde's past employment with companies in similar businesses, such as Success Display Limited and Wing's Success Limited), but I find it difficult then to understand why Tarsem Chand, who Mr. Hunt and Mr. Wilson admit lacked any qualifications, was then hired.

The Production Planner before Mr. Van Der Linde applied, one Alan Aimer, lacked qualifications; the man hired as Production Planner after Mr. Van Der Linde applied, Tarsem Chand, lacked qualifications. Mr. Van Der Linde, who had extensive related past experience on at least some of the specifics sought in the Company's Work Order, is rejected in between and the ostensible explanation is that he is unqualified. I cannot accept it.

(d) *Timing:* The respondent's explanation is that sometime after Mr. Van Der Linde's application (August 14) but before his second conversation with Mr. Hunt

345. These decisions are discussed in Chapter 7.
346. (1982), 3 C.H.R.R. D/685 (Ont. Bd. of Inquiry).

(August 17) the Company changed its plans and decided to fill the Production Planning position internally. Yet, it is significant that the Company did not cancel the Work Order. In fact, there was evidence of a telephone call between the respondent and Canada Manpower on August 29, 1979 during which the respondent indicated that the Work Order was still open and they had not made any decision. . . . The Work Order was not cancelled until September 19, 1979 when the Company advised Canada Manpower that they had changed their plans and no longer needed anyone.

For all of the foregoing reasons, I do not believe the respondent's explanation of the sequence of events leading to Mr. Van Der Linde's refusal.[347]

The board in *Van Der Linde* based its conclusion in part on the "mixed motive" doctrine, discussed above.

Another board relied on a more succinct statement of factors in the assessment of credibility:

> An assessment of the credibility of Mrs. House's testimony versus what little testimony the Board received from Mr. Wilcock is central to the decision of this Board. In cases such as this, the courts have set out standards for the assessment of witness credibility. In *Faryna v. Chorny* (1952), 2 D.L.R. 354 (B.C.C.A.), at pp. 356-357, the Court stated that
>
> > Opportunities for knowledge, powers of observation, judgement and memory, ability to describe clearly what he has seen and heard, as well as other factors, combine to produce what is credibility. . . . In short, the real test of the truth of the story of a witness in such a case must be its harmony with the preponderance of the probabilities which a practical and informed person would readily recognize as reasonable in that place and in those conditions.
>
> This passage is very often cited in human rights cases as a basis for assessing witness credibility (see for example, *Forsyth v. Matsqui (Dist.)* (1988), 10 C.H.R.R. D/5854 at D/5859 (B.C. H.R.C.); *Humble v. Parsad & Co.* (1988), 9 C.H.R.R. D/5057 at D/5060 (B.C. H.R.C.); *Penner v. Gabriele* (1987), 8 C.H.R.R. D/4126 at D/4128 (B.C. H.R.C.); *Lindahl v. Auld-Phillips Ltd.* (1986), 7 C.H.R.R. D/3396 at D/3398 (B.C. H.R.C.); *Langevin v. Engineered Air Div. of Air Tex Industry Ltd.* (1984), 6 C.H.R.R. D/2552 (B.C. H.R.C.).[348]

Documentary Evidence

(a) Statutory Provisions: Both the *Code* and the *Statutory Powers Procedure Act* contain provisos that affect the admissibility of documentary evidence. The *Statutory Powers Procedure Act* provides:[349]

> (2) Nothing is admissible in evidence at a hearing,
> (a) that would be inadmissible in a court by reason of any privilege under the law of evidence; or
> (b) that is inadmissible by the statute under which the proceeding arises or any other statute.
>
> (3) Nothing in subsection (1) overrides the provisions of any Act expressly limiting the extent to or purposes for which any oral testimony, documents or things may be admitted or used in evidence in any proceedings.

---

347. *Ibid.*, at D/687-8.
348. *Grant v. Willcock* (1990), 13 C.H.R.R. D/22, at D/24.
349. R.S.O. 1990, c. S.22, s. 15.

(4) Where a tribunal is satisfied as to its authenticity, a copy of a document or other thing may be admitted as evidence at a hearing.

(5) Whether a document has been filed in evidence at a hearing, the tribunal may, or the person producing it or entitled to it may with the leave of the tribunal, cause the document to be photocopied and the tribunal may authorize the photocopy to be filed in evidence in the place of the document filed and release the document filed, or may furnish to the person producing it or the person entitled to it a photocopy of the document filed certified by a member of the tribunal.

(6) A document purporting to be a copy of a document filed in evidence at a hearing, certified to be a copy thereof by a member of the tribunal, is admissible in evidence in proceedings in which the document is admissible as evidence of the document.

Section 33(13) of the *Code* contains a provision relating to documents removed for copying in the course of an investigation.

(13) Copies of, or extracts from, documents removed from premises under clause 3(c) or subsection (7) certified as being true copies of the originals by the person who made them, are admissible in evidence to the same extent as, and have the same evidentiary value as, the documents of which they are copies or extracts.

(b) Notice: A board of inquiry has declined to grant a request for advance notice of documentary evidence.[350] The admission of affidavit evidence concerning similar facts was challenged because notice had not been given under section 8 of the SPPA as to allegations with respect to character. The Divisional Court held that the affidavit was properly admitted where the evidence arose out of issues raised by the opposing party at the hearing.[351]

Section 12(1)(b) of the *Statutory Powers Procedure Act* authorizes the board to compel the production of documents and other things provided they are relevant and admissible.[352] The *Code* authorizes the board, when exercising this power, to adjourn the proceedings upon production of the documents or things to permit the parties to examine them.[353]

The board's discretion, under the previous *Code*, in the granting of *subpoenas duces tecum* was recognized in *Metropolitan Toronto Board of*

350. *Nembhard v. Caneurop Manufacturing Ltd.* (1976), unreported (Ont. Bd. of Inquiry).
351. *Olarte v. Commodore Business Machines Ltd.* (1983), 4 C.H.R.R. D/1705 (Ont. Bd. of Inquiry), affirmed (1984), 49 O.R. (2d) 17 (Div. Ct.).
352. S. 12 states:
    "12.—(1) A tribunal may require any person, including a party, by summons, . . .
        (b) to produce in evidence at a hearing documents and things specified by the tribunal,
relevant to the subject-matter of the proceeding and admissible at a hearing." And see *Ryckman v. Board of Commissioners of Police (Kenora)* (1987), 8 C.H.R.R. D/4138 (Ont. Bd. of Inquiry).
353. "39.—(4) Where a board exercises its power under clause 12(1)(b) of the *Statutory Powers Procedure Act* to issue a summons requiring the production in evidence of documents or things, it may, upon the production of the documents or things before it, adjourn the proceedings to permit the parties to examine the documents or things."

Commissioners of Police v. Ontario Human Rights Commission,[354] in which the Ontario Divisional Court upheld a board's decision to refuse to quash a subpoena requiring a respondent to produce certain documents and to adjourn the proceedings to permit counsel for the board to examine the documents. With respect to the adjournment, the court said that the board had the power to determine its own procedure and that the court would not review a decision to grant an adjournment unless the board violated the principles of fairness or exceeded its jurisdiction.

As discussed above in the section on discovery, boards of inquiry have refused to allow *subpoenas duces tecum* to be used for discovery.

A test that has been used by boards is that stated in *Dalgleish v. Basu:*[355]

(1) The witness must be fairly informed in advance what he is to produce. He must be asked to produce documents rather than to make discovery of documents.

(2) Greater latitude will be permitted in describing the documents where there is no prior compulsory discovery of documents and where voluntary disclosure has been refused.

(3) Greater latitude will also be permitted where the witness in question is a party or agent and can be taken to know the issues reasonably well.

(4) The issues involved in the proceedings must be considered. The broader the scope of the hearing, "the greater should be the permissible breadth of a *subpoena duces tecum.*"

Cases in which this test has been applied are discussed above in the section on notice and discovery.

In many of the cases in which confidentiality of documents has been discussed, the discussion has arisen because of an attempt by the respondent to subpoena the contents of Commission files. Generally, boards have refused to allow such documents to be subpoenaed.

In *Gares v. Board of Governors of Royal Alexandra Hospital,*[356] an Alberta board denied the respondent access to the Commission's files on the grounds that they were confidential and protected by Crown privilege.

In *Linton v. Nabob Foods Limited,*[357] a British Columbia board of inquiry refused to compel the production of the investigating officer's report to the Director of the Human Rights Branch. The board said:

In our opinion, the disclosure of such internal communications would impede the Branch in investigating and endeavouring to effect settlement of Complaints, and contribute little to assist the Board in dealing with the issues before it. While the opinions of the investigating officer may be necessary to those engaged in evaluating the investigation and in determining what further efforts should be made to resolve the dispute, the Board must formulate its own opinions, based on the facts and not the opinions of others.

---

354. (1979), 27 O.R. (2d) 48 (Div. Ct.).
355. (1974), 51 D.L.R. (3d) 309 (Sask. Q.B.).
356. (1974), unreported (Alta. Bd. of Inquiry).
357. (1977), unreported (B.C. Bd. of Inquiry).

Furthermore, the efforts of the Branch to settle Complaints would be imperiled if a Board of Inquiry could subsequently compel disclosure of the details of such efforts. The facts surrounding the investigation which can and should be disclosed can be adduced through the evidence of the investigating officer.[358]

The board also refused to permit the respondent to question this officer, while on the witness stand, with respect to statements made during settlement negotiations on the grounds that these statements were privileged. The board agreed with the policy of encouraging parties to attempt to settle by protecting from disclosure communications made with a view to settlement.

In *Naugler v. New Brunswick Liquor Corporation*,[359] the board briefly noted that any matter related to conciliation should be excluded from the hearing because, otherwise, the process of conciliation would be unworkable.[360]

The respondents in *Benet v. G.E.C. Canada Limited*[361] had served on two human rights officers *subpoena ad testificandum* containing directives to produce documents in Commission files as well as to testify. As the knowledge of these officers pertained only to the inquiry and conciliation proceedings the board quashed these subpoenas, finding such information privileged. The board, in an interim decision, noted:

> Documents are privileged when they are prepared in contemplation of litigation. Such materials are privileged in law because a party to litigation should be able to assess and determine his position without fear of disclosure, and material prepared in this regard is not really relevant to the factual evidence culminating in the event which has given rise to litigation.
>
> A second basis of privilege is that the objective of conciliation of the *Code* would be compromised if discussion and knowledge gained in that process could be forced through a subpoena to be divulged at a subsequent hearing. It is in the public interest that discussions as to conciliation and settlement of a complaint take place, and the *Code* requires the Commission's officers to "endeavour to effect a settlement" — s. 14(1). This possibility is maximized if the discussions in the conciliation stage are without prejudice, and it seems to me to be implicit to the *Code*, at least as a general proposition, that such discussions are without prejudice, that is, a subpoena to compel a human rights officer to testify as to his or her knowledge of such discussions will be refused. Confidentiality is implicit to the conciliation process. One can conceive of exceptions, for example, if it is alleged that there is fraud or coercion in effectuating a settlement, but such is not, of course, suggested in the instant situation. The protected privilege of the confidentiality is stated by Wigmore *On Evidence*, 3rd ed. (1940), vol. 8, para 2285 to rest upon the following requirements:
>
> > (1) The communications must originate in a confidence that they will not be disclosed.

---

358. *Ibid.*, pp. 21-22 (transcript). A similar finding was made in *Stairs v. Maritime Co-op. Services* (1975), unreported (N.B. Bd. of Inquiry).

359. (1976), unreported (N.B. Bd. of Inquiry).

360. Also see *Bulger v. Branch No. 4, Royal Can. Legion* (1978), unreported (N.B. Bd. of Inquiry) discussed below.

361. (1981), unreported (Ont. Bd. of Inquiry).

(2) This element of confidentiality must be essential to the full and satisfactory maintenance of the relation between the parties.

(3) The relation must be one which, in the opinion of the community, ought to be sedulously fostered.

(4) The injury that would inure to the relation by the disclosure of the communications must be greater than the benefit gained for the correct disposal of litigation.

In my opinion, the conciliation process pertaining to a human rights' complaint more than meets the standards for requiring confidentiality of discussions and documents pertaining thereto. I would quash the Gaspar and Stratton subpoena.[362]

The board also quashed a *subpoena ad testificandum* directed to independent legal counsel who had been retained by the Commission for the purposes of obtaining advice with respect to the complaint. The board held that any testimony this witness might give is privileged "as being professional communications between solicitor and client of a confidential character which took place for the purpose of obtaining legal advice."[363]

In *Morgan v. Toronto General Hospital*,[364] the board denied the respondent's request to compel the production of the investigating officer's report. The board said that this report would contain notes, with respect to attempts to effect a settlement, which are not admissible, and other information, which is privileged, included for the purposes of obtaining a legal opinion as to whether a board of inquiry should be appointed. The board was of the opinion that these materials cannot be separated from other materials in the file.

Most recently, in *Solomon v. Searchers' Paralegal Services*,[365] a board of inquiry declined to order the attendance of a commission officer with various documents from the Commission's file, including the intake records, an analysis of investigation findings, and a list of witnesses' names, citing the privilege established in regard to lawyers' "work product."[366]

The issue of privilege has also been raised in respect of various types of correspondence. In *Bezeau v. Ontario Institute for Studies in Education*,[367] the respondent claimed privilege for correspondence between the respondent and third parties concerning information about persons being reviewed for tenure. Some of the third parties had been told that their letters would be kept confidential. The board applied the Wigmore criteria mentioned in *Benet* and found that, in the circumstances, the broader public

---

362. *Ibid.*, pp. 9-11 (transcript).

363. *Ibid.*, p. 12.

364. (1977), unreported (Ont. Bd. of Inquiry).

365. (1984), unreported (Ont. Bd. of Inquiry).

366. The Board cited *Hickman, Administrator v. Taylor* 329 U.S. 495 (1947), and *Steeves v. Rapanos* (1982), 140 D.L.R. (3d) 121 (B.C. S.C.), affirmed (1983), 142 D.L.R. (3d) 556 (B.C. C.A.).

367. (1982), 3 C.H.R.R. D/874 (Ont. Bd. of Inquiry).

interest embodied in the preamble to the *Code* tipped the balance in favour of disclosure. The board noted that, while confidentiality is very important in the peer-evaluation process of universities, the letters, in this case, were written by persons outside the university and the importance of confidentiality was not so great. The board considered

> the importance to the individual being assessed of knowing the evidence which has been considered in making decisions which may have adversely affected an important area of his life, namely, his career. There is a danger that peer evaluation may, from time to time, drift into a highly subjective and, indeed, arbitrary exercise. The application of the administrative law principle of fairness to many aspects of these decisions could be largely emasculated in this area of decision-making through reliance upon the concept of privilege. Members of the academic community should not necessarily be considered to be above carelessly critical comments, exaggerated demonstrations of brilliance, petty jealousies and other human weaknesses.[368]

The board questioned whether confidentiality is really necessary in the peer-evaluation process, noting that academics often publicly criticize each other's work in journals or public forums.

The chairman found that, under the Wigmore formulation, disclosure is the rule, and the privilege of confidentiality is the exception. The chairman also reviewed recent Supreme Court and court of appeal decisions on the issue. In summing up, he noted:

> the courts have been reluctant to extend the operation of the doctrine of privilege and, it might be said that reluctance is certainly understandable. If not applied with restraint, the concept of privilege could greatly diminish the capacity of the courts to resolve disputes with a corresponding decrease in public confidence in the administration of justice.[369]

In conclusion, he noted that any adverse consequences of disclosure could be prevented by holding the hearing *in camera*.

In *Bulger v. Royal Canadian Legion*,[370] the respondent attempted to introduce into evidence correspondence between itself and the Commission. The Commission objected, as the correspondence related to the process of settlement and was written "without prejudice." The board ruled that it was entitled to inspect the correspondence to determine whether the necessary conditions existed to render it non-admissible under the "without prejudice" restriction. The correspondence consisted of two letters from the Commission stating that the Commission's investigation had revealed a violation of the Code and requesting that the complainant be reinstated in her job and be compensated, and two letters from the respondent explaining its actions. The board held that the correspondence at issue was not protected.

---

368. *Ibid.*, at D/879.
369. *Ibid.*, at D/880.
370. *Ante*, note 360.

Finally, in *D.D. v. R.*,[371] the respondent objected to the admission of a summary of a probation officer's notes taken after an interview with the complainant. The original notes had been destroyed by the probation officer after she had summarized them for her file. The respondent objected to the notes' admission on the ground that their introduction would impair communications between probation officers and their clients. The board said:

> As to the second objection, it is of interest to note that the claim of privilege was asserted by the respondent and not the complainant who might have an even greater interest in preserving the confidentiality of his communications with his probation officer. Moreover, the privilege was claimed only in connection with the introduction of the summary and not the other evidence given by Ms. Rousse concerning her dealings with the complainant. The board appreciates that disclosure of private communications between probation officers and their clients or of evaluations made by probation officers of their clients might, in some circumstances, be injurious to the public interest. The argument for exclusion of such evidence is equally compelling whether the communications or evaluations are recorded in writing or otherwise. The Board's ruling, however, was specifically restricted to notes of the events which happened at the meeting. It did not extend to Ms. Rousse's evaluations of the complainant or to any private conversations. We do not feel that our ruling violates the confidential nature of the relationship between Ms. Rousse and the complainant.[372]

The board also held that the fact that the notes were a summary of the original notes went to their weight and not to their admissibility.

Where a person who is subject to a subpoena refuses to comply, section 13 of the *Statutory Powers Protection Act* provides that the board may state a case to the divisional court. After a hearing, the divisional court may deal with the matter as contempt of court.

In *D.D. v. R.*,[373] the probation officer, who was called as a witness, was permitted to read into evidence parts of a summary of notes she had made while interviewing the complainant. She had destroyed the original notes after making a summary of them for her case file. The board held that the fact that these were not the original notes, and the fact that this summary was not made immediately after the probation officer's interview with the complainant, went to weight rather than admissibility. The board said:

> The question of accuracy of the original notes and the possibility of distortion during transcription into summary form are two factors which we considered in evaluating the evidence.[374]

The board also rejected the respondent's argument that these notes were privileged, on the ground that the privilege in this case was the complainant's.

---

371. (1976), unreported (B.C. Bd. of Inquiry).
372. *Ibid.*, p. 11 (transcript).
373. *Ibid.*
374. *Ibid.*, pp. 10-11 (transcript).

In *Ali v. Such*,[375] the complainant had left the country and did not attend the hearing. The board admitted her affidavit into evidence even though the respondent had had no opportunity to cross-examine her on it. The board took this factor into account when assessing the evidence.

In *Jahn v. Johnstone*,[376] the board permitted the complainant, as a witness, to refresh her memory from notes she had made shortly after the events surrounding the alleged discrimination occurred. At the request of the respondent these notes were admitted into evidence and the respondent was permitted to cross-examine her on them. The board noted that it relied on the oral evidence rather than on the notes in making its finds of fact.

In a recent board of inquiry, a previous board called to hear the same matter had heard ten days of evidence before resigning. The Chair appointed to replace the previous Chair ruled upon request of the respondent that the transcripts of the previous board, and exhibits, were to be entered in their entirety.[377]

Taking a View

Section 39(5) of the *Code* permits the board to adjourn the proceedings so that the board, the parties and their counsel may attend at another place for the purpose of taking a look at something.[378] Prior to the passage of the present *Code* this had been done only on consent.[379] This provision will presumably be used by boards where entry to premises has been refused in the investigative phase of a complaint.

In *Singh v. Domglas Ltd.*,[380] a decision under the previous *Code*, the board discussed whether it had the power to view the respondent's premises to determine whether the decisions of the respondent employer's management with respect to the alleged acts of discrimination were reasonable. The board decided that its power, under the *Statutory Powers Procedure Act*, to compel the production of evidence[381] only extended to physical objects that could be brought to the hearing, and did not permit the board to compel the taking of a view. However, the board held that its power to admit into evidence "any document or other thing"[382] was broad enough to permit the

---

375. (1976), unreported (Alta. Bd. of Inquiry).

376. (1977), unreported (Ont. Bd. of Inquiry).

377. *Kafato v. Halton Condominium Corp.* (1991), 14 C.H.R.R. D/154 (Ont. Bd. of Inquiry).

378. "39.—(5) The board may, where it appears to be in the interests of justice, direct that the board and the parties and their counsel or representatives shall have a view of any place or thing, and may adjourn the proceedings for that purpose."

379. See *Ingram v. Natural Footwear Ltd.* (1980), 1 C.H.R.R. D/59 at D/61 (Ont. Bd. of Inquiry).

380. (1980), 2 C.H.R.R. D/285 (Ont. Bd. of Inquiry).

381. *Statutory Powers Procedure Act*, R.S.O. 1990, c. S.22, s. 12(1).

382. *Ibid.*, s. 15(1).

board to take a view provided the board had the consent of all parties. The board required consent because of the practical difficulties of taking a view of a party's premises without the party's consent. Furthermore, the board held that it could draw inferences from a party's refusal to consent.[383] The board, however, declined to make adverse inferences because no submissions were made on this point, the respondent had supplied photographs and blueprints of the site, and the board was of the belief that, in light of the evidence already adduced, it was unlikely that a view would add much in the way of clarification.

Motion for Non-Suit

Obviously, the motion for non-suit is based on the allegation that a *prima facie* case has not been made out. Given that the *prima facie* case has been discussed previously in this chapter, and more specifically in Chapters 2, 4, 6 and 7, it will not be further discussed here.

In *Harris v. Bouzide*,[384] such a motion was brought with the respondent arguing that no evidence had been presented that would tend to show that the respondent knew that the complainants were "negroes," a necessary element of the case. Counsel for the Commission replied, first, that there was evidence of at least associated knowledge which had not yet been adduced but which would be introduced if the respondent elected to call no evidence and, second, that, as the Commission's powers of investigation were limited under the 1962 *Code*,[385] the board ought to exercise its powers to call the respondent as a witness for the purposes of obtaining the required evidence. After the board ruled that it could call the respondent as a witness on the Commission's behalf, the respondent withdrew his motion and elected to call evidence.

In *Nimako v. C.N. Hotels*,[386] the board compared the contrasting procedures followed in civil and criminal trials and decided that, as boards of inquiry are fundamentally civil in nature, the board ought to put the respondent to an election as to whether to call evidence, unless the circumstances were exceptional. The respondent's view that the Commission's case was weak did not constitute exceptional circumstances, nor did consideration of expense.

The board took a different view in *Abary v. North York Branson Hospital*.[387] The respondent's counsel's application was characterized as one of "no case to meet," and the board ruled that in such cases the respon-

---

383. The respondent in *Singh v. Domglas* had objected to the board taking a view.
384. (1971), unreported (Ont. Bd. of Inquiry).
385. S.O. 1961-62, c. 93.
386. (1985), 6 C.H.R.R. D/2894.
387. (1988), 9 C.H.R.R. D/4975

dent need not elect whether to call evidence prior to the board's decision. However, the board relied on *Dubois v. The Queen*[388] in ruling that in such cases,

> the evidentiary threshold is very low, i.e.: "any" evidence capable of supporting the adverse finding. Moreover, the credibility of evidence is not to be weighed at this stage in the absence of the extreme situation of testimony which is so far-fetched as not to be capable of belief by any reasonable person.[389]

The board dismissed the application.

Order of Presentation of Evidence

Clearly the general rule in litigation is that the evidence of the proponent is presented first in its entirety. An issue in this regard has arisen before boards of inquiry dealing with complaints of constructive discrimination. The board in *Gohm v. Domtar Inc.*[390] set out the problem as follows:

> At the outset of the hearing of evidence, counsel for the Commission asked for directions from the board on this point. The issue arose because this complaint alleged adverse effect discrimination on the basis of religion, contrary to s. 4 of the Ontario *Human Rights Code*, R.S.O. 1980, c. 340 [now R.S.O. 1990, c. H.19]. The Commission sought directions on the propriety of its proposed course of action, which was to present evidence only about the allegation of adverse effect discrimination and discussions held about reasonable accommodation, and not to call any evidence about whether the Company or Union could have reasonably accommodated the complaint without incurring undue hardship.
>
> The Commission proposed to establish a prima facie case of adverse effect discrimination, mainly through testimony by the complaint. This, it argued, would shift the onus to the respondents to establish that reasonable accommodation was not possible in this case because the accommodation would cause undue hardship. The Commission sought to be in a position to respond to the Company and Union on this point, by calling further evidence on possible accommodation of the complainant. And the Commission acknowledged that this might entail re-calling the complainant as a witness.
>
> The essence of the problem identified by counsel for the Commission, Mr. Lepofsky, was that if evidence on reasonable accommodation and undue hardship was called by the Commission in its case in chief, and later called into question by evidence presented by the Company, the Commission would be barred from calling further corroborative evidence on these points in reply under the usual rules concerning case splitting. And so the Commission was in the position of having to anticipate the Company's and Union's evidence on this point without the benefit of particulars or formal disclosure, such as are available in civil actions. Counsel for the Commission argued that its proposed course of action would not cause either respondent hardship because he offered to undertake to recall the complainant in reply if the respondents undertook not to cross-examine her during the case in chief on the issue of where accommodation were possible or feasible. Thus he submitted both respondents were guaranteed an opportunity to cross examine the complainant on this issue, and to challenge the Commission's evidence on the matter.

---

388. [1985] 2 S.C.R. 350
389. *Ante*, note 387 at D/4975
390. (1990), 12 C.H.R.R. D/161

The Commission argued that under the law established by the Supreme Court of Canada in *Ontario Human Rights Commission v. Simpsons-Sears Ltd.*, [1985] 2 S.C.R. 536 (the O'Malley case), it merely had to establish a prima facie case of adverse effect discrimination on the basis of creed, and then the legal onus shifted to the respondents to call evidence to defend its conduct by establishing that reasonable accommodation was not possible. This legal framework was invoked by the Commission to support its position with respect to the presentation of evidence.[391]

The board ruled that the Commission should put all of its evidence in at once, rather than proceeding to divide the case between evidence about adverse effect discrimination and requested accommodation, and evidence about possible accommodation and undue hardship, stating that, although in law a board of inquiry is not bound by the formal rules of evidence or civil procedure, these rules offer a convenient and appropriate guideline to the resolution of an issue such as this. It did not appear to the board to create an unfair advantage for any party to require the Commission to call all of its evidence about adverse effect discrimination and to address the issue of accommodation and undue hardship in its case in chief. The board ruled that it would permit the Commission or the complainant to call evidence in rebuttal of specific evidence called by the respondents with respect to undue hardship.[392]

The board's rationale for this ruling was that it was convenient and appropriate to hear as much evidence as possible from the complainant and the Commission about the key issues in the case, which involved both adverse effect discrimination and reasonable accommodation short of undue hardship. On the basis of the outline of the case presented by the Commission, it was evident that the key issue in the case was the extent to which accommodation of the complainant was possible, or available, or tried, or refused, and who bore responsibility for that. Thus the board ruled that the Commission should lead evidence about all of these elements of the case during its case in chief.

In a subsequent case, *Roosma v. Ford Motor Co. of Canada*,[393] the board, while emphasizing that the burden is not on the Commission to show that the respondent could reasonably have accommodated the complainant, made the same ruling, and indicated that "because the burden is on the respondent to prove accommodation . . . the Commission will be entitled to recall the complainant or adduce other evidence in reply except to the extent that reply evidence would simply reiterate other testimony."[394]

The issue of case-splitting was raised most recently in *Tomen v. Ontario Teachers' Federation*,[395] a case which was not a complaint of con-

---

391. *Supra*, at D/163-4.
392. *Ibid.*
393. (1988), 10 C.H.R.R. D/5766 (Ont. Bd. of Inquiry).
394. *Ibid.*, at D/5769.
395. (1989), 11 C.H.R.R. D/104 (Ont. Bd. of Inquiry).

structive discrimination. In that case, the respondent intended to rely on section 13 [now s. 14] of the *Code* as a defence to an allegation of sex discrimination, and it suggested that the Commission was obliged to lead evidence, as part of the *prima facie* case, to rebut this defence. The board ruled that there was no such obligation on the part of the Commission before the respondent had produced evidence in defence.

FINDINGS AND AWARDS BY A BOARD OF INQUIRY

A board must make a "finding and decision" within thirty days after the conclusion of the hearing.[396]

The award powers of a board are set out in the *Code* in section 41. That section may be roughly divided into four categories: subsection 1 sets out general remedies; . . . subsection 2 allows a board, where harassment has been found, to make orders for the prevention of future harassment; and subsection 4 allows for an award of costs against the Commission in certain circumstances. These categories are dealt with below.

General Award Power: Section 41(1)(a)

Where a board finds that a party has breached section 8[397] it may, by order,

> (a) direct the party to do anything that, in the opinion of the board, the party ought to do to achieve compliance with this Act, both in respect of the complaint and in respect of future practices.

It would be difficult to conceive of an award power more broadly drafted than that found in section 41(1)(a). Obviously, the legislature intended to encourage board creativity in the area of awards.

Non-monetary awards have included the following directions to the respondent:

1. to make a written apology to the complainant;[398]

2. to offer the complainant an opportunity to apply for the next job opening or vacancy in rental accommodation;[399]

---

396. S. 41(5). Where the board is unable to do this, or to exercise its award powers for any reason, "the Commission may request the Minister to appoint a new board of inquiry in its place." (s. 41(3)).

397. See Chapter 2 for a discussion of the meaning of a breach of s. 9.

398. See, for example, *Hendry v. Ontario (Liquor Control Board)* (1980), 1 C.H.R.R. D/160 (Ont. Bd. of Inquiry); *Khalsa v. Co-op. Cabs* (1980), 1 C.H.R.R. D/167 (Ont. Bd. of Inquiry); *Wan v. Greygo Gardens* (1982), 3 C.H.R.R. D/812 (Ont. Bd. of Inquiry) *cf. Cinkus v. Diamond Restaurant & Tavern* (1980), 2 C.H.R.R. D/339 (Ont. Bd. of Inquiry).

399. See, for example, *Copenance v. West* (1979), unreported (Ont. Bd. of Inquiry); *Segrave v. Zellers* (1975), unreported (Ont. Bd. of Inquiry); *Bone v. Hamilton Tiger Cats* (1979), unreported (Ont. Bd. of Inquiry).

3. to reinstate the complainant in employment;[400]

4. to undo the damage caused by a discriminatory competition for promotion by awarding the promotion to the complaint (displacing the person who had received the promotion);[401]

5. to send a revised version of the complainant's record of employment, stating the discriminatory reasons for dismissal, to the same authorities as those to whom the original, which alleged incompetency, had been sent;[402]

6. to place advertisements for employment or rental accommodation with minority group organizations or newspapers, or to submit advertisements to the Commission for approval;[403]

7. to post a copy of the Ontario *Human Rights Code* in the place of employment or rental accommodation;[404]

8. to desist from breaching the *Code.*[405]

The board has also used the offices of the Commission as a monitoring agency in case of repetition of discriminatory behaviour. In *Sharp v. Seasons Restaurant,*[406] a sexual harassment case, the board ordered the respondent to notify the Commissioner every time a female employee left his employ, for a period of two years.[407]

---

400. See, for example, *Singh v. Security & Investigation Services* (1977), unreported (Ont. Bd. of Inquiry). See *Obdeyn v. Walban Machine Products of Canada Ltd.* (1982), 3 C.H.R.R. D/712 (Ont. Bd. of Inquiry), for remarks on when reinstatement is not suitable.

401. In *Karumanchiri v. Ontario (Liquor Control Board)* (1987), 8 C.H.R.R. D/4076, the board ruled that, having twice been passed over for promotion due to his race and ethnic origin, monetary damages would not adequately compensate the complainant. The order was upheld by the Divisional Court: (1988), 9 C.H.R.R. D/4868, additional reasons at (1988), 27 O.A.C. 246 (Div. Ct.)

402. *Cuff v. Gypsy Restaurant* (1987), 8 C.H.R.R. D/3972 (Ont. Bd. of Inquiry).

403. See, for example, *Mitchell v. O'Brien* (1968), unreported (Ont. Bd. of Inquiry); *Boyd v. Mar-Su Interior Decorators* (1978), unreported (Ont. Bd. of Inquiry).

404. See, for example, *Hendry v. Ontario (Liquor Control Board)*, ante, note 398; *Mitchell v. Nobilium Products Ltd.* (1982), 3 C.H.R.R. D/641 (Ont. Bd. of Inquiry); *Wan v. Greygo Gardens* (1982), 3 C.H.R.R. D/812 (Ont. Bd. of Inquiry); *Cf. Cousens v. Nurses Association (Canada)* (1980), 2 C.H.R.R. D/365 (Ont. Bd. of Inquiry); *Morano v. Nuttall* (1988), 9 C.H.R.R. D/4876 (Ont. Bd. of Inquiry); *Noffke v. McClaskin Hot House* (1989), 11 C.H.R.R. D/407 (Ont. Bd. of Inquiry); *Blainey v. Ontario Hockey Association* (1987), 9 C.H.R.R. D/4549 (Ont. Bd. of Inquiry); *Booker v. Floriri Village Investments Inc.* (1989), 11 C.H.R.R. D/44 (Ont. Bd. of Inquiry).

405. See, for example, *Dhillon v. F. W. Woolworth Co.* (1982), 3 C.H.R.R. D/743 (Ont. Bd. of Inquiry); *Dubniczky v. J.L.K. Kiriakopoulos Co.* (1981), 2 C.H.R.R. D/485 (Ont. Bd. of Inquiry).

406. (1987), 8 C.H.R.R. D/4133 (Ont. Bd. of Inquiry).

407. Also see *Morano* and *Nofke, ante,* note 404.

Boards of inquiry have also fashioned orders that have an ongoing impact on the respondent's business practices.

In *Singh v. Security and Investigation Services*,[408] a case in which the respondent had constructively discriminated against Sikhs by enforcing dress regulations that required its officers to be clean-shaven and to wear uniforms, the board ordered:[409]

> Security is to make an exception, for Mr. Singh and for any other sincere, practising member of the Sikh faith who is a prospective employee of Security, in respect of Security's employment regulations of requiring all their guards to wear caps while on duty and to be clean-shaven. Security must accommodate prospective Sikh employees in respect of their religious practices by not requiring them to dispense with their turbans and beards as a prerequisite to employment as security guards with Security.

In *Hendry v. Ontario (Liquor Control Board)*,[410] on a finding of sex discrimination, the board made an order

> that the Respondent co-operate with the Human Rights Commission and the Women's Bureau of the Ministry of Labour in designing a program to take such steps as are appropriate to reduce the imbalance between men and women employed by the Respondent.
>
> And it is further ordered that the Respondent provide the Human Rights Commission with sufficient information on employment practices and statistics to permit the Human Rights Commission to monitor the employment practices of the Respondent insofar as they relate to the *Human Rights Code*, for a period of twelve months from the date of this order.[411]

In *Dhillon v. F.W. Woolworth Company*,[412] in which the board had found racial harassment, an order was made for the organization and supervision of a Race Relations Committee in the respondent's place of business:

> The Respondent shall forthwith constitute an *ad hoc* Management-Employees Race Relation Committee (hereinafter called "the Committee") for its warehouse, consisting of an equal number of three groups: a management group, an East Indian employees group, and a non-East Indian employees group, and the said Committee, together with an *ex officio* member of the Committee appointed by the Ontario Human Rights Commission from its staff (which member of the Committee is hereafter called the "Commission representative") shall meet together on company time at least once a month for the next four months, or more often if and when requested by the Commission representative, with the Committee's objectives being, first, to establish effective communications on the general issue of inter-race relations within the warehouse, and second, to suggest to the management of the Respondent such reasonable measures as seem appropriate and necessary from time to time to remove verbal racial harassment from within the Respondent's warehouse, and the Respondent shall implement such reasonable measures as are recommended by the Committee and are feasible from a practical standpoint from time to time.

---

408. *Ante*, note 400.
409. *Ibid.*, p. 37 (transcript).
410. *Ante*, note 398.
411. *Ibid.*, at D/166.
412. *Ante*, note 405.

In the event that, in the opinion of the Commission representative the Committee is not functioning in a manner and making such appropriate recommendations as meet the intent of this Order of removing verbal racial harassment within the Respondent's warehouse, and/or the Respondent is not implementing reasonable measures necessary to achieve the intent of this Order, being the removal of verbal racial harassment within the Respondent's warehouse, the Ontario Human Rights Commission may, upon giving written notice to the Respondent, request of this Board of Inquiry that it reconvene to hear such further representations as the Ontario Human Rights Commission considers necessary and the Board of Inquiry deems appropriate.

In the event that the Respondent is unwilling or, in its opinion, unable to implement the reasonable measures contemplated by this Order to meet the intent of this Order, being the removal of verbal racial harassment within the Respondent's warehouse, the Respondent may, upon giving written notice to the Ontario Human Rights Commission, request of this Board of Inquiry that it reconvene to hear such further representations as the Respondent considers necessary and the Board of Inquiry deems appropriate.

The Committee constituted by section 3 of this Order shall function as set forth for not less than four months from the date of this decision, and this Board of Inquiry shall remain seized of jurisdiction for six months from the date of this decision to reconvene the Inquiry as contemplated in sections 4 and/or 5 of this Order, and on such reconvened Inquiry, make any such further Order it sees fit, within its powers, in respect of the subject matter of this Inquiry, to implement this decision.[413]

In *Hickling v. Lanark, Leeds & Grenville County Roman Catholic School Bd.*,[414] a board ordered the respondent to make changes in its staffing, staff training, and amenities to provide for the integration of the developmentally handicapped into regular primary schools for part of the school day.

In *Booker v. Floriri Village Investments Inc.*,[415] the landlord was ordered both to change his rental application and to allow the Commission to inspect his rental rolls for a two-year period.

In *Morgoch v. City of Ottawa*,[416] the respondent was ordered to change the health standards adhered to in the recruitment of firefighters.

In *Blainey v. Ontario Hockey Association*,[417] the respondent was ordered to make extensive changes to sexually discriminatory practices relating to the organization and implementation of hockey games.

There has always been a question as to whether subsection 41(1)(*a*) empowers a board to order an "affirmative action" program[418] in an appropriate case. In *Action Travail des Femmes v. Canadian National Railway Co.*,[419] a board of inquiry under the federal *Human Rights Act*, finding

---

413. *Ibid.*, at D/763-4.
414. (1986), 7 C.H.R.R. D/3546 (Ont. Bd. of Inquiry), reversed on other grounds (1987), 8 C.H.R.R. D/4235 (Ont. C.A.).
415. *Ante*, note 404.
416. (1989), 11 C.H.R.R. D/80 (Ont. Bd. of Inquiry).
417. *Ante*, note 404.
418. The various definitions of "affirmative action" are discussed in Chapter 6.
419. (1984), 5 C.H.R.R. D/2327 (Cdn. Human Rights Trib.).

widespread discriminatory employment practices by the respondent, made a detailed order including numerous modifications to the way in which CN tested for entry level positions, to job requirements, and to the dissemination of employment information and hiring practices. In addition, it ordered a temporary recruitment campaign aimed at women, and a special hiring program involving the hiring of at least one woman to every four positions not traditionally held by women, until a level of 13% of women in non-traditional positions was achieved.

The appeal in *Action Travail* reached the Supreme Court of Canada. The court considered the award power set out in the *Canadian Human Rights Act*, subsection 41(2):

> If, at the conclusion of its inquiry, a Tribunal finds that the complaint to which the inquiring relates is substantiated, subject to subsection (4) and section 42, it may make an order against the person found to be engaging or to have engaged in the discriminatory practice and include in such order any of the following terms that it considers appropriate:
>
>> (a) that such person cease such discriminatory practice and, in consultation with the Commission on the general purposes thereof, take measures, including adoption of a special program, plan or arrangement referred to in subsection 15(1), to prevent the same or a similar practice occurring in the future;
>> (b) that such person make available to the victim of the discriminatory practice on the first reasonable occasion such rights, opportunities or privileges as, in the opinion of the Tribunal, are being or were denied the victim as a result of the practice;
>> (c) that such person compensate the victim, as the Tribunal may consider proper, for any or the wages that the victim was deprived of and any expenses incurred by the victim as a result of discriminatory practice; and
>> (d) that such person compensate the victim, as the Tribunal may consider proper, for any or all additional costs of obtaining alternative goods, services, facilities or accommodation and any expense incurred by the victim as a result of the discriminatory practice.

In the court below, the judge had drawn a distinction between "prevention" and cure, holding that the provision could not be used for an order that would rectify past wrongs. However, the Supreme Court, using the purposive approach it had taken in other human rights cases, pointed out that the purpose of human rights legislation as a whole is to prevent discrimination, and that the interpretative approach to the purpose of a particular section should take the broader purpose of the Act into account. Subsection 41(2) should therefore be interpretated to allow for a remedial order of the nature of the board made. In the words of Chief Justice Dickson, "there simply cannot be a radical disassociation of remedy and prevention. Indeed there is no prevention without some sort of remedy."[420]

It is interesting to examine subsection 41(1)(*a*) in the light of the *Action Travail* decision. The argument against the validity of affirmative

---

420. (1987), 8 C.H.R.R. D/4210 (S.C.C.).

action orders under the Ontario *Code* would, presumably, be similar to that which was accepted by the federal court, that is, that the wording of subsection 41(1) limits the order to achieving "compliance with" the *Code*, and that since the undertaking of a special program as described in section 14 of the *Code* is purely voluntary, a true special program goes beyond "compliance." However, it would seem likely that this argument would be unlikely to meet with success when held against the Supreme Court of Canada's analysis in *Action Travail*. Subsection 41(1)(*a*) speaks of "future practices"; more importantly, the *Code*'s wide-ranging preamble, coupled with the Court's express position in regard to human rights legislation, seems likely to result in a "fair, large and liberal" ruling of the type expressed in *Action Travail*.

Another interesting question arises as to balancing interests when the effect of an order of a board is to make changes to the seniority system of a respondent employer. No Ontario boards have yet addressed this question, but in *Canadian Human Rights Commission v. Dalton*,[421] the federal Court of Appeal overturned an injunction against the implementation of a settlement that would affect the appellant's seniority. The court found that the union and the Commission had been entitled to negotiate the settlement at issue.

When the union is not a party to the proceedings, a difficulty may arise in obtaining an order that would disturb existing seniority. Such was the case in *Chapdelaine v. Air Canada*,[422] and the board refused the order. However, in *Hamlyn v. Cominco Ltd.*[423] the board declined to accept an argument of the respondent employer that the union should be given the opportunity to make a submission prior to such an order being issues. The board made the order, holding that no evidence had been adduced that union members would be affected by the order, and that the union had not applied to make a submission. The board also relied on the *Etobicoke*[424] pronouncement that parties cannot "contract out" of the provisions of human rights legislation.

Monetary Compensation: Section 41(1)(b)

Section 41(1)(*b*) of the *Code* states that a board of inquiry may

> (*b*) direct the party to make restitution, including monetary compensation, for loss aris-
> ing out of the infringement, and, where the infringement has been engaged in wil-
> fully or recklessly, monetary compensation may include an award, not exceeding
> $10,000, for mental anguish.

---

421. (1986), 7 C.H.R.R. D/3189 (Fed. C.A.), leave to appeal to S.C.C. refused (1986), 67 N.R. 158 (note) (S.C.C.).

422. (1987), 9 C.H.R.R. D/4449 (Cdn. Human Rights Trib.), varied (June 19, 1991), Doc. No. T.D. 8/91 (Cdn. Human Rights Review Trib.).

423. (1989), 11 C.H.R.R. D/333 (B.C. Council of Human Rights).

424. (1982), 3 C.H.R.R. D/781 (S.C.C.).

Special or Compensatory Damages

Complainants in human rights cases have recovered lost earnings and potential earnings, lost pension plan contributions and welfare plan contributions[425] loss of accumulated entitlement in a profit-sharing plan,[426] travel costs,[427] and the cost of hockey school.[428]

Boards have stated that there is a duty to mitigate damages in most circumstances,[429] but have taken into account that prompt efforts to mitigate are not always to be expected.[430]

---

425. See for example: *Torres v. Royalty Kitchenware Ltd.* (1982), 3 C.H.R.R. D/858 (Ont. Bd. of Inquiry); *Cuff v. Gypsy Restaurant* (1987), 8 C.H.R.R. D/3972 (Ont. Bd. of Inquiry); *Almeida v. Chubb Fire Security* (1984), 5 C.H.R.R. D/2104 (Ont. Bd. of Inquiry); *Scott v. Foster Wheeler Ltd.* (1985), 7 C.H.R.R. D/3193 (Ont. Bd. of Inquiry); varied (1987) 8 C.H.R.R. D/4179 (Ont. Div. Ct.); *Olarte v. DeFilippis* (1983), 4 C.H.R.R. D/1705 (Ont. Bd. of Inquiry); affirmed (1984), 6 C.H.R.R. D/2833 (Ont. Div. Ct.); *Whitehead v. Servodyne Canada Ltd.* (1986), 8 C.H.R.R. D/3874 (Ont. Bd. of Inquiry); *Morano, Noffke, ante,* note 404; *Shaw v. Levac Supply Ltd.* (1990), 91 C.L.L.C. 17,007 (Ont. Bd. of Inquiry); and *Heinke v. Emrick Plastics* (1990), 91 C.L.L.C. 17,010 (Ont. Bd. of Inquiry); *Szabo v. Atlas Employees Welland Credit Union* (1988), 9 C.H.R.R. D/4735 (Ont. Bd. of Inquiry).

426. *Shaw, Szabo, ibid.*

427. *Morgoch, ante,* note 416.

428. *Blainey v. Ontario Hockey Assn. (No. 2)* (1986), 9 C.H.R.R. D/4972.

429. See *Almeida v. Chubb Fire Security Ltd., ante,* note 425; *Cuff v. Gypsy Restaurant, ante;* note 425; *Grasser v. Porto* (1983), 4 C.H.R.R. D/1569 (Ont. Bd. of Inquiry); *Scott v. Foster Wheeler Ltd., ante,* note 425.

430. In *Almeida v. Chubb Fire Security Ltd., ibid,* the board commented on the difficulties facing a complainant who suspects that he or she was refused promotion through discrimination:

"It may easily be seen that the Imposition of such a duty may impose considerable hardship. An individual may not be at all confident that a refusal to promote was based on discriminatory grounds. Or, alternatively, the victim of discrimination may feel that the most prudent course of action is to remain with the present employer and attempt to earn the respect of those who are currently operating on the basis of discriminatory attitudes. Moreover, the individual may well fear that this problem is not one which is exclusive to his or her current employer but is a problem likely to be encountered elsewhere, and accordingly that there is no point in seeking employment at an equivalent level elsewhere in the hope that a promotion will ultimately be forthcoming. In circumstances such as these, one could easily understand that a reasonable victim discrimination might not decide to attempt to minimize his or her losses by seeking employment with another employer."

See also *Scott v. Foster Wheeler Ltd., ibid.,* (board noting circumstances in which it was reasonable for the complainant to refuse another job offer); *Cuff v. Gypsy Restaurant Ltd., ibid.* (board concluding that complainant had reason to believe that she had been laid off rather than fired, but after a certain period of time complainant should have ascertained her status and commenced search for other employment); and *Engell v. Mount Sinai Hospital* (1989), 11 C.H.R.R. D/68 (Ont. Bd. of Inquiry), in which complainant was pregnant and had multiple sclerosis when she was discharged. Also see *Whitehead v. Servodyne Canada Ltd., ante,* note 425.

In respect of a complaint of loss of employment due to discrimination, the board in *Piazza v. Airport Taxi Cab (Malton) Assn.*[431] awarded eleven weeks wages to an employee with four years' experience who had been employed by the respondent for only two and a half months at the time of her dismissal. On appeal, the Divisional Court reduced the award, stating that the appropriate guideline for compensation was that used in wrongful dismissal cases — reasonable notice. In that case the Divisional Court determined that the appropriate period of notice was four weeks.[432] However, on appeal, the Court of Appeal restored the order of the board.[433]

Also in the context of damages for loss of employment, a respondent unsuccessfully raised the "work now, grieve later" rule of labour relations in an attempt to avoid liability for employment discrimination. In *Engell v. Mount Sinai Hospital*,[434] the complainant had been refused permission to take vacation at a specific time, in part because she had lost considerable work time in sick leave. She took the vacation despite the fact that she had been warned that she would be fired if she did. The respondent argued that her resulting loss of income would not have occurred had the complainant acceded to her employer's refusal to permit her to take vacation at that time. In respect of the "work now, grieve later" rule, the board ruled as follows:

> Human rights law . . . is not an attempt to accommodate or balance the interests of institutions and workers. Instead it is designed to protect the rights of individuals who tend to be discriminated against by institutions and other individuals. The focus is the protection of disadvantaged individuals and groups, not the efficient functioning of industry or employment relations. While the latter may at times enter into human rights analysis, it is safe to say that these are not the foremost driving components of the legislation. While human rights adjudicators may recognize the need for hierarchical structures and measurable production quotas, we must be vigilant to ensure that the human rights of employees are preserved regardless of conflicting institutional interests.
>
> This conclusion is strengthened by the special status the courts have accorded human rights legislation. Mr. Justice McIntyre, writing for a unanimous Supreme Court of Canada, has stated: "Legislation of this type is of a special nature, not quite constitutional, but certainly more than the ordinary and it is for the courts to seek out its purpose and give it effect. The *Code* aims at the removal of discrimination." *Ontario Human Rights Commission v. Simpsons-Sears Ltd.*, [1985] 2 S.C.R. 536 at 546-7. Legislation of a quasi-constitutional nature, which seeks to accord rights and opportunities to disadvantaged groups, should be interpreted in a manner which upholds those rights even where labour relations rulings might hold differently.
>
> This position is further buttressed by the fact that the complainant was not a unionized employee, and did not have access to a union grievance procedure. As a result of the Supreme Court ruling in *Seneca College of Applied Arts and Technology v.*

---

431. (1986), 7 C.H.R.R, D/3196 (Ont. Bd. of Inquiry).
432. Varied (1987), 9 C.H.R.R. D/4548 (Ont. Div. Ct.).
433. (1989), 69 O.R. (2d) 281 (C.A.); see also *Whitehead v. Servodyne Canada Ltd., ante,* note 425.
434. *Ante,* note 430.

Bhadauria, [1981] 2 S.C.R. 181, her only remedy for discrimination was through the auspices of the Commission under [the] Ontario *Human Rights Code*. The limited resources at the Commission result in protracted delay for most human rights litigants, delay which is more extensive than that generally seen in the labour relations setting. The concept of "grieving later" takes on a different ring within a human rights process which can take years for resolution.[435]

General Damages

The 1981 *Code* placed a financial cap of $10,000 on the amount of damages awarded under this heading, and added a requirement that the board find "wilfull or reckless" infringement before making such an award. ✔ This has not noticeably diminished the number of awards in the nature of general damages issued by boards. Awards for injuries to the feelings and pride of complainants have steadily risen in quantum.[436] In regard to harassment cases, in which general damages can be expected to be higher, the board in *Torres v. Royalty Kitchenware Ltd.*[437] set out a list of considerations that has been used by boards in similar cases:

1. The nature of the harassment, that is, was it simply verbal or was it physical as well?

2. The degree of aggressiveness and physical contact in the harassment.

3. The ongoing nature, that is, the time period of the harassment.

4. The frequency of the harassment.

5. The age of the victim.

6. The vulnerability of the victim; and

7. The psychological impact of the harassment upon the victim.

A recent Divisional Court judgment took an extremely restrictive approach to the complainant's right to damages in human rights cases. In *York Condominium Corporation No. 216 v. Dudnik*,[438] the board had found discrimination on the ground of age and family status against certain condominium corporations whose by-laws prohibited occupancy by children. One complainant, Mr. Ramdial, who had an agreement to sell his unit, had allowed the prospective purchaser, Ms. Salmon, to withdraw from the agreement because he had notice that the condominium would enforce its rule by injunction. Mr. Ramdial later sold the condominium for a higher

---

435. *Ibid.*, at D/73-D/74.
436. See: *Sharp v. Seasons Restaurant* (1987), 8 C.H.R.R. D/4133 (Ont. Bd. of Inquiry); *Whitehead, Morano, Noffke, Shaw, Heinke, Morgoch, ante,* note 416; *Blainey, ante,* note 404; *Cuff, ante,* note 402; *Booker, ante,* note 404; *Rossetti v. Montgomery* (1987), 9 C.H.R.R. D/4498 (Ont. Bd. of Inquiry).
437. (1982), 3 C.H.R.R. D/858; and see *Cuff, ibid.*
438. (1991), 3 O.R. (3d) 360 (Div. Ct.).

price, but Ms. Salmon, a single mother, lost her chance to purchase a home and was unable to find another suitable home at the price. The board awarded Mr. Ramdial special damages of $4,000, taking into account the expenses he had incurred by reason of his not having completed the transaction with Ms. Salmon, balanced against the further profit he had realized in the later sale. In regard to Ms. Salmon, the board noted that the market in housing was rapidly rising at the time of the aborted transaction, and that the condominium corporation's action had caused her a significant opportunity loss. The board awarded general damages of $25,000.

The other two complainants had purchased condominiums in which they lived with children under the prohibited age. The Condominium Corporation's actions under the *Condominium Act* to prohibit their continued occupancy resulted in one of these complainants moving. Both adult complainants were awarded $1,000, and smaller awards were given to their children. The board did not make these awards under subsection 41(1)(*b*), although it had found that, in acting intentionally to enforce the "adults only" rule, the corporations had acted "wilfully." The board cited stress to the complainants and their families as the reason for the awards.

In a decision characterized by a marked lack of curial deference, Carruthers, J. disallowed the damage award to Ramdial, taking the view that no right of his had been infringed. He went in *obiter* to express the view that the Commission should be obliged to give notice in any case in which it intends to ask for "damages fashioned by common law principles." Turning to the Salmon award, Carruthers, J. appeared to take the position that there was no opportunity loss flowing from the discriminatory action of the Corporation:

> If her object was profit through her purchase of the unit and subsequent sale in a rising market, then she was free to complete the transaction with Ramdial. And if she had done that, then insofar as the provisions of s. 2(1) of the *Code* are concerned, her right would have remained. Then, if it was found to have been breached, the object of the exercise before the board would have been to determine her loss, economic or otherwise due to her not residing in the premises she purchased with her son, or residing there but without him.
>
> As I have noted she chose, and I have said it was reasonable for her to have done so, to walk away from her transaction with Ramdial and continue to live with her sister. Having reached that conclusion, then the question is what amount of monetary compensation should be given to Salmon for having been effectively denied the right to have her child live with her in the accommodation of her choice.[439]

Carruthers, J. then went on to impose an extremely narrow definition of the term "wilfully" as used in subsection 41(1)(*b*):

> To the extent that the Board appears to treat "wilfully" and "intentionally" as being synonymous, I cannot agree. In my opinion, while the act upon which it is founded must be

---

439. *Ibid.*, at 373-374.

intentional, the infringement must be the purpose of that act in order to be wilful within the meaning of s. 40(1)(*b*) [now 41(1)(*b*)]. I do not think that the circumstances of this case permit that conclusion.[440]

In the result, Carruthers, J. did not disturb the *Cryderman* and *Dudnik* awards. He reduced Ms. Salmon's award to $1,000 and her son's to $500. Having ruled out compensation for stress except as "mental anguish" under subsection 41(1)(*b*), and denied the applicability of the notion of opportunity loss, it is not clear on what basis Carruthers, J. made this award.

The *York Condominium* decision is disturbing on a number of points. In the first place, it appears not to recognize the very real deterrent posed by the actions of the Corporation to the sale of the Ramdial unit. Secondly, in denying compensation to Mr. Ramdial, the court appeared not to give due weight to section 11 of the *Code*. Finally, the insistence that "wilful" infringement of the *Code* encompasses only situations where the intention is to discriminate, the court seems to restrict recovery only to cases in which "animus" can be proved, which is in direct opposition to the thrust of human rights jurisprudence in recent years.

The Commission has applied for leave to appeal the decision.

Interest

Boards currently seem to differ on the issue of whether monetary awards should attract interest. In a number of early cases, interest was awarded on the total of special and general damages; in two such cases the award was confirmed by the Divisional Court.[441] The current debate seems to focus on whether interest should be awarded in regard to general with some boards making the quantum their general damage awards reflect mental anguish up to the date of the inquiry, rather than awarding interest.[442]

Costs

Neither the previous nor the present *Code* contains any provision directing a board as to an award of costs to the successful complainant.

---

440. *Ibid.*, at 377.
441. See *Cameron v. Nel-Gor Castle Nursing Home* (1984), 5 C.H.R.R. D/2170 (Ont. Bd. of Inquiry); *Cuff v. Gypsy Restaurant* (1987), 8 C.H.R.R. D/3972 (Ont. Bd. of Inquiry); *Scott v. Foster Wheeler Ltd.*, *ante*, note 405; *Tabar v. Scott* (1982), 3 C.H.R.R. D/1073 (Ont. Bd. of Inquiry); *Olarte v. DeFillips*, *ante*, note 405. The award of interest in *Tabar* was specifically confirmed by the Divisional Court in *West End Construction Ltd. v. Ontario (Ministry of Labour)* (1986), 57 O.R. (2d) 391 (Div. Ct.) and the one in *Olarte*, without comment, by the Divisional Court in *Commodore Business Machines v. Ontario (Minister of Labour)*, *ante*, note 405.
442. See especially *Noffke v. McClaskin Hot House* (1989), 11 C.H.R.R. D/407 (Ont. Bd. of Inquiry); and *Morgoch*, *ante*, note 416.

In *Amber v. Leder*,[443] the board suggested that, in some circumstances, it might award a complainant costs but that, in the case at hand, costs were not appropriate. After the board of inquiry had been appointed, the Commission decided that the respondent's offer of settlement was reasonable and that, therefore, the hearing before the board should not proceed. The complainant insisted that the hearing proceed and, believing the Commission's position to be contrary to her own, hired her own counsel to represent her before the board. The board decided that once a board of inquiry had been appointed by a minister it could not be terminated by the Commission. However, the board denied costs to the complainant because it found that the Commission had not acted unreasonably and that the hearing, although it had been allowed to proceed at the request of the complainant, had really been unnecessary.

In *Hadley v. Mississauga*,[444] the board of inquiry also suggested that costs might be awarded, but that they were not appropriate in that case. The board said:

> The Ontario Human Rights Commission is compelled by s. 14b(1)(a) [now 18(1)(a)] to have carriage of the complaint and, in this inquiry, the matter was prosecuted by very able counsel on behalf of the Commission. In the usual case the interests of the Commission and the Complainant are the same. That was the situation here as there was no conflict in the position taken by the Commission and the Complainant. Although the Complainant is entitled to be represented by counsel, in the instant case, it was somewhat redundant to have two counsel present as there was an identity of interests between the two parties. If the positions had been diverse, then an award as to costs with respect to the complainant's personal counsel might have been justified.

In *Wan v. Greygo Gardens*,[445] the board of inquiry decided that costs could not be awarded under the previous *Code*. One of the complainants had requested that she be reimbursed for her travel expenses to attend the hearing. The board concluded:

> With respect to Mrs. Chen's claim for train fare, I would observe that this item related to the conduct of the hearing and not directly to the Respondent's wrongful acts. In ordinary civil litigation it would be regarded as a matter of costs, rather than as part of the claim for damages. There is no express provision for an award of costs under the *Human Rights Code*. In my view, the distinction between a compensation for loss and the costs of a legal action is sufficiently well-known that the legislature would have expressly provided for recovery of costs under the *Code* had it intended to authorize such an award. Since section 19(b) of the *Code* provides only for compensation, I conclude that an award for an item in the nature of costs, such as Mrs. Chen's train fare to attend the hearing, is not within my jurisdiction.[446]

---

443. Ont. Human Rights Comm. Bd. of Inquiry, Tarnopolsky (1970) (unreported).
444. (1976), unreported (Ont. Bd. of Inquiry).
445. (1982), 3 C.H.R.R. D/812 (Ont. Bd. of Inquiry).
446. *Ibid.*, at D/816.

In *Karumanchiri v. Ontario (Liquor Control Board)*,[447] the Divisional Court confirmed that, absent a specific statutory provision, the board has no jurisdiction to award costs.

Costs against the Commission are specifically provided for in the *Code* and will be discussed later in this chapter.

Vicarious, Corporate Liability

The 1981 *Code* statutorily extended corporate responsibility by providing that any act or thing done or omitted to be done in the course of his or her employment by an officer, official, employee or agent of a corporation, trade union, trade or occupational association, unincorporated association or employers' organization shall be deemed to be an act or thing done or omitted to be done by the corporation trade union, trade or occupational association, unincorporated association or employers' organizations.[448]

This section of the *Code* specifically excludes vicarious responsibility in regard to the harassment and prosecution section of the *Code*. However, a number of boards of inquiry dealing with harassment have held corporations responsible for the acts of employees, which such employees were "directing minds" of the corporation, or where "directing minds" authorized, condoned, adopted or ratified the actions of an employee.[449] A board has also, in *obiter*, expressed the opinion that corporate liability might arise through the common law in respect of agency.[450] More recently, in imposing

---

447. (1987), 8 C.H.R.R. D/4076 (Ont. Bd. of Inquiry), application for judicial review refused (1988), 9 C.H.R.R. D/4868 (Div. Ct.), additional reasons at (1988), 27 O.A.C. 246 (Div. Ct.).

448. Section 45(1), applied in *Booker v. Floriri Village Investments Inc.* (1989), 11 C.H.R.R. D/44 (Ont. Bd. of Inquiry).

449. *Olarte v. DeFillips* (1983), 4 C.H.R.R. D/1705 at D/1737 to D/1746 (Ont. Bd. of Inquiry), affirmed (1984), 6 C.H.R.R. D/2833 (*sub nom. Commodore Business Machines v. Ontario (Minister of Labour)* (Ont. Div. Ct.); *Cox v. Jagbritte Inc.* (1981), 2 C.H.R.R. D/609 (Ont. Bd. of Inquiry); *Dhillon v. F. W. Woolworth Co.* (1982), 3 C.H.R.R. D/743 (Ont. Bd. of Inquiry) were decided under the pre-1981 legislation. While the liability theory was not specifically discussed by the court, the damages award against the corporate respondent was confirmed in the *Commodore Business Machines* judgment. In *Wei Fu v. Ontario Government Protective Services* (1985), 6 C.H.R.R. D/2791 (Ont. Bd. of Inquiry), the board considered, in *obiter*, both the statutory provisions governing an award in cases of harassment and the "organic theory of corporate responsibility" developed in the above noted boards of inquiry (paras. 22919-22926). *Cuff v. Gypsy Restaurant* (1987), 87 C.L.L.C. 17,015 (Ont. Bd. of Inquiry) (corporate respondents found liable for the harassment under 1981 *Code*); *Piazza v. Airport Taxi Cab (Malton) Assn.* (1987), 7 C.H.R.R. D/3196 (Ont. Bd. of Inquiry), varied (1987), 24 Admin. L.R. 149 (Ont. Div. Ct.), reversed (1989), 69 O.R. (2d) 281 (C.A.); *Boehm v. National System of Baking Ltd.* (1987), 87 C.L.L.C. 17,013 (Ont. Bd. of Inquiry); *Broere v. W.P. London & Associates Ltd.* (1987), 87 C.L.L.C. 17,026 (Ont. Bd. of Inquiry); *Rampersad v. 547440 Ontario Ltd.* (1987), 16 C.C.E.L. 209 (Ont. Bd. of Inquiry).

450. See *Wei Fu v. Ont. Government Protective Services, ibid.*

strict liability on the employer in the absence of a specific statutory provision, the Supreme Court of Canada has rejected employer liability based on theories arising from tort, criminal or quasi-criminal matters, choosing instead to determine liability through a purposive interpretation of the Act in question.

In *Robichaud v. Brennan*[451] a board had found that an employee had been sexually harassed by her supervisor. The issue was whether the corporate employer was responsible for unauthorized discriminatory acts by its employee in the course of employment. The Supreme Court took a broad and purposive approach to the interpretation of the Act. LaForet, J. stated that the theory of employer liability in these situations did not have to be based upon fault nor upon the theories developed under the law of tort. The issue of whether the theory of employer liability in *Robichaud* is applicable to the Ontario *Code*, is discussed in Chapter 7.

Prevention of Harassment: Section 41(2)

Section 41(2) sets out a procedure whereby an order can be made against a person who is able to penalize or prevent harassment, but fails to do so:

> (2) Where a board makes a finding under subsection (1) that a right is infringed on the ground of harassment under subsection 2(2) or subsection 5(2) or conduct under section 7, and the board finds that a person who is a party to the proceeding,
>> (a) knew or was in possession of knowledge from which the person ought to have known of the infringement; and
>> (b) had the authority by reasonably available means to penalize or prevent the conduct and failed to use it,
> the board shall remain seized of the matter and upon complaint of a continuation or repetition of the infringement of the right the Commission may investigate the complaint and, subject to subsection 36(2), request the board to re-convene and if the board finds that a person who is a party to the proceeding,
>> (c) knew or was in possession of knowledge from which the person ought to have known of the repetition of infringement; and
>> (d) had the authority by reasonably available means to penalize or prevent the continuation or repetition of the conduct and failed to use it,
> the board may make an order requiring the person to take whatever sanctions or steps are reasonably available to prevent any further continuation or repetition of the infringement of the right.

The subsection is discussed in Chapter 7 and therefore will not be dealt with here.

---

451. (1987) 8 C.H.R.R. D/4326 (S.C.C.); and see discussion in Chapter 7.

Costs Against the Commission: Section 41(4)

Section 41(4) provides:

> (4) Where, upon dismissing a complaint, the board of inquiry finds that,
>
> (*a*) the complaint was trivial, frivolous, vexatious or made in bad faith; or
>
> (*b*) in the particular circumstances undue hardship was caused to the person complained against,
>
> the board of inquiry may order the Commission to pay to the person complained against such costs as are fixed by the board.

An award of costs against the Commission is clearly not to be made lightly. The import of the terms "trivial, frivolous, vexatious" and "in bad faith" has been discussed in Chapter 8. Suffice it to say, here, that an award of costs under the first test in subsection 41(4) will be made only when the Commission has acted in a way that is completely unjustified, in bringing a complaint. Where a board is inclined to make such a finding, it is suggested that one factor that should be considered is whether the respondent was so uncommunicative or so misleading in its actions that the Commission's decision to proceed with the complaint was justified.

An example of this type of assessment can be seen in the remarks of the board in *Rawala v. DeVry Institute.*[452] In that case, three students had cheated on an exam. All three admitted, at the board of inquiry, to having both shared and copied answers, although not all three of the students had been so candid when caught by school officials. Two of the students, who were members of visible minority groups, were dealt heavier punishments than the third, a white student.

At the board of inquiry, the discrepancy in treatment was explained by the respondents in a manner that satisfied the chairman. However, the chairman made the following remarks about the Commission's justification for bringing the matter to the board:

> Although I have . . . concluded that a factual basis for these two complaints has not [been] established, there are a number of suspicious circumstances arising in the present case which should be addressed. Counsel for the respondent has suggested that not only are the complaints brought in the present case groundless but the investigation and handling of these matters by the Ontario Human Rights Commission and its staff have been, in some sense, irresponsible. In my view, the conduct of the officials and staff of DeVry in the present case is such that it is not at all surprising that the complainants reached the view that DeVry was motivated by bias and that the Commission, in the course of its inquiries, developed the view that there was some basis for this concern.
>
> The dealings between DeVry officials and Mr. Souza and Mr. Rawala could not have been better designed to provoke suspicion of this kind. Having meted out a lesser sanction to Mr. Roy, whom both Souza and Rawala knew to have engaged in similar conduct to their own, DeVry officials refused to give any explanation to Souza and

---

452. (1982), 3 C.H.R.R. D/1057 (Ont. Bd. of Inquiry). This case is discussed above in the section on circumstantial evidence.

Rawala of this differential treatment. Further, the explanations offered to Mr. Sackrule, the Commission's investigator, did not ring true.

. . . .

I accept the evidence of various members of the Committee who indicate that no attempt was made to assess the respective abilities of three students during the Committee meeting. But I also accept Mr. Sackrule's evidence that he received the impression that the DeVry officials with whom he had [been] in contact . . . justified the differential treatment on a basis which had no grounding in fact. Mr. Dykstra's misconception of Roy's abilities may, of course, have resulted from knowledge of Roy's performance on the supplemental. But it is not [at] all surprising that Mr. Sackrule felt that so obviously inadequate an explanation for the differential sanctions was a suspicious circumstance.

A second explanation offered by Mr. Sackrule was similarly groundless. It is suggested that the fact that Roy had been an unwilling participant in the cheating episode was a material consideration. Mr. Sackrule explored this question with Mr. Lehtila and the latter quite properly confirmed that he did not view Mr. Roy's participation as unwilling. . . . Further suspicions were raised by the seemingly *ad hoc* nature of the decision-making processes established by DeVry to deal with this matter and an apparent failure to follow the procedures described in the DeVry Calendar. . . .

Further, the manner in which the investigation was conducted by the Committee gave rise to some suspicion that no sincere attempt was made to authenticate Mr. Souza's allegation concerning Mr. Roy. If the respective records of the students were examined, it would have been revealed that both Mr. Rawala and Mr. Souza were significantly better students than Mr. Roy. Either of them could have passed the AIE course without writing the final examination at all because of their high standing in previous assignments. It would have been evident that Mr. Roy was more likely to be in need of assistance than they. No attempt was made to contact Mr. Souza with a view to identifying the question or questions on which Mr. Roy had obtained information from the others. As has been indicated, the mode of investigation by comparison of answer papers left much to be desired. Although it is perhaps all too easy for individuals trained in the drawing of inferences from circumstantial evidence to criticize the efforts of individuals without such training, the investigation conducted by the Committee was by any measure incompetent in the extreme. For the reasons advanced above, I am satisfied that this was an exercise in incompetence rather than improper bias. Again, however, it is not surprising that others took a different view of the matter.[453]

Clearly, the board in *Rawala* suggests that the Commission is not to be faulted for being properly suspicious of circumstances that appear discriminatory, where no reasonable explanation is given in the course of the usually lengthy conciliation process.

Commenting in *obiter*, one board suggested that an award of costs should not be made simply because a previous arbitration board had found the complainant incredible, where there was no evidence of unsatisfactory handling of the complaint by the Commission and where the complainant was sincere in his complaint.[454] In another case, the board refused an application for costs where, although the complainant may have acted in bad faith, the Commission did not and the circumstances were not trivial,

---

453. *Ibid.*, at D/1069–D/1070.
454. *Hyman v. Southam Murray Printing Ltd.* (1981) 3 C.H.R.R. D/617 (Ont. Bd. of Inquiry).

frivolous or vexatious.[455]

One board declined to award costs even where it was less than satis-fied with the Commission's investigation, finding it "rather selective" in some respects. In that case the board stressed that the complaint itself could not be said to be frivolous, trivial, vexatious, or made in bad faith.[456]

Costs were awarded against the Commission where certain allegations were deleted from the complaint at the start of the hearing, and the board found that they had been made in bad faith. The board found that the Commission had assessed the complaint on the basis of a biased report by an improperly appointed investigating officer. The board also found that the respondent suffered undue hardship due to false, bad faith allegations.[457]

In a more recent case, costs were awarded where the board found the complaint to be trivial and frivolous, with an absence of facts necessary to prove the allegations.[458]

Enforcement of an Order

The order of a board of inquiry may be enforced in two ways. Section 19(1) of the *Statutory Powers Procedure Act* provides:

> A certified copy of a final decision and order of a tribunal in any proceeding may be filed in the Ontario Court (General Division) by the tribunal or by a party and, if it is for the payment of money, it may be enforced at the instance of the tribunal or of such party in the name of the tribunal in the same manner as an order of that court, and in all other cases by an application by the tribunal or by such party to the court for such order as the court may consider just.

Section 44 of the *Code* provides that, with the consent of the Attorney General, a prosecution under the Provincial Offences Act may be launched against anyone who contravenes the order of a board of inquiry. If the person is convicted he or she may be fined up to $25,000.[459]

APPEALS

Any party may appeal the decision or order of a board of inquiry to the divisional court. Section 42 sets out the relevant provisions:

> (1) Any party to a proceeding before a board of inquiry may appeal from a decision or order of the board to the Divisional Court in accordance with the rules of court.

455. *Nimako v. Canadian National Hotels* (1985), 6 C.H.R.R. D/2894 (Ont. Bd. of Inquiry).
456. *Adams v. Bata Retail* (1988), unreported (Ont. Bd. of Inquiry).
457. *Pham v. Beach Industries Ltd.* (1987), 8 C.H.R.R. D/4008 (Ont. Bd. of Inquiry).
458. *Ouimette v. Lily Cups Ltd.* (1990), 12 C.H.R.R. D/19 (Ont. Bd. of Inquiry).
459. "44.—(1) Every person who contravenes section 9, subsection 33(11), or an order of a board of inquiry, is guilty of an offence and on conviction is liable to a fine of not more than $25,000.

(2) No prosecution for an offence under this Act shall be instituted except with the consent in writing of the Attorney General."

(2) Where notice of an appeal is served under this section, the board of inquiry shall forthwith file in the Divisional Court the record of the proceedings before it in which the decision or order appealed from was made and the record, together with a transcript of the oral evidence taken before the board if it is not part of the record of the board, shall constitute the record in the appeal.

(3) An appeal under this section may be made on questions of law or fact or both and the court may affirm or reverse the decision or order of the board of inquiry or direct the board to make any decision or order that the board is authorized to make under this Act and the court may substitute its opinion for that of the board.

The "record of proceedings" mentioned in the section is kept by virtue of section 40 of the *Code*:

The oral evidence taken before a board at a hearing shall be recorded, and copies of a transcript thereof shall be furnished upon request upon the same terms as in the Ontario Court (General Division).

INDEX